G000139750

27 SEP 2001

MELBOURNE AIRPORT
050Y

AUSTRALIA

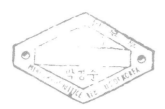

DEPARTMENT OF IMMIGRATION
PERMITTED TO ENTER
AUSTRALIA

24 APR 1996

For stay of *12 Month*

SYDNEY AIRPORT 54

IMMIGRATION DIVISION BANGKOK, THAILAND
A
72
DEPARTED
-6 FEB 1998
SIGNED

ETHNIC AFFAIRS

.... Person
30 OCT 1999
DEPARTED
AUSTRALIA

SYDNEY 32

T R A V E L E R ' S
AUSTRALIA
C O M P A N I O N

上陸許可
ADMITTED
15. FEB. 1996
4
Status: 4-1-
Duration: 90 days
NARITA(N)
Immigration Inspector

日本国

ADMITTED
20. OCT. 1998
Status: 4-1-16
Duration   *180 days*
Port: HANEDA

Signature

№ 011278

THE UNITED STATES
OF AMERICA
NONIMMIGRANT VISA

USSED
Air Port

U.S. IMMIGRATION
170 HHW 1710

JUL 2 0 1998

HONG KONG
(1038)
-7 JUN 1997
IMMIGRATION
OFFICER

The 2001–2002 Traveler's Companions
ARGENTINA • AUSTRALIA • BALI • CALIFORNIA • CANADA • CHILE • CHINA •
COSTA RICA • CUBA • EASTERN CANADA • ECUADOR • FLORIDA • HAWAII •
HONG KONG • INDIA • INDONESIA • IRELAND • JAPAN • KENYA •
MALAYSIA & SINGAPORE • MEDITERRANEAN FRANCE • MEXICO • NEPAL •
NEW ENGLAND • NEW ZEALAND • NORTHERN ITALY • PERU • PHILIPPINES •
PORTUGAL • RUSSIA • SOUTH AFRICA • SOUTHERN ENGLAND • SPAIN • THAILAND •
TURKEY • VENEZUELA • VIETNAM, LAOS AND CAMBODIA • WESTERN CANADA

Traveler's AUSTRALIA Companion

First published 1998
Second Edition 2001
The Globe Pequot Press
246 Goose Lane, PO Box 480
Guilford, CT 06437 USA
www.globe-pequot.com

© 2001 by The Globe Pequot Press, Guilford, CT, USA

ISBN: 0-7627-0950-2

Distributed in the European Union by
World Leisure Marketing Ltd, Unit 11
Newmarket Court, Newmarket Drive,
Derby, DE24 8NW, United Kingdom
www.map-guides.com

Created, edited and produced by
Allan Amsel Publishing, 53, rue Beaudouin
27700 Les Andelys, France.
E-mail: AAmsel@aol.com
Editor in Chief: Allan Amsel
Editor: Anne Trager
Picture editor and book designer: Roberto Rossi
Original design concept: Hon Bing-wah

Printed by Samhwa Printing Co. Ltd., Seoul, South Korea

TRAVELER'S
AUSTRALIA
COMPANION

by Samantha Wauchope

Photographed by Roberto Rossi

Second Edition

The
Globe
Pequot
Press

GUILFORD
CONNECTICUT

Contents

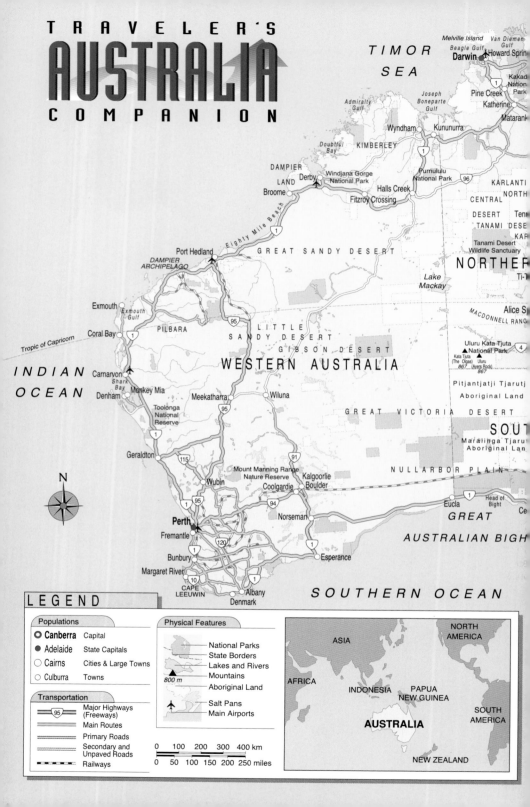

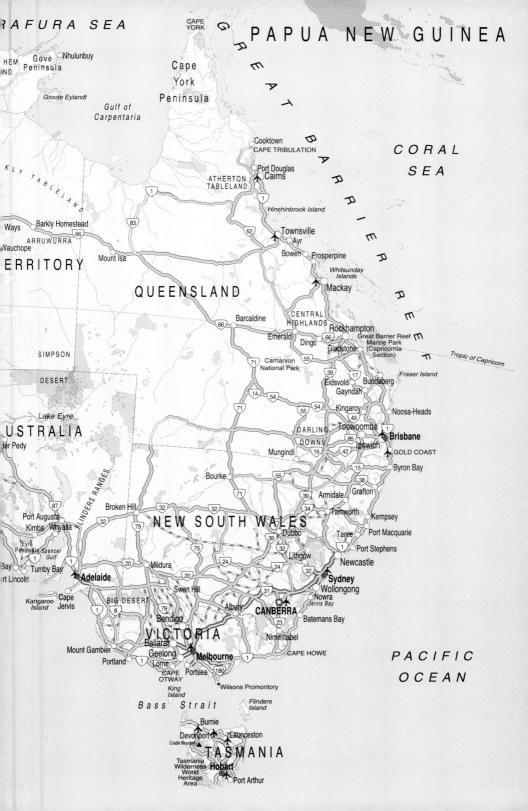

TOP SPOTS

Buzz the Bungle Bungles

WE COULD HAVE BEEN APPROACHING AN ALIEN PLANET. Our helicopter hovered above a barren, arid landscape scattered with thousands of surreal, striped "bee-hives": the Bungle Bungles, relics of an enormous coral reef system in the far north of Western Australia. When we looped down among the huge ember-like domes, though, narrow passages of bright green appeared here and there. Closer in, we saw moist, shaded gullies with crystal-clear rock-pools and tall palms.

From the ground, the Bungle Bungles are strange and formidable mountains. Twenty million years of uplift and erosion produced these distinctive landforms, whose crumbly sandstone is protected to some degree by bands of red silica and black lichen. As we landed and set up camp, sunset transformed the Bungles briefly into fiery striped visions.

The next morning we set off for a seven-day exploration of the gullies and hidden worlds of this strange wilderness, once a refuge for outlaws, escaped convicts, and Aboriginal people fleeing white man's law. Much of this labyrinth is inaccessible, its ravines protecting plants and animals that have vanished elsewhere. Of great spiritual significance to the Kija people, who named the area Purnululu ("soft stone"), these domes are also rich in Aboriginal art and sacred sites. But even the Kija respected the dangers of this place. Few others knew of its existence until the mid-1980s, when a 1982 documentary film brought it to public attention.

April, just at the beginning of the dry season, is the perfect time to visit the Bungle Bungles. The shaded gullies are cool and the creeks have dried, leaving occasional deep rock-pools with plate-sized, waxy pink water lilies. The ravines are lined with beautiful tropical ferns, vines and soaring Livistona palms.

From November to March, however, huge downpours create great torrents through these gullies and road access is impossible. Most sightseers choose to view the Bungle Bungles from the air, and in the Wet this is the only option. Even in the Dry, when the few tracks into the area are open to four-wheel-drive vehicles, negotiating boulders and narrow ravines makes trekking hard going. And a helicopter tour offers a view quite different from the ground perspective.

A combination of a flight and a trek is perhaps the most rewarding way to visit the Bungle Bungles. A half-hour helicopter tour costs $130, and passengers can opt to fly with the helicopter doors removed — a boon for photographers. The Western Australian Tourism Commission ((08) 9220 1700 WEB SITE www.westernaustralia.net organizes scenic flights and tours of Purnululu with experienced guides. They are also a vital resource for anyone considering a driving tour of this remote region.

OPPOSITE and ABOVE: The striped domes of the Bungle Bungles conceal crystalline rock-pools .

The Great Barrier Reef

FISH, BRILLIANT AS JEWELS, GLIDE BETWEEN WAVING SPONGES AND DELICATE CORAL FORMATIONS. On the sea floor, starfish and sea urchins forage in underwater grottoes. Queensland's Great Barrier Reef, a World Heritage Site, is a veritable underwater Garden of Eden, home to over 500 different species of coral and 2,000 species of fish. Over thousands of years, millions of minute coral polyps have lived and died here, leaving behind calcium skeletons. New coral grows on these remains, nurtured by the warm, clear, shallow and nutrient-rich waters unique to the eastern coastal strip.

Although reef trips sometimes include glass-bottomed boats and visits to underwater observatories, to examine this wonderland at close quarters you need to get wet. Snorkeling is the easiest way to explore shallower parts of the reef, and requires no special skill or training; just a mask, flippers and a snorkel (usually provided free-of-charge by reef tours and at resorts). Wetsuits are not needed in North Queensland's warm tropical waters, and underwater visibility is generally excellent. You need a boat to access the reef from the mainland, but on many of the coral cays and islands you can literally walk off the beach into a coral wonderland.

Scuba diving allows you to see the reef at its dazzling best. If you ever thought about taking up this sport, what better time to start than during a visit to the Great Barrier Reef? For those who have never dived before, learn-to-dive courses are offered at most resorts and towns along the reef coast. If your time is limited, brief supervised dives for novices are offered as an extra on many of the day-trips that visit the reef, such as those run by Ocean

Spirit Cruises ((07) 4031 2920 out of Cairns. Most boats and camera stores rent out underwater cameras.

Visit the World's Oldest Art Galleries

THE IMAGES TELL STORIES OF THE DREAMING, OF HOW ANCESTRAL BEINGS SHAPED THE WORLD. Or they depict hunting tales or battles between different clans. Many tell stories of sacred sites. And among the thousands of Aboriginal art sites throughout Australia — some sacred places closed to outsiders — are paintings that date from 20,000 to 65,000 years ago, predating even the Paleolithic paintings found in France. These oldest of the world's art galleries also represent the oldest continuing art tradition on earth, kept alive today by Aboriginal and Torres Strait Islander artists. Many designs, iconography and pigments have changed little over the centuries, and today's visitors can learn about their significance from the land's Aboriginal custodians.

Some of the galleries show animals long extinct, others show obsolete weapons and implements, or ceremonial dress unknown today. Highly stylized " X-ray" art portrays the organs and skeletons of animals and people. "Contact" paintings describe visits by Macassan fishermen from Sulawesi 400 years ago, and eighteenth- and nineteenth-century Western sailing boats. White men are easily identified by their hats, pipes, and hands in pockets. A figure near the East Alligator River crossing has a gun and long pigtails down his back, a reminder of the Chinese laborers who worked in the area's mines in the late nineteenth century.

More controversial rock art recently found in the Kimberley region of Western Australia depicts groups of men rowing peculiar high-bowed canoes, in paintings estimated to be up to 40,000 years old. In Arnhem Land, paintings often portray the stick-like Mimi, spirits that inhabit sacred sites and are so thin they can slide between cracks and fissures. Attempts at dating Mimi art have confirmed it to be the oldest on the continent — and in the world.

There are over 200 modest Aboriginal art sites in the Sydney area alone. However, a guided visit to the maze of caves in Arnhem Land's Mount Borradaile area or into the heart

ABOVE and BOTTOM RIGHT: Scuba diving is the best way to view the coral gardens of the Great Barrier Reef. TOP RIGHT: Bradshaw cave painting in Western Australia's Kimberley.

of the Kimberley offers the richest experience of Aboriginal art. Always ask your guide before swimming or taking photos; sometimes even certain landforms and trees are sacred. For more on Australia's Aboriginal art sites see CULTURAL KICKS, page 42 in YOUR CHOICE.

Ferry Across Sydney Harbour

TO UNDERSTAND SYDNEY, BEGIN WITH THE HARBOR, WHICH DIVIDES THE CITY IN TWO. And to experience the harbor the way the locals do, head to Circular Quay and take a commuter ferry. The views are breathtaking.

The first ferry, the *Rose Hill Packer*, began running in 1789, only a few years after Sydney was founded. While early ferries were no more than large rowing boats, by 1909, 51 steam-powered ferries were carrying over 40 million passengers a year. State Transit now operates hundreds of trips around the harbor every day, from the lumbering green-and-gold Sydney Ferries to speedy jetcats, most leaving from Circular Quay. Private ferry companies and water taxis add to commuter options.

For an introductory 40-minute trip, consider one of the four Manly ferries — *Queenscliff, Narrabeen, Collaroy* and *Freshwater* — which are named after the city's northern beaches. As the ferry leaves Circular Quay and enters broad Port Jackson, it skirts around the sculpturally brilliant Sydney Opera House, with the majestic Harbour Bridge to the left. Not far offshore is Fort Denison on tiny Pinchgut Island. The fort was built in 1857 as a response to the Crimea War, although the chance of a Russian frigate straying from the Black Sea to Australia was quite remote. Once used as a place of

leads up to the end of the peninsula and some of the best views of the inner harbor. Back through the park, another pathway cuts through scenic bush along the foreshore. Kookaburras, rainbow lorikeets and sulfur-crested cockatoos lurk in the grassy knolls. In winter, coral trees burst full of red blooms.

Secluded Whiting Beach provides another stop and an opportunity for a quick dip. The walk ends at Tooronga Zoo, only a few minutes by ferry from Circular Quay.

Sydney Ferries provide transport maps and information on harborside walks, and John Gunter's *Sydney by Ferry and Foot* outlines an excellent selection of scenic tours around the foreshore.

Walk with the Animals

DAWN AND DUSK ARE THE BEST TIMES TO SEE MARSUPIALS — kangaroos, tammar wallabies, sooty dunnarts, ring-tail, brushtail and little pygmy possums and southern brown bandicoots — although sleeping koalas can be seen at any time of day. And Kangaroo Island — where else? — is the place to get a close look. Isolated from the mainland and largely undeveloped, Kangaroo Island teems with unique Australian wildlife. The absence of dingoes, foxes and rabbits has protected many of the island's species from extinction. The tiny human population live mainly in fishing villages along the eastern coast, leaving the rest of the island to the animals. More than half of Kangaroo Island has never been cleared, and today a third of it is national parkland, where the animals roam freely.

At the western end of the island, Flinders Chase National Park harbors a prolific population of Kangaroo Island kangaroos, a smaller and furrier sub-species of the western gray. A few tend to hang out around the headquarters area. Although feeding the kangaroos, and in fact any of the island's animals, is prohibited, they're likely to steal food from unsuspecting picnickers. Kangaroo Island also has a large population of pretty tammar wallabies, an endangered species once found throughout the continent, but now restricted to here and to small pockets of Western Australia. Koalas are widespread throughout the island, with the largest colony around Rocky River. You might see a shy duck-billed platypus swimming in the streams; they live in semi-submerged burrows dug into the muddy banks.

temporary exile for recalcitrant convicts, the island earned its name because prisoners sent here were left with only a meager supply of bread and water.

The ferry bends to the left as it approaches the mouth of the harbor and enters Manly Cove. The subsequent whiling away of an afternoon in Manly is part of understanding this city. It's a three-minute walk across the peninsula to popular Manly Beach, the first of Sydney's northern beaches. A walking tour around the foreshore offers great views. From Manly Wharf, a scenic walkway skirts the high cliffs of Dobroyd Head along the water's edge to Spit Bridge, passing through sections of Sydney Harbour National Park before crossing over to Balmoral Beach at Mosman.

A shorter walk links the wharves of Cremorne Point and Tooronga Zoo. From the ferry stop at Cremorne Point Wharf, a path

There is no better way to see Sydney than from the water — Sydney Harbour ferries provide a relaxed and inexpensive cruise.

Rare Australian sea lions sun themselves on the white beaches of Kangaroo Island's Seal Bay. The adults tend to languor, occasionally heading into the waves for a splash or a surf, but otherwise content to roll over and continue sleeping. The pups have a lot more energy. Rangers make sure that tourists keep their distance: however awkward looking, a bull seal can give a good chase down the beach when disturbed.

At Cape du Couedic, fur seals take a breather on the rocks from fishing expeditions that can take them far out to sea. Fur seals are not as tolerant of humans as sea lions, but visitors can watch them at a safe distance from the viewing platform on the cliff above the rocks.

Little (or fairy) penguins are also common on Kangaroo Island. The National Parks and Wildlife Service ((08) 8553 2381 leads guided tours of penguin colonies at Penneshaw and Kingscote every evening. Tours aside, don't be surprised to see penguins waddle across the main street on their way to the beach.

Kangaroo Island lies just off the tip of South Australia's Fleurieu Peninsula, an hour's drive south of Adelaide. Ferries cross regularly from Cape Jervis, or there are flights from Adelaide. Guided tours of the island can be booked through Tourism Kangaroo Island ((08) 8553 1185 WEB SITE www.tourkangarooisland.com.au.

Drive Victoria's Surf Coast

HALFWAY UP THE MOUNTAIN, NOTHING BUT A LOW RAILING SEPARATED US FROM A SHEER DROP INTO THE OCEAN. Around another bend, the road descended to a narrow bridge where a river flowed into a cove and out into the ocean. Suddenly the road was so close to the beach we could step from the car directly onto the sand. But before we knew it we soared once again above vast expanses of ocean and seemingly endless lengths of honey-colored cliffs. The real skill, though, while negotiating hairpin bends and steep ascents and descents is coping with the endless appeals from passengers. No, we can't reverse to that last bend to take a photo, or go back for the sunglasses that just slid across the dashboard and out the window.

Victoria's Great Ocean Road was designed to be spectacular, which it is from start to finish. Returned servicemen began carving into the cliffs and mountains in 1919, often using picks and shovels. Work continued through the great depression, the project providing much-needed employment, and the Great Ocean Road officially opened in 1932.

ABOVE: Life can be a bit tiring for the sea lions of Kangaroo Island. OPPOSITE: The many turns of Victoria's Great Ocean Road reveal endless breathtaking scenery.

From the seaside town of Torquay, the 280-km (170-mile) drive soars along dizzying limestone cliffs, through ferny gullies and tracts of dense rainforest, past picture-perfect bays — including those of the popular seaside towns of Anglesea, Aireys Inlet, Lorne and Apollo Bay. If you're lucky you might spot whales and their calves frolicking in the deep inlets along this beautiful stretch of coastline during Australia's winter months. One thing for sure, though, no matter what time of day or year, you'll see surfers making the most of the onshore winds and massive waves. Victoria's West Coast is a surfing Mecca. While many of the beaches are ideal for beginners, the real acrobatics are to be seen at more challenging breaks. Jan Juc and Bell's Beach — home to the Bell's Beach Surf Classic — are the most famous, but there are hundreds of lesser-known breaks popular with locals. Regular viewpoints are thoughtfully positioned along the route.

After cutting the corner through the Cape Otway rainforest, the road returns to the coast at the eastern end of the dynamic stacks, arches and gorges that make up the Port Campbell National Park. Three lookouts provide unforgettable views of the Twelve Apostles, enormous columns of rock carved by the crashing sea and the winds that whip the coast. Sunsets at the Apostles are worth waiting for.

There are, in fact, only nine still standing, the others having been claimed by the sea. In geographic terms they're surprisingly young. As recently as 1990 "London Bridge," a hair-raising limestone arch that connected one pillar to the mainland, fell into the waves, leaving astonished tourists stranded for several hours until they were airlifted off the new-born Apostle.

While the best way to appreciate Victoria's spectacular West Coast is with your own car, for solo travelers, Otway Discovery Tours ((03) 9654 5432 operates day tours from Melbourne visiting most of the major attractions, with the option of stopping overnight along the way. Other companies have similar one- to three-day tours; for more information contact Tourism Victoria (132 842 FAX (03) 9653 9744 WEB SITE www.visitvictoria.com. Great Ocean Road Airtours ((03) 5261 5100 FAX (03) 5261 5797, at Tiger Moth World, Blackgate Road, Torquay, offers joy-flights over Bell's Beach and Point Addis, as well as one-hour flights along the ocean road to Port Campbell National Park and the Twelve Apostles. For those fit enough, Topbike WEB SITE www.topbike.com.au organizes eight-day cycling tours of the coast, with transport to help riders through more difficult stretches. Make sure your break pads are in good condition.

Amble Through the Outback

THE CAMELS' LARGE, PADDED FEET MOVED NOISELESSLY THROUGH THE GRASSLANDS AND SCRUB. From time to time the silence was broken by the metallic screeching of flocks of pink galahs. Otherwise the only sound was the occasional cameleer's call as we traveled by caravan through the Aboriginal land of the Iwupataka people, part of the vast, arid outback of Australia's harsh interior.

The center of Australia offers the continent's greatest challenge to explorers, artists, and anthropologists, and to all those who love scenery and wilderness. Great desert plains and salt lakes stretch for huge distances in all directions from Alice Springs. This is one of those few areas where, in spite of modern road, rail and air travel, there remains the distinct possibility of getting irrevocably lost. Hazards include lack of water and extremes of temperature. But the rewards of a guided inland trek are unforgettable: a serrated landscape of red quartzite ranges on the horizon, the absolutely flat grassland of Missionary Plain — beautifully suited to camel travel — and multicolored seas of wildflowers in spring.

Camels, I found out, have quite distinct personalities. Mine was friendly and gentle-natured, although she liked to gallop off to nibble juicy leaves. No biting or spitting, though. "It's all about upbringing," explained Steve, the cameleer. Treated with kindness, camels become the most amiable of domestic animals, quite unlike the herds of wild camels roaming Central Australia, descendents of Afghan camels brought to the country a century and a half ago. Our steeds were bred from captured wild camels.

We rode and walked five hours a day, leaving time to unload the camels, set up camp and do some exploring. By the third day we were following the edge of some of the most ancient mountains in the world. The MacDonnell and James ranges have weathered and eroded to a series of steep-sided ridges. Gorges, ravines and gullies harbor pockets of rainforest vegetation with lush grass for the camels. We bypassed famous Standley Chasm and Serpentine Gorge, sticking to places that cannot be reached by road.

Rock-pools provided a welcome drink or a quick bathe during the heat of the day, but at dusk temperatures fell quickly, and we moved in closer around the campfire. The camels have to be hobbled in the evenings, as they can wander vast distances. Each night, riders were rostered to watch over them — a pleasant occupation out on the plains around sunrise and sunset, watching the glorious color changes on the ridges.

The Queensland-based Outback Camel Company ((07) 3854 1022 FAX (07) 3854 1079 WEB SITE www.outbackcamel.com.au runs 12-to 23-day safaris deep into Australia's deserts and outback, including more challenging expeditions across the Simpson Desert to the Indian Ocean. To get a taste of camel riding, Frontier Camel Tours ((08) 8953 0444 FAX (08) 8955 5015 WEB SITE www.cameltours.com.au offers short camel rides along the Todd River and sunrise or sunset rides near Uluru.

Under the Canopy

THE NINETEENTH-CENTURY TRAIN TREMBLED AND SLOWLY MOVED OFF TOWARDS THE GREAT DIVIDING RANGE, doing little to alleviate the heavy, damp heat of tropical North Queensland. Fifteen hand-cut tunnels and 40 trestle bridges later, we would reach, by way of the dense forest along the edge of the dramatic Barron River Gorge, the village of Kuranda. The spectacular 90-minute journey runs through one of the most biologically diverse — and oldest — rainforests in the world, World Heritage listed since 1988.

As our train climbed upward, panoramic views over sugarcane fields and out across the Coral Sea to the Great Barrier Reef gradually gave way to a natural greenhouse within the vine-draped tropical forest. Opal-winged butterflies and tiny finches darted from tree to tree, feeding on new blossoms above the forest canopy. Rainbow lorikeets occasionally showed vivid flashes of yellow, blue, red and a fluorescent apricot. Butcher birds, which impale their prey on thorny bushes, joined the incessant chorus of tree frogs, fruit bats, king parrots and sulfur-crested cockatoos.

Breaking through the dense canopy, frequent switchbacks offered views across the vibrant green treetops to the indigo and cobalt peaks of the Atherton Ranges. In a sweeping coastal panorama, the occasional bottle-green island, licked in white, broke up the endless blue. The small train clung to the edges of the gorge as it climbed past majestic Stoney Creek Waterfall, the water crashing far below. We paused briefly at Barron Falls to take in impressive views of Glacier Rock and Red Bluff before finally lumbering on to Kuranda.

The Kuranda railway opened in 1891 to transport supplies to the tin mines of the Atherton Tableland. For most of the twentieth century the train ran weekly; Kuranda was little more than a post office and a pub servicing local farmers. But in the 1970s, this village in the rainforest became a magnet for alternative lifestylers, who were soon joined by like souls from the United States and Europe. Kuranda became something of a tropical Big Sur. Its renowned market, vegetarian cafés and art and craft galleries reflect the town's essentially alternative identity, and the local amphitheater still hosts regular workshops in tai chi, aerobics and "Open Circus." Houses are built from local cedar, with shady verandas opening onto verdant gardens: everywhere you look tropical plants, flowers, birds and butterflies seem to be trying to reclaim their land. Kuranda has an impressive walk-through aviary and a butterfly sanctuary containing more than

---

OPPOSITE: Bird's-nest ferns high in the tropical rainforest canopy create mini-ecosystems harboring frogs, insects and tiny orchids. ABOVE: A caravan of linked camels makes its way across a desert plain.

2,500 tropical butterflies. There is even a "noctarium," where nocturnal rainforest and wetlands animals can be viewed in their natural habitats.

An alternative to taking the train back to Cairns is to return via the Skyrail cableway. Designed to lessen the impact of visitors on the rainforest's sensitive ecology, the six-person gondola wafts silently above the treetops, giving a bird's-eye view of the living canopy just below. There are two optional stops along the way: a rainforest ecosystem display and a boardwalk through a section of the forest.

Adventure Connection ((07) 3876 4644 WEB SITE visitors@greatbarrierreef.aus.net in Cairns operates small-group tours to Kuranda and the rainforest, with botanists and zoologists as guides. Other guided tours into the rainforest from Kuranda or Cairns can be organized through Tourism Tropical North Queensland ((07) 4051 3588 FAX (07) 4051 0127 E-MAIL information@tnq.org.au WEB SITE www.tnq.org.au in Cairns, who also book tickets on both the Kuranda Railway and Skyrail.

Beguiled by the Kings of the Sea

IN THE CRYSTALLINE WATERS OF MONKEY MIA, UNDER THE FORGET-ME-NOT-BLUE WESTERN AUSTRALIAN SKY, DOLPHINS SWIM AROUND MY LEGS. A young male, hardly more than a pup, throws his head out of the water, laughs at our blundering movements, then veers onto his side and jets into deeper water a few meters away. A playmate joins him, and together they show off their skills, propelling themselves out of the water in unison.

Dolphins have been coming into the shallows of Monkey Mia beach since a pair were befriended by a fisherman's wife in the 1960s. Their antics and obvious enjoyment of human company quickly dispel thoughts that they're just looking to be fed. In fact, the protected waters of Shark Bay World Heritage Area are home to such a multitude of fish that the 40 or so dolphins who frequent Monkey Mia today have been known to offer their own catch to human visitors.

Elsewhere in Shark Bay, sea-grass growing in the calm waters of Eagle Bluff attracts dugongs — sea cows — in the summer months, infants often catching a ride on their mothers' backs.

Visitors can row small boats out for a closer view of these shy, prehistoric-looking mammals, which can reach four meters (13 ft) in length.

Australia's waters are home to dozens of species of marine mammals, including dolphins, seals, sea lions, dugongs and whales. In all seven states, government initiatives protect marine animals and the sensitive marine ecology while promoting responsible tourism. From April to October, humpback, minke, Bryde's, southern right, killer and gray whales migrate along Australia's coasts, traveling up from Antarctica to the warmer waters to mate and give birth, returning to colder waters at the end of the austral spring. The whales pass very close by prominent headlands, such as Cape Byron in New South Wales, Cape Otway in Victoria, or North West Cape in Western Australia.

Up to five southern right whales give birth each season in the waters off Warrnambool, on Victoria's West Coast. The whales can often be seen from the shore and headlands, resting with young calves in shallow water just beyond the surf line. Named by whalers because they were the "right" whales to hunt, these whales are slower swimmers than most and yield high amounts of oil and baleen. Their numbers were dwindling rapidly until whaling ceased, but conservation efforts are now bringing a steady increase in the population.

A second breeding ground for southern right whales is off Head of Bight in South Australia. This area is Yalata land, and permits are required to leave the highway. The Yalata people have a strong association with the whales, which are celebrated in song, dance and painting.

Humpbacks mate and breed along the Great Barrier Reef. Before beginning their return journey to Antarctica, they spend four or five days in Hervey Bay resting or feeding their newborn calves; males often sing long and complex songs, clearly audible to swimmers. Reaching up to 19 m (63 ft) in length, the humpback's exceptionally long flippers — measuring up to a third of its total body length — allow it to perform spectacular aerial leaps. The marine park of Hervey Bay is also home to hundreds of bottlenose dolphins, large turtles, dugongs, long-fin pilot whales, and even the occasional minke whale.

But the most playful animals I have met underwater are the Australian sea lions of Baird Bay on South Australia's Eyre Peninsula. It's hard to keep up with the younger ones' antics in the water: they circle swimmers, peer into masks, and even rest their flippers across your back.

OPPOSITE: The Kuranda Skyrail soars above the dense rainforest. RIGHT: Playing with the dolphins at Monkey Mia on Western Australia's Shark Bay.

YOUR CHOICE

The Great Outdoors

For lovers of the great outdoors, Australia is one of the world's top destinations. Divers can explore colorful coral reefs with their exotic aquatic life, while walkers and hikers can revel in an array of wilderness areas including deserts, alpine high-country and tropical rainforest. Animal-lovers can have close encounters with creatures seen nowhere else in the world — including 48 species of kangaroo. Fishermen, sailors and surfers will find the waterways and waves among the world's most challenging. A surprising outdoor attraction are the world's oldest art galleries (see VISIT THE WORLD'S OLDEST ART GALLERIES, page 14 in TOP SPOTS). And star-gazers will revel in the sky in the southern hemisphere, where most of the stars visible from earth can be seen and the southern cross is clearly visible.

Australia values its natural heritage highly and has over 800 national parks. In recognition of their significance, natural value and uniqueness, 14 areas have been given UNESCO World Heritage listings. The most accessible to visitors are Queensland's Wet Tropics, the Great Barrier Reef and Fraser Island, the Tasmanian Wilderness Area, Shark Bay in Western Australia, Kakadu and Uluru-Kata Tjuta national parks in the Northern Territory, and the Blue Mountains just outside Sydney.

National parks are managed by the states, apart from the Great Barrier Reef, which is managed by the Federal Government. Local and state national parks offices and tourist information centers generally provide maps and extensive information on park entry requirements, visitor facilities, essential seasonal information, and guides to flora and fauna.

NEW SOUTH WALES
New South Wales has extensive areas of forested national parks along the spine of the Great Dividing Range. The **Blue Mountains** World Heritage Area just west of Sydney is the most famous, with its deep green chasms, vertiginous rock formations and caves with extraordinary stalactites and stalagmites. Other beautiful forested areas are **Ku-ring-gai Chase National Park** just north of Sydney, and **Barrington Tops National Park** further north, which harbors an extraordinary array of wildlife.

New South Wales' coast is peppered with beautiful coves, harbors and beaches. While some have developed into resorts with innumerable possibilities to experience the area from land, sea or air; many are only visited by local anglers and surfers.

VICTORIA
Victoria's national parks include **Wilsons Promontory**, **Croajingolong** and the **Otway**

OPPOSITE: The crystalline waters of Dove Lake, at Cradle Mountain in Tasmania. ABOVE: A sleepy koala fights to keep his eyes open.

clothes and enough food for the whole trip. You should report to the ranger's office before you leave, and beware of unpredictable weather. There are also easy day-trips from Cradle Mountain Lodge or Lake St. Clair.

The **Franklin River**, part of the Tasmanian Wilderness World Heritage Area — the best example of pristine temperate rainforest in Australia — attracts rafters from around the world.

SOUTH AUSTRALIA

The **Heysen Trail**, a sensational walk through the center of South Australia, crosses 1,500 km (932 miles) of wilderness, from the coastal beaches of **Cape Jervis**, where sea eagles soar overhead, through the **Mount Lofty Ranges** to spectacular **Parachilna Gorge** in the northern **Flinders Ranges**. The trail is well-marked with red blazes, and accommodation is available in numerous huts and youth hostels; there are also plenty of places to camp along the way. Winter is the best time to tackle the Heysen Trail. Maps can be obtained from Friends of the Heysen Trail ((08) 8212 6299.

WESTERN AUSTRALIA

Almost as big as Texas, the **Kimberley** in Western Australia is one of the last great wilderness frontiers. Guided tours from Broome, Kununurra or Darwin take visitors deep into the Kimberley's unique and spectacular landscapes to visit the **Bungle Bungles** of Purnululu National Park (see BUZZ THE BUNGLE BUNGLES, page 13 in TOP SPOTS) and the otherworldly isolation of the **Mitchell Plateau**, with soaring ravines and oases of rock pools surrounded by palms and wildflowers. At **Mitchell Falls**, four sets of falls plunge from one dark-red rocky plateau to the next.

Roads in the Kimberley are treacherous at any time. All but the major Broome–Darwin route require four-wheel-drive vehicles during the dry season (from April to October), and are often impassable during the wet season (from November to March). The best time to visit is late April, when grevillea and wattle trees blossom, grassy plains fill with wildflowers, and pink water-lilies float among the red rocks in post-monsoon waterfalls and rock pools.

There are 70 species of native mammals in the Kimberley. Many are nocturnal, but colorful rock wallabies and numerous goannas and lizards are usually out and about. Freshwater crocodiles abound in the inland area of the Kimberley, although these are timid

coastal parks, and the inland reserves of the **Grampians** and the **High Country**. Wilsons Promontory is particularly popular with animal watchers and walkers, with over 80 km (50 miles) of marked walking tracks. The five-kilometer (three-mile) Lilly Pilly Gully Trail passes through bushland and lush pockets of temperate rainforest with spectacular old tree ferns. Other walks follow coastal cliffs and cut through salt marshes, perfect for birdwatchers.

TASMANIA

At the other end of the country, Tasmania's **Cradle Mountain** is rated as one of the great walking areas in the world. The six-day Overland Track, for the fit, takes hikers past jagged peaks, through heath and dense beech forests, across high alpine moorlands and over fast-flowing streams. There are catered tours run by experienced guides and outfitters; try Cradle Huts ((03) 6260 4094. The best part of this trip is that hikers are only expected to carry a light backpack with sleeping bag, lunch, and the bare minimum of clothes. Accommodation is provided in comfortable cabins along the route, which are well-stocked with food and complete with hot and cold running water, showers and toilets. Walking the track without a guide is much cheaper, but you need to carry tents, plenty of warm

ABOVE: The Kimberley's vast plains are carpeted with wildflowers in spring. RIGHT: Cooling off in a ravine of the Mitchell Plateau.

YOUR CHOICE

and do not attack humans. Coastal Kimberley and its tidal estuaries harbor saltwater crocodiles, a genuine hazard for tourists. It is dangerous to swim in its rivers and creeks, or even to walk in many areas, as the crocodiles will go on land to attack a human.

The rich bird life of the Kimberley (some 241 species) includes red-tailed black cockatoos, blue-winged kookaburras, little black grass-wrens and superb little rainbow bee-eaters, which dart about the river surface.

NORTHERN TERRITORY
Several tour companies offer four-wheel-drive day tours around the waterfalls of **Kakadu National Park**. You can tour the park in your own vehicle (four-wheel drive only), but the track is very rough and a good command of off-road driving skills is essential. The spectacular permanent waterfall of **Twin Falls** lies deep within a steep gorge, accessible only by swimming or paddling a raft upstream from the lower reaches of the creek (the freshwater crocodiles prolific in these waters are, supposedly, harmless).The narrow stream finally widens into a large pool, fringed by white, sandy beaches and pockets of monsoon forest, palms and ferns.

Saltwater crocodiles can be seen on the floodplains of Kakadu's **Yellow Water Billabong**, on the Upper South Alligator River, an area renowned for the richness and variety of its wildlife. The cool, clear, still waters of the lagoon may tempt you to dive in for a quick and refreshing swim, but once you have seen your first "salty" at close quarters, and taken note of its huge, powerful jaws, strong teeth and hungry grin, your enthusiasm will quickly disappear. Water birds here include the majestic and graceful jabiru, after which Kakadu's main town is named. Take the sunrise or sunset cruises to see the bird life at its most plentiful, and to avoid the hot midday sun.

QUEENSLAND
The **Great Barrier Reef** has been described as one of the seven wonders of the natural world, a claim endorsed enthusiastically by anyone who has visited it. This diverse ecosystem has the largest collection of coral in the world (500 species in all), and living off the coral are 2,000 fish species of every shape and color imaginable. The water is warm, averaging about 18°C (64°F), an ideal temperature for the maintenance of this natural wonderland and perfect for visitors who want to explore the reef either using scuba gear or snorkels. The waters around the reef are clear, with visibility on the order of 50 m (164 ft) not uncommon.

It is difficult to comprehend the size of the Great Barrier Reef, which stretches over 2,000 km (1,200 miles), covers an area of 350,000 sq km (130,000 sq miles), and is visible from space. The composition of the reef varies over its length, and in fact it is not one structure but a series of 2,900 individual reefs.

Port Douglas, in far north Queensland, is one of the closest towns to the reef. Quicksilver Connections ((07) 4099 5500 has two vessels that leave daily for Agincourt Reef, the only ribbon reef accessible for day-trips. Snorkeling gear and life jackets are supplied. The company also organizes dives, which vary according to your experience. Those who don't want to get wet can view the coral from a glass-sided submarine.

The **Daintree Rainforest**, part of Queensland's Wet Tropics World Heritage Area, contains one of the oldest surviving tracts of rainforest anywhere on earth, with spectacular waterfalls cascading off steep escarpments. The rainforest is populated by colorful butterflies and tropical birds — along with snakes and crocodiles. The lowland rainforest can be explored along the lower reaches of Mossman Gorge, 15 km (10 miles) from Port Douglas, however you'll need to rent a four-wheel-drive vehicle or take an organized tour.

Sporting Spree

Australia is one of the world's most sports-crazy societies. The warm, sunny climate draws Australians out-of-doors whenever possible, and there's always plenty of space to spin a Frisbee, have a hit of cricket, or start up an impromptu football match.

Introduced in 1912 by Hawaiian legend Duke Kahanamoku, **surfing** is a way of life for many Australians, and Australia has some of the best surf beaches in the world. Victoria's Bells Beach, off the Great Ocean Road, is the world's only Surfing Recreation Reserve, and hosts the International Bells Beach Surf Classic at Easter. Experienced surfers who want the thrill of the big wave should try the area around Port Campbell in Victoria, justifiably nick-named the Awesome Coast. The best swells are from February to May. Other top surf beaches are at Noosa Heads in Queensland, Byron Bay in New South Wales and Margaret River in Western Australia — where the Margaret River Masters event draws crowds in March.

TOP: Cooling off in Litchfield National Park in the Northern Territory. BOTTOM: Beach volleyball championships at the St. Kilda Festival, Melbourne.

From September to the end of May, Australian Surfing Adventures TOLL-FREE (1800) 113 044 WEB SITE www.surfadventures .com.au operates a surfing trip (for novices and more experienced surfers) to breaks along New South Wales' north coast. The five-day trip departs from Circular Quay, Sydney, every Monday and Tuesday and costs $440, including accommodation at beachside bunk-houses, board rental, wetsuits, lessons and all meals. Surfaris TOLL-FREE (1800) 007 873 WEB SITE www.surfaris.com has a similar package, with accommodation in beachside tents (with mattresses). Theirs leaves Sydney's Central Station every Monday morning, and costs $395. For more information about surfing in Australia contact the Surf Life Saving Association ((02) 9597 5588.

Yachting enthusiasts won't want to miss the annual Sydney-to-Hobart race, which takes place between Christmas and New Year. In addition, most seaside towns and resorts have yacht clubs, and it is usually possible to find someone looking for crew members for the day. For more information contact the Australian Yachting Federation ((02) 9922 4333.

It is usually easy to rent **sail boards**, **jet skis** or **power boats** at beach resorts. There are special sections of beach for these activities, and the rental company should be able to fill you in on local rules. Tour operators at the more popular beaches offer **water-skiing** or **parasailing**.

Luxurious reefs, rich sea life and a fair share of wrecks make Australian off-shore areas ideal for **scuba diving**. The Exmouth Diving Centre ((08) 9949 1201 organizes dives at Ningaloo Reef off the Western Australian coast between April and June that offer a close look at whale sharks, 12-m (36-ft) gentle giants of the sea. The greatest underwater sex show in the world occurs at the Great Barrier Reef in November when the coral spawn *en masse* in an explosion of color. Tusa Dive ((07) 4031 1248 runs night dives out of Cairns. Good dive sites in this area are listed in Neville Coleman's book *Dive Sites of the Great Barrier Reef*.

Cycling is another popular sport in Australia and combined with rail travel makes an interesting way to see the country. Bikes can be rented in all capital cities and many tourist destinations. Most capital cities are reasonably flat, except for Sydney which presents cyclists with numerous challenging hills. Canberra provides the most extensive cycle tracks of any major city, with a network that covers 130 km (81 miles). A popular ride is around Lake Burley Griffin, which takes about two hours.

Favorite routes outside the major cities, selected for their lack of hills and good sightseeing, include the wine-producing areas of Rutherglen (Victoria), Barossa Valley (South Australia), and Hunter Valley (New South Wales). Near Canberra, Thredbo is a Mecca for Australian mountain bikers. The Crackenback and Snowgums chairlifts, open to bikers from the beginning of November to mid-May, give riders an indulgent ascent before a mostly downhill ride through some of Australia's best alpine country. Note that it is compulsory to wear an approved helmet when cycling in Australia.

Golf courses are plentiful in Australia, where there is no lack of open space and outdoor beauty. Paradise Palms Golf Course ((07) 4059 1166 near Cairns challenges players of all standards with an intricate network of pebbly creeks, a vast array of grass bunkers and hollows and a total of 90 sand traps. In New South Wales, the Ocean Shores Country Club ((02) 6680 1008, Orana, 20 km (12.5 miles) north of Byron Bay, has a par-72 course with immaculately maintained greens and an ocean backdrop. Victoria's Cape Schanck Golf Course ((03) 5950 8100 also offers awe-inspiring views with rocky cliffs overlooking the foaming ocean waves below.

Victoria's high county cattlemen are renowned for their horsemanship, and a number of **horseback riding** tours are organized in the area. Out of Mansfield, Stoney's Bluff & Beyond Trail Rides ((03) 5775 2212 offers day and overnight rides in the Howqua Valley and through the Bogong and Dargo High Plains. Join the cattle muster for something different. Spring and autumn are the main **horse racing** seasons in Australia. In the capital cities racing events fill the calendar most weekends and sometimes during the week. The Australian obsession with horse

racing reaches a peak with the Melbourne Cup at Flemington on the first Tuesday of November — the entire nation stops for three minutes as the horses race for the coveted cup. You don't have to be a horse-racing fanatic to enjoy the Melbourne Cup; many people spend most of the day in the car park drinking champagne and enjoying themselves. Some don't even get to the race track.

Rock climbing and **abseiling** off the plateau or cliffs of the Blue Mountains provide both an adrenaline rush and spectacular views of the plain below. The Australian School of Mountaineering ((02) 4782 2014, in Katoomba, runs tours for both beginners and the more experienced. Transport, food, and specialist clothing and equipment are provided. For experienced rock climbers challenging cliff faces can be found in the Grampian Mountains (Victoria), Moonarie in the Flinders Ranges (South Australia), Bobs Hollow near Margaret River (Western Australia), and Frog Buttress (Queensland). Nowra in New South Wales has the best crags in Australia, some of which were not conquered until 1989.

The best places for **whitewater rafting** are in the Tasmanian highlands, with Franklin River offering an exciting ride through some truly magnificent scenery. In New South Wales, the fast-flowing Snowy and Mitta Mitta rivers in the higher regions of the Great Dividing Range provide for hair-raising whitewater rafting. Peregrine Adventures ((03) 9663 8611 runs rafting expeditions on all these rivers. Another excellent rafting location is the Tully River in northern Queensland.

OPPOSITE: Casting a line at Venus Bay, on South Australia's Eyre Peninsula. ABOVE: A hang-glider soars above the coastal rainforest near Port Douglas in northern Queensland.

Deep-sea fishing for prize fighting fish such as marlin, mackerel, barracuda and sailfish is available along the eastern coast. The Great Barrier Reef is one of the more popular destination; organized fishing trips out of Cairns seek giant black marlin. No fishing license is required, provided your catch is for your own consumption.

There are some world-class spots for **freshwater fishing** in Australia. In central Tasmania, the Land of Three Thousand Lakes is stocked with wild brown trout, and around Darwin, barramundi run from June to November. Fishing licenses may be required; ask at the local angler's shop or contact the State Fisheries Department.

Not many people would associate Australia with **skiing**, but New South Wales and Victoria's ski slopes are open from the Queen's Birthday long weekend in early June until

October. There are some reasonable downhill runs, and the cross-country ski touring is world-class.

Australia has produced more than its fair share of **tennis** greats, and the temperate climate means you can have a game all through the year. The Australian Open Tennis Championship, one of the four Grand Slam events (along with the United States' Open, the French Open, and Wimbledon), is played in Melbourne over two weeks in January. Day-passes for the earlier matches can be purchased at the venue; these are relatively inexpensive and allow access to all games except those on center court. For the finals, you need to book in advance ((03) 9286 1234.

Motor racing enjoys a high profile in Australia. The Grand Prix is raced around Melbourne's Albert Park Lake in March; early reservations are essential ((03) 9258 7100.

where fanaticism is at its height and state pride is at stake, are held in May and June. **Soccer** is the fourth football code played in Australia, and is gaining in popularity. It is played mainly in Melbourne, Sydney and Adelaide.

In summer **cricket** takes over from the football. One-day games provide excitement for the novice, but for the connoisseur there is no substitute for a five-day test match, particularly if England is in town for an Ashes series.

The Open Road

Driving in Australia often entails long distances, but fortunately most regions have excellent roads. Adventurous drivers who long to get off the beaten track need a four-wheel-drive vehicle, and in the outback vast distances between towns make it essential to take adequate provisions, particularly drinking water.

Gregory's and UBD produce a series of excellent fold-out road maps of all capital cities and popular tourist regions. For touring, a better option is Robinson's *Road Atlas of Australia*. If you're planning any off-the-road, four-wheel-drive touring, consult the two-volume Gregory's *4WD Escapes*, which provides detailed maps of treks and GPS readings on all major routes across Australia. Driving the Australian outback presents its own unique hazards (see GETTING AROUND, page 320 in TRAVELERS' TIPS).

Short trips out of the capital cities are possible, but the truly great routes can take days to complete and cover 1000 km (over 600 miles) or more.

The **Nullarbor Plain** offers a memorable driving experience, albeit a test of endurance. The plain runs along the Great Australian Bight, between Ceduna in South Australia and the mining town of Norseman in Western Australia. It covers 200,000 sq km (77,400 sq miles), an area similar to that of the British Isles. The name Nullarbor, from the Latin "no trees," aptly describes this arid limestone plain where nothing but low-lying bushes grow. The road, however, is south of the true plain, so you will see trees on the route. Further north a railway line runs through the center of the plain in a dead straight line. If you are excited by featureless

The race coincides with the city's Moomba festival, and there are sporting events and entertainment for those looking for a break from mainlining on exhaust fumes. In late September, the Bathurst 1000 Road Races (held 221 km/137 miles west of Sydney) feature production cars and motorbike racing. The 500cc Motorcycle Grand Prix takes place on Phillip Island in late October.

As winter approaches men, women and children across the country don scarves and woolen caps, grab flags in club colors and make a pilgrimage to the local oval to watch **Australian Rules Football**, referred to simply as "footy." This unique code of football was born in the inner suburbs of Melbourne and spread to all other states. It is a fast-running game in which large men launch themselves high above the pack to pluck the ball out of the air, or kick it over 60 m (180 ft) with ease. Combatants also engage in bone-crushing physical encounters, all without padding (take note, gridiron fans). League games are played in most capital cities. The ultimate experience is to watch an Australian Football League Grand Final in late September, when over 100,000 fans cram into the Melbourne Cricket Ground (MCG). Tickets are almost impossible to get, although some travel agents may be able to secure them for you if you make your request early enough.

Rugby union and **league** are also played in Australia, mainly in New South Wales and Queensland. State of Origin test matches,

OPPOSITE: Staying fit, Sydney style, against the ivory sails of the Sydney Opera House. ABOVE: A quiet back road in rural Victoria.

expanses of flat terrain, then a 1,300-km (800-mile) drive along the Eyre Highway through parts of the Nullarbor Plain should be on your agenda. Crossing the Nullarbor is the most direct land route from Adelaide to Perth.

On the route, subterranean rivers running into large lakes have carved cathedral-like caves out of limestone. The Nullarbor is a treasure trove for archaeologists, and the earliest human footprints, 5,500 years old, have been discovered there. A well-preserved 4,600-year-old specimen of the now-extinct Tasmanian tiger was discovered in a cave called Thylacine Hole, and is on show at the Western Australian Museum in Perth. And since the Eyre Highway is never far from the Great Australian Bight, sightings of southern right whales add interest to the crossing. The whales come to this area to breed, and 20-m (60-ft) whales and their calves can be seen off the coast between June and October. The lookouts are off the highway on Aboriginal land and permits, costing $2 per person, can be obtained from Yalata Roadhouse ((08) 8625 6807 or 8625 6986 and the Nullarbor Hotel-Motel Inn ((08) 8625 6271.

If you want to get off the main road, then look no further than Queensland's **Fraser Island**. The largest sand island in the world, it's 120 km (75 miles) long and 50 km (30 miles) wide. There are no paved roads on the island, but the beach provides a driving track like no other. Buses and four-wheel-drive wagons

whip along its hardened sand. Colored sand cliffs are backed by the largely unspoiled rainforest that covers the hinterland. The beach is an official road, and although it may not have a white line painted down the middle, all the usual road rules apply.

A car ferry runs from the mainland at Hervey Bay. A four-wheel-drive vehicle is essential. You can rent one from Island Explorers 4WD Hire ((07) 41254 3770, in Hervey Bay. If you wish to camp on the island, Fraser Island Backpacking Safaris ((07) 4125 3933 organizes very popular trips and supplies both vehicle and camping gear. There are over 40 freshwater lakes on Fraser Island, formed in depressions in the sand dunes and home to thousands of water birds. A large community of dingoes, native Australian dogs, roam Fraser Island's beach. While generally harmless, they have become persistent in begging for food, spoiled by generations of tourists.

Most people who visit **Alice Springs** focus their attention on traveling an additional 400 km (250 miles) to Uluru (Ayers Rock). However, there is an interesting drive into the western MacDonnell Ranges much closer to Alice. The scenery is as spectacular, with a series of deep gorges cutting through the hills. Take Scenic Drive west out of Alice Springs into the West MacDonnell National Park. You are likely to spot plenty of rock wallabies in the forests of stately ghost gums. A turn-off goes to Standley Chasm, which is best seen at midday when its walls flame red. Back to the main road, the right fork runs along Namatjira Drive for 82 km (50 miles) to the Ormiston Gorge turn-off. The road curves round to the south to join Larapinta Drive. At Hermannsburg Mission there is a turn-off to Palm Valley, an oasis of ancient cycads that are part of the Finke Gorge National Park. The gorge can only be explored by foot, and after rain a series of rock pools form along its length. Return to Larapinta Drive for the trip back to Alice Springs.

The **Great Ocean Road** hugs Victoria's western coastline, overlooking sheer cliffs and offering breathtaking coastal scenery. It plunges down to empty bays and slow flowing streams, and passes through delightful tiny seaside resort towns. Occasionally the road takes a turn inland, passing through virtually untouched remnants of dense rainforest (see DRIVE VICTORIA'S SURF COAST, page 18 in TOP SPOTS). This section of coast is called the Shipwreck Coast, as over 30 ships foundered here in the nineteenth and early twentieth centuries. Some can still be seen today between Warrnambool and Port Fairy.

Backpacking

With a little preplanning and organization Australia can be a backpacker's paradise. Countless enterprises have realized the enormous business potential of catering to backpackers, resulting in an explosion of inexpensive options in all capital cities and favorite tourist destinations. A number of free newspapers and magazines are produced for backpackers. *TNT Magazine* is a small quarterly booklet packed with lots of useful information, while the *Aussie Backpacker*, a bimonthly newspaper, has information on tours, special deals, travel information and accommodation; its classified pages contain job advertisements for casual work. Both publications are readily available in hostels and bus terminals.

Backpackers World outlets can be found in Sydney ((02) 9380 2700, 212 Victoria Street, Kings Cross; in Byron Bay ((02) 6685 8858, Byron Street; in Melbourne ((03) 9329 1990, 167 Franklin Street; and in Cairns ((07) 4041 0999, 12 Shields Street. They offer an enormous range of budget tours throughout Australia, from treks across Cradle Mountain in Tasmania and safaris in Central Australia or Kakadu to dive courses on the Great Barrier Reef and

cruises in Queensland's Whitsundays. This a good place to find low-priced bus or flight packages. Another source of information is the **Backpacker Travel Centre** in Sydney ((02) 9231 3699, Pitt Street Level, Imperial Arcade; Melbourne ((03) 9654 8477 Shop 19, Centre Place, 258 Flinders Lane; and Brisbane ((07) 3221 2225, Brisbane Arcade, Queen Street Mall.

The most extensive hostel network is offered by **Youth Hostels of Australia (YHA)** WEB SITE www.yha.org.au, where beds usually cost $10 to $24 per night. There's a small annual membership fee. Information and reservations are available through YHA offices in every capital city, or from the larger hostels in the network. The standard at YHA hostels is consistently good. If you intend to use YHA extensively then it is worth getting one of their accommodation packages: 20 nights for $250, valid for six months, or 10 nights for $130, valid for two months. There are also cut-price tickets to the movies, bike rental and some excellent tours arranged out of YHA hostels.

OPPOSITE: Shopping for a didjeridu at the Eumundi Village Market in Queensland. ABOVE: Cruising the Whitsunday Passage in comfort after a day snorkeling the reef.

Main cities have private backpacker hostels, which charge between $12 and $25 a night, depending on the location and the level of competition. A number of independent hostels have banded together to form the **VIP Backpackers Association** ((07) 3268 5733 WEB SITE www.backpackers.com.au. A membership fee of $25 includes discount cards for $1 per night off accommodation. Another popular backpacker organization is **Nomads** TOLL-FREE (1800) 819 883, WEB SITE www.nomadsworld.com/oz, which provides a hostel discount card (Nomads Adventure Card) to members. Most of their hostels offer a choice of dorms, singles or doubles, and provide a range of services and tours for guests, including Internet facilities. Linen is provided, and airport and train transfers are often included. For more on Australia's youth hostel associations, see under ACCOMMODATION, page 327 in TRAVELERS' TIPS.

In cities, rooms can be rented in student households for about $60 to $100 a week. Advertisements are usually posted on university notice boards and in bookshops and cafés frequented by students.

In the countryside, **campsites** are the cheapest option, but many also have on-site caravans and cabins at very reasonable prices. These places fill up quickly during summer, Easter and school vacations, so book ahead. For groups of three or more travelers, **renting an apartment** can be cheaper than staying in a hostel, particularly during the off season. Along the Queensland coast I've found two-bedroom apartments with fully-equipped kitchens and a private swimming pool for as little as $50 a night. Local tourist information services usually have details on available apartments. State-wide accommodation guides are easy to come by in most tourist areas.

coach companies, Greyhound Pioneer and McCafferty's, offer special tourist passes, which allow unlimited travel for a fixed number of days. There are also smaller regional operators that offer good deals on limited routes. Information for these is usually posted on bulletin boards of backpacker lodgings and hostels.

For long stays in Australia, **purchasing a car** can be an economical option; a reasonable second-hand car costs $2,000 to $5,000. Private sales are advertised in Saturday newspapers. It helps to know something about cars to avoid buying a lemon, but in any case ensure that a Roadworthy Certificate is provided.

If you've come to Australia for a working vacation, it is essential that you have a working visa before seeking employment (see ARRIVING AND LEAVING, page 318 in TRAVELERS' TIPS). Casual work is fairly easy to find in major cities, and on farms and orchards during the picking seasons. Popular locations include Mildura, Bundaberg, Kununurra, and the grape-growing areas of South Australia and Victoria.

Living It Up

Exceptional hotels and restaurants can be found in many parts of Australia, although few can compete with the absolute luxury of Queensland's tropical island and coastal resorts along the Great Barrier Reef.

Fringed by powder-white beaches, **Hayman Island** is one of the most beautiful of the Whitsunday Islands. Guests choose between a French provincial suite, Italian palazzo, Japanese suite, a Grecian villa or a contemporary Southern Californian scheme — all overlooking tropical gardens. Lagoon-style swimming pools are delicately lit at night, and palm-shaded beaches lead down to crystal-clear waters where snorkelers are treated to shoals of iridescent fish. Beautiful paths run through tropical gardens. Hayman Island Resort has six exceptional restaurants, or guests can order a gourmet picnic hamper complete with a chilled bottle of champagne. Activities include sailing, scuba-diving and water-skiing, and sailing to nearby reefs and other islands. Saunas, massages and beauty treatments are available in the extensive Jacuzzi. Hayman is just one of a number of excellent resorts in the Whitsundays, all of which have a slightly different feel and focus.

If you don't mind getting your hands dirty, then try "WWOOFing." The **Willing Workers on Organic Farms (WWOOF)** program gives travelers interested in environmentally sensitive agricultural practices an opportunity to work on an organic farm. Travelers get free board in exchange for a few hours work a day. To join, contact ((03) 5155 0218 E-MAIL wwoof @wwoof.com.au WEB SITE www.wwoof.com.au, Mount Murrindal Coop, Buchan, Victoria 3885. Membership costs $45 for individuals and $50 for a couple.

For long trips, **buses** are the cheapest means of transportation, and it is possible to travel from, say, Sydney to Darwin — a distance of 4,060 km (2,540 miles) — for about $300. The cost of plying the more popular routes, such as Melbourne–Sydney, is significantly cheaper because of the amount of competition, and fares can be as low as $30. The two largest

Just a section of the gargantuan lagoon swimming pool at Port Douglas' luxurious Sheraton Mirage Resort in Tropical North Queensland.

Bedarra Island in Tropical North Queensland is the most exclusive of the island resorts. The emphasis here is on luxury, relaxation, exquisite dining and the sense that you have the island to yourself. Guests are limited to 15 at any one time, and children under 15 are not permitted. The priveleged few stay in secluded serviced villas, all with private balconies, hammocks, slate bathrooms, and aromatherapy burners. Motor-powered dinghies are provided to explore the many deserted beaches, with delicious gourmet picnic hampers included. Daily activities include catamaran sailing, private game fishing, yacht charters, and walks through the island's rainforest. The cabana-style central bar remains open day and night — guests just help themselves.

Port Douglas, north of Cairns, boasts the most luxurious resorts on mainland Australia. These include the **Sheraton Mirage Resort** — where Bill Clinton chose to unwind after winning a second term in 1996 — set in 120 ha (300 acres) of tropical gardens, with a massive saltwater lagoon. Another is the **Radisson Treetops Resort**, whose miniature waterfall, cascades into rock pools surrounded by a serene garden with a restaurant on stilts among the tree tops. Nearby is the Daintree Rainforest, where the rooms of the **Silky Oaks Lodge**, located in its midst, blend into the lush greenery.

For those wanting to visit Australia's Great Barrier Reef and isolated tropical islands in absolute luxury without having to unpack and repack their luggage, **Captain Cook Cruises** offers three-, four- or seven-day voyages on the

Reef Endeavour. The cruise includes snorkeling or scuba-diving adventures and sorties into the rainforest of the Cape York Peninsula. The ship is fitted with swimming pools, Jacuzzis and saunas, and a smaller glass-bottomed boat provides a dry introduction to the reef. In May the *Endeavour* undertakes a seven-day golf cruise along Queensland's coast.

EXCEPTIONAL RESTAURANTS

A high level of competition among Australia's chefs — especially in Melbourne, Sydney, Canberra and Brisbane — has resulted in an inordinate number of world-standard restaurants. Although not cheap, prices at these cities' best restaurants are very often far lower than at restaurants of a similar standard in European and American capitals.

Sydney's most refined dining experience is the set-menu-only extravaganza offered by **Tetsuya's** ((02) 9555 1017. Lunchtime diners choose between an eight-course or a 13-course meal; at night it's the 13-course option only. Don't panic though, courses are small and the menu perfectly balanced. Tetsuya Wakuda has created a French–Japanese–Australian cuisine that he pairs with fine Australian wines. His signature dish is a shimmering confit of Tasmanian ocean trout with marinated celery, seaweed and trout roe.

The most romantic restaurant in Sydney though, with unerringly prepared French classics and an unparalleled ocean view, is a 45-minute drive from town. In fact, the restaurant provides the perfect excuse to stay the night at **Jonah's** ((02) 9974 5599, 69 Bynya Road, Palm Beach. To really live it up, **Sydney Harbour Seaplanes** TOLL-FREE (1800) 803 558 has package sightseeing-and-lunch flights to Jonah's for around $200 per person, including lunch and wine.

Chefs to watch out for in Melbourne include **Jacques Reymond** ((03) 9521 1552, whose restaurant of the same name provides perhaps Australia's most formal dining experience. For a true gastronomical fix, **Let's Eat** ((03) 9520 3287 merges high-quality market and delicatessen shopping with a simple but excellent restaurant. Diners can discuss their meals with the chef and create pretty well whatever they feel like from the enormous range of fresh ingredients sold in the store; and once you've ordered, you're give a pager so that you can continue shopping until the meal is ready.

Chris's Beacon Point Restaurant ((03) 5237 6411 is a gem of a restaurant deftly producing mediterranean-style dishes with a decided French-Greek slant. Chris Talihmanidis makes the most of Apollo Bay's excellent fish and local produce in a balanced menu that changes daily.

Family Fun

AUSTRALIAN ANIMALS

What child wouldn't like to cuddle a koala or pat a kangaroo? Every state has at least one major wildlife park, and it is becoming

increasingly popular to allow visitors to come in personal contact with Australian native animals. Only 65 km (41 miles) northeast of Melbourne, **Healesville Sanctuary** is one of Australia's best native animal parks. Opened in 1934, the sanctuary is home to more than 200 species of native birds, mammals and reptiles, displayed in a natural bush setting. A path weaves through the park taking visitors through large habitat areas where colorful birds swoop overhead, kangaroos and emus stroll among the visitors, while dingoes howl and birds of prey display their hunting skills. This is a true sanctuary, and contact with the animals isn't encouraged. Wardens do walk friendly dingoes around the park on leashes and there are different activities throughout the day — from feeding the koalas to meeting a baby wombat. Healesville has Australia's best platypus display.

Waratah Park, just north of Sydney, was made internationally famous by the *Skippy the Bush Kangaroo* television series. There are plenty of gentle Skippies to play with here as well as koalas to cuddle, along with not-so-cuddly Tasmanian devils, friendly dingoes, jaw-snapping crocodiles and a variety of colorful Australian birds.

OPPOSITE: Sunset over Apollo Bay mimics the soft hues of the rose garden at Chris's Beacon Point Restaurant in Victoria. LEFT: A mob of kangaroos graze at dusk in Ben Boyd National Park, New South Wales. ABOVE: Australia's native dog, the dingo.

While petting and cuddling animals is a memorable experience, seeing them in the wild is another thing altogether, and not be missed. **Kangaroo Island** off the coast of South Australia is one huge nature reserve. Every evening little penguins waddle up the beaches at several locations. Further inland, koalas hide in gum trees. Elsewhere, adult Australian fur seals bask in the sun, while pups chase seagulls (see WALK WITH THE ANIMALS, page 17 in TOP SPOTS).

Australia has some of the best aquariums in the world. At **Oceanworld Manly**, a fun 30-minute ferry ride from Circular Quay in Sydney, children can walk through a clear plastic tunnel to view, among other fish, stingrays, gray nurse sharks up to three and a half meters (10 ft) long, and a giant cuttlefish with three hearts and green blood! The more adventurous parents and kids over 12 can scuba-dive with the sharks, an activity which is (fortunately) held after feeding time. More popular with smaller children is the seal area, where Australian and New Zealand fur seals can be seen at play. Children can handle a number of harmless sea creatures in touch pools. Other top-notch aquariums are the **Melbourne Aquarium**, the **Sydney Aquarium** and **Great Barrier Reef Wonderland** in Townsville.

If ever the opportunity arises to secretly observe a "mob" of wild kangaroos in Australia, you are guaranteed an unforgettable memory. Kangaroos are absolutely harmless, unless you get between a mother and her joey (a baby kangaroo), or try to approach a buck. Stay a few feet back and these gentle marsupials won't mind the company at all. Ask a local where a mob is likely to graze; go out just before dusk and wait quietly in some tall grass. Soon enough you'll hear the rumbling thunder of them hopping together, then sudden stillness as they stop to graze, standing proud and larger than life.

THEME PARKS

Queensland's Gold Coast, with its numerous theme and amusement parks alongside long stretches of safe swimming beaches, is the popular choice with most kids. At **Dreamworld**, the rides are guaranteed to elicit delighted screams from children. Kids can enter the world of the Eureka gold rushes, and take a cruise on Captain Sturt's paddle-steamer. At nearby **Sea World**, in Surfers Paradise, dolphins and whales perform and sea lions lounge around on rocks. There are also numerous rides here, all with a nautical theme. **Warner Bros. Movie World**, 20 miles north of Surfers Paradise, produced special effects for films such as *Mission Impossible*, *Twenty Thousand Leagues under the Sea* and

Flipper. Children can see how stunt men ply their trade and unravel the mysteries of special effects. Rides range from pleasant to terrifying. For the smaller children, Tweety Pie, Bugs Bunny, and a host of other Warner Brothers cartoon characters wander the streets. Across the road, **Wet 'n' Wild Water World** is a paradise for kids who like getting wet, and for families wanting to cool off in the Queensland heat. There are water slides and pools of all varieties, including a film pool, where you can watch kid-friendly movies from the comfort of a floating air mattress.

Fox Studios Backlot brings the theme park to central Sydney, with every element of the film-making process explored and explained — from sound effects to stunts and sets.

SCENIC TRAIN RIDE

Puffing Billy is a lovingly restored steam train that is made for children. It winds around the hills of the Dandenong Ranges, just outside Melbourne. The view from the windows is quite pretty, but the real hit is that children are allowed to sit on the carriage window sills, dangling their feet outside the train. Puffing Billy starts its journey at Belgrave and passes through fern groves and spectacular mountain ash forests before arriving at Emerald Lake — a popular picnic spot, with gas barbecues and picnic tables.

MUSEUMS

All of Australia's capital cities have good museums, with educational and interactive displays for children. The country's newest and largest museum, the **Melbourne Museum** is a stimulating experience with a heavy slant towards the natural environment and new technology. Challenging and exciting interactive experiences include the "Immersion Reality Theater," a "Living Forest Gallery," and a special exhibition for three- to eight-year olds, the "Children's Museum Big Box." **Powerhouse**, on the edge of the central Sydney area, is a large hangar-like building full of video special effects and computer games to surprise and enthrall even the most jaded kid. **Scienceworks** in Spotswood, an inner suburb of Melbourne, has loads of hands-on science and technology displays. In Canberra, **Questacon**, the National Science and Technology Centre's museum, is an interactive science center with cutting-edge exhibitions. Children can play music with light beams or control a computer with their thoughts.

TOP: Enjoying an old-time drive at Fox Studios Backlot in Sydney. BOTTOM: Children experience the thrill of a downriver ride in an inflatable raft.

Cultural Kicks

ABORIGINAL ART

Paintings by modern Australian Aborigines belong to a tradition over 40,000 years old, making it the oldest living art tradition in the world. Primarily social and religious in nature, Aboriginal art often tells of the Dreamtime, when creation ancestors traveled across the land, creating the seasons, forming the land and clashing with other creatures. It is used to explain the laws that govern ceremonies and the day-to-day life of family groups. It records happenings such as the killing of an animal for food, the passing of a family group, and in more recent times the arrival of white man. Rock art is part of a spectacular array of art forms that include ground sculpture, body painting, wood carving and bark painting, not to mention rich oral traditions and elaborate songs and dance styles.

Like their ancestors, modern artists combine traditional motifs and Dreamtime stories with day-to-day life issues, including dispossession, racism and cultural identity. Work by modern artists is displayed in galleries throughout the country.

To visit traditional art sites requires a little more effort. Kundjehmi cave paintings at Nourlangie Rock in **Kakadu National Park** depict Namarrgon, the Lightning Man, and six-fingered Namandi spirits. Ubirr (Obiri) Rock, in the East Alligator River floodplains at the northern end of Kakadu, has Aboriginal rock paintings dating back at least 20,000 years, with several smaller sites nearby. X-ray style paintings in red and yellow ocher show wallabies, turtles, goannas, snakes and great shoals of barramundi. Ancient carvings of

animal tracks, snakes, and spirals at **Ewaninga Rock Carvings**, 35 km (22 miles) south of Alice Springs, include a depiction of unusual creature with a fern-like tail. Two gorges within **N'Dhala Gorge Nature Park**, 92 km (57 miles) east of Alice Springs, are decorated with nearly 6,000 rock carvings.

Enormous **Quinkan Reserve**, 314 km (195 miles) north of Cairns, is perhaps the most abundant Aboriginal art site in Australia. It's named after the elongated spirit figures that predominate in the paintings. The thousand or so art sites contain many other colorful depictions of spirit beings, local wildlife, humans, and contact paintings including a six-meter-long (20-ft) horse. Aboriginal stencil art at **Carnarvon Gorge National Park**, in the heart of Queensland, dates back 18,000 years. There are stencil frescoes up to 137 m (449 ft) long, and an enormous painting of the sacred Rainbow Serpent. Cathedral Cave, the Amphitheater and the Art Gallery feature images of emu and kangaroo feet, boomerangs, and human hands and feet.

In Western Australia, many of the **Kimberley's** caves hide Aboriginal rock art dating back thousands of years. There are literally thousands of Aboriginal art sites here, representing a multitude of different forms, styles and periods. Very few of them have ever been seen by white people. Bradshaw figures are delicate and decorated with elaborate headgear. These figures carry tools, dilly bags and weapons thought to date back from 4,000 to 35,000 years. Wandjinas are a more modern tradition — going back only 2,000 or 3,000 years. Wandjinas represent powerful spirits that control the elements, particularly water, storms and lightning. They are often depicted as large-headed, haloed human-like figures, with eyes and nose, but no mouth. According to local belief, to show the mouth would bring excessive and persistent rain.

Within **Royal National Park**, 36 km (22 miles) south of Sydney, are Dharawal rock engravings up to 7,000 years old. Rock engravings at Jibbon Beach, near the park's northern tip, show dolphins, whales and kangaroos and a six-fingered male figure. Rock engravings in dramatic **Ku-ring-gai Chase National Park**, 24 km (15 miles) north of Sydney, depict spirit entities, human figures and animals including fish and whales — some eight meters (26 ft) long.

South Australia's **Flinders Ranges** shelter 100 recorded Aboriginal sacred sites, many with superb rock art. Among the best are Arkaroo Rock, Sacred Canyon, Yourambulla Cave and Chambers Gorge.

Gariwerd, or Grampians National Park, in Victoria has art sites decorated with motifs styled in clay, ocher and charcoals. Ngamadjidj, or "Cave of Ghosts," features figures painted in white clay, while the "Cave of Hands" fresco in Gulgurn Manja is made of hundreds of stenciled hand prints of Koori children.

NON-ABORIGINAL AUSTRALIAN ARTISTS

Australia's non-Aboriginal artists have also managed to create works that are uniquely Australian. Works are touched by the open and exuberant youthful spirit of modern Australia and the exceptionally clear light and vivid colors of the Australian bush and wilderness areas. Well-known artists are represented in Australia's major galleries — the three biggest are the **National Gallery of Australia** in Canberra, Melbourne's **National**

Gallery of Victoria, and the **Art Gallery of New South Wales** in Sydney. These artists include Sidney Nolan (1917–1992), whose series of expressionist portraits of bushranger (outlaw) Ned Kelly and vivid images of the Australian outback have garnered considerable international success. Arthur Boyd's (1924–1999) works range from earlier more realistic landscapes through to later lyrical and colorful works. Like Boyd, Brett Whitely (1939–1992) traveled widely, producing intense and often sensuous works drawing on European, Japanese and Australian Aboriginal cultures. Fred Williams (1927–1982) produced large canvasses exemplifying the broad spaces and vivid colors of the Australian bush and outback.

Traditional rock art has inspired modern Aboriginal artists to produce highly stylized contemporary works.

PERFORMING ARTS

The renaissance in Australian drama began in small fringe theaters such as **La Mama** in Melbourne and the **Nimrod Theatre** in Sydney. It was in these places that the twang of the Australian accent was heard and robust slang used to wake up the audience to the richness of their language and confront them with contemporary problems of everyday Australian life. Some plays, like Jack Hibberd's *Stretch of the Imagination* and David Williamson's *The Removalist*, have become modern mainstream classics. La Mama is still going, and has been joined in Melbourne by the **Courthouse** and **Budinsky** theaters. Sydney's Nimrod has competition from the **New Theatre** and **Stables Theatre** where the latest plays, often premiers, are shown.

All state capitals have opera seasons, during which all the old favorite Italian, German and French operas are performed. There are also some Australian operas joining the repertoire, such as *Voss*, based on the novel by Nobel Prize winner Patrick White, *Summer of the Seventeenth Doll*, and an opera about the construction of the Sydney Opera House called *The Eighth Wonder*, which, naturally, premiered there. Dance and ballet troupes tour the country. The best are the Sydney Dance Company and the Australian Ballet Company.

To find out **current arts information**, visit WEB SITE www.stateart.com.au, which reviews the latest in opera, dance, music, theater, film and visual arts. **Citysearch**

WEB SITE www.citysearch.com has links to the individual city sites with useful information on the arts. State tourist information offices also publish **cultural guides**: the *Sydney Arts & Cultural Guide* is biannual, as is the *Victoria &Melbourne Cultural Guide*. Tourist information offices' web sites are another good source of information. The WEB SITE www.ticketek.com has an excellent booking service with info on upcoming events across the country.

Shop till You Drop

ABORIGINAL ARTS

A new generation of Aboriginal artists render traditional motifs and styles onto canvasses in a unique visual expression which is becoming highly prized among art lovers. Other works range from traditional bark paintings to more modern silks and screen prints using traditional earth pigments. You'll also find hand-decorated jewelry and beautiful wood carvings, often combining both traditional and contemporary styles. Painted boomerangs and coolamons (bowls) and didgeridoos (or didjeridus) are sold throughout Australia, with the decoration differing from one Aboriginal community to another.

Aboriginal communities often have stores selling arts and crafts. **Visual Arts and Specialist Tours (** (08) 8952 8233 E-MAIL pyvast @ozemail.com.au, PO Box 2432, Alice Springs NT 0871, runs personally designed buying

trips to many remote Aboriginal art centers accompanied by a specialist art advisor. Darwin, Alice Springs, Cairns, Sydney, Brisbane and Melbourne all have good stores selling high-quality works, many Aboriginal-owned. Tourist information offices in these cities can help find reputable retailers.

Sydney's **djamu Gallery** shop ℂ (02) 9320 6431, in the Customs House at Circular Quay, has a comprehensive range of books on Aboriginal art and culture, and stocks a selection of traditional and contemporary works. Another reliable vendor is nearby **Gannon House Gallery** ℂ (02) 9251 4474, 45 Argyle Street, The Rocks. In outer Melbourne, **Mia Mia Gallery** ℂ (03) 9846 4636, Westerfolds Park, Templestowe, is a café, a performance art space and a gallery. Contemporary and traditional works are displayed and sold. **Tjapukai Aboriginal Cultural Park** ℂ (07) 4042 9999 WEB SITE www.tjapukai.com.au, near Cairns, has an excellent art shop, selling high-quality art and decorated pieces at very reasonable prices.

CLOTHING
While most Australians live in cities, bush "clobber" has become very fashionable both in urban Australia and worldwide, particularly gear with the R.M. Williams label. An Akubra hat, traditionally made out of rabbit pelts, a Dri-az-a-bone waterproof jacket and stockman's boots will have you looking like an outback character, but may set you

back a cool $600 or more. Blundstone and Redback boots are hardy classics at more competitive prices.

Bush clothing is sold throughout Australia, with some good bargains in tourist areas where competition is high. Cairns and nearby Kuranda, and Noosa or Byron Bay further down the coast are all good places to find this generally high-quality, 100 % cotton clothing, along with hats and classically styled leather belts, jackets, shoes and boots. Most items are exceptionally long-wearing. Another good buy are broad-brimmed straw or cotton sun hats for both men and women.

MARKETS
Throughout Australia, in sizeable towns and cities, you'll find markets: farmers' markets, alternative-life markets, or established daily markets. Major cities have weekly art and craft markets. **Paddington Village Bazaar** is held every Saturday in Sydney at Eastside Parish Church, on the corner of Oxford and Newcombe streets. There you will find everything from bric-a-brac to antiques, books, handicraft and homemade food. In Melbourne, on the Esplanade overlooking the **St. Kilda** foreshore is a Sunday market which mainly sells art, crafts and handmade furniture.

OPPOSITE: Kuranda Market features local arts and crafts as well as bush clothing and crocodile- and kangaroo-leather goods. ABOVE: Aboriginal carvings and artworks are sold throughout Australia.

Australian paintings and jewelry can be bought here directly from the artists. Near Perth, the **Fremantle Market** on South Terrace, is held Friday to Sunday and sells all manner of goods and crafts. **Darwin's night market** reflects the laid-back nature of the town. Held every Thursday night, it is as much a social meeting place as a market, with food stalls set up along Mindil Beach. Try barbecued kebabs featuring emu and kangaroo meat, or famous Mindil Market croc-burgers.

At Sydney's **Fish Market** you can buy lunch and eat it on the docks outside. Left of the front entrance is an irresistible souvenir store — anything fishy goes, from big plastic lobsters and octopuses to handcrafted ceramic bowls and platters painted with denizens of the deep.

On Queensland's Sunshine Coast, the **Eumundi Village Market** draws thousands of people every Saturday morning, as the town's streets and parks are turned into a marketplace. Many of the foodstuffs and handicrafts for sale are produced locally. Beautifully crafted turned-wood bowls and jewelry boxes are made from rainforest timber. Handmade pottery, glassware and needlework are among the items on offer.

Another country market that has a strong following is the **Red Hill Market**, which is 80 km (50 miles) south of Melbourne. It is held the first Saturday of the month from October to May. The market circles a cricket oval — there's usually a game in progress. The market has a reputation for excellent locally produced foods, especially breads, pickles and sauces.

GEMS

The Argyle diamond mines are in the Kimberley region of northwestern Australia. Gems found here, particularly the "champagne" and "cognac" varieties, are much prized for their subtle colors and high quality. At the bottom of the Kimberley, in Broome, pearl diving is an important industry, while gold is mined at Kalgoorlie in the southwest. Local gems and gold jewelry can be bought in all of these areas, and in larger cities, particularly Perth. **Linney's Jewelers of Subiaco** ℂ (08) 9382 4077, in Perth's inner suburbs, sells select hand-crafted Western Australian pearls, diamonds and gold.

Australia supplies 95% of the world's commercial opal, most of it from the 70 opal fields around Coober Pedy in the outback of South Australia. The opal is Australia's official gemstone, and opal jewelry can be bought in most places. To get the best quality stones it is wise to shop in established jewelry shops rather than in souvenir or tourist shops.

Not surprisingly, Coober Pedy's shops have more opals on display than anywhere else in the world.

Opals are composed of silica and water. Ninety percent of all opals, called "potch," are without fiery colors and are considered worthless. Colored opals, on the other hand, can fetch good prices. The most valuable is the black opal with its dark base. The almost transparent crystal opal displays colors ranging from fire-red — the rarest and therefore most prized — to the less preferred green and blue gems. Swirls of color in the opal are more valuable than pinfire opals, which have small specks of color.

Festive Flings

Australians look for any excuse for a party, and a multitude of festivals and special events are held throughout the year. They vary from festivals celebrating the cultural diversity of Australia to boat races along dry river beds. The following is sample of some of the innumerable festivals and sporting events held in Australia. For a full list of events in a particular region contact the respective state tourist bureau.

JANUARY
The **Sydney Festival** WEB SITE www.sydneyfestival .org.au takes over the city for three weeks in January, combining high-brow and low-brow.

Many outdoors activities take advantage of Sydney's great weather. The festival culminates on Australia Day with fireworks over the harbor.

Australia Day, January 26, commemorates the landing of the first British colonists in Sydney. Sydney's celebrations include a re-enactment of the First Fleet sailing into the harbor, a tall-ships race and a ferry race, and military aerial and parachutist displays. Australia's biggest music festival, the **Big Day Out** WEB SITE www.bigdayout.com is held in Sydney on Australia Day, moving around the country in the weeks that follow. **Survival Day** WEB SITE www.adc.nsw.gov.au /indig is an alternative celebration honoring the resilience of Aboriginal culture and identity. Initiated and coordinated by Sydney's Aboriginal community it is one of the biggest Aboriginal cultural events of the year.

In mid-January, **Summer Dreaming** WEB SITE www.summerdreaming2000.com is a three-day no-holds-barred dance extravaganza in rural New South Wales featuring DJs, music and visual artists from around the globe. The location varies from year to year.

The **Australian Country Music Festival** WEB SITE www.countrymusic.asn.au is held at Tamworth in the last two weeks of January. Tamworth, 440 km (275 miles) north of Sydney, is to Australian country music what Nashville is in the United States, and 600 events are programmed over the 10-day festival.

FEBRUARY

The **St. Kilda Festival** WEB SITE www.portphillip .vic.gov.au/events/festival, in Melbourne kicks off in mid-February with a variety of events including live music, DJs, performance art and sporting competitions — all for free. In Western Australia the **Perth International Arts Festival** WEB SITE www.perthfestival.com.au provides an extensive program of music, film, theater and dance at a variety of venues around the city.

Womadelaide WEB SITE www.afct.org.au is a biennial (odd years) world music event held in late February, with over 200 artists from 20 different countries converging on Adelaide for three days of music, dance, arts, and food. Over the last weekend of February, vintage bike enthusiasts gather for the **Village Fair and National Penny-farthing Championships** WEB SITE www.launceston.tas.gov.au, at Evandale, 20 km (12 miles) south of Launceston in Tasmania. The festivities also include market and craft stalls, and for the kids silly side-shows and amusing street entertainment.

Melbourne's **Food and Wine Festival** WEB SITE www.foodwine.yellowpages.com.au gives the city's best chefs and Victorian winemakers the chance to show off their skills from late February through early March.

OPPOSITE: Stiltwalkers at Melbourne's Moomba Parade. ABOVE: On the starting block at Evandale's Village Fair and National Penny-farthing Championships.

MARCH

For the entire month of March, the Sydney gay and lesbian community show off their culture during the **Gay and Lesbian Mardi Gras** WEB SITE www.mardigras.com.au, with live theater, music, film, visual arts, street performance, sports and community events filling the calendar. (The festival begins in the last week of February.) Its climax is an all-night street parade that blends imagination, exhibitionism, hedonism and humor, attracting crowds of up to 1,000,000. After the parade there is a monster party. The Mardi Gras Party is a private event for members of Sydney Gay & Lesbian Mardi Gras and their guests, but anyone, anywhere can become a full member if nominated by two other current full members. People living within Australia but more than 150 km (93 miles) from the Sydney GPO can also become associate members, while others can become international members. Both associate and international members can buy just one party ticket. For membership applications E-MAIL members @mardigras.com.au, or call ((02) 9557 4332. For party tickets call ((02) 9266 4222 or E-MAIL www.ticketek.com.au/ticketek/mardigras.

The **Adelaide Festival** WEB SITE www. adelaidefestival.telstra.com.au is the oldest and best-known festival of culture, performance and the arts in Australia. It is held every even year in early March. Coinciding with the Adelaide Festive, the **Adelaide Fringe Festival** sees avant-garde performers taking over the streets, small theaters and pubs.

Melbourne's **Moomba** WEB SITE www .melbournemoombafestival.com.au usually starts in the first week of March, and includes water-skiing on the Yarra River, fireworks, food and entertainment. Also in March, the **Canberra Festival** is a 10-day party that features outdoor concerts and art exhibitions. A highlight of the festival is the Birdman Rally, where hopeful aviators try out their homemade human-powered flying machines over Lake Burley Griffin. The winner gets $20,000 prize money — the losers get wet as their creations plunge into the lake.

APRIL

Sydney's **Royal Easter Show** WEB SITE www .eastershow.com.au is the foremost agricultural show in Australia. Ten days of displays of rural produce, rodeo events, fireworks and rides.

Melbourne has a strong tradition of rearing great comedians. Their talents are showcased during the **Melbourne Comedy Festival** WEB SITE www.comedyfestival.com.au, which starts on or near April Fool's Day (April 1), and has the place in stitches for four weeks.

The **Barossa Valley Vintage Festival** web site www.barossa-region.org/vintagefestival is held every odd year. Winemaking and tasting festivities are combined with great food and live music in the vineyards.

MAY TO AUGUST

The **McLaren Vale Gourmet Weekend** WEB SITE www.tourism.sa.gov.au provides an ideal opportunity to taste over 100 local wines, with food stalls serving dishes that are usually only seen in fine restaurants. McLaren Vale is on the Fleurieu Peninsula, 30 km (20 miles) south of Adelaide.

Being denied a white Christmas, Australians gather in mountain resorts to celebrate Christmas in June where, with luck, snow may fall. One of the most organized mid-year Christmas-style events is **Yuletide** WEB SITE www.blue.mountains.com.au, held in the Blue Mountains near Sydney. The **Wintersun Festival** WEB SITE www.wintersun.org.au is a 10-day festival held in Coolangatta on the border of New South Wales and Queensland. This is Australia's leading 1950s and 1960s rock-and-roll nostalgia festival.

In Alice Springs the brave mount camels for July's **Camel Cup** WEB SITE www.nttc.com.au, held along the dry bed of the Todd River. The day usually includes a few other novelty events.

As the weather improves in late August, Sydney's annual **City to Surf** WEB SITE www .voyeurmagic.com.au/citysurf fun run attracts thousands of runners to battle the 14 km (nine miles) from Sydney Town Hall to Bondi Beach, with the famous Rose Bay Hill testing runners to their limit.

In Broome, the **Festival of Pearl** WEB SITE www.broomewa.com/shinju (or **Shinju Matsuri**) lasts nine days, beginning at the end of August; its concluding beach carnival coincides with the September full moon. August also sees the **Melbourne Fringe Festival**, with alternative theater, music and performance art.

SEPTEMBER

The Fringe Festival is followed in September by Melbourne's **International Festival of the Arts** WEB SITE www.melbournefestival.com.au, which brings local and overseas artists to the city for 17 days of dance, theatre, opera, music and visual arts.

Birdsville Picnic Races WEB SITE www .queensland-holidays.com.au/pfm/menu/evts is a horse-racing event renowned throughout the country. Birdsville is 1,569 km (973 miles)

TOP: Dancing at Darling Harbour during January's Sydney Festival. BOTTOM: Alice Springs' Henley-on-Todd Regatta, held along the dry bed of the Todd River.

west of Brisbane near the South Australian border, in the middle of nowhere. Every September this tiny town with a population of approximately 30 attracts thousands of race fans, who fly in from all over Australia.

The **Tasmanian Tulip Festival** WEB SITE www.tased.edu.au/tasonline is celebrated in the Royal Tasmanian Botanical Gardens in Hobart and in Wynard on the north coast, where the theme is Dutch culture, with music, dancing, and of course, thousands upon thousands of beautiful blossoms.

In late September or early October the Commonwealth Park in Canberra is transformed for the **Floriade** WEB SITE www .floriadeaustralia.com. About half a million flowers provide a floral display unmatched anywhere else in the country. Private gardens are opened up and there are talks and demonstrations on every aspect of gardening.

OCTOBER

Those who prefer their music cool should look no further than the **Manly Jazz Festival** WEB SITE www.manly.nsw.gov.au, when the best musicians from Australia and around the world arrive to perform at this bustling Sydney seaside suburb.

NOVEMBER

The **Fremantle Festival** WEB SITE www.fremantle .wa.gov.au turns the port city over to 10 days of culture, ending in a street parade and all night party.

As the water warms up with the coming of spring, Mount Gambier's famous volcanic lake (in South Australia) turns a vivid blue, and the town celebrates the **Blue Lake Festival** WEB SITE www.bluelake.org.

DECEMBER

Most cities and towns in Australia gather outdoors for **Carols by Candlelight**. In Melbourne it's held at the Myer Music Bowl and in Sydney on The Domain.

The **Sydney-to-Hobart Yacht Race** leaves Sydney on Boxing Day (December 26) — huge harborside picnics and live music accompany the event. The yachts sail into Hobart's Constitution Dock around New Year's Eve, coinciding with Hobart's food and wine celebration, **Taste of Tasmania**, and the start of the **Hobart Summer Festival**.

PUBLIC HOLIDAYS

In addition to the following national holidays, each state has an additional two or three days given over to such events as Melbourne Cup (the first Tuesday in November), Labor Day and bank holidays.

New Year's Day	January 1
Australia Day	January 26
Good Friday	Friday before Easter
Easter Monday	Monday after Easter
Anzac Day	April 25
Queen's Birthday	Second Monday in June
Christmas Day	December 25
Boxing Day	December 26

Galloping Gourmet

Australia boasts a virtually limitless culinary variety, from the "bush tucker" of its indigenous population to new takes on classic Mediterranean, Middle Eastern, and Asian dishes. Year-round quality produce and a polyglot population has given rise to excellent restaurants, particularly in Melbourne and Sydney, that would be at home in Los Angeles, New York or London. Australian chefs combine fresh local ingredients, whether they be indigenous or introduced, with both classic techniques and bold, inventive cooking styles to create a cuisine that is particularly Australian.

Food does become plainer (and more British in style) as you move further from the urban centers, although good restaurants can be found in the most surprising places: some of the best are in the wine regions of South Australia, the Hunter Valley, or rural Victoria. Wherever you go though, the quality of the produce can be outstanding. Across the county, the most humble pub may surprise you with an unforgettable T-bone steak or Sunday lamb roast. In coastal areas it is worth finding out what is caught locally. Try barramundi caught in estuaries and rivers of the north or plump Tasmanian salmon. Queensland is known for its mud crabs and Moreton Bay bugs (a delicious, prehistoric-looking crustacean) while Sydney rock and

Tasmanian oysters are much prized. Pacific sea urchins also make their way onto Australian plates.

BUSH TUCKER

When Captain Cook visited Australia in 1770, he wrote: "The Land naturally produces hardly anything fit for Man to eat." How wrong he was. The Aboriginal diet at the time was composed of an estimated 10,000 plants and animals. Although the macadamia nut quickly became a profitable export for Australia, it is only in the last 20 years that white Australia has begun to experiment with the bush's wealth of native meats and indigenous plants.

Kangaroo and wallaby meat are low in fat and cholesterol and high in iron. Long, lean, strip loin fillets are best quickly seared over high heat so as not to dry out, and topside kangaroo roast can be delicious; some chefs soak the meat in milk for a few hours to soften its gaminess. Wallaby has a lighter color, a finer texture, and a sweeter flavor; it is regarded by many as the "veal" of kangaroo. Both meats are excellent smoked, as is emu. Crocodile meat is also becoming available in butcher shops far south of the reptile's tropical habitat. Its strong, slightly fishy flavor is

OPPOSITE: A stall at Sydney's lively Fish Markets does a roaring trade in rock oysters, Moreton Bay bugs and other crustaceans. ABOVE: South Australia's Barossa Valley produces many of Australia's finest wines.

wonderful grilled or barbecued, and is often served with a light sauce based on berries or citrus fruits. Yabbies (small freshwater crayfish) are found throughout the country, and a large variety of native herbs, seeds and fruits are used in increasingly inventive ways.

Sydney's Lillipilli on King uses bush tucker to great effect. Lilli-pillis (a purplish native berry) and other fruits are combined with bush herbs and local meats and fish in 100% Australian dishes. Edna's Table uses Asian-inspired techniques in preparing Australian native meats like emu, wallaby and kangaroo, and even crocodile, with bush herbs and fruits. Melbourne's Jarrah Room is an inexpensive place to sample bush tucker, with dishes like kangaroo fillet, emu and crocodile pie, or yabbie salad flavored with indigenous wattle seed, lemon myrtle and munthari berries. In Adelaide, Alice Springs and Cairns, the Red Ochre Grill specializes in bush foods, using native herbs fruits, nuts and spices and indigenous meats.

WINES
Wine entered Australia's history with the arrival of the first European settlers. Vines were included in the cargo of the First Fleet in 1788, and the colony's governor, Captain Arthur Phillip, had a private vineyard planted on his property. The first issue of *The Sydney Gazette* in 1803 carried an article, written by a French viticulturist, entitled "Method of Preparing a Piece of Land for the Purpose of Forming a Vineyard."

Australia's wines are often compared to those of their New World counterpart, California. However, generally lower levels of tannin in reds and oak in whites, along with a slightly lower alcohol content, often bring them closer to the Old World wines of France. Most vineyards are open to the public, and a tour of one of the major regions can be a memorable part of the traveler's itinerary (see TAKING A TOUR, below). Wherever you are in Australia, even smaller restaurants and hotels often have excellent wine lists.

WHITES
Exceptional Semillon and Sauvignon Blanc grapes are grown in Western Australia's Margaret River and South Australia's Coonawarra and Padthaway regions. Alone or blended (sometimes with Chenin Blanc) they produce fresh, concentrated whites. Like California, Australia's Chardonnays range from golden, buttery wines full of ripe fruit — similar to the gutsy wines of the Sonoma and Napa Valleys — to the newer, often unoaked, crisp, dry Chardonnays of the cooler vineyards in southernmost Victoria and northern Tasmania. The hot, damp climate of New South Wales' Hunter Valley produces particularly rich Semillons and Chardonnays, while Victoria's wonderfully aromatic Chateau Tahbilk Marsanne is in its own category: it is perhaps the world's only wine made solely from Marsanne grapes. South Australian Rieslings have leaped ahead over the past decade. Look out for Petaluma, Henschke, and the delicate Rieslings produced in the Eden and Pewsey valleys.

REDS
Big, round Cabernets — sometimes blended with Syrah or Merlot — are produced in all of Australia's wine-growing areas. Margaret River's intense Moss Wood and Leeuwin are classic examples; South Australia has the glorious Wirra Wirra, Pewsey Vale and Petaluma; and in western Victoria Taltarni consistently produces beautifully balanced, firm reds. But while Cabernets account for two-thirds of Australia's red wine, the most exceptional reds are the deep, powerfully structured Syrahs (or Shirazs, also called Hermitage). The very best come from Barossa Valley vineyards Henschke, Penfold's, St. Hallett and Peter Lehmann. These earthy, spicy wines often need at least eight to ten years to fully develop their silky complexity.

Coonawarra, the Hunter and Barossa Valleys, and the temperate Margaret River region all produce fine, balanced Bordeaux-like Syrahs. As winemakers realize the potential of some of Australia's cooler regions, Pinot Noir too is beginning to make its mark. Victoria's Yarra Valley produces Australia's finest — clean, crisp and well-defined — although Tasmanian Pinots are improving every year.

SPARKLING WINES AND DESSERT WINES
Most of Australia's sparkling wines come from the Great Western region of Victoria, although the best is from Moët and Chandon's vineyards in Victoria's Yarra Valley. Newer vineyards on the cool slopes of Tasmania, however, have recently been putting out Pinot-Noir–Chardonnay blends that suggest the island has a big future in the sparkling market. Golden, honeyed botrytis-affected Rieslings are produced by a number of Riesling growers: try those of Barossa's Henschke or Petaluma.

Victoria's Murray River region is world-famous for its velvety fortified dessert wines, made from Muscat de Frontignan and Muscadelle grapes (these are sometimes called Tokays, although there is no relation to the Hungarian Tokay).

Special Interests

ABORIGINAL AUSTRALIA

Tourist information offices will often organize bush-walks with Aboriginal guides and other ways of meeting with and learning from local Aboriginal people. A longer visit to an Aboriginal community can be a memorable experience, though, and a way to learn first-hand the lifestyle, culture and problems faced by Australia's indigenous people today. The Northern Territory has the greatest number of possibilities for visitors to learn from Aboriginal people, who comprise 25% of its population and own nearly 50% of the land. A visitor permit is required to enter Aboriginal lands, although most tour operators will organize this for you. Photography is often restricted at sites of spiritual significance, and some can be visited only by members of one sex. The **Northern Territory Tourist Commission** ((08) 8951 8492 TOLL-FREE (1800) 621 336 FAX (08) 8951 8550 WEB SITE www.nttc.com.au, 43 Mitchell Street, Darwin NT 0800, can book tours throughout the territory. For information on obtaining permits see ABORIGINAL LANDS, page 319 in TRAVELERS' TIPS.

TOP END

Traveling through Aboriginal-owned Arnhem Land without a guide is not only difficult and potentially dangerous, it means missing out on the cultural significance of the area and the

chance to spend some time with the people who know it best. **Umorrduk Safaris** ((08) 8948 1306 FAX (08) 8948 1305 E-MAIL bbrookes @ozemail.com.au runs one-day or two-day, two-night tours through Gummulkbun people's land. Tours leave from Darwin, an hour's flight from the camp, visiting superb rock art galleries and introducing the traditional lifestyle and spiritual beliefs. An associate company, **Brookes Australia Tours** (same contact details) provides a range of tours across the Top End for individuals and small groups, all with knowledgeable Aboriginal guides.

The Top End is virtually impassable during the wet season, and most tours operate from April to November only. One exception is **Davidson's Arnhemland Safaris** ((08) 8927 5240 FAX (08) 8945 0919 E-MAIL dassafaris @onaustralia.com.au WEB SITE www.allaust .com.au, PO Box 41905, Casuarina NT 0811, who offer spectacular tropical summer safaris traveling by airboat and cruise boats over the vast wetlands. Tours visit sandstone outcrops harboring some of the most extensive rock art in Australia. This is an outstanding wilderness experience; along with the crocs and wallabies, the wet season floodplains attract a wide variety of birds and bring out brilliant tropical flora.

The most exclusive tourist option is **Dreamtime Safari in Arnhem Land** (/FAX (08) 8948 0333, PO Box 1545, Katherine NT 0851. Frenchman François Giner has lived with the

Dancers at Tjapukai Aboriginal Cultural Park, Cairns.

Ngalkbon people in central Arnhem Land for over a decade. His Bodeidei Safari Camp offers the chance to share this unique relationship, with traditional dance, demonstrations of art and craft techniques and storytelling. Dreamtime Safari also runs **Wadda Safaris** ((0417) 815 682 FAX (08) 8948 0333, PO Box 4286, Darwin NT 0801; four-day camping safaris out of Katherine for the budget traveler, with young Ngalkbon guides teaching bush skills and showing remote art sites.

Kakadu Parklink Tours ((08) 8979 2303 TOLL-FREE (1800) 089 113 E-MAIL kakair.com.au offers fascinating eight-hour tours into Arnhem Land from Jabiru or Cooinda in Kakadu to rock art sites and billabongs. They also run 75-minute cruises of East Alligator River.

In Katherine, **Travel North** ((08) 8972 1044 TOLL-FREE (1800) 089 103 E-MAIL travelnorth @pobox.com runs a wide range of guided walks through Nitmiluk (Katherine Gorge) and neighboring Manyallaluk ("Frog Dreaming") — where guests are encouraged to participate in traditional bark painting, fire lighting, spear throwing, and didgeridoo playing.

THE RED CENTRE

The **Central Australian Tourism Industry Association** ((08) 8952 5800 E-MAIL visinfo @catia.asn.au WEB SITE wwwcatia.asn.au, 60 Gregory Terrace, Alice Springs NT 0870, can advise on different tours in the Red Centre, from 20-minute bush-tucker walks to longer stays with Aboriginal groups.

The **Aboriginal Art and Culture Centre** ((08) 8952 3408 E-MAIL aborart@ozemail.com.au WEB SITE www.aboriginalart.com.au, 86-88 Todd Street, PO Box 130, Alice Springs NT 0871, offers day tours to Uluru, Kings Canyon and Aboriginal communities in Central Australia. The **Institute for Aboriginal Development** ((08) 8951 1311 FAX (08) 8953 1884, PO Box 2531, Alice Springs NT 0800, runs Aboriginal cultural awareness bush camps from March to October. **Kamiku Arangka** ("Grandmother's Way") ((08) 8953 0946, PO Box 8723, Alice Springs NT 0871, has similar courses on Central Australian Aboriginal culture. Both teach bush medicine and tucker, tracking skills, history, kinship, language and dance.

John and Rex Spencer combine their experience as cattlemen with the knowledge taught to them by their Aboriginal elders in four-day "back-track magic" visits to Uluru. They also specialize in personally designed private tours. Contact **Spencer Tours** (/FAX (08) 8952 2639, PO Box 8057, Alice Springs NT 0871. **Desert Tracks** ((02) 6680 8566 FAX (02) 6680 8567, PO Box 1285, Byron Bay NSW 2481, is another Aboriginal-owned company that takes small groups on one- to eight-day visits to communities in Pitjantjatjara Lands near Alice Springs. **Rod Steinert Tours** ((08) 8558 8377 TOLL-FREE (1800) 679 418 E-MAIL rstours@cobweb .com.au organizes short "Dreamtime and Bush Tucker" visits to Warlpiri bush camps near Alice Springs, where Dreaming stories are told through dance and explanations of local art.

A unique way to visit some of Australia's most remote Aboriginal communities is to join the outback mail flight from Alice Springs. Aboriginal-owned **Ngurratjuta Air** ((08) 8953 5000 flies four times a week delivering mail and passengers throughout the Red Centre, with half-day flights Tuesdays and Thursdays, full-day flights Wednesdays and Fridays, from $240.

NOODLING FOR OPALS
There are few places more remote than the town of Coober Pedy, 863 km (535 miles) northwest of Adelaide and 687 km (430 miles) south of Alice Springs. Opal was first discovered here by teenager Jim Hutchison in 1915. After World War I, returned soldiers drifted to the fields to seek their fortune. The town was named in 1922, from the Aboriginal words "Kupa Piti," meaning "white man's burrow." Most of its residents live underground to escape the searing heat. Temperatures regularly reach 45°C–50°C (113°F–122°F).

Visitors can noodle (fossick) for opals in the discarded mullock heaps still containing opals missed by miners. Always ask permission if you want to noodle a mullock heap next to a miner's claim, though, as some miners reserve this right for themselves.

Noodling is hot work, but the hope of uncovering a valuable opal makes this a popular activity. While it is possible to noodle without a guide, the best way to undertake the full outback experience is on a **Coober Pedy Discovery Tour** ((08) 8672 5028. The well designed tour includes tips on noodling, visits to an underground house and the Coober Pedy Underground Catacomb Anglican Church, and a free opal gift.

VISITING VINEYARDS
Small boutique wineries is where you'll find wines that have real regional character. Most vineyards are open to the public for tastings and sales. Often choice vintages can be picked up at a discount. Just drop in and try the latest vintage. The leading wine-producing regions are in Coonawarra, Clare Valley, McLaren Vale and Barossa Valley in South Australia, Cowra and Hunter Valley in New South Wales, Rutherglen, Yarra Valley and Mornington Peninsula in Victoria, Margaret River in Western Australia, and northeastern Tasmania.

Gourmet Tours of Australia ((03) 5777 3503 runs bicycle tours of wineries in all states, combining wine sampling with visits to the best regional restaurants. Tour guides talk as authoritatively about a suitable wine to complement your dinner as they do about front and rear sprocket gear ratios.

Taking a Tour

The range of tours available in Australia is mind-boggling. You can do anything from droving with cattlemen in the outback to sailing around the Whitsunday Islands. There are bus tours across the country, covering great distances, or you can tackle the arduous Overland Track at Cradle Mountain on foot.

MAINSTREAM TOURS
Organized tours are an ideal way to see large tracts of the country efficiently and in comfort. Tours are usually booked through travel agents.

The largest and oldest tour company is **AAT King's** TOLL-FREE (1800) 334 009 FAX (03) 9274 7400, which operates a fleet of luxury buses the length and breadth of Australia. Accommodation is included in packages and is usually in good quality hotels. Even its camping safaris include a few nice touches such as wine with dinner.

Australian Pacific Tours TOLL-FREE (1800) 675 222 FAX (1800) 655 220 offers fully accommodated coach tours, camping safaris and four-wheel-drive adventure tours, from half-day city tours to 38 round-Australia trips.

Scenic Tours Australia ((02) 4929 4333 TOLL-FREE (1800) 022 488 provides a more limited range of bus safaris and camping tours. Australia's major domestic airlines, **Qantas** and **Ansett**, both offer tour packages combining flights with bus, cruise and train trips. For airline details see under GETTING AROUND page 20 in TRAVELERS' TIPS.

ADVENTURE TOURS
One of the most experienced adventure tour companies is **Peregrine** ((03) 9662 2700 FAX (03) 9662 2422, 258 Lonsdale Street in Melbourne. Possible tours include rafting down the Franklin River and trekking in the Flinders Ranges.

Raging Thunder ((07) 4030 7990 FAX (07) 4030 7911 guarantees an adrenaline rush whitewater rafting down grade-4 rapids on the Tully River. They also offer rafting trips down North Johnson River, which is so remote it is accessed by helicopter. While the company specialty is rafting, they also offer sea kayaking and diving trips along the Great Barrier Reef, camel-back tours and cross-country cycling.

OFF THE BEATEN TRACK
There are a number of tour companies that take you off the beaten track. They are usually local, and provide very special trips in an

Australian wines are making a splash worldwide.

area they know a lot about. For tours into Aboriginal Lands of the Northern Territory, see SPECIAL INTERESTS, above.

There are few places in Australia more remote than its northern tip, Cape York, which is known as Quinkan Country, after an Aboriginal Dreamtime figure. Cairns-based **Oz Tours Safaris (** (07) 4055 9535 TOLL-FREE (1800) 079 006 E-MAIL oztours@internetnorth.com.au WEB SITE www.oztours.com.au has run wilderness safaris deep into Cape York Peninsula and to the Torres Strait Islands for over 15 years. Tours last from six to 16 days, visiting crystal-clear jungle streams, isolated Aboriginal art sites and the northernmost tip of the continent.

Nevis Tedoldi has developed an impressive network among Aboriginal people and her **Cultural Connections (** (03) 9349 4233 FAX (03) 9349 4211 offers cultural tours to remote parts of the country. She can organize visits to contemporary artists and galleries to see and buy indigenous paintings, or wilderness experiences with local Aboriginal people.

Bogong Jack ((08) 8383 7198 FAX (08) 8383 7377 is one of the few tour operators that has adventure tours into places such as the Flinders Ranges, Kangaroo Island, the wild Snowy River and the alpine areas of Victoria.

ORGANIZED BIKE TOURS

Cycling Australia, with its great distances, presents a formidable challenge. A number of small companies provide organized tours, with support vehicles should the effort become too arduous. **Remote Outback Cycles (** (08) 9244 4614 FAX (08) 9244 4615 E-MAIL roc @cycletours.com.au WEB SITE www.cycletours .com.au, in Western Australia, provides mountain bikes which are up to the task of traversing wilderness areas such as the Great Victoria Desert, MacDonnell Ranges in Central Australia and Margaret River in Western Australia.

There are bicycle clubs in most states, with regular rides organized every weekend. If you don't mind a crowd, then join 5,000 cyclists on the **Great Victorian Bike Ride** in November/ December each year, a 16-day tour that takes in some lovely countryside. Routes range from easy to medium, and the tour cost includes campsite, most meals and, best of all, a support vehicle. Contact Bicycle Victoria **(** (03) 9328 3000 FAX (03) 9328 2288 or E-MAIL bicyclevic @bv.com.au to book a tour. The **Great Tasmanian Bike Ride** in January, the **Great Queensland Bike Ride** in August/September and the **Great South Australian Bike Ride** in September are run along similar lines. Reservations can also be made through Bicycle Victoria. Bicycle NSW organizes a nine-day, 500-km (310-mile) tour,

the **Great New South Wales Bike Ride**, through country towns and inland countryside. Reservations can be made at **(** (02) 9283 5200.

INTERNATIONAL TOUR OPERATORS

Below are several operators with offices in the United Kingdom and the United States.

Abercrombie and Kent TOLL-FREE IN THE UNITED STATES (800) 323-7308 FAX (630) 954-3324 E-MAIL info@abercrombiekent.com WEB SITE www.abercrombiekent.com, 1520 Kensington Road, Oak Brook, Illinois 60523-2141, organizes tailored luxury tours with some reasonable deals to Australia. In the United Kingdom, they can be contacted at Abercrombie and Kent Travel **(** (020) 7730 9600 FAX (020) 7730 9376 E-MAIL info@abercrombiekent.co.uk, Sloane Square House, Holbein Place, London SW1W 8NS. In Australia contact Abercrombie and Kent **(** (03) 9536 1800 FAX (03) 9536 1805 E-MAIL contact@abercrombiekent.com.au, Berkeley Hall, 11 Princes Street, PO Box 327, St. Kilda, Melbourne, Victoria 3182.

Dreamtime Travel ((014) 2473 4747 FAX (014) 2473 1818 E-MAIL sales@dreamtime-uk.com WEB SITE www.dreamtime-uk.com, 10 Regency Arcade, Devonshire Road, Bexhill-on-Sea, East Sussex TN40 1BD, United Kingdom, is an Australian specialist that can organize just about anything anywhere in Australia at any budget.

Australian Pacific Tours ((416) 234-9676 TOLL-FREE IN THE UNITED STATES (800) 290-8687 FAX (416) 234-8385 E-MAIL reservations @aptours.com, Suite 620, 4605 Lankershim Boulevard, North Hollywood, California 91602, is a reputable company that runs tours throughout Australia for people of all ages and tastes at very reasonable prices. They also have an office in the United Kingdom **(** (020) 8879 7444 FAX (020) 8944 9329 E-MAIL ukinfo@aptours.com.au, Second Floor, William House, 14 Worple Road, Wimbledon, London SW194DD.

Absolute Australia ((888) 285-6094 or (212) 627-8258 FAX (212) 627-4090 E-MAIL info @absoluteaustralia.com WEB SITE www .absoluteasia.com, 180 Varick Street, New York, New York 10014, offers luxury tours including a 19-day Australia Overview Tour taking in Sydney, Tasmania, Melbourne, Uluru, Darwin, Kakadu, Daintree Rainforest, and the Great Barrier Reef.

Introduced by early explorers and settlers, camels thrive in Australia's central deserts and arid lands.

Welcome
to
Australia

VAST AND ISOLATED, AUSTRALIA OFFERS A VARIETY OF MOODS AND BEAUTY THAT IS HARD TO EXPRESS. It is the only country that is also a continent, albeit the world's smallest. It is a land of sweeping golden beaches and forested mountain ranges, of coral reefs and tropical rainforests teeming with life, and of endless, barren deserts. Here towering natural sculptures wrought by wind and rain and geological upheavals are matched by ambitious urban structures. And Australia averages only six people per square mile — but what a mix of people you find!

Australia's Aboriginal people have occupied the country for over 60,000 years, developing a phenomenal diversity of languages, cultural and spiritual beliefs, ceremonies and art forms. Alongside this ancient culture is the newest of the New World, descendants of the predominantly Anglo-Celtic colonists, gold diggers and early settlers and of more recent arrivals. Post-war immigrants came from southern and eastern Europe; later tensions and wars in Asia brought people from farther east. More than 160 different ethnic groups are represented in Australia today, making it one of the most ethnically diversified countries in the world.

Somehow, though, Australians *do* have some things in common. Only two percent are of Aboriginal or Torres Strait Islander descent — 98% are immigrants, or have descended from immigrants recently enough to retain strong cultural memories. Almost a quarter of all Australians were born overseas. Perhaps this is what makes for the widespread understanding of humankind's capacity to break new frontiers, to develop a new life in a new land, to take risks and nurture self-resilience. Australians admire those who overcome great odds to achieve success, and who aren't afraid to get their hands dirty. They're renowned both for supporting the underdog and for cutting "tall poppies" down to size — anyone whose success or attention swells the ego too much. Perhaps above all, many Australians share a striking independence of spirit, and an avoidance of any suggestion of weakness — a machismo shared by women as much as by men.

And as any traveler will vouch for, an inordinate number of independent young Australians pack their backpacks and tour the furthest corners of the planet — there are only 19 million people in the country, after all.

With its warm, sunny climate Australians spend much of their free time out of doors — from playing or watching team sports to surfing, sailing or bush walking, or just dining or sipping lattes in its ubiquitous sidewalk cafés. While most Australians today live in cities and large towns along the southeastern coast, these cities border on vast areas of wilderness. Even in the heart of Sydney, a sense of the sheer size and power of the natural environment pervades the Australian psyche.

The visitor must also contend with the enormousness and diversity of the country — one must make choices. Most won't want to miss out on the country's must-sees — the kaleidoscopic beauty of Queensland's Great Barrier Reef, the other-worldly strangeness of Uluru (Ayers Rock) and the Red Centre, and sparkling, stylish Sydney, with its enviable lifestyle. But every state has much to offer. The exotic scenery and wildlife of Western Australia's Kimberley and Shark Bay or the swollen rivers deep in the Tasmanian Wilderness World Heritage Area can add an exciting element to the more adventurous traveler's itinerary. The most common complaint I hear from tourists is that they tried to fit too much into a single limited

vacation. In the hope that visitors will take the time to explore parts of Australia in greater depth, I have included in this guidebook not only the country's more famous destinations, but also some lesser-known places that offer another viewpoint, another Australia.

OPPOSITE TOP: Children and their dog explore a tranquil stretch of beach at Twofold Bay, on New South Wales' southern coast near Eden. BOTTOM: A road train on the dusty Bourke Cobar Highway. ABOVE: Stallholders at the Sunday Esplanade Market, St. Kilda, Melbourne.

The Country and Its People

AUSTRALIA IS THE LARGEST ISLAND IN THE WORLD, covering an expanse of almost eight million square kilometers (three million square miles). That makes it roughly the same size as the United States, excluding Alaska, with a northernmost point that reaches up towards the equator and a chilly southern tip of Tasmania at a latitude equivalent to that of Toronto.

From tropical Cape York Peninsula to the Grampians west of Melbourne, the Great Dividing Range runs the entire length of the east coast — mountainous Tasmania in fact forms the southern reaches of this ancient range. The "Great Divide" catches most of the country's rain, allowing very little to fall on the rest of the continent. The Top End is an exception: it is watered by monsoons.

West of the Divide, much of the country is inhospitable: a broad, flat landscape with a perennial heat haze rising from the parched earth. The ocher-colored soil matches the fur of its red kangaroos. Huge central lakes Torrens, Eyre and Frome can be salt pans for years on end, where fish lie dormant, deep below the dry surface, until rain finally fills the waterways and cloaks the plains in pale yellow and blue wildflowers.

The dense vine-clad jungle of Cape York's tropical rainforests, with spectacular waterfalls that plummet into bottomless lakes, is about as far as it gets from the arid Red Centre. Home to giant pythons and crocodiles, sparrow-sized butterflies and crested cassowaries the height of a man, under the rainforest canopy, bird's-nest ferns form mini pond-ecosystems high in the treetops, complete with luminous green tree frogs and broad-footed tree kangaroos — which rarely touch down on solid ground. Strangler figs and tenacious sticky vines make much of this jungle impenetrable.

The southeast seaboard offers the most hospitable climate, making it home to all but a fraction of Australians. Winters are crisp (with good skiing in New South Wales and Victoria), autumns often wet, and spring and summer sunny and dry, resulting in an informal lifestyle and a general appreciation of nature and the environment.

Climate and way of life conspire to make Australia a country of hedonists with a penchant for outdoor activities year-round. Urban Australia, however, also nurtures a vibrant and exciting arts culture. All capital cities host art and film festivals annually, fine places to sample the best of the country's culture.

Out of the city and into the outback, both perspective and lifestyle change. The wit can be as dry as the red dust in the street. Social life in the bush revolves around the pub, which serves also as information office, lending bank and local committee room. Local dances draw crowds from out yonder; farmers travel hundreds of kilometers for the agricultural show.

Aboriginals and Torres Strait Islanders remain the country's most disadvantaged group, suffering from an unemployment level well in excess of the national average, below average education, and poor health and living conditions. Across the country, Australians from all backgrounds have in recent years begun to recognize these disparities, and ever-increasing numbers support the country's original inhabitants as they struggle to renew ties to their traditions and to have their say in shaping the country's future.

ABORIGINAL HISTORY

Aboriginal history is the story of the Dreamtime. It recounts the origins of the land and the people who inhabited it for hundreds of generations, how every river, mountain and gorge came into existence, carved out of the terrain by ancestral beings. These creators also made birds, animals, plants and all other living creatures, including man. Dreamtime stories and Aboriginal Dreaming — a specific concept that encompasses beliefs, values and spirituality — establish the relationships Aborigines maintain with every element of their environment.

Archaeological evidence indicates that the Aboriginal people migrated from the north at least 50,000 and probably over 60,000 years ago. They might have crossed a land bridge that linked Southeast Asia to Australia or used boats to traverse the relatively short distance, hopping across the numerous islands scattered between the two land masses. Some scholars suggest they originated in Sri Lanka.

Once they arrived on the Australian continent, Aborigines adapted to the often harsh conditions and spread into every corner of the vast continent. There is no written Aboriginal language, and history was told around the fire, passed on through stories, songs, art and dance from one generation

ABOVE: A member of Arnhem Land's remote Yolngu community, at Nhulunbuy on the Gove Peninsula. OPPOSITE: Beautifully textured Aboriginal paintings decorate Obiri Rock in Arnhem Land.

to the next. Yet most of the 600 to 700 tribes spoke different dialects and languages and rarely met except on ceremonial occasions. Dreamtime, however, was a unifying force, and rock paintings depicting this creation period can be found throughout the country.

Although Aboriginal people did not cultivate the land, they did master it through controlled burning of the bush to encourage regrowth, which in turn attracted animals. Sophisticated weapons such as the boomerang were developed to hunt kangaroos and other wildlife, some to extinction. In Victoria, an area rich in wildlife and fish all year round, Aborigines established permanent stone settlements, and in coastal areas they built intricate structures to trap fish.

Before the arrival of British settlers, Aboriginal people had reached an equilibrium with the land. This balance was based on a profound knowledge of the seasons and how to survive in a country that could appear to outsiders to be poor in natural resources.

VOYAGES OF DISCOVERY

There is evidence that the first visitor to Australia after the original migration of the Aboriginal people was the Chinese admiral Zheng He, who explored waters south of the Indian Ocean between 1405 and 1432. A Chinese statuette and sandstone carvings have been discovered near Darwin, confirming other evidence of visits by northern fishermen.

Subsequent visits were by European sailors — Dutch, English and French — blown off course on their way to the Spice Islands. Other explorers went in search of *Terra Australis*, "the land to the south," which might offer similar riches to those discovered in the nearby East Indies. What they saw disappointed them, and the great southern land was left alone.

These explorers had landed on Australia's more barren northern and western shores. In 1770 British Captain James Cook, on the other hand, sailed the length of the continent's fertile eastern seaboard. He christened the land New South Wales and claimed it for England in the name of King George III. Cook chartered the coast, naming the Great Barrier Reef and islands, mountains, rivers and inlets — including Botany Bay and nearby Port Jackson.

At first Britain had little use for a country some months' sail from home. It had recently lost the American colonies in the 1776 War of Independence, and by the 1780s, overflowing prisons and workhouses in London had led the government to keep convicts locked in hulks moored along the River Thames. In 1787, King George III instructed Captain Phillip to found a penal colony at Botany Bay.

EUROPEAN SETTLEMENT

Now all you young viscounts and duchesses
Take warning by what I do say,
And mind it's all yours what you touches-es
Or you'll land down in Botany Bay.

— From "Botany Bay," a convict ballad

On January 26, 1788, Captain Arthur Phillip established his penal colony at Port Jackson, on what he described as "one of the finest harbors in the world," finding Botany Bay unsuitable. Phillip's "First Fleet" carried in 443 seamen, 568 male and 191 female convicts, 160 marines and 51 officers. Further penal colonies were established for recidivist offenders in godforsaken places such as Port Arthur in 1830, and Norfolk Island and Moreton Bay in 1824. On Norfolk Island, prisoners were known to draw lots to decide who would kill whom, because murder meant a trial in Sydney and some hope of escape.

After a shaky start as settlers adapted to an unfamiliar land, the settlement at Sydney Cove grew rapidly in the early years of the nineteenth century, as thousands of free settlers took advantage of land grants and promised riches. Britain's stringent inheritance laws, under which firstborn sons claimed all land titles, led second and later sons in particular to grasp the chance to strike out for themselves in this land of opportunity. Adelaide, in 1836, and Melbourne, in 1837, were settled by just such opportunists.

Transportation of convicts ended in 1864. It is estimated that around 160,000 convicts were sent to Australia over 76 years, most of whom stayed on once they were freed. While the number of convicts was insignificant when compared to the free settlers who streamed into Australia in the latter half of the nineteenth century — attracted by gold, cheap land, and the promise of a new life — convict labor played a major role in building Australia's nascent cities.

Strict inheritance laws saw that land in Britain was passed from father to eldest son, and could not be subdivided. Younger sons traditionally entered the clergy or the military. The promise of generous land grants in New South Wales drew the younger sons of England's wealthy to emigrate and establish stock stations of a magnitude they could never have imagined back home — many of which still exist today. As freed convicts joined the increasing number of settlers attracted to the promise of this burgeoning southern land (where labor was in great demand), many began to appreciate that they were better off than if had they stayed in an overcrowded and recently industrialized England.

Together, these disparate colonials and their children battled hostile environments to establish an indigenous culture based on solidarity and a distaste for authority.

Dust rises as stockmen round up cattle on the dry expanse of a Northern Territory ranch.

BOOM AND BUST

The colonies experienced a major boost to their economies when gold was found, first in New South Wales in 1851 and then in prodigious quantities in Victoria. The ensuing gold rush had a dramatic effect, as men left the land and crews jumped ship to seek riches on the gold fields. Fortune-seekers arriving in overcrowded ships came from all corners of the globe. At its peak during the year 1852, over 86,000 people arrived from England alone.

Untamed shanty towns were populated by men who worked hard during the day and at night dreamed of great fortunes, as they sat around the

his plough-share mask they shot at his feet, which were unprotected. Captured, Kelly was sentenced to death and hanged in Melbourne on November 11, 1880. His last words were: "Such is life."

The prosperity that gold brought to Australia accelerated the country's development. Roads and railway lines were laid down, linking the colonies and creating a new-found confidence around the nation. People began talking about an Australian identity that incorporated the ideas — born in the gold fields — of mateship and egalitarianism. A sense was developing that Australia, rather than Britain, was now home.

After the gold rushes Australia went through several cycles of boom and bust, and the Depression

campfires or huddled in pubs to discuss their day with the other diggers. During this period, colonial Australia's first "heroes" were born — bushrangers, who were admired for challenging authority. The term was coined in 1805 to describe escaped convicts who had turned to robbery to survive in the bush. Many poor farmers and laborers also tried their hand at bushranging. Some with colorful sobriquets such as "Yankee" Jack Ellis, Captain Moonlight and "Mad Dog" Morgan became household names, while songs celebrating their exploits became popular. The best known bushranger was Ned Kelly who, after his mother was wrongfully arrested, ambushed and killed three troopers. Outlawed in 1878, he and his gang held up banks and successfully evaded the police for two years. Ned Kelly was finally trapped in Glenrowan in June, 1880, where he defied the police, protecting himself with home-made armor. Realizing that they could not penetrate

of the 1890s saw the growth of new unions and their political arm, the Australian Labor Party, which protected worker's rights within Parliament and was the most successful social democratic party in the world, forming a government in 1908.

Australian men at the turn of the last century were called "Cornstalks." The Cornstalk was typically two meters (six feet) tall, wearing corded pants, red shirt, a wide blue sash and a cabbage tree hat, high boots and a stock whip wrapped around his arm. His character was described by a contemporary source as "slow, easy, indolent in the ordinary way, proud of his country and himself and capable of holding his own in anything in which he is interested." This popularly accepted view of Australians as country types was at odds with the trend towards urbanization — by the start of the twentieth century nearly half the population lived in the six capital cities.

COMING OF AGE

Australia's six independent colonies came together in 1901 to form the Commonwealth of Australia. On the first day of the New Year a procession snaked its way through the streets of Sydney to the wild cheering of 150,000 celebrating onlookers. After Queen Victoria's proclamation was read in Centennial Park, a 21-gun salute announced the birth of the new nation. But despite its independent status, Australia remained loyal to the British Empire, and imperial foreign policy was slavishly followed. The fireworks that saw Australia's true coming of age happened

fourteen years later on the bloody battlefields of World War I.

In the first major encounter involving Australian troops, they lost 8,000 men against a strong Turkish force on the beach at Gallipoli. This battle is remembered on Anzac Day (April 25), when veterans march through the streets of every capital city and major town. Australian soldiers, who in a nod to the country's gold-rush years were known as "diggers," went on to fight on the battlefields and in the trenches of France and Belgium. By the end of the war Australia had lost 59,000 men.

Along with many other countries, Australia's fortunes slumped in the 1930s. The Depression set in, scarring a generation of Australians. Many men without permanent employment took to the road to survive, finding odd jobs as sheep shearers, cattle rustlers and laborers. Known as "swagmen," their swag being the small sack in which they kept all their worldly goods, they had a healthy disregard for authority. Their exploits were celebrated in folk songs, the most famous being *Waltzing Matilda*.

World War II helped end the Depression. Japan conducted bombing raids against Australia's northern coastline between March, 1942 and November, 1943. With Britain fighting for its very survival and unable to help, the entry of the United States into the Pacific theater of war in 1941 was welcomed.

Within weeks of Japan's attack on Pearl Harbor, 4,600 American troops arrived in Australia. On March 17, 1942, General Douglas MacArthur arrived to establish headquarters in Brisbane, and over the next few years hundreds of thousands of American troops passed through. Although American GIs were criticized as being "over-sexed, over-paid and over here" — mainly because of their reputation for being free-spenders and their success with local women — a lasting bond and mutual respect developed between the fighting men of Australia and the United States.

In the aftermath of the war, the debate on Australia's future turned to its pitifully small population. To overcome this weakness the catch-cry was coined "populate or perish." And so the great postwar period of immigration began.

MULTICULTURAL AUSTRALIA

Every aspect of contemporary Australian life has been influenced by the influx of immigrants over the past fifty-odd years. The first wave came from Europe: Britons who had seen their homes demolished during the Blitz and the Continent's displaced people and refugees who desperately wanted an opportunity to build a new future.

Change came, albeit in very small ways. Immigrants established restaurants that allowed them to enjoy foods from their homelands. For a few years they had these to themselves, but in the late 1960s students would hunt out Balkan or Greek restaurants, which were not only exotic but cheap.

As ethnic communities gathered in different suburbs, the character of neighborhoods began to change. Walking through Cabramatta in Sydney is like visiting an Asian city, while Johnston Street in Melbourne, with its tapas bars, is a little piece of Spain. In a number of capitals Chinatown is a major tourist attraction, with restaurants that employ the best chefs from Hong Kong, Shanghai and Singapore. Whereas once Australians might venture to the local Chinese restaurant for some chow mien, today you are more likely to find diners arguing the relative merits of Cantonese regional cooking and the more spicy Sichuan cuisine.

The stamp of immigration goes deeper than the pleasures of the table. Although Australians were

OPPOSITE: Introduced by early explorers, camels thrive in the Red Centre. ABOVE: Newlyweds on Hamilton Island, part of the Whitsunday chain

at first unused to non-English speakers, the initial cultural shock gave way to a liberalization and an acceptance that Australia was a multicultural society. Newcomers have widened Australian perspectives of the world. Just as the continent itself lies over a tectonic plate sluggishly moving a few millimeters each year towards Asia, so also are Australia's attitudes and policies looking towards the Orient.

The Vietnam War brought home to Australia that it was geographically part of Asia, and Australia's involvement there provided the first local in-depth reporting of that part of the world. It was the Whitlam government of the early 1970s that turned the country's foreign policy towards its neighbors. The slow continental drift is now

CONFLICT AND RECONCILIATION

Captain Cook, on his voyage of discovery, wrote in his journal that the Aborigines "appear to be the most wretched people upon the Earth, but in reality they are far happier than we Europeans." Despite Cook's insight, it did not stop him basing his claim on the eastern seaboard of Australia on the legal fiction that he had discovered a *terra nullius* — a land without people.

At the time of Cook's visit the Aboriginal population was probably between 500,000 and one million. The subsequent interaction between white settlers and Aborigines almost turned Cook's legal

being overtaken by a profound cultural shift, as Australia embraces more immigrants from Southeast Asia. Although they compose just five percent of the population, East Asians are the fastest growing immigrant group.

Although nearly 23% of the current population was born overseas, Australia remains a monarchy, and Queen Elizabeth II of Great Britain is also the Queen of Australia. A few changes have occurred. In 1984, "Advance Australia Fair" replaced "God Save the Queen" as the national anthem, although the Union Jack still occupies a corner of the national flag. Over the last few decades the belief that Australia should become a republic has become almost universal, although a 1999 referendum rejected the alternative, presidential model proposed by the sitting conservative government. Most political commentators believe it is only a matter of time before the Republic of Australia becomes a reality.

fiction into fact. Disease, high child mortality rates and persecution of the local inhabitants dramatically reduced their numbers during the eighteenth and nineteenth centuries. At the beginning of the twentieth century the Aboriginal population was as low as 50,000. Today it is estimated that there are about 230,000 people of Aboriginal descent living in Australia.

Aborigines were displaced, often by force, by early white settlers who spread out from their first settlements to secure grazing land for sheep. In Tasmania dispossession turned to genocide, nearly wiping out it's indigenous population. Only a few survived on offshore islands.

The settlers' weapons easily overpowered those of the indigenous people, but the Aborigines did not simply give up their land without a fight. In many areas of the country guerrilla warfare tactics were used by Aboriginal people in retaliation for the white settlers' transgressions of tribal law. In some areas with a high Aboriginal population, such as near Hobart and Sydney and Cooktown on Cape York, different tribes united to launch attacks on the colonists. The expansion of the colony, however, was not greatly hindered by Aboriginal resistance, much weakened by the diseases brought by Europeans. The introduction of alcohol further debilitated their society.

In 1905, the government adopted a policy of "protecting" the Aborigines by segregating them from the influences of European society. This formalized and accelerated a movement initiated in the 1870s of moving Aboriginal people to missions and reserves. This was in fact a reaction to widespread concern that Australia had witnessed the destruction of a race with the death of Truganini — purportedly "Tasmania's Last Aborigine" — in Hobart in 1876. Aborigines were removed from their traditional territories and different tribes were moved onto the same reserves without any regard to kinship or relationships. The Aboriginals Ordinance in 1918 placed many Aboriginal children of white fathers in the foster care of white families, as a way of ensuring the "purity" of Aboriginal communities. This institutionalized racism continued until the 1930s, and in some cases into the 1960s, resulting in a "stolen generation" of people, forcibly cut off from their Aboriginal heritage.

There is a saying among Aborigines that he who loses his dreaming is lost. The arrival of Europeans almost ended the traditional Aboriginal way of life, and today most live in cities and towns or in isolated settlements near tribal lands. In the outback and urban communities, though, elders are making every effort to ensure that their children are told the secrets of the Dreamtime so they do not lose touch with their religious and spiritual values. Although few continue their nomadic ways, many of Australia's Aboriginal people still speak traditional languages at home, and there is a growing interest among younger people to learn more about the life, art, stories and music of their forefathers.

In recent years, Australia has become more sensitive to the plight of Aborigines, resulting in increased health and educational services, greater recognition of Aboriginal land rights and a growing appreciation of Aboriginal culture.

Aborigines' claims to their traditional lands remains a festering sore. The Aboriginal Lands Rights Act of 1976 returned large tracts of land to traditional owners, including over 50% of the Northern Territory. A High Court decision in the 1990s overturned the legal concept that Australia was occupied as *terra nullius* and opened the way for Aboriginal land rights. While "white mans' law" remains valid on Aboriginal lands — this is another point of contention among many groups — individual Land Councils evoke their own supplementary laws which must be respected by

residents and visitors. Such laws restrict access to sacred sites, promote respect for the land and its people, and respond to particular needs and beliefs of their communities.

There are other changes heralding a period of reconciliation: school programs devote increasing attention to Aboriginal history and culture, contemporary Aboriginal art is shown in the best galleries and the relationship traditional Aborigines have with their land is starting to be appreciated by a world that has shown itself incapable of reaching a balance with nature.

Reconciliation between the Aboriginal people and the rest of the country has only just begun. There is a tentative optimism among Aborigines,

but one tempered by 200 years of accumulated disappointments. In 2000, "walks for reconciliation" were held across the country, drawing unprecedented numbers of protestors from all political streams, demanding a formal apology from the federal government to Australia's indigenous people. Although the retrogressive "One Nation" party regularly makes the headlines with their confrontational and racist assertions, the truth is they receive only a tiny percentage of the national vote, and that only in the north and far west of the country. The true political force that the two major parties have been obliged to acknowledge is the voice of the Greens, who in the 2001 elections emerged as a viable third alternative.

As hosts of the 2000 Olympic Games, Australia entered the twenty-first century on a wave of optimism, amid a growing appreciation of the comfortable lifestyle shared by most Australians. But across the country this is tempered with a widespread sense of the need to face up to unanswered questions, to acknowledge past mistakes and present inequities, and to work together to ensure that all Australians are given a "fair go."

OPPOSITE: Aboriginal activists outside South Australia's Government House in Adelaide, protesting against the state's mining activities. ABOVE: Taking a break in the outback.

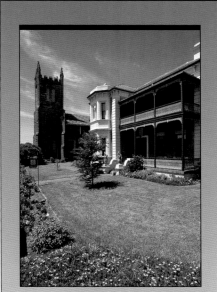

Sydney
and
Northern
New
South
Wales

CREATIVE, ELOQUENT AND VIVIDLY DESCRIPTIVE, Captain James Cook must have had an off day when he named New South Wales in 1770. The man who came up with "Botany Bay," "Cape Tribulation," "Whitsunday Passage," "Glass House Mountains," and "Magnetic Island," might have been overwhelmed by the responsibility of attaching a label to the 4,000 km (2,500 miles) of lushly forested tropical and subtropical coastline, sandy coves and coral islands and cays he had spent four months navigating. The new-found land was neither new nor more than vaguely resembled South Wales, but the misnomer stuck.

Britain showed little interest in the far-off land at first — giving the Yura and Dharuk Aboriginal people of the lands around Botany Bay and Port

ski fields of the Snowy Mountains near the Victorian border, including Australia's highest peak, Mount Kosciusko at 2,228 m (7,310 ft).

The Great Dividing Range's proximity to the coast gives birth to broad fast-flowing rivers, carving the deep bays and magnificent harbors that are the most identifiable feature of the New South Wales coast. Along the north coast the blue-green eucalyptus forests mingle with the more extraverted colors of the subtropical rainforest. Cooler coastal weather patterns rarely make it across the divide; sudden downpours are common in Sydney — when it rains it pours — but over the mountains, the dry western plains of the wheat belt gradually merge into the legendary outback.

Jacksona few years grace. But by the mid-1780s, following the loss of their colonies in the 1776 American War of Independence, London's prisons and workhouses were overflowing. The solution chosen by the British dramatically and irrevocably altered Aboriginal history. The first fleet of convicts and settlers arrived at Sydney Cove in 1788, and the colony of New South Wales grew rapidly to cover over half of Australia — encompassing modern-day Queensland, Victoria and parts of South Australia. Although today the state occupies only 10% of the continent — it's roughly the size of California — over a third of Australia's population live here, 96% of them within an hour's drive of the coast.

Geographically, New South Wales has a bit of everything. The rugged Great Dividing Range stretches along the state's eastern seaboard. Marked by vertiginous outcrops, deep gorges, and rich soil supporting diverse vegetation, it rises to form the

For many visitors New South Wales is a land of perfect beaches, great surf and outstanding nature (its 70 national parks cover nearly 40,000 sq km, or 15,400 sq miles). Yet the state has a rich, multifaceted and often brutal history. Archeological relics, Dreamtime stories and rock paintings remind visitors of the complex culture of the numerous Aboriginal clans who lived freely on these lands until 1770. The early penal colony, which eventually became the city of Sydney, constructed solid Georgian buildings that remain today — inmates' quarters, churches and government buildings. The subsequent era of exploration, free settlement and westward expansion, followed by the colorful gold rush years, left in its wake historic townships and tall tales throughout the state.

Fireworks on Sydney Harbour Bridge welcome in the new millenium, showering above a fleet of pleasure boats and the Sydney Opera House.

Sydney and Northern New South Wales

SYDNEY

Canberra may be Australia's capital, but Sydney is its heart. Most flights to Australia arrive at its Kingsford–Smith Airport, looping down over the city on their final descent towards runways that jut into Botany Bay. On a clear day, this is the best introduction to Australia. Against a backdrop of densely forested mountains and fronted by the Pacific Ocean, leafy suburbs and red-tiled rooftops gradually give way to the urban landscape of inner Sydney. The first fingers of water seem unconnected: spots of deep blue edged with parkland that break up the concrete and traffic. But quickly the water widens out to the expanse of Port Jackson, held together at its narrowest point by the arch of the Sydney Harbour Bridge. Near the bridge, flashes of sunlight on the oversized seashell that is the Sydney Opera House shine white against the blue of the harbor's deep waters, which are dotted with islands and peppered with sailing boats, ferries, windsurfers, motorboats and tilting seaplanes.

Sydney is a sprawling city with over four million inhabitants. It was Australia's first city and remains its largest, measuring 70 km (43.5 miles) from north to south and 55 km (34 miles) east to west. To the rest of Australia it's a fast-paced urban jungle. By international standards, however, Sydney is definitely laid-back. Far more San Francisco than New York, and with a better bay. Sydneysiders enjoy almost year-round sunshine, without the tropical humidity of Brisbane and Cairns — or only rarely. With such a combination of climate and topography, it's hardly surprising they are such outdoors fanatics.

The never-ending estuaries, coves, islands and inlets of Port Jackson (or Sydney Harbour) form a watery maze that divides the city in two, and today's Sydneysiders live by, on, in, above and occasionally below the sparkling waters of its harbor. They commute by ferry or drive over its soaring bridge. They rollerblade, skateboard, cycle, jog or simply lunch along its banks. Office parties and even weddings are frequently held on boats, and cafés along Bondi and Manly beaches open early to serve coffee and breakfast to the body-conscious who brave the surf from sunrise year-round. For all its legitimate claims as a cosmopolitan, multicultural, innovative and exciting city, Sydney is above all the best this planet has to illustrate the maxim most dear to sun-seekers: "life's a beach." It has 70 of them.

BACKGROUND

Captain Cook sailed into Botany Bay in 1770, naming it after botanist Joseph Banks' excitement at the strange and lush plant growth. Cook noted what he thought was a smaller harbor a little further north, and named this Port Jackson. When

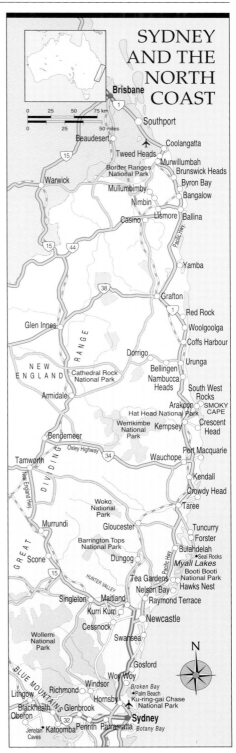

Britain later decided to establish a penal colony in New Holland, as Australia was then known, Cook proposed Botany Bay as an ideal site. But on arriving with the First Fleet in 1788, Captain Arthur Phillip was apparently not convinced of Cook's choice. The fleet waited six days while Phillip explored the surrounding coastline, until finally, on January 26, 1788, he declared Port Jackson to be "the finest harbor in the world" and sailed the fleet through its headlands. Once ashore, Phillip raised the Union Jack and proclaimed the Colony of New South Wales in the name of King George, and himself Governor of it.

Phillip established his colony on lands controlled by Yura (alternatively spelt Eora or Iora) clans — some of the rock carvings in Sydney are over 40,000 years old. Although he endorsed a policy of non-violence towards the Aborigines, the settlers cleared the Yura's forests, restricted their access to traditional hunting and fishing grounds, and even pilfered their fishing nets and baskets and eventually their women. Retaliation was inevitable. Isolated attacks were prevented from escalating into full-blown warfare by a smallpox epidemic in 1789, which almost annihilated the Aboriginal population (influenza, pneumonia and tuberculosis added to the devastation). Guerrilla attacks continued, though, led by angered warriors like Pemulway, who speared the Governor's gamekeeper in 1790 and fought against the New South Wales Corps until he was killed in 1802.

Although Britain continued to transport convicts to Sydney until 1840, the colony's steady growth owed more to land grants and other schemes that attracted thousands of free settlers. Convicts provided necessary labor (just below convicts on the social scale, young Aborigines were employed as servants and farmhands). Pioneers built homesteads up and down the coast, and in 1813 a track was finally cleared through the Blue Mountains, opening up the fertile plains to the west. But in 1850–1851, the news of sizeable nuggets of gold found near Bathurst changed the face of the new colony. Fortune-seekers the world over set sail for Sydney Harbour. Sydney's population doubled over the next 10 years.

GENERAL INFORMATION

Sydney's main tourist information office is the **Sydney Visitor Centre** ((02) 9255 1788 WEB SITE www.sydneycity.nsw.gov.au, 106 George Street, The Rocks, open 9 AM to 6 PM daily; it's often referred to by its former name, The Rocks Visitor Centre. Other helpful centers are **Bondi Visitors Information Centre** ((02) 9130 5311, corner of Campbell Parade and Roscoe Street, Bondi Beach; **Darling Harbour Visitors Centre** ((02) 9268 0111, Palm Grove, Darling Harbour; and **Manly Visitors Information Bureau** ((02) 9977 1088, on South

Steyne, Manly Beach. To make travel arrangements in New South Wales contact the **Countrylink NSW Travel Centre** ((02) 9224 4744 TOLL-FREE 132 077 WEB SITE www.tourism.nsw.gov.au, 31 York Street. **Travelers Information Service** ((02) 9669 5111 books accommodation and tours, and helps with travel passes.

Sydney's **GPO** ((02) 9244 3700, 159–171 Pitt Street, is open Monday to Friday from 8:15 AM to 5:30 PM, Saturday 8:30 AM to noon. Open 24 hours, **Kinko's** ((02) 9267 4141, 175 Liverpool Street, and ((02) 9252 3245, 58 Pitt Street, has copy, fax, computer and Internet facilities. The **Telstra** center at 130 Pitt Street also has fax services.

Most city banks have foreign exchange facilities. **Westpac** ((02) 9215 3366, 60 Martin Place, usually has good rates and doesn't charge to cash travelers' checks. **American Express** ((02) 9239 0666 is at 92 Pitt Street.

There are Internet cafés at every turn in Sydney. A popular one is the **Well Connected Coffee Shop** ((02) 9566 2655, 35 Glebe Point Road. The Hotel Sweeney's **Internet Café** ((02) 9261 5666, located at 236 Clarence Street, is also well managed. For a **city guide** covering upcoming events, concerts, and restaurants and cafés, visit WEB SITE www.sydney.citysearch.com.au.

All public hospitals have emergency rooms open 24 hours. The most central is **Sydney Hospital** ((02) 9382 7111, on Macquarie Street. The Wayside Chapel ((02) 9358 6577, 29 Hughes Street, offers crisis counseling and assistance, and telephone counseling is also offered by **Lifeline** (131 114. For medical and other **emergencies** throughout Australia dial (000, Australia's equivalent of the United States' 911 service.

New South Wales tourist information is also handled by the Sydney Visitor Centre (132 077 WEB SITE www.tourism.nsw.gov.au. For bus and rail information throughout New South Wales, call **Countrylink** (132 232 or the Sydney Visitor Centre.

GETTING AROUND

Sydney has a very efficient, if complicated, public transportation system. State Transit runs Sydney Buses, Sydney Ferries and CityRail. In addition, there are 37 private bus lines and eight private ferry operators. Information on all public transportation services can be found on the Internet at WEB SITE www.sydneytransport.net.au, or pick up a copy of the excellent **Sydney Public Transport Map** at Manly Wharf, The Rocks Visitor Centre, Circular Quay or Bondi Junction. Far more than just a map, it manages to make the system seem almost comprehensible. Call **Infoline** (131 500 (lines open 6 AM to 10 PM) for State Transit queries.

Travel passes not only lower costs considerably, they're a good way to avoid the long Sydney queues — a DayRover, a SydneyPass or a weekly

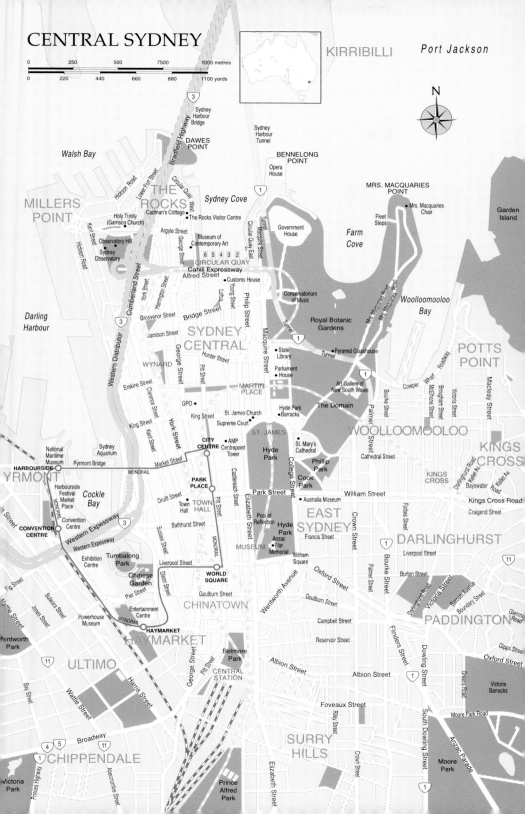

TravelPass covers unlimited use of State Transit services; a DayPass is for their buses and ferries only. Family passes allow all the kids to travel for the price of one.

Sydney Ferries operate **jetcats and ferries** from 6 AM to midnight seven days a week, linking the city terminus at Circular Quay with north and south Sydney ports. Their office is on Circular Quay, opposite Wharf 4. Hegarty's Ferries ((02) 9206 1167 and The Rocket ((02) 9264 7377 also provide regular ferry services in the harbor, and a number of private companies have services reaching as far as Palm Beach (see TOURS AND CRUISES, below).

The **CityRail** network operates between 4:30 AM and midnight. Lines are color-coded. They also have trains to the Blue Mountains and Hunter Valley. For other rail or bus travel you'll need **Countrylink** (132 232. Curving above the city center, the futuristic 3.6-km (2.2-mile) **Monorail** ((02) 9552 2288 links a number of sights, including the Sydney Aquarium and the Powerhouse Museum. It offers good views of the harbor. Locals tend to disparage it, but the ride is pretty cool. Tickets cost $2.50, a day-pass $6.

Displays at most **bus** stops provide timetable information, and **Nightride** services take over from midnight. Night buses have radio links to taxi companies, so you can arrange for a cab to meet you at your destination. Bright green and yellow **Airport Express buses** run every 10 minutes between 7 AM and 7:30 PM on weekdays, less often at other times. Route 300 runs from Circular Quay via George Street, Town Hall and Sydney Central stations, route 350 from Kings Cross via Oxford Street. Star City Casino operates a covey of free shuttle buses throughout Sydney so that punters can hang onto their cash until they get there — the casino is conveniently located at Darling Harbour, so make use of the free ride. Ask if one runs nearby.

It's usually easy enough to flag down a taxi in Sydney, and there are cab ranks outside most train stations and wharves. The 20-minute drive from central Sydney to the airport will cost around $20, unless it's peak hour, when you can double that. Be sure to tell the driver clearly whether you're going to the domestic or the international terminal; the free shuttle service connecting the terminals takes 20 minutes. Larger companies include **Yellow Cabs** TOLL-FREE 131 924, **ABC Cabs** TOLL-FREE 132 522, **Premier Taxis** ((02) 9897 4000, **RSL Cabs** ((02) 9699 0144, and **Taxis Combined Services** ((02) 8332 8888. Water Taxis are costly but fun. Try **Harbour Shuttles** ((02) 9810 5010, **Harbour Taxi Boats** ((02) 9555 1155, or **Taxis Afloat** ((02) 9955 3222.

There are plenty of car rental companies throughout the city. **Bayswater Car Rental** ((02) 9360 3622, 180 William Street, Kings Cross, offers among the best value. **Dollar Rent a Car** ((02) 9955 3970, 5 McLaren Street, North Sydney, offers free car delivery and pretty good rates. Both have one-way rentals, as do Avis, Budget, Hertz and Thrifty, which all have desks at Kingsford–Smith airport and branches in William Street, Kings Cross. **Avis** ((02) 9357 2000 is at No. 214, **Budget** ((02) 9339 8888 at No. 93, **Thrifty** ((02) 9380 5399 at No. 75, and **Hertz** ((02) 9360 6621 at No. 65.

Bicycles can be rented from **Centennial Park Cycles** ((02) 9398 5027 or (02) 9398 8138, 50 Clovelly Road, Centennial Park.

WHAT TO SEE AND DO

The Rocks and Circular Quay

Australia's first permanent British settlement grew on Sydney Cove's rocky peninsula. Hence **The**

Rocks. Australia's oldest precinct is built around winding streets connected by flights of narrow stone steps. Its scrubbed cobblestone streets, converted warehouses, historic buildings and convict-built terraces now draw in the tourists with an exhausting number of art, craft and souvenir shops and tempting cafés and restaurants. The Sydney Visitor Centre in George Street provides useful maps and staff are exceptionally helpful.

A six-story art deco building along the waterfront, the **Museum of Contemporary Art** ((02) 9252 4033 or (02) 9241 5892 (24-haur recorded information), 140 George Street, is bright and stylish. Its permanent displays covers painting, sculpture and mixed media, as well as cutting-edge computer animation. They have an energetic program of temporary exhibitions. Aboriginal artists are particularly well represented. Closed Tuesdays; otherwise it's open daily 9 AM to 4 PM; entry $9.

Inner Sydney's oldest surviving house, **Cadman's Cottage ℂ** (02) 9247 8861, 110 George Street, was built on the original shoreline in 1816 — John Cadman moored his boat out front, which gives an idea of how much today's Circular Quay encroaches on the harbor. Open 9 AM to 5 PM; free entry. Further down George Street, colonial warehouses dating from 1830 make up Campbells' Storehouse, now a row of interesting-but-expensive waterfront restaurants. The fabulous views of Sydney Cove, the Harbour Bridge and the Opera House are well worth the price of a coffee and cake though. Nearby Macquarie Point is the place for the classic snapshot of Sydney Opera House and the Harbour Bridge.

apparently the exhilaration can go to your head: over 100 marriage proposals have been made at the summit so far.

Views from under the Moreton Bay fig trees on **Observatory Hill**, the highest point in the city, are especially lovely at dusk, which is also the best time to visit the 1858 **Sydney Observatory ℂ** (02) 9217 0485. Its heritage exterior belies the twenty-first-century technology within. During the day visitors can view solar systems up to 4.5 million light years away and at night zoom in on Neptune. The permanent exhibition includes interactive displays and compares the Greek mythology of the northern sky with the Aboriginal mythology of Australia's southern sky. Free entry 2 PM to 5 PM

The **Sydney Harbour Bridge** took nine years to build, and 11 workman fell to their deaths during construction. It opened in 1932. The two pylon lookouts ℂ (02) 9218 6888 are open daily, 10 AM to 5 PM — it's a 200-step climb to the top. Enter via stairs on Cumberland Street, The Rocks, or from Milsons Point on the North Shore. Crocodile Dundee actor Paul Hogan once worked as a Harbour Bridge painter, and returned to inaugurate the vertigo-inducing **Harbour Bridge Climb** ℂ (02) 8274 7777 E-MAIL admin@bridgeclimb.com WEB SITE www.bridgeclimb.com, 5 Cumberland Street. Outfitted in stylish blue overalls and a chunky harness, climbers edge their way over arches, ladders and catwalks to the summit, 134 m (440 ft) above the water. They're rewarded with 360-degree harbor views and the right to say "I did it." Prices vary from $100 and $150 per climb (it's cheaper to do it during the week). But be careful,

weekdays, 10 AM to 5 PM weekends, night programs vary but generally cost around $7.

The inside of the nearby pseudo-Gothic **Garrison Church**, built between 1840 and 1843, is adorned with the dusty flags of the British regiments who once worshiped here; the church is still used by the Australian Army.

The main commuter terminal for harbor ferries, **Circular Quay** is also the only place Sydney's bus, ferry and train services intersect (it was originally called Semi-Circular Quay, which makes a lot more sense). To confuse visitors, its five wharves are numbered from two to six — Wharf 1 having succumbed to the gentrification of Circular Quay East. Opposite the wharves, the imposing colonial **Customs House** building is now a cultural and gallery

For those who dare, the Harbour Bridge Climb affords unparalleled views across central Sydney and the Opera House on Bennelong Point.

space; its **djamu Gallery (** (02) 9247 2285 — *djamu*
means "I am here" in the language of Sydney's traditional owners, the Yura — houses the Australian
Museum's collection of indigenous art and cultural
exhibits from Australia and the South Pacific, the
largest of its kind in Australia. From time to time
the gallery hosts free cultural programs, including
concerts and Aboriginal storytelling.

Past Circular Quay, on Bennelong Point are the
pearl-like sails of Australia's most famous urban
icon, the **Sydney Opera House (** (02) 9250 7111
FAX (02) 9251 3943. Inlaid in the paving from the
Quay towards the Opera House are tributes to writers who are from or have written about Australia, among them Banjo Patterson, Robert Louis
Stevenson, Ted Hughes (of *The Fatal Shore*), Mark
Twain, and dozens of others. Although the first
Opera House performance was in 1960, when
militant unionists invited black American singer
and activist Paul Robeson to sing at the building
site, work wasn't completed until 1973. The building has weathered heavy criticism over its design,
its cost ($105 million vs. an original budget
of $6.7 million) and its acoustics. The design has
since grown on Sydneysiders, the interior has recently been overhauled and its acoustics fine-
tuned. In addition, free lunchtime organ recitals
in the 25-m-high (85-ft) Concert Hall, which seats
2,700, have opened it to the public. The Opera
House now holds 3,000 opera, theater, dance and
concert performances a year. Guided one-hour
tours depart from the tour office on the lower
forecourt from 9 AM to 4 PM, except during performances or rehearsals. Call in advance; adults
$12.90, children $8.90.

Built during the Crimean War in 1857 as a defense post against any possible Russian invasion,
Fort Denison sits incongruously on tiny Pinchgut
Island, east of the Opera House. Its One O'clock
Cannon is still fired daily. The island was once used
to punish recalcitrant convicts. Marooned here in
chains, they were given meager supplies of bread
and water, hence the island's name. There are tours
to the island from Circular Quay, but you get a
reasonably good view of it from the Manly, Rose
Bay or Watsons Bay ferries.

Darling Harbour

A lot of money has been spent on attracting tourist dollars to the newly developed Darling Harbour area, easily reached by Monorail from the city
center. It suffers a little from its very commercial
orientation, and the monolithic Star City casino
complex (** (02) 9777 9000, 80 Pyrmont Street, open
24 hours, adds little charm to the area. Nevertheless, some of Sydney's must-sees are in the Darling Harbour area. Although the restaurants in the
Harbourside Marketplace are average and overpriced, the wide boardwalk is pleasant on a warm
evening, with the city skyline sparkling across the

small harbor. Across the Monorail walk-bridge,
the Cockle Bay development boasts better restaurants and a couple of urban-chic bars.

A celebration of science, technology and popular culture, the ever-changing **Powerhouse Museum (** (02) 9217 0111 WEB SITE www.phm.gov.au,
500 Harris Street, Ultimo, is housed in a converted
power station. Its dynamic exhibitions include
hands-on interactive displays often combining
videos and computer gadgetry. Open daily 10 AM
to 5 PM; adults $8, children $5. Exhibitions at the
National Maritime Museum ((02) 9298 3777 or
(005) 562 002 (recorded information) WEB SITE
www.anmm.gov.au, 2 Murray Street, range from
Aboriginal canoes to First Fleet and more modern naval vessels. Most memorable, though, are
tours on the working vessels moored outside: a
Vietnamese refugee boat, the 1983 America's
Cup-winning *Australia II* racing yacht, the evoca-
tively named HMAS *Vampire* naval destroyer

(nicknamed "The Bat"), and a military submarine. Open 9:30 AM to 5 PM daily; adults $10, children $6.

Plexiglas tunnels give a fish-eye view of the harbor at the **Sydney Aquarium** ((02) 9262 2300 WEB SITE www.sydneyaquarium.com.au, Aquarium Pier, Darling Harbour. There are three floating oceanariums to wander through. One contains a consternating array of Australia's native sharks and enormous rays, some measuring more than an impressive two meters (seven feet) across. Other tanks include a seal sanctuary, kaleidoscopic fish partying around a live section of coral reef, and displays of Sydney Harbour marine life. It's open 9:30 AM to 10 PM every day; adults cost $19 and children $9.

Large-scale, high-tech (and high-decibel) rides and virtual reality games at **Sega World** ((02) 9273 9273, 1–25 Harbour Street, are generally a hit with older kids, particularly if the weather lets you down. Adults $28, children and accompanying

adults $22, Sega World opens weekdays at 11 AM, weekends at 10 AM, and closes at 10 PM Fridays and Saturdays, other nights 8 PM.

Sydney's Chinese population numbers around 300 000. With the influx of capital from ex-Hong Kong Chinese, **Chinatown** has grown rapidly over the last decade. Its red gates are in Dixon Street, under which soil, sand and rock from Guangdong Province have been buried. Sussex Street is the center of it all though, between Goulburn and Hay streets, and many of its restaurants are open all night long (see WHERE TO EAT, below). Interspersed with the restaurants and teahouses are jewelry stores and upmarket designer boutiques. The lakes, bridges and waterfalls of the serene **Chinese Gardens** on Harbour Street are a welcome change from the bustle.

Many of Darling Harbour's restaurants offer convivial outdoor areas, perfect to make the most of Sydney's balmy evenings.

West of Darling Harbour, on Blackwattle Bay, the **Sydney Fish Markets** are reputed to be second only to Tokyo's Tsukiji. Morning auctions sell premium tuna, barramundi, trevally and snapper to Japan; local restaurateurs and Sydneysiders join in or shop at the many stalls. A number of stalls prepare sushi and sashimi on the spot, others sell fishy dishes from steaming mussels to fish and chips. Or just buy a dozen Sydney rock oysters and a chilled bottle of wine and make the most of the quayside tables.

City Center

The haphazard layout of roads in Sydney and its inner suburbs owes its pattern to random paths created by meandering the bullock carts that once moved goods between the business district and Sydney Cove. Today's high-rise buildings make central Sydney's streets appear even narrower. Streets to the south of the city are more orderly, with **Pitt**, **George** and **Castlereagh** streets forming the heart of the shopping district.

Australia's tallest building, the 305-m (1,000-ft) **Centrepoint Tower** ((02) 9229 7444, at the corner of Castlereagh and Market streets, provides panoramic views of Sydney and the harbor. Open Sunday to Friday 9:30 AM to 10.30 PM and Saturday to 11:30 PM; admission $10 adults, $5 children. Centrepoint is pretty much at the heart of downtown. Catch the Monorail at the corner of Market and Pitt streets and weave your way among buildings along the 3.6-km (2.2-miles) loop that links Darling Harbour to the city center.

Hyde Park Barracks was built as a dormitory for 600 male convicts, and later used to house the New South Wales Regiment. The building was designed by ex-convict Francis Greenway, convicted for forgery. The barracks now house a museum with rooms devoted to different aspects of Sydney life from the colonial period to modern times, including a room on women and how they made their way to Australia over the last two centuries. Convict dormitories have been reconstructed on two floors. Greenway also designed the adjacent **St. James' Church**. It was originally intended to be a courthouse, changing identity during construction. From Hyde Park, Macquarie Street passes several neoclassical buildings associated with the early history of the colony. The oldest section of **Parliament House** was built between 1811 and 1816 as a hospital and then donated to the state in return for a concession on importing rum. Open Monday to Friday, 10 AM to 4 PM, admission free. Almost next door, the Doric-colonnaded **State Library** contains Captain Cook's original ledgers, along with diaries and letters written by early explorers, governors and settlers — including Captain Bligh's log books.

East of Macquarie Street, the **Royal Botanic Gardens** extend from the peninsula above the Opera House to Mrs. Macquaries Road on the far side of Farm Cove, the Domain running along its eastern and southern limits and extending the green belt through to Hyde Park. This is the site of the colony's first attempt at growing vegetables, and the tiny farm has been preserved. Within the gardens is the ebullient, Gothic-revival **Government House**, atop the hill overlooking the Opera House. The interior has been lavishly restored to its original opulence. Open 10 AM to 3 PM Fridays, Saturdays and Sundays only — the upside is that entrance is free. Governor Macquarie's wife had a seat hewn into the rock of the opposite headland: a prime spot for a picnic, with views of Farm Cove, Government House and the Opera House.

The **Art Gallery of New South Wales** ((02) 9225 1744, in the neighboring Domain, houses one of Australia's finest collections of Australian, European and Asian art. Its **Yiribana Gallery** displays an extensive permanent exhibition of Australian Aboriginal art which is free of charge. The gallery hosts excellent temporary exhibitions too. Open 10 AM to 5 PM. Another good gallery of Aboriginal art is **Jinta Desert Art** ((02) 9290 3639 WEB SITE www.jintaart.com.au, 154 Clarence Street, open 10 AM to 6 PM Monday to Saturday, 1 PM to 6 PM Sunday, which exhibits and sells a wide selection of traditional and contemporary bark paintings and artifacts.

Inner East

East of the Domain is the buzzing inner-city pocket of **Kings Cross**, **Darlinghurst**, **Woolloomooloo** and **Surry Hills**, and the residential harbor-side (and thus elite) **Potts Point** and **Elizabeth Bay**.

The liveliest street in Sydney is **Oxford Street**. From Hyde Park in the city it cuts through the inner east and runs all the way to Bondi Junction. This long street is lined with artsy shops, alternative businesses, and funky cafés and pubs. There are dozens of gay bars and clubs along the Darlinghurst strip of Oxford Street — Sydney's equivalent of San Francisco's Castro district. Known as "The Golden Mile," it really fires up for the flamboyant **Gay and Lesbian Mardi Gras Parade** on the first Saturday of March, and the ensuing **Mardi Gras Party** (see FESTIVE FLINGS, page 46 in YOUR CHOICE). Appreciating Sydney's generally relaxed and tolerant attitude to its enormous up-front and out gay and lesbian population is essential to understanding the city — the Mardi Gras is Australia's largest outdoor event. While most of the inner east residential neighborhoods (and Newtown to the west) have large gay populations, "Darlo's" queer society is Sydney's strongest, rivaled only by neighboring Surry Hills. There's also a strong lesbian community here, but Sydney's true lesbian turf is Leichhardt to the west — often referred to as "Dykeheart." For an online guide to Oxford Street go to WEB SITE www.toolkit.com.au/OxfordNet.

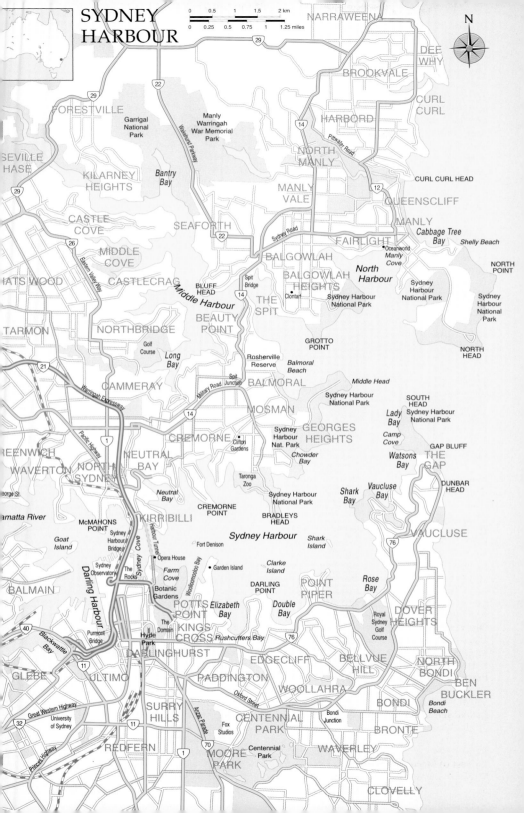

The **Sydney Jewish Museum** ((02) 9360 7999, 148 Darlinghurst Road, Darlinghurst, chronicles the Holocaust and Australia's Jewish history with exhibits, videos and audiovisual displays. The museum contains a series of displays on the history of Jewish life in the city and settlement of Australia generally, as well as a multi-level remembrance of the Holocaust, exceptionally well done and effective. The docents are, in some cases, survivors of the death camps and offer first-hand reports of their history.

North of Oxford Street off William Street, the **Kings Cross** neighborhood has been a locally notorious red-light district since United States soldiers were based nearby during World War II.

cafés are interspersed with clothes and designer homeware stores, arthouse cinemas, and good book stores. A number of successful Australian fashion designers began with stalls among the wind-chimes and crafts of **Paddington Village Bazaar**, held every Saturday in St. John's Churchyard on the corner of Oxford and Newcombe streets.

There are over 70 art galleries in the Paddington area. Most are included in the *Guide & Map to Art Galleries in Eastern Suburbs & Inner City* — ask for a copy at the Sydney Visitors Center. **Hogarth Galleries** ((02) 9360 6839, 7 Walker Lane, is one of the country's foremost galleries representing Aboriginal and Torres Strait Islander artists (closed Monday). **Coo-ee Aboriginal Art** ((02) 9332 1544,

Characterized by strip joints and porn shops, the Cross is a colorful mix of student travelers, bearded bikers, prostitutes, young kids sitting on the curbs smoking and drinking, and budget tourists toting dusty backpacks. During the day it's crammed with tourists along for the show. The area also hosts a dense selection of inexpensive hotels, cheap eating places, and other resources for the traveler, often on quiet tree-lined side streets. Only five minutes from Kings Cross, a leafy park skirts the water and expensive sailboats bob at the marinas of picturesque **Rushcutters Bay**, home to the Cruising Yacht Club ((02) 9363 2399. The cove fills with sails on Boxing Day (December 26) for the launch of the Sydney to Hobart Yacht Race.

Paddington

Paddington is Sydney's most fashion-conscious suburb. Here, Oxford Street's modern-Mediterranean

98 Oxford Street, carries paintings, sculpture and limited edition prints by traditional and urban Aboriginal artists and sells Aboriginal art, artifacts, gifts, and music CD-ROMs. The **Five Ways** junction area, a block back from Oxford Street, is peppered with small galleries, inviting shops and friendly pubs. Paddington is also known for its rows of Victorian terrace houses decorated with intricate wrought iron balconies, or "Paddington lace." Glenmore Road at Five Ways shows off some particularly lacy creations.

Centennial Park

Sydney's answer to New York's Central Park is a 220-ha (550-acre) complex of sporting fields, rose gardens, bridle paths and ornamental lakes, open from 6 AM until sunset. Centennial Park opened in 1888 to commemorate Sydney's first hundred years. On weekends Sydneysiders swarm in to picnic, cycle, rollerblade, fly kites, play chess, sunbathe, jog and just play. **Centennial Park Cycles** ((02) 9398 5027, 50 Clovelly Road, rents bicycles and roller-blades. **Centennial Park Horse Hire and Riding School** ((02) 9361 4513 offers horseback riding and private or group lessons for all ages, as does **Moore Park Stables** ((02) 9360 8747, in the Centennial Park Equestrian Centre.

The old Royal Agricultural Society Show Grounds alongside the park have been redeveloped by Fox Studios into a complex comprising film studios, cinemas, and a theme park. The **Fox Studios Backlot** ((1300) 369 849 WEB SITE www .foxstudios.com, Driver Avenue, Moore Park, shows how it is all done, with film sets and props to explore. Participation-orientated visits cover sound studios, make-up rooms and film and television studios. Wandering minstrels and street performers ensure all children partake in the fun. The marketing team have successfully honed in on the young punters' psyches: it's promoted as "a unique dining, entertainment and retailing experience." Don't say you weren't warned. Open 10 AM to 6 PM daily.

South Head

South Head's high sandstone cliffs and 180-degree views of the ocean and back across the harbor to the city make it one of the best spots to watch the beginning of the Sydney-to-Hobart Yacht Race on Boxing Day. Gun placements once used by early colonists in zealous defense of the harbor's narrow entrance are now part of the extensive **Sydney Harbour National Park**. A walking path leads to the popular beach at **Camp Cove**, then continues along to **Lady Bay**, Sydney's only *official* nude beach.

The sheer precipice at **The Gap** is notoriously popular for flamboyant suicides. From Gap Bluff, a six-kilometer (3.7-mile) walk follows the cliffs all the way to Bondi, passing the lovely **St. Peter's Church**, whose pipe organ dates from 1796 and was once lent to the exiled Napoleon.

Bondi

It's crowded, it's noisy, and on a sunny day there's hardly room in the water to practice your Australian crawl. Just seven kilometers (four miles) from the city, Bondi Beach has become synonymous with sun-bronzed Australians. Australia's first lifesaving club was established here in 1906. Drop in for an invigorating morning dip along with octogenarian surfers, body-beautiful urbanites and post-nightclub revelers. The **Bondi Iceberg Club** saltwater lap pool is at the southern end of the beach, barely contained by low concrete walls worn down by the surf's endlessly crashing over them. The pool is open to all, but membership involves mid-winter swims with ice added to the water for extra shivers. A scenic walkway leads around sandstone boulders to Bronte Beach next door.

Bondi's foreshore is a lively mixture of good cafés, cool wine bars, predominately Thai and Italian restaurants, shops selling swimwear and surfing gear, and crowds of people. Rollerblades, surf-boards and skateboards can be rented or bought from **Bondi Boards and Blades** ((02) 9130 3325, 230 Oxford Street, Bondi Junction. Across from the center of the beach, **New Zealand Natural** sells the best ice cream in town.

Taronga Zoo

Worth visiting for its glorious site alone, no matter where you are in Taronga Zoo ((02) 9969 2777, Bradleys Head Road, Mosman, on the harbor's north shore. The glorious backdrop of the harbor and city skyline makes this a particularly Sydney experience. The ascent from the Athol Wharf entrance can be exhausting, so board the Arial Safari Cable Car instead, and stroll back down to the ferry. Marsupials are the stars at the Australian Walkabout area, a good place to begin sorting out your wallabies from your kangaroos.

Manly and North Head

Manly's harbor-side cove was named by Governor Phillip after noting the "confidence and manly behavior" of a group of Aborigines on its shore. On a small peninsula leading to Sydney Harbour's **North Head**, Manly is the gateway to the northern beaches. Appropriately, it has both surf beaches (Queenscliff break is arguably Sydney's best) and harbor beaches popular with windsurfers. In all Manly has 18 beaches, coves and inlets, including Ocean Beach, Shelly Beach, Little Manly and Fairlight. By car, Manly can be reached via the Harbour Bridge or tunnel but the best way across is by ferry, a leisurely 45-minute journey. Alternatively, take the jetcat and whiz across in 20 minutes. The Corso pedestrian mall links Manly Cove on the harbor side of the peninsula and Manly Beach on the Pacific Ocean side.

Manly Beach is lined with tall Norfolk pines, and it's an easy walk from the surf lifesaving club at the southern end along the ocean front to tiny **Fairy Bower Beach** and on to the more sheltered **Shelly Beach**. From here to North Head, Manly Peninsula is largely devoted to the one of the biggest sections of the **Sydney Harbour National Park**, against the backdrop of the Pacific Ocean on this side and the harbour along the southwest coastal — the tourist information office can provide details of the many walks trough the park. Tea trees and banksias in on North Head shelter a colony of indigenous long-nosed bandicoots. For more adventurous walkers, the **Manly Scenic Walkway** follows the edge of the harbor from Manly Wharf, skirting the high cliffs of Dobroyd Head through quiet inlets and bush reserves to

---

The best known beach of them all: Bondi.

Spit Bridge, then crosses over to **Balmoral Beach** at Mosman. Pick up a free map at the **Manly Visitors Information Bureau** ((02) 9977 1088 on the beach end of the Corso. The Sydney Harbour National Park continues along the banks of the harbor to Taronga Zoo.

Manly Surf School ((02) 9977 6977 WEB SITE www.manlysurfschool.com is based at the North Steyne Surf Club, in the middle of the beach. It has patient instructors, teaches to groups of no more than six and is highly recommended. A two-hour lesson costs $40, which includes wetsuit and board rental; prices drop if you book three or more lessons. **Manly Blades** ((02) 9976 3833 WEB SITE www.manlyblades.com.au, opposite the beach, rents rollerblades and skateboards, popular pastimes along the broad beachfront promenade. **Oceanworld Manly** ((02) 9949 2644, on the West Esplanade near Manly Wharf, is more than an excellent aquarium of Australian sea life: twice a day the sharks are hand-fed by scuba-diving keepers. If the 110-m (365-ft) Plexiglas tunnel isn't close enough for you, adults and children over 12 can dive with the sharks. Their beautiful WEB SITE www.oceanworldmanly.com is worth checking out too.

TOURS AND CRUISES

Sydney's biggest lure is its beautiful harbor. Thousands of pleasure craft, yachts and commuter ferries sail it every day. The options for harbor cruising are numerous. The easiest (and cheapest) way to explore Sydney's waters is to take public transportation—buy a TravelPass and you can cruise to your heart's content. But why not sail on a tall ship, a racing yacht, a paddle-steamer or a sea kayak? I give some suggestions below; pick up *The Complete Guide to Harbour Cruises* from Wharf 6, Circular Quay, for more possibilities.

Captain Cook Cruises ((02) 9206 1111, Wharf 6, Circular Quay, operates the largest fleet of harbor cruises. As they are cheaper than most, they can be rather crowded. The two-hour Coffee Cruise departs at 10 AM and 2:15 PM. It circles the harbor from Middle Harbour to the Heads and back past the gracious mansions on the north shore. The Explorer Cruise leaves every two hours from 9:30 AM to 3:30 PM and makes a circuit stopping at major attractions. Passengers can hop off at any stop and catch the next ferry to continue the tour. Captain Cook also has dinner and lunch sailings, and sunset-and-champagne cruises. **Sydney by Sail** ((02) 9247 5151, also at Wharf 6, offers yacht cruises with the option of taking the helm or just enjoying the view. **Sail Venture** ((02) 9264 7377 operates relaxed catamaran cruises four times a day, leaving from Aquarium Wharf, Darling Harbour and the Eastern Pontoon at Circular Quay. **Sydney Showboats** ((02) 9552 2722 has paddle-steamers touring the harbor during the day, with cabaret and

dinner cruises in the evening. For those who'd prefer the freedom of renting their own yacht, **Sunsail** ((02) 9955 6400, in Lavender Bay, operates a sailing school. They also offer skippered or bare-boat charter of small to medium sailboats; their prices are reasonable, particularly if you can get a small group together (see SPORTS AND OUTDOOR ACTIVITIES, below, for more on sailboat charters). Lunch or dinner cruises on Australia's largest tall ship, the *Bounty* ((02) 9247 5151, crewed by pirates, are a definite hit with the kids — let them help sail it with the crew while you enjoy the views and the excellent menu.

Australian Travel Specialists (ATS) ((02) 9555 2700 WEB SITE www.atstravel.com.au, Unit 5, 5 Parsons Street, Rozelle, is a free-of-charge booking service for most tour operators. Ask about half-day sails on America's Cup yacht *Gretal* or the *Ocean Spirit III*, a 26-m (86-ft) catamaran. ATS has branches at Wharf 2, Circular Quay; Shop 208, Manly Wharf; Harbourside, Darling Harbour; and in Centrepoint Tower. ATS also organizes land-based Sydney Sites tours and tours of the Homebush Bay Olympic site.

And then there's the **Duck** ((02) 9251 7774 or 131 007 (ticket hotline) WEB SITE www.aussieduck.com, Clocktower Square, 35 Harrington Street, The Rocks. This amphibious bus tours The Rocks and inner Sydney, then splashes into the harbor for an hour-long cruise.

Sydney Harbour Seaplanes TOLL-FREE (1800) 803 558 take up to six passengers on 15-minute scenic flights from Rose Bay out through Sydney Heads, past Bondi Beach then back over the Harbour Bridge and the Opera House ($55 per person). Combination sightseeing-and-lunch flights to restaurants include a stop at the exquisite Jonah's in Palm Beach ($175 to $210 per person including lunch and wine). **Above and Beyond Sydney** ((02) 9317 3402, at Mascot Airport, has exhilarating helicopter tours of Sydney, flying over the Opera House, the Harbour Bridge, Bondi and the city center for $100 per person.

Sydney Buses runs two **guided bus tours** (131 500. The red *Sydney Explorer* leaves every 20 minutes from 9 AM to 5:15 PM, stopping at 22 of Sydney's more popular attractions. The blue *Bondi and Bay Explorer* passes through Kings Cross, Double Bay, Vaucluse and Watsons Bay, returning via Bondi Beach, Centennial Park and Oxford Street. Both cost around $30 and depart from Circular Quay; passengers can stop as many times as they like along the way.

Two groups can take you the back of a Harley roaring over the bridge, along cliff tops and along the beaches: **Easyrider Motorbike Tours** ((02) 9247 2477, at The Rocks Market, and **Thunder Down Under Harley Tours** ((02) 9294 5353, 1–25 Harbour Street, Darling Walk. Most Sydney neighborhoods organize **walking tours**. Visitors information centers can provide details.

SPORTS AND OUTDOOR ACTIVITIES

All of Sydney's **beaches** are patrolled, so swim between the flags. There is a danger of sharks — albeit extremely slight — at harbor-side beaches, but the twin beaches at Balmoral, near Mosman, are lovely, and part of the northern one is protected by a shark-net. For waves, head to the ocean beaches. The closest is Bondi, though Manly is well worth the extra traveling time. For **lap-swimming**, try Manly's free lap pool, Fairy Bower Rock Pool, Cabbage Tree Bay, off Bower Street, or Bondi Beach's saltwater lap pool, which is something of an icon. Or go swim with the pros in the 2000 Olympics' International Aquatic Centre ((02) 9752 3666, Sydney Olympic Park, Homebush Bay.

to the 2000 Olympics, **Cook and Phillip Park** ((02) 9326 0444, 4 College Street, is between Hyde Park and the Domain. Facilities include a 50-m (164-ft) lap pool, a leisure pool and a hydrotherapy pool, as well as a state-of-the-art fitness and recreation center. The **City Gym** ((02) 9360 6247, located at 107-113 Crown Street, has been going for close to 30 years, and is more popular than ever. Both offer personal trainers and a multitude of classes.

The harbor's convoluted banks provide the city with 240 km (149 miles) of shoreline. Nearly every cove and inlet has its own marina, most of which offer all types of **sailing** boat and cruiser rental. Pacific Sailing School ((02) 9326 2399 at the Cruising Yacht Club ((02) 9363 2399 on Rushcutters

Most surf lifesaving clubs rent surfboards and bodyboards ("boogie boards") for around $15. Many also have surf schools; Palm Beach, Cremorne and Manly are all particularly recommended. The New South Wales Surfriders Association ((02) 9970 7066 has lists of all **surfing** schools. The two harbor-side beaches at Balmoral, past Mosman, are ideal for **windsurfing**. Balmoral Windsurfing ((02) 9960 5344 WEB SITE www.sailboard.net.au, on the beach next to the boat shed, rents equipment and offers lessons in windsurfing, kitesurfing and sailing.

The main venue for the **Sydney 2000 Olympics**, Homebush Bay is 15 km (nine miles) west of the city center. The SuperDome hosts major sporting events. Tours of the site leave the Visitors Centre ((02) 9752 3666 regularly. Many of the Olympics facilities are open to the public. Built in the lead-up

Bay teaches sailing on boats from seven meters (23 ft) to 20 m (66 ft) long. Week-long courses, with three hours of sailing a day, cost around $500. The NSW Canoe Association ((02) 9660 4597 can provide details of the many marinas offering canoe or sea-kayak rentals. Charter Boat Information Service ((02) 9552 1827 can help with chartering sailboats and **houseboats**, and provide information on sailing lessons, skippered boat rental or organized **fishing trips**. The 17-m (57-ft) *Mystery Bay* ((02) 9969 6482 leaves Mosman Bay on open-sea fishing trips at 6 AM Saturdays and Sundays.

Sydney Hang-gliding Centre ((0418) 419 914, Stanwell Park, Bald Hill, gives one-to-one lessons and classes, and rents gliders. Air Support ((02) 9450 2674 also organizes **hang-gliding** and **paragliding** classes. Beginners can opt for tandem rides

Passionate about their harbor, sailing is enormously popular among Sydneysiders.

with experienced fliers, gliding above the northern beaches. A cheaper, and safer, thrill is to hook yourself to a parachute and soar behind a speedboat. Sydney Harbour Paragliding ((02) 9977 6781, or (02) 9977 5296, at Manly Wharf, will have you flying for $49, children $39.

Sydney follows three **football** codes — Rugby League, Rugby Union and Australian Rules. Rugby League WEB SITE www.arl.organization.au is by far the most popular sport in New South Wales. Friday's newspapers detail the weekend's offerings. When the football season is over in September, **cricket** begins — the best games to see are the international sides against Australia, guaranteed to attract a crowd. The New South Wales Cricket

Bay Olympic site Tennis Centre ((02) 9735 4306 hosts major tennis events, including the Adidas International Tennis Tournament in January, but at other times the courts can be used by the public. In leafy surroundings behind Fox Studios, the courts at Centennial Parklands Sports Centre ((02) 9962 7033, on the corner of Anzac Parade and Lang Road in Moore Park, are particularly lovely and well looked after. Sydney's historic White City Tennis Club ((02) 9360 4113, 30 Alma Street, Paddington, is currently being revamped, but its 24 grass and hard-surface courts are still open to the public.

Bicycles and **rollerblades** can be rented in Centennial Park; this is also the place to go for **horseback riding** (see CENTENNIAL PARK, page 84).

Association ((02) 9261 5155 can fill you in on upcoming matches. Tickets for all major sporting events can be booked through Ticketek ((02) 9266 4899.

Golf is popular in Sydney. There are 69 golf courses open to the public. A round costs $15 to $30, and courses are generally quiet on weekdays. Woollahra Golf Course ((02) 9327 1943, in O'Sullivan Road, Rose Bay, is well-maintained and fairly central. Contact the New South Wales Golf Association ((02) 9439 8444 or (02) 9264 8433 for details of other public courses and information on Sydney's private links, including the Royal Sydney Golf Course. Private links generally only allow members to play, although if you're keen you can sometimes talk them into letting you in.

There are hundreds of public **tennis** courts throughout the city. Most charge around $15 an hour, and it's always advisable to book ahead. Ask the tourist office for ones close to you. The Homebush

SHOPPING

The multi-domed **Queen Victoria Building**, on George Street, houses 200 shops in opulent surroundings of sweeping staircases and stained-glass windows. Many of them are upscale fashion outlets and tourist magnets. It is considered by some (including Pierre Cardin — although he did have a vested interest, so to speak) to be the most beautiful shopping center in the world. The building started life as a farmers market, until designer and City Architect George McRae vamped it up in 1898. The huge clock hanging over the atrium shows scenes from the history and colonization of Australia, with moving mechanical figures about one-twelfth scale.

A particularly pleasant place to shop, **The Rocks'** upmarket stores sell opals, Aboriginal artworks — both traditional and contemporary —

along with other gifts and souvenirs from the playful and the tacky to stylish designer pieces. **Gannon House Gallery** ((02) 9251 4474, 45 Argyle Street, stocks genuine Aboriginal artwork and crafts, and they freight worldwide. They've a wide range of beautiful didgeridoos, and offer free lessons with each sale. **Opal Minded** ((02) 9247 9885, 36-64 George Street, sells unset stones and contemporary opal jewelry. Two other recommended opal specialists are **Flame Opal** ((02) 9247 3446, 119 George Street, and **Opal Beauty** ((02) 9264 8772, 5 Argyle Street. On weekends, George Street, just under the bridge, transforms into a crowded open-air **craft and gift market**. The **djamu Gallery Shop** ((02) 9320 6431, Level 2 Customs House, Circular Quay, has a com-

prehensive range of books on Australian and Pacific Islander art and culture, as well as a good selection of traditional and contemporary arts.

Another good weekend market is the **Manly Arts & Crafts Market**, along Sydney Road and Market Lane in Manly. But Sydney's best market is its oldest. The lively **Paddington Village Bazaar** sells clothes, antiques, jewelry, crafts and bric-a-brac, and much more.

Australia produces a number of excellent hiking and worker's boots. Although they're only a necessity if you're planning any real bush-walking, they double up as a fashion statement back home. **Hylands Boot City** ((02) 9555 1400, 104-108 Victoria Road, Rozelle, stocks most brands, with prices a lot lower than those of more tourist-orientated stores. My favorite all-purpose eclectica shop, **Gowings**, on George Street, sells outdoor clothing, backpacking equipment, fishing tackle, travelers'

books and supplies, sundries and underwear, collectible miniature ships, model cars and airplanes, jeans, and expensive brass compasses and sextants.

WHERE TO STAY

Very Expensive

Large marble bathrooms, beautifully decorated and spacious rooms, and balconies overlooking either Walsh Bay or the parkland on Observatory Hill make staying at the **Observatory Hotel** ((02) 9256 2222 FAX (02) 9256 2233 E-MAIL observatory@mail .com, 89–113 Kent Street, The Rocks, a sophisticated experience. The hotel's health club is the best I've seen in Sydney. The Observatory is a member of the Orient Express group, and service here is impeccable. The glorious **Park Hyatt Hotel** ((02) 9241 1234 E-MAIL sydney@hyatt.com.au, 7 Hickson Road, The Rocks, boasts one of the most coveted locations in town. The rooms with the most panoramic views are the Executive Opera Studios (rooms 43 and 44) and the $5,000-a-night Governor's Suite — with the Opera House and Harbour Bridge outside your window, you save on the cost of a cruise.

Expensive

Several good "boutique" hotels — smaller hotels that combine luxury with intimacy — provide more personal service than do the larger luxury hotels. Classy wooden floors and fixtures, high ceilings and an overall chic appeal make the 29-room **Russell Hotel** ((02) 9241 3543 FAX (02) 9252 1652 E-MAIL russhtl@zip.com.au, 143A George Street, The Rocks, an attractive choice. Located in a row of charming nineteenth-century terrace houses, the **Kendall Historic Hotel** ((02) 9357 3200 FAX (02) 357 7606, 122 Victoria Street, Potts Point, is another boutique hotel with lots of character and attention to detail. **Cremorne Point Manor** ((02) 9953 7899 FAX (02) 9904 1265, 6 Cremorne Road, is a Federation mansion on the edge of the harbor with million-dollar views; it is only a short distance from the Cremorne ferry terminal.

Moderate

Staying close to the city center is generally expensive as moderately priced hotels are thin on the ground. One excellent exception to this rule, though, is **Victoria Court** ((02) 9357 3200 TOLL-FREE (1800) 630 505 E-MAIL info@VictoriaCourt.com.au, Victoria Street, Potts Point, which offers remarkable value. The hotel comprises two elegant terrace houses built in 1881, restored and modernized. Rooms are decorated with detailed attention to the hotel's nineteenth-century trimmings. Breakfast is served in an elegant inner courtyard. The owners' personal approach makes this a hotel guests tend to return to. Book well ahead.

Moreton Bay fig trees shade the green lawns of Rushcutters Bay, only minutes from busy Kings Cross.

The **Cambridge** ((02) 9212 1111, 212 Riley Street, Surry Hills, is close to the funky Oxford Street area and a pleasant walk through Hyde Park to downtown. It's part of the Flag Inn chain. Prices can move into the expensive category. Just back from Darling Harbor, rooms at **Aarons Hotel** TOLL-FREE (1800) 101 100 E-MAIL aarons@acay.com.au, 37 Ultimo Road, are basic but clean and comfortable. Staff are helpful, and it's close to the Monorail and central Sydney. For an authentic Aussie pub atmosphere try **O'Malley's Hotel** ((02) 9357 2211, 228 William Street, Kings Cross. This Victorian-era hotel has been carefully restored and provides B&B accommodation in a great location.

Periwinkle ((02) 9977 4668 FAX (02) 9977 6308, 19 East Esplanade, Manly, offers B&B in a nineteenth-century guesthouse. In Paddington, stay at **Paddington Terrace** ((02) 9363 0903 FAX (02) 9327 1476, 76 Elizabeth Street. Hosts Dianne and Ron are friendly and helpful, and their restored Victorian terrace house provides a comfortable and homey atmosphere. The **Garden Studios** ((02) 9356 2355 FAX (02) 9356 4943, at the corner of Bourke and Plunkett streets, Woolloomooloo, are self-contained units a 10-minute walk from the city through the Domain. Opposite the University of New South Wales, **Barker Lodge Motor Inn** ((02) 9662 8444 FAX (02) 9662 2363, 32 Barker Street in Kingsford, is midway between the city and airport. The **Rooftop Motel** ((02) 9660 7777 FAX (02) 9660 7155, 146 Glebe Point Road, Glebe, is near the University of Sydney and close to good inexpensive restaurants. The **Metro Inn** ((02) 9319 4133 FAX (02) 9698 7665, 1 Meagher Street, Chippendale, is close to Chinatown and handy to Central Station.

Inexpensive

Kings Cross is an excellent area for budget accommodation. The **Springfield Lodge** ((02) 9358 3222 FAX (02) 9357 4742 E-MAIL springfieldlodge@wheretostay.com.au, 9 Springfield Avenue, Kings Cross, charges $80 for a spare but clean double with bath, $55 with shared facilities. It's convenient and unlike some reasonable quiet. **Astoria Hotel** ((02) 9356 3666 FAX (02) 9357 1734, 9 Darlinghurst Road, and **Barclay Hotel** ((02) 9358 6133 FAX (02) 9358 4363, 17 Bayswater Road, are both very close to everything, as is the **Wynyard Hotel** ((02) 9299 1330 (established in 1873), at the corner of Clarence and Erskine streets.

New backpacker's lodges seem to pop up every other week in Sydney in anything from converted tenement buildings to purpose-built beachside resorts. The **Sydney Beachouse** ((02) 9981 1177 WEB SITE www.sydneybeachouse.com.au, 4 Collaroy Street, Collaroy Beach, is the latter, with lovely sunny balconies, a swimming pool, Internet access, and free use of surfboards, bodyboards, snorkeling gear, bicycles and volleyballs. Rooms have a maximum of six beds; there are private rooms too. The drawback: it's a little far from the center. **Nomads' The Palms** ((02) 9357 1199 TOLL-FREE (1800) 737 773 FAX (02) 9331 3854, 23 Hughes Street, Potts Point, offers particularly attractive and comfortable budget lodging in one of the more beautiful parts of town. Close to Bondi Beach and the city center, private doubles with bathrooms cost $50. All rooms are heated in winter and air-conditioned in summer. The lodge has fully equipped laundry and kitchen facilities, Internet and cable television, and offers free airport and rail transfers.

WHERE TO EAT

Sydney's chefs are probably Australia's most innovative. With a warmer climate than Melbourne and all that water around, seafood predominates here. In a city with such a beautiful harbor, though, splendid views can be considered justification for an unreasonably high bill. Beware!

Very Expensive

Tetsuya's ((02) 9555 1017, 729 Darling Street, Rozelle, is consistently voted not only Sydney's best restaurant, but Australia's. It's an exceptional place for a really special night out. Tetsuya Wakuda blends French with Japanese to create a blissful fixed-price tasting menu in which diners receive small servings of several entrees, main courses and dessert. He is famous for slow-cooked salmon. Dishes balance each other perfectly, and unusual combos like grilled fillet of veal with wasabi and sea urchin butter somehow work wonderfully under Tetsuya's deft touch. Open for dinner Tuesday to Saturday, lunch Wednesday to Saturday. Book weeks ahead.

The Bathers Pavilion ((02) 9969 5050, 4 The Esplanade, Balmoral, offers a bold Mediterrasian menu in a magical beach-side setting. The subtle luxury of the decor includes leather banquettes and exotic flowers. The Bathers Pavilion has built up its reputation over the last decade, and the chefs aren't afraid of daring ingredients. It's worth visiting just for their poached black-lipped abalone with thrice-cooked pork ear, served on a bed of black wood fungus and surrounded by shimmering salted jellyfish. This is possibly the most fashionable locale in town.

The decor at **Ampersand** ((02) 9264 6666, Roof Terrace, Cockle Bay Wharf, is worth seeing in itself. Rich browns create an inviting ambiance in the bar area, with a sloping glass wall looking onto the timber decking outside and across Darling Harbour. The marble bar is inset with aqua lighting, offsetting the otherwise neutral tons of the rich brown carpeting and velvet seating. The cuisine is invariably exemplary, which it should be at this price. This is the place for a special meal, but book well ahead.

Expensive

Alio ((02) 8394 9368, 5 Baptist Street, Surry Hills, is one of the newer breed of classy Sydney restaurants that incorporate international experience with the best local produce to create simple but perfect food. The predominately traditional Italian peasant food includes tasty risottos, rich saltimbocca and a bolito misto of a quality you won't find elsewhere in Australia. The well-chosen wine list represents a good selection of Australian finest. Pre-dinner cocktails at the designer bar are the best in Sydney. Open for lunch Tuesday to Saturday, dinner Monday to Saturday.

Edna's Table ((02) 9267 3933, 204 Clarence Street, combines bush herbs and fruits with emu, kangaroo and crocodile to create an Asian-inspired, truly Australian cuisine. Vegetarians are well-catered to, and seafood and other meats also have their place on the menu. Moderate prices sometimes move into the expensive category, or try the six-course native Australian tasting menu for $75. You may need good connections to get a window seat with a bird's-eye view of the Harbour Bridge and Opera House at **No. 7 at the Park** ((02) 9256 1630, in the Park Hyatt Sydney, 7 Hickson Road, The Rocks. The views are good from anywhere in the restaurant. Jutting out over the water at Rose Bay, **Catalina** ((02) 9371 0555, 1 Sunderland Avenue, Rose Bay, is the epitome of harbor-side restaurants. Its voguish design makes the most of harbor views, its modern Australasian food relies on fresh ingredients and subtly balanced flavors.

Doyles on the Beach ((02) 9337 2007, 11 Marine Parade, Watsons Bay, may still be a Sydney institution, but it hasn't really kept up with the changing tide. The cuisine would these days be best described as simple and fresh seafood. The best view of the city is from the **Centrepoint** ((02) 9233 3722 revolving restaurant, with an à la carte menu upstairs and a moderately priced bistro below. On a clear day you can see as far as the Blue Mountains west of the city. Another fine restaurant with a bay view, **The Boathouse** ((020 9518 9011, at the end of Ferry Road, Blackwattle Bay, Glebe, serves French-style dishes, with the occasional Australian classic. The staff are well informed, so let them help you choose. At these prices it's worth booking well ahead to make the most of the view; the back room is far less appealing. **Bennelong** ((02) 9250 7578 is under the smaller sails at the back of the Opera House and offers pre-theater meals and supper upstairs.

Moderate

At the top end of the moderate range, but certainly worth the extra, **MCA Fish Café** ((02) 9241 4253, Circular Quay West, does include a few vegetarian and meat dishes, but excellent seafood is obviously their thing. Another stylish choice is the **Café at the Bathers Pavilion** ((02) 9968 1133, 4 The Esplanade, which looks out over Balmoral Beach. The emphasis is on fresh ingredients, in simple seafood preparations. For an oyster fix try **Bayswater Brasserie** ((02) 9357 2177, 32 Bayswater Road, Kings Cross, with a daily selection from New South Wales, Tasmania and Victoria. They also serve aged beef and classic Italian and Greek dishes with a twist.

For something uniquely Australian, **Lillipilli on King** ((02) 9516 2499, 441 King Street, Newtown, combines fresh local produce with native ingredients used in traditional Aboriginal cuisine to create innovative and delicious takes on bush tucker. Lilli-pillis are white to purplish berries of the indigenous lilli-pilli tree — these and other fruits, along with bush herbs, emu, kangaroo and wallaby meat, and local seafood are balanced with vegetables and meats introduced by Europeans. Open dinner only, seven days a week.

Le Kiosk ((02) 9977 4122 on Shelley Beach at Manly is an old standard. On hot days the crowded outdoor tables are worth waiting for. Another good restaurant with a view, **Wharf Restaurant** ((02) 9250 1761, Pier 4, Hickson Road, Walsh Bay, looks across to Sydney's old Luna Park. The clientele is predominately regulars, the cuisine an inspired blend of Italian and Provençal. Location is also the key word for the **Concourse Restaurant** ((02) 9250 7300 within the Opera House, which serves a wide selection of meals from snacks to a full dinner.

The menu at **Milson's** ((02) 9955 7075, at the corner of Broughton and Willoughby Streets, changes weekly, making the most of seasonal produce. The freshly shucked oysters are always the best available, and the balanced but small menu blends Asian and Mediterranean influences.

For tasty Cantonese cuisine try Chinatown's **Marigold's** ((02) 9264 6744, 299–305 Sussex Street. You'd better believe that the seafood is fresh at this restaurant, as you can choose your dish (alive) from large tanks; a few minutes later the lobster or crab will appear (cooked) in front of you. It brings tears to my eyes. Cantonese *yum cha*, consisting largely of steamed and fried dumplings, has become very popular in Sydney and is traditionally served as a brunch. **East Ocean** ((02) 9212 4198, 421 Sussex Street, offers a wide selection of dishes which come around on trolleys for you to select. At 149 Oxford Street, **Jo Jo's** ((02) 9331 3293 (moderate) serves traditional North Indian cuisine.

Inexpensive

The **Siam Restaurant** ((02) 9331 2669, 383 Oxford Street, serves excellent classic Thai dishes at bargain prices. An excellent takeaway with a split personality, **Chopsticks and Cutlery** ((02) 9261 0622, 511 Kent Street, has something for almost everyone. Choose between classic Anglo sandwiches and burgers — fillings include grilled vegetables, fresh parmesan, smoked ham or rare roast beef, on white, wholemeal, sourdough or rye bread

— or aromatic Asian dishes like Peking duck pancakes, Singapore noodles, or Thai laksas. The variety of stalls in **Dixon House Food Hall** on Dixon Street prepare the kind of dishes typically sold from street-stalls in Southeast Asia. Dishes from a dozen Asian countries are served with prices ranging from a low $9 to $14. The center of the hall has long tables populated with hungry dinners. There is probably no cheaper or more interesting place to dine in Chinatown.

The choice of restaurants widens around Oxford Street between the city and Paddington, where the best places to eat have good views of Oxford Street. The active street-life adds spice to the meal. A good spot to pause for a light meal or a *café au*

performances of opera and ballet, good plays and concerts are always on the program at one of its various halls. While the interior of the Opera House has its detractors, the location is unsurpassed and the views at night are bewitching.

Numerous playhouses are found in the suburbs of Sydney. The **Stables Theatre** ((02) 9361 3817, 10 Nimrod Street, Kings Cross, and the **Belvoir Street Theatre** ((02) 9699 3444, which is situated in a converted tomato sauce factory at 24 Belvoir Street in Surry Hills, both show good plays in season. **Sydney's Original Comedy Store** ((02) 9565 3900, 450 Parramatta Road in Petersham, showcases Australia's best humorists — Tuesday nights new talent is let loose on the audience.

lait is **Café Flicks** ((02) 9331 7412, 3 Oxford Street, Paddington, next to the Academy Twin Cinema. **Freckle Face** ((02) 9957 2116, 32 Burton Street, makes the perfect coffee and homemade biscotti to follow its light meals. **Billi's** ((02) 9955 7211 at 31A Fitzroy Street is bright and cheery, with good snacks and cakes.

Glebe Point Road is a bit of a mixed bag, with a number of inexpensive restaurants. **Borobudur** ((02) 9660 5611, at No. 125, has delicious, spicy Indonesian food. Very good Indian cuisine is served at **Flavour of India** ((02) 9692 0662, at No. 142.

NIGHTLIFE

Sydney at night can be loud and wild or quiet and cultured, but never dull.

Lovers of music and traditional performing arts can enjoy the **Opera House**. In addition to fine

Half-price tickets for some plays are available on the day of performance from the **Halftix** booth in Martin Place which is open on weekdays from noon to 5:30 PM and Saturday from 10:30 AM to 4 PM.

For cabaret try the **Sydney Show Club** ((02) 9552 2592, at the corner of Pyrmont and Allen streets in Darling Harbour. Sydney has long been a stronghold of jazz and many well-established clubs are situated near The Rocks. **Soup Plus** ((02) 9299 7728, 383 George Street, and the **Basement** ((02) 9251 2797, 29 Reiby Place, are venues that dish out supper with hot music. A number of pubs have live music at night. Try the **Mercantile Hotel** ((02) 9247 3570, 25 George Street, The Rocks, and the **Cock 'n' Bull** ((02) 9389 3004, in the Grand Hotel at 89 Ebley Street, Bondi Junction. Depending on the band, some pubs may charge admission. **The Bridge** ((02) 9810 1260, 135 Victoria Road, Rozelle, is well known for its rock music.

Information on what's on in Sydney can be found in the Metro section of Friday's *Sydney Morning Herald*, which can also be found on WEB SITE www.smh.com.au. On the streets of inner Sydney you can pick up a free copy of *Beat* newspaper.

HOW TO GET THERE

Sydney is the major international gateway to Australia and the hub of the transport network along the eastern seaboard.

By air, Sydney is an hour from both Melbourne and Brisbane and two hours from Adelaide, transferring from an international to domestic flight at Sydney's Kingsford–Smith Airport ((02) 9667 9111

requires a short bus trip between terminals — when connecting to a domestic flight allow yourself at least 30 minutes, as the quite often undermanned and overworked transfer desks can cause missed flights.

Greyhound Pioneer and McCafferty's have coaches throughout Australia. The bus takes 17 hours from Brisbane, 13 hours from Melbourne, 23 hours from Adelaide and two and half days from Perth, which is on the other side of the continent. Sydney is the eastern terminus for the transcontinental *Indian–Pacific* rail line, linking the two oceans. If you fancy long-distance train-travel, this 62-hour trip is one of the world's last great train journeys.

It's a reasonably easy drive on good roads to Sydney from Brisbane or Melbourne, although either destination will take 10 to 12 hours, including the neccessary rest stops.

AROUND SYDNEY

NORTHERN BEACHES

The surf beaches of Freshwater, Curl Curl, Dee Why, Collaroy, Narrabeen and Avalon that thread along Sydney's north coast from Manly to Palm Beach are all patrolled and have reliable breaks and surf lifesaving clubs that rent out boards.

Palm Beach

Sydney's most northern cove, Palm Beach's picture-perfect beach is the setting for Australia's original seaside soap opera, *Home and Away*. A thin strip of land separates the beach from the broad Pittwater Basin — here you can catch a ferry across to The Basin wharf, where there are some interesting Aboriginal rock carvings nearby. The ferry driver can point out the path.

Past the shops, towards the south end of the beach, the 1930s-style Palm Beach Surf Lifesaving Club features in *Home and Away* as Summer Bay Surf Club (the shop used in the series as Alf's Boat Shed can be seen from the Palm Beach Public Wharf on the Pittwater side). There is a pretty sea-pool at the south end of the beach for swimming laps. A sandy peninsula links Barrenjoey Headland to Palm Beach. The 40-minute climb up to Barrenjoey Lighthouse, built at the north end of the beach in 1881, is rewarded by views of ocean, national parks and lovely Palm Beach itself — this is the place for panoramic shots. If you're here around sunrise or sunset, you may spot a wallaby.

There's a string of good cafés along the beachfront at Palm Beach. Higher up, the fabulous ocean view at Jonah's ((02) 9974 5599, 69 Bynya Road, Palm Beach, almost takes the attention away from the perfectly cooked lamb *noisettes* and thick, tender cuts of beef. Jonah's has excellently executed seafood dishes, including juicy seared scallops, and an excellent wine list; expensive. Opened in 1929, Jonah's also offers B&B accommodation.

Ku-ring-gai Chase National Park

Bordered by Pittwater to the east, Broken Bay to the north and Sydney's suburbs towards the south, the Ku-ring-gai Chase National Park contains rivers, gorges and more than 100 km (62 miles) of navigable water. The caves and sheltered overhangs provided protection for the Aborigines who once lived there. Rock engravings of kangaroos, dolphins, emus and sharks are their memorial. Maps pointing out Aboriginal paintings can be obtained from the Bobbin Head Information and Retail Centre ((02) 9457 9322, or from Kalkai Visitor Centre ((02) 9457 9853, both open 9 AM to 5 PM daily.

Eating Sydney rock oysters alfresco at Circular Quay, with the Harbour Bridge in the background.

The original *Skippy the Bush Kangaroo* television series was filmed at **Waratah Park (** (02) 9450 2377, Namba Road, Duffy's Forest, atop the Ku-ring-gai Chase escarpment. This sanctuary is home to more than kangaroos though, with koalas, emus, tree-climbing kangaroos, dingoes, crocs, Tasmanian devils and numerous native birds. Used to strangers, the sleepy koalas don't seem perturbed by visitors giving them a cuddle. A dinky "Bush Railway" takes the load off your feet.

How to Get There
A ferry to the park leaves from Palm Beach, or follow the signs from the Berowra, Ku-ring-gai or Cowan railway stations.

THE BLUE MOUNTAINS

The Blue Mountains World Heritage Area, a leisurely hour-and-a-half drive from Sydney, was *the* vacation spot for locals before the advent of inexpensive overseas air fares. Fifty years ago the Blue Mountains were lauded for their healthy "mountain air." These days their vistas have been rediscovered by day-trippers and weekenders from Sydney, attracted by the region's beauty. Make the trip in a day or stick around and explore the surrounding countryside.

From a distance the mountains really appear blue due to eucalyptus vapor from the gum trees, which absorbs the red component of sunlight. Grand escarpments form dramatic backdrops in every direction. The area's early popularity influenced people to build a great number of lovely old guesthouses and hotels, usually surrounded by English cottage gardens and renowned for their gracious hospitality.

General Information
Information on touring around the Blue Mountains can be obtained from the **Blue Mountains Tourist Authority (** (02) 4739 6266, on the Great Western Highway, Glenbrook. They also have an information booth at Echo Point, two kilometers (one mile) from Katoomba, with a good collection of books about the area and walking guides for sale. **Ropewerx (** (02) 4787 6236 organizes abseiling, bush-walking, canyoning, and rock climbing within the region.

New South Wales tourism puts out a number of excellent guides to the Blue Mountains, available at any of Sydney's or the Blue Mountain's tourist information offices; one of the best is *The Blue Mountains Holiday Book*, which includes five different self-drive itineraries — all of which are magic — plus info on accommodation, events, bushwalks, tours, restaurants and attractions. The *Blue Mountains Wonderland Visitor's Guide* is local publication (free) with detailed maps and loads of advice.

What to See and Do
Man's encroachment on the sandstone ramparts is confined to the procession of small towns and villages straddling the Great Western Highway, which links the mountains to Sydney. The Blue Mountains are really a 1,000-m (3,280-ft) sandstone plateau. Millions of years of erosion have created a scenic wilderness of valleys, ravines and cliffs.

Most of the area is a conservation region. Numerous walking tracks run parallel to the edge of the escarpment and lookouts are clearly signposted. They provide breathtaking panoramas of the harsh but spectacular land. Walking tracks within the national park lead to more than 40 waterfalls.

There are several pretty villages along the Great Western Highway: **Leura**, **Blackheath** and the village of **Springwood**.

For over 50 years, World famous author and artist Norman Lindsay (1879–1969) lived at Faulcon-

bridge, Springwood, etching and painting satyrs and nude women in compositions of Bacchanalian revelry. His works scandalized his generation, although they are now appreciated without the tut-tutting of that sanctimonious age. His homestead has been converted into the **Norman Lindsay Gallery and Museum** ((02) 4751 1067, on Norman Lindsay Crescent, Faulconbridge, Springwood. His studio has been preserved exactly as it was when he died.

The main town in the Blue Mountains is **Katoomba**, perched near cliffs which rise from the Jamieson Valley. What is claimed to be the world's steepest railway plunges 250 m (820 ft) down the cliff wall on a 400-m (1,300-ft) track. A cable car also sways out over the valley to give a truly heartstopping ride. Both the **Scenic Railway** and **Skyway** ((02) 4782 2699 start at the corner of Cliff Drive and Violet Street.

Katoomba is best known for the **Three Sisters** rock formation, with good views from Echo Point or Queen Elizabeth Lookout. Rising out of the Jamieson Valley, these three sheer rock columns are steeped in Aboriginal folklore. Three maidens, Meenhi, Wimlah and Gunedu were menaced by a witch doctor. Their father saw their plight from the valley below and — to protect his daughters — turned them to stone using a magic stick. However, in his excitement the father dropped his stick and the witch doctor turned him into a lyrebird. The sound of the lyrebird is believed by Aborigines to be the girls' father looking for his magic stick so that he can bring his daughters back to flesh and blood.

Katoomba and surrounding villages are also the place for a mid-year Christmas. Australians are

North Sydney's Palm Beach: a sickle of surf beach backing onto the tranquil waters of Pittwater Basin.

used to celebrating Christmas at the height of summer. Nevertheless, the mounain communities have come up with a solution for the missed snow-related northern hemisphere traditions. In June the area celebrates Yuletide. There are Christmas decorations in the streets, including a Christmas tree in Katoomba, and a snowman in Leura. More than 30 guesthouses, restaurants, hotels and resorts in the Blue Mountains serve the full traditional Christmas dinner to the accompaniment of carol singing, open fires and mulled wine.

Horseback riding through the Kanimbla Valley is a memorable way to appreciate the mountain environment. Day-trips can be organized through the **Centennial Glen Horse and Sulky Hire** ((02) 4787 7179, Blackheath. The picturesque greens and fresh mountain air at **Leura Golf Club** ((02) 4782 5011, on Sublime Point Road, will have you at the eighteenth hole well before you begin to wilt.

About an hour and a half west of Katoomba are the limestone caverns of the **Jenolan Caves**, open daily. The best way to see these natural lime cathedrals is to join a guided tour, which leave every 30 minutes from the Jenolan Caves Reserve Trust ((02) 6332 5888.

Where to Stay

There are some wonderful guesthouses and hotels in the Blue Mountains, although they're not cheap. Rates usually go up over weekends.

With million-dollar views over sheer cliff faces into pretty valleys below, one of the most interesting hotels in the Blue Mountains is the **Hydro Majestic Hotel** ((02) 4788 1002, at Medlow Bath, with a striking art nouveau-inspired domed front entrance. Windows fill the wall that faces the Megalong Valley. The Hydro Majestic Hotel started out as a health resort, but when the promises of bowel kneading, enemas and centrifugal douching lost their attraction, the resort was turned over to vacationers and the inside remodeled to take on the appearance of a grand hotel. Expensive.

In Katoomba, also in the expensive category, the **Cecil** ((02) 4782 1411 FAX (02) 4782 5364, 25 Lurline Street, is a traditional guesthouse built more for comfort than style.

Leura is one of the prettiest towns in the area, without the hustle and bustle of Katoomba. It has a number of appealing and moderately priced B&Bs. At **The Greens** ((02) 4784 3241, 24 Grose Street, hosts Jean and Peter provide a friendly welcome; facilities include a spa, library and full-size billiard table. **Where Waters Meet** ((02) 4784 3022 FAX (02) 4784 3343, 15 Mount Hay Road, is an elegant and secluded guesthouse about three kilometers (two miles) out of town. In the same price category, **Jenolan Caves House** ((02) 6359 3322 FAX (02) 6359 3227, near the caves, has the relaxed atmosphere of a country homestead.

For inexpensive accommodation try **Sky Rider Motor Inn** ((02) 4782 1600 at the intersection of Scenic Cliff Road and the Great Western Highway, Katoomba. In nearby Blackheath, **Jemby-Rinjah Lodge** ((02) 4787 7622 FAX (02) 4787 6230, 336 Evans Lookout Road, set into the bush adjacent to the Grose Valley, has large comfortable rooms at inexpensive to moderate prices.

Mid-year Yuletide accommodation packages are available at the Cecil guesthouse, the Hydro Majestic, and Jenolan Caves House.

Where to Eat

While in Katoomba a drop into the **Paragon Café** at 65 Katoomba Street, for some tea or a light meal, is a gauranteed pleasurable break. This charming 1916 art deco café serves interesting, wholesome food and has a great selection of cakes. Try the specialty homemade chocolates, which are displayed in leadlight cabinets that date back to 1925. For light meals, snacks and coffee, a good choice is the **Parakeet Café** ((02) 4782 1815, in Katoomba. In Leura, **Gracie's on the Mall** ((02) 4784 1973 serves homemade pies, soups and flower-pot dampers, as well as a hearty breakfast every day. For a superb meal in a charming setting and relaxed atmosphere, have dinner at **The Ferns** ((02) 4784 3256, 130 Megalong Street, where the unique seafood sausage is a favorite. If you are traveling with kids, or to revive your own memories of childhood, go to the **Candy Store Old Time Lolly Shop** ((02) 4782 5190, inside Leura's Strand Arcade, where you can select from over 1,000 jars of your favorite old-fashioned candy— called "lollies" in Australia — including hard candies, nougats, toffees and chocolates.

How to Get There

Katoomba is about two hours by train from Sydney. The drive along the M4 Highway from the outskirts of Sydney takes one and a half hours, slightly longer on the Great Western Highway.

Trains to the Blue Mountains leave from Sydney's Central Station hourly (platforms 12 and 13), stopping at Springwood, Leura, Katoomba, Mount Victoria and Lithgow. A one-day return to Katoomba costs $11.80 and connects with the Blue Mountains Explorer Link bus — a continual service that tours the major sights, returning to Katoomba for the return train to Sydney. For timetables call (1300 300 915 or State Transit's **Infoline** (131 500.

Local bus lines connect with the train services, running frequent services on weekdays and Saturday morning.

Daily tours from Sydney are offered by **Australian Pacific Tours** (131 304, and **AAT King's Tours** ((02) 9252 2788, with stops at popular lookouts in the Blue Mountains and the Jenolan Caves.

In Aboriginal legend, the Three Sisters were turned to stone by their father to protect them from a witch doctor.

BRISBANE WATER AND WOLLEMI NATIONAL PARKS

Brisbane Water National Park ((02) 4324 4911 is nine kilometers (five miles) southwest of Gosford and 60 km (37 miles) north of Sydney, off the Pacific Highway. Aboriginal engravings can be seen on the sandstone landscape at Bulgandry on Woy Woy Road. The 100-m-high (300-ft) cliffs overlooking the Hawkesbury River at Warrah Trig and Staples lookouts provide panoramic views, and the displays of Christmas Bells and flowering Waratah are stunning in November and December.

Wollemi National Park, 100 km (62 miles) northwest of Sydney, is New South Wales' second largest park and contains the state's largest wilderness area. A maze of narrow canyons and gorges channel through a region of precipitous basalt mountains covered with thick, undisturbed rainforest. Abundant fauna live in their native habitat. Although the extremely rugged terrain makes access difficult, the park offers plentiful rewards for the properly equipped and experienced bush-walker. Bob Turners Track descends toward the beaches along the Colo River, through one of the state's longest and most scenic gorges. Other attractions include whitewater canoeing down the Colo, Wolgan, and Capertee rivers and a glow worm-filled railway tunnel near Newnes. There are camping areas at Newnes, Wheeney Creek and Dunns Swamp.

THE HUNTER VALLEY

Only an hour and a half from Sydney, the Hunter Valley is the most northerly producer of wines of any quality in Australia. Hunter Valley vineyards were established to introduce a less-intoxicating drink into the rum-dependant colony.

While the climate north of Sydney verges on subtropical, the Hunter Valley's has an unusual microclimate with a cloud cover in the summer months that shelters the vines from the sun and lengthens the grape-ripening period, which results in complex and intense reds and whites. The most successful red grape grown here is Syrah — known as Shiraz in Australia, and sometimes called Hermitage. The best Hunter Shirazs are earthy and spicy, they age reasonably well, and are often blended with Pinot Noir. Hunter whites can be excellent too, particularly the broad, round, golden Semillons.

The Hunter Valley sees more tourists than any other wine area in the country because of its proximity to Sydney. For the visitor this means plenty of choice in accommodation and restaurants, and plenty of different activities to choose from. Wineries, cafés, and guesthouses have generally been prettied up with climbing roses and classy woodwork, while a lot of the accommodation is of the romantic B&B ilk (and can be rather pricey). Some

of Sydney's best chefs have set up restaurants here. The valley's popularity also causes Hunter wines to be overpriced in comparison with the, generally better, wines from South Australia. This is particularly true in Sydney.

GENERAL INFORMATION

The **Wine Country Visitor Information Centre** ((02) 4990 4477 FAX (02) 4991 4518 WEB SITE www.winecountry.com.au, Turner Park, Aberdare Road, Cessnock, can help with information and bookings, and provide a comprehensive list of upcoming events throughout the Hunter Valley. For an **on-line booking** and information service, go to WEB SITE www.hunter-region.org.au.

If you're wine tasting and driving, it may be better to park the car and call the **Vineyard Shuttle Service** ((02) 4991 3655 or **Cessnock Radio Cabs** ((02) 4990 1111. A variety of tours are also available, see TOURS, below.

WHAT TO SEE AND DO

Wineries

There are over 80 wineries in the area, although not all are open to the public. The oldest and biggest are **Lindemans** (now owned by Penfolds) ((02) 4998 7684, McDonalds Road, Pokolbin; **Tyrrell's** ((02) 4993 7000 WEB SITE www.tyrrells.com.au, Broike Road, Pokolbin; **McWilliams Mount Pleasant** ((02) 4998 7505, Marrowbone Road, Pokolbin; and **Wyndham Estate** ((02) 4938 3444, Dalwood Road, Dalwood via Branxton. Of these, Tyrrell's and Wyndham produce the better wines. Tyrrell's opens Monday to Saturday, 8 AM to 5 PM, with tours of their 100-year-old vats at 1:30 PM. Wyndham's tasting and sales area — known in Australian wineries as the "cellar door" — opens from 10 AM to 4:30 PM every day; tours at 11 AM feature their Cellar Reserve Winery, which uses open vat fermentation.

Rothbury Estate ((02) 4998 7363, Broke Road, Pokolbin, produces some of the Hunter's best wines, and is well worth visiting. Its Semillon is close to perfect and its long, complete reds are firmly structured and rich on the palate — they're often at their best only after eight to ten years. The cellar door is open seven days a week, from 9 AM to 5 PM; their café is a pleasant place to stop for lunch.

A number of smaller and newer winemakers are also making outstanding wines. **Brokenwood** ((02) 4998 7559, McDonalds Road, Pokolbin, opens daily from 10 AM to 5 PM, were only established in 1970, but they're now one of the best in the valley. Even newer on the block, **Pepper Tree Wines** ((02) 4998 7539 WEB SITE www.peppertreewines.com.au, Halls Road, Pokolbin, is beginning to make their mark on the Hunter. Surrounded by flower gardens, Pepper Tree's cellar door is among the prettiest. Their beautiful guesthouse, The Convent, overlooks the vineyards, and their restaurant, Robert's, is definitely the best in the Hunter (see WHERE TO EAT, below). **Hungerford Hill** ((02) 4998 7666, McDonalds Road, Pokolbin, produces some very interesting wines too. Their cellar door was previously the village church.

Events

Tourism is big business here, although essentially catering to day-trippers and weekenders from Sydney and Newcastle. Concerts, fairs and festivals are put on throughout the year. For information on the following events, and on others throughout the year, contact the Wine Country Visitor Information Centre (see above), or visit their web site. The biggest events include the April **Harvest Festival**, celebrating the end of the Hunter's late harvest with different musical acts to accompany the offerings of local winemakers and restaurateurs. For the annual **Opera in the Vineyards** in October, Australian and international opera singers perform in an amphitheater in the middle of Wyndham Estate's vineyard. Also in October, **Jazz in the Vines**, held in Tyrrell's Long Flat Paddock, attracts thousand to enjoy the wine, food and jazz music. The four-day **Wollombi Folk Festival** in September can be fun, and includes music, Aboriginal cultural performances, comedians and a film festival.

TOURS

A number of operators offer tours around the vineyards, both from Sydney and locally. From Sydney, **Hunter Valley Wine Tours** ((02) 9498 8888, 84 Pitt Street; **Grape Expectations** ((02) 9692 9494, 5A Gladstone Street, Lilyfield; and the **Scenic Winetasting Tour** ((02) 9967 3238, 2 Windsor Road, Willoughby, know the vineyards particularly well. All have daily tours from $90 to $100, including lunch. Ask about two-day packages including accommodation, which can be good value. Qualified winemaker Richard Everett runs **Wine Country Tours** ((02) 9484 1109 E-MAIL winecountrytours @bigpond.com.au. Richard adapts his tours to his passengers, conducting wine tastings at the cellar doors, and generally helping his guests to make the most of their visit. His tours cost more than the others, but include lunch at wonderful Robert's.

Local operators include **Hunter Valley Day Tours** ((02) 4938 5031 WEB SITE www.daytours @hunter-region.org.au, in Paterson, and **Hunter Vineyard Tours** ((02) 4991 1659, 26 Mountview Road, Cessnock, who both offer pickup and return to and from Newcastle, Maitland and local guesthouses. The **Vineyard Shuttle Service** ((02) 4991 3655 in Cessnock will stop at any Vineyard in the Lower Hunter, at passengers' discretion. For complete control, **Cessnock Radio Cabs** ((02) 4990 1111 operates both normal taxi services and private vineyard tours.

Grapemobile Bicycle & Walking Tours ((02) 4991 2339 WEB SITE www.grapemobile.com.au, in Pokolbin, organizes one- and two-day tours of the valley on bicycle or on foot, with a support bus available if the wine takes effect. They also rent out bikes for $25 a day. **Pokolbin Horse Coaches** ((02) 4998 7765 E-MAIL pokolbin@aljan.com.au, McDonalds Road, Pokolbin, have full- and half-day horse-and-carriage tours (drawn by magnificent, heavy-footed Clydesdales), with drivers who understand both horsemanship and viticulture. They also offer courtesy pick-up from your hotel or guesthouse.

SPORTS AND OUTDOOR ACTIVITIES

For those interested in **fishing** the tidal estuaries of the lower Hunter, Auz Wiz Guided Fishing ((02) 4932 4068, 6 Adelong Close, Rutherford, organizes private full- and half-day trips on a Webster Twinfisher catamaran, with a highly experienced local fisherman. There are no less than three good 18-hole **golf** courses in the area. Cypress Lakes Golf and Country Club ((02) 4993 1800 TOLL-FREE (1800) 465 318, at the Cypress Lakes Resort, is a par-72 course, the front nine tree-lined with sloping fairways and undulating greens, the back nine in a links-style layout. The Oaks Golf and Country Club ((02) 4990 6703, 49 Lindsay Street, Cessnock, is slightly smaller and has competitions every day but Tuesday and Thursday; visitors are welcome to join in. The Portofino Golf Course ((02) 4991 4777 is at the corner of Allandale and Lovedale roads, Pokolbin.

The **New South Wales Tandem and Skydiving Centre** ((02) 4990 1000 WEB SITE www.tandem skydive.com, lot 210 Allandale Road, Cessnock (behind the Chardonnay Sky Motel), caters to tandem-diving beginners right through to free-fall certification seekers. Tandem dives for absolute beginners cost $239, for experienced divers prices fall to $49 including equipment rental, $22 if you have your own. The facility includes a swimming pool and tennis courts, and motel or youth hostel accommodation. Right next door, Australia's most experienced **ballooning** company, Balloon Aloft ((02) 4938 1955 TOLL-FREE (1800) 028 568 WEB SITE www.balloonaloft.com, Lot 1, Main Road, North Rothbury, will carry you above the vineyards and hills for a memorable start to your day. Flights leave at sunrise every day (weather permitting). A hearty breakfast (wine included, of course) follows. Prices range from $150 to $225, children $130.

The Hunter River Retreat ((02) 4930 1114, 1090 Maitland Vale Road, Rosebrook, offers **horseback riding** for all levels through the scenic Rosebrook and Moonabung ranges. Horseback riding is also offered at the picturesque village of Wollombi, through the **Wollombi Horse-riding Centre** ((02) 4998 3221.

WHERE TO STAY

Glamorous resorts and guesthouses abound in the Hunter Valley. Most are fairly expensive, but prices often drop dramatically mid-week. Many have a two-night minimum stay requirement. The visitor information office has listings of guesthouses and B&Bs in the region, many at moderate prices.

Expensive

For true decadence, the **Kirkton Park Country House Hotel** ((02) 4998 7680 E-MAIL kirkton.park @hunterlink.net.au, Oaky Creek Road, Pokolbin, features a beautiful central rose garden and a

away. Tastefully decorated with polished wood floors, Indian rugs and period furniture, rooms are large and comfortable and some of the guest facilities include tennis court, swimming pool and Jacuzzi.

Moderate

The **Woolshed Hill Estate** ((02) 4998 7685, Deasys Road, Pokolbin, offers B&B at moderate prices, with dinner an option. It has its own nine-hole golf course and a golf driving range and practice net. Other facilities include tennis court and a saltwater pool.

Inexpensive

The **Chardonnay Sky Motel** ((02) 4991 4812 E-MAIL chardsky@bigpond.com, Lot 210 Allandale

Grecian-style indoor swimming pool and spa surrounded by broad, arched windows with sweeping views of the valley. More of a mini-resort, there is also a gym, a sauna and tennis court, and rooms are beautifully appointed with antique and period furniture. Its restaurant, Leith's, offers stylish French-inspired cuisine; service is excellent.

Cypress Lakes Resort ((02) 4993 1555 WEB SITE www.cypresslakes.com.au, corner of McDonalds and Thompsons roads, Pokolbin, has its own 18-hole golf course, a 25-m (82-ft) heated swimming pool and a lagoon pool, a spa, two lighted tennis courts, and a gym and sauna with beauty treatments and massage services. Choose between a suite or a two- or three-room villa. The resort has three bars and two restaurants.

The Convent ((02) 4998 7764 at Pepper Tree Wines is housed in a beautiful old convent transported from Coonamble, over 600 km (373 miles)

Road, Cessnock, has both inexpensive motel accommodation and a separate youth hostel section alongside its skydiving school. It's a little stark and can be crowded with potential skydivers, but the rooms are large, the swimming pool inviting, and it's as close to the vineyards as any.

A number of hotels in Cessnock offer inexpensive basic accommodation, often with shared bathrooms. One of the cheapest is the friendly **Royal Oak Hotel** ((02) 4990 2366, 221 Vincent Street, Cessnock (from $35 double). Just down the road the **Black Opal Hotel** ((02) 4990 1070, 220 Vincent Street, Cessnock, has rooms from $75 a double. The National Trust-classified **Neath Hotel** ((02) 4930 4270, Cessnock Road, Neath, restored to its original state and containing an interesting antique collection, also has inexpensive rooms, as does the attractive **Hotel Beatty** ((02) 4938 9451, 52 Park Street, East Gresford, a little further north.

WHERE TO EAT

Eating out in the Hunter can be pricey. A lot of the wineries have their own restaurant or café, although most open for lunch only.

Robert's Restaurant ((02) 4998 7330 at Pepper Tree Wines is housed in a picture-postcard heritage cottage decorated with period furniture and fittings. Chef and owner, Robert Molines uses his classic French training to create dishes that wouldn't be out of place on the Rue de Rivoli: duck *confit* with *choucroute*; bouillabaisse of blue-eye cod, shrimp, mussels and crab, with croutons and garlic *rouille*; or venison pie with roasted mushrooms and spinach and a red-wine *jus*. Not only does Robert's serve Pepper Tree's excellent wines, this is one of the few restaurants in the Hunter to offer wines from the rest of Australia and France. It's expensive but well worth the price; open for lunch and dinner.

Wyndham Estate has both an inexpensive café and a moderately priced restaurant, where the food is reliable without being adventurous. **Elizabeth's Café** ((020) 4998 7280, at Mount Pleasant Estate, serves lunches and morning and afternoon teas, with good sandwiches and salads and a few simple hot meals at inexpensive prices. **Rothbury Estate** has a café with similar food, but prices are a little higher here.

Classic pub food at the **Royal Oak Hotel** ((02) 4990 2366 includes hearty steaks and big salads (moderate). Another good choice in the moderate range is **Blue** ((02) 4990 2573, Mount View Road, Cessnock; open lunch and dinner, Thursday through Sunday. Good Italian food at **Il Cacciatore** ((02) 4998 7639, at Hermitage Lodge, ranges from an extensive northern Italian dinner menu (moderate) to inexpensive pizza, pasta and salads for lunch. Open for dinner seven days a week, lunch Friday to Sunday.

HOW TO GET THERE

Driving north along the Sydney–Newcastle F3 Freeway, the turnoff to Cessnock is eight kilometers (five miles) past Morisset, 130 km (81 miles) north of Sydney. Cessnock is another 30 km (19 miles) along.

Trains from Sydney to Moree or Armidale stop at Maitland, from where there are buses to Cessnock. Countrylink (132 232, or the Sydney Visitor Centre can provide train and bus information. There are two daily buses to Cessnock from Sydney, the service is operated by **Batterhams Express** TOLL-FREE (1800) 043 339.

The Hunter Valley can also be easily reached from Port Stephens (see following page). A number of tour operators offer combined day or weekend trips to Port Stephens and the Hunter.

Sydney and Northern New South Wales

BARRINGTON TOPS NATIONAL PARK

World Heritage-listed **Barrington Tops National Park** is 96 km (60 miles) northwest of Newcastle and 35 km (22 miles) west of Dungog. It has widely differing ecosystems, including a high plateau where snow gums and Antarctic beech proliferate, and a plain at 1,550 m (5,000 ft) above sea level with subtropical vegetation. The park's eucalypti run from tall wet stands of Sydney blue gum on the valley slopes to silvertop and messmate stringybarks and brown barrel at higher altitudes. Snow gums, black Sally and mountain gums dominate the sub-alpine areas.

This unusual combination of forest ecosystems provides habitats for around 38 threatened species. Some of them take an expert to track down — among them some of Australia's rarest natives, like red-legged pademelons, rufous scrub-birds, masked owls and glandular frogs — but bush turkeys, lyrebirds, bowerbirds, wombats, red-*necked* pademelons and red-necked wallabies are all pretty commonly seen, particularly if you visit around dawn or dusk. Pademelons, which look a lot like small wallabies with a weight problem, are creatures of habit. They sleep in the dense forest during the day, but forage in clearings or on roadsides at night, generally returning to the same grounds every evening.

Camp Cobark ((02) 6558 5524, on Scone Road, Barrington, a family-run horse farm, take visitors on trail rides through the forest, crossing through streams and stopping for a picnic lunch.

The Barringtons Country Retreat ((02) 4995 9269 WEB SITE www.thebarringtons.com.au, Chichester Dam, Dungog, has an array of lodges and cottages, many with private spas, some with billiards tables, some nested in the forest, others overlooking the lagoon, and many with lovely views. There's a small swimming pool, a tennis court and a two-hole chip and putt golf course. Activities include fishing, scenic horse trail rides and mountain biking. Prices vary within the moderate category and are lower mid-week. Their restaurant is better than average and serves Hunter Valley wines, of course.

The **Gloucester Visitor Information Centre** ((02) 6558 1408, Denison Street, Gloucester, can provide details about other accommodation options in the area and realms of information on Barrington Tops and its flora and fauna. Tourist offices in Sydney, the Hunter Valley, Newcastle and Port Stephens also have plenty of information on the park.

Pepper Tree Wines cellar door and the vineyard's excellent restaurant, Robert's, are among the most welcoming in the Hunter.

PORT STEPHENS AND THE GREAT LAKES

The beautiful seaside resorts on Port Stephens are only an hour from Cessnock and can be used as a base to visit the Hunter. The harbor is home to around 140 resident bottlenose dolphins that live in family groups, and whales migrate close by in spring and autumn. There are some glorious beaches here, with white volcanic sand and aquamarine waters, enclosed by two volcanic headlands. The magnificent 32-km (20-mile) stretch of Stockton Bight is backed by natural bush, while good surf beaches include One Mile Beach, Birubi Point and Fingal Beach, or Hawks Nest Beach on the northern Yacaaba Head. Stockton Beach has the largest expanse of sand dunes on the east coast of Australia. Nelson Bay, on the southern headland, is the largest resort and the main anchorage.

From pretty Hawks Nest, a small coastal road squeezes between beaches and the Myall River. In the nearby Great Lakes National Park, marshes and rainforest separate long expanses of near-empty beaches — some with dramatic dune formations — from Broadwater, Boolambayte, Myall and Wallis lakes. It has over 1,300 sq km (495 sq miles) of cruising and fishing waters.

With dense tracts of rainforest and some of the largest stands of flooded gums in the state, a drive through Wang Wauk and Bulahdelah state forests, inland from Myall Lake, provides a pleasant change from the beach. If you're walking here though, apply insect repellent and wear long trousers and socks — leeches thrive in the forest's damp heat. Within Wang Wauk Forest, Stoney Creek Road is an 11-km-long 6.8-mile) unpaved road connecting the Pacific Highway, seven kilometers (four miles) north of Bulahdelah, with Great Lakes Way. Halfway along Stoney Creek Road, a short boardwalk leads to "The Grandis;" a 76-m (249-ft) flooded gum and the tallest tree in New South Wales. Watch out for meter-long (three-foot) goannas.

The lakes end at the twin towns of **Forster–Tuncurry**, smaller beach resorts with excellent surfing on Tuncurry Beach in particular.

GENERAL INFORMATION

The **Port Stephens Information Centre** ((02) 4981 1855 TOLL-FREE (1800) 808 900 WEB SITE www.portstephens.org.au helps with advice, accommodation and bookings. They have an abundance of information, from detailed maps to tide charts and fishing guides. Just behind the information center, **Port Stephens Boat Hire** ((02) 4984 3843 or (02) 4984 3224 has a floating office at D'Albora Marina. They handle everything from yacht charter, cruise bookings and deep-sea fishing trips to rental of small boats, runabouts or Hydro-bikes.

Tea Gardens Information Centre ((02) 4997 0111 TOLL-FREE (1800) 802 692 is in Myall Street, Tea Gardens. It and the **Great Lakes Tourism Office** ((02) 6554 8799 WEB SITE www.greatlakes.org.au, in Little Street, Foster, at the other end of the lakes, produce information sheets covering walking and camping, surf breaks, fishing spots and local flora and fauna. **Port Stephens Ferry Service** ((02) 4981 3798 and **Simba Cruises** ((02) 4997 1084 both run daily ferry services between Tea Gardens and Nelson Bay. Timetables vary seasonally, they say dolphins are sighted on 95% of the crossings.

WHAT TO SEE AND DO

The sight of a 15-m (49-ft), 48-ton humpback whale propelling itself skyward with powerful thrusts of its tail and crashing back into the sea is unforgettable. Here, approximately 3,500 humpback whales migrate north along the coast from late May to July, returning in September to November. They swim in very close to Port Stephen's headlands and the off-shore islands. Bryde's, minke and killer whales are also seen regularly between May and October. The best way to see the whales is to take a **whale-watching** cruise, and there are plenty of operators to choose from. **Dawsons Scenic Cruises** ((02) 4982 0444 depart from the Cruise Passenger Terminal in Nelson Bay; other larger operators include **Moonshadow Cruises** ((02) 4984 9388 E-MAIL moonshadow@hunterlink.net.au and **Spirit of the Bay Cruises** ((02) 4984 1004. Smaller sailing vessels take visitors out too: *Imagine* ((02) 4984 9000 WEB SITE www.imagineportstaphens.com.au, *Advance II* ((02) 49841 0399 and **Waywind Charters** ((02) 4982 2777. Most operators also offer **dolphin-watching** cruises year-round, and one departs daily from Tea Gardens, operated by **Simba Cruises** ((02) 4997 1084.

The twin villages of **Tea Gardens** and **Hawks Nest**, on either side of the Myall River mouth, are linked by the Singing Bridge (I've yet to hear a note, but apparently it sings when there's a strong southwesterly wind). Hawks Nest has two lovely beaches, with an attractive golf course alongside the northern end of the surf beach. Sailing, boating and fishing are big attractions here too, with the choice of the river and lake system, Port Stephens, and the Pacific. The small reserve on the corner of Ibis and Kingfisher avenues, on the left after you've crossed the bridge into Hawks Nest, is home to a large population of **koalas**.

One third of the Great Lakes has been set aside in national parks or state forests, and the region has 27 beaches along its 145 km (88 miles) of Pacific coastline. There are some excellent **walks** on the coastal side of the Great Lakes. Maps are available from the tourist offices, who also produce the free *Walkers Guide to the Great Lakes*. My favorite is the 16-km (10-mile) Mungo Track Nature Walk, which passes through dense rainforest. It doesn't stray far from Mungo Brush Road, meeting it in four places, so it's easy to walk a shorter section. I'd recommend the northern few kilometers. Gray kangaroos, swamp and red-necked wallabies, gliding possums and bandicoots are all frequently spotted along the way. Swamp mahogany and paperbark are koala food trees: you may just spot one sleeping above you.

Mungo Brush Road ends at the Bombah Ferry, taking cars and walkers across to Lakes Road every half hour or so. There are a number of unsealed roads and four-wheel-drive tracks here too, the tourist offices have good maps of roads and walking tracks, and know the area well. Black swans, cranes, pelicans and numerous ducks populate the lakes.

Both Pro Dive Nelson Bay ((02) 4981 4331 E-MAIL prodive@dialix.com.au at the d'Albora Marina, and Dive Nelson Bay ((02) 49981 2491 E-MAIL divenbay@oze-mail.com.au, 5/35 Stockton Street, Nelson Bay, offer **scuba diving** trips and PADI certification. Bay Barefoot and Waterski School ((02) 4981 9409, 30 Albert Street, Taylors Beach organize **water-skiing** lessons for children and adults. Jimmy's Beach in Hawks Nest, on the Port Stephens side, is a good place to take up **windsurfing**. Jimmy's Beach Watercraft Hire ((02) 4984 3735 rents canoes, catamarans, sea kayaks, surf skis and windsurfers, and gives lessons.

There are a number of **golf** courses at Port Stephens. Horizons Golf Club ((02) 4982 0502, an

Great Lakes Seaplanes ((02) 6555 8771, at the Pacific Palms Recreation Club, offers scenic flights over the lakes and beaches for $45 per person.

SPORTS AND OUTDOOR ACTIVITIES

Fishing is a big drawcard throughout this area, with its extensive river and lake system linked to deep Port Stephens and opening into the Pacific Ocean. Flathead, bream and whiting are common, and catches include mulloway, tailor, rock blackfish, trevally, luderick, kingfish, tuna and perch. Marlin, swordfish and sharks are fished from January to March. Boats can be rented almost anywhere. Try Jimmy's Beach Watercraft Hire ((02) 4984 3735 in Hawks Nest, Tea Gardens Boatshed and Marina ((02) 4997 0307, or Port Stephens Boat Hire ((02) 4984 3843 or (02) 4984 3224, at D'Albora Marina in Nelson Bay.

18-hole championship course in Salamander Bay, is considered the best. Watch out for the kangaroos. Hawks Nest Golf Club ((02) 4997 0145, in Sanderling Avenue, is a friendly club with ocean views.

Sahara Horse Trails ((02) 4981 9077, Port Stephens Drive, Anna Bay, and Horse Paradise ((02) 4965 1877, Nelson Bay Road, Williamtown, organize **horseback riding** along Port Stephens' beaches and dunes. **Walkabout Camel Adventures** ((02) 4965 0500 takes small groups on camelback along the beach or into surrounding forests.

WHERE TO STAY

Accommodation here ranges from luxury resorts to campgrounds and includes some ugly high-rise condos. Houseboat rental is obviously a popular

Camping on the banks of Myall Lake.

choice, particularly for families. Again, there are numerous operators to choose from. The tourist information office has details, or try **Houseboats on Port Stephens** TOLL-FREE (1800) 620 202 WEB SITE www.houseboat-hire.com.au or **Boats on Port Stephens** TOLL-FREE (1800) 262 871 WEB SITE www.boatsonportstephens.com.au. Self-contained and serviced apartments can offer very affordable accommodation and many have ocean views and private swimming pools. Most apartments are rented through local letting agents, although the tourist information office and web site list them too. They also list a large number of privately run B&Bs. **PRD Realty Port Stephens** ((02) 4984 2000 WEB SITE www.prd.com

luxury accommodation at moderate prices. Rooms look out to a terraced swimming pool area shaded by swaying palm trees, a chorus of native birds serenading you through breakfast. Beyond the pool is the bay and pretty Dutchies Beach. Thurlows has only two suites, so book ahead.

Shoal Bay Country Club Hotel TOLL-FREE (1800) 040 937 WEB SITE www.shoalbaycountryclub.com.au, Shoal Bay Road, Shoal Bay, has two restaurants and a wood-fired pizza bistro. Children up to 14 stay for free. In the same street, at No. 59, **Shoal Bay Motel and YHA (backpackers)** ((02) 4981 1744, Shoal Bay, has moderately priced units.

There is a clothing-optional resort set in attractive parklands only a 10-minute walk from Port

.au/portstephens, Shoal Bay Road, Shoal Bay, has some attractive apartments, as does **K.D. Winning** ((02) 4981 1999 WEB SITE www.kdwinning.com.au, Bay Village Shopping Mall, Shoal Bay, or 19 Stockton Street, Nelson Bay. In Hawks Nest, try **Hawks Nest Accommodation Centre** ((02) 4997 0755, 166 Myall Street.

Expensive

Peppers Anchorage Port Stephens ((02) 4984 2555 TOLL-FREE (1800) 809 142 E-MAIL anchorage@peppers.com.au has beautifully appointed spa suites overlooking the marina.

Moderate

A five-minute walk from Nelson Bay along a shaded foreshore path, **Thurlows** ((02) 4984 3722 E-MAIL thurlows@castle.net.au, 60 Thurlow Avenue, Nelson Bay, is a tranquil B&B providing

Stephens' only official clothing-optional beach, Samurai Beach. **Bardots Resort** ((02) 4982 2000 WEB SITE www.bardots.com.au, 288 Gan Gan Road, Anna Bay, has comfortable bungalows and a swimming pool area with outdoor spa. They offer free transfers to and from the beach. **One Mile Beach Holiday Park** ((02) 4982 1112 WEB SITE www.onemilebeach.com, on Gan Gan Road, Anna Bay, has accommodation from beach houses or villas with spas to inexpensive campsites and cabins, all with use of the saltwater pool and outdoor spa.

Inexpensive

Dolphins Motel ((02) 4981 1176, on Shoal Bay Road in Nelson, offers simple units, a swimming pool and an outdoor barbecue area. It is close to Little Beach. **Bahama House B&B** ((02) 6554 4843, 2 Bahama Place, Tuncurry, has a saltwater pool and comfortable rooms. **Shoal Bay Backpackers** ((02)

4981 0982, 59 Shoal Bay Beachfront Road, doesn't have a pool, but there is a sauna.

A number of caravan parks have inexpensive on-site vans and cabins, only minutes from the beaches. Good ones to try are **Hawks Nest Beach Caravan Park** ((02) 4997 0239, Booner Street, Hawks Nest; **Treachery Camp** ((02) 4997 6138, Treachery Head (said to have the best surf); and **Palms Oasis Caravan Park** ((02) 6554 0488, Boomerang Drive, Pacific Palms.

WHERE TO EAT

Peppers Anchorage Port Stephens has the best restaurant in town — they even run cooking classes here. The cuisine is French/Polynesian emphasizing seafood (expensive). My favorite of the string of restaurants at D'Albora Marina is the inexpensive **Rob's on the Boardwalk** ((02) 4984 4444, which serves delectable salads, simply prepared seafood and tasty range-grazed Hunter beef. Opposite Shoal Bay Beach, **Marco's Restaurant** ((02) 4981 2980 prepares hearty Italian food and tempting desserts (inexpensive). **Moffats Famous Oyster Barn Restaurant** ((02) 4997 5605, Moffats Road, Swan Bay, has the freshest oysters around, served 13 to the dozen.

The string of waterfront cafés in Tea Gardens offer beautiful sunset views of the marina. They're all friendly and serve home-style food at outdoor tables. Swiss-run **Tillermans Café Restaurant** ((02) 4997 0138 is a little more expensive than the others, but still in the inexpensive–moderate range. **Lane's Rest Café** ((02) 4997 1899 serves cheap lunches.

HOW TO GET THERE

Port Stephens is just over 200 km (124 miles) from Sydney. Take the F3 Sydney–Newcastle freeway to the New England Highway, where it ends and meets the Pacific Highway. The intersection here is fairly confusing, just look out for signs to the Pacific Highway or Raymond Terrace. Six kilometers (four miles) along the Pacific Highway, the Raymond Terrace bypass branches off to the right. Take this bypass, then take the first road off it, a kilometer or so further. This is Richardson Road and leads to Nelson Bay, 50 km (31 miles) away.

Port Stephens Coaches ((02) 4982 2940 depart from Eddy Avenue, Central Station in Sydney, daily at 2 PM. There are frequent trains from Sydney to Newcastle, from where Countrylink runs a connecting bus service to Corlette and Nelson Bay. **Newcastle Airport** ((02) 4965 1925 is halfway between Newcastle and Port Stephens, with direct flights from Sydney, Melbourne, Brisbane and Canberra. A direct **seaplane service** ((02) 9388 1978 to Port Stephens also operates daily from Sydney.

PACIFIC HIGHWAY

The countryside becomes increasingly lush and subtropical north along the New South Wales coast as you travel the 900 km (560 miles) that separate Sydney from the Queensland border. The Pacific Highway branches off from the New England Highway at Hexham, near Newcastle, and continues on to Brisbane in Queensland. Along the way broad cultivated valleys mark a succession of wide rivers that flow into bays and coves and out to the Pacific Ocean. Towns in the valleys prosper from farming and timber, while small fishing villages cluster around the river mouths. In summer these villages attract thousands of vacationers from the south who come to the excellent beaches or to try some angling.

Although the highway follows the seaboard and brushes a number of its broad harbors, it only really hugs the coast for 85 km (53 miles) between Nambucca Heads, a small resort town best-known for its surf, and Corindi Beach, not meeting it again until 15 km (nine miles) from the Queensland border. The section from Bulahdelah to Coolongoolook cuts through timberland and the Bulahdelah State Forest, and is particularly lovely.

PORT MACQUARIE

Founded as a convict settlement in 1821, the resort town of Port Macquarie is very popular with anglers and offers an array of family-oriented activities.

General Information

Port Macquarie-Hastings Tourism TOLL-FREE (1800) 025 935 on Horton Street is open daily from 9 AM to 4:30 PM.

What to See and Do

Several examples of colonial architecture have survived in Port Macquarie, including **Saint Thomas Church** at the corner of William and Hay streets. It was designed by convict architect Thomas Owen and built by convicts in 1828.

This part of the coast has Australia's most concentrated population of koalas. The **koala hospital** and study center at Roto House ((02) 6584 1522 is open 9 AM to 5 PM daily. Visitors can pat the koalas and learn more about their habits and habitats. **Billabong Koala Park** ((02) 6585 1060 and **Kingfisher Park** ((02) 6581 0783 are other wildlife centers where visitors can get close to a koala, which will most likely be snoozing.

Sea Acres Rainforest Centre ((02) 6582 3355, on Pacific Drive just south of town, comprises more than 30 ha (73 acres) of littoral rainforest. Visitors can wander along a 1.3 km-long (three-quarter-mile) multi-level boardwalk where strangler figs,

Houseboat rental is a popular accomodation option in the Great Lakes National Park.

native olives, brush bloodwood and shining leaf stinger trees support epiphytic ferns and draping vines. Native fruits attract rufous fantails, satin bowerbirds, white-eared honeyeaters and tawny frogmouths. Open daily from 9 AM to 4:30 PM. Admission $12. **Fantasy Glades** ((02) 6582 2506, in Parkland Close, is a theme-park that introduces children to the wonders of the rainforest. It's something of a miniature eco-Disneyland, with a pink-painted castle and a yellow monorail gliding through the forest. Open from 9 AM to 5 PM daily.

Fresh to saltwater, the waters around the Port Macquarie estuary offer sensational **fishing**, with good catches of bass, flathead, bream, and black-fish. Both SeaQuest Fishing Charters ((02) 6583

Where to Stay and Eat

Sails Resort ((02) 6583 3999 TOLL-FREE (1800) 025 271 FAX (02) 6584 0397, on Park Street, has luxury accommodation, a good restaurant and laidback bars, with a wide range of sporting facilities for guests. Motels further back from the beach offer more moderately priced alternatives. These include **Arrowyn** ((02) 6583 1633, 170 Gordon Street, and almost next door, **Bel Air** ((02) 6583 2177 FAX (02) 6583 2177, 179 Gordon Street. The **Port Macquarie Hotel** ((02) 6583 1011, Horton Street, has run-down but inexpensive rooms with ocean views. For longer stays, you can rent a self-contained unit at **Beach House Holiday Apartments** TOLL-FREE (1800) 025 096, 50 Owen Street.

3463 and Port Macquarie Estuary Sports Fishing ((02) 6582 2545 rent boats and equipment, take visitors out on fishing trips and provide extensive information on what's biting where. **Cruises** along the Hastings and Maria rivers are organized by Waterbus Everglades Tours ((0412) 363 418 and Port Venture River Cruises ((02) 6583 3058.

Surfing is big here too, with good waves at Flynns Beach. A regular vehicle ferry crosses Hastings River at Settlement Point — the service continues round the clock. An unsealed road leads to Point Plomer, 15 km (nine miles) north of Port Macquarie in the Limeburners Creek Nature Reserve. There's excellent surfing here, and the beach stretches for kilometers. If you don't have four-wheel drive, ask the tourist office road conditions.

Skydive Port Macquarie ((02) 6584 3655, at Port Macquarie Airport, offers tandem dives and free-fall lessons.

MACLEAY VALLEY

The meandering Macleay River has carved a broad valley running from Kempsey to the coastal towns of South West Rocks and Grassy Head, with scenic river flats leading to sandy beaches. Over 80% of the coastline is protected national park, and there are some impressive walking tracks along these craggy headlands. The half-hour walk to **Korogoro Arch and Cave** at Hat Head is best at low tide, when the cave is fully accessible. Another easy walk is the circular track in the **Arakoon State Recreation Area**, which leads to some beautiful views.

Kempsey Visitor Information Centre ((02) 6563 1555 TOLL-FREE (1800) 642 480 WEB SITE www.kempsey.midcoast.com.au, South Kempsey Park, South Kempsey, or **South West Rocks Visitor Information Centre** ((02) 6566 7099, 1 Ocean Drive, can provide maps and book accommodation.

South West Rocks

South West Rocks is surrounded by eight beautiful beaches, numerous river tributaries, and Arakoon State Recreation Area. The ruins of **Trial Bay Goal**, which opened in 1886 as a rehabilitation prison, are pleasant to explore. Sea eagles are often seen soaring on thermal air currents along the coastal bluffs here. Trial Bay's calm waters are perfect for **windsurfing** and **sailing**, while around the point, Gap Beach has good surf.

There are some good **snorkeling** and **scuba diving** locations here too. The best is **Fish Rock Cave**, one of the largest ocean caverns in the southern hemisphere. It is surrounded by reefs, sponge gardens and harbors a variety of marine creatures,

of champagne and a fruit platter on arrival, teas, plunger coffee and homemade cookies, and a delicious (huge) breakfast. Shaded by the tall eucalypti of Hat Head National Park, the three Garden Suites ($90 single, $180 double) have French doors opening to the verandah and double spa baths (bath oils and robes supplied). Bicycles are available free of charge, and your hosts Ken and Mary Markwell can organize fishing trips.

COFFS HARBOUR

Coffs Harbour was named by Captain John Korff, who sheltered here during a violent storm in 1847. Spelling perhaps wasn't a strong point among the

including loggerhead turtles and friendly bat fish. Fish Rock Dive Centre ((02) 6566 6614, 332 Gregory Street, or South West Rocks Dive Center ((02) 6566 6474, 5/98 Gregory Street, will take you cave diving, or to explore the wreck of the *Agnes Irving*. They also offer accommodation packages and accredited dive courses.

Trial Bay Fishing Charters ((0427) 256 556 can provide gear, bait and tackle and take individual or group bookings. **Hat Head National Park** extends from Arakoon State Recreation Area south to the village of Hat Head at Korogoro Point. There are magnificent views from Captain James Cook Lookout at Smoky Cape lighthouse, and camping is allowed in two areas.

One relaxing place to stay here is the **Smoky Cape Retreat Guesthouse** ((02) 6566 7740 FAX (02) 6566 7840, Cockatoo Place, Arakoon Road, South West Rocks, whose moderate prices include a bottle

early settlers. This is the largest banana-producing area in New South Wales, and Coffs is surrounded with banana groves. Its first, famous, tourist attraction is just north of town: a 13-m (40-ft) fibro-cement Big Banana, built in 1964, that fronts a quirky theme park. The banana industry has attracted a large Indian community, and Woolgoolga, 10 km (six miles) north of Coffs Harbour, has the highest concentration of Sikhs in Australia.

Coffs Harbour is something of a party place. With plenty of cheap accomadation and a plethora of inexpensive outdoor activities it has gained a reputation as a backpacker and adventure travel center. Competition is high among the dozens of operators, and prices for activities from scuba-diving to whitewater rafting or sky-diving tend to be lower here than elsewhere.

Stupendous promotion in the banana-growing region of Coffs Harbour.

General Information

Coffs Harbour Tourist Information Centre ((02) 6652 1522, on the corner of Pacific Highway and Marcia Street, is open weekdays from 8 AM to 5 PM, and from 8 AM to 6 PM on weekends.

What to See and Do

While the walk-through **Big Banana** itself is not that awe inspiring, except perhaps as a kitsch icon, the complex includes a train-ride through a banana plantation with stops at displays on all aspects of banana growing. There's a restaurant at the top of the hill (bananas a specialty) and a lookout with free telescopes and panoramic views of the valley.

Animals at the **Pet Porpoise Pool Oceanarium** ((02) 6652 2164 — a refuge for hurt or abandoned sea lions, fur seals, dolphins and penguins — are used to being petted and appear to enjoy the interaction. The twice-daily seal and dolphin show is old-fashioned entertainment for all age groups. **Muttonbird Island** rises out of the harbor like an egg covered in a tangle of vines (not really an island anymore, as you can walk across to it from the end of the marina). An estimated 25,000 mutton birds live on the island, although they migrate north for three months in winter (June to August). In spring, the birds lay their eggs in burrows dug a meter or so into the cliff-side, sheltering the opening with overhanging creepers. Chicks start to appear around Christmas. A viewing platform allows visitors to watch the birds without encroaching on their space, and is a great place to whale-watch during the annual migration periods from May to October/November. Also on the island are a butterfly house, tearoom, and a maze.

Whitewater rafting the rapids of the Goolang and Nymboida rivers is a thrilling way to get more exercise than you'd expect. Day-trips start at around $100, including lunch, rafts, wet-suits and helmets and transport. One of the least expensive operators is **Rapid Rafting Co.** TOLL-FREE (1800) 111 514 E-MAIL barracud barracud@key.net.au, run by Barracuda Backpackers. **Wow Rafting** ((02) 6654 4066 in Coffs also runs one- and two-day trips ($139 and $295), meals included.

Learn to Dive ((02) 6685 8333 TOLL-FREE (1800) 223 203 has scuba-diving lessons at the Solitary Island Marine Park, home to turtles and psychedelic fish. Four-day PADI certification courses, including accommodation, start at only $150. **Divers Depot** ((02) 6651 3514 TOLL-FREE (1800) 111 514 has a similar four-day course for $200.

Yuraygir and **Bundjalung** national parks stretch 80 km (50 miles) along the shore north of Coffs Harbour and feature secluded beaches, untouched coastline and wetlands full of water birds. There is good surfing at **Angourie Beach**. The area can be explored from one of the many tracks that meander along the coast.

Where to Stay

Set in a subtropical valley on Charlesworth Bay, three kilometers (two miles) north of Coffs Harbour, the **All Seasons Premier Pacific Bay Resort** ((1300) 363 360 WEB SITE www.pacificbayresort .com.au has its own beachfront and a nine-hole golf course. Moderate to expensive rates include access to tennis and squash courts, a gym, three swimming pools, and a beauty salon. There are two restaurants and a children's club, and a walking trail through the surrounding rainforest.

Santa Fe ((02) 6653 7700 is like a slice of New Mexico only five minutes north of Coffs. It's a bit of a walk to Sapphire Beach, but the sunken swimming pool, generous landscaped tropical gardens, and zappy decor are good value at moderate prices.

Contact **Variety Holidays Information and Booking Service** ((02) 6651 2322, 23 Vincent Street, for self-contained and serviced apartments and houses. During summer demand is high so reserve early. **Bo'suns Inn Motel** (/FAX (02) 6651 2251, 37 Ocean Parade, and **Midway Motor Inn** ((02) 6652 1444, on the Pacific Highway, are inexpensive and convenient to the city center.

Not far from the main beach, **Barracuda Backpackers** TOLL-FREE (1800) 111 514 WEB SITE www .barracudabackpackers.com has a swimming pool and spa, offers free use of fishing equipment, flippers, surfboards and boogie boards, and has Internet facilities.

Where to Eat

My favorite of the string of cafés and restaurants along the marina is friendly **Passionfish** ((02) 6652 1423, 384A High Street. The menu is Thai-ish, their sweet curry laksa of snapper, Moreton Bay bug tails and squid, and delicious home-made noodles. It is one of the best around (moderate). The busy **Tide and Pilot Brasserie** ((02) 6651 6888, at the marina, serves four types of oysters, golden seared scallops, and a wide variety of local fish grilled, baked, sautéed or fried (moderate). The $25 three-course dinner menu is good value.

Star Anise ((02) 6651 1033, 93 Grafton Street (Pacific Highway), looks like any other small-town café. But chef Gary Tyson trained at the Bather's Pavilion in Sydney, and his modern Australian cuisine draws on Greek, Japanese and Italian influences to create perfectly executed strong-flavored dishes. Tyson is renowned for his desserts, although I've never had room to test them (moderate). **Annie's** ((02) 6652 7555, at the Aanuka Beach Resort, serves modern Australian classics at fairly expensive prices. It has ocean views, a good wine list and attentive service; open for dinner only, Tuesday to Saturday.

Around Coffs Harbour

The lush green hills behind Coffs Harbour can provide a good alternative to the beach. A pretty village

15 km (nine miles) inland from the Pacific Highway and 50 km (31 miles) from Coffs Harbour,
Bellingen is the gateway to the World Heritage-
listed Dorrigo and New England national parks and
has a thriving arts community, galleries along the
main street and some wonderful rainforest walks.

The mountainous drive from Bellingen to the
entrance of **Dorrigo National Park** cuts through
the rainforest's edge. Griffith Lookout, 26 km
(16 miles) after Bellingen, offers spectacular views
down to the coast. The unsealed road into the park
begins two kilometers (one mile) further on.
Dorrigo National Park is famous for its native orchids in the spring months from September to
December, and its rare ringwood trees, found only
in this area. It offers excellent bush-walking trails
— pick up a walking map from the **Rainforest
Centre (** (02) 6657 2309 at the park entrance — and
picnic areas. There's a suspended boardwalk path
for shorter sorties. Wildlife includes the nocturnal
tiger quoll, a carnivorous marsupial the size of a
cat (if you hear a derisive sneer coming from the
bushes, it's probably one of these harmless creatures). Although **New England National Park**
begins only 20 km (12.5 miles) from Dorrigo National Park, the meandering mountain drive circles
through Fernbrook and Ebor, and takes well over
an hour. Most of the park is accessible only to experienced hikers, and there is a campsite near the
entrance. Just south of tiny Ebor are the 450-m
(1,476-ft) **Ebor Falls**.

A little piece of India has been transplanted to
Woolgoolga, 26 km (16 miles) north of Coffs. The
white-domed **Guru Nanak Sikh Temple** at the top
of the hill greets visitors driving in from the south.
Turbaned men and women in saris are part of the
local color, and there are some good Indian eateries in town and near the temple.

HOW TO GET THERE

Although the Pacific Highway begins in central
Sydney, the first section meanders along the coast
to Newcastle — a beautiful drive, but not the route
to take if you want to head further north in a hurry.
It's much faster to take the Sydney–Newcastle
Freeway until it meets the Pacific Highway near
Hexham, 150 km (93 miles) north. From here the
route to Brisbane is one of the easiest drives in
Australia. The road is good, the views often su-
perb, and you're never far from a gas station or a
store. Coffs Harbour is 555 km (335 miles) from
Sydney, 427 km (265 miles) from Brisbane.

The Sydney–Queensland train stops at Taree,
Kendall, Wauchope (for Port Macquarie), Kempsey,
Eungai, Macksville, Nambucca Heads, Urunga,
Sawtell and Coffs Harbour. From there it cuts in-
land via Grafton City and Casino. For train time-
tables call **Countrylink (** 132 232. Greyhound
Pioneer, Lindsay Coach Service, Kirklands and

McCafferty's all operate daily bus services along
the Pacific Highway between Sydney and Brisbane.

There are daily flights from Sydney to Coffs
Harbour and Port Macquarie on **Eastern Austra-
lia Airlines (** 131 313. **Impulse (** 131 381 flies from
Sydney to Coffs Harbour via Port Macquarie. They
also have flights via Newcastle to Port Macquarie,
Coffs Harbour and Coolangatta, and flights from
Brisbane to Coffs Harbour. Coast to Coast fly to Port
Macquarie from Brisbane, Lismore and Newcastle.

BYRON BAY

Australia's easternmost tip, Cape Byron was named
after the poet's grandfather, John "Foulweather Jack"
Byron, who circumnavigated the globe in 1766,
becoming governor of Newfoundland in 1769. Byron
Bay, which was originally a whaling station, is the
gem of the New South Wales coast. Its idyllic subtropical climate hosts a rich creative culture, eclectic boutiques and eateries and beautiful seascape.

BACKGROUND

The coastline around Byron Bay has been called the
Rainbow Country since hippies flocked into the area
in the late 1960s and 1970s. Later they were followed
by disciples of the New Age. Byron Bay's alterna-
tive-lifers and local residents pretty well kept their
crescent-shaped beach and crystalline coves to themselves until the mid-1990s, when what had been a
steady trickle of tourists swelled into a full fledged
flood. Local resistance to development, however,
has kept out any Gold Coast-style high rises or tacky
Big Bananas. As a result, Byron's natural beauty is
paired with an attractive, laid-back town that has
become a second home to many of Australia's artistic elite. Actors and film producers, fashion designers and interior designers mingle reasonably
comfortably with flower children, surfers and European backpackers. The atmosphere livens up in
the evening, with live music in pubs and cafés. The
surf is excellent, the waters clear and not too cold,
and the hinterland clad in rainforest.

GENERAL INFORMATION

The **Byron Bay Tourist Association (** (02) 6685 8050
is at 80 Jonson Street. Almost next door, at 84 Jonson
Street, **Byron Bus and Backpacker Centre (** (02) 6685
5517 has information on rail and bus services and
car rental; they also book local tours and activities.
Part of the same center, you can surf the web or catch
up on your e-mail at **Global Gossip (** (02) 6680 9140,
open from 8 AM to midnight every day. They have
sound-proof phone booths and cheap national and
international call rates. For a cab call **Byron Taxis
(** (02) 6685 5008.

The Byron Echo and *Byron Shire News* have weekly
guides to what's on in and around Byron.

WHAT TO SEE AND DO

Get oriented with a drive, walk or cycle to lovely **Cape Byron Lighthouse**, where generally a few wallabies hang out at dawn and dusk. A three-kilometer (two-mile) walk from the lighthouse through **Cape Byron Headland Reserve** skirts Cape Byron's craggy cliffs and sheltered coves, passing through rainforest vegetation that opens into fantastic coastal views. Look out for dolphins, and whales in season.

Jonson Street, Byron's main drag, leads onto the southeastern end of the long **Main Beach**. There's a patrolled swimming area here and a park with plenty of shade and play equipment for children. Main Beach becomes **Belongil Beach** as it approaches the white-sand Belongil Creek estuary. This end is quieter, and the curving estuary is safe for small children to paddle.

There are 60 or so wrecks in the waters around Byron. The hull of the SS *Wollongbar* lies in the bay off the end of Jonson Street — it's responsible for the unusual surf break here known as "**The Wreck**." Southeast from Main Beach, picturesque **Clarks Beach** curves around the headland, with **The Pass**, a popular surf break for long boarders, at its eastern extremity. There are shady picnic areas here, and a walking track leads to a small lookout platform. At the bottom of the Cape Byron Headland Reserve, two smaller sandy beaches lead from The Pass to the tip of the cape: **Wategos Beach** and **Little Wategos Beach. Tallow Beach** begins past the cliffs at Cosy Corner, and stretches for seven kilometers (four miles) to Broken Head.

The Byron Bay scene attracts well-known Australian bands. Music runs from rock to techno, from blues and jazz to ambiance and alternative. The **East Coast Blues and Roots Festival**, held in Byron Bay

Pighouse Flicks Cinema ((02) 6685 5833 are big cushions (socks obligatory), other seating is in black-and-white-spotted lounge chairs.

Meet the locals at the Byron area's **Sunday markets** selling arts and crafts and homegrown produce. Byron Bay's market is the first Sunday of the month, Channon's on the second Sunday, Ballina's the third, and both Bangalow and Nimbin have markets on the fourth Sunday.

Godwana Gifts ((02) 6685 8866, Shop 6, Middleton Street, sells Aboriginal artworks, boomerangs and didgeridoos, and offer free didgeridoo lessons.

Alternative therapies are the norm in Byron. In a fairytale subtropical garden setting five minutes from Byron, **Magical Garden** ((02) 6684 7630 E-MAIL magicalgarden@hotmail.com combines eastern and western methods including acupressure, therapeutic bodywork, a variety of massage techniques, sea-weed and clay scrubs, aromatherapy and Ayurveda. They offer an enormous range of pampering and beauty treatments, all using natural products, and have accommodation packages. **Osho's House, Healing for Mind Body & Soul** ((02) 6685 6792 or (015) 299 258 E-MAIL oshos@nrg.com.au, 1/30 Carlyle Street, has flotation tanks and specialize in massage, reflexology, and Faura Soma (color therapy). They also offer Tarot readings. Even the backpackers' lodge at Belongil Beach has a flotation tank and offers shiatsu massages (**Relax Haven** ((02) 6685 8304).

SPORTS AND OUTDOOR ACTIVITIES

Byron can sometimes make your dreams come true — even your childhood dreams. I heartily recommend Byron's **Flying Trapeze and Circus School** ((02) 6685 8000 E-MAIL beachclub@byron-bay.com, at the Byron Bay Beach Club, whose patient instructors make it all so easy at only $25 for two hours. Before you know it you'll be leaping, with a safety harness and net, from a six-meter (20-ft) platform and swinging high above the palms into the ever-blue skies to be caught, Tarzan-style, in the arms of a pro.

With eight surf breaks close by, including "The Wreck" at the bottom end of Main Beach, Byron is a good place to try your hand at **surfing**. Byron Bay Surf School TOLL-FREE (1800) 707 274 WEB SITE www.byronbaysurfschool.com, Shop 5/84 Jonson Street, offers group lessons three times daily, as well as private lessons and board and wetsuit rental. A single three-hour lesson is $33, three lessons are $77. Style Surfing ((02) 6685 5634 or (0416) 162 969 is another good school, owned and operated by longtime Byron Bay resident and surfer, Gary Morgan.

Byron Bay Dive Centre ((02) 66 858 333 TOLL-FREE FAX (02) 66 855 750 E-MAIL byronbaydive@yahoo.com, 9 Marvel Street, runs **scuba** courses through to instructor level and offers recreational dives to the Julian Rocks Marine Reserve, an aquatic reserve

in April, features Dixieland, New Orleans and mainstream jazz and blues, with international and Australian bands.

As Australia's most easterly point, Byron Bay is the first to see the dawn of the new year, and their New Year's Eve "**Last Night, First Light**" celebrations are legendary. The crowds are enormous, but a large number of attractions and activities during the night keeps everyone absorbed — alcohol is not permitted on Byron's streets, parks or beaches. As the sun sets, the Hare Krishna Rathayatra procession heads along the beach and into town, with hundreds of devotees dancing and chanting about the red and yellow, glowing, six-meter-high (nearly 20-ft) cloth image of Lord Jagannath on his chariot.

Next door to the Arts Factory Lodge on Skinners Shoot Road, a pig abattoir has been converted into a vegetarian restaurant and cinema, know collectively as the **Piggery**. The first four rows of funky

---

Sun and surf at Byron Bay.

established in 1982 that harbors a diverse array of warm-temperate and tropical marine life. The first dive is $70, subsequent dives only $40, and courses are taught in either SSI or PADI standards. They also take **snorkelers** out for $40 per day, including gear.

Sea-kayaking tours around Wategos Beach and Cape Byron is especially exciting during the gigantic humpback whale migratory season (from May to October/November). The thrilling experience of cutting through the surf next to a couple of bottlenose dolphins can, however, be enjoyed all year-round. Byron Bay Sea Kayaks (/FAX (02) 6685 5830 has two tours daily. Dolphin Kayaking ((02) 6685 8044 E-MAIL mark@dolphinkayaking.com.au is also a recommended group.

WHERE TO STAY

Expensive

A gargoyle-flanked tunnel leads to the Gilligan's Island-like retreat of the **Garden Burée of Byron** ((02) 6685 5390, a five-minute walk from the village center. The individual *burées* are two-story bamboo and glass cottages, each with a spiral staircase that leads to an arched woven-grass cathedral ceiling. Amenities are definitely modern and include a large bathroom with a double spa downstairs and private outdoor showers. Prices vary seasonally, with good deals if you book for a week. Just seconds from Main Beach **Waves Motel** ((02)

Skydiving and parachuting have been popular in Byron for 20 years. Byron Bay Skydiving Centre ((0412) 392 273 E-MAIL skydive@norex.com.au caters to all levels, and offers training towards certification. They have a free pickup service for their customers within the Byron Bay area. Both Byron Bay Hang Gliding School ((015) 257 699 and Flight Zone Hang-gliding ((02) 6685 8768 give **hang-gliding** instruction and take passengers on tandem flights, while Skylimit Sports Aviation ((02) 6684 3711 offers joy-flights on powered hang-gliders.

Byron Bay Golf Club ((02) 6685 6470 on Broken Head Road is an attractive and well-kept **golf** course. There's also a nine-hole course at Byron Bay Beach Club ((02) 6685 8000, on Bayshore Drive and a beautiful par-72 course near Ocean Shores, 20 km (12.5 miles) north of Byron at the Ocean Shores Country Club ((02) 6680 1008, Orana (considered one of the best courses in New South Wales).

6685 5966 E-MAIL info@byronwaves.com, 35 Lawson Street, is only a short stroll to the heart of Byron Bay. Deluxe suites feature marble bathrooms with king-sized baths.

Five minutes out of town, **Byron Bay Rainforest Resort** ((02) 6685 6139 WEB SITE www.rainforest resort.com.au, 39–75 Broken Head Road, has cottages, cabins and guesthouses in a rainforest setting with good weekly rates. Originally designed as a resort for wheelchair-users and mobility impaired travelers, facilities still include a swimming pool with ramp and submersible wheelchair and a spa with a hydraulic lift.

Moderate

One of the most relaxing guesthouses I've ever stayed in, the lovely **Byron Bay Guest House** ((02) 6680 8886 FAX (02) 6685 5673 E-MAIL byronguest @one.net.au, 70 Kingsley Lane, puts toned-down

Balinese decor in an airy federation cottage. The spacious rooms have polished teak floors, bathrooms have free-standing baths, slate wall and floor tiles, and French doors leading to a leafy private court yard. It's two streets back from the beach, and close to the center of town. In the same area, **Avalon Guest House** ((02) 6685 8143 FAX (02) 6685 8001 E-MAIL avalon@byron-bay.com, 47 Carlyle Street, has a range of rooms, all originally, and tastefully, decorated. Another moderate option is the **Bay Mist Motel** ((02) 6685 6121, 12 Bay Street, opposite Main Beach.

Three kilometers (two miles) northwest of town, **Byron Bay Beach Club** ((02) 6685 8000 FAX (02) 6685 6916 TOLL-FREE (1800) 028 927 E-MAIL beachclub @byron-bay.com, Bayshore Drive, is set on 568 ha (230 acres) of parkland with two kilometers (one mile) of beach frontage. Cabins are fairly basic, shaded by native trees that attract birds and wallabies. Not only does it offer two swimming pools, tennis courts, a bar and restaurant and free use of bicycles and canoes, the Beach Club runs Byron's Trapeze and Circus School and has a nine-hole golf course. Rates are moderate, becoming inexpensive for groups of four or more.

Inexpensive

Nanette's ((02) 6685 6895 or (0408) 740 963 E-MAIL nanette@byron-bay.com is a small guesthouse with a pretty garden that backs onto a nature reserve. It's only a short walk to the beach, and at $30 a night, or $120 a week (per person, in double rooms), Nanette's cozy homelike atmosphere is a steal. There are only five rooms, so book ahead. The **Magical Garden** ((02) 6684 7630 E-MAIL magicalgarden @hotmail.com has inexpensive B&B accommodation and offer packages that include beauty and health treatments.

Aquarius Backpackers Motel TOLL-FREE (1800) 028 909, 16 Lawson Street, Byron Bay, just back from Main Beach, has singles, doubles, and group rooms as well as cheaper dorms. They're close to everything, have a solar-heated pool, Internet facilities, a bar/café, attractive home-style rooms and units, and palm-shaded gardens. They offer free pickup. **Belongil Beachouse** ((02) 6685 7868, in Childe Street, is another friendly and well-kept backpackers', with similar facilities minus the pool. The chilled-out **Arts Factory Lodge** ((02) 6685 7709, on Skinners Shoot Road, is a 10-minute walk from the town center, with dorms, teepees and cheap tent sites. They offer free use of their bicycles and have a regular-ish shuttle service into Byron.

WHERE TO EAT

Most of the larger resorts have their own restaurants, generally in the moderate to expensive bracket, but to get a feel for Byron it's better to check out the local eateries.

For lovers of Asian flavors, Byron is close to heaven. A string of cafés crush together along Bay Lane, behind the Beach Hotel. **Red, Hot & Green** ((02) 6685 5363, Lawson Arcade, Bay Lane, is one of the best. At inexpensive to moderate prices, the essentially Japanese–Thai offerings are unerringly fresh and delicious. It's small and doesn't take bookings: be prepared for a wait on Friday and Saturday nights. Another good one in this strip, **Thai Lucy** ((02) 6680 8083, 4 Bay Lane, uses lots of lemongrass and coconut to produce spicy Thai dishes at similar prices. Again, it's small and often crowded. Closed Mondays. More upmarket, **Orient Restaurant** ((02) 6685 7771, on the corner of Jonson and Lawson streets, offers delicious moderately priced modern Asian dishes. The bar area has simpler versions at inexpensive prices. Hideki and Mayami Takagi have been serving sushi and sashimi at **Misaki Byron** ((02) 6685 7966, 11 Fletcher Street, for 13 years (moderate). The beautiful **Byron Thai** ((02) 6685 8453, 31 Lawson Street, run by Vinya Chantra, serves authentic Thai food using herbs and vegetables from his own garden. Prices are at the low end of moderate.

With sweeping views of the beach, the best wine list in town and knowledgeable waitstaff, **Fins** ((02) 6685 5029, in the Beach Hotel, serves excellent seafood inspired by food from the ports of Portugal, France and Greece. Prices are moderate to expensive. This is the place to come for a special meal, but reserve ahead. Groovy **Fresh** ((02) 6685 7810, 7 Jonson Street, uses organic produce, a lot of it grown on their own farm, to create inventive vegetarian dishes and several tasty fish and chicken courses. It's a popular place for breakfast (moderate). A stylish late-night café, **The Latin** ((02) 6680 9188 serves South American food at inexpensive prices until 3 AM, and features Latin dancers on weekends. Inexpensive takeaway or eat-in fish and chips (gourmet style) have never been better than at **Mongers Fish Takeaway** ((02) 6680 8080, Shop 1, Bay Lane, where the batter is a delicate tempura and only the freshest fish and seafood are used. **Piggery Supernaturalfood** ((02) 6685 5833 is a funky and inexpensive vegetarian restaurant in a converted piggery at Skinner's Shoot.

Ten minutes inland from Byron, the pretty hinterland village of Bangalow has become something of a gourmet retreat. Housed in a nineteenth-century terrace, **Baci** ((02) 6687 1133, 24 Byron Street, Bangalow, serves predominately seafood, in a Mediterrasian cuisine pared down to a Japanese-Italian cross (moderate). **Ruby's** ((02) 6687 2180, at the Bangalow Hotel in Byron Street, serves generous portions of modern Australian cuisine in the old hotel dining room and along its broad verandah.

After a few lessons with a pro, surfing at Byron is a breeze.

How to Get There

Byron Bay is 800 km (497 miles) from Sydney, and 200 km (124 miles) from Brisbane. Trains from Sydney to the Queensland border pass by Casino, where there is a connecting train to Lismore, Byron Bay, Mullumbimby and Murwillumbah. For train timetables call **Countrylink (** 132 232.

Greyhound Pioneer, Lindsay Coach Service, Kirklands and McCafferty's operate daily coach services to Byron from both Sydney (around $70) and Brisbane (around $30). A number of coach operators have attractive three- to five-day Sydney-to-Byron deals, some specializing in surfing lessons, others tour the Hunter and include whitewater rafting (see BACKPACKING, page 35 in YOUR CHOICE).

Byron is only two-and-a-half hours' drive from Brisbane, and is 85 km (53 miles) south of Coolangatta. Although Ballina's small airport is closer to Byron Bay, there are far more flights into Coolangatta's busy Balinga airport. Ansett and Qantas have regular flights to Coolangatta from all capital cities, and Kendell flies Sydney–Ballina three times a week. **Byron Bay Airporter (** (02) 6680 8726 or (0414) 608 660 runs a shuttle service between Byron Bay and Coolangatta, and will drop you at your hotel. **Byron Bay Airbus (** (02) 6681 3355 or (0417) 813 355 operates a similar service to and from Ballina.

AROUND BYRON BAY

National Parks

Mountainous **Whian Whian State Forest** is a remnant of the forests that blanketed the coastal hills before loggers arrived in the nineteenth century. **Nightcap Forest Drive** loops through the forest from the tiny town of Repentance Creek, 20 km (12.5 miles) inland from Byron, ending at the Big Scrub Flora Reservation, and passing within meters of the 120-m (394-ft) Minyan Falls. A detour leads towards **Peates Mountain Lookout**, with views down to Cape Byron. There are numerous good walking tracks in the forest, some leading into the adjacent **Nightcap National Park**.

An hour northeast of Byron Bay, **Mount Warning National Park** is dominated by Mount Warning, a volcanic plug named by Captain Cook. Despite Byron's claims, it is this 1,160-m (3,805-ft) summit that sees the sun's rays before anywhere else in the country. Enormous ferns grow in the stunning rainforest here, which is home to lyrebirds, scrub turkeys, and pademelons. To reach the park, head north along the Pacific Highway, turning left nine kilometers (five and a half miles) past Burringbar, in the direction of Stokers Siding. Turn left at the T-intersection, then follow the road around to Dum Dum. The five-kilometer (three-mile) road into the park from Dum Dum is signposted.

Nimbin

The 1973 Aquarius Festival put Nimbin on the hippie map, bringing the counter culture to this quiet dairy township, sister village to Woodstock (officially). Today, Nimbin is still considered the headquarters for alternative lifestylers in Australia; it's also the undisputed marijuana capital of Australia. The main street is a hive of activity, its façades adorned with psychedelic murals. Men and women wear long, flowing clothes and play drums and chant along the street. Art, music, street theater and poetry have lived hand in hand with a culture of healthy living, social reform, healing and environmental awareness for almost 30 years, although in recent years harder drugs have clouded the picture. The **Nimbin Shuttle (** (02) 6680 9189 has daily round-trip service from Byron Bay or Nimbin.

Nimbin Museum ((02) 6689 1764, 2/80 Cullen Street, explains it all, promising to "follow the Rainbow Serpent's journey through time" as it presents "the Aboriginal, pioneer and hippie eras of Nimbin's history." A few doors down from the museum, the **Rainbow Café** is the center of the town's social life. Locals meet here, trade produce and occasionally share a joint. The vegetarian food isn't bad either, and the cakes are delicious. The fourth Sunday of the month, locals come to sell tropical fruit, homespun garments and handicrafts at the **Nimbin Market**. If you're around at the end of April, though, Nimbin's well-organized **Mardi Grass Festival** swells the town's population as people come from all over for the evening's **Marijuana Harvest Ball**.

Nimbin's commercial enterprises include the **Rainbow Power Company Ltd. (** (02) 6689 1430, at 1 Alternative Way, which displays different sources of sustainable energy. **Phantom Possum Design (** (02) 6689 1911, produces hand-painted silk and hemp creations tagged "wearable art for your home or body."

Grey Gum Lodge ((02) 6689 1713, 2 High Street, offers inexpensive B&B accommodation in a beautiful old house with a swimming pool.

Tours

Forgotten Country Ecotours ((02) 6687 7845 has tours into the rainforest and to Nimbin from Byron Bay and Ballina. Trips, from one day to one week, include bush-walking, canoeing, horse riding, gold panning, mountain biking, bird watching and fishing. Owner-operators Paul and Jenny Massies' local knowledge is invaluable. **Jim's Alternative Tours (** (02) 6685 7720 E-MAIL jimstours@byron-bay.com also has day-trips to Nimbin and the rainforest. **Byron Bay to Bush Tours (** (02) 6685 6889 has similar day-trips, and visit alternative farms and communes in the rainforests. **Pioneering Spirit (** (02) 6685 7721 organizes climbs to the summit of Mount Warning.

The Grandis, New South Wales' tallest tree.

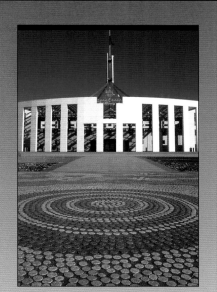

Canberra
and
Southern
New
South
Wales

WHEN IT CAME TIME TO PASS POWER FROM THE HANDS of individual states to a federal government, a prickly question arose: Which city, Melbourne or Sydney, was to be honored with the title of Australia's Capital? Australia's fledgling constitution, a document representing a myriad of compromises between state and federal powers, included one named "The Australian Capital Territory." When the first federal legislature convened in 1901 in Melbourne's Parliament House it was with the understanding that in future a new and permanent location would be found between that city and Sydney.

The site was not chosen until 1908. In 1911, 35-year-old American architect Walter Burley Griffin won an international competition to design the national capital. The city was officially named Canberra — an Aboriginal word for "meeting place" — at the laying of the foundation stones in March 1913. Griffin, with considerable input from his wife, architect Marion Mahoney Griffin, designed the street plan and building placement to take full advantage of the natural amphitheater formed by the surrounding mountains. The Griffins' vision of a city in harmony with nature was realized in 1926.

East of the capitol New South Wales's southern coast, punctuated with inlets, bays, lagoons and estuaries, beautiful white-sand beaches and large tracts of national park, is largely overlooked by foreign visitors. Away from the main centers, there is often barely a footprint on the glaringly white beaches.

CANBERRA

Like Washington, DC, Canberra is a planned city, purpose-built to be the nation's capital. It's role is unavoidable — at every turn there seems to be a national monument or museum commemorating Australia's foundations and heritage. The city showcases some of the most impressive public architecture in Australia. Centered on Lake Burley Griffin, each public edifice has been carefully positioned among Canberra's broad thoroughfares and manicured gardens. Buildings are set well back from the roads, parklands break up the neat rows of houses, and no building is taller than six stories.

Canberra is also a city of great natural beauty. Surrounded by rolling hills and native bush, its climate is more temperate than most other Australian cities. Spring arrives with a blaze of golden wattles in August, and trout to fish in the Murrumbidgee. Summers are hot — in January, half the population seems to escape to Batemans Bay and New South Wales' southern beaches, only an hour and a half away. In autumn a canopy of reds, yellows, greens and oranges covers the boulevards; days are bright and clear, nights cool and crisp. And by June the hills surrounding Canberra are capped with snow — Australian Capital Territory borders on New South Wales' Kosciusko ski fields, part of the Snowy Mountain Range.

GENERAL INFORMATION

The **Canberra Visitor Information Centre** ((02) 6205 0044 TOLL-FREE (1800) 026 192 WEB SITE www .canberratourism.com.au, is at 330 Northbourne Avenue, Dickson. Their web site is excellent, with maps, an extensive "What's On" section, and a good accommodation service. Another useful **web site** is www.canberra.citysearch.com, with restaurant reviews and a booking service.

The main bus terminal is at the **Jolimont Travel Centre** on Northbourne Avenue. For bus information and timetables contact **Action Bus Service** ((02) 6207 7611.

A Canberra **Privileges Card**, available at the tourist information center for $25, gives half-price entry to many major attractions, discounts at others, savings on sightseeing tours, cruises, cinemas, theaters and concerts, and discounts at over 80 restaurants — good value if you're in town for more than a day or two. Internet access, light meals and coffee are available at **Cyberchino Café** ((02) 6295 7844, 33 Kennedy Street, Kingston.

GETTING AROUND

Navigating Canberra's convoluted whorls is a skill that takes decades to acquire. Invest in a good map and, when driving or walking, always allow time to lose your way and find it again at least once.

Canberra's **public bus service**, ACTION ((02) 131 710, is based around the four town center interchanges — City, Woden, Tuggeranong and Belconnen. An adult day-ticket costs $8.40. Canberra City Sights and Tours ((02) 6294 3171 FAX (02) 6294 4010 has two-hour **bus tours** of the lake and Canberra's major attractions for $22.

Canberra has 150 km (93 miles) of cycle paths, and one of the best ways to get a feel for the city is to **rent a bike**. Try Mr. Spoke's Bike Hire ((02) 6257 1188, Barrine Drive, Acton, Wombat Mountain Bikes ((02) 6285 4058 or 6288 2753, based at Lyons Shops in Woden, or Canberra YMCA ((02) 6248 9155, Dryandra Street, O'Connor.

The major **car rental agencies** have offices in Canberra: Budget ((02) 6257 1305 or 132 848, Canberra Airport, Pialligo; Avis ((02) 6249 1601 Canberra Airport, Pialligo; Hertz ((02) 6257 487732 Mort Street, Braddon; and Thrifty ((02) 6247 7422, 29 Lonsdale Street, Braddon.

For **taxis** call Arial Taxi Cabs ((02) 6285 9222.

WHAT TO SEE AND DO

At Canberra's center, **Lake Burley Griffin** was created in 1964 by damming the Molonglo River. From the air, Burley Griffin resembles an elaborate

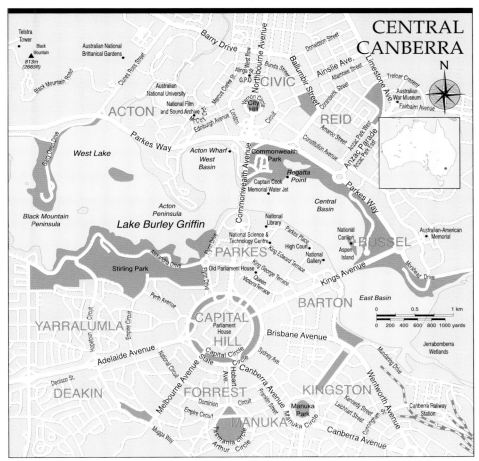

Chinese dragon (turn your map upside down). At its head is **Government House** — home to the Governor General, the Queen's official representative in Australia. It is not open to the public, but if you look into its gardens you might spot the resident colony of kangaroos. At the lake's eastern tail the **Jerrabomberra Wetlands** bird sanctuary is home to a diverse array of resident and migratory bird species. This isn't a place to come for peace and quiet. Listen for the eastern yellow robin's high bell-like piping and the bell-miner's echoing chime.

Lake Burley Griffin is bisected by Commonwealth Avenue, which runs through the city's two foci: Civic, the main business and shopping center, and Capitol Hill, dominated by grass-topped **Parliament House (** (02) 6277 5399. Many of the most interesting things to see in Canberra are found along the stretch of lake between Commonwealth and Kings avenues.

An 81-m (265-ft) flagpole forms the centerpiece of Parliament House, which opened in 1988. The building itself is understated, and part of it is underground to maintain the original topography of Capitol Hill. A walkway on the grassed roof provides good views over the city. In the forecourt, a mosaic by Northern Territory artist Michael Tjakamarra Nelson represents an Aboriginal meeting place. A magnificent tapestry designed by Arthur Boyd hangs in the Great Hall, while paintings by leading Australian artists hang in the Foyer and around the building. Tours of the building leave every 30 minutes. Parliament is open daily 9 AM to 5 PM, or later when the legislature is sitting; entry is free.

More than 70 countries have diplomatic representation in the national capital. Lovers of kitsch will find themselves in paradise in this architectural hodgepodge: the Japanese embassy is set in traditional gardens, the Thai embassy is a landmark with its elevated roof and gold-colored tiles, and the Italian embassy blends modern design with inspiration from ancient Rome.

Questacon — National Science and Technology Centre ((02) 6270 2800 WEB SITE www.questacon .edu.au, King Edward Terrace, Parkes, is an interactive science center with cutting-edge hands-on exhibitions. Visitors can play music with light beams or control a computer with thoughts. There's a very realistic simulated guillotine.

Overlooking the lake, the **National Gallery of Australia** ((02) 6240 6502, Parkes Place, holds an outstanding collection of over 70,000 paintings: including some exceptional Aboriginal bark paintings and the works of foreign masters from Jackson Pollock's controversial *Blue Poles* to paintings by Picasso, Warhol and Matisse. The chimes of the imposing **National Carillon** ((02) 6271 2888 waft to the gallery across the placid waters of Lake Burley Griffin. Built on three pillars, this 50-m (150-ft) structure houses 53 bronze bells. Depending on the season, several recitals are held here every day.

Next door to the gallery is the **High Court** ((02) 6270 6811, King Edward Terrace, Parkes, where judges deliberate constitutional disputes. Tours are organized daily. Further along the lake shore is the **National Library of Australia** ((02) 6262 1111, in Parkes Place, with one and a half million books and thousands of audio recordings. A changing exhibition of rare and historic documents in the library's collection is on display in the Exhibition Gallery. Entry is free, but call ahead for opening hours.

The **Australian National Botanic Gardens** are on the lower slopes of Black Mountain, three kilometers (two miles) west of central Canberra. It has the largest collection of native flora in Australia, with more than 170,000 plant species from every corner of the country. Open 9 AM to 5 PM daily, entry is free. Above the gardens, the 195-m (640-ft) **Telstra Tower** provides a panoramic view of Canberra and the surrounding landscape, the best views though are from its revolving restaurant.

WHERE TO STAY

Expensive
Built in the 1920s, the art-deco **Hyatt Hotel Canberra** ((02) 6270 1234 FAX (02) 6281 5998 WEB SITE www .canberra.hyatt.com, Commonwealth Avenue, Yarralumla, has enormous rooms with mable bathrooms and high-quality fittings. Rolling landscaped gardens add to the tranquility of this lovely hotel. **Olims Canberra** ((02) 6248 5511 TOLL-FREE (1800) 020 016 FAX (02) 6247 0864 WEB SITE www.olims .cafesydney.net, at the corner of Ainslie and Limestone avenues, Braddon, is set around a flowery and sunny courtyard. Rooms are comfortable and spacious, and most have garden views.

Moderate
Only a five-minute walk from the lake, the **York** ((02) 6295 2333 FAX (02) 6295 9559, 31 Giles Street, Kingston, has bright and airy contemporary suites with a very good restaurant (Artespresso) and bar downstairs. **Telopea Park Motel** ((02) 6295 3722

FAX (02) 6239 6373, 16 New South Wales Crescent, Forrest, and the **Quality Hotel Diplomat** ((02) 6295 2277 TOLL-FREE (1800) 026 367 FAX (02) 6239 6432, Canberra Avenue, Barton, are two reasonably priced, modern hotels on the Parliament side of Lake Burley Griffin, back from Parliament House. On the city side of the lake, **Acacia Motor Lodge** ((02) 6249 6955 FAX (02) 6247 7058, 65 Ainslie Avenue, Reid, is a friendly motel in a quiet leafy neighborhood only a five-minute walk from the center of town.

Inexpensive
Kambah Inn ((02) 6231 8444 FAX (02) 6231 2450, on Marconi Crescent, is off the main highway in a

quiet suburban setting. A little further out, in Queanbeyan, **Burley Griffin Motel** ((02) 6297 1211 FAX (02) 6297 3083, 147 Uriarra Road, has simple but large rooms at similar prices.

WHERE TO EAT

The presence of 70 diplomatic missions, four universities, and an educated, well-traveled and well-paid population is reflected in the extensive choice of high quality restaurants and cafés throughout Canberra.

Expensive
One of this city's best Italian restaurants, **Tosolini's** ((02) 6232 6600, 2 Furneaux Street, Griffith, offers antipasto, excellent home-made pasta, imaginative pizzas and perfect risotto, along with a comprehensive wine list. The menu at the extremely

popular **Juniperberry** ((02) 6295 8317, in Red Hill Shopping Center, Red Hill, changes regularly and always offers good vegetarian options. Their seven-page wine list is well-chosen, with wines from all major Australian grape-growing regions. Book well ahead. **Fringe Benefits** ((02) 6247 4042, 54 Marcus Clarke Street, remains one of the best restaurants in Canberra with an imaginative menu of Mediterranean dishes. Surprisingly, you're not just paying for the view at the revolving **Tower Restaurant** ((02) 6248 6162, Telstra Tower, Black Mountain. The menu includes creative indigenous meals, including crocodile soufflé with yabbie consommé, and flambéed, gin-marinated seared wallaby.

Inexpensive

Gus's Café ((02) 6248 8118, on Bunda Street, serves a good choice of reasonably-priced light meals, and is extra pleasant if the weather permits dining in their attractive leafy outdoor area. **Zefferelli** ((02) 6262 5500, 5/55 Woolley Street, Dickson, not only has the cheapest pizza in town but they make one of the best as well. They also have a good selection of fresh seafood and an assortment of classic Italian dishes. **Beat Café** ((02) 6295 1949, 21 Kennedy Street, Kingston, has a mixed menu that includes pizzas, burgers, nachos and pasta. Their beer garden is casually comfortable, and on weekends free live entertainment gets the place buzzing.

Moderate

The **Antigo Café and Bar** ((02) 6249 8080, London Cirt, Civic Square, has a large outdoor terrace, a good selection of pasta and risotto, and well-prepared fresh seafood. Their dinner banquet menus are especially good value. In between perusing the Old Parliament House, on King George Terrace, Parkes, stop in at **Backbenches Café and Bar** ((02) 6270 8156, a friendly place for a light lunch. If you want to make a night of it more substantial meals are served at dinner. Joseph Cotter at **Geetanjali** ((02) 6285 2505, in Duff Place, Deakin, is a Canberra fixture, widely respected as one of the city's best Indian chefs. He specializes in dishes from northern India. **La Rustica** ((02) 6295 0152, 35 Kennedy Street, Kingston, has a good selection of Italian classics plus some great daily specials. Their antipasto is particularly good, as are their pizzas.

How to Get There

Canberra is 286 km (177 miles) from Sydney and 653 km (404 miles) from Melbourne. The fastest route between Sydney and Melbourne by road is the Hume Highway, which passes within 50 km (31 miles) of Canberra. From Melbourne, turn off the Hume Highway at Yass onto the Barton Highway. From Sydney, turn off the Hume just after Goulburn, onto the Federal Highway. Both routes are well marked. Canberra is also easily reached from New South Wales's south coast, and from Cann River in Victoria.

Both major domestic airlines run frequent **flights** into Canberra from both Melbourne and Sydney, with less-frequent flights from other Australian cities.

Australia's Old Parliament House, on the shores of Lake Burley Griffin in Canberra.

Greyhound Pioneer stops at Canberra on their Melbourne–Sydney route, and has connections to Adelaide. The trip takes three and a half hours from Sydney, eight hours from Melbourne, and 16 hours from Adelaide. **Murray Australia** (132 251 runs coach service into Canberra from the Snowy Mountains and from Sydney and the coast between Narooma and Nowra.

AROUND CANBERRA

Tidbinbilla Nature Reserve is part of a eucalyptus-forested mountain range 35 km (22 miles) southwest of Canberra. The reserve has large walk-through enclosures of Australian wildlife in a gentle mountain landscape. Residents include kangaroos, koalas, wombats, emus and water birds.

Near the reserve, the **Canberra Deep Space Communication Complex** ((02) 6201 7880 FAX (02) 6201 7975 E-MAIL cdscc-prc@anbe.cdscc.nasa.gov WEB SITE www.cdscc.nasa.gov, Discovery Drive (Tourist Drive 5), Tidbinbilla ACT, is one of just three tracking stations in the world linked to NASA's Deep Space control center — the others are in California and Spain. The station is run jointly by Australia and the United States. Its giant "antennae" — the largest is 70 m (230 ft) across and weighs more than 1.9 million kg (861,834 lbs) — monitor spacecraft such as Voyager and Galileo, and NASA's Pathfinder mission to Mars. The center's 26-m (85-ft) antenna was the first to pick up the pictures of Neil Armstrong's historic "giant step for mankind" on the moon. Appropriately enough, a sizeable piece of the moon is on display at the visitors' center. You can also see other space memorabilia, check out what the well-dressed astronaut wears on the moon, and get the latest space news on-line from NASA. Open daily 9 AM to 5 PM (8 PM during daylight saving).

Round About Tours ((02) 6259 5999 does day-trips from Canberra to Tidbinbilla Nature Reserve and the Space Center.

KIAMA TO NOWRA

Traveling south along the Princes Highway from Sydney, the first seaside town is tiny Kiama, 117 km (73 miles) south of Sydney. Small villages in the nearby southern highlands region retain their early nineteenth-century feel, nestled in subtropical rainforest.

GENERAL INFORMATION

Kiama Visitor Centre ((02) 4232 3322, at Blow-hole Point, Kiama, and the **Shoalhaven Tourist Centre** ((02) 4421 0778, 254 Princes Highway, Bomaderry, are both open daily 9 AM to 5 PM. **Terry's Cycling Adventures** at **Shoalhaven Bike Hire** ((0412) 603 831, PO Box 258, Nowra, rents bikes

and offers day, weekend and longer cycling and mountain bike tours throughout southern New South Wales.

WHAT TO SEE AND DO

Kiama is a good place to stop for lunch, where the **Terraces**, a row of verandahed timber cottages built in 1886, have been restored into a string of art galleries, craft shops and cafés. Behind the stores, a pretty wooden church with rolling lawns backs onto a tranquil harbor, at the end of which an impressive **blowhole** spurts ocean spray up to 60 m (197 ft) into the air when the sea is rough and the wind is blowing from the southeast. The blowhole is floodlit at night. There are two splendid walks along the cliffs to **Cathedral Rocks** and **Kaleula Head** from here — maps of the trails are available from the visitor center. Fifteen kilometers (nine miles) west of Kiama, a few kilometers past the sleepy village of Jamberoo, is **Minnamurra Rainforest**, within **Budderoo National Park**. **Minnamurra Falls** drop 50 m (164 ft) to a rocky gorge in the heart of this subtropical rainforest. The falls are only a short walk from the car park and visitor center, and an elevated boardwalk takes you up into the rainforest canopy among giant stinging trees and strangler figs. Don't worry, it's safe.

Inland from Kiama are the small towns of Berrima and Bowral. **Berrima** has changed very little since it was settled; in fact virtually no buildings have been erected here since 1890. There are numerous restaurants, tea rooms, antique stores and galleries in town. **Bowral** too has retained its buildings from the late nineteenth century, many on Winge-carribee and Bendooley streets. Bowral is frothing with tributes to its favorite son, Donald Bradman: the greatest batsman Australian cricket has ever produced, who died in February 2001. A **museum** in St. Jude Street dedicated to this cricketing immortal includes an oak bat from the mid-eighteenth century and mementos from the current test team. Open daily, 10 AM to 3 PM. In September and October, Bowral hosts a spectacular **Tulip Festival**, when a profusion of flowers daubs the town.

From Kiama, the Princes Highway swings inland to **Berry**, which also has some interesting small antique stores. Alternatively, seven kilometers (four miles) out of Kiama, take a left turn towards Gerringong. There is a lovely view of the length of **Seven Mile Beach National Park** from **Kingsford–Smith Lookout**, three kilometers (two miles) past Gerringong. From here a picturesque coastal road passes through **Gerroa** to **Shoalhaven Heads**, popular small resorts at either end of the national park. The beach's sandy dunes are backed by tea-trees, coast wattle and tall eucalyptus forest. It's seven kilometers (four miles) back to the Princes

New South Wales' eucalypt forests support almost half the country's koalas.

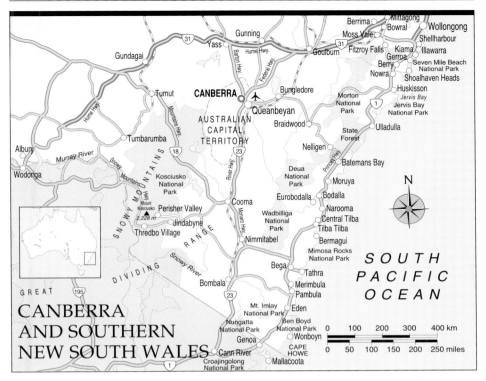

CANBERRA AND SOUTHERN NEW SOUTH WALES

Canberra and Southern New South Wales

Highway at Berry via Beach Road in the middle of the park, or 22 km (14 miles) from Shoalhaven Heads along Shoalhaven River to Nowra.

Nowra is the administrative center of the area, but there's not a lot here for visitors. The Fleet Air Arm of the Royal Australian Navy is based at nearby HMAS *Albatross*, and aviation enthusiasts might want to drop in on the **Naval Aviation Museum** ((02) 4421 1920, Albatross Road, Nowra Hill, which showcases military models and memorabilia along with one of the finest collections of military aircraft in Australia. The **Nowra Animal Park** ((02) 4421 3949, Rockhill Road, on the banks of the Shoalhaven River, set in lush rainforest, is home to friendly wallabies and curious emus. Visitors can feed them, as well as wombats and kangaroos. **Morton National Park**, high on the tableland 28 km (17 miles) from Nowra, features the spectacular **Fitzroy Falls** and is a haven for a large number of indigenous animals and wild birds.

WHERE TO STAY

In Kiama, the **Grand Hotel** ((02) 4232 1037, in Bong Bong Street, and the **Kiama Inn Hotel** ((02) 4232 1166 FAX (02) 4232 3401, 50 Terralong Street, are moderately priced and comfortable. **Berrima Bakehouse Motel** ((02) 4877 1381 FAX (02) 4877 1047, Wingecarribee Street, Berrima, is another good option in the moderate range. At the south end of Seven Mile Beach, **Coolangatta Estate** ((02) 4448 7131 FAX (02) 4448 7997, 1335 Bolong Road, Shoalhaven Heads, is on the site of the first settlement on the South Coast in 1822. The property includes its own winery, with cellar-door tastings and sales. There is also a golf course, tennis courts, croquet, a solar-heated pool, two restaurants and a pleasant outdoor café. Rates include dinner and breakfast, at $180 to $220 for a double during the week, $240 to $260 on weekends and Christmas/New Year; children up to 13 are only $30 extra per day. The knowledgeable staff is a big plus.

Staying in Bowral can be expensive, but the accommodation available is special. **Milton Park** ((02) 4861 1522 FAX (02) 4861 4716, Hordern's Road, has beautifully fitted rooms and serves good meals, with an outstanding wine selection. Just out of town, **Craigburn Resort** ((02) 4861 1277 FAX (02) 4862 1690 has been providing accommodation since 1910 and has its own nine-hole golf course. Both are expensive. **Bunyip Inn Guest House** ((02) 4464 2064, 122 Queen Street, Berry, a converted turn-of-the-twentieth-century bank, is classified by the National Trust. It tends to be booked out on weekends and holiday periods (moderate). If you're curious, a bunyip is a mythical bush spirit, mainly associated with rivers. The **Riverhaven Motel** ((02) 4421 2044 FAX (02) 4421 2121, 1 Scenic Drive, Nowra, on the banks of the Shoalhaven River, has good-value weekend packages.

WHERE TO EAT

Like most of southern New South Wales' small coastal towns, Kiama's restaurants are friendly, filling and generally inexpensive. A favorite with the locals, **Chachis** ((02) 4233 1144 makes good pastas and seafood combo dishes. Chachis is essentially Italian, but a few select tropical ingredients thrown in give it a touch of originality. The sandstone **Surveyor General Inn** in the main street of Berrima has been pulling pints since 1834. It also serves good-value pub meals, and has Guinness on tap. The tiny **Marmalade Café** ((02) 4861 3553, 362 Bing Bong Street, Bowral, serves delicious homemade food, including the tastiest hot scones in the district. The moderately priced **Baker and Bunyip Restaurant** ((02) 4464 1454, 23 Prince Alfred Street, Berry, serves freshly caught fish, hearty vegetarian meals, and prime local beef.

JERVIS BAY

Strangely enough, and unknown to most Australians, Jervis Bay is officially part of the Australian Capital Territory — it was for some time considered a potential site for the capital, and evidently the federal government felt they had the right to claim at least one port. Since 1915, the Royal Australian HMAS Cresswell Naval College has shared the south end of the bay with the many playful dolphins that frequent the area. Jervis Bay's 56 km (35 miles) of shoreline forms one of the most beautiful and undisturbed coastal areas in Australia, and the sand on Hyams Beach is regularly touted as the brightest and whitest in the world.

The **Jervis Bay Visitors Centre (** (02) 4443 0977 on Village Road, Jervis Bay, can direct you to the best spots, whether it be fishing, surfing, sailboarding, snorkeling or scuba you desire.

WHAT TO SEE AND DO

Fabulously clear waters make Jervis Bay a wonderful snorkeling and scuba location, and Australian film and television makers' preferred place for underwater shoots. Six villages line the shores of the bay. **Huskisson**, the main village, has a strip of stores selling souvenirs, beachwear and sun hats. There are also some cool surf-style cafés at the beach end. **Jervis Bay Seasports (** (07) 3844 7429 FAX (07) 3844 1669, 47 Owen Street, rents and sells diving equipment, and organizes classes or private lessons. Dive charters start from $57 and fishing charters from $60.

The waters of Jervis Bay are home to several pods of dolphins, and whales migrate through from late September to November. Fur seals and

The sweeping curve of the breakwater in Kiama Harbour reflects the tranquility of this small township.

penguins are also regular visitors. **Dolphin Watch Cruises** ((02) 4441 6311, 50 Owen Street, Huskisson, takes guests out on a sleek 17-m (55-ft) catamaran to spot dolphins and whales. Cruises operate year-round, subject to weather conditions. Fishing is very popular here too — the tourist information center has good maps and a guide to what's biting where. Only three kilometers (two miles) south, **St. Georges Basin**, connected to the sea by narrow Sussex Inlet, also has excellent fishing. Boats can be rented from the many jetties. The Basin is also popular with windsurfers. There's an 18-hole **golf** course six kilometers (nearly four miles) south of Huskisson, above Plantation Point, and another at St. Georges Basin East.

4441 5781, Owen Street, has moderate rates and large, somewhat stark rooms. **Huskisson Beach Motel** ((02) 4441 6387, 9 Hawke Street, also moderately priced, is friendly but can be noisy on Friday and Saturday nights. **Paperbark Lodge and Camp** ((02) 4441 6066, on Wollamia Road, offers inexpensive accommodation in a natural environment.

FAR SOUTH COAST

The lovely coastal strip from Ulladulla (a corruption of the Aboriginal *Ullatha Ullatha* or *Ullada Ullada*, meaning "safe harbor") to Cape Howe and the Victorian border was among the earliest settled by Europeans, with the arrival of whalers

On the south headland of Jervis Bay, **Booderee National Park** — jointly managed by the Wreck Bay Aboriginal Community Council and the Commonwealth Government — provides a sanctuary for wombats, wattlebirds, honeyeaters and large flocks of crimson rosellas and sulphur-crested cockatoos. The park extends to Wreck Bay, where perpendicular cliffs plunge sheer for 90 m (296 ft) and continue for another 60 m (197 ft) underwater. Camping is permitted in the park, but you should book a site ahead through the park's **visitor center** ((02) 4443 0977, who also organize guided nature walks in the summer and Easter vacations.

WHERE TO STAY

Local resistance has thankfully kept development around the bay to a minimum. Most of the accommodation is in Huskisson. The **Jervis Bay Motel** ((02)

and sealers early in the nineteenth century. Visitors today can go on whale-spotting sorties during the annual migration of southern right, humpback, blue, pilot and killer whales from September to November. The many white-sand beaches and deep bays and inlets waiting for surfers, swimmers, windsurfers and keen anglers attracts quite a few tourists in summer and at Easter, but for the rest of the year the pace slows down a few notches.

Logging took off quickly here, where the cooler climate supported spotted gum, blackbutt and many other hardwoods. The coast's deep harbors proved invaluable to early loggers, and the cleared soil formed some of the richest dairy land in the country (Central Tilba, Bodalla and Bega still produce much of Australia's cheese). Fishing was, and still is, another important industry. Author and fishing enthusiast Zane Grey put

Bermagui on the world game-fishing map when he visited in the 1930s to tackle the formidable black marlin. Oyster and mussel farms are plentiful too, with Moruya, Pambula and Eden all famous for their oysters. Unopened dozens sell for under $10.

Over the last 15 years, environmental activists and increased local appreciation of bushland and indigenous wildlife have managed to restrict logging activities. Faced with the resulting increased unemployment and regular population drain to Melbourne and Sydney, many see tourism as the answer to the area's future. The result so far is an endless logging–unemployment–tourism debate, as locals struggle to retain their piece of paradise.

ULLADULLA

The small township of Ulladulla, 70 km (44 miles) south of Jervis Bay, offers beautiful beaches and some lovely walks around **South Pacific Headland Reserve** and **Ulladulla Wildflower Reserve**, but is mostly known for its incomparable fishing opportunities and a string of close-to-perfect surf breaks. Fishing has attracted a sizeable Italian community to the town, with the result that Ulladulla's restaurants are the best on the south coast. On Easter Sunday, the **Blessing of the Fleet Ceremony** is held to pray for the safety of the fishermen over the coming year, with music, entertainment and beach parties well into the night.

Twenty kilometers (12 miles) south of Ulladulla is the turn-off to **Bawley Point, Kioloa,** and **Merry Beach.** There is a string of superb beaches here, and a meandering path between Kioloa Beach and

Bawley Point through the **Murramarang Aboriginal Area,** a rocky headland with a midden and other archeological evidence of Aboriginal occupation dating back 12,000 years. Merry, Pretty, Pebbly and Depot beaches back onto **Murramarang National Park.** Pebbly Beach is renowned for the kangaroos who bound along the edge of the surf to cool down on hot days. There are generally a few friendly roos around the picnic area here — but please don't feed them.

The **Ulladulla Visitors Centre (** (02) 4455 1269 TOLL-FREE (1800) 024 261 is in the Civic Centre on the Princes Highway.

Where to Stay and Eat

One of Ulladulla's restaurants I always like returning to is **Tony's Seafood Restaurant (** (02) 4454 0888, on the harbor at 30 Wason Street, which serves the best of the fish caught daily on the family's trawler. Another favorite with locals, also on the waterfront, is the **Harbourside Restaurant (** (02) 4455 3377. Both are moderately priced. Although **Supreeya's Thai Restaurant (** (02) 4455 4579, upstairs at the corner of Deering and St Vincent streets, is back from the harbor, its hilltop location affords magnificent views across to the Pacific Ocean. The inexpensive red chicken or fish curries are superb, with a good choice of vegetarian dishes too. The **Fisherman's Co-op,** next to the jetty, sells freshly caught fish, raw or cooked.

Albacore Motel ((02) 4455 1322, on Boree Street, just back from the jetty, has airy rooms at inexpensive to moderate prices. **Beach Haven Holiday Resort (** (02) 4455 2110 WEB SITE www.beachhaven.com.au offers inexpensive cabins and vans with facilities including two swimming pools (one with a water-slide), a spa, sauna, volleyball and games room. It's an especially good choice for those travelling with children.

BATEMANS BAY

Flanking the Clyde River estuary, Batemans Bay is a popular seaside resort where rumor has it you can simply pick up oysters on the shore. It's probably easier to buy a couple of dozen famous Clyde River oysters — or a crayfish — and picnic with a bottle of Chablis on the foreshore. On the coast north of Batemans Bay is **Murramarang National Park,** with broad beaches and towering headlands.

The **Batemans Bay Visitor Centre (** (02) 4472 6900 is at the corner of the Princes Highway and Beach Road.

Murramarang Caravan and Camping Resort ((02) 4478 6355 FAX (02) 4478 6230 has inexpensive self-contained bungalows on the beach in Murramarang National Park, 10 km (six miles) from Batemans Bay. In Batemans Bay itself, the

Ulladulla's white-sand beaches invite sporting activities on and off the water.

Coachhouse Marina Resort ((02) 4472 4392 FAX (02) 4472 4852 offers accommodation from inexpensive cabins to moderately priced villas. For a little luxury try the **Old Nelligen Post Office Guest House** ((02) 4478 1179, 7 Braidwood Street, Nelligen, inland from Batemans Bay, which has attractive weekend "getaway" deals. There's also a **YHA hostel and caravan park** ((02) 4472 4972 on the Old Princes Highway at Batemans Bay.

CENTRAL TILBA AND TILBA TILBA

Central Tilba, 79 km (50 miles) south of Batemans Bay, is surrounded by rugged coastal mountains. Frozen in time, this village of 25 wooden buildings was built between 1889 and 1906 during a short-lived gold rush and has remained unaltered to this day. Its tiny wooden stores sell local cheese, alpaca wool knits, and calorie-laden homemade fudge. **Tilba Woodturning Gallery** showcases the work of local artisans using the area's beautiful hardwoods. Stop for a light lunch at the pretty wooden **Tilba Bakery**, which serves pies and other pastries, sandwiches and rolls and city-style expresso coffee.

Tilba Tilba has some attractive B&Bs, and lovely flower gardens at **Foxglove Spire Cottage** ((02) 4473 7375, on Corkhill Drive. The town is at the base of **Mount Dromedary**; sacred to the Yuin people, who call it Gulaga and still perform ceremonies on its slopes. The entire mountain is a flora reserve, with lush ferns and subtropical vegetation and large numbers of wallabies and foxes (introduced by British hunting fans, foxes thrive in the cooler forests of Southern New South Wales and Victoria). The climb to the top (two hours) is rewarded with 360° views. **Mount Dromedary Trail Rides** ((02) 4476 3376 takes small groups up on horseback from Tilba Tilba.

Off the coast near Narooma, 14 km (nine miles) from Central Tilba, **Montague Island Nature Reserve** harbors large populations of Australian fur seals and little penguins. The clear waters here are popular with divers. Narooma Charters and **New South Wales Parks and Wildlife Services Narooma** ((02) 4476 2888 runs regular tours to the island and its century-old lighthouse.

MERIMBULA AND EDEN

Merimbula is one of the most popular resort areas on New South Wales' south coast, with excellent surf, safe beaches, and good fishing and shrimping in its relatively shallow saltwater lake. This small town has embraced tourism more wholeheartedly than its neighbors, and in season has a lively nightlife and a multitude of generally family-orientated activites. **True Blue Cruises** ((02) 6495 1686 E-MAIL starfish@acr.net.au take two-hour dolphin watching cruises year-round, and four-hour whale-watching cruises from September to November, departing from Merimbula jetty. They also offer half- and full-day reef and game-fishing trips.

A small township with a long stretch of safe swimming beach, Eden is a few kilometers around deep Twofold Bay from the site of Ben Boyd's 1840s whaling town: Boydtown. Eden, too, was established on the strength of its whale population, and during their migrations (September to November), humpbacks, blue whales, southern right whales and minke's pass close by the heads of Twofold Bay, some entering the harbor. Whale-watching cruises operate during this period — ask at the tourist information center. Eden's carefully-tended **Killer Whale Museum** ((02) 6496 2094, in Imlay Street, includes the skeleton of "Old Tom," a killer whale that reputedly guided whalers to their prey. It also recounts the tale of a local Jonah, swallowed alive in 1891. He survived 15 hours in the belly of the beast, the stomach acids bleaching his hair and skin to a snowy white.

Ben Boyd National Park lies along the coast both to the north and south of Eden. There are some isolated coves and beaches in both sections. **The Pinnacles** and **Haycock Point** in the north and **Green Cape Lighthouse** in the south are good places to watch migratory whales. **Saltwater Creek** and **Brittangabee Bay** in south Ben Boyd National Park have bush camping areas and networks of walking tracks.

The **Merimbula Tourist Information Centre** ((02) 6495 1129 TOLL-FREE (1800) 633 012 is on Beach Street, Merimbula, and the **Eden Tourist Information Centre** ((02) 6496 1953 TOLL-FREE (1800) 633 012 is on the Princes Highway, Eden.

Where to Stay and Eat

Most of Merimbula's accommodation is in the form of holiday apartments, which can be booked through **Sapphire Coast Accommodation Centre** TOLL-FREE (1800) 246 778 WEB SITE www.acr.net.au/~starfish, a free service for accommodation and tours in the Merimbula and Eden area. **Merimbula Beach Cabins** ((02) 6495 1216 E-MAIL jaybee@acr.net.au, back onto bushland right on Short Beach, a pleasant stretch of beach a little away from central Merimbula, and far quieter than the main Merimbula Beach.

There's not a great deal of accommodation available in Eden, as Merimbula is more set up to attract tourists. One friendly option is **Bellevue Lodge B&B** ((02) 6496 1575 MOBILE (018) 489 575 E-MAIL bellevuelodge@highwayone.com.au, 13 Bellevue Place, which offers moderately-priced B&B in a quiet location with sea views. They also organize whale-watching cruises. Another good B&B is the **Crown and Anchor** ((02) 6496 1017, 239 Imlay Street, which serves a cooked breakfast on their sunny veranda overlooking the sea.

There is a string of reliable restaurants along Merimbula's main street, and a couple of excellent fish-and-chip outlets right on the wharf in Eden. Eden's **Wheelhouse Restaurant** ((02) 6496 3392, Main Wharf, has views across Snug Cove and Twofold Bay. The menu is, as you'd expect, predominately seafood, but meat courses are hearty and well-prepared.

How to Get There

Most of the sights on the south coast are on or near the Princes Highway (Highway 1), which begins 82 km (51 miles) south of Sydney at Shellharbour and follows the New South Wales coast south until it crosses the Victorian border near Genoa, following Victoria's east coast to Melbourne.

Regular **trains** run from Sydney's Central Station to Kiama and Bomaderry, just north of Nowra. Motor Services of Nowra operates a **bus** service

connecting with trains from Sydney and following the route along the 325-km (200-mile) coastline to the Victorian border. For details contact **Countrylink** ((02) 9224 4744 TOLL-FREE 132 077 WEB SITE www.tourism.nsw.gov.au. Greyhound Pioneer have services from Sydney to Melbourne along the Princes Highway.

THE SNOWY MOUNTAINS

While most parts of Australia are hot and dry, the alpine regions — the higher peaks along the Great Dividing Range — are much visited by skiers and other winter sports enthusiasts. The best skiing areas are the Snowy Mountains, 200 km (124 miles) south of Canberra along the Monaro Highway.

Snow gums bent by the strong alpine winds at Mount Kosciusko National Park. Some of Australia's major ski resorts are located within this region of the Snowy Mountains.

In winter, the high peak of Mount Kosciusko glitters with snow or disappears in a shroud of mist. There are beautiful passes through the mountains and some good ski resorts in the area. In summer the high country is a favorite haunt for trout fishing. Spring is flower-hunting time.

GENERAL INFORMATION

The **Tourist Information Centre** ((02) 6947 1849, on the Snowy Mountains Highway at Tumut, provides useful advice on current road and skiing conditions. Other useful centers are the **Snowy Region Visitor Centre** ((02) 6450 5600, on the Kosciusko Road at Jindabyne, and **Cooma Visitor Centre** ((02) 6450 1740, at 119 Sharp Street, Cooma.

WHAT TO SEE AND DO

Skiers pack the slopes of **Thredbo**, **Perisher**, **Blue Valley**, **Selwyn**, **Smiggins Holes**, **Charlotte Pass** and a few other resorts on the mountains from June to September. There is also cross-country skiing throughout the whole area, and the major ski fields are in the **Kosciusko National Park**. The park covers 690,000 ha (1,700,000 acres), making it the largest national park in New South Wales.

In summer the mountains' slopes are a tapestry of yellow, white and purple wildflowers, making this alpine region almost as popular as it is in winter. The moment the snow recedes hikers take to the tracks, climbers head for sheer rock walls, and anglers cast lines for trout in clear alpine streams and lakes.

Mount Kosciusko, dominates the Snowy Mountains at 2,228 m (7,307 ft) above sea level. Although modest by world standards, this is Australia's highest peak. Take a chairlift (which operates year-round) from Thredbo or hike up a leisurely eight-kilometer (five-mile) track through alpine meadows. A more challenging 20-km (12-mile) walk begins at the information office at Sawpit Creek, making its way up Perisher Valley.

It's great fun to explore the mountains on horseback. **Reynella Kosciusko Rides** TOLL-FREE (1800) 029 909 FAX (02) 6454 2530 offers three- to five-day rides from November to May into the high country where wild horses roam the meadows.

WHERE TO STAY

In winter it is essential to book well ahead. Rooms above the snowline can be expensive and some places will only accept reservations in blocks of a week or more. Summer tariffs can drop to half price.

There are several reservation services both on and off the mountains which can save you the bother of hunting around for lodging. Contact the **Snowy Mountains Reservation Centre** ((02) 6456 2633 TOLL-FREE (1800) 020 622 FAX (064) 561 207,

Shop 16, Town Centre, Jindabyne; **Kosciusko Accommodation Centre** ((02) 6456 2022 TOLL-FREE (1800) 026 354 FAX (02) 6456 3945, at Shop 2, Nugget's Crossing, Jindabyne; or the **Thredbo Accommodation Services** ((02) 6457 6387 TOLL-FREE (1800) 801 982 FAX (02) 6457 6057, at Shop 9 Mowamba Place, Thredbo Village.

In the center of Thredbo Village, **Thredbo Alpine** ((02) 6459 4200 TOLL-FREE (1800) 026 333 FAX (02) 6459 4201 has expensive but welcoming accommodation; some rooms with spas. **Bernti's Mountain Inn** TOLL-FREE (1800) 500 105 FAX (02) 6456 1669, 4 Mowamba Place, is moderately priced and comfortable.

Alpine Resort ((02) 6456 2522 FAX (02) 6456 2854, 22 Nettin Circuit, Jindabyne, has moderate rooms **Lakeview Plaza Motel** ((02) 6456 2134 FAX (02) 6456 1372, 2 Snowy River Avenue, is a little cheaper. **Kosciusko Chalet** TOLL-FREE (1800) 026 369 FAX (1800) 802 687 is a rambling luxury guesthouse in Charlotte Pass, above the snowline in winter, and expensive.

If you have a car, save on accommodation by staying in one of the lowland towns. In Cooma, the **Bunkhouse** ((02) 6452 2983, 28 Soho Street; the **Hawaii** ((02) 6452 1211, 192 Sharp Street; and the old-style **Cooma Hotel** ((02) 6947 1040 all offer inexpensive accommodation.

HOW TO GET THERE

Car access is by way of the Snowy Mountains Highway, the Alpine Way and Kosciusko Road. During winter, carry tire chains. Greyhound Pioneer have regular services from Melbourne and Sydney.

Skitube trains to Perisher, Smiggins Holes and Blue Cow Mountain leave Bullock's Flat in Jindabyne every twenty minutes in winter and on the hour in summer. Savings can be made by purchasing a return Skitube pass and chair-lift ticket package. For details contact **Countrylink** ((02) 9224 4744 TOLL-FREE 132 077 WEB SITE www.tourism .nsw.gov.au.

Qantas has daily flights to Cooma from both Sydney and Melbourne; Kendell Airlines flies from Melbourne daily.

BROKEN HILL

Western New South Wales is flat, arid and sparsely populated, a land of endless red plains, dotted with clumps of mulga bushes and rocky outcrops. For those who really want get off the beaten track, New South Wales' vast outback can be rewarding, but like all of Australia's arid inland areas, visiting it takes preparation, an appropriate vehicle and good detailed maps.

The journals of explorers Leichhardt and Eyre inspired Patrick White's epic 1957 novel *Voss*, which describes an ill-fated voyage into just such an interior. Prussian-born naturalist and explorer Ludwig Leichhardt was awarded medals by the Geographical Societies of Paris and London following long explorations in Australia's north. He disappeared in 1848 while attempting a transcontinental journey from Sydney. Despite extensive searches as recently as 1953, no further trace of him was ever found.

Broken Hill is the most user-friendly town in New South Wales' west, and the easiest place to base your visit. In 1883, Charles Rasp discovered rich lead, silver and zinc deposits here, and the town almost immediately became a mining center. Broken Hill Proprietary formed to exploit the mine, and then used their wealth to invest in steel manufacture and petroleum exploration. Today BHP is Australia's largest multinational company.

The **Broken Hill Visitor Information Centre** ((08) 8087 6077 is at the corner of Bromide and Blende streets.

WHAT TO SEE AND DO

Broken Hill could justifiably be known as "Silver City" — its mines once produced a third of the world's silver. At **Delprats Underground Tourist Mine** ((08) 8088 1604, in Crystal Road, a 120-m (400-ft) drop in a cage takes visitors into the heart of the mine. Tours are taken at 10:30 AM weekdays and 2 PM on Saturday, and meander though the labyrinth of tunnels.

The arid, otherworldly landscape around Broken Hill has inspired a generation of bush painters, some among Australia's most successful. The most famous, Pro Hart, has a gallery at 108 Wymam Street; Jack Absalom at 638 Chapple Street is also highly regarded. Works by other painters calling themselves "brushmen from the bush" can be seen at the **Ant Hill Gallery**, 24 Bromide Street.

To gain some understanding of the wealth generated in the area visit the **Broken Hill City Art Gallery** ((08) 8088 9252, at the Entertainment Centre in Chloride Street. The pride of the Silverwork collection is *The Silver Tree*, commissioned by Charles Rasp. An admission fee is charged, and the gallery is open Monday to Saturday.

If you really want to get off the beaten track, book a seat on the **Bush Mail Run**, a light aircraft that delivers post and supplies to 25 remote sheep stations in outback New South Wales. It leaves Broken Hill Airport Tuesday and Saturday mornings on a round-trip of approximately 1,100 km (680 miles), taking about 10 and half hours. Morning tea and lunch at a homestead are included. Traveling only a few thousand meters above the endless plain you begin to truly appreciate the forbidding hinterland — harsh and desolate. The airplane can hold up to five passengers. Reserve through **Crittenden Airlines** ((08) 8088 5702.

Broken Hill's Outback Tours ((08) 8087 7800, in Crystal Street, takes small groups on four-wheel-drive tours to explore the surroundings areas, including **Mootwingee** and **Kinchega national parks**, along with White Cliffs and its opal fields. Alternatively, rent a four-wheel-drive vehicle from **Silver City Vehicle Hire** ((08) 8087 3266 FAX (08) 8088 5775, 320 Beryl Street, and explore the outback at your own pace.

About 25 km (16 miles) from Broken Hill is the "ghost town" of **Silverton,** which was deserted when the silver mines in the area were exhausted. The population now stands at around 100 and it is not unusual to see a camel walking down the main street.

A three-hour drive from Broken Hills is **White Cliffs**, a town built underground to avoid the searing heat of the outback. This area is Australia's oldest opal field, and visitors have been known to pick up valuable opals by fossicking around the old diggings. Local guide **Ross Jones** ((08) 8091 6607 will show you the best places to fossick for blue-green opals, tell tall tales and truths about local history, and arrange a visit to an underground home. While in White Cliffs you could always improve your golf game on the local course, which has no green fees because it has no greens. The sand-traps, however, are something else! Indeed, the whole place is… something else.

WHERE TO STAY

There is a good choice of moderately priced motels in Broken Hill. The **Charles Rasp** ((08) 8088 1988, 158 Oxide Street, and the **Old Willyama Motor Inn** ((08) 8088 3355 FAX (08) 8088 3856, 30 Iodide Street, are near the center of town. The **Tourist Lodge** ((08) 8088 2086, 100 Argent Street, and the **West Darling Hotel** ((08) 8087 2691, 400 Argent Street, both offer inexpensive accommodation.

In White Cliffs, the **Underground Motel** ((08) 8091 6647 TOLL-FREE (1800) 021 154 FAX (08) 8091 6654, may not have any views but will nevertheless, provide a memorable stay. The enterprising proprietor, Leon Hornby, excavated all the 32 rooms himself. Vertical shafts provide natural light.

HOW TO GET THERE

A number of airlines fly into Broken Hill. Ansett flies from Sydney and Melbourne via Mildura; Kendell flies in daily from Adelaide. There is direct train service between Broken Hill and both Sydney and Adelaide.

Victoria

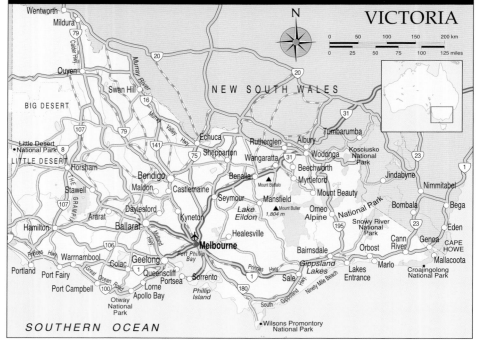

VICTORIA, AUSTRALIA'S MOST DENSELY POPULATED STATE and, per capita, its wealthiest, is blessed with a breathtaking western coastline, historic gold towns and spa towns, excellent vineyards and outstanding national parks with an abundance of indigenous fauna — all within a few hours drive of Melbourne. Settled in 1834–1835 by private enterprise, Victoria challenged the Sydney-based government's perception of Australia's evolving role and identity, and Victoria hasn't looked back since. Rivalry between Melbournians and Sydneysiders is as strong as ever: the difference in character between Australia's two major cities is tangible.

Victoria was one of the last Australian states to be colonized, which is surprising given its hospitable climate and proximity to Sydney. Although the New South Wales government twice attempted to establish settlements on the south coast, they failed to find an adequate source of fresh water. When entrepreneurial John Batman applied in 1827 for permission to start a new colony on Port Phillip Bay (having been unsuccessful in obtaining a land grant in Tasmania), the New South Wales governor ruled that the lands were not to be settled. His reasons were political: Sydney was demoralized and discontent. Convicts and naval officers comprised most of her population and the nearby Hobart Town was experiencing astounding growth. The New South Wales government feared a new colony based on free settlers would incite a repeat of the rebellion that had deposed Governor Bligh in 1808.

In November 1834, Edward Henty ignored the governor's mandate and settled at Portland Bay. Batman almost immediately sailed across Bass Strait himself, and in June 1835 "purchased" the land on the western shore of Port Phillip Bay from the local Aborigines. This made Victoria the only state whose settlers acknowledged the Aboriginal inhabitants' ownership of the lands.

This isn't to suggest that Batman's 1835 treaty with eight clan chiefs from the Boonwurrung and Woiworung peoples was in any way equitable. To the Aboriginal people, the *tanderrum* ritual gave the whites only the rite of passage through their lands. In the short term, though, the misunderstanding satisfied both parties immensely. Batman believed he was purchasing 243,000 ha (600,000 acres) of arable land, including a 70-km (43.5-mile) stretch of the broad Yarra River and a deep sea-port, for the price of 20 blankets, 30 knifes, 12 red shirts, four flannel jackets, 50 handkerchiefs and a medley of tools and household items. He boasted "I am the greatest landowner in the world." The clan chiefs thought they had negotiated a high price to welcome their white guests.

At first the New South Wales government refused to recognize Batman's purchase, but settlers streamed in anyway. Robert Hoddle devised the outline of Melbourne in 1836, his vision for what was then only a village of a few makeshift houses and muddy streets was of a city with wide avenues laid out in a neat grid. In 1837 Batman named his city Melbourne, after Britain's prime minister, and explorers rapidly settled the lands from the Murray River south to the Pacific Ocean and Bass Strait, and west to Portland. The New South Wales administration was forced to accept Victoria as a successful, semi-autonomous, colony with its own customs office, police force and lands office, officially proclaiming the colony of Victoria on July 1, 1851. It was already home to more than 80,000 settlers.

MELBOURNE

Writing about the Melbourne of 1856, a contemporary admired "its wide and spacious thoroughfares, fringed with edifices worthy of the wealth of its citizens, and corresponding in architectural pretensions to their occupants." Fortunately much of Melbourne's architectural heritage remains intact in its dozens of lavishly embellished buildings from the mid-1850s, a taste that became more outrageous during the boom years of the 1880s and 1890s. Melbourne's economic growth over the last decade has similarly left its mark on the face of the city, with towering high-rises and ambitious architectural projects.

Today the city of 3.2 million is the youngest of its size in the world. Melbournians comprise over 110 ethnic groups, an exceptional diversity of traditions and culture that is felt throughout the city, by far the most multicultural in Australia. It has the largest Italian community of any city outside Italy, the largest Greek community outside Greece (it is the third largest Greek city in the world). And nowhere is Melbourne's diversity more apparent than in the overwhelming variety of authentic cuisines found in even the most suburban parts of town.

Melbournians' enthusiasm for spectator sports is unmatched. This is the birthplace of Australian Rules football — the season runs from March, fans' ardor reaching fever pitch by the Grand Final in September. It is home to Grand Slam tennis at the Australian Open in January, the Australian Grand Prix Formula One Championship in March, and cricket over summer. Horse-racing is another passion: the first Tuesday in November is a state-wide holiday in honor of the Melbourne Cup, a 3.2-km (two-mile) race that has been held at the inner-city Flemington Racecourse since 1874. Fashion-watching, celebrity-spotting and champagne-sipping often take attention away from the horses.

BACKGROUND

Melbourne's entrepreneurial spirit shaped the nascent colony and continues to do so today. When E. H. Hargraves discovered gold near Bathurst in New South Wales in 1851, Melbourne's founders responded by offering a reward to anyone who could find gold within 300 km (186 miles) of Melbourne. They had to pay up only five days later. Victoria's gold-rush was on, its mines the most

productive ever found, and for almost a decade close to 1,800 people a week sailed into Melbourne's port. Overnight Victoria became Australia's wealthiest state, Melbourne the financial and administrative capital of Australia. In 1853 alone 1,000 buildings were erected in the city center — this only 18 years after John Batman stood in the forest alongside the Yarra river and famously declared "This is the site for a village."

Wealth and confidence led to encouragement of the arts. At a Melbourne theater in 1856, actors "were obliged to appear before the footlights to bear a pelting shower of nuggets — a substitute for bouquets — many over half an ounce, and several of which fell short of the mark into the orchestra." Opera singer Nellie Mitchell, born in Melbourne in 1861, became the world's leading prima donna in 1888 and took the name Melba in honor of her home town (hence Peach Melba and Melba Toast).

The city's cultural diversity began early, with a rough start. An estimated 12,000 Aboriginal people, in 38 tribal groups, populated Victoria when Batman negotiated his "treaty" in 1835. By 1856 disease and clashes with land-hungry settlers had reduced the state's indigenous population to around 2,000.

The gold-rush brought with it a melting-pot of treasure-seekers. The Polish and Irish suffered racial slurs, but it was the state's almost 20,000 Chinese who bore the brunt of the fear and bigotry that grew as the gold fields dried up, culminating in the establishment of racist immigration and property laws. Inevitably though, this heterogeneous citizenry was to become more tolerant. Industrial and manufacturing growth after World War II attracted large numbers of southern and eastern European settlers, refugees from the wars in Vietnam and Cambodia altered the face of the city yet again. As the children and grandchildren of these immigrants percolate through Melbourne's business, political, and cultural communities, Melbourne's multiculturalism is becoming ever more indelible.

GENERAL INFORMATION

The **Victoria Visitor Information Center** ((03) 9658 9972 or (132 842 FAX (03) 9654 1054 WEB SITE www .visitvictoria.com, in the Melbourne Town Hall on the corner of Swanston and Collins streets, can book tours and accommodation and has extensive information on Melbourne and Victoria and current attractions. Open 9 AM to 6 PM weekdays, and 9 AM to 5 PM weekends and public holidays. Ask for a copy of their useful *Melbourne Visitors Map*, also available at the three central Melbourne Visitor Information booths located in the Bourke Street Mall, Swanston Street's City Square and in the Rialto complex at 525 Collins Street.

The City of Melbourne publishes the monthly *Melbourne Events*, free from information centers and most hotels.

The **General Post Office (GPO)** and **Poste Restante** on the corner of the Bourke Street Mall and Elizabeth Street, City, is open from 9 AM to 5 PM. New Internet cafés are continually popping up all over town. Even the corner store is likely to have a terminal, but may not be too reliable at times. Open 24 hours, 7 days a week, **Kinko's** ((03) 9650 3255, 136 Exhibition Street, City, handles e-mails and all office needs. Also in the City is **Global Gossip** ((03) 9663 0511, 440 Elizabeth Street. **Cyber Chat** ((03) 9534 0859, first floor Acland Court, Acland Street, St. Kilda, has great rates, reliable terminals and offers services including faxing, cheap long distance calls and most business services. Staff are friendly and helpful.

For medical assistance during normal working hours, the **Traveler's Medical and Vaccination Center** ((03) 9602 5788, Level 2, 393 Little Bourke Street, can answer queries and help find a doctor. For emergencies call the **Royal Melbourne Hospital** ((03) 9342 7000, Royal Parade, Parkville.

Affiliated with AAA, the **Royal Automobile Club of Victoria (RACV)** ((03) 9642 5566, 360 Bourke Street, can also help with information and reservations and is the place to go for road maps and driving information. **Victorian National Parks Association** ((03) 9650 8296 FAX (03) 9654 6843 organizes walks every weekend around Victoria's parks. Non-members pay $5 and transportation to the park can usually be arranged. Reservations, however, need to made two to four weeks ahead.

GETTING AROUND

Melbourne's city center (inevitably referred to as the City) is not enormous, and most sites of interest to visitors are easily accessible by foot. The **subway** consists of one loop around this center, with only five stops. Melbourne's public transportation system — a combination of trains, buses, and of course trams (streetcars) — essentially radiates out from the grand, domed Flinders Street Station.

One of the few cities in the world to have retained **trams** as an intrinsic part of the transport network, a trip to Melbourne would not be complete without a ride on one — it's also a relaxing and fun way to tour the city and inner neighborhoods. A good way to get your bearings is to hop aboard the maroon-colored **City Circle Tram**, a free circuit of the city center that runs continually from 10 AM to 6 PM daily, traveling in both directions along Spencer, Latrobe, Spring and Flinders streets every 10 minutes. If you're intending to drive in Melbourne, remember that you can never pass a tram on the right, nor pass a stationary tram if its doors are open. When passing a stationary tram with its doors closed, the speed limit is five kilometers per hour (three miles per hour).

Melbourne's public transportation system, the **Met**, operates between 5 AM and midnight Monday to Saturday and 8 AM to 11 PM Sundays (on weekends the **Nightrider Bus** departs hourly from the City Square between 12:30 AM and 4:30 AM to most suburbs). Two-hour tickets, 60 Plus tickets (for seniors) and Short Trip tickets can be purchased on trams and buses. Daily or weekly tickets, valid for travel on all trains, trams, and buses within the zones and time-limits that suit your needs, are often the best option, however. A Zone 1 daily card, which covers the city center and inner suburbs, costs $4.40, a weekly ticket is $19.10. These are sold at train stations, and at newsagents, milk bars (corner stores), and pharmacies displaying a Metcard sign. The **City Met Shop** WEB SITE www.vitrip.vic.gov.au, 103 Elizabeth Street, City, sells tickets and provides transport maps and timetables. The **Met Information Center** (131 638 operates from 7 AM to 9 PM daily.

The **Melbourne City Explorer Bus** ((03) 9650 7000 circuits the city six times daily, taking in most of Melbourne city's highlights. One- or two-day passes allow you to get off and re-board at any of the designated stops during operating hours. Tickets can be purchased on board — a one-day pass is $22 for adults, $10 for children. Stop 1 is at the Melbourne Town Hall in Swanston Street, but you can start the tour at any one of the sixteen stops.

Skybus ((03) 9335 3066 operates transfers to and from Melbourne's Tullamarine Airport 24 hours a day, seven days a week, with drop-offs and pick-ups at central hotels and Spencer Street Station. The cost is $9 for adults and $4.50 for children. Taxis from the airport to central Melbourne cost between $25 and $35, depending on the traffic; the drive takes about 45 minutes. The three biggest cab companies are **Silver Top** (131 008, **Black Cabs** (132 227, and **Yellow Cabs** (131 924.

V/Line (136 196 operates a network of trains and buses throughout Victoria and to several interstate destinations.

WHAT TO SEE AND DO

To appreciate today's Melbourne, you'll need to explore some of its idiosyncratic neighborhoods, particularly Fitzroy, St. Kilda, Carlton and South Yarra, all central and convenient by public transportation from the City. Melbourne's love affair with bold architectural statements dates back to the brash confidence of its early boom years. Many beautiful old buildings remain, mostly in the city center and in stately homesteads soon engulfed by the town's rapid expansion. Inner city neighborhoods are characterized by Victorian terrace houses decorated with ornate wrought-iron lacework, and sculpted ceiling roses, cornices and fireplaces. Many have been converted into cafés, stores and restaurants.

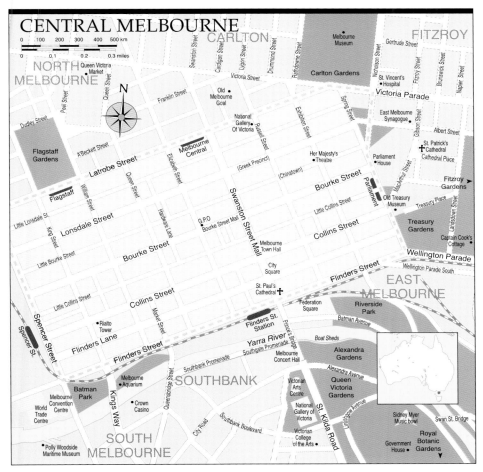

CENTRAL MELBOURNE

City Center

Melbourne's more temperate climate is kind to gardeners, and while many of the best gardens are those of the city's stately homes, the most magnificent by far are the Royal Botanic Gardens.

City Center

Flinders Street Station, at the corner of Swanston Street, is traditionally the hub of Melbourne. The yellow sandstone building is decorated with domes, turrets and arches. Meeting "under the clocks" over the main entrance at the top of the steps (they once announced upcoming departure times) is a Melbourne tradition. When railway management threatened to remove the clocks, the city blew its collective stack. They remain.

Melbourne's **Aquarium** ((03) 9620 0999, on the corner of Flinders and King streets, spreads out over four levels. An impressive 2.2-million-liter (483,942-gallon) oceanarium tops the show. The Coral Atoll, on ground level, brings visitors face-to-face with spiny lobsters, king crabs, coral reef and thousands of tropical fish. Upstairs other tanks

hold saltwater and freshwater marine life. A long Plexiglas tube called the Badlands runs through a tank of sharks, manta rays, and enormous groupers. Open every day of the year from 9 AM to 6 PM and in January from 9 AM to 9 PM, the tour is strictly one direction only, no backtracking.

Housed in Melbourne's original Customs House on the corner of Flinders and William streets, the **Immigration Museum** ((03) 9927 2700 WEB SITE www.mov.vic.gov.au/immigration uses multimedia to explore Victoria's immigration history. The Schiavello Access Gallery features changing exhibitions by community groups and there is also a program of traveling exhibitions from Australia and overseas. Open daily from 9 AM to 5 PM.

The "top end" of Collins Street, towards Russell and Spring streets, is shaded by plane trees that light up at night with fairy lights. On Spring Street facing down Collins, the classical Renaissance style **Old Treasury Building** (1858) now houses an exhibition on Melbourne's history. Open 9 AM to 5 PM,

Monday to Saturday. The observation deck on the fifty-fifth floor of the **Rialto Tower (** (03) 9629 8222, 525 Collins Street, (promoted as "the tallest building in the southern hemisphere") offers a spectacular 360-degree panorama of the city and the Yarra River. Come to its licensed café at twilight to watch the city lights blink on. They've recently installed "Zoom City" live action cameras. Open every day, 10 AM until late.

Guided tours of the richly adorned **Parliament House of Victoria (** (03) 9651 8911 in Spring Street are offered weekdays when Parliament is in recess. The building was constructed in stages between 1856 and 1930, and technically remains unfinished. The original design featured a domed roof, and every few years there is talk of actualizing it. The highlight at the moment, though, is the Legislative Council Chamber, with an ornately painted vaulted ceiling.

On the corner of Little Bourke Street, the **Princess Theatre (** (03) 9299 9850, 163 Spring Street, built in 1854 as Astley's Amphitheatre, has survived periodic and extensive renovations, with complete facelifts in 1857, 1865, 1886, and 1922. The façade of this ludicrously decorated piece of Victoriana includes figures of the Muses, urns, lions and a golden angel tooting a trumpet.

Australia's most comprehensive art collection, the **National Gallery of Victoria (** (03) 9208 0356 WEB SITE www.ngv.vic.gov.au was, at the time of writing, temporarily housed in the old gallery building at 285–321 Russell Street (the refurbished St. Kilda Road gallery is slated to reopen late in 2002). This is Australia's oldest public art gallery, originally founded as the Melbourne Museum of Art in 1861. The National Gallery Art School, established in 1870, trained many of the country's best known painters, including Tom Roberts, Frederick McCubbin, Arthur Streeton, Arthur Boyd and Sidney Nolan. Today the gallery houses over 70,000 works, including vast Aboriginal and non-Aboriginal Australian collections and an excellent collection of Chinese robes and ceramics. Open from 10 AM to 5 PM daily.

The remains of the **Old Melbourne Gaol (** (03) 9663 7228, on Russell Street, are now a penal museum, open to the public. Australia's best known bushranger (outlaw), Ned Kelly, was hanged here on November 11, 1880. Self-guided tours operate daily from 9:30 AM to 4:30 PM, with theatrical tours by candlelight Wednesday, Friday and Sunday evenings.

Lonsdale Street between Russell and Swanston streets is known for its Greek cafés and delis. It's also home to the **Antipodes Festival** in March, a month-long celebration of Greek dancing, food and entertainment.

Swanston Street leads from Flinders Street Station north through to Carlton and Melbourne University. The first few blocks are a pedestrian

mall known as Swanston Walk. Beware of trams and bikes though — they are still allowed along it. **Saint Paul's Cathedral (** (03) 9650 3791, at the start of Swanston Street, is a good example of Gothic transitional architecture, consecrated in 1891. Organ recitals are an integral part of the cathedral's life, as are other music recitals, drama and art exhibitions. Bell ringers practice on the cathedral's 13 bells Wednesday evenings from 6:30 PM to 9 PM. The cathedral opens 7 AM daily and closes after evensong.

Completed in 1924, the **Capitol Theatre (** (03) 9925 1986 is back in business after lying idle for several years. At the peak of their careers at the time, architects Walter Burley Griffin and his wife Marion Mahoney Griffin, who together designed Australia's capital, Canberra, spared no extravagance on this grand building. The 2,000-seat cinema has 6,000 colored lights on the ceiling,

programmed to recreate the effect of light refracting through crystal.

On Swanson and Collins, water cascades around the boundary of Melbourne's **City Square**. During the week the plaza is often a venue for free entertainment, while at weekends skateboarders and rollerbladers turn it into an unofficial acrobatics track.

The heart of Old Melbourne lies at the corner of Collins and Queen streets. Elaborate financial institutions are reminders of the early colony's wealth — each building tried to outdo its neighbor in ostentation. Many have spires and turrets more suited to a Bohemian castle, and interiors resplendent with ceiling paintings and gold trimmings. At 388 Collins Street, griffins guard the entrance of what was once the **E.S.&A. Bank**, built in 1883. Its embellishments pushed it to the limits of outrageousness, even for a neo-Gothic building.

The enormous **Queen Victoria Market** ((03) 9320 5822 resounds with vendors competing for shoppers' attention. There are similar markets throughout Melbourne, but the "Vic Market," inaugurated in 1878, has the largest stock of fresh produce at the best prices in town. Over 1,000 stalls sell clothes, antiques, art and craft and a little bit of just about everything. The market is bounded by Peel, Franklin, Victoria and Elizabeth streets. Open 6 AM to 5 PM, Tuesday, Thursday, Friday and Saturday, the food halls are closed on Sunday but the rest of the market opens at 9 AM.

East Melbourne

Behind Parliament House, **St. Patrick's Cathedral** is a classic example of English Gothic Revival architecture — set in tranquil gardens it's an ideal

Melbourne's skyline, seen from the Yarra River.

place to take a rest from the noisy city center. The original blue-stone building has been extended some since the first section was blessed in 1858. Other denominations have built places of worship nearby. The sturdy **Lutheran Church** (24 Parliament Place) opened in 1853, **Baptist Church House** (486 Albert Street) in 1859, and the **East Melbourne Synagogue** (488 Albert Street) in 1877.

Carlton

Carlton, just north of the City, can be reached by tram No. 1 or No. 15 along Swanston Street, but it's close enough for a pleasant walk. **Lygon Street** ("Little Italy") is a hub of activity day and night. In true Italian fashion, boisterous conversation resounds from the many cafés and restaurants lining the wide pavement. The smell of coffee and Italian food is a temptation that's hard to resist, and on warm summer nights families stroll by enjoying the best *gelati* in town. A steady flow of students from nearby Melbourne University, Victoria College, and the Royal Melbourne Institute of Technology liven up the scene. There are several good alternative cinemas here, a variety of clothing stores, and excellent delis and bookstores. Over Alexander Parade in North Carlton, tree-lined **Rathdowne Street** is considerably quieter and has a wonderful assortment of cafés, restaurants, bookstores and tiny boutique stores.

There's so much to see at the immense new **Melbourne Museum** ((03) 8341 7777 WEB SITE www.melbourne.museum.vic.gov.au (book tickets online through Ticketek WEB SITE www.ticketek .com.au) in Carlton Gardens, schedule at least a few hours to take it in. The museum highlights cutting-edge interactive technology and enormous natural exhibits. Open 10 AM TO 6 PM daily.

Parkville begins two blocks west of Lygon Street, at Melbourne University on Swanston Street. More than 450 animal species from Australia and around the world are housed in the **Melbourne Zoo** ((03) 9285 9300, Elliott Avenue. Zoo-keepers successfully breed rare animals, including giant pandas, snow tigers and the western lowland gorilla. Open every day of the year 9 AM to 5 PM, and on selected summer evenings until 9:30 PM.

Fitzroy

Most of the activity in Fitzroy centers on the bohemian strip of **Brunswick Street**. Lined with eateries of all kinds, its stores have a distinct hippie-chic, retro-ethnic thrust along with young designer labels, music stores, bookshops and small art galleries. Fitzroy's pubs are rated some of Melbourne's best; many put on live music a few nights a week. Although locals will bemoan the area's gentrification over the last decade or so, reminiscing about just how cool it used to be (and how you could once find a park here), Brunswick Street remains Melbourne's hipsters' haven.

Brunswick Street begins at Victoria Parade in Fitzroy — tram No. 11 east along Collins Street will get you there, and it's a short walk from Parliament House. The beginning of the street takes in Melbourne's first suburb, Newtown, which was established in the 1840s. The oldest houses in the street are **Mononia** at No. 21 and **Dodgshun House** at No. 9, both built in 1851.

Founded in 1981 by a group of art school graduates, **Roar Studios** ((03) 9419 9975, 115A Brunswick Street, provided them with a place to show works rejected by mainstream galleries. Many artists from Roar have gained recognition and moved on, replaced by a new generation. Open Tuesday to Sunday, 11 AM to 5 PM. Non-profit **200 Gertrude Street** ((03) 9419 3406, a contemporary art complex, features work by emerging and innovative Australian and international artists. The **Centre for Contemporary Photography (CCP)** ((03) 9417 1549, 205 Johnston Street, is a publicly funded gallery that exhibits innovative, experimental and contemporary photo-based artwork. **The Artists' Garden** ((03) 9417 7705, tucked above Fitzroy Nursery at 390 Brunswick Street, is a small gallery that promotes local artists. Not all of Fitzroy's artwork is indoors, though: brightly painted street furniture and whimsical statues fill Brunswick Street with color; the nursery is a masterpiece in itself.

The coolest of Melbourne's public parties, September's **Brunswick Street Festival** attracts hordes of people for contemporary music and arts events. **Johnston Street** comes to life with Spanish dance and music during the **Spanish Festival** in November.

Southbank

South from Flinders Street Station, Princes Bridge crosses the Yarra River to St. Kilda Road, where Melbourne's arts complex includes the **Victorian Arts Centre**, the **Melbourne Concert Hall** and the **National Gallery of Victoria**. At the time of writing the Gallery was undergoing extensive renovations, and the bulk of the collection was being housed in the old National Gallery building on the corner of Russell and Latrobe streets, City, until 2002 (see above). The Concert Hall houses three theaters with a full program of theater, music, opera, and dance. To find out what's on here and at other Melbourne venues, or to book tickets, see NIGHTLIFE, below. Within the Arts Centre, the **Performing Arts Museum** ((03) 9281 8263 has eclectic exhibitions dealing with all aspects of entertainment, past and present. **Melbourne River Cruises** ((03) 9629 7233 depart from below the Princes Bridge; their Ticket Kiosk is on the bridge.

Past Southgate, the behemoth **Crown Entertainment Complex** includes a 24-hour casino, a Planet Hollywood restaurant and numerous bars, restaurants and stores.

Diners enjoy a leisurely meal at one of the many sidewalk restaurants that line Southbank Promenade.

The Royal Botanic Gardens

The Royal Botanic Gardens, across St. Kilda Road just south of the Arts Centre, are by far the queen of Melbourne's many gardens. The gardens were laid out in the first 20 years of the colony. They include lakes, hills, rolling lawns and dense forest sections. There's a pleasant café in the center, alongside the major lake. The gardens are home to the elegant native black swan, which sports a white line across the tip of its red beak, and a variety of ducks and storks. Near the southeastern exit, large native fruit bats hang out in the dark and damp fern gully. Open daily from 7:30 AM to sunset.

The Botanic Gardens form part of the larger Kings Domain. Victoria's governor lives in **Government House**, a turreted building alongside the Botanic Gardens. Tours run from February to December, on Monday, Wednesday and Saturday. They cost $8, $4 for children and are booked through the National Trust ((03) 9654 411. Not far from its front gates, the original, temporary government house, **Governor Latrobe's Cottage** is open daily, except Tuesday and Thursday, from 11 AM to 4:30 PM. Admission is $3.

St. Kilda

Acland Street, St. Kilda, is where Haight-Ashbury meets Miami Beach. Groovy cafés, bookstores, surfwear and hippie-wear outlets line the street provides. Things get pretty crowded on weekends, when an outdoor table becomes a valuable commodity. **Linden**, 26 Acland Street, a brick mansion built in 1870, houses a gallery showcasing local artists; admission is free. At the other end of the Esplanade, the slightly seedier **Fitzroy Street** is lively 24 hours a day. Opened in 1911, **Luna Park** ((03) 952 5033, Lower Esplanade, with its gaudy four-meter (24-ft) entrance in the shape of a laughing clown, has mostly tame family rides. The Ferris wheel provides good views of St. Kilda and the bay.

The end of the pier, with its domed buildings and a foreshore fringed with palm trees, is a good place to survey St. Kilda's Moorish skyline. The historic **St. Kilda Pier Kiosk**, an upmarket café with outdoor seating, serves great light food and tempting cakes (specializing in seafood, of course). The pier ends at the kiosk, but a breakwater continues out to a small marina (closed to the public). There's a small colony of little penguins here, with boat tours from the pier. Along the Upper Esplanade, back from the beach, St. Kilda's Sunday **art and craft market** can be fun.

The walking track and bicycle/skateboard/rollerblade lane running along the beach continues for 22 km (14 miles). **Rock 'n' Roll**, 11A Fitzroy Street, rents rollerblades and boards. Staff will help the inexperienced with an impromptu lesson.

In the heat of late February, the **St. Kilda Festival** brings music and a carnival atmosphere to Acland Street and St. Kilda beach.

Williamstown

On weekends there's a ferry from St. Kilda pier to Williamstown on the other side of the bay; it leaves St. Kilda every hour, from 9 AM to 5 PM. There's also a regular ferry to Williamstown from Southgate, doing the return trip four times daily. For timetables call ((03) 9506 4144, a 24-hour a day information service. Despite its proximity to Melbourne, Williamstown has a village feel. It started life as a port town in 1837, but fell into disuse as the Port of Melbourne developed. Williamstown's streets are lined with Edwardian laborers' cottages. On the last Sunday of every month a market is held in the park opposite Nelson Place.

Stately Homes

Built between 1869 and 1887, **Rippon Lea** ((03) 9523 6095, 192 Hotham Street, Elsternwick, is a grand Romanesque building surrounded by a lush garden. The house is beautifully furnished and decorated, and the Victorian Pleasure Garden includes a lake, islands and bridges and a large Victorian fernery. The gardens are popular with picnickers. Open Tuesday to Sunday, 10 AM to 5 PM, and Mondays if it's a public holiday. **Como** ((03) 9827 2500, Como Avenue, South Yarra, was built in the 1840s and retains its original furnishings. The graceful house overlooks the Yarra River.

Werribee Park ((03) 9741 2444, a 30-minute drive from Melbourne, is an imposing 60-room Italianate mansion built in 1874, with 12 ha (30 acres) of gardens and an ornamental lake. Adjacent to it is the **Werribee Zoo** ((03) 9742 7933, where lions, hippos, giraffes, rhinoceroses and other animals can be seen close up during an exciting safari bus ride.

SPORTS AND OUTDOOR ACTIVITIES

From March to September Melbourne goes **football** crazy, with league games on Friday nights and Saturday afternoons. The best stadiums to go to see a game and soak up the atmosphere are the Melbourne Cricket Ground (MCG) in Brunton Avenue, Jolimont, and Waverley Park in Wellington Road, Mulgrave. Special trains and buses are brought into service for these games.

In the summer **cricket** takes over from football at the MCG, for tense one-day matches and the more drawn-out World Series Test matches.

There is **horse racing** at Flemington, Caulfield and Moonee Valley all year long, with the main season coming in spring. The highlight of the Spring Racing Carnival is the Melbourne Cup. Many punters get no further than enjoying chicken and champagne in the car park, dressed up in zany outfits and strange collections of hats.

The Australian **Tennis** Open (a Grand Slam tournament) is held at Melbourne Park each January, and **car racing** enthusiasts flock to Albert Park for the Australian Grand Prix in March, the first event in the annual FIA World Championship.

Melbournians love **cycling**: bike paths line many of its wide streets, beaches, rivers and parks. And Melbourne is relatively flat. From the city center you can peddle along the River Yarra for miles along green parks and around, but not through, the Botanic Gardens. Along the bay you may have to compete with hoards of rollerbladers, but if you have the energy you can ride from Port Melbourne to Brighton on an almost uninterrupted path, a distance of over 20 km (12.5 miles). When riding on the streets, particularly around the city center, beware of tram tracks: a hazard to cyclists at any time, they're like ice to bikes when wet. As

wave-jumpers. Young entrepreneurs with trailers of boards for rent at inexpensive rates dot practically the whole of the bay these days. Popular spots for beginners are the small coves found at St. Kilda, Brighton and Hampton beaches. Most rental operators are helpful if they notice you are a novice.

Tennis has always been popular in Melbourne and public courts are scattered throughout the city and suburbs. In the City, Melbourne Park ((03) 9286 1234, Batman Avenue, hosts the Australian Open Tennis Championships. It has 21 outdoor courts and five indoor, but bookings are essential. Of the suburban courts, my favorite is the Tulip Street Tennis Center ((03) 9584 7684, 107 Tulip Street Sandringham, which has 13 synthetic grass courts,

in most of Australia, bicycle helmets are required by law and fines apply. Many bicycle stores rent bikes — from mountain to tandem — at very reasonable rates. To find one near you, contact Bicycle Victoria ((03) 9328 3000, 19 O'Connell Street, North Melbourne, a non-profit organization that conducts regular tours and events and can supply helpful information.

Rollerblading fever took a hold of Melbourne many years ago and has now become a basic means of transportation for hundreds of Melbournians. Weekend skaters compete with the cyclists for space on the St. Kilda beachfront, although on weekdays you can skate along here without much fear of a messy pile-up. Blades can be rented from Rock 'n' Roll, 11A Fitzroy Street, St. Kilda.

The generally calm waters of Port Phillip Bay are perfect for beginner **windsurfers**, and when the wind picks up, loads of fun for experienced

all with competition night lighting. The relaxed atmosphere and licensed café can make for a fun social event. Rackets and balls can be rented for a small fee. Open daily from 7 AM to 11 PM.

Golfing enthusiasts need only go two kilometers (one mile) from the city center to reach the 18-hole Albert Park Golf Course ((03) 9510 8144 Queens Rd, which is kept in immaculate condition. Visitors can rent all the necessaries and a few extras like golf buggies and cars. The Royal Melbourne Golf Club ((03) 9598 6755, Cheltenham Road, Black Rock, is one of the largest golf courses in Victoria. Its two completely separate 18-hole links form a composite course with a number of possible permutations. It is a favorite for many international tournaments. Huntingdale Golf Club ((03) 9579 4622, Windsor Ave, Oakleigh South,

A grand final Australian Rules football match in Melbourne.

home to the Australian Masters, is one of the most prestigious and beautiful golf courses in Melbourne. Some professionals have described the final hole of the course as one of golf's toughest.

SHOPPING

Melbourne Central, Swanston Street, a popular shopping complex dominated by the **Daimaru** department store, contains over 150 specialty shops. Entertainment is often provided at lunchtime under its conical skylight, which encloses a shot tower built in 1889.

South Yarra is a short journey from the City by tram No. 8 from Swanston Street, and only two stops from Flinders Street Station by train. The two main strips are chic **Toorak Road**, which becomes more exclusive as it moves into Australia's most expensive neighborhood, Toorak, and suave **Chapel Street**, which grunges down a little as it heads north into Prahran. Toorak Road is *the* upmarket shopping precinct of Melbourne, lined with exclusive fashion boutiques, specialty gift and antique stores, cafés and some of Melbourne's most expensive restaurants. The **Prahran Market** on Commercial Road is a lively place to wander around and stock up on produce and fresh fruit and vegetables. **Greville Street**, off Chapel Street, is the groovy part of the neighborhood. It's a relaxed mix of good cafés, retro and contemporary clothes stores, bookshops and music stores. On Sundays a small crafts and clothes market pops up in the square halfway along the street, with music performed in the small belvedere.

Other good areas for clothes and accessories are **Lygon Street** in Carlton; **Brunswick Street** in Fitzroy, for young designers and retro stores; **Swan Street** in Richmond for factory outlets; and the **City**, particularly around the major department stores, Myers and David Jones, both on Bourke Street.

Gallery Gabrielle Pizzi, 141 Flinders Lane, sells works from major Aboriginal artists and has taken many of its exhibitions on overseas tours. Paintings and artifacts from Central Australia are sold at the **Gallery of Dreamings**, 73 Bourke Street.

The **Meat Market Craft Centre**, 42 Courtney Street, North Melbourne, is just a short walk from Victoria Market. Its name hardly conjures up a craft shop, but it was originally a meat market. It showcases pottery, hand-painted fabrics, woodcrafts and leatherwork by contemporary artists and has regular exhibitions of other crafts, also for sale.

WHERE TO STAY

Probably the most important consideration when booking a hotel in Melbourne is location. The city is bisected by the Yarra River, and the few bridges crossing it are notorious for traffic jams. It's best to decide which side of the river you want to be

(Melbourne residents are known for refusing to cross the Yarra, mourning the loss of friends who rashly make the big move). For a short visit I'd suggest staying close to the city center, which is an efficient hub for Melbourne's public transportation system.

Very Expensive
Overlooking the historic Fitzroy Gardens, five-star **Hilton on the Park** ((03) 9419 2000 WEB SITE www.hilton.com/hotels/MELHITW/, 192 Wellington Parade, East Melbourne, has excellent facilities and views of the city. The hotel has a large outdoor heated pool, gymnasium, spa and sauna. The Hilton has a formal dining room, its own café, hairdresser, florist and gift shop. Enjoy uninterrupted views over the Yarra River promenade at the **Sheraton Towers Southgate** ((03) 9696 3100 WEB SITE www.sheraton-towers.com.au/, 1 Southgate Avenue, Southbank, in totally luxurious surroundings only a short stroll from the heart of the city. Go all the way with one of their 11 ultra-luxury suites — full personal butler service is included. All rooms are lavishly appointed and spacious, service is impeccable, and the hotel has three restaurants and an elegant cocktail lounge.

Expect the very best at **Como** ((03) 9825 2222 WEB SITE www.hotelcomo.com.au, 630 Chapel Street, South Yarra, one of *the* deluxe hotels in Australia. The Como comprises 36 studio rooms as well as 71 suites with terrace garden views, fully equipped kitchens and the option of a private office fitted out with computer, printer, modem and fax. If you require all this you may as well take the optional secretarial and butler services. Special leisure facilities include a pool with retractable glass roof, a gymnasium, spa and sauna.

Expensive
Le Meridien at Rialto ((03) 9620 9111 WEB SITE www.lemeridien-melbourne.com, 495 Collins Street, is distinguished by its elaborate nineteenth-century venetian façade. The property began its life as wool stores and offices in 1891, and the historical architecture remains today, featuring stained-glass windows, wrought-iron balustrades and blue cobblestone pathways. A spectacular nine-story glass atrium soars above the hotel's Café Rialto, joining the century-old Rialto and Winfield buildings. Rooms combine modern-day appointments with European-style interior furnishings and paintings. A rooftop heated pool, spa, sauna, gymnasium and sun deck add the final touch.

Created out of an old city warehouse, the slick **Adelphi Hotel** ((03) 9650 7555, 187 Flinders Lane, City, incorporates muted colors, swathes of burnished steel and subdued designer features in all of its 34 big and very livable rooms (book well ahead). The Club Bar continues the minimalist, designer feel, with fab city views. They also have the most original lap pool in town: the last few meters are clear-bottomed and extend out above the busy street!

Moderate

The hyper-stylish **Hotel Lindrum** ((03) 9668 1111 WEB SITE www.small-hotel.com/lindrum/, 26 Flinders Street, is one of the most centrally located hotels in Melbourne. The high-ceilinged, spacious bedrooms are decorated in rich, warm colors. Refined is the word here. Rooms include fax machine, modem outlet and complimentary in-house movies.

Belying its ornate Italianate façade, **King Boutique Accommodation** ((03) 9417 1113, 122 Nicholson

Street, Fitzroy, combines the elegance of grandly proportioned rooms with an airy minimalist interior to create sophisticated and modern B&B-style accommodation. Close to lively Lygon Street, **Rydges Carlton** ((03) 9347 7811 E-MAIL reservations_carlton@rydges.com, 701 Swanston Street, offers stylish and comfortable hotel accommodation without the hefty price tag. Rydges has a sauna and a heated, rooftop swimming pool.

Overlooking Port Phillip Bay at St. Kilda Beach, **Novotel St**. **Kilda** ((03) 9525 5522 WEB SITE www.novotel-stkilda.citysearch.com.au, 16 The Esplanade, offers the choice of standard, deluxe, family rooms, suites and interconnecting rooms. Facilities include a heated salt-water swimming pool, a gymnasium, sauna and spa. Not far away, **Brooklyn Mansions B&B** ((03) 9537 2633, Residence 5, 95 Fitzroy Street, St. Kilda, represents a part of the area's history. One-time boarding house,

brothel, backpacker hostel and squat, today four-poster queen-sized beds and homey hospitality are the norm. Prices include a cooked breakfast which, weather permitting, can be enjoyed on the first floor deck with its novel tableaux of the NYC skyline, Tuscany and the Australian Rainforest. There are only three rooms and one executive apartment, so book well ahead.

The **Tilba** ((03) 9867 8844, 30 Toorak Road West, South Yarra, is an elegant little hotel in a turreted Victorian home close to the Botanic Gardens and South Yarra's shopping and café precinct. Rooms have lofty ceilings embellished with intricate roses and cornices and decorated in period furnishings.

Inexpensive

One of the most remarkable backpacker lodges in Melbourne is **The Nunnery** ((03) 9419 8637, 116 Nicholson Street, Fitzroy, in a beautiful nineteenth-century terrace building. Rooms, once the nuns' cells, range from six-bed dormitories to singles and doubles. Television is discouraged in the communal lounge because it stifles conversation, and this friendly B&B is a great place to meet other travelers and swap traveling tips. In groovy St. Kilda, **Leopard House** ((03) 9534 1200, 27 Grey Street, and **Enfield House** ((03) 9534 8159, 2 Enfield Street, are two more popular budget options. The **Olembia Private Hotel** ((03) 9537 1412, 96 Barkly Street, St. Kilda, is a good inexpensive B&B.

There are two YHA hostels in North Melbourne, the enormous, modern **Queensberry Hill YHA** ((03) 9329 8599 FAX (03) 9326 8427, 78 Howard Street, and the quieter and more intimate **Chapman Gardens YHA** ((03) 9328 3595, 76 Chapman Street. In the City, the **Hotel Y** ((03) 9329 5188, 489 Elizabeth Street, is often crowded, but it's conveniently located.

WHERE TO EAT

Melbournians love to dine out. Be prepared to eat extremely well for relatively little money. Its multitude of cafés, wine bars, restaurants, delicatessens, pub restaurants and markets reflect the city's multicultural diversity while drawing on Victoria's staggering variety of fresh produce.

Different nationalities concentrate in different neighborhoods. Lygon Street houses a lively Little Italy, Lonsdale Street has classic Greek. You'll find authentic Asian in Little Bourke Street's Chinatown or Richmond's Little Vietnam on Victoria Street. For a taste of Spain go to Johnston Street, Fitzroy. Jewish bakery cafés line Acland Street, St. Kilda. Other areas are defined more by their "feel." Funky Brunswick Street, Fitzroy, has excellent affordable cuisines of all types, Toorak

Tiny Jerry's Milk Bar in Elwood is a friendly and popular locale.

Road and Chapel Street offer cool inner city cafés and more expensive haute cuisine. St. Kilda has the largest concentration of cafés, restaurants and bars in Melbourne. Throughout the city though, alfresco dining is the go in summer, when tables line many of the city's streets.

Chefs compete with each other avidly, continually trying something new and innovating to keep their already spoiled clientele satisfied. For a few dollars more (true, in some cases considerably more) dining takes on a level that sets world standards. For the most comprehensive guides to eating in Melbourne pick up a copy of the *Age Good Food Guide* or the *Age Cheap Eats in Melbourne* — they help narrow down choices a little.

as *bœuf bourguignon, filet de bœuf béarnaise, escargots* and *crème brûlée* are expertly and authentically prepared. The kitchen is open late, making it ideal for after show dining.

Overlooking the splendid Royal Botanic Gardens, **Lynch's** ((03) 9866 5627, 133 Domain Road, South Yarra, features an outside front courtyard or winter garden and a uniquely Parisian-style interior. With an emphasis on French style, the menu covers a broad range of revitalized traditional fare as well as regular new creations.

Jacques Reymond ((03) 9521 1552, 78 Williams Road, Prahran, is housed in a restored Victorian mansion, where clients dine in intimate individual rooms. Since being introduced to Asian ingredi-

Expensive

Winner of many prestigious awards, **Chinois** ((03) 9826 3388, 176 Toorak Road, South Yarra, combines traditional French techniques with exotic Asian flavors to produce original haute cuisine. Take predinner drinks in the well-stocked café bar downstairs then make your way to the intimate upstairs dining room. In the evening, the upstairs restaurant menu can also be mixed and matched with the café menu, bringing the price closer to the moderate range. Classics include delicate sashimi, aromatic noodle dishes, corn-fed chicken or perfect roast duck on braised red cabbage. A wine suggestion is made for every dish. The staff are some of Melbourne's best, the atmosphere relaxed and unpretentious. **France-Soir** ((03) 9866 8569, 11 Toorak Road, South Yarra, a bustling Parisian-style bistro, is well known for its wine list, featuring almost 1,500 different wines. French classics such

ents, Reymond has subtly integrated them into his repertoire to produce some of the more innovative cuisine in town. Quail terrine, duck *foie gras*, scallop and baby octopus tart or roasted wild barramundi fillet coated with mild spices are just a few tempting dishes from the extensive menu. The five-course vegetarian menu and fixed-price lunch menu are great value for money.

Once a grungy alternative music venue, **Circa** ((03) 9536 1122, in the Prince Hotel, 2 Acland Street, St. Kilda, has been transformed into the most *in* restaurant in Melbourne. Starters might include Jerusalem artichoke soup with a hint of truffle oil, served over a tender piece of rabbit *confit*. For main course try poached fillet of blue-eye trevally, served on a bed of spinach with a herb, tomato and parmesan crust, or local pheasant. The wine list is comprehensive, with over 600 varieties to choose from. Staff, including a professional sommelier, are discreet, well informed and efficient. Like the rest of the Prince, Circa is ultra-stylishly decked out, with soft banquettes along three walls of the large dining area and pink silk room-dividers. For pre-dinner drinks drift out to the courtyard or take your time at the bar. Book at least two weeks ahead; it will be well worth the wait.

For the best in bayside dining try **Donovans** ((03) 9534 8221, 40 Jacka Boulevard, St. Kilda. Relax in the large comfortable sofas by the fireplace, amongst book collections, mismatched chairs, and photo's, with views of Port Phillip Bay. Donovans serves predominately seafood, but carnivores are also well looked after. Start with hearty fish soup with croutons, gruyere and *rouille*, or young fresh

squid with parsley stuffing and anchovy sage fritters. Many of their mains evoke Italy — the shrimp risotto with saffron threads and cognac is particularly good, as is the barramundi fillet steamed under a blanket of seaweed and served with pippis and clams. Donovans also offers a selection of perfectly grilled fish and meats. Upstairs at the **Stokehouse** ((03) 9525 5555, 30 Jacka Boulevard, St. Kilda, is one the of the most beautiful sea-side restaurants in Melbourne. Looking out though swaying palms across St. Kilda Beach, the converted timber teahouse offers specialty seafood dishes and succulent char-grills. Try the blue swimmer crab salad or the roast barramundi and spicy calamari. Book well ahead.

Considered by many to be the best Italian restaurant in Melbourne, **Café Di Stasio** ((03) 9525 3999, 31 Fitzroy Street, St. Kilda, continues to pack them in. Di Stasio's sophisticated simplicity is

probably its key to enduring success. Quality ingredients are expertly prepared to produce dishes such as legendary fresh crayfish omelet with a bisque sauce, sea urchin risotto or tender baby octopus cooked in red wine and chilies. For a real bargain try their $20 two-course lunch special, which includes a glass of wine.

The **Flower Drum** ((03) 9662 3655, 17 Market Lane, City, has been one of Australia's greatest Chinese restaurants for almost 30 years. The menu has hardly changed in this time, although there are always some pleasant surprises. Service is meticulous as is the attention to detail. Their Peking duck is legendary.

A much-loved establishment for several decades now too is the excellent **Grossi Florentino** ((03) 9662 1811, 80 Bourke Street, City. The downstairs bar and grill offers traditional Italian fare while the elegant upstairs dining room produces more sophisticated dishes. Long-time favorites include oven-roasted suckling lamb, marinated garfish fillets and slow-cooked ox tripe. Bookings are essential for upstairs dinner.

Toofey's ((03) 9347 9838, 162 Elgin Street, Carlton, serves some of the best seafood in Melbourne. Dishes are not overly adventurous, but for perfectly cooked fish or succulent meaty crayfish you can't go wrong. Beware, they are ludicrously generous with the seafood in the spaghetti marinara. Desserts are usually something special too.

For splendid river and city views combined with adventurous dining, **Blakes Restaurant** ((03) 9690 9621, Ground Level, Southgate, puts on a good show. Follow kangaroo prosciutto with rocket (arugula), reggiano, beetroot crisps and white truffle oil with char-grilled garfish on a braised artichoke salad. Each dish has a recommended wine by the glass. Upstairs, **Scusa Mi** ((03) 9699 4111, Mid Level, Southgate, serves contemporary Italian cuisine in smart surroundings. The ricotta-filled gnocchi is really something special, as is the crisp roasted duck. The dessert menu is irresistible and the cheese selection well chosen. Bookings are essential, particularly for a balcony table.

Est Est Est ((03) 9682 5688, at 440 Clarendon Street, South Melbourne, has received much well-deserved critical acclaim. The owners have trained with some of the world's best, using their experience to create modern takes on classic dishes. Pigeon, hare, veal and barramundi feature regularly, but the menu changes often. Starters of scallops in a black sauce or Moreton Bay bug tortellini are seafood treasures. Pace yourself for one of their fabulous desserts. Open for dinner only Monday to Saturday from 6:30 PM.

Vlado's ((03) 9428 5833, 61 Bridge Street, Richmond, has been serving prime beef and little else

At the end of the long wooden pier, diners at St. Kilda Pier Kiosk enjoy lunch with a view.

for 40 years. The $52 set menu starts with home-made sausages and continues with a choice of beef cuts — cooked to perfection — and a basic side salad. For dessert, it's pancakes. That's it. After a meal in this unpretentious steak house you will understand why Vlado has had no reason to change his simple formula.

The burgundy-colored **Colonial Tramcar Restaurant** ((03) 9696 4000, allows you to combine lunch or dinner with relaxed sightseeing. The tram leaves from Clarendon Street (Corner of Normanby Road), South Melbourne and passes through the City, South Yarra, and St. Kilda. The food is better than you might expect and diners loosen up quickly, creating a lively atmosphere.

buy kitchen utensils (the mezzanine also regularly hosts cooking demonstrations, wine tastings, and book signings).

For authentic Greek cuisine the **Greek Deli & Taverna Restaurant** ((03) 9827 3734, 583 Chapel Street, South Yarra, has all the dips, grilled meats and seafood you could imagine. The enormous seafood platter could feed a family of four. The gracious hosts are warm and friendly, creating an all-round pleasant dining experience.

With over 700 wines on their list, it's no wonder **Syracuse** ((03) 9670 1777, 23 Bank Place, City, has for several years cleaned up in local wine list awards. Syracuse's grand Victorian dining room in the city's financial district is not the least bit

Moderate

Occupying what was once a supermarket, **Let's Eat** ((03) 9520 3287, 163–185 Commercial Road, South Yarra, is now a gleaming renovated warehouse at the back of Prahran Market. About half the floor-space is devoted to groceries, with local and imported goods, fresh meats and fish, a delicatessen and fruit and vegetables. There's also a wine bar, a sushi bar, a sandwich bar, a coffee and cake outlet and the main café. Order from the menu or pick out some fresh produce and for $5 more they will cook it any way you like. There are pads of tear-off recipes tacked to the walls, free to take for good cooking suggestions. After ordering you are given a vibrating pager, which lets you do your shopping until your meal is ready (sometimes quite a while). There are tables outside in the courtyard, inside on the shop-floor or near the wine store and bar, and upstairs in the mezzanine, where you can

stuffy. The food is essentially a selection of gourmet snacks, plus a small list of heartier meals and desserts. You can choose just a single char-grilled lamb cutlet or a slab of divine pan-fried saganaki (sheep's milk cheese) while experimenting with the wines, or totally indulge in copious mains such as char-grilled marlin. At the top end of the moderate price range but worth every cent is Italian-influenced **Becco Produce Store Restaurant Bar** ((03) 9663 3000, 11–25 Crossley Street, City. For mains try roast duck, which is perfect with a glass of Pinot Noir, or the excellent pumpkin-and-marscapone ravioli with marjoram butter. Becco also does nourishing takeout.

Jimmy Watsons Wine Bar & Restaurant ((03) 9347 3985, 333 Lygon Street, Carlton, is into its third generation of family-run quality wining and dining. The remarkable wine list warrants a visit in itself, but the food is also consistently good here.

The restaurant draws the academic crowd from nearby Melbourne University, so book in advance for the out-door courtyard. **Il Primo** ((03) 9663 6100, 242 Lygon Street, is a converted Victorian terrace with a courtyard out front. Crowded every night, it serves classic Italian at its best, although prices can climb into the expensive range.

Due to its enormous popularity, **Guernica** ((03) 9416 0969 257 Brunswick Street, Fitzroy, has grown from a casual local café into a highly respected restaurant. It follows the modern Australian style of combining different cuisines with fresh and intense flavors and follows up with a well thought-out wine list. Further along at 413 Brunswick Street, **Retro Café** ((03) 9419 9103, has comfortable couches for pre-dinner drinks and a menu that's far from retro.

Spargo's Café Bar ((03) 9428 2656, 288 Bridge Road, Richmond, has a large outdoor eating area and a spacious and lively interior. Choices run from full breakfasts to pastas, wood-fired pizzas and other hot meals, salads and gourmet sandwiches and calorie-laden cakes and desserts, all at reasonable prices.

The **Isthmus of Kra** ((03) 9696 3805, 50 Park Street, South Melbourne, serves modern Thai in an atmosphere of subtle lighting decorated with wonderful Asian antiques. Start with oysters in a claypot or the Gado Gado. For mains try the Fiendishly Thai Green Curry or Beef Pai Nai — beef pieces slowly cooked with vegetables in a fragrant cinnamon and bay leaves, spiced coconut stock. Their dessert platter of Thai sweets and fresh fruit is a cut above desserts served in most Asian eateries.

Madame Joe Joe ((03) 9534 0000, 9 Fitzroy Street, St. Kilda, is a perennial local favorite for its simple Mediterranean dishes made from only the freshest available ingredients. Tiger-prawn tortellini or yabbie bouillabaisse finished off with a double-baked chocolate soufflé leaves most guests more than satisfied. Downstairs at the **Stokehouse** ((03) 9525 5555, 30 Jacka Boulevard, St. Kilda, right on St. Kilda Beach, serves sizeable portions of good quality meat and seafood along with pastas and vegetarian dishes. They have a well chosen wine list, with many wines served by the glass. This is hearty home-style food, a St. Kilda classic after a day at the beach.

Inexpensive

Rhumbarella's ((03) 9696 2973, 342 Brunswick Street, Fitzroy, has a huge and casual dining area downstairs, a progressive art gallery upstairs, and a fine reputation for serving wholesome fresh food and outrageously decadent cakes. Rhumba's, as it is affectionately known by its many regulars, is a gregarious and friendly spot and well worth checking out for its bohemian atmosphere. The **Provincial** ((03) 9417 2228, 299 Brunswick Street,

Fitzroy, offers bar, lounge and restaurant dining. The menu is modern with a Tuscan feel, inexpensive in the Provincial's bar area, moving up a little in the restaurant. The dessert selection is probably the best on the strip, so don't miss out.

The **Galleon** ((03) 9534 8934, 9 Carlisle Street, St. Kilda, has been a favorite of mine for many years, serving eclectic healthy light lunches in a relaxed atmosphere. Long-time standards are chicken and leek pie and spanakopita, or classic vegetarian stir-fried noodles. For imaginative vegetarian meals, try **Wild Rice** ((03) 9534 2849, 211 Barkly Street, St. Kilda. Though free of dairy, sugar and animal products, dishes manages to stay tasty and varied. The predominately Asian influenced weekly specials include some surprising alternatives. **Big Mouth Cafe** ((03) 9534 4611, 168 Acland Street, St. Kilda, enjoys a fine reputation for both its downstairs café and its upstairs restaurant. Downstairs puts on a hearty breakfast and is ideal for light lunches and afternoon cake and coffee. Upstairs has a spacious food hall feel to it with a diverse menu that offers nourishing vegetarian alternatives. But my favorite place for a light lunch or afternoon snack in Melbourne is **St. Kilda Pier Kiosk** (no phone). Sitting on the end of St. Kilda pier, diners are surrounded by bobbing boats, with views across the beach and city.

Little has changed over the years at **Tiamo Restaurant & Bistro** ((03) 9347 0911, 303 Lygon Street, Carlton, a favorite among nearby Melbourne University students and professors. Expect generous portions of wholesome classic Italian meals selected from the blackboard menu. The decor is a mishmash of the owners' memorabilia, the pastiche of posters making this a fun and casual place to eat. Open until 2:30 AM. The **University Café** ((03) 9347 2142 257, Lygon Street, Carlton, has tasty snacks and rich Italian patisseries downstairs and more substantial pastas and meat dishes upstairs. It's always alive with the buzz of students and locals enjoying meals just like mama used to cook. Open 7 AM through to midnight.

The café at **Lounge** ((07) 9663 2916, First Floor, 243 Swanston Street, City, serves flavorsome and healthy food on the club's balcony overlooking busy Swanston Street. Hearty burgers and salads, focaccias, a good selection of vegetarian options and some shareable choices such as nachos and dips complement the laid-back and cool nature of the place. The popular **Nudel Bar** ((03) 9662 9100, 76 Bourke Street, City, is one of the best value Asian fusion restaurants in town. For under $20 you can enjoy a great meal including a glass or two of wine. The green-tea noodles with or without poached squid are always good, as are any of the noodles in broth. Open untill late the **Supper Inn** ((03) 9663 4759, 15 Celestial Ave, City,

Brunswick Street, Fitzroy, has an eclectic mix of shops, art galleries, cafés and restaurants.

is well known for its congee — rice cooked to porridge consistency and flavored according to taste — which comes in 15 different varieties. They also offer an assortment of fresh seafood dishes. **Café Segovia** ((03) 9650 2373, 33 Block Place, City, is a perfect resting point for weary shoppers who appreciate its friendly service, relaxed atmosphere and healthy snacks. Their foccacias are excellent. The **Jarrah Room** ((03) 9629 5255, 44 Spencer Street, City, is a home-like establishment with an emphasis on bush tucker. Choices include kangaroo fillet, emu and crocodile pie and yabbie salad. Dishes are flavored with indigenous plants such as wattleseed, lemon myrtle and munthari berries and your meal begins with three different types of damper (Australian bush bread). The Jarrah is also a good place to satisfy your meatier needs, with large steaks and copious mixed grills. Open for lunch and dinner.

The **Globe Café** ((03) 9510 8693, 218 Chapel Street, Prahran, does quite a sophisticated and eclectic menu for the low price and has a mouthwatering display of cakes. It's always full on weekends for their ridiculously huge breakfasts. There's also an upstairs bar, and from Wednesday to Saturday they open a back bar from 7:30 PM until late. The post-modern decor, cruisy music and piles of magazines lying around give the feel of visiting a friend's lounge room sometime in the 1950s.

The **Southgate** complex in Southbank houses 15 cafés and restaurants and a busy **Food Wharf** where you can buy a glass of wine at one bar, a main dish from elsewhere and sit yourself almost anywhere in the huge downstairs dining area. Stalls run from Thai to Sushi to vegetarian and juice bars, with a couple of good Italian delis thrown in. Needless to say the atmosphere is upbeat and busy, day or night, seven days a week.

NIGHTLIFE

The Victoria Visitor Information Centre put out a helpful *State of the Arts* leaflet listing higher-profile Melbourne music, dance and theater events, but the best all-round source of information is Friday's *EG* (Entertainment Guide) section of *The Age* newspaper. The *EG* is also on the web at WEB SITE www.theage.com.au. The *Hit* section of Thursday's *Herald-Sun* newspaper is useful too.

All-nighters are the rage in Melbourne, with most clubs offering Sunday "recovery parties" — basically an excuse to party on right through the weekend. New venues seem to pop up regularly, offering entertainment at all hours, every day of the week. For gig listings and venues check out the free papers *Beat* and *In Press* magazine, found in cafés, bars and pubs throughout the inner city. *Beat*'s WEB SITE is at www.beat.com.au.

Bars, Clubs and Pubs

Lounge ((07) 9663 2916, first floor, 243 Swanston Street, City, is a bar, club and café that, since opening in 1990, has consistently showcased some of the most diverse acts and artists around to establish itself as one of the most alternative venues in Melbourne. Today it draws more of a techno-crowd, but as Lounge seems to stay in the fore-front of what's happening, who knows what interesting shift next month will bring. Lounge is open from 10 AM until late seven days a week. Gin is the thing at the **Gin Palace** ((03) 9654 0533, 90 Little Collins Street, City, a bar-club where people go to be seen in a setting suggestive of Melbourne's golden years. If you're up for a night on the town this is as good a place as any to get started. **Spleen Central** ((03) 9650 2400, 41 Bourke Street, City, is a hip four-roomed bar in the heart of busy Bourke Street. The often crowded entrance has comfortable stools and designer lamps, while the back room is dimmer with simple wooden chairs and tables. In between is a small stage where, on weekends, jazz players perform. Go upstairs for a more intimate atmosphere.

The **Velour Bar** ((03) 9663 5589, 121 Flinders Lane, City, with its mirror balls, fluorescent walls, loud music, and dancing is really more of a night-club than a bar. A no-queue, no-entry-charge policy and subtle security make it more welcoming than some of the other clubs, though. Open early evening until late, seven nights a week. **Tony Starr's Kitten Club** ((03) 9650 2448, Level 1, 267 Little Collins Street, City, is another friendly nightclub with innovative food, great cocktails and live music. With weathered floorboards and a huge semicircular window looking out across to Parliament House, the **Melbourne Supper Club** ((03) 9654 6300, 161 Spring Street, City, is a wonderful long, narrow room full of battered leather arm-chairs and couches with their stuffing poking out. This is a good place to wind up the night and at-tracts a slightly older arty crowd. The well-stocked bar has a great selection of digestives, ports and Cuban cigars — the special ventilation makes it bearable — and simple but tasty snacks. Open seven days to 5 AM.

The **Night Cat** ((03) 9417 0090, at 41 Johnston Street, Fitzroy, offers live entertainment four nights a week and features a mixture of acid-jazz through to retro outfits. This spacious haven for the young and trendy has two bars, decorated in 1950s kitsch, and a large dance floor. The **Perseverance Hotel** ((03) 9417 2844, 196 Brunswick Street, Fitzroy, has live music, a bistro, and a bar serving Guinness on tap and a large selection of Australian and New Zealand wines, while the **Punter's Club** ((03) 9417 3006, 376 Brunswick Street, Fitzroy, is a fix-ture for the alternative crowd who come to see

The Esplanade Hotel in St. Kilda, Melbourne's most popular bayside pub.

anything from art auctions to roof-raising rock. The quieter front bar is a good place to relax over a game of billiards with the locals.

The **Victorian Cigar Room** ((03) 9827 3135, in the Como Centre, 299 Toorak Road, South Yarra, is open Monday to Saturday and stocks cigars from around the world. **Chasers Nightclub** ((03) 9827 6615, 386 Chapel Street, South Yarra, is one of the oldest nightclubs in Melbourne and still packs them in most nights. Open late seven nights a week, until 7 AM Friday to Sunday. Down the road, **Revolver Nightclub** ((03) 9521 5985, 229 Chapel Street, Prahran, combines a live performance area and a large, relaxed lounge filled with tatty old sofas where the laid-back cool hang out and play chess and billiards. Local and international DJ's and artists present predominantly electronic-based grooves seven days a week. Open from noon on weekdays, serving light snacks and Thai meals, on weekends it's 24-hour action with breakfast served from 5 AM. Just off Chapel, the **Continental Café** ((03) 9510 2788, 132 Greville Street, Prahran, displays art exhibitions in the café, has DJs in the cocktail bar and showcases local and international musicians and the occasional comedy act in the upstairs club.

A St. Kilda institution, the **Esplanade Hotel** ((03) 9534 0211, upper Esplanade, St. Kilda, is a perfect place to watch glorious sunsets from the huge bay window of the front bar and to eat an inexpensive pub meal. After sunset, local and international bands fire up and it's standing room only. Out back, the Gershwin Room has become synonymous with stand-up comedy. Grungy and in need of repair the Espy may be, but that's the way everyone likes it.

Of the many gay bars in Melbourne that are loads of fun, one longstanding venue is the **Sir Robert Peel** ((03) 9419 4762, Peel Street, Collingwood, known for late-night dancing and drinking and relaxing Sunday cocktail nights. The **Xchange Hotel** ((03) 9867 5144, 119 Commercial Road, South Yarra, has wild drag shows five nights a week, where almost anything goes. All performances are free and begin at 10:30 PM. Melbourne's newest dance and drag venue, **Priscillas Nightclub** ((03) 9629 8505, 14 King Street, City, puts on drag talent nights Friday and Sunday, followed by recovery on Saturday and Sunday mornings. A good web site for what's happening within the gay community in Australia is the **Australian Gay Venue Guide** at www.oz.dreadedned.com.au.

Theater and the Arts

The **Victorian Arts Center** ((03) 9281 8000 WEB SITE www.artscenter.net.au, 100 St. Kilda Road, City, a modern complex dominated by its metal spire, includes theaters, a museum and arty gift stores. It is the home to the Australian Ballet, Opera Australia, the Melbourne Symphony and the Melbourne Theatre Company. The National Gallery of Victoria is normally here too, although it was closed for redevelopment at the time of writing, its collection temporarily housed in the old National Gallery in Russell Street, City (see WHAT TO SEE AND DO, above).

The downstairs theater at the **Athenaeum** ((03) 9650 1500, 188 Collins Street, City, presents a selection of work from popular performances by the Bell Shakespeare Company to high-caliber comedy during the hugely popular Melbourne Comedy Festival (see FESTIVAL FLINGS, page 46 in YOUR CHOICE). The smaller upstairs theater shows a selection of more independent and alternative works from dance performance to progressive theater. Dame Nellie Melba sang her first full-scale opera at **Her Majesty's Theatre** ((03) 9663 3211, 219 Exhibition Street, City. Opera, ballet, musical comedy, pantomime, and cinema have all been shown here. These days it's a wonderful venue to see lavish musicals in a fabulously ornate old theater.

In 1929 Sidney Myer instituted free concerts by the Melbourne Symphony Orchestra in Melbourne's Royal Botanic Gardens. The **Sidney Myer Music Bowl** ((03) 9281 8360, 21 Linlithgow Avenue, in the Kings Domain, next to the Botanic Gardens, is a venue for music of all types and special festive occasions. The Melbourne Symphony Orchestra continues to hold free concerts here throughout summer.

La Mama ((03) 9347 6142, 205 Faraday Street, Fitzroy, showcases plays by new writers, as well as poetry and play readings. **Theatreworks** ((03) 9534 4879, 14 Acland Street, St. Kilda, puts on ground-breaking new Australian plays, such as the novel *Storming St. Kilda By Tram*, performed entirely on a tram in transit.

HOW TO GET THERE

Most international airlines that fly into Australia have direct flights into **Melbourne's Tullamarine Airport** ((03) 9297 1600, although a few smaller carriers will pass by Sydney first, which adds another hour to the flight to Melbourne. Ansett and Qantas have flights between Melbourne and all major Australian cities.

V/Line (132 232 WEB SITE www.vline.vic.gov.au operate trains and buses from Melbourne to Adelaide and Sydney and to country Victoria. All long-distance trains leave from Spencer Street Station. Buses leave from outside the station. A few other bus companies also use this coach terminal. McCafferty's has a large number of services to destinations as far-flung as Cairns and Perth, and **Firefly** ((03) 9670 7500 runs regular coaches to Adelaide and Sydney.

By car, the trip from Sydney takes about 12 hours; allow 10 hours from Adelaide.

AROUND MELBOURNE

THE DANDENONG RANGES

Melbournians love to take the family for a drive to
the Dandenong Ranges. In summer cool temperate
rainforest, deep gullies, sassafras trees and kangaroo ferns provide respite from the city heat. In winter mist creates an enchanted forest. The lookouts
provide expansive views of Melbourne and the Yarra
Valley. European trees have been introduced to the
hamlets and villages of these hills and provide colorful displays in autumn. Laughing kookaburras,
gangs of crimson rosellas and mobs of sulphur-
crested cockatoos thrive in the diverse ecosystems.
Most of the area's native animals — owls, possums,
bats and gliders — are nocturnal. In daylight hours,
however, you could come across an echidna or
wombat scratching along the forest floor.

General Information

At the foot of the Dandenongs is the entrance to
**Ferntree Gully National Park and Dandenong
Ranges Tourist Information Service** ((03) 9758
7522, 1242 Burwood Highway, Upper Ferntree
Gully, which provides walking maps of the area
free of charge, and a wealth of useful information.
Open from 9 AM to 4:30 PM daily.

What to See and Do

Before white settlers established themselves in the
Dandenongs, this was an important area for the
Yarra Yarra tribe. Monbulk, from the Aboriginal
word *monbolloc*, meaning "hiding place in the hills,"
was reputed to contain healing springs.

In 1935, sculptor William Ricketts retired here
to live as a hermit and shape native animals and
Aboriginal figures from clay. In 1964, the Victorian Government acquired Ricketts' superb property and opened it to the enjoyment of the general
public. **William Ricketts Sanctuary** ((03) 9751
1300, 92 Mount Dandenong Tourist Highway, just
past Kalorama, is an enchanted place where sculptures have been molded into rocks or set into fern-
lined nooks and grottos where water trickles over
carved possums and kangaroos.

Tearooms are part of the Dandenongs experiences. Just outside Sassafrass, **Henry the Eighth
Tearoom** ((03) 9755 1008 has open fires in winter, and in town is **Miss Marple's Tearoom** ((03)
9755 1610, with a quaint English interior. Both
specialize in Devonshire teas, served with scones,
fresh cream and jam, an indulgence that can only
be justified after a brisk walk in the nearby
Sherbrooke Forest Reserve. The very lucky may
see a shy, flightless lyrebird in the forest's shady
glades. The male lyrebird displays its large tail —
resembling a lyre — during the mating dance.
Sherbrooke Falls are an easy two-and-a-half-

kilometers (one-and-a-half-mile) walk from the
Sherbrooke Picnic Grounds.

In spring the **National Rhododendron Gardens**
off Falls Road near Olinda, come to life in a vivid
display of 15,000 rhododendrons and 12,000 aza-
leas against a backdrop of countless daffodils.

Starting at Belgrave, the narrow-gauge steam
railway **Puffing Billy** ((03) 9754 6800 WEB SITE
www.pbr.organization.au runs 13 km (eight miles)
to **Emerald Lake Park** through beautiful fern
glades, over ancient wooden bridges and across
farmland. The line closed in 1954, but was restored
by steam enthusiasts. They also offer lunch and
dinner "journeys" in red-curtained carriages.

There are many tracks designated for **mountain bikes** and over 300 km (186 miles) of **walking tracks** meandering though the hills parks. Most
walks start from the picnic grounds.

How to Get There

The park is 35 km (22 miles) east of Melbourne.
Driving. Take the Burwood Highway to Upper
Ferntree Gully, then follow the Mount Dandenong
Tourist Drive. Trains leave Flinders Street for
Belgrave Station every hour or so, where the train
connects with buses to all the main attractions.

HEALESVILLE SANCTUARY

Healesville Wildlife Sanctuary ((03) 5962 4022 is
one of the best places in Australia to view native
wildlife in simulated natural enclosures. About
200 species, many of them rare or endangered, live
in a 30-ha (77-acre) bush habitat.

Displays include walk-through aviaries, wetlands, a billabong, a flying fox enclosure, Tasmanian devils, snakes and an exciting birds of prey
demonstration. Healesville is 65 km (40 miles)
northeast of Melbourne along State Route 34, the
Maroondah Highway. Open 9 AM to 5 PM daily,
admission $13 for adults and $7 for children.

MORNINGTON PENINSULA

The Mornington Peninsula — the neck of land that
makes up the eastern side of Port Phillip Bay —
combines calm bay waters on the "front beaches"
with good surf and rugged coastline walks on the
"back beaches," making it a very popular vacation destination in the summer months and ideal
for day-trips all year round. The area has some
reputable wineries, many open to the public, and
a well-preserved national park. Activities include
horse riding along the beach, sailing, swimming
with dolphins, coastal walks, and fine golfing.

General Information

The **Greater Peninsula Visitor Information Center**
((03) 5987 3078 FAX (03) 5987 3726, Point Nepean
Road, Dromana, provides information and booking

services for Mornington Peninsula and Port Phillip Bay activities. **Mornington Peninsula Tourism Inc.** have a WEB SITE at www.travelbook.com.au. During summer and Easter vacations, book well ahead for accommodation anywhere on the peninsula.

What to See and Do

The best wineries are found at the start of the peninsula, in Dromana. With its generally cool climate and fertile soils, exceptional Pinot Noir and Chardonnay are produced here. Two particularly good wineries are the **Dromana Estate** ((03) 5987 3800, Harrisons Road, open 11 AM to 4 PM, which serves lunch daily, and **Hickinbotham of Dromana** ((03) 5981 0355, 194 Nepean Highway, third-gen-

for Queenscliff every two hours from 8 AM to 8 PM daily (6 PM in winter). This is an ideal alternative for getting to the Bellarine Peninsula and the west coast (see page 157). Based in Sorrento, **Rip Charters** ((03) 5984 3664 takes fishing trips around Port Phillip Bay and Bass Strait and organizes snorkeling adventures with the bay's dolphins and seals. **Polperro Dolphin Swims** ((03) 5988 8437 also organizes dolphin encounters.

At the end of the highway, **Portsea**, a resort popular with Melbourne's well-to-do, has some impressive vacation mansions in prime ocean-watching locations. The deepwater front beaches support excellent diving while the back beaches' pounding surf never stops. Widely regarded as the

eration winemakers who make some interesting blends and spark up a wonderful open fire in winter. From Dromana take the scenic drive 305 m (1,000 ft) up to **Arthurs Seat** (a chairlift operates daily between September and mid-June) for great bay views. There are picnic facilities here, as well as the excellent Arthurs Peak Restaurant and Bistro (see WHERE TO STAY AND EAT, below). Terry and Bev who run **Gunnamatta Trail Rides** ((03) 5988 6755, TOLL-FREE (1800) 801 003, Truemans Road, Rye, have outstanding horses and organize beach rides and winery tours on horseback.

Sorrento is the site of Victoria's hasty first settlement in 1803, which survived only six months. The early settlers' graves and a memorial can be found on the picturesque cliff-top overlooking **Sullivan's Bay**. Today Sorrento is dotted with vacation homes, cafés and historical blue-stone hotels. A **car and passenger ferry** ((03) 5258 3244 departs Sorrento

most well-manicured course on the peninsula, the **Portsea Golf Course** ((03) 5984 2909 is a short course by today's standards, but tight fairways and thick trees require pinpoint placement.

The **Mornington Peninsula National Park** has some splendid walks. **Point Nepean** was off limits for 100 years, but is now open and the best place to view the turbulent entrance to the Port Phillip Bay. Within the park the weather-beaten **London Bridge** rock formation on the Portsea back beach and surrounding coast is well worth a look. The 30-km (19-mile) **coastal walk** begins here — it is best done in stages — and ends at the **Cape Schanck Lighthouse** ((03) 5568 6411, built in 1859. There is a museum here, and the lighthouse keeper's residence has been converted to accommodate guests and is moderately priced. Take a handy supply of spare balls to the **Cape Schanck Golf Course** ((03) 5950 8100, 150 Boneo Road,

WHAT TO SEE AND DO

situated along the ocean (with great views) and open to the elements. The strong variable winds carry many a ball into the sea.

Where to Stay and Eat

The **Portsea Hotel (** (03) 5984 2213, Point Nepean Road, right on the beach, serves great meals and has comfortable accommodation at inexpensive to moderate rates.

Arthurs Peak Restaurant and Bistro ((03) 5981 4444, Scenic Drive, Dromana, has the best vantage points on the peninsula. The cuisine is predominantly French, incorporating the best of local produce and featuring peninsula wines. One of the newest restaurants in Sorrento, **Opus (** (03) 5984 1770, 145 Hotham Road, is also proving to be one of the peninsula's best. Local produce meets modern cuisine. The homemade gnocchi is particularly good. Dinner for two can easily creep into the expensive range and bookings are definitely recommended. Along the foreshore the **Sorrento**, the **Continental** and the **Koonya** were all built in the 1870s and serve pub meals at reasonable prices.

The **Castle Restaurant (** (03) 5984 4000, Point Nepean Road, combines modern European and traditional Asian to produce some adventurous meals, such as steamed sand-crab custard on sweet pork. It is expensive, but really very good.

PHILLIP ISLAND

Phillip Island has long been a favorite summer vacation destination for Melbournians for its fine surf beaches and decent rock fishing. It has a koala conservation center and a large permanent fur seal colony. Its nightly parade of little penguins has international renown.

GENERAL INFORMATION

Open daily the **Phillip Island Tourist Information Center (** (03) 5956 7447, Newhaven, provides visitors with maps of the island, takes reservations for the penguin parade and can offer accommodation suggestions.

WHAT TO SEE AND DO

Every evening at dusk, little penguins (also known as fairy penguins) make their way across **Summerland Beach** to burrows found further up the shore. These days hundreds of tourists watch from terraces built along the foreshore. Penguin numbers vary from just handful to a few hundred in the cooler months.

The island's endangered koala population has been given a safe haven at the **Koala Conservation Center**, where visitors can see these lazy characters at eye level from raised platforms. The new **Seal Rocks Sea Life Center (** (03) 5952 9333 at the

Knobbies allows a close-up view of Australia's largest fur seal colony. Live, remote-controlled footage is transmitted from the seals' habitat one and a half kilometers (one mile) away and viewed in a comfortable theater.

Just to the south of Newhaven is the **Cape Woolamai State Fauna Reserve**, which has good walking tracks and is an important nesting ground for mutton birds. Try not to disturb them: migratory travel has carried these birds up to 30,000 km (19,000 miles) in a round-trip voyage to and from the northern hemisphere.

HOW TO GET THERE

Phillip Island is a pleasant 140 km (87 miles) drive from Melbourne. By car, take the South Eastern Arterial (M1) from Melbourne and follow signs to Cranbourne where Phillip Island signposts begin. The South Gippsland Highway (M420) links up with the Bass Highway (A420), which continues to San Remo and then across the bridge onto Phillip Island.

WILSONS PROMONTORY

At the southernmost tip of the Australian mainland, Wilsons Promontory is Victoria's largest and most popular national park. More than 80 km (50 miles) of walking tracks — some short, some overnight — offer open heaths, salt marshes, long drifts of sand dunes, tree-ferned valleys and forested slopes. The "prom" has it all.

GENERAL INFORMATION

Parks Victoria (131 963 WEB SITE www.parks.vic .gov.au manages Wilsons Promontory. Their office at Tidal River (** (03) 5680 9555 TOLL-FREE (1800) 350 552 opens daily and has excellent displays on the prom and its flora and fauna, along with detailed walking guides. Accommodation consists of cabins, huts and lodges at prices to suit most budgets. Camping is permitted at Tidal River and remote locations on overnight walks (permits required). Wilsons Promontory is extremely popular all year round so book well ahead.

WHAT TO SEE AND DO

A wealth of birds and wildlife inhabits the park. Laughing kookaburras, multi-colored lorikeets and rosellas are common while emus, kangaroos and wallabies roam unperturbed by people. At night, with a good flashlight, wombats, possums and the smaller bush creatures can be spotted.

Favorite short walks include the one-kilometer (half-mile) **Leo-Errn Track** and the five-kilometer

A baby possum found in Wilsons Promontory National Park is fed on nuts and fruit blossoms.

(three-mile) **Lilly Pilly Gully Trail**. The Lilly Pilly Gully Trail is particularly interesting, passing through typical bush where koalas are easily spotted and through lush rainforest with spectacular old tree ferns. Overnight walks include **Sealers Cove** and **Waterloo Bay** on the east coast and the **Lighthouse Track**, 38 km (24 miles) to the south, which ends at a lighthouse constructed in 1859. Accommodation in the lighthouse is sometimes possible; ask. On this track you could also veer slightly at **Roaring Meg** and continue to **South Point**, the southernmost point of the Australian mainland. The two-hour walk to **Mount Oberon Summit** at 558 m (1,830 ft) rewards with superb views of the western coast.

rainforest, woodland, ocean beaches, rocky promontories, inlets and coves. Several rare species of wildlife inhabit the park, including the smoky mouse and the ground parrot. The park's rivers support a wide variety of native fish, reptiles and amphibians. Colorful displays of wildflowers such as boronia, banksia and Victoria's floral emblem, common heath, flourish throughout the year, encouraging unusual varieties of butterflies and other invertebrates.

Southern right and humpback whales pass by here in autumn and spring, with dolphins and seals around throughout the year. A series of tracks in the park and the adjoining state forest are suitable for mountain bike touring or four-wheel-drive

Norman Bay, on the east coast near Tidal River, has safe swimming, windsurfing, beginner surfing and boat launching. **Picnic Bay** and **Squeaky Beach** are great for snorkeling, and you can surf and fish off nearby **Whisky Bay**.

HOW TO GET THERE

The park is 200 km (124 miles) southeast of Melbourne. Take the South Gippsland Highway (B440), turning south at Meeniyan and again at Fish Creek or Foster. The route is well signposted.

CROAJINGOLONG NATIONAL PARK

Croajingolong National Park stretches over 100 km (62 miles) from Cape Conran to the New South Wales border and contains virtually undisturbed

vehicles. Check ahead for road conditions and seasonal closures.

GENERAL INFORMATION

For campsite bookings, road and weather conditions and all general inquiries contact the **Parks Victoria Information Line ℂ** 131 963 WEB SITE www .parks.vic.gov.au.

WHAT TO SEE AND DO

To reach **Thurra River**, take the Tamboon Road from Cann River and turn off at the Point Hicks Road. Along the river, you will find some great camping spots with basic amenities, good fishing and several easy nature walks. Close by is **Point Hicks Light Station**. The point was named after Lieutenant Hicks of Captain Cook's *Endeavour*, the first to sight the new land. It is possible to stay in the light station if you reserve well in advance. For inquiries call ((03) 5158 4268.

Further east, West Wingam Road will take you to wonderfully secluded **Wingam Inlet** on the edge of the **Sandpatch Wilderness Area**. You'll have to rough it here, since there are only basic camping facilities, but the isolation and serenity of this spot are worth it.

The turnoff south from Genoa leads onto **Mallacoota** and its placid lakes, a popular sailing destination, well known for excellent inland fishing. The **Mallacoota Accommodation Hotline** ((03) 5158 0654 E-MAIL fegwa@mallacoota.org can provide a list of accommodation options.

Close to the New South Wales border is **Gabo Island**, an isolated reserve 10 km (six miles) off the coast. A lighthouse keeper and his family live out here, but the other two houses — originally there were three full-time keepers stationed on the island — accommodate guests. Gabo has the largest colony of little penguins in the world, and in spring whales are often spotted playing with their calves near the island. Call ((03) 5158 0219 to reserve a house and for details on getting across from the mainland.

HOW TO GET THERE

The park commences about 450 km (280 miles) east of Melbourne along the Princes Highway (A1). Access is via a number of unsealed roads starting from the highway between Cann River and the New South Wales border, or from Mallacoota.

BELLARINE PENINSULA

At the tip of the Bellarine Peninsula, and today only a 90-minute drive from the heart of Melbourne city, **Queenscliff** has been a well-established holiday resort since before 1900. Back then visitors arrived by steamship from Melbourne. Numerous towns and vacation resorts now dot the coast, with Geelong the nearest city (25 km / 16 miles to the northwest of the peninsula).

Connected to the mainland by an isthmus called "The Narrows" at the entrance to Port Phillip Bay, Queenscliff is a perfect town to stroll around, with grand Victorian buildings, cottages, museums, surf beaches, bay beaches, art galleries and craft and antique shops offering plenty of distractions. The army once used Queenscliff as a sentry post to guard the bay; **Fort Queenscliff** ((03) 5258 0730, King Street, was built in 1882 in response to fears of Russian invasion following the Crimean War. Its **Black Lighthouse** is one of only three in the world this color. Guided tours of the fort leave at 1:30 PM weekdays, and at 1 PM and 3 PM weekends ($6 adults, $3 children). The **Marine Discovery Center** ((03) 5258 3344, Weeroona Parade, a non-profit educational facility, promotes awareness of southern Australia's marine environment.

Ocean Grove, approximately 25 km (16 miles) from Geelong, and **Barwon Heads**, situated at the mouth of the Barwon River are two popular beach resorts on the Bellarine Peninsula. Both have large patrolled safe swimming areas in summer and good sand breaks for surfing.

One of Australia's best known small restaurant-hotels, **Mietta's Queenscliff Hotel** ((03) 5258 1066 WEB SITE www.miettas.com.au, 16 Gellibrand Street, has been wooing its guests with Old World accommodation and superb dining for many years now. Within the hotel, built in 1887, are two bars, two dining rooms, three sitting rooms, three gardens and verandas upstairs and downstairs. Although chef and doyenne of all things culinary Mietta O'Donnell was tragically killed in a car accident in January 2001, the restaurant continues to serve exceptional food. Dining here is a wonderful experience (expensive to very expensive), and it is well worth inquiring about their accommodation/dining packages.

The **Queenscliff–Sorrento ferry** ((03) 5258 3244 is an excellent means of avoiding driving through Geelong and along the underinspiring Melbourne–Geelong Highway. The first 40-minute voyage leaves Queenscliff at 7 AM daily, then every odd hour until 7 PM (5 PM in summer), the return journey leaving Sorrento every even hour from 8 AM to 8 PM (6 PM in summer). Cars $38, $7 foot passengers, $9 with a bike.

Croajingolong National Park features long stretches of soft sandy beaches, often without a footprint.

THE GREAT OCEAN ROAD

Most of the formidable Great Ocean Road can be driven in a day, but to fully appreciate all this spectacular coast has to offer you'll need at least two or three days. Along the way you are bound to want to stop regularly to take in the breathtaking coast and country vistas, to explore the unique abundance of flora and fauna and to simply relax in the many laid-back towns.

TORQUAY TO LORNE

The Great Ocean Road driving adventure begins at the sleepy surf town of Torquay — the perfect spot to rent a board or take a lesson. **Surfcoast Plaza** houses cheap cafés and a string of shops selling surfwear, boards, good quality beachwear and watersports accessories. The **Surfworld Museum** here is one-of-a-kind, and open daily.

Surfers are spoilt here with a cluster of excellent breaks facing different angles: as long as there's an offshore breeze of some kind, and there almost always is, there'll be some waves. Ask a local which one to head for. A good beginners' surf school, **Go Ride a Wave** ((03) 5263 2111 gives informative two-hour lessons to get you on your feet. You can catch the pros at it every January, when the world surfing championships take place at nearby **Bells Beach**.

From Torquay the road begins its steep and winding path through Anglesea and Aireys Inlet on to Lorne, which is probably best known for the **Angahook-Lorne State Park**, a cool and temperate forest of blue gum, mountain ash, messmate and mountain gum. Rewarding walking tracks often end at falls and cascades that pour into refreshing rock pools. Of the park's excellent camping grounds, my favorite at **Kennett River** ((03) 5289 0272, just off the main road next to the river. If it is too early in the trip to stop for the night, then stop for a picnic at **Erskine Falls**. Lorne is also the best place on the coast to buy beach clothing and surfing accessories thanks to its several nearby factory outlets, with retail stores within the shopping complex. Anglers are often spotted along this stretch of coast.

Lorne Tourist Information Center ((03) 5289 1152 FAX (03) 5289 2492 is at 144 Mountjoy Parade.

Where to Stay and Eat

In Torquay, moderately priced, comfortable rooms can be found at the **Surf City Motel** ((03) 5261 3492 FAX (03) 5261 4032, 35 The Esplanade.

The large unavoidable complex in Lorne, the **Cumberland Resort** ((03) 5289 2400 FAX (03) 5289 2256 WEB SITE www.cumberland.com.au, has one- and two-bedroom suites all with a spa and a balcony overlooking the sea. The accommodation is in the expensive category, but some of their

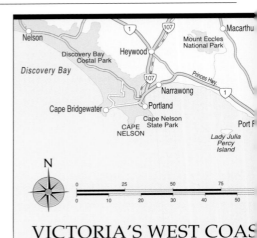

VICTORIA'S WEST COAS

package deals offer moderate prices. A restored 1930s-style guest house, **Erskine House B&B** ((03) 5289 1209 WEB SITE www.erskinehouse.com.au has moderately priced rooms and wonderful Old World extras on offer such as tennis, croquet and bowls. Opposite the pier, the **Grand Pacific Hotel** ((03) 5289 1609 has inexpensive, very basic rooms; the wonderful waterfront views and low price make up for the slight shabbiness.

The Mediterranean influenced **Marine Café** ((03) 5289 1808, 6A Mountjoy Parade, is the best place to eat the freshest and most interesting seafood in Lorne. The fettuccine marinara is generous, the calamari tender, and the lamb souvlaki authentic. Prices are in the moderate range and especially reasonable as you can BYO (bring your own bottle).

For hearty, inexpensive cooked breakfasts, try **Kafe Kaos**, 50 Mountjoy Parade, which also makes gourmet sandwiches and vegetarian burgers. A Lorne institution with surfers since the 1950s, the **Arab**, 94 Mountjoy Parade, serves filling and inexpensive breakfast, lunch and dinner.

APOLLO BAY AND THE OTWAYS

The next leg of the drive twists even more and takes you past **Wye River** to the fishing village of **Apollo Bay**, with its majestic back-drop of the **Otway Ranges**. Between the picture-postcard bay with colorful fishing boats and the scenic drives through the rainforest, Apollo Bay rates as my favorite spot on this coast. The town offers ample choice of fishing charters and tours and some of the best accommodation and eating options on the coast. Call Mark at **Apollo Bay Boat Charters** ((03) 5237 6214 to be taken to the best fishing spots or for an informative and relaxing marine-life cruise.

Scenic **Wild Dog Road**, between Apollo Bay and Skenes Creek in the **Otway State Forest**, runs

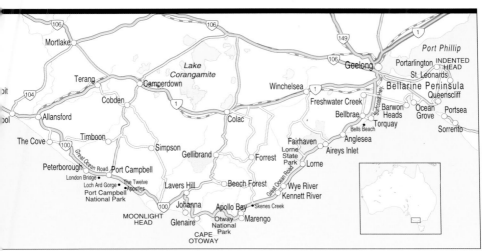

through hilly green farmland with superb views. At **Tanyburn Junction** take a left and follow the road north until you reach the sign for **Turtons Track**. Tree-ferns form an arch over the road, and numerous thoughtfully placed parking spots allow visitors to explore the dense forest. If you've come this far, definitelty take a look at the splendid **Beauchamp** and **Hopetown Falls**, one and a half kilometers (one mile) east of Beech Forest via the Aire Valley Road south.

A little further on, the **Otway National Park** teems with unique wildlife inland, while its 60-km (37-mile) stretch of rugged coastline is some of the most inaccessible in Victoria. Many lives were lost off this coast until the **Cape Otway Lighthouse** ((03) 5237 9240 WEB SITE www.lightstation.com was completed in 1848. Still functioning today, guided and self guided tours operate daily between 9 AM and 5 PM. Many other historic buildings are preserved within the precinct making this a very worthwhile detour. Old World accommodation is provided in some of the restored sandstone residences on the grounds.

The excellent **Great Ocean Road Visitor Information Center** ((03) 5237 6529 FAX (03) 5237 6194, 155 Great Ocean Road, Apollo Bay, opens 9 AM to 5 PM, seven days a week. They not only have information on food and accommodation, but provide free walking, surfing, driving and fishing guides; present displays of the rainforest vegetation and ecosystems; and have brochures on the area's geology, history and flora and fauna.

Where to Stay and Eat

Chris Talihmanidis, a renowned chef in Australia, is the most gracious host I have ever known. A trip to this coast would not be complete without dinner at **Chris's Beacon Point Restaurant and Villas** ((03) 5237 6411 FAX (03) 5237 6930, 280 Skenes Creek Road (expensive). His signature dish of

kakavia — a hearty Greek seafood soup — is unparalleled. The slow-cooked duck for two is tender, juicy, and simply perfect. The fine wine list is carefully chosen to match Chris's dishes, so don't hesitate to ask for recommendations. Five beautifully appointed villas have panoramic views down to Apollo Bay; they're also in the expensive range, but worth every cent.

High above the Great Ocean Road is one of the more romantic B&Bs that I've stayed in, **Wongarra Heights** (/FAX (03) 5237 0257 E-MAIL wangarrabb @primus.com.au, Sunnyside Road, 12 km (seven miles) east of Apollo Bay. The guesthouse dates from 1890, with an unmatched 180-degree view of this beautiful coastline: sweeping views from Cape Patton to Apollo Bay. The bedrooms are fitted with antique furniture and iron beds, the house a combination of warm wood and long verandahs. Moderate. Not so high up but still with impressive views, **Seafarers Retreat** ((03) 5237 6507 FAX (03) 5237 7061, Ocean Road, Apollo Bay, has clean and comfortable, self-contained studios and beach lodges (inexpensive) or, for a more romantic get-away, lodges higher in the hills (moderate). All the lodges have fire places and all rooms have huge bay windows.

In town, **Sea-Grape Wine Bar and Grill** ((03) 5237 6610, 141 Great Ocean Road, specializes in freshly-caught local seafood, cooked simply but perfectly. The wine list would rival most city joints, and they also have the best desserts in town. From 9 AM the Sea-Grape whips up a hearty breakfast for hungry surfers. Of the numerous cafés my favorite is friendly **Café Nauti'gals** ((03) 5236 7058, 58 Great Ocean Road. Decorated with women's swimwear from the 1940s and 1950s, they serve an interesting assortment of burgers (try Shark Attack), freshly prepared gourmet sandwiches and pies, and make the best coffee in town. They also have the only public Internet access.

PORT CAMPBELL NATIONAL PARK AND WARRNAMBOOL

The road meets the coast again at Glenaire but immediately veers north to Lavers Hill, where the **Melba Gully State Park** is a must-see. This lush green forest is filled with myrtle beeches, blackwoods and tree ferns, with a ground-cover of low ferns and mosses. Take the 35-minute **Madsens Nature Walk** from the car park to the **Big Tree**, a 300-year-old messmate, 27 m (88 ft) in circumference. At night glow-worms faintly light the trail, weaving webs to trap small insects. As it's the wettest place in the state, the park is home to huge biting mosquitoes, so don't forget the repellent.

Once back on the main road the drive stays pretty well inland until Princetown where it meets Port Campbell National Park and what is known as the **Shipwreck Coast**. Between here and Port Campbell stands an Australian landmark: the **Twelve Apostles**. Only ten of these ancient limestone stacks remain, eroded from the cliffs by the pounding seas and buffeting winds. They are best seen from viewing platforms built around the cliff tops. Sunsets here are a photographer's dream. While waiting for sunset, go on a little further to **Loch Ard Gorge** and the **Blowhole**. The gorge is the site of an 1878 maritime disaster when the *Loch Ard*, a three-masted square rigger, struck **Mutton Island**, killing all but two of the 54 people aboard. A stairway down to the beach accesses several interesting sign-posted walks.

Port Campbell itself is a small town with safe swimming and good snorkeling but not a great deal else. Most of the accommodation is budget standard and very often booked out.

It is worth driving a further 66 km (41 miles) to Warrnambool, a prettier and more historic township. In the winter months, nearby **Logans Beach** is best place to view southern right whales calving. All-season attractions include the **Flagstaff Hill Maritime Village**, which depicts life in an Australian seaport in the nineteenth century. On display is a famous earthenware peacock that was recovered several days after the *Loch Ard* disaster. The town's **botanic gardens** have remained virtually unchanged since the nineteenth century; they're well worth a look. Only a 15-minute drive northeast is **Hopkins Falls** — tumultuous in winter — while a little west off the main road is the **Tower Hill State Game Reserve**. Here you can drive around an extinct volcano. You are likely to see koalas, kangaroos, echidnas and many varieties of water birds in the reserve.

The **Warrnambool Information Center** ((03) 5561 7837 FAX (03) 5561 2133, 600 Raglan Parade, opens weekdays and school and public holidays from 9 AM to 5 PM, weekends 10 AM to 12 PM and then again from 1 PM to 4 PM

Where to Stay and Eat

For accommodation, B&B is the best option. Many offers are in beautifully restored nineteenth-century homes, with very reasonable prices. **Merton Manor** ((03) 5562 0702 WEB SITE www.ansonic .com.au/merton, 62 Ardlie Street, an 1880 Italianate villa, has six moderately priced suites superbly furnished in antiques and looking out over a landscaped rose garden. **Wollaston** (/FAX (03) 5562 2430, 84 Wollaston Road, dates back to 1854 and is located on the banks of the Merri River (moderate). Guests can choose between the homestead and the historic, self-contained, Governor's cottage.

PORT FAIRY

The Great Ocean Road ends halfway between Warrnambool and the historic fishing village of Port Fairy. Port Fairy's Old World streets are lined

with restored buildings dating from its bountiful years between the 1850s and 1880s, when whaling and rich farmland made it the second-busiest port in Australia. A short walk from town over a causeway is **Griffith Island**, home to tens of thousands of mutton birds between October and May. The 22-km (14-mile) **Mahogany Walking Track** begins at Griffith Island car park, but there are plenty of access trails along the way for shorter walks. The walk is named after the wreck of what was thought to be a Spanish vessel, spotted by sealers from the 1830s until its disappearance in the 1890s. Historians now believe it was a Portuguese wreck from the 1500s, suggesting Australia was visited 250 years before Captain Cook. The **Port Fairy Information Centre** ((03) 5568 2682 FAX (03) 5568 2515, Bank Street (open weekdays 10 AM to 4 PM and weekends 10 AM to 12:30 PM and 1:30 PM to 4 PM) can provide a map.

Talara House ((03) 5568 2575, Princes Highway, a magnificent two-story blue-stone home, circa 1856, has three B&B rooms, all with their own individual character. The four-course breakfast combines the best of local produce — it is well worth going hungry the night before. Prices are moderate to expensive. **Merrijig Inn** ((03) 5568 2324, on King George Square, is Victoria's oldest. The attractive suites (moderate) have open fireplaces; there are also slightly cheaper rooms in the attic. Room rates include breakfast. With five bright and airy rooms overlooking the yachts and fishing boats moored on the Moyne River, **Shearwater House** ((03) 5568 1081 E-MAIL shearwbb @standard.net.au, 53 Gipps Street, is another good choice in the moderate range.

A small fishing village on Victoria's West Coast, Apollo Bay nestles into the slopes at the start of the Otway Ranges.

How to Get There

There are three ways to drive to the Great Ocean Road from Melbourne. The quickest is to head out along the Princes Highway (National Route 1) over the West Gate Bridge to the bayside city of Geelong. From here, follow signs south along the Surf Coast Highway to Torquay. The Surf Coast Highway does a 90-degree turn to the right at the coast, becoming the Great Ocean Road in the process. From Warrnambool or Port Fairy, the return trip can be made via the second route: inland through Colac on the Princes Highway — about two hours faster than returning along the coast. For those with time to explore, the third option is to drive southeast from Melbourne to Sorrento and catch the ferry across to Queenscliff (see page 157 for details).

V/Line ((03) 136 196 operates a bus service from Melbourne to the Geelong railway station, connecting with a coach along the Great Ocean Road to Apollo Bay. On Mondays and Fridays in December and January the bus continues on to Port Campbell. There are three daily V/Line trains between Melbourne and Warrnambool via Geelong, with V/Line buses on to Port Fairy, Portland and Mount Gambier in South Australia.

Otway Discovery Tours ((03) 9654 5432 run day tours from Melbourne visiting most of the major attractions. Several other companies organize similar one- to three-day tours along the coast, with many returning inland via Ballarat. Tourist information offices in Melbourne have details. The **Wayward Bus** TOLL-FREE (1800) 882 823 offers a three-day one-way trip for $180, including campsite accommodation, home-cooked meals and sightseeing. The same company runs a similar six-day trip that takes in the Grampians, Ballarat and Sovereign Hill.

GOLD FIELDS

Melbourne was founded on the wealth of Victoria's gold fields, which sprang to life in the rush of 1851 around Ballarat and Bendigo. In the following decade, miners extracted 1,000 tons of gold, 40% of the world's total production for the same period.

To help the successful prospectors spend their hard earned money, townships such as Ballarat, Bendigo, Castlemaine and Maldon sprouted like toadstools, satisfying the needs of the miners with banks, stores hotels and brothels. Bars and grog shops did a bustling trade quenching parched throats everywhere. Many of the gold mining towns continued to prosper after the gold ran out, although their populations today are a fraction of what they were during the rush.

The gold fields are about two hours from Melbourne. V/Line runs regular train services from Melbourne Spencer Street Station to Bendigo and then has bus connections to the main towns.

General Information

The tourist information centers in the major towns are **Ballarat Visitor Information Center** ((03) 5332 2694, 39 Sturt Street; **Castlemaine Tourist Information Center** ((03) 5470 6200, Duke Street; **Bendigo Tourist Information Center** ((03) 5444 4445, Pall Mall Center; and **Maldon Visitor Center** ((03) 5475 2569, High Street.

BALLARAT

Ballarat, the state's largest inland metropolis with a population of 64,000, lies 112 km (70 miles) from Melbourne. It has matured from a rough tent city during the gold rush into a provincial center with pretensions to style and graciousness. Ballarat's mid to late nineteenth-century architecture keeps the National Trust busy — over 60 buildings have been classified for their historical importance.

What to See and Do

Buildings in the old part of town are decorated with the cast-iron verandah friezes and balustrades common to all British colonial architecture from Calcutta to Cape Town. Take a look in the shops at the north end of Lydiard Street for some typical examples of lacy embellishments. The lovely **Botanic Gardens** are on the shores of **Lake Wendouree**.

The **Sovereign Hill Gold Mining Township** ((03) 5331 1944, on the corner of Main Road and Bradshaw Street, recreates a gold rush township. The main drag represents the Main Street of Ballarat as it was 150 years ago. This award-winning living museum contains over 40 buildings including a forge, bakery, a post office, a confectioner, a Chinese joss house and a hotel, all operational and open for business. You can pan for gold at Red Hill Gully in the township, or explore the nearby underground mine. In the evening a sound and light show, *Blood on the Southern Cross*, relates the drama of the Eureka Stockade of 1864, a strike against police brutality and lack of miners rights. The 20-minute battle grabbed the sympathy of all Victorians and miners were awarded all their due rights. A replica of the **Eureka Stockade** "fortification" stands at the corner of Stawell and Eureka streets, and a memorial in the park is dedicated to the 30 miners and five soldiers who died during the rebellion. Entrance costs $20 adults and $10 children.

The **Gold Museum** ((03) 5337 1188, Bradshaw Street opposite the Sovereign Hill Township, houses an extensive and valuable collection of gold nuggets, alluvial deposits, gold ornaments and coins and is a good place to glimpse Ballarat's history and the struggles of early miners, desperate to strike it rich. Open 9:30 AM to 5:20 PM seven days a week.

Set in 40 ha (16 acres) of beautiful peppermint gum woodland, the **Ballarat Wildlife Park** ((03) 5333 5933, corner of Fussell and York streets, specializes in close contact with koalas, kangaroos, emus and other native animals and not so close contact with crocodiles, Tasmanian devils, goannas, giant tortoises, wedge-tailed eagles, and snakes. They have a wonderful exhibit of the delicate quokka, an irresistible small wallaby found in southwestern Australia, and displays of Australian native fish and aquatic plants. Open 9 AM to 5:30 PM everyday, admission costs $11 for adults and $5.50 for children.

For those interested in art the **Ballarat Fine Art Gallery** ((03) 5331 5622, 40 Lydiard Street North, is a must-see. This gallery's collection constitutes a significant number of Colonial and Heidelberg school paintings, Australian prints, watercolors and drawings from 1770 to the present. In addition, the gallery's collection includes medieval and Renaissance manuscripts, oriental rugs, nineteenth-century European paintings and decorative arts. A number of artworks relating to the gold fields and Ballarat are on display, such as the original Eureka flag. Open daily from 10:30 AM.

Where to Stay and Eat

For comfortable Old World accommodation **Craigs Royal Hotel** ((03) 5331 1377, 10 Lydiard Street South, built in 1867 (and a National Trust classified building), has comfortable rooms with spa bath (high end of moderate). The **Ballarat Heritage Homestay** ((03) 53 328296 FAX (03) 5331 3358 has several historical homes and cottages with the convenience of modern facilities and the ambiance of a bygone era (moderate to expensive).

Ballarat has a good selection of restaurants and cafés covering most tastes and budgets. The **Ansonia Hotel** ((03) 5332 4678, 32 Lydiard Street South, set in a classic Victorian building, is a popular and well-reputed restaurant with a seasonal menu and fine regional wines served in a relaxed atmosphere. They also have luxury suites and studio accommodation. The moderately priced **Café Pazani** ((03) 5331 7100, at 102 Sturt Street, has a varied international menu which also caters to vegetarians. Along with good alfresco dining, they make great freshly baked cakes. **Dyers Steak Stable** ((03) 5331 2850, 28 Little Bridge Street, has been serving perfectly cooked prime beef and game for 25 years. They also have some pleasing seafood starters and options for non beef eaters.

BENDIGO

North of Ballarat, Bendigo was once nicknamed Queen of the Gold Fields. The magnificent **Alexandra Fountain** stands at the crossroads at the center of town, a testament to Bendigo's former wealth. Nearby, the elegant **Shamrock Hotel**, at the intersection of Pall Mall and Williamson Street, once served hooch to the many Irish miners of Bendigo. It was said that the owner of the hotel earned himself an extra £4 each day by sweeping the floor and collecting gold dust brought in on his customers' boots. On a warm night there is still no nicer place to be than on the balcony of this fine hotel enjoying a tall cold ale. Almost across the road, on Pall Mall, the old **Post Office**, built in 1887, is now the tourist bureau. It is well worth a visit, as the interior has been lovingly restored to its former splendor.

Chinese indentured laborers also left their mark on Bendigo. The **Chinese Joss House** ((03) 5442 1685, in Finn Street, Emu Point, is a temple built in the 1860s by the lonely men of See Yup to honor their ancestors. The best way to get there is on the vintage **Talking Tram** ((03) 5443 8070, which waxes lyrical about Bendigo's history. It starts in the center of town. The tram takes visitors to the **Central Deborah Mine** ((03) 5443 8322, in Violet Street, a 422-m-deep (1,385-ft) gold mine with 17 levels, which operated in the 1940s and 1950s and is linked to shafts sunk a century earlier. Tours are conducted daily.

For a bit of luxury and a glimpse of history spend your night at the **Shamrock** ((03) 5443 0333, at the corner of Pall Mall and Williamson Street, which also serves excellent meals. For something a little more romantic and peaceful, try the moderately priced **Nanga Gnulle** (/FAX (03) 5443 7891, 40 Harley Street, which has welcoming open fires in the cooler months and a beautiful garden. Eight kilometers (five miles) out of Bendigo is one of my favorite getaways: the moderately priced **Skye Glen Llama Farm** ((03) 5439 3054, which overlooks peaceful Mandurang Valley. Scottish Ron and Heather McLeod serve hearty highland breakfasts and shortbread for afternoon tea. They've even given the llamas Scottish names.

MALDON

Gold was mined continually at Maldon from 1854 until the 1930s, and the National Trust protects much of the town's goldrush streetscape. A blacksmith restores nineteenth-century wagons at the **Blacksmith and Wainwright Shop** in High Street and a candlelit tour of **Carmans Tunnel** ((03) 5475 2656, a 570-m-long (1,870-ft) horizontal shaft two kilometers (one mile) from town off Parkin's Reef Road, runs on weekends and public holidays.

A steam train to Muckleford leaves from the **Maldon Tourist Railway** ((03) 5475 2966 at Maldon Station in Hornsby Street on weekends and during national and school holidays.

In Main Street, Maldon, **Lemonwood Cottage** ((03) 5475 2015 offers historic cottage accommodation at moderate prices.

CASTLEMAINE

The rush at Castlemaine started about a year after the first diggings at Ballarat. Today it's a leisurely country town, justifiably proud of its gardens and galleries. The **Castlemaine Art Gallery and Museum** ((03) 5472 2292, 14 Lyttleton Road, has a good collection of art dating from the late nineteenth century to the mid-twentieth. Open from 10 AM to 5 PM. In Mostyn Street the **Market Museum** ((03) 5472 2679, built in 1861, has exhibitions and audio-visual displays telling the story of the Castlemaine gold rush. Daily opening hours are from 10 AM to 5 PM. Good private galleries show contemporary arts and crafts. Try **Federation Fine Art Gallery** ((03) 5472 2025, 8 Parker Street.

The **Buda Historic Home and Garden** ((03) 5472 1032, corner of Hunter and Urquhart streets, is open for inspection daily. The house was built in 1861 and has been furnished to re-create the nineteenth-century colonial style; on display is silverware by the Hungarian silversmith Ernest Leviny, who once owned Buda.

In Castlemaine the luxury-priced **Midland Private Hotel** ((03) 5472 1085, 2 Templeton Street, retains much of its late nineteenth-century interior, while the **Coach and Rose** ((03) 5472 4850, 68 Mostyn Street, is a small and cozy moderately priced B&B.

GARIWERD NATIONAL PARK (THE GRAMPIANS)

In 1991 the Grampians, in western Victoria, officially reverted to its original Aboriginal name of Gariwerd. The range includes some of the oldest land on earth and is one of the most scenic areas in Victoria. It comprises a series of dramatic sandstone ridges with sheer waterfalls, vast lakes, 10,000-year-old Aboriginal rock art sites and plenty of unspoiled native flora and fauna. Over 1,000 km (621 miles) of walking tracks and nearly the same amount of primary and secondary roads crisscross the park, providing excellent scenic cycling, conventional vehicle touring, and four-wheel driving opportunities. Over 900 native plants species have been identified here — between August and November each year the widest variety of them are in full bloom.

General Information

Grampians Region Tourism ((03) 5358 2314 TOLL-FREE (1800) 246 880, 54 Western Highway, Stawell, has up-to-date information on activities and sights. Sporting activities, from abseiling to

The gold rush days live on at Sovereign Hill, a reconstructed mining town in Ballarat.

canoeing in Gariwerd/The Grampians National Park, can be booked at the **Center of Activities** ((03) 5356 4556 in the Stony Creek Stores Center in Halls Gap.

What to See and Do

Halls Gap is the main tourist center in Gariwerd/ The Grampians, and has caravan parks, shops, cafés, restaurants, motels and guesthouses, making it the best base. Sporting options include abseiling, horse riding, tennis, fishing, swimming and canoeing. Other places of interest are the **Wallaroo Wildlife Park** ((03) 5356 4346, Halls Gap–Ararat Main Road, and the **Brambuk Aboriginal Cultural Center** ((03) 5356 4452, Dunkeld Road (behind the visitors center), which has exhibitions, talks and traditional dances showcasing the Koori communities of southwest Australia. Inexpensive dorm accommodation, hot meals and snacks are available.

The park's geological formations include the **Balconies**, **Elephant's Hide**, and **Wonderland Forest Park**. There's an oppurtunity to meet a colony of tame kangaroos in a paddock beside the road at **Zumsteins** and the koalas that abound in the tall manna gums can usually be heard grunting in the night, as they wake up a little. Nearby the spectacular **McKenzie's Falls** plummets down in torrents all year round, with many other smaller falls visible from the McKenzie River track.

There are a dozen wineries in the area, the best known being **Seppelts Great Western** ((03) 5361 2222 where thousands of bottles of sparkling wine mature in enormous tunnels left over from gold mining days.

In the township of **Stawell** at the southern end of the ranges, the **Stawell Gift** foot race, run each Easter, draws competitors from all over the world. Just south of Stawell is **Bunjil's Shelter**, one of Victoria's most important Koorie art sites. There is great fishing and golf in **Horsham**, as well as a fine art gallery, some interesting antique shops and the old **Dooen Pub**, a good place for dinner. Horsham's **Botanic Gardens** and the nearby **Wimmera Lakes** are both pleasant places to take a break. Horsham is the nearest large town to **Mount Zero**, which is a popular spot for abseiling enthusiasts.

Where to Stay

Halls Gap offers the widest variety of accommodation in the Grampians. The **Kookaburra Lodge Motel** ((03)5356 4395 FAX (03) 5356 4490, Heath Street, has inexpensive comfortable basic rooms within walking distance of the town's amenities. A little further out of town, **Boroka Downs** ((03) 5356 6243 FAX (03) 5356 6343 WEB SITE www.grampians .org.au/boroka, Birdswing Road, has five secluded boutique residences on 754 ha (305 acres) of undulating land. The modern cottages include large

circular spa, open wood fire, hand-crafted furniture, and fully-equipped kitchen and laundry. This is possibly the most comfortable place to stay in the area (expensive).

There are more than 15 camping grounds scattered around the park, all with basic amenities, and most with fresh water. There is no booking system but the visitors center sells permits. Bush camping is permitted anywhere outside of designated camp areas.

How to Get There

The Grampians can be reached in three to four hours from Melbourne. Take the Western Highway (National Route 8) northwest to Ballarat and continue through to Ararat, where you can turn west into the park. Alternatively, continue on into Stawell then head southwest to Halls Gap.

SPA COUNTRY

An hour's drive or so from Melbourne, the spa towns of Daylesford and Hepburn Springs have been health resorts for Melbournians since the gold rush. The therapeutic spring water is said to relieve a variety of complaints. Today spa baths, aromatic oils, massage and walking tracks add to the natural attributes of these twin watering holes. Spa Country is an easy day-trip from Melbourne, but an overnight stay allows you to make the most of the area's good restaurants, and complete the rest-cure with old-fashioned pampering in one of its many guesthouses.

GENERAL INFORMATION

The **Daylesford Tourist Information Center** ((03) 5348 1339 is in Vincent Street, the main thoroughfare in Daylesford. The center is open seven days a week.

WHAT TO SEE AND DO

It takes a good leisurely hour to walk around Daylesford's two lakes, **Jubilee Lake** and **Lake Daylesford**. Numerous birds live in the surrounding parkland, including playful willy wagtails and black-fronted dotterels. The **Boathouse Café** ((03) 5348 1387 rents boats and canoes. If the weather lets you down drop into the **Bookbarn** next to Lake Daylesford. Owner Kerry Bolton invites browsers to sit around the potbellied stove and dip into any books they are considering purchasing.

A Catholic convent imaginatively converted to a restaurant–gallery, the **Convent Gallery** ((03) 5348 3211, 7 Daly Street, on Wombat Hill, Daylesford, exhibits pottery, paintings and jewelry from over 600 artists. The Mediterranean-style restaurant is an attractive place for lunch and looks out into the gallery's beautiful gardens.

WHERE TO STAY AND EAT

The most stylish place in Daylesford is **Lake House** ((03) 5348 3329, King Street, where reservations are essential (expensive). Lake House also offers accommodation overlooking Lake Daylesford, at moderate to expensive rates; package deals bring the cost down a bit. For an inexpensive meal try **Sweet Decadence** ((03) 5348 3202, 57 Vincent Street, named after the chocolate made on the premises. In Hepburn Springs, **Cosy Corner Café** ((03) 5348 3825, Tenth Street, has a friendly ambiance and an open fire in winter.

Old style luxury accommodation is available in Hepburn Springs at the **Linton House** ((03) 5348 2331, 68 Central Springs Road, while the comfortable **Dudley House** ((03) 5348 3033, 101 Main Road, is moderately priced. For inexpensive accommodation, the slightly rundown but welcoming **Continental Guesthouse** ((03) 5348 2005, 9 Pine Avenue, Hepburn Springs has doubles for $50 and dorm beds for around $20. The Continental runs a vegan café on Saturday only.

HOW TO GET THERE

Daylesford is 109 km (68 miles) northwest of Melbourne, off the Midland Highway. Hepburn Springs is a further four kilometers (two and a half miles) north. V/Line has a train to Woodend, where a bus connects to Daylesford.

MURRAY RIVER PORTS

Over a century ago, before railways and paved roads, the Murray formed an essential trading artery for the entire southeast part of the continent. Hundreds of riverboats plied its 2,590-km (1,610-mile) length. The Murray forms most of the border between Victoria and New South Wales, and continues into South Australia to Encounter Bay. Today, the Snowy Mountain scheme manipulates the level of the Murray's waters to provide hydroelectric power and irrigation for southeastern Australia, greatly reducing its size along the South Australian section. The three states debate heavily over the sharing of the river.

One of the best web sites in Australia is the Murray River site at **www.murray-river.net**, which contains everything you could possibly want to know on the region.

SWAN HILL

In the nineteenth century, Swan Hill served as a great river port. The **Pioneer Settlement** ((03) 5032 1093 at Horseshoe Bend recreates a riverside port town, centering on the *Gem*, which in its day was the biggest and most powerful paddle-steamer on

the river. Nowadays the *Gem* is a floating restaurant, which serves juicy local yabbie, witchetty grubs and kangaroo tail soup. Around the settlement, bakers dressed in period costume slide damper from wood ovens, printers compose type, blacksmiths forge iron, and confectioners make authentic boiled sweets. Old-time stores line the streets of Swan Hill.

The **Swan Hill Regional Art Gallery** opposite the settlement has some interesting exhibitions and the **Manatunga Aboriginal Artefacts Shop** ((03) 5026 4799, George Street in nearby Robinvale, sells some of the better souvenirs available.

Two large homesteads open to the public, border either side of the Murray: the **Murray Downs** and **Tyntyndyer**. They highlight home life in the early 1800s with furnishings and other implements spanning back about 130 years. The Tyntyndyer homestead is reputed to be the first brick veneer home built in Australia.

The **Swan Hill Regional Tourist Information Center** ((03) 5032 3033, 306 Campbell Street, is open daily.

Where to Stay and Eat

In Swan Hill, two good motels in the moderate price range are the **Swan Hill Motor Inn** ((03) 5032 2728, 405 Campbell Street, and **Paruna Motel** ((03) 5032 4455 TOLL-FREE (1800) 810 445, at 386 Campbell Street, both with swimming pool. Those interested in renting a houseboat in Swan Hill should contact **Kookaburra Houseboats** ((03) 5032 0003 E-MAIL kookabur@swanhill.net.au.

Carriages ((03) 5032 2017, 421 Campbell Street, Swan Hill, at the Pioneer Motor Inn has a good varied menu, while **Silver Slipper** ((03) 5032 2726, at the Swan Hill Motor Inn, specializes in fresh river fish. Both are moderately priced.

MILDURA

Mildura, the river's garden city and center of the Sunraysia fruit-growing district, lies another 250 km (155 miles) downstream. Sunny mild winters and picturesque locations on the banks of the Murray make Mildura a pleasant oasis in the dry region. For water enthusiasts, the Murray and Darling rivers support canoeing, water skiing and safe swimming. There are lots of shady spots for those who prefer to just go fishing.

Mildura Arts Center, 199 Cureton Avenue, houses a colonial museum and an art gallery. Ask at the **Mildura Alfred Deakin Visitor Information Center** ((03) 5021 4424, 180–190 Deakin Avenue, for a walking tour brochure. Trail sights include the **Psyche Pump Station** designed by George Chaffey and operated from 1891 to 1959; **Old Mildura Homestead**, a reconstruction of the first home built in Mildura; and the **Mildura weir and lock**.

There are a number of wineries in the area including **Lindemans**, established in 1843, **Mildura Vineyards** and **Deakin Estate**. All have cellar door sales. The irrigated vines of this region produce vast quantities of well-made, fruity, ready-to-drink wines that represent great value for money.

Mildura has two **paddle-boats**: the steam-driven PS *Melbourne* runs daily two hour cruises, and the PV *Rothbury* makes day-trips to **Golden River Zoo** and **Trentham winery**.

Where to Stay and Eat

Accommodation options in Mildura include motels and holiday apartments, well-equipped caravan parks and a huge choice of houseboat rental.

The **7th Street Motel** ((03) 5023 1796 E-MAIL sevmomil@ruralnet.net.au, 153 Seventh Street, is centrally located and has clean and comfortable inexpensive rooms, a swimming pool and a grassed barbecue area. The Budget chain of motels keeps a high standard and has two good inexpensive motels in central locations in Mildura. The **Mildura Park Motel** ((03) 5023 0479, 250 Eighth Street, and **Sunraysia Apartments** ((03) 5023 0137, 441 Deakin Avenue, have good facilities including swimming pools. The **Acacia Holiday Apartments and Park Cabins** ((03) 5023 3855, E-MAIL acacia@vic.ozland .net.au, 761 Fifteenth Street (Calder Highway), offers three different styles of accommodation set in gardens with grassed areas (inexpensive to moderate rates).

A gracious old-style hotel just back from the river, the **Mildura Grand Hotel** ((03) 5023 0511, Seventh Street, is now more renowned for its restaurant, **Stefano's**, touted as one of Australia's best. The restaurant's $50 set menu includes antipasti, risotto, homemade pasta, a main course and dessert. Many of Mildura's visitors come just for the pleasure of eating here. On street level the hotel has a casual and inexpensive wine bar/café that makes great pizza.

There is also a string of restaurants and cafés along Langtree Street; **Langtree** at No. 34 and **Liasons Bistro** right next door are the best of the bunch.

HOW TO GET THERE

There are direct flights into Mildura from Adelaide, Broken Hill, Melbourne and Renmark. V/Line runs train service from Melbourne to Swan Hill and a rail/coach service to Echuca.

Greyhound Pioneer buses bound for Broken Hill pass through Echuca and Swan Hill, their buses to Deniliquin also stop at Echuca. **Australian Pacific Tours** ((03) 9277 8555 E-MAIL info@aptours .com.au operates coach tours to Echuca.

The Murray Princess paddle-steamer trundles its way towards Mildura.

Tasmania

TASMANIA IS PRIMARILY A LAND OF WILDLIFE AND WIL-DERNESS. Almost a third of the island's landmass is protected in national parks and reserves. Craggy mountains provide plenty of dramatic panoramas to reward those who undertake one of its more than 200 km (125 miles) of world-class walking tracks. In southwestern Tasmania a group of national parks — Southwest, Franklin–Gordon Wild Rivers, Cradle Mountain–Lake St. Clair, Hartz Mountains and Walls of Jerusalem national parks protect the world's last great temperate rainforest, the Tasmanian Wilderness World Heritage Area. Here, Australia's most famous walk, the Overland Track from Cradle Mountain to Lake St. Clair, takes at least five days to complete.

The state's colonial heritage is hard to escape. Well-preserved historic villages dot the island, historic houses and colonial cottages, often built by convicts, host many of Tasmania's small hotels and B&Bs. Tea rooms and bakeries here replace the mainland's Continental cafés, and Tasmanians seem to slip into nineteenth-century dress for every town fair and harvest festival.

As Australia's only island state, Tasmania's climate and culture are distinct from those of the mainland. The post-war immigration boom hardly registered here. More than any other state, Tasmanians remain predominately of Anglo-Irish heritage. But although Tasmanians like to make comparisons with England, the island's vegetation, predominately mountainous terrain and rugged wilderness bear far more in common with New Zealand. Isolated when sea-levels rose 8,000 to 13,000 years ago, Tasmania's seclusion and cooler climate have also preserved many plants and animals that have since disappeared from the mainland. Among these the Tasmanian devil, Australia's largest carnivorous marsupial, thrives throughout the state.

Tasmania was probably the last part of Australia to be inhabited. Anthropologists believe the ancestors of its Aboriginal population arrived around 20,000 years ago and developed a culture and social system somewhat different from those on the mainland. The island was first recorded by Europeans in 1642, when Dutch navigator Abel Tasman named it Van Diemen's Land after Anthony van Diemen, governor of the Dutch East Indies. More European explorers visited in the eighteenth century, but it was not colonized until Hobart became Australia's second penal settlement in 1804 (although whalers and sealers had set up isolated camps from around 1800). Tasmania's penal colonies were escape-proof prisons for convicts who had committed serious crimes, and for repeat offenders from the mainland colonies. They were notoriously the harshest in Australia, particularly those at Sarah and Maria islands. Port Arthur, Tasmania's ultimate penal settlement, was founded on the Tasman peninsula. Across its narrowest point — Eaglehawk Neck — ferocious dogs were chained in line to discourage prisoners from escaping.

As throughout Australia, European settlers quickly took over traditional Aboriginal hunting grounds and spiritual sites, fencing lands off and preventing the Aboriginal people from entering them. Although Tasmania's Aboriginal people fought back through guerilla-type raids, attacks on cattle and crops and organized warfare, they were systematically killed or sent to camps such as those on Bruny and Flinders islands and at Oyster Cove, near Hobart, to be taught Christianity. Separated from their land and clans, many were forced to live with members of traditionally enemy tribes. Camps lacked clean water and medical supplies, and the death rate was high. Colonists' efforts to remove indigenous people from mainland Tasmania culminated in the death of Truganini in Hobart in 1876, considered at the time to have been the "last Tasmanian Aborigine."

Tasmania continued to officially deny the existence of its original Aboriginal people until the 1970s. Truganini's skeleton was on show at the Hobart Museum until 1976 as an example of a supposedly extinct race. Hobart's Aboriginal community, many of whom are descendents of Aboriginal women taken as wives by nineteenth-century sealers and whalers to live on islands in Bass Strait, finally managed to have Truganini cremated a century after her death. Her ashes were scattered over the waters of the D'Entrecasteaux Channel.

HOBART

Snuggled between Mount Wellington and the banks of the Derwent River, Hobart is Australia's smallest state capital, with a population of just 160,000. Beautiful Georgian buildings cluster around the docks, whose sandstone merchant warehouses are now home to galleries and small boutiques. Waterfront cafés and restaurants add to the general sparkle, and a colorful art-and-craft-and-whatever-else market is held along the wharves every Saturday.

Hobart's modern role as the departure point for Antarctic voyages and supply vessels reflects its seafaring past. It is also the finishing point of the Sydney-to-Hobart Yacht Race. The yachts leave Sydney on Boxing Day (December 26) and generally sail into Constitution Dock around New Year's Eve. This is definitely the time to visit Hobart, as it coincides with the food and wine celebration, Taste of Tasmania (December 28 to January 3), and the start of the Hobart Summer Festival (December 28 to the end of January).

Only five minutes from the center, the suburbs climb the lower slopes of Mount Wellington. Ten minutes more and you're in the bush, with sweeping views of Hobart and the pretty Derwent River

TASMANIA

estuary, backed by green pastures and apple orchards. Hobart's climate is mild. Temperatures drop below 0°C (32°F) in winter and rarely exceed 25°C (77°F) in summer. Always pack a sweater.

BACKGROUND

Hobart was the second city founded in Australia, 16 years after Sydney and a year after Tasmania's first colony was settled at nearby Risdon Cove. The decision was strategic, with the intention of thwarting French designs on the island. The importance of whaling and shipbuilding in Tasmania made the deep harbor of the broad Derwent River estuary an obvious site for the city. Many of Hobart's beautiful colonial buildings were built by the convicts who formed the majority of the first settlers.

For the first half of the nineteenth century Hobart was a whaling center and a bustling port for the burgeoning wheat, wool and timber industries. By 1860, however, its wealth was declining. Hobart saw far less growth in the twentieth century than other Australian cities. As a result, Hobart's gracious colonial and Georgian mansions, tiny mariners' cottages, honey-colored sandstone warehouses and ornate public buildings not only remain intact, they haven't been overshadowed by modern high-rises. More than 90 buildings in Hobart are classified by Australia's National Trust.

GENERAL INFORMATION

The **Tasmanian Travel and Information Center** ((03) 6230 8233 WEB SITE www.tas.gov.au/tourism/tasman.html, 20 Davey Street, has good maps and can book tours, transportation and accommodation. This is also the place to pick up copies of the *Treasure Islander* and *Tasmanian Travelways* WEB SITE www.travelways.com.au, free newspapers with up-to-date information on accommodation, transportation and car rental throughout Tasmania, including comprehensive bus timetables. Another free publication, *This Week in Tasmania* has well-written, informative articles on current and upcoming events.

A **walking tour** of Battery Point leaves from the wishing well here at 9:30 AM Monday to Friday, run by the National Trust ((03) 6223 7570 ($5, no booking necessary).

There are several good Internet cafés in central Hobart. Their rates are the same, $10 an hour. **Internet Central** ((1300) 655 633 E-MAIL info@tassie .net.au, Level 1, 29 Elizabeth Street, and **Southern Internet Services** ((03) 6234 7444, second floor, 4 Liverpool Street, are both open 9 AM to 5 PM weekdays, and on Saturday mornings. A friendly local café with great Colombian coffee is **Drifters Internet Café** ((03) 6224 3244, 33 Salamanca Place. Drifters opens Monday to Saturday 9 AM to 5 PM, Sunday 11 AM to 5 PM, and reopens 10 PM to 5 AM from Thursday to Saturday.

The **GPO** is on the corner of Elizabeth and Macquarie Streets. The **Wilderness Society** ((03) 6234 9366 is at 130 Davey Street.

The **Royal Automobile Club of Tasmania (RACT)** (132 722 WEB SITE www.ract.com.au has its head office on the corner of Murray and Patrick Streets. For **roadside assistance** throughout Tasmania call (131 111.

GETTING AROUND

City and suburban **bus services** in Hobart are run by Metro (132 201. Their offices are in the Metro City bus station at 18 Elizabeth Street, opposite the GPO. The City Explorer leaves from here and stops at most major sites; you can break your journey as often as you like. Day Rover tickets can be bought on any bus, and allow an unlimited number of off-peak trips (weekdays 9 AM to 4:30 PM and after 6 PM, and all day on weekends).

Evening **coach tours** of Hobart are offered by City Sights Under Lights ((03) 6231 1187 or (0418) 538 018. The two-and-a-half-hour tour includes a light supper and explores Hobart's history, heritage and culture. Adults $30, $15 for those under 16. Tasmanian Redline Coaches ((03) 6231 3233 offer numerous day-trips from Hobart.

Two **car-rental companies** with exceptionally low prices in Hobart are Advance TOLL-FREE (1800) 030 118 E-MAIL rentals@advancecars.com.au and Lo•Cost ((03) 6231 0550 E-MAIL locost@tassie .net.au. Budget ((03) 6234 5222 has an office at the airport, as does Delta ((1300) 131 390 and Thrifty TOLL-FREE (1800) 030 730. All three offer drop-off services at any airport. Tasmania Camper Van Hire TOLL-FREE (1800) 807 119 has camper-vans with microwaves, heating, linen and color televisions from $90 a day.

Tas Vacations TOLL-FREE (1800) 030 160 E-MAIL holidays@tasvacations.com.au offers a variety of attractively priced **self-drive packages** that include accommodation and car rental from $60 a day (Kendell Airlines have similar packages including airfare, see HOW TO GET THERE, page 179).

WHAT TO SEE AND DO

Hobart is an excellent city to walk around: it's small and most sights are within a short distance from the wharves. A good starting point is the former maritime village of **Battery Point**, perched between the city docks and Sandy Bay. Once home to sailors, fishermen, shipwrights and merchants, Battery Point's pubs, churches, houses and winding lanes have all been lovingly preserved. The name comes from a battery of cannons the British colonials set up on the promontory in 1818 to repulse potential French invaders. The cannons are gone, but the **signaling station** — Battery Point's oldest building — remains. There are great views from here of the Derwent and the wharf area.

Castray Esplanade bends southward from the signaling station to become Hampton Road. Take first turn to the left to visit **Secheron House**, classified by the National Trust and home to the **Maritime Museum of Tasmania** ((03) 6223 5082, 21 Secheron Road. The museum has an interesting collection of photos, paintings and models and the house itself is worth the minimal entry fee ($4). Open daily from 10 AM to 4:30 PM.

Battery Point's village green, **Arthur's Circus**, is just a few meters along pretty Runnymede Street. Nineteenth-century pastel-painted stone cottages garnished with pockets of colorful flowerbeds ring this small circular park. The spire of **Saint George's Anglican Church** on nearby Saint George's Terrace dominates Battery Point; its bells chime on the hour.

Hampton Road has a few friendly cafés, restaurants and antique shops. The **Van Diemen's Land Folk Museum** ((03) 6234 2791 at No. 103 is the oldest in Australia, established in 1834. Set in picturesque "Narryna," a stately Georgian home, the museum displays a fascinating collection of heirlooms, antiques and curios from Tasmania's pioneering days. Open Tuesday to Friday 10 AM to 5 PM, weekends from 2 PM to 5 PM. Admission is $5 for adults, $2 for children.

Kelly Street runs from Hampton Street to the steep **Kelly Steps**, which descend to tree-lined **Salamanca Place**, dating back to the whaling days of the 1830s. Its old sandstone warehouses now house some good cafés and bar-restaurants and a variety of craft and tourist-orientated shops, most open every day. Saturday's **Salamanca Market** adds hundreds of outdoor stalls covered by bright umbrellas. Good buys include hand-knitted, hand-spun sweaters and beautifully turned bowls and platters made from native timbers.

Antarctic Adventure ((03) 6220 8220 WEB SITE www.antarctic.com.au in Salamanca Square offers over 50 different activities. Kids can try downhill skiing on the blizzard simulator ride, play in the snow in Antarctic weather conditions in the "Cold

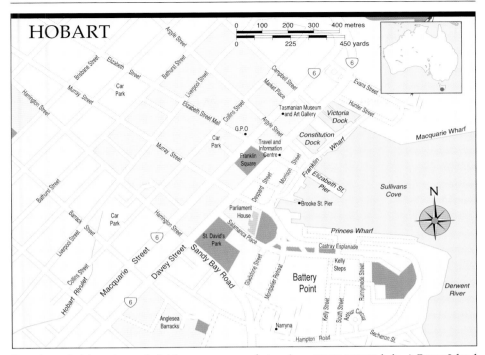

HOBART

Experience," visit an Antarctic field camp or see the southern night sky at the planetarium. Open daily 10 AM to 5 PM; $16 adults, $8 children and $40 a family.

Tasmania's **Parliament House**, at the western end of Salamanca Place, was built by convicts between in 1841 as Hobart's original customs house. The deep-red velvet benches and ornate painted ceiling of the tiny Legislative Council Chamber date from the mid-nineteenth century. Hobart Town's first burial ground is opposite, in **St. David's Park**, with pioneer gravestones dating back to 1804.

The old boathouses and warehouses along **Elizabeth Street Pier** are now a series of excellent restaurants, including the two Mures (see WHERE TO EAT, below). Elizabeth Pier is also "home port" to the *Lady Nelson*, a replica of the ship that helped found Hobart — on weekends she opens her sails for 90-minute cruises on the Derwent at $5 per person. Just past the pier is **Constitution Dock**, the center of attention when competitors in the Sydney-to-Hobart Yacht Race arrive in late December. Stalls here sell fresh and cooked seafood and fish year-round.

Cruisers leave from adjacent Franklin Wharf on tours of the Derwent River. A vintage ferry, the *Emmalisa* ((03) 6223 5893 runs lunch cruises twice daily, departing at 11:30 AM and 1:30 PM, and the **MV** *Commodore* ((03) 6234 9294 has regular cruises along the river to the Cadbury Chocolate factory just north of town, including a tour of the

factory (see AROUND HOBART, below). **Bruny Island Charters'** ((03) 6234 3166 *On the Edge* sails on day-trips to Bruny Island from here for a six-hour cruise and a gourmet seafood lunch on the island. Keen anglers can fish from the boat in the morning and a crew member will cook their catch up for lunch.

A beautiful example of colonial architecture, the **Tasmanian Museum and Art Gallery** ((03) 6211 4177, 5 Argyle Street (entrance at 40 Macquarie Street), houses an interesting collection of Aboriginal artifacts, convict relics and early colonial prints and paintings. Open seven days a week from 10 AM to 5 PM, free admission. Free guided tours Wednesday to Sunday at 2:30 PM.

Hobart's **Royal Theatre**, 29 Campbell Street, is the oldest in Australia, having been built in 1837. Its perfectly preserved interior exemplifies the harmony of Georgian architecture, based on classical Roman principles. Open Monday to Saturday, 9 AM to 4:30 PM.

The sprawling Queen's Domain, a large parkland with sporting facilities and an adventure playground for the kids, flanks the river north of central Hobart. Within the Domain, Hobart's **Royal Botanic Gardens** ((03) 6234 6299 put on a spectacular display of begonias in summer, and there's a pretty restaurant-café. Open 8 AM to 4:45 PM daily, admission is free. The gardens' Botanical Discovery Center organizes multimedia tours of "Australian wilderness and flora" every day from 10 AM to 4:30 PM; $6 per adult, and $3 per child.

Antarctic Cruises

As Australia's southernmost city, Hobart is the point of departure for research and tourist voyages to the Australian Antarctic Territory. Members of the International Association of Antarctic Tourist Operators (IAATO) encourage minimal impact tourism and an awareness of the fragility of the Antarctic environment, where heavy-footed moon-boots could destroy mosses and lichen, and penguin or seal colonies must be approached with particular care.

Most operators include on-board lectures by wildlife experts. **Aurora Expeditions** ((02) 9252 1033 TOLL-FREE (1800) 637 688 WEB SITE www .auroraexpeditions.com.au, Level 1, 37 George Street, Sydney, NSW 2000, offers highly recommended true adventure voyages from Hobart which include overnight camping on the ice and forays into the Ross Sea and along the coast of Oates Land — areas first chartered in the 1950s and 1960s.

One of the world's most powerful icebreakers, the *Kapitan Khlebnikov*, operated by **Adventure Associates** ((02) 9389 7466 TOLL-FREE (1800) 222 141 FAX (02) 9369 1853 E-MAIL mail@adventureassociates .com, 197 Oxford Street Mall, Bondi Junction NSW 2022, runs 25-day voyages from Hobart deep into the Antarctic pack ice, visiting scientific research stations as well as historic sites and expedition huts associated with the great Antarctic explorers. The thoroughly refurbished ship accommodates passengers in comfort, carries both Zodiac landing craft and helicopters for excursions, and sails with a highly experienced team of naturalists, geologists and historians.

Specifically designed for expeditionary cruising, the comfortable 100-passenger *Explorer* also takes passengers on adventures to the Australian Antarctic, departing from Hobart or Melbourne. Distinguished guides and lecturers and highly experienced crew take passengers onto the ice in the ship's fleet of Zodiacs. For details contact **Abercrombie & Kent** ((03) 9699 9766 TOLL-FREE (1800) 331 429 FAX (03) 9699 9308 E-MAIL contact @aandktravel.com.au.

WHERE TO STAY

Hobart is more popular than ever, particularly from December through April, when it's wise to book ahead. For a comprehensive and up-to-date guide to accommodation in Hobart and throughout Tasmania, pick up a free copy of *Tasmanian Travelways* at any tourist office, or visit their WEB SITE www .travelways.com.au.

Expensive

It's hard to miss the imposing **Hotel Grand Chancellor** ((03) 6235 4535 WEB SITE www.hgchobart .com.au, 1 Davey Street. Towering over the waterfront, it has all the modern amenities of a first-class international hotel and a choice of mountain view and water view executive suites, priced accordingly (for special deals check out the "Grand Indulgence" packages on their web site). Although not overly inspired, staff are welcoming and more than efficient. Its restaurant, Meehan's, is a plus (see WHERE TO EAT, below).

Slightly incongruous in the quiet beach-side suburb of Sandy Bay, the redeveloped **Wrest Point Hotel Casino** ((03) 6225 0112 WEB SITE www .wrestpoint.com.au, 410 Sandy Bay Road, offers unsurpassed views of the city and easy access to the gaming rooms. Although the building can't escape its dated exterior, the views are fab and the interior and facilities have kept up with the times.

There is a variety of bars and restaurants, including a revolving restaurant (see WHERE TO EAT, below), a disco, and live showroom entertainment. **Salamanca Inn** ((03) 6223 3300 WEB SITE www .salamancainn.com.au, 10 Gladstone Street, has attractively furnished and roomy one- and two-bedroom suites. It could be worth the bit extra to be only a two-minute walk from the happening Salamanca Market area.

Moderate

At the top end of the moderate range, **Lenna of Hobart** ((03) 6232 3900 FAX (03) 6224 0112, 20 Runnymede Street, in Battery Point, is a stately mansion steeped in history. Once the home of whaling magnate Alexander McGregor, its sumptuous interior, beautifully decorated rooms and ideal location, just above the Salamanca Market, make for a memorable stay in Hobart.

A romantic way to spend your stay is in one of the many colonial B&Bs dotted around Hobart. A favorite is the well positioned and homey **Jarem Waterfront Guest House** ((03) 6223 8216, 8 Clarke Avenue, Battery Point, which has wonderful views and very reasonable rates, even in the high season. Their full breakfasts can include berry pancakes, smoked salmon with scrambled eggs and spinach brioche. As it caters to a maximum of only six people at a time, it is advisable to book well ahead. The **Colonial Battery Point Manor** ((03) 6224 0888, 13 Cromwell Street, has spacious rooms with views over the Derwent Estuary, and serves a generous breakfast in their historic cellar.

For something a little more modern, **Oakford** ((03) 6220 6600, on Elizabeth Street Pier, has stylish apartments, some with broad balconies (closer to expensive prices) but all looking out over the pier and the Derwent River.

Inexpensive

In and around the city, Hobart has no shortage of conveniently located hotels, motels, B&Bs, vacation flats and hostels offering comfortable budget accommodation. The centrally located **Astor Private Hotel** ((03) 6234 6611 FAX (03) 6234 6384, 157 Macquarie Street, has clean, comfortable rooms with more personal service than most larger hotels. Prices start at $50 a single and $65 a double.

Barrack Street Colonial Cottage ((03) 6224 1054 FAX (03) 6224 1754, 55 Barrack Street, is a fully self-contained two-story convict-built brick cottage where you can relax in front of an open fire or in your own secluded courtyard, sipping on the complimentary port and listening to cathedral bells chime in the distance. Nestled in between parkland and only five minutes south of the city center, **Amberly House** ((03) 6225 1005 WEB SITE www .view.com.au/amberly, 391 Sandy Bay Road, Sandy Bay, was built in the late 1890s. All rooms are decorated in period style, with a choice of water, mountain or garden views, deluxe (double spa) or standard rooms. **Cottages of the Colony Past and Present** TOLL-FREE (1800) 804 613 WEB SITE www .view.com.au/cottages, and the **Tasmanian Colonial Accommodation Association** TOLL-FREE (1800) 815 610 can provide other options; pick up their brochures at any Tasmanian Travel Centre.

In the same area, the **Black Prince** ((03) 6234 3501, 145 Elizabeth Street, has large modern rooms with bathroom and television starting at $50 a double. If you want to be by the water without having to spend a fortune, then the **Customs House Hotel** ((03) 6234 6645, 1 Macquarie Street, offers only basic amenities but good views of the waterfront at only $70 for a double with bath. The **Hobart Tower Motel** ((03) 6228 0166, 300 Park Street, Newtown, has neat en-suite rooms starting at a very reasonable $54. The **Waratah Motor Hotel** ((03) 6234 3685 FAX (03) 6234 3502, 272 Murray Street, offers modest accommodation close to the city center.

The best of Hobart's hostels is **Central City Backpackers** ((03) 6224 2404, 138 Collins Street, which is clean, quiet, secure and friendly. Dorms

The 1830s sandstone wharehouses at Salamanca Place have been converted into restaurants and shops.

start at $16, and for a single room you pay $30. You can camp in a wonderful location less than three kilometers from the city center at the **Sandy Bay Caravan Park** ((03) 6225 1264, 1 Peel Street, Sandy Bay, which has campsites for $12, on site vans for $32, and cabins for $50.

WHERE TO EAT

For a relatively small city, Hobart has an impressive variety of restaurants; making the most of the high quality local produce. In general, Tasmanian wines are expensive compared to mainland prices, but they are definitely well worth trying, particularly the Pinot Noirs and Reislings. Local beers too

pancetta or the simple but perfect steamed Tasmanian salmon on puréed potatoes are both highly recommended. The three-course Waterfront Menu is excellent value at $35. Dinner is served from Tuesday to Saturday, with dancing on Friday and Saturday nights. In historic Battery Point, **Alexander's** ((03) 6232 3900, 20 Runnymede Street, uses the best local produce to create modern Mediterrasian dishes such as pan-fried scallops with kumquat and ginger butter. They have an exceptional wine list, with many Tasmanian wines available by the glass.

Revolving on the seventeenth floor of the Wrest Point Casino, the views from **The Point** ((03) 6225 0112 are matched by an impeccable wine list.

are excellent — Tasmania's Cascade and Boag's are two of the best.

Expensive

Overlooking the Victoria docks, **Mures Upper Deck** ((03) 6231 1991, Victoria Dock, is a Hobart institution. Meaty local oysters or Mures' own smoked salmon are a great starter. If your waiter mentions striped trumpeter as the fish of the day, order it. It is found only in Tasmania and is superb. Open seven days noon until late. The nearby **Drunken Admiral Restaurant** ((03) 6234 1903, at 17 Hunter Street, serves an excellent bisque to a very loyal clientele, its interior a maze of nets and seafaring memorabilia. Open every evening.

For modern Australian fine dining, **Meehan's** ((03) 6235 4583, at the Hotel Grand Chancellor, 1 Davey Street, with views of Victoria Dock, is my perennial favorite. The milk-fed veal wrapped in

Surprising for a restaurant that could draw customers on the strength of the panoramic views alone, the food is also excellent. For a closer view of the Derwent, the signature chili prawns at **Prosser's on the Beach** ((03) 6225 2276, on Beach Road, Long Point, are perfectly complemented by a cool Riesling from the restaurant's cellar of select Tasmanian wines.

Moderate

The spacious **Gastrodome** ((03) 6224 7557, 24 Salamanca Square, is a restaurant, bar and café with a predominantly modern Italian menu, which includes homemade pasta and risotto and a select choice of four smoky wood-fired pizzas. They also do a capacious weekend brunch and have a particularly inviting cake selection. Nearby, at 87 Salamanca Place, the **Ball and Chain Grill** ((03) 6223 2655 serves generous portions from its charcoal grill. In summer its courtyard is a relaxing place to enjoy an extended dinner.

Mures Lower Deck ((03) 6231 1991, Victoria Dock, is a less formal version of their Upper Deck seafood restaurant. The fish and chips are the best in town, while adjacent **Orizuru** ((03) 6231 1790 is an excellent sushi bar on the dock side. **A Splash of Paris** ((03) 6224 2200, Elizabeth Street Pier, guarantees just what the name implies: classic French dishes with particularly good daily specials. Also found on Elizabeth Street Pier, the stylish **Tavern 42 Degrees South** (03) 6224 7742 has an eclectic but appealing menu that ranges from a superbly garlicky Greek fish stew to Thai laksas and pan-fried local fish with couscous. Book ahead and ask for an outside table in summer. **Sisco's** ((03) 6223 2059, Level 1, Murray Street Pier, has an international menu, but stick to their Spanish dishes and you can't go wrong. Leave room for one of their legendary desserts.

There is a wide choice of restaurants in Elizabeth Street, North Hobart, of which the most popular is the highly awarded **Mit Zitrone** ((03) 6234 8113, 333 Elizabeth Street, North Hobart. Set in picturesque surroundings, Mit Zitrone serves innovative dishes in a casual atmosphere and represents some of the best value in town. Book ahead. It's BYO and open from 10:30 AM to late (closed Sundays). Authentic Thai, Indian and Indonesian cuisine, any of which goes well with one of Tasmania's home-grown beers, can be found just down the road at **Vanidol's** ((03) 6234 9307, 353 Elizabeth Street.

Inexpensive

Spend half an hour checking your e-mail and enjoy a tasty foccacia or an all-day breakfast at the same time at **Drifters Internet Café** ((03) 6224 6286, 33 Salamanca Place, and you would be pushed to spend over $12. Open 10 AM to 6 PM Monday to Saturday, and 11 AM to 5:30 PM Sundays. Similarly, the **Machine Laundry Café** ((03) 6224 9922, 12 Salamanca Square, serves good, cheap food while your washing tumbles in the dryer. If you're not pressed try one of their tasty tarts and cakes, which are baked on the premises. **Panache** ((03) 6224 2929, 89 Salamanca Place, is a simple café in a historic sandstone building; the outdoor dining area is very pleasant.

Rockerfeller's ((03) 6234 3490, 11 Morrison Street, on the waterfront in an 1856 flourmill, is one of Tasmania's most popular restaurants. Tapas and a varied à la carte menu are available, while live jazz adds to the active atmosphere. Save a lot of room for the delicious and copious desserts. Open for lunch Monday to Friday 12 PM to 2 PM and dinner seven nights 6 PM until late. BYO and licensed, reservations are recommended.

In the heart of the city is **Aromas** ((03) 6223 4355, 34 Murray Street, an informal and friendly café, set in an airy open atrium. The coffee is always excellent here. A house of ill repute in the 1890s, **Shearers** ((03) 6235 5246, 19 Macquarie Street, is nowadays best known for their char-grilled beef and extensive Tasmanian wine list at affordable prices.

HOW TO GET THERE

Qantas (131 313 and **Ansett** (131 300 have frequent flights to Hobart from all Australian capitals and Launceston. Ansett's subsidiary, **Kendell Airlines** (131 300, has direct flights from Sydney, Melbourne and Adelaide, at more than competitive prices. The best deals combine airfare, car rental and accommodation. Find out what's on offer from Tasmanian Travel and Information centers in other Australian states or the Australian Tourist Commission abroad (see TOURIST INFORMATION, page 320 in TRAVELERS' TIPS), or try Tourism Tasmania's WEB SITE www.tas.gov.au/tourism/tasman.html.

As the *Spirit of Tasmania* and the *Devil Cat* both arrive in the north of the island, many visitors enter Hobart by road. **Tassielink** ((1300) 300 520 provides a statewide bus service that is ideal for independent travelers. The daily service links towns, the more popular wilderness areas, national parks and heritage sites, and a flexible Explorer Pass is available in 7-, 10-, 14- and 21-day blocks. Pre-programmed itineraries can be supplied or travelers can create their own vacation plan around the statewide timetable. Pass holders also receive discounts on Tigerline day tours, and $10 cash back on return of their pass. **Hobart Coaches** TOLL-FREE (1800) 030 620, 4 Liverpool Street, Hobart, run services in southeast Tasmania.

Hobart and Launceston are only 200 km (124 miles) apart and connected by the Heritage Highway. The drive is an easy two hours. If you're coming in from the west on the A10 though, be aware that roads are mountainous and driving slow. The 250-km (155-mile) drive from Queenstown to Hobart will take at least four hours.

AROUND HOBART

There are dozens of glorious scenic drives and lookouts around Hobart. **Mount Wellington** (1,300 m or 4,200 ft) is often shrouded in clouds, but on a clear day the panoramas are inspiring. From central Hobart, take Davey Street south for 10 km (just over six miles), then turn right, following signs to "The Pinnacle," 12 twisting kilometers (seven and a half miles) further on. After driving through dense temperate rainforest into alpine vegetation above the snowline you are rewarded with fine views of the Derwent Valley to

Hobart's busy Franklin Wharf.

the north, Hobart to the east, and across the islands and peninsulas south to the Tasman Sea. Bring jackets, as the summit is usually cold and windy, even in the height of summer. The peak is closed to cars in winter. Walking maps and tours are available from the Travel Center in Hobart.

A great family outing is to visit the **Cadbury Chocolate Factory** ((03) 6249 0111, in Claremont, 14 km (just under nine miles) north of Hobart on the Lyell Highway. The 40-minute tour follows the chocolate-making process, with stops along the way for tasting. Tours operate Monday to Friday from 8 AM to 1 PM. For an added treat, combine your tour with a boat cruise with **The Cruise Company** ((03) 6234 9294, Brook Street Pier.

Tours of Australia's oldest working brewery, **Cascade Brewery** ((03) 6221 8300 operate weekdays at 9:30 AM and 1 PM. The brewery is 10 minutes out of Hobart on Cascade Road, buses leave from the Metro City bus station on Elizabeth Street. Bookings are essential, and can be made at the Travel Center on Davey Street.

THE HUON TRAIL

The Huon Trail is a wonderful day's drive south of Hobart. Take the Channel Highway through to Taroona where it is worth a stop to take in the fine views from **Taroona Shot Tower**, a manageable 318-step climb to the top. The Southern Outlet Highway leads on to the Huon Highway at Kingston, passing through the apple-growing country of picturesque **Hounville** on the Huon River. Following the river south into **Franklin**, boat builders can be seen learning the traditional skill of shaping Huon pine. The fishing village of **Dover**, 44 km (27 miles) further south, was once a convict station — with the old commandants office still standing. **Southport** was established in the whaling and sealing days and has good fishing, surfing, swimming and bush-walking. Not far from here is Lune River, where the **Huon Magical Mystery Tours** ((03) 6298 3117 E-MAIL luneriver@trump.net.au take small groups deep into the area's many cave systems. Glow-worms add a touch of magic. Locals rent out sea kayaks or canoes to paddle the estuary, and fishing tackle for those who want to dangle a line. **Cockle Creek**, on the shores of **Recherche Bay**, is literally the end of the road — this is the farthest south it is possible to drive to in Australia. Walk on for two hours and you are at the southernmost tip of Australia.

RICHMOND

Half an hour from Hobart, beyond Coal River, Richmond is one of Australia's finest examples of a nineteenth-century village, with more than 50 intact Georgian buildings, mostly built by convicts. To enhance the Old World charm at night the streets

are lit by gas lamps. Richmond Bridge is Australia's oldest, built in 1823 as part of the old route between Hobart and Port Arthur. The town was an important military post and convict station during the 1830s but after the completion of the Sorrel Bridge in 1872 it lay dormant for 100 years.

Richmond Goal, the oldest in Tasmania, was built in 1825 to temporarily house those going on to Port Arthur. Go into a cell to experience a taste of solitary confinement. The wooden triangle in the Flogging Yard is an example of the harshness of convict life. The reputedly haunted **Prospect House** ((03) 6260 2207, 1384 Richmond Road, a grand two-story Georgian mansion built in 1830 and set in country grounds, has a restaurant and moderately priced accommodation. Other fine architectural examples are **Saint John's Roman Catholic Church** (1831), **Saint Luke's Church of England** (1834) and the **court house**, which is still used today. Kids and the young at heart should check out **Old Hobart Town** ((03) 6260 2502, in Bridge Street, a scale model village that depicts Hobart in the 1820s. Set outdoors, it covers 600 sq m (6,458 sq ft).

A handful of tea rooms offer country-style hospitality. The **Maze and Tearooms** ((03) 6260 2451, 13 Bridge Street, has two mazes to temporarily lose the kids in while parents enjoy a Devonshire tea. There is also the new **Zoo Doo** ((03) 6260 2444, 620 Middle Tree Road, which has miniature horse racing and exotic animals to keep the young ones entertained.

Coal River Wine Tours (/FAX (03) 6248 1377 E-MAIL crvwinetours@bigpond.com offers daily tours that include a gourmet lunch, wine tasting at three local vineyards and a stopover in Richmond, for $78 per adult.

The free brochure *Let's Talk About Richmond* details the history of most of the inns, shops and houses and provides a useful map. It's available in shops all over town.

BRUNY ISLAND

Gentle Bruny Island is a popular weekend getaway spot for Hobart residents, and makes a relaxed day or overnight trip from Hobart. Idyllic ocean beaches along the east coast and in Cloudy Bay are balanced by the fertile fishing grounds of the more sheltered west coast, where sea eagles hover in the updrafts off the coastal cliffs.

Bruny skirts the coastline south of Hobart for almost 50 km (31 miles), sheltering the waters of the D'Entrecasteaux Channel and so creating ideal breeding grounds for crayfish, scallops and oysters. Bruny would be two islands were it not for an improbably thin isthmus called The Neck. Right in its center is a penguin rookery where fairy penguins can be seen around dusk every evening between July and April.

GENERAL INFORMATION

Before boarding the ferry, stop in at the **Bruny D'Entrecasteaux Visitor Center (** (03) 6267 4494, 81 Ferry Road, Ferry Wharf, Kettering. Here you can organize to explore Bruny's Beaches on a camel track expedition with **Camel Tracks (** (03) 6260 6335, in Great Bay, North Bruny.

WHAT TO SEE AND DO

Bruny is actually a misspelling: the island was named after French Admiral Bruni d'Entrecasteaux who surveyed it in 1792.

her on the island, just out of Alonnah, the main town on the island, on the southern end of the west coast.

Discover Bruny's rich heritage at the **Alonnah History Room** in the Old Court House, which has comprehensive displays on the island's Aboriginal people and its whaling, coal and timber industries. Open seven days a week from 10 AM to 4 PM. The **Bligh Museum of Pacific Exploration (** (03) 6293 1117, in Adventure Bay, South Bruny, was built in 1954 from convict-made bricks dating from the 1840s. The museum has a number of interesting and unusual artifacts including a remnant of a tree on which Captain Cook carved "Cook 26th January 1777" and some interesting memorabilia relating to Captain Bligh. Open from 9 AM

Although Abel Tasman had sighted the island (known to local Nuenonne people as Lunawannaalonna) in 1642, he didn't go ashore. Those who did land included Furneaux in 1773, Cook in 1777, and Bligh in 1778. (Australia's first apple trees were planted here, at Adventure Bay, by a botanist sailing with Bligh's expedition.)

But Bruny Island's history wasn't always peaceful. Early hostilities were provoked by whalers and sealers kidnapping Nuenonne women. Then, from 1829 the island was used by the colonial government as an experiment in converting Aboriginal people to European beliefs and practices. The experiment was deemed a failure after continued conflicts with the whaling community at Adventure Bay. The Aborigines, including Truganini, were removed from the island in 1831. Truganini's ashes were finally scattered over the D'Entrecasteaux Channel in April 1976, and there is a memorial to

to 5 PM in summer and 10 AM to 4 PM in winter; $2.50 admission fee.

Three ships were wrecked in D'Entrecasteaux Channel in 1835, with a total loss of over 150 lives. This led to action, and the **Cape Bruny Lighthouse** in the **South Bruny National Park** was constructed in 1838. Today it's the second oldest lighthouse in Australia, and it operated continuously until 1996. The lighthouse has been a popular sightseeing and picnic destination since the mid-nineteenth century, providing wonderful views of the rugged coastline. There are a number of good walking tracks throughout the park. From July to April little penguins can be seen waddling on the south coast. Other fauna likely to be encountered are mutton birds, seal colonies, dolphins, sea eagles, and occasionally whales.

Hobart and wintry Mount Wellington. The Tasman Bridge is one of 5,000 bridges on the island of Tasmania.

WHERE TO STAY AND EAT

As most of the accommodation on Bruny island is in cottages and guesthouses, it is necessary to book ahead. The secluded **Mavista Cottages (** (03) 6293 1347, 120 Resolution Road, Adventure Bay, each have a spa, log fires and a homey attic bedroom with polished pine floors and peaked pine ceilings at $125 a double, including breakfast (no smoking). At **Morella Island Retreats (** (03) 6293 1131, 46 Adventure Bay Road, Simpson's Bay, "Poppies" and "Angel's Retreat" are cozy beachside bungalows, while "The Shed" is a pretty cottage with a hot tub, in the midst of the verdant Morella Gardens. All cost $140 and have fully equipped kitchens and wood fires. For $195 you move up the hill and into the rainforest at "The Cockpit," which has glorious panoramic views of D'Entrecasteaux Channel.

For inexpensive accommodation, try one of the island's simple guesthouses: **Rosebud (** (03) 6293 1325, on Lorkin's Road; **Barnes Bay Villa (** (03) 6260 6287, 315 Missionary Road; or **Mill Cottage (** (03) 6293 1217 or (015) 875 052, on Cloudy Bay Road, are all friendly and clean. Other options are the **Adventure Bay Caravan Park (** (03) 6293 1270 has neat little cabins for only $45 and campsites for $10. The **Lumeah YHA Hostel (** (03) 6293 1265, Main Road, Adventure Bay, has dorm beds for $15 and private rooms for $42. **Bruny Hotel (** (03) 6293 1148, on Main Road, has simple rooms for $50, and serves old-fashioned pub meals.

The **Penguin Tea Room** in Adventure Bay is a friendly place with generous meals, good fresh fish and home-style cakes. A little more expensive, the **Hothouse Café** at the Morella Island Retreat also has excellent fresh seafood, and is licensed. Most of the accommodation on Bruny island is

TASMAN PENINSULA

The Tasman Peninsula is connected to the rest of Tasmania by a narrow isthmus named Eaglehawk Neck. In 1830 Governor Arthur selected it for a penal colony for criminals convicted of the most violent crimes, and for convicts charged with repeat offences in colonial Australia. The last prisoners left Port Arthur in 1877. Port Arthur Historic Site is both lovely and unsettling. The peninsula is particularly lush, with forests ending at small coves and some interesting caves and rock formations.

Just nine kilometers (five and a half miles) past Eaglehawk Neck, **Tasmanian Devil Park ℂ** (03) 6250-3230, Arthur Highway, Taranna, has a large number of devils as well as other indigenous species. Tasmanian devils are the largest of the carnivorous marsupials, although they reach only 60 cm (two feet) in length, and were named because of their vicious-sounding snarls and growls. They kill and eat small mammals and reptiles and as renowned scavengers are most often seen on roadsides eating roadkill. Devils are particularly impressive when eating; they are fed at 10 AM and 11 AM daily at the Taranna park.

PORT ARTHUR

Port Arthur was originally established as a timber station using convict labor. It became a prison settlement for male convicts, especially for repeat offenders, and promoted severe punishments such as flogging. These severe measures gave way eventually to more humane reform methods.

With over 2,000 convicts and staff by 1840, Port Arthur was also a major industrial settlement, producing timber, ships, clothing, shoes, furniture, coal, vegetables and many other goods. Between 1830 and 1877 about 13,000 convicts served sentences at Port Arthur.

General Information

For information and bookings within the Port Arthur Historic Site, including restaurants and tours, contact the **Port Arthur Information Office** TOLL-FREE (1800) 659 101 WEB SITE www. portarthur .org.au at the entrance to the Port Arthur Historical Site. Admission into the site is $12.50 per person.

What to See and Do

The Port Arthur historic site is not by any means all gloom and doom. It is an extremely tranquil spot and perfect for picnics. The **Commandants House** (*circa* 1848) sits on a high point overlooking **Carnarvon Bay** and **Mason Cove**, offering wonderful views of the entire grounds. A variety

self-catering; if you're not planning to do any fishing you can buy fresh fish along with other groceries at Adventure Bay or Alonnah.

HOW TO GET THERE

Bruny Island is reached by a 20-minute ferry from Kettering, 35 km (22 miles) south of Hobart. The first crossing is at 6:50 AM Monday to Saturday and 8 AM on Sunday. The last is at 6:30 PM (7:30 PM Fridays). The ferry costs $18 return per car on weekdays, $23 on weekends, and $3 for cyclists. Hobart Coaches' Kettering **bus** service connects with the ferry, for bookings call the Tasmanian Travel and Information Center in Hobart.

Bruny Island Charters ℂ (03) 6234 3166 runs popular day-trips from Hobart's Franklin Wharf to Bruny Island (for details see WHAT TO SEE AND DO, page 174 in HOBART).

The convict settlement at Port Arthur was built to withold the most intractable of New South Wales convicts.

of birds, including large numbers of crimson rosellas, feed on the fruit trees planted by the colonial housekeeper in the now somewhat overgrown gardens. Down the hill from here the **Guard Tower** (1835) is still a prepossessing structure.

The dominate **Penitentiary** was built as a granary and flour mill in 1842 and was converted to lodge about 500 prisoners in 1857. One floor housed the prisoners' library, another has the remains of a series of bathrooms where prisoners were treated with warm baths once a week.

A number of the grounds' cottages and houses have been furnished in period pieces. In the **Junior Medical Officers House** (1848) I suddenly came upon a gentleman who seemed to be writing his memoirs and was only too happy to stop and explain some enthralling historical facts. Personal tourism or one of the many ghosts renowned to haunt the area? To find out take the spooky one-and-a-half-hour **Historic Ghost Tour** which departs from information office at dusk. Bookings at the office are essential.

Prisoners who misbehaved or tried to escape were sent to the **Separate Prison** (also known as the Model Prison) for anything from a day to two months, where experimental methods were used in line with new ideas on reforming prisoners. Prisoners were subjected to sensory deprivation in the soundproof and darkened cells. Essentially reform was seen as a question of instilling or reinforcing Christian virtues and morals, and lessons in reading and understanding the bible were part of the experiment. A chapel in the Model Prison allowed prisoners to participate in church services, each pew separated by a high wooden wall.

The remnants of the large **church** (1837) are testament to the convicts' skills. The youths in the **boys' prison** carved the stone blocks and some of its fittings.

Over 1,000 convicts and freemen are buried on the **Isle of the Dead**, which is reached by ferry from the jetty. The tombstones of the freemen were carved by prisoners, complete with spelling errors. The **Asylum** (1867) was the last building built before the closure of the settlement. It is now a museum.

Transportation ended in 1853 and the number of convicts began to decline. The settlement closed in 1877 and then fell into disrepair through neglect and fires. Many buildings were sold off and torn down but eventually hotels and guest houses were built and a thriving tourist industry established. In the 1980s a government funded program restored the remaining buildings. For an idea of what conditions were like when Port Arthur was a penal settlement, read *For the Term of his Natural Life* by Marcus Clark, a classic of Australian literature.

Port Arthur became the site of a modern tragedy in April 1996, when a lone gunman opened fire on visitors and staff in and around the park's coffee shop. Eventually he took hostages at a guest-house where he doused himself in gasoline and set it alight, intending to kill himself. He was captured as he ran from the burning building. A total of 35 people were killed and many more were injured. Visitors should be aware that the Tasman Peninsula is home to a very small and close-knit population, and most people working in the tourism industry here are locals. Questions about the 1996 shootings can be very disturbing. The coffee shop has been replaced by a memorial garden, a new café and restaurant complex has been built nearby.

Where to Stay and Eat

With over 30 buildings, ruins, and sites to see, an interactive interpretation gallery, harbor cruises (not in winter) and optional one-hour Isle of the Dead tours or scenic flights, Port Arthur really is at least a full day's excursion from Hobart. Tickets are valid for 48 hours and it's definitely worth staying in the area overnight.

Just up the hill from the prison settlement, **Port Arthur Motor Inn** ((03) 6250 2101 FAX (03) 6250 2417 overlooks the ruins and has rooms from $100 a night. Diners in either the restaurant or the cheaper bistro area can watch the sun set over the ruins while enjoying a hearty meal. The wallaby stew is excellent. A reasonably priced à la carte menu with good regional wines by the glass makes this a very pleasant way to finish a day at Port Arthur.

Port Arthur Villas ((03) 6250 2239 FAX (03) 6250 2589 doesn't have a view but does have clean, self-contained one- and two-bedroom units for around $70 a double. **Port Arthur Caravan and Cabin Park** ((03) 6250 2430 FAX (03) 6250 2509, Garden Point, two kilometers (a little over one mile) before entering Port Arthur has cabins for $50, or campsites for $11. There are numerous guest houses and other lodgings a little further out at places such as Nubeena, 11 km (seven miles) west of Port Arthur on the B37 and Koonya, 20 km (12.5 miles) northwest of Port Arthur on the A9. The **Tasmanian Travel and Information Center** in Hobart or the Information Office at the entrance to the Port Arthur Historic Site have information on accommodation in the area.

Langfords licensed restaurant in the restored policeman's residence on the grounds is a convenient spot for lunch or tea and cake. There is also a cafeteria in the new main entrance building that serves lunch and snacks. A separate licensed restaurant within the same building, **Felons**, specializes in local seafood and game and serves dinner from 5 PM. Felons looks directly onto the settlement.

HOW TO GET THERE

The Tasman Peninsula is 100 km (62 miles) southeast of Hobart, a one-and-a-half-hour's drive through farming country. Take the A3 Highway from Hobart, which changes at Sorell into the A9 the rest of the way south to Port Arthur. Several companies run organized tours from Hobart — these can be booked at the visitor center in Hobart.

THE EAST COAST

Far less visited than the more spectacular west, Tasmania's sparsely populated east coast has a tranquil beauty, with softly rolling forest-covered hills descending to tiny fishing villages and untouched beaches. Freycinet Peninsula and its national park form one of the most spectacular and beautiful areas in Tasmania. Further south, the remains of the Darlington penal colony on Maria Island are surrounded by a wildlife reserve.

MARIA ISLAND

Maria Island is best known for its penal settlement which, although older and a lot smaller than Port Arthur, is remarkably intact. No cars are allowed on the island. Walkers are rewarded with beautiful coastal views and wildlife including an unusually large population of emus and Forester kangaroos. There are some lovely stretches of beach here, and the fairly dry forests hide ferny glens.

Visitors can stay in basic hostel accommodation within the old penal settlement, but most people stay on the mainland and come across for a day-trip. Orford is the closest town to Maria Island. It has a small beach and inexpensive motel accommodation at the **Blue Waters Motor Inn** ((03) 6257 1102. Moderately priced accommodation is available at the **Eastcoaster Resort** ((03) 6257 1564, four kilometers (three and a half miles) north of Orford. The resort operates a ferry service ((03) 6257 1589 to Maria Island three times daily, four times in summer.

FREYCINET PENINSULA

Green lichen cloaks pink granite peaks and vertical cliffs drop straight into the sea at Freycinet Peninsula National Park, one of the most tranquil places in Tasmania. There is no easy way to explore Freycinet, however, since no roads go past the entrance to the park. Until recently walking was the only option, although kayaking and boating are now also possible. The tiny town of Coles Bay is at the neck of the Freycinet Peninsula, backed by the Hazards — a 300-m-high (1,000-ft) pink granite outcrop.

General Information

The post-office-*cum*-general-store in the main street of Coles Bay is open daily. It also provides tourist information. A shuttle bus leaves from here to the entrance of Freycinet National Park, six kilometers (just under four miles) away, at 9:40 AM daily.

There are two buses a day between Coles Bay and Bicheno; they too leave from the general store.

What to See and Do

It's a steep three-kilometer (just under two-mile) walk across the peninsula to idyllic **Wineglass Bay**, where a perfect arc of white-sand beach backed by hills covered in native bush meets deep-blue and usually icy waters. One of the most popular hikes is the 25-km (16-mile) circuit of the peninsula. The coastal scenery is magnificent, and tracks cut through tall eucalyptus forests leading to Wineglass Bay, the **Lighthouse** and the pink granite Hazards, colored with orange and green lichens. On the other side of the peninsula is **Hazards Beach**. Just off shore from here, **Promise Rock** and **Refuge Island** are protected bird rookeries where cormorants and red-lipped Pacific gulls roost. Early in the morning the beach is often marked with the busy paw prints of Tasmanian devils, with the occasional kill carelessly tossed to one side in the sand. The nocturnal devils themselves are hard to spot; patience and a flashlight are needed.

Bennetts wallabies are common throughout the peninsula and often come down onto the sands of Wineglass Bay, and wombats scurry around in search of food at dusk. Walkers during the day usually see a variety of different birds, with flashes of color as green and crimson rosellas shoot past. The mischievous-looking black cockatoo is never far away.

Visitors rarely make it to the pristine **Schouten Island** off the southeast coast, a true paradise lost surrounded by the cleanest of turquoise water where dolphins love to frolic and whales drop by in April and November.

One of the best eco-friendly and peaceful ways to enjoy Freycinet is on a kayaking adventure. At a leisurely pace kayakers can reach spots inaccessible by foot, sometimes drifting gently to approach uninhabited wildlife. **Coastal Kayaks** ((03) 6257 0500 WEB SITE www.view.com.au/coastalkayak has half-day, full-day ($110), three-day ($560) and five-day ($820) all-inclusive tours operating all year round, though it's recommended to go between October and April to avoid Tasmania's chilly and wet winter. **Freycinet Experience** ((03) 6223 7565 TOLL-FREE (1800) 506 003 E-MAIL walk@freycinet .com.au organizes four-day eco-nature walks from November to April which include a night on Schouten Island and a night at comfy Freycinet Lodge.

Where to Stay and Eat

Freycinet Lodge ((03) 6257 0101 WEB SITE www .busker.trumper.com.au/frey, at Friendly Beaches within the national park, has won numerous environmental and tourism awards. It has two restaurants, a comfortable and spacious lounge and bar with an open fireplace and 60 cabins separated by native bush. Moderate to expensive. They can arrange a host of activities including abseiling, windsurfing, mountain bikes, kayaking, scenic flights, guided walks, penguin tours, whale and dolphin watching. There's also a **camping** ground along Richardsons Beach from Freycinet Lodge, and free campsites further in the national park. Inexpensive accommodation in Coles Bay is provided by **Iluka Holiday Centre (** (03) 6257 0115 on Muirs Beach, which has campsites, on-site caravans, cabins and even hostel accommodation. **Madge Malloys (** (03) 6257 0399, 3 Garnet Avenue, serves excellent fresh local seafood.

BICHENO

Originally a whaling town, Bicheno is a good base from which to visit Freycinet or the **Douglas-Apsley National Park**, which begins at Apsley Gorge, 10 km (six miles) north of town. It's reached by taking the Rosedale Road off the Tasman Highway (A3) three kilometers (just over one mile) north of Bicheno. There are three small waterfalls in the park, and a marked two-day walking path.

Just past the turnoff to the park, the **Eastcoast Birdlife and Animal Park (** (03) 6375 1311 gives visitors the opportunity to pet and hand-feed kangaroos, wallabies and wombats. There are also Tasmanian devils here, but they're not quite as friendly. Open 9 AM to 5 PM daily.

A colony of **little penguins** lives at the northern end of Redbill Beach. Tours leave the information office **(** (03) 6375 1333 at dusk every evening. A footway extends from Redbill Point north of Bicheno to the **blowhole** at the south. Whalers Lookout provides good views of the coast, and in October and November native rock orchids bloom here.

ST. HELENS

The largest town on the east coast, St. Helens, on the shores of **Georges Bay**, is renowned for its crayfish, flounder and game fishing. The **Visitor Information Centre (**/FAX (03) 6376 1329, 20 Celia Street, can book game-fishing charters. An assortment of private boats at the main jetty take bay cruises. There's good fishing from one of the many jetties in Georges Bay, and tackle is available for rental or purchase from several shops in town.

The St. Helens **History Room (** (03) 6376 1744, 57 Celia Street, next to the library and opposite the post office, details the history of the area and has information on walking tracks and eco-tourism. The foreshore playground has a safe swimming for children and a sheltered barbecue area, but **Beerbarrel Beach** is the place to go for surf. **East Coast Scuba Center (** (03) 6376 1720, Celia Street, offers scuba-diving rental and information.

Several interesting drives north of the area include **Binalong Bay**, the **Bay of Fires Coastal Reserve** and **The Gardens**, which in springtime is covered with colorful wildflowers, flowering heath and wattles.

St. Columbia Waterfalls are the highest falls in Tasmania and are well worth the pleasant 20-minute drive from Pyengana along the windy St. Columbia Falls Road, from where it's a short 10-minute walk to the viewing platform. And do try the tasty local cheese made at the **Pyengana Cheese Factory** along the way.

Beaumaris, only 11 km (seven miles) south of St. Helens, has magnificent beaches with surfing and surf fishing the popular activities. A further nine kilometers (five and a half miles) south, **Scamander** is situated on pounding ocean beaches and the **Scamander River**, which is famous for its trout and bream fishing.

LAUNCESTON

Huddled among the mountains and the hills at the head of the picturesque Tamar Valley, Launceston, with a population of 70,000, is the largest city of northern Tasmania. It is a quiet place known for its numerous parks, in which European trees such as ash, oak and elm thrive. It also has some marvelous Victorian streetscapes to enjoy and makes an excellent base for exploring the northern part of Tasmania, with its historic villages, fine wineries and national parks.

GENERAL INFORMATION

The **Tasmanian Travel and Information Centre** ((03) 6336 3122, at the corner of St. John and Paterson streets, is open from 8:45 AM to 5 PM weekdays, and from 9 AM to noon weekends. The

Launceston Lending Library ((03) 6336 2625 in Civic Square offers **Internet** access and is open Monday to Thursday from 9:30 AM to 6 PM, Friday 9:30 AM to 8 PM, and Saturday 9:30 AM to 12 PM.

WHAT TO SEE AND DO

Launceston's most outstanding natural beauty spot is only a few minutes' walk from the center of town. Surrounded by parklands, the South Esk River plunges through **Cataract Gorge** into the Tamar River, with spectacular ferocity after heavy rain. A walking path follows the nearly vertical cliff face up to **First Basin**, from where a 300-m (985-ft) chairlift offers a breathtaking ride over the deep water. There's a café and a restaurant here, with quite a few peacocks ready to pick up any crumbs.

Hiking into Freycinet Peninsula is rewarded with clear views across Wine Glass Bay.

Second Basin is half an hour further upstream, with good views of Launceston and the Tamar River along the way.

Launceston was founded just a few months after Hobart, and its natural beauty is complemented by elegant Victorian buildings, a number of which line St. John and George streets. The **Old Umbrella Shop** ((03) 6331 9248, 60 George Street, built from Tasmanian blackwood in the 1860s, is an excellent example of an original Victorian shopfront and interior.

Only six kilometers (just under four miles) south on the Midland Highway, **Franklin House** ((03) 6344 7824 was built by convicts in 1838. Its beautiful furnishings include an eighteenth-century mahogany clock, an organ, and some fine portraits. The house and garden are open to the public 9 AM to 5 PM, Monday to Friday; an admission fee is charged.

Opened in 1891, the **Queen Victoria Museum and Art Gallery** ((03) 6331 6777, on Wellington Street, houses a fine collection of colonial and Aboriginal art and a planetarium. The museum incorporates **Macquarie House**, built by local merchant, Henry Reed, in 1830.

Penny Royal ((03) 6331 6699, 147 Paterson Street, is a commercial tourist attraction that recreates colonial industrial practices. A water mill has been restored to working order, along with a corn mill, windmill, cannon foundry and arsenal. A nineteenth-century Launceston No. 16 tram operates every 10 minutes between the water mill and the windmill. The *Lady Stelfox* paddle-steamer leaves from here on a 45-minute cruise of the Tamar River and Cataract Gorge. **Boag's Brewery** ((03) 6331 9311, on the Esplanade, beer was voted Australia's best beer of 1999 and has tours Monday to Friday.

Devils Playground Ecotours ((03) 6343 1787 WEB SITE WWW.tassie.net.au/devilsplayground, have some great day-tours of Launceston and the region west as far as Cradle Mountain and east as far as Freycinet Peninsula.

WHERE TO STAY

Many of Launceston's nineteenth-century houses and cottages have been converted into tourist accommodation, generally within the moderate price range. A large weeping willow shades **The Shambles** ((03) 6334 2231, 121–129 Balfour Street, where guests sleep in old-fashioned four-poster beds. **Airlie** ((03) 6334 2162 FAX (03) 6334 3195, 89 Margaret Street, and **Thyme Cottage** ((03) 6398 5129 FAX (03) 6398 5164, 31 Cimitiere Street, are two other nineteenth-century-cottage B&Bs.

Just a few minutes' walk from Cataract Gorge, the imposing Federation-style **Turret House** ((03) 6334 7033 FAX (03) 6331 6091, 41 West Tamar Road, has large comfortable rooms. At the corner of

Margaret and York streets is the **Old Bakery Inn** ((03) 6331 7900 FAX (03) 6331 7756, which has been restored to its nineteenth-century condition. Some of the original ovens remain.

Fiona's B&B ((03) 6334 5965 FAX (03) 6331 1709, 5/141As George Street, comprises a group of two-story modern cottages at only $60 a single and $80 a double. The price includes a copious cooked breakfast cooked and served by two of the most gracious hosts on the isle. If you want to really pamper yourself, right next door are the **Aquarius Roman Baths** ((03) 6331 2255, 127-133 George Street, a luxurious spa complex decorated with white marble statues and pillars. Entrance costs $20, or $32 a couple, with optional extras like massages and facials.

Eight kilometers (five miles) southwest of Launceston is the **Country Club Casino** ((03) 6344 8855 FAX (03) 6335 5788 in Prospect Vale. Along with its gaming tables the hotel offers a restaurant, an 18-hole, par-72 golf course and nightly live entertainment.

For comfortable and inexpensive motel-type accommodation try the **Great Northern Hotel** TOLL-FREE (1800) 030 567 FAX (03) 6331 3712, 3 Earl Street, or **North Lodge** TOLL-FREE (1800) 006 042 FAX (03) 6334 2810, 7 Brisbane Street.

WHERE TO EAT

The cliffs surrounding the **Gorge Restaurant** ((03) 6331 3330 (moderate) at Cataract Gorge are illuminated at night, giving diners a sense of distance from downtown Launceston. During the day, light meals and afternoon tea are served on outside tables.

The moderately priced **Fee & Me** ((03) 6331 3195, 190 Charles Street, is housed in an elegant two-story mansion built in 1835 and is well known for its excellent cellar of Tasmanian wines. All courses are offered at starter size, allowing guests to sample several different dishes. Nearby is **Elm Cottage** ((03) 6331 8468, 168 Charles Street (moderate), a quaint restaurant near the middle of Launceston. **Quigley's Balfour Terrace** ((03) 6331 6971, 96 Balfour Street (moderate), is notable for its game and fish dishes. **Arpar's** ((03) 6331 2786, ont the corner of Charles and Patterson Streets, serves authentic and inexpensive Thai. Their tasty selection is large and caters well to vegetarians.

HOW TO GET THERE

Ansett and Australian Airlines have flights from most state capital cities to Launceston, although direct service is only available from Melbourne and Sydney. Kendall have flights from Melbourne. **Airlines of Tasmania** TOLL-FREE (1800) 030 550 flies between Hobart and Launceston.

Penny farthings on parade at Evandale's annual Town Fair and Penny-farthing World Championships.

THE CENTRAL NORTH

EVANDALE

Twenty kilometers (12 miles) south of Launceston is the tiny township (population 700) of Evandale. Well worth a visit anytime for its wonderfully preserved historic buildings, Evandale is particularly lively during its **Town Fair and Penny-farthing World Championships** held in late in February. Locals turn out in period costume with vintage cars, food and craft stalls, entertainment and the thrilling eliminations and final. Turning sharp corners at break-neck speeds and dangerously close to one another makes for exciting viewing. As well as the championship title there are tandem races, relays (including the father and son and mother and daughter events), and over-55s titles. The day ends with a vintage car and bicycle parade.

Off the main road eight kilometers (five miles) from town, **Clarendon House** ((03) 6398 6220 would not have been out of place on a grand plantation in old Virginia. A long curving driveway leads to the two-story mansion, built in 1838 by wealthy wool grower and merchant James Fox. The house is furnished in the style of the period and is open for visits daily from 10 AM to 5 PM.

LONGFORD

Longford, 25 km (16 miles) south of Launceston, is a fine example of a Georgian town with many of its original buildings still in use. The **Corner Shop Café** (early 1830s), corner of Wellington and Marlborough streets, offers snacks and light lunches. It also sells local handicrafts and connects with an interesting curio shop. If you need to check your e-mail go into the **regional library** (*circa* 1858) on Wellington Street and take in the old interior while contemplating your electronic responses. On the way pop into the enchanting antique doll restorers shop a few doors up. A short drive away is **Woolmers Estate** ((03) 6391 2230 WEB SITE WWW.vision.net.au/woolmers, in Woolmers Lane, a colonial homestead (*circa* 1816) kept in the same family for six generations. Visitors can stay in wonderfully restored self-contained cottages (moderate) set in beautiful gardens and farmland. The house itself has been meticulously restored and furnished and is one of the best examples of this period in Tasmania. There are guided tours twice daily.

January and February are Tasmania's peak inland trout-fishing months. **Davidsons Wild Trout Tasmania** ((03) 6391 2220 WEB SITE www.wildtrout tasmania.com.au, 51 Marlborough Street, Longford, takes trips into the central highland lake country to enjoy some of the greatest trout fishing spots in the world. Their lodge includes modern fishing equipment and is set on a private lake.

PERTH

Perth, along the Midland Highway only 20 km (13 miles) south of Launceston, also has strong nineteenth-century connections. The **Leather Bottell Inn** ((03) 6398 2248, 55 Main Road, built in 1830, has been converted into an excellent restaurant and is open daily for morning and afternoon tea and lunch, and for dinner from Thursday to Saturday. Take a look at the **Baptist Tabernacle** in Clarence Street, constructed in 1889. It's an ornate octagonal brick building with a domed iron roof and large paneled doors.

LIFFEY VALLEY STATE RESERVE

Thirty kilometers (19 miles) west of Longford via Bracknell, **Liffey Valley State Reserve** on the slopes of the Great Western Tiers is a cool temperate

rainforest shaded by myrtle, sassafras and leatherwood. A nature walk leads through forests of towering eucalypti and tree ferns, past a number of smaller falls, finally leading to the impressive **Liffey Falls**. Rosellas, pink robins and fairy-wrens are common here and at night Tasmanian devils, quolls, bandicoots and wallabies come out to feed.

The area is also great for fishing. The **Tasmanian Fly Fishing and Guiding School** ℂ (03) 6362 3441 FAX (03) 6362 3441, 118 Emu Bay Road, Deloraine, can provide personalized tuition in the art of fly fishing and in guiding skills, with half-day to five-day packages.

For refreshments and great views stop at the wonderful **Liffey Tea Gardens and Bush Cabins** ℂ (03) 6397 3213, built from shingle and pine and set in a wattle glade and gardens at the foot of **Dry's Bluff**, the highest peak of the **Great Western Tiers**. Open weekends 10 AM until 4 PM.

MOLE CREEK

Mole Creek lies 72 km (46 miles) west of Launceston along the Bass Highway. Delicious leatherwood honey is made here from the blossom of leatherwood trees that exist only in the rainforests of the west coast of Tasmania. A group of over a dozen caves **limestone caves**, 15 km (nine miles) west of Mole Creek, are among the best in Australia. Kubla Khan, Genghis Khan, Croesus, Lynds and Haile Selassie all require permits, and with the exception of Lynds are all locked. The larger of the caves is **Marakoopa Cave**, which has some beautiful wax-like formations and a series of small pools. It and **King Solomon's Cave** are open to visitors, and have safe pathways and lighting.

Gentle Liffy Falls are tucked away in a leafy gully not far from Mole Creek.

For permits and information on touring the caves or organizing caving visits, contact **Parks and Wildlife Service's Marakoopa Base** ((03) 6363 5182. **Wild Cave Tours** ((03) 6367 8142 E-MAIL wildcavetours@vetas.com.au explore a number of the lesser-known "undeveloped" caves here. The most popular with experienced cavers is Kubla Khan, although permits are only given to groups accompanied by a qualified local guide. Visitor numbers to these caves are limited, and trips should be booked ahead.

TAMAR VALLEY WINE REGION

Tasmania's major wine-producing region, the Tamar Valley, has really taken off over the last 10 years. The cool climate here is best suited to whites, especially Riesling, Chardonnay and Pinot Noir. **Pipers Brook** ((03) 6382 7527, 1216 Pipers Brook Road (east of the river), produces excellent sparkling wines and Riesling. Nearby is the quaint **Brook Eden Vineyard** ((03) 6395 6244, 167 Adams Road, Lebrina, which has particularly good Pinot Noir. Both have cellar doors, open daily 10 AM to 5 PM. While there, ask to try the excellent **Ashgrove Farm** cheeses which go incredibly well with the wines. **Marion's Vineyard** ((03) 6394 7473, Foreshore Drive, Deviot, produce some good wines too — the bonus here is the chalet style accommodation (moderate) with amazing scenery of the river and hills. Their wood-fired pizzas are pretty amazing as well.

To get to the wine region take either the East Tamar Highway (A7) (direction Beauty Point) or the West Tamar Highway(A8) (direction Lilydale) north from Launceston. For more information on the vineyards and their wines pick up a copy of *Tasmanian Wine Route* and *Taste Tasmania Cellar Door and Farm Gate* guides from any tourist information office, or browse Tourism Tasmania's WEB SITE www.tourism.tas.gov.au.

THE NORTHWEST

DEVONPORT

Devonport, situated at the mouth of the Mersey River, is the largest and most important port on Tasmania's north coast. Even so most people hop off the ferry and continue on their journey without giving it much regard. There are several interesting things to see and do here, though, warranting at least a few good hours.

The **Tiagarra Aboriginal Interpretive Center** ((03) 6424 8250 FAX (03) 6427 0506, Mersey Bluff, Devonport, displays well-documented information on Tasmania's Aboriginal people, including their first encounters with Europeans and the tragic events that followed. There are many authentic Aboriginal crafts for sale here.

A five-minute drive west from the ferry terminal, **Don River Railway** (/FAX (03) 6424 6335 displays a large collection of locomotives and passenger carriages dating from 1869 up to 1961. Take the 30-minute round trip to **Coles Bay** or disembark and return on a later train. Open daily with trains running hourly from 11 AM to 4 PM. An interesting historical attraction is **Home Hill** ((03) 6424 3028, 77 Middle Road, the home of Dame Enid and Sir Joseph Lyons and their 12 children. Sir Joseph Lyons was the only Australian prime minister (1932–1939) to have also served as premier of his state, and Tasmania's only prime minister. In 1949, 10 years after his death, Dame Enid Lyons was the first woman to become a member of the House of Representatives. The carefully preserved building, built in 1916, has impeccable manicured gardens, with some fine Queen Anne furniture and many unusual artifacts given to Lyons during his career.

Situated in the Old Harbour Master's residence, the **Tasmanian Maritime and Folk Museum** ((03) 6424 7100, in Gloucester Avenue, West Devonport, was built in 1920 and has extensive displays of maritime memorabilia, with some detailed models of ships that visited the island. It is open every day of week (except Mondays) from 10 AM to 4:30 PM.

BURNIE

Burnie, found on a narrow coastal plain skirting Emu Bay, is one of the major industrial centers on Tasmania's north coast. It's not a great introduction to Tasmania, although it does have a couple of lovely gardens and parks. Not far from the town center, **Burnie Park** has a wildlife sanctuary in the center with a walking track to Oldaker Falls and **Burnie Inn;** the first licensed pub in Burnie, the inn was built in 1847 and has been relocated to the park, where it now operates as a tearoom. Burnie's Agricultural Show is combined with the Rhododendron Festival and held in October.

The **Pioneer Village Museum** ((03) 6430 5746, on Little Alexander Street, Civic Centre Plaza, is an impressive recreation of life in Burnie at the turn of the century.

On route from Burnie to Cradle mountain, **Annsleigh Gardens and Tea House** (/FAX (03) 6435 7229, 4 Metaira Road, nine kilometers (five and a half miles) south on the B18, is a beautiful English-style tea garden and a haven for local bird life. The gardens are renowned for their thousands of rhododendrons, and are open to the public from September until March.

WYNARD AND BOAT HARBOUR

Sleepy, picturesque Boat Harbour, 10 km (six miles) west of Wynard on the Bass Highway, offers a pleasant alternative to accommodation in either

Burnie or Wynard, and it is handy to Wynard Airport (sometimes referred to as Burnie Airport). **Boat Harbour Beach** has a string of houses and a good fish and chip shop overlooking a crescent of white sand beach and the cold blue waters of Bass Strait. It has reasonable surfing with board hire available on the beach.

Just out of Wynard at **Table Cape** are cliff-top **tulip** and **poppy farms** (the flowers blossom late September to mid-October). An alternative seven-kilometer-long (four-mile) coastal road from Wynard passes along Table Cape and joins the Bass Highway four kilometers (two and a half miles) before the Boat Harbour turnoff. The coastal road is a lovely drive, and early in the morning or around dusk you're sure to see quite a few wallabies hopping across the road and nibbling in the locals' front gardens. This is not a road to speed along.

Killynaught Spa Cottages ((03) 6445 1041 FAX (03) 6445 1556, Bass Highway, Boat Harbour, comprises five luxuriously appointed, self-contained, Victorian and Edwardian cottages filled with antiques and memorabilia. This moderately priced accommodation looks across rolling pastures and out to sea and provides a comfortable base to explore the northwest; it is only 40 minutes from Stanley.

For an aerial perspective of the region, **Tasmanian Scenic Flights** ((03) 6442 1111 runs from Wynard to several locations in Tasmania, including Cradle Mountain ($90 per person) and the southwest wilderness area ($180).

STANLEY

The fishing village of Stanley is nestled under a 13-million-year-old, 152-m-high (500-ft) rocky outcrop known as the **Nut**. Known as Moo-Nut-Re-ker by Tasmanian Aborigines, by 1851 settlers had come to know it simply as the Nut. It's a steep, 20-minute walk up the Nut, but better still to take the chair-lift and enjoy the breezy panorama. The **Nut Chairlift and Information Centre** ((03) 6458 1286 is on Brown's Road.

Stanley is a classified historic town full of beautifully preserved buildings that has changed very little since 1825. The **Discovery Centre Folk Museum** ((03) 6458 1145, in Church Street, can supply walking maps of the area and other local information. It's open daily from 10 AM to 4:30 PM. The **Plough Inn** was built in 1842 and operated as a hotel until the license expired in 1876, when it became a branch of the National Bank of Tasmania. It has been restored and furnished with antiques and is open to the public. **Lyons Cottage** in Church Street is the birthplace of Joseph Lyons (born in 1879), who was Australia's only Tasmanian prime minister (from 1932 to 1939). The cottage is open to the public and contains interesting memorabilia. **Saint James' Presbyterian Church**

is an early example of a prefabricated building; it was transported from England to Stanley in 1853.

Historic **Highfield Estate**, near Stanley, was built in 1832 as headquarters for the Van Diemen's Land Company, which had been set up 10 years previously to exploit the northwest coast's wool-growing potential. Although a large farm was established here, financial losses forced the company out within 30 years.

Stanley Guest House (*circa* 1909) ((03) 6458 1488, 27 Main Road, has a friendly relaxed atmosphere, centered on the guest lounge and open log fire. Rooms are elegantly furnished and spacious, with views of the Nut.

HOW TO GET THERE

Kendell Airlines (131 300 TOLL-FREE (1800) 338 894 has direct flights from Melbourne to Devonport and Wynard (Burnie). They also have some great package deals which include return flights, accommodation and car rental with unlimited miles.

The Spirit of Tasmania ferry leaves Melbourne at 6 PM on Monday, Wednesday and Friday, arriving at Devonport the next morning. A bus connection meets the ferry and arrives in Launceston at 10 AM.

THE TASMANIAN WILDERNESS WORLD HERITAGE AREA

The group of national parks that make up the Tasmanian Wilderness World Heritage Area feature rugged terrain and a remote, untouched coastline, with pristine highland tarns and lakes. The deep green forests contain some of the world's most ancient trees — Huon pines, gums and sassafras — and ferny glades straight out of the *Jungle Book*. There are enough peaks and crags here to keep the keenest walkers and climbers busy for a lifetime.

The Tasmanian Wilderness World Heritage Area comprises the following national parks: Southwest, Franklin–Gordon Wild Rivers, Mount Field, Cradle Mountain–Lake St. Clair, Hartz Mountains and Walls of Jerusalem.

GENERAL INFORMATION

There is an entry charge for all 16 national parks in Tasmania. A daily pass is $5 and a two-month pass $30. For information on national parks and the World Heritage Area contact the **Tasmanian Conservation Trust** ((03) 6234 3552.

CRADLE MOUNTAIN–LAKE ST. CLAIR NATIONAL PARK

Cradle Mountain–Lake St. Clair National Park contains an extensive network of walking tracks, from a boardwalk with wheelchair access to the at-least-five-day Overland Track. All are clearly marked on a map that can purchased from the visitors' center. The weather can be extremely unpredictable in this part of the world, changing from sun to snow in one day, so be prepared. Walker registration is essential, even for short walks, and there are registration booths at Waldheim and Dove Lake car parks.

General Information

Cradle Mountain Visitor Center ((03) 6492 1133, just inside the national park entrance, has informative displays, an art gallery, videos and reference books. Open daily 8 AM to 5 PM. There are picnic shelters and electric barbecues here too. The **Park Shop** sells postcards, books, film and clothing suited to mountain trekking.

Lakeside St. Clair Wilderness Holidays ((03) 6289 1137 FAX (03) 6289 1250 WEB SITE www .view.com.au/lakeside, in Derwent Bridge books cruises and accommodation in the area.

What to See and Do

The most popular destination in the park is undoubtedly rugged but serene **Cradle Mountain**, with its crystal-clear **Dove Lake**, razored mountain peaks and an assortment of excellent walking tracks. Wedge-tailed eagles soar overhead while tiny echidnas furrow in the ground. Enormous snow gums and thousand-year-old King Billy pines tower above necklace fern, pandani, kangaroo fern and colorful wildflowers. The mountain is a nature lover's paradise.

The two- to three-hour **Dove Lake Circuit Track** is a great introductory walk to the park. It leaves from the Dove Lake car park.

In the northern end of the park, several bushwalker huts mark the location of the old **Waldheim Chalet**, tucked in among Cradle Valley's myrtle and King Billy pines. Gustav Weindorfer, an Austrian who fell in love with the area, built Waldheim (German for "forest home") here in 1912. There's a visitor center here too, with environmental displays and an audio presentation of the early days of Cradle Mountain. In the late afternoon you're likely to see Bennetts wallabies and wombats pottering around the valley floor.

At the southern end of the park, at an altitude of 737 m (2,418 ft), **Lake St. Clair** is the source of the River Derwent, and Australia's deepest natural freshwater lake. It stretches over 17 km (10.5 miles) into the depths of Tasmania's Wilderness World Heritage Area. Dominated by **Mount Olympus** at 1,447 m (4,747 ft), the shoreline is forested with sassafras, myrtle, native pines and beeches. The five- to eight-day **Overland Track** begins (or ends) here and passes through alpine shrubbery to glacial lakes, waterfalls and forests, en route to Cradle Mountain. Although this is one part of Australia where independent walks are entirely possible, a knowledgeable guide adds to the experience.

Several companies offer guided walks. One reputable company is **Craclair Tours** ((03) 6424 7833 E-MAIL craclair@southcom.com.au, which runs all inclusive eight-day walks and five-day combined sailing and walking tours. Walkers register at the information center and ranger station ((03) 6289 1172 at the southern end of the lake. There's a kiosk nearby where small boats can be rented for fishing or exploring the lake. A ferry leaves from here, making three return trips a day to the northern end of the lake. **Seair** ((03) 6492 1132 has several daily scenic flights of the region, weather permitting.

Bordering Cradle Mountain on the eastern side is the less accessible **Walls of Jerusalem National Park**, where steep mountains create a natural amphitheater of sub-alpine wilderness, and ancient pencil pine forests border a number of glacial lakes. It can snow here at any time of the year and you need to be a competent and prepared bushwalker to take this one on.

Where to Stay and Eat

Cradle Mountain Lodge ((03) 6492 1303 TOLL-FREE 132 469 FAX (03) 6492 1309 WEB SITE www.usp.com .au/P&O, Cradle Mountain Road, via Sheffield, offers accommodation ranging from deluxe cabins with spas (expensive) or standard open-plan (moderate) to budget rooms (two only). The complex comprises 96 timber cabins, plus two rooms on the second floor of the lodge. Cabin facilities are good and all include a log fire. The lodge has both a licensed restaurant (moderate to expensive) and a bar area serving wholesome inexpensive bistro-style food.

Several nearby towns are pleasant to stay in. **Lemonthyme Lodge** ((03) 6492 1112 FAX (03) 6492 1113, Dolcoath Road, at Moina, is 35 km (22 miles) from Cradle Mountain off Cradle Mountain Road. It offers luxurious (expensive) accommodation in a rustic rainforest setting. A bit further on in Staverton, the **Cradle Vista Guest House** ((03) 6491 1553 FAX (03) 6491 2380, 1030 and 978 Staverton Road, combines horseback riding with comfortable accommodation (moderate) and authentic country meals.

How to Get There

The northern entrance to Cradle Mountain–Lake St. Clair National Park is a 30- to 40-minute drive from Burnie and a little more than an hour from Launceston. Tassielink ((1300) 300 520 has daily bus services from both towns, and connecting buses from the park visitor center to Strahan and Hobart.

MOUNT FIELD NATIONAL PARK

On the Lyell Highway only 80 km (50 miles) northwest of Hobart, **Mount Field National Park** contains beautiful forests and crystal-clear (and icy) lakes. Snow cloaks a windswept highland plateau

in winter, making it perfect for cross-county skiing. More than 25 species of eucalyptus co-exist on the lower slopes, while on the higher slopes there are snow gums, pencil pines, sassafras and dwarf mountain pines. Of the many good bush-walks, the most popular in summer is the short 10-minute walk to **Russell Falls**, which drop 50 m (164 ft) into a gorge lush with ferns and rainforest.

SOUTHWEST NATIONAL PARK

Covering nearly 5,400 sq km (2,085 sq miles) Tasmania's Southwest National Park is the largest of Tasmania's national parks. It comprises some of the most rugged and wild untouched wilderness in the world, usually only seen by the most intrepid bush-walkers. Many pockets of dense temperate rainforest contain trees only found in Tasmania, including ancient Huon and towering King Billy pines. The park encompasses several

mountain ranges. **Federation Peak** may be only 1,425 m (4,675 ft) in altitude, but scaling it challenges even the best climbers, particularly over the last section of sheer, steep rock face. For experienced hikers a 150-km (93-mile) bush-walking track runs from Geevestown to Bathurst Harbour and then follows the coast to Hastings.

The park also contains lakes **Pedder** and **Gordon**, which together comprise the largest inland freshwater catchment in Australia. Lake Pedder was flooded in 1972 as part of the Gordon River power development project, although this sparked the enormously strong environmental campaign that led to the creation of the Tasmanian Wilderness World Heritage Area and saved the surrounding forests from similar destruction. There is now a strong movement pushing to drain the artificial lake and restore the valley to its former beauty.

Cradle Mountain is Tasmania's most popular destination, especially for hikers.

Only worldwide pressure will convince the government to do so. Environmentalists and biologists argue that if done soon the submerged forest will quickly regenerate. For more on the campaign have a look at the **Wildernesss Society** WEB SITE www.wilderness.org.au

FRANKLIN–GORDON WILD RIVERS NATIONAL PARK

The isolated Franklin and Gordon rivers have some of the most spectacular temperate rainforest in the world just off their banks. In the late 1970s, these rivers were the scene of much controversy when Tasmania's then conservative government decided

to dam the Franklin River, in the process destroying this unique wilderness area. Local environmentalists, led by Bob Brown, convinced the Federal Labor Government to halt the destruction, and a decision from the High Court in Canberra in 1983 eventually saved the Franklin and the Wild Rivers area. The publicity boosted tourism in Tasmania and interest in its wilderness areas, irrevocably, changing the incumbent state government's perception of its priorities.

The raging Franklin River begins in the Cheyne Range west of Lake St. Clair, flowing south until it meets at the Gordon and Olga River junction. The Franklin passes the Lyell Highway about 100 km (62 miles) east of Strahan, where the adventurous begin exciting whitewater rafting trips. Only fully experienced rafters should attempt this trip alone, although several companies operate rafting tours.

Tasmanian Expeditions ((03) 6334 3477 TOLL-FREE (1800) 030 230 WEB SITE www.tassie.net.au/tas_ex, 110 George Street, Launceston, run four- to 11-day rafting tours of the Franklin, the shorter ones taking in the lower Franklin and Gordon Rivers, while extended trips start in the upper Franklin, including a two-day hike to Frenchman's Cap. Based in Melbourne **Peregrine Adventures** ((03) 6231 0977 WEB SITE www.peregrine.net.au/rafting, 258 Lonsdale Street, have similar five- to 10-day rafting tours.

Beret-shaped **Frenchman's Cap**, known for its excellent bush-walking and flora, has hikes that last several days and shorter walks starting from the Lyell Highway. The best of the shorter walks are to **Donaghys Hill**, with views of Frenchman's Cap and the Franklin River, and the splendid **Nelson Falls**. The longer hike to the Cap takes a minimum of three days, and passes forests and buttongrass, lakes and bogs, and crags and valleys. Expect sudden weather changes. The **Lodden Plains**, on route to the Cap, are notoriously wet throughout the year. Camping areas are limited but there are good huts at **Vera** and **Tahune** lakes.

Strahan

Strahan, on Tasmania's far west coast, is the starting point for cruises and flights along the Gordon River into the heart of the Franklin–Gordon Wild Rivers National Park. Established in 1883, Strahan soon became the starting point for inland expeditions. The discovery of gold, silver and copper gave birth to the nearby inland towns of **Queenstown** and **Zeehan**, with Strahan being the only port servicing the new mining fields. It wasn't long before steamers operated from here to Melbourne, Launceston and Hobart. Today Strahan is a working fishing port that processes crayfish, shark, abalone, salmon and rainbow trout and a popular base for visitors to the World Heritage Area. Visit the **Strahan Visitors Center** ((03) 6471 7622 FAX (03) 6471 7020 on the Esplanade.

The **Strahan Wharf Centre** ((03) 6471 7488 presents the history of the southwest through well-presented displays. The center's marvelous reception desk is built from local Huon pine and the foyer is clad in river gravel. At the northernmost end of **Strahan Harbour** is the **People Park**, a blend of natural forest and botanical gardens with picnic and camping facilities. From here the 45-minute walk to **Hogarth Falls** passes through rainforest typical to the region with many trees clearly identified for budding botanists. The old carved headboards at the **Cemetery** on **Regatta Point** have some interesting occupants. If you're fortunate enough to strike warm weather, the **West Strahan Beach** is ideal for swimming.

To appreciate the vast size of the **Henty Dunes** (14 km or eight and a half miles from Strahan on the Zeehan Road) don't try to walk it, but instead try a four-wheel motorbike tour. For bookings call ((0419) 508 175. It's a lot of fun, and an experienced guide can point out sacred Aboriginal sites and several significant environmental points of interest without causing damage to them. A current driver's permit is necessary. **Dune surfing** is also fun here, boards are rented out daily from the car park.

In 1821, an expedition of 110 people including 74 convicts were sent to **Sarah Island** to harvest Huon pine and establish a shipbuilding industry and penal settlement. It was these convicts who named the entrance to the harbor **Hells Gates**. Tasmania's first and most brutal penal colony, it really was the entrance to hell for most. Out of the 182 prisoners, 169 received a total of

Where to Stay and Eat

A cozy place to stay is the **Strahan Wilderness Lodge and Bay View Cottages** (/FAX (03) 6471 7142, located behind the sawmill on Smugglers Cove. They have one-, two- and three-bedroom self-contained cottages and cabins starting at a very reasonable $60 to $80 depending on the season. Excellent facilities include an indoor heated pool and spa set inside the natural bush. Accommodation in the lodge costs from $40 to $55 a double including breakfast. For a luxurious stay at moderate prices, try **Franklin Manor** ((03) 6471 7311. As the base for visits to the Gordon and Franklin Rivers, Strahan has become a very popular destination, so it is wise to book well ahead.

7,000 lashes between them. Not many survived, and the colony closed in 1832.

Gordon River Cruises ((03) 6471 7187 FAX (03) 6471 7317 and **World Heritage Cruises** ((03) 6471 7174 WEB SITE WWW.worldheritagecruises.com.au, both in Strahan, operate cruises up the Gordon River. Tours include a stop at Sarah Island, a Heritage Rainforest Walk and views of Hells Gates. **Wild Rivers Jet** ((03) 6471 7174 runs 50-minute rides up the King River daily from 9 AM to 5 PM, from $36. Bookings can be made at the wharf. Another popular way of seeing the World Heritage Area is by seaplane with **Wilderness Air** ((03) 6471 7280. The planes take off from Strahan's wharf every one and a half hours from 9 AM until 3:30 PM (extended hours in January and February) and fly up the river to Sir John Falls, where they land so that you can take a walk in the rainforest. It's a breathtaking flight at only $99 for adults and $22 for children.

There is a string of cafés along the waterfront esplanade, and a pub with a good bistro menu.

How to Get There

Strahan is 298 km (185 miles) west of Hobart on the Lyell Highway, 41 km (25 miles) past Queenstown. **Tigerline** ((03) 6272 6611 FAX (03) 6272 7555 www.tigerline.com.au runs a bus service between Hobart, Strahan and Launceston.

MIDLANDS

The Midland Highway, Route 1, runs 198 km (123 miles) between Hobart and Launceston, and is Tasmania's main artery. Although not as spectacular as a coastal or mountain route, it is much

OPPPOSITE: Fun on the slopes at Henty Dunes.
ABOVE: Strahan is the base for cruises along the wild Gordan River.

more direct and bypasses many historic villages, allowing them a peace that has been lost elsewhere with the advent of cars. Many townships just a short distance off the highway have early histories as coaching stops and military depots, and are rich in colonial character. The trip can be made in two hours by car, but it's worth taking your time.

ROSS

The splendidly preserved village of Ross, a living museum of nineteenth-century colonial architecture, stretches along the banks of the Macquarie River, 122 km (76 miles) from Hobart. Its streets are lined with historic homes and public buildings, many of which have been restored and now house hotels, museums, and shops catering for tourists.

The **Ross Bridge** spans the river. Built with convict labor in 1836, it's not quite as old as the bridge at Richmond, but is certainly one of the most beautiful in Australia. The convicts, the majority of them Irish, carved 186 stones over the sandstone arches with images inspired from Celtic folklore. It is rumored that some of the figures are caricatures of local colonial "deities." The head stonemason, a convict named Daniel Herbert, was pardoned in recognition of his detailed work.

The main intersection of Bridge and Church streets was known locally as the "four corners of Ross" — Damnation (a corner occupied by a women's prison, now gone), Recreation (the Town Hall), Salvation (Lady of Sacred Heart Catholic Church) and Temptation (Man O'Ross Hotel). Of the four buildings, only the 1817 hotel survives, its interior richly paneled with Tasmanian oak and blackwood.

The **Village Bakery and Tea Room** serves light refreshment opposite St. John's Church on the main street. The tea rooms also display and sell local craft works.

CENTRAL HIGHLANDS

An alternative route through the center of Tasmania crosses the **Land of Three Thousand Lakes**. The roads here are neither as good nor as direct as the Midland Highway, but the scenery more than justifies getting off the beaten track to see this seldom-visited area.

From Launceston, drive along the Bass Highway to Deloraine and then turn onto the scenic Lake Highway, which takes you onto the windswept central plateau with its scurrying clouds, gnarled pencil pines, moorland and mountains. Glacial lakes pockmark the terrain. Often no larger than a football field, some of them are so shallow that it's possible to walk right across.

Visit one of the 40 major lakes or hundreds of creeks, tarns or highland rivers and cast a line for a wild Tasmanian trout. Reeling in a two-kilogram (four-and-a-half-pound) trout is an everyday event and in some lakes four-kilogram (nine-pound) trout are not uncommon. Brown trout dominates throughout the region, and some of the best places to fish are **Arthurs Lake**, **Macquarie River**, **Bronte Lagoon**, **Little Pine Lake** and **Great Lake**. Sea-run trout are found in estuaries. The best times to fish is from the beginning of October to late March. A fishing license can be purchased from most sports stores. Organized tours by locals who know the best places to fish are available from **Peter Hayes Guided Fishing**, which operates out of the **Compleat Angler Lodge** ((03) 6259 8295, in Miena. **Ausprey Tours** ((03) 6330 2612 is organized out of Launceston and specializes in fly fishing.

WHERE TO STAY

Ross has a good selection of colonial accommodation. The **Man O'Ross** ((03) 6381 5240 is inexpensive and feeds you a hearty breakfast. There are several charming, moderately priced self-contained cottages, dating back as early as 1850, which can be reserved through the **Colonial Cottages of Ross** ((03) 6381 5354 FAX (03) 6381 5408, in Church Street. Each is furnished with furniture from the mid-nineteenth century.

There are few places to stay along the Lake Highway, but some moderately priced accommodation is available in Bothwell. **Whites Cottages** ((03) 6259 5651, in Queens Street, provides B&B accommodation while eight kilometers (five miles) out of town is the quaint **Mrs. Woods Farmhouse** ((03) 6259 5612.

The **Compleat Angler Lodge** ((03) 6259 8179, on Haddens Bay, and **Great Lake Hotel** ((03) 6259 8163 FAX (03) 6259 8147, on Swan Bay, are moderately priced and generally cater to those on fishing vacations.

HOW TO GET THERE

Tasmanian Redline Coaches run a daily service between Hobart and Launceston along the Midland Highway. There are no regular buses for transportation along the Lake Highway, the only way to explore this area is by car or bicycle.

Tasmania is Australia's most mountainous state. The Highland Lakes region offers the best trout fishing opportunities in Australia — straight from the horse's mouth.

South Australia

SOCIAL THEORIST EDWARD GIBBON WAKEFIELD ARGUED in the 1820s that colonies could grow on the capital raised from the sale of Crown land to free settlers. Wakefield, who hatched his scheme while spending time in Newgate Prison for abducting a 15-year-old heiress, maintained that a civilized community could only thrive with such colonists. Initially rejected by the government, Wakefield soon lost interest in the idea. His supporters remained committed though, and on August 15, 1834, Westminster passed the Act for the Establishment of the Colony of South Australia.

South Australia prides itself as being the only state never to have accepted convicts (Victoria had a short-lived penal colony at Sorrento in 1803, although it lasted fewer than six months). Its free settlers built churches and beautiful colonial sandstone buildings, and in its capital, Adelaide, extensive parklands were established along the Torrens River. In the twentieth century a love for culture was added, with the inauguration of the Adelaide Arts Festival, the first such event in Australia. To complete the picture of an entirely civilized place, South Australians acquired an appreciation of fine wines. Australia's best wines, as any South Australian will quickly tell you, are made exclusively in this state's Clare, Eden and Barossa valleys, McLaren Vale and Coonawarra.

ADELAIDE

Situated on the Torrens River plain between St. Vincent's Gulf and the Mount Lofty Ranges, Adelaide's wide tree-lined streets and fine colonial buildings are surrounded by a green belt of parklands. The large number of churches throughout the city have earned Adelaide the nickname "City of Churches," while the Mediterranean climate makes Adelaide ideal for the many outdoor festivals that run throughout the year, attracting artists from all over the world. Beyond the city, the suburbs stretch to the low sand dunes of the Gulf St. Vincent in the west, and up into the green folds of the Adelaide Hills to the east. Many immaculate beaches are only a short drive from the city, the most famous at Glenelg. Another short drive from the city and you are in rolling hills and farmland; a little further still is Australia's premier wine region. The range and quality of its produce are reflected in the city's many fine restaurants, which represent some of the best value for money in Australia. Adelaide has a laid-back country feel, its people relaxed and open, but nevertheless has historically been one of Australia's most progressive cities, being the first to give women the vote and to grant land titles to Aborigines.

All in all, Adelaide is one neat package, without the stress of the larger cities, but with a lively modern edge that doesn't let it fall into the "big country town syndrome."

BACKGROUND

In 1836 Colonel William Light, the first Surveyor-General, chose the location for Adelaide. Later that year Governor Hindmarsh arrived to administer the new colony. A raging quarrel erupted between the two men who disagreed on where Adelaide should be sited. To onlookers this squabble was out of place in the civilized colony both men wished to found. Following his run-in with Colonel Light, the volatile Hindmarsh's petty disputes with land developers led to his recall by the Imperial Government in 1838.

Surviving without convict labor proved difficult and only copper discoveries, in Kapunda in 1842 and Burra in 1845, provided the economic stimulus that allowed Adelaide to embark on an ambitious building program. Fortunately many of these churches, public buildings and houses built in the late nineteenth century survive today.

GENERAL INFORMATION

The **South Australian Tourism Commission Travel Centre** ((08) 8212 1505 TOLL-FREE (1800) 882 092 WEB SITE www.tourism.sa.gov.au, 1 King William Street, is open weekdays from 9 AM to 5 PM and provides information, books accommodation and can arrange a variety of interesting tours throughout the state. On weekends it closes at 2 PM. In Glenelg, the **Tourist Information Centre** ((08) 8294 5833 on the foreshore at Bayworld Museum is open daily.

The **Royal Automobile Association of South Australia** ((08) 8202 4540, 41 Hindmarsh Square, sells maps, offers information about road conditions and reserves accommodation.

For emergency **medical service** call ((08) 8223 0230 or (08) 8216 2222.

The best Internet café and a great place to just hang out is **Ngapartji** ((08) 8232 0839 WEB SITE www.ngapartji.com.au, 211 Rundle Street, where you can surf the net or check your e-mail on the many indoor terminals, or wait to use one of the free terrace terminals — they have a time limit though.

GETTING AROUND

The TransAdelaide Information Centre ((08) 8210 1000, on the corner of King William and Currie streets, can provide **bus** timetables and maps of Adelaide's bus system. The center is open 7 AM to 8 PM. For information on country and interstate **trains** phone Adelaide Rail Station ((08) 8231 4366 from 8:30 AM to 5:30 PM weekdays.

Three good city **taxi** services are: Suburban (131 008, Adelaide Independent (132 211, and Access Cabs ((1300) 360 940.

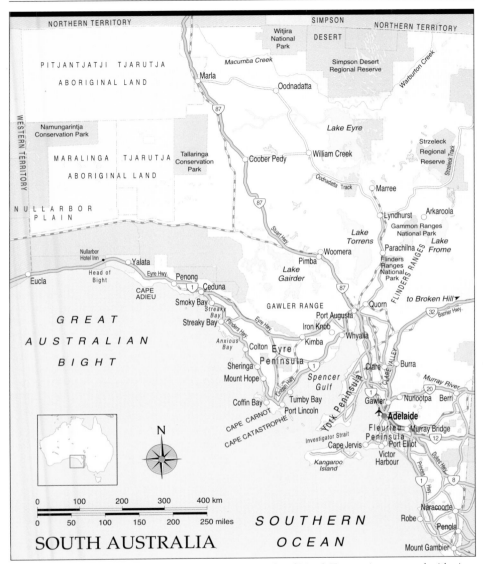

SOUTH AUSTRALIA

WHAT TO SEE AND DO

City Center

Adelaide Explorer Bus provides an easy way to discover Adelaide. The relaxing two-and-a-half-hour round-trip journey, which starts at the travel center at 1 King William Street, encompasses both Glenelg and the city center. Passengers can get on and off the bus as often as they like on the same ticket. Colonel Light's well structured layout for Adelaide and its flat topography makes the city center highly walkable.

South Australia's seats of political power, learning and culture are conveniently distributed along

tree-lined **North Terrace**, interspersed with nineteenth-century churches. West of King William Street, **Old Parliament House** ((08) 8226 8555, built in 1855, is now a constitutional museum. Adelaide has led the world in many social reforms and these and other historical items of interest are documented here. Next door is the "new" Parliament House. Just behind these two buildings, the **Adelaide Casino** ((08) 8218 4111 is housed in the restored Adelaide Railway Station. It's one of the most elegant casino buildings in Australia. East of King Street and next door to the Museum of Adelaide, the **Art Gallery of South Australia** ((08) 8207 7000 has an excellent collection of Aboriginal and non-Aboriginal Australian art, as well as works from Europe and Asia. The gallery has some inspiring works by Hans Heysen, who painted the Flinders Range's multi-hued rocks and enormous ghost gums.

The **University of Adelaide** sits crammed between North Terrace and the Torrens River. The overcrowding, however, has not robbed the predominantly neo-Gothic campus of its academic repose. The on-campus **Museum of Classical Archaeology (** (08) 8303 5239, on the second floor of the Mitchell Building, exhibits artifacts from ancient Rome, Greece and Egypt, some dating back 5,000 years. The museum is open weekdays from noon to 3 PM and admittance is free.

Further east along North Terrace, the **Botanic Gardens and State Herbarium (** (08) 8228 2311 provide relaxing shady lawns and promenades to escape Adelaide's heat. Magnificent 120-year-old Moreton Bay fig trees line the avenue down the center of the gardens to the Main Lake. In the giant glasshouse **Bicentennial Conservatory** near the Plane Tree Drive entrance a fine spray of water nourishes lush rainforest, beautiful flowers and wetlands plants.

Ayers House, 228 North Terrace, just opposite the **Royal Adelaide Hospital**, was built in 1855. The stately mansion, home to Sir Henry Ayers, who was elected Premier of South Australia for a record seven times, is open to the public Tuesday to Sunday. Off East Terrace, the **Tandanya National Aboriginal Cultural Institute (** (08) 8224 3200, 253 Grenfell Street, supports Aboriginal culture, art and dance, and its activities and exhibitions are open to the public. Authentic Aboriginal art and artifacts can be purchased from the center, which is open from 10 AM to 5 PM. The center includes a performing arts area, a museum and art gallery, art and craft workshops, and a café that serves native foods. *Tandanya* is the name given to the Adelaide area by the Kaurna Aboriginal people — it means "place of the red kangaroo."

Grenfell Street leads into **King William Street**, which, at 42 m (140 ft), is the widest of any Australian city thoroughfare. It bisects the city and continues into North Adelaide.

The center of Adelaide is marked by **Victoria Square**, at the junction of Grote, Wakefield and King William streets. Just north of Victoria Square is the **Post Office**, built in 1867, and the imposing Renaissance-style **Town Hall** built between 1863 and 1866, inspired by public buildings in Florence and Genoa. There are one-hour tours of the interior of the Town Hall every Tuesday and Thursday at 10:30 AM and 2:30 PM.

Festival Centre

Overlooking the Torrens River, just off King William Street north of the city, Adelaide's Festival Centre (** (08) 8226 8111, opened in 1973, the same year as the Sydney Opera House. The focus of Adelaide's cultural life, its concert halls have excellent acoustics. The superb complex houses the Festival Theatre, the Playhouse, an amphitheater for outdoor performances and a plaza for informal cultural gatherings.

The Festival Centre is the main venue for the **Adelaide Festival of the Arts (** (08) 8216 4444 E-MAIL afa@adelaidefestival.net.au, held every second March (even years), which attracts Australian and international performing artists, writers and visual artists, and incorporates a **WOMAD** world music event. It started in 1960 mainly as a hometown affair; today, however, interstate visitors attracted by its reputation pack Adelaide for the three-week festival.

Coinciding with the Adelaide Festival, the **Fringe Festival** WEB SITE www.adelaidefringe.com.au features alternative contemporary performance art and music.

Port Adelaide

Port Adelaide was established in 1840. As the once-thriving maritime heart of the developing colony, it boasts some of the finest historic buildings in South Australia. Solid stone warehouses, workmen's cottages, traditional old hotels and wharves recall an era when the port was kept busy with clippers and steamships. Explore the area bounded by Nelson Street, Saint Vincent Street, Todd Street and McLaren Parade for intact nineteenth-century streetscapes. The area's history is on display at the **South Australian Maritime Museum (** (08) 8240 0200, 126 Lipson Street, which extends over several sites, including an 1850s bond store, the 1869 lighthouse, and a wharf with vessels tied alongside. Open 9 AM to 5 PM daily.

Glenelg

The first settlement in Adelaide was at Glenelg, which today is an attractive seaside suburb, 12 km (seven miles) from the city center, with some excellent cafés and restaurants. To get there take a pleasant 30-minute ride on Adelaide's only tram from Victoria Square to Jetty Road, Glenelg's main thoroughfare.

In Macfarlane Street, Glenelg North, a **plaque** marks the spot where Governor Hindmarsh proclaimed South Australia a British colony, in December 1836. A replica of Hindmarsh's ship, the **HMS** *Buffalo*, has been converted into a museum with illustrations and extracts from log books, original diary notes, sketches and photographs. The boat is moored at **Patawalonga Boat Haven (** (08) 8294 2122, on Adelphi Terrace.

OPPOSITE, TOP: Victorian terrace houses have been converted into colorful shops. BOTTOM: The Art Gallery of South Australia.

SHOPPING

Broad **Rundle Mall** buzzes with activity on week days at least. Its department stores, coffee shops and cinemas, fountain and colorful flower stalls make it a pleasant setting to shop or to sit back in an outdoor café and be entertained by buskers. A number of arcades lead off the mall, often with interesting smaller stores. The **Myers Centre** fronts the mall — its food hall on the lower ground floor is perfect for picnic supplies.

Specializing in fresh foodstuffs, **Central Market** has operated from its site in Grote Street for over 120 years. Fresh kangaroo and emu meat is sold here daily, as well as an enormous variety of European, Australian and Asian produce. The weekend **East End Market** in Rundle Street near Frome Street has an enormous food hall which can seat 150 people, and offers a choice of Chinese, Italian and other cuisines from around the world, but its main attraction is its stalls selling crafts, clothing and souvenirs.

At **Opal Field Gems (** (08) 8212 5300, 33 King William Street, you can watch stones being cut and learn about the history of opal mining. **Olympic Opal (** (08) 8267 5100, 142 Melbourne Street in North Adelaide, sells a range of opal jewelry, and **Bartram Opals (** (08) 8223 3684, 30 Gawler Place, sells sought-after black opals.

The **Jam Factory Contemporary Craft and Design Centre (** (08) 8410 0727, 19 Morphett Street, a government-sponsored project, exhibits contemporary craft works. Visitors are free to visit the studios to watch artists at work, and the retail shop sells pieces produced by craftspeople in the Jam Factory's studios.

WHERE TO STAY

Expensive

For something a little different, **North Adelaide Heritage Apartments (**/FAX (08) 8272 1355 WEB SITE www.adelaide-heritage.com.au offers a choice of coonial cottages. Many of the apartments are fitted with colonial antique furnishings, while the newest addition, the **Fire Station Inn**, has a vintage fire truck parked in the apartment! There are hundreds of rooms with great ocean views at the **Stamford Grand Hotel (** (08) 8376 1222 TOLL-FREE (1800) 882 777 E-MAIL hotels@accomline.com, in Moseley Square, Glenelg. The hotel is also handy to the airport, just five minutes away.

Moderate

The well-located **Adelaide Meridien (** (08) 826s7 3033 TOLL-FREE (1800) 888 228 WEB SITE www.hotelbook .com.au, 21–37 Melbourne Street, North Adelaide, has helpful, attentive staff and spacious, airy rooms. The upstairs rooms out back have great views of the Adelaide Hills and even the executive suites, with separate lounge and bar, are moderately priced. The **Grosvenor Vista (** (08) 8407 8888 TOLL-FREE (1800) 888 222 E-MAIL reservations @grosvenorvistahotel.com.au, 125 North Terrace, is conveniently located across from the casino and their standard rooms, all with large private bath, are good value. **Largs Pier (** (08) 8449 5666 E-MAIL info@postcards.sa.com.au, 198 The Esplanade, Largs Bay, built in 1883, is an impressive three-story hotel with wide colonial verandahs. In North Adelaide, the **Old Adelaide Inn (** (08) 8267 5066 TOLL-FREE (1800) 888 378 FAX (08) 8267 2946, 160 O'Connell Street, is actually only about 25 years old, but it's stylish, and the rooms are large and comfortable

Inexpensive

Princes Lodge ((08) 8267 5566, 73 Lefevre Terrace, North Adelaide, offers budget accommodation within walking distance of the city. By the sea at Glenelg, **St. Vincent (** (08) 8294 4377, 28 Jetty Road, and the **Norfolk Motel (** (08) 8295 6354, 69-71 Broadway, are both cheap and cheery.

WHERE TO EAT

Adelaide may not be able to boast the vast array of restaurants found in Australia's larger cities, but locals are justifiably proud of the ones it has. Visitors can enjoy a wide variety of cuisines, expertly prepared, to match the high caliber of South Australia's world-renowned wines, and for considerably less than in Sydney or Melbourne. A few streets in particular are renowned for their eating spots. Gouger Street, near the Central Market, is traditionally Adelaide's dining central, with cafés, restaurants and wine bars of all persuasions and in all price ranges. Hindley Street is another good one to try for its good seafood and authentic Lebanese and Indian restaurants. Rundle Street has some more urban and Mediterranean-inspired bistros. North Adelaide is an attractive area with excellent cafés. O'Connell and Melbourne streets in particular have a number of interesting eateries serving a variety of cuisines from around the world, generally at inexpensive to moderate prices.

Expensive

The Harris sisters of Sydney fame recently brought their skills to Adelaide and are captivating a loyal clientele with their unique brand of modern Australian fusion food at **Nediz (** (08) 8223 2618, 170 Hutt Street. **Eccolo (** (08) 8410 0102, 22 Grote Street, serves possibly the best Italian cuisine in town. Roasted-pumpkin-filled ravioli and the incredible broccoli soufflé demonstrate their creativity. For the best in East-meets-West dining, **The Grange (** (08) 8237 0698, Hilton International, Victoria Square, has been described by many **Pie** reviewers as sensational. The set menus are worth every dollar. Suitable wines are recommended with all meals.

Moderate

Well known for their imaginative menus, **The Chifley** ((08) 8223 4355, 226 South Terrace, represents great value for money. Try the broccoli, camembert and cashew strudel followed by the grilled kangaroo fillet with tatsoi, beetroot *confit*, wild rice and port wine *jus* for something really different. The **Botanic Gardens Restaurant** ((08) 8223 3526, Botanic Gardens, North Terrace, has a totally serene ambiance amid the garden's manicured lawns, overlooking the duck pond. Their

a delicious meal try the char-grilled emu medallions or Murray cod garnished with bush herbs. Right on the water in the seaside village of Glenelg, **Lido Caffe Ristorante** ((08) 8294 0111, 2 Marina Pier, Holdfast Shore, serves a huge variety of well prepared classic Italian dishes.

Inexpensive

There are some good, inexpensive restaurants at the western end of Hindley Street; most are noisy and full of life. As this is also the entertainment center of the city, restaurants begin serving meals in the late afternoon and keep filling with customers during the evening. **Quiet Waters** ((08) 8231 3637, 75 Hindley Street, and **Jerusalem**

two set menus are great value. It is well worth paying the extra for one of their delicious desserts, such as the quince (*Cydonua vulgaris*) *tarte tatin* with cardamom ice-cream.

For an authentic taste of Argentina **Gaucho's** ((08) 8231 2299, 91 Gouger Street, cooks most meals on the charcoal grill, basting them in *chimichurri*, a traditional sauce of olive oil, lemon juice, garlic, herbs and spices. The menu is predominantly meat but there are several appetizing seafood plates as well. For water views, **Jolleys Boathouse** ((08) 8223 2891, Jolleys Lane, across the road from Adelaide's Festival Theater complex, overlooks the river. Its appealing menu changes regularly. **Bacall's** ((08) 8267 2030, 149 Melbourne Street, serves Cajun fish and the exotic flavors of Creole cooking. The **Red Ochre Grill** ((08) 8212 7266, 129 Gouger Street, has a café that opens up into a formal restaurant. For

Sheshkabab ((08) 8212 6185, 131B Hindley Street serve good Lebanese food. The amazingly cheap **Ceylon Hut** ((08) 8231 2034, 27 Bank Street serves tasty Sri Lankan. Run by Vietnamese Buddhists, **Blossom's Vegetarian** ((08) 8212 7805, 167 Hindley Street, gives interesting twists to humble bean curd. The **Red Rock Noodle Bar** ((08) 8223 6855, 186 Rundle Street, is another café serving great Asian meals in a bustling, lively atmosphere. Their *laksa* was recently voted best in town; the Thai green chicken curry is even better. They've opened eateries at four other locations in Adelaide, proof of their popularity.

Visitors to Adelaide might be dared by locals to try South Australia's national dish — the pie floater — a meat pie sitting in green pea soup. Should you feel both peckish and brave, **Cowley's**

A Coopers Ale buggy trots down Rundle Mall.

Cart opens after 6 PM outside the Post Office on Franklin Street, while **Balfour's** is outside the casino on North Terrace.

NIGHTLIFE

Adelaide's major daily newspaper, the *Advertiser*, is a good source of information on what's happening in and around town. On Thursday, the *Guide* section provides information on theater and band venues. The free newspaper *Rip It Up* WEB SITE www.ripitup.com.au is distributed in pubs, cafés and music shops, and contains a wealth of information on the local music scene. Most magazine and book stores have copies of the free *Adelaide Review*, which provides an excellent and critical guide to theater, concerts and dance. The radio station SAFM ((08) 8272 2990 has a recorded gig guide service.

Adelaide has a decent selection of pubs with live music on selected nights. The **Earl of Aberdeen**, in Carrington Street, a laid-back pub with a loyal local crowd, is a venue for local bands. University students tend to hang out at the **Exeter**, 246 Rundle Street, which alternates live music and DJs. The **Universal Wine Bar**, 285 Rundle Street, pumps a vibrant blend of current music, and has loads of character. The most popular club is **Heaven**, in the old Newmarket Hotel at the corner of West and North Terraces, which has DJs from Wednesday to Saturday and live bands nightly in the adjoining **Joplins Nightclub**. **Cartoons Nightclub**, 145 Hindley Street, puts on live music most nights of the week and has a dance club, while **Rio's International**, 111 Hindley Street, is more of an upmarket venue.

HOW TO GET THERE

A number of international flights include stopovers in Adelaide, and there are direct flights from Melbourne, Sydney, Darwin, Perth and Canberra. Adelaide is a fine starting point for exploring the outback, with direct flights to Alice Springs, Uluru (Ayers Rock), Broken Hill, Ceduna, Coober Pedy, Katherine, Mount Gambier and Tennant Creek.

Greyhound Pioneer and McCafferty's have regular bus services from Alice Springs, Darwin, Perth, Sydney and Melbourne.

The *Indian–Pacific* train passes through Adelaide on Tuesdays and Fridays on its journey from Perth to Sydney. The famous *Ghan* makes a weekly 20-hour journey from Alice Springs to Adelaide, departing Alice every Monday, with an extra train running from April to November. Book well ahead for both. The *Overland* runs four times a week between Melbourne and Adelaide. The three trains are operated by **Great Southern Railway Ltd.** (132 232, check out their WEB SITE www.gsr.com.au for exact timetables and fares.

ADELAIDE HILLS

In 1838, 52 Lutheran families fleeing Prussia settled in the hills that rise out of the central plain, 30 km (19 miles) east of Adelaide. The community prospered creating many picturesque villages and hamlets worth visiting. The **Adelaide Hills Tourism Information Centre** ((08) 8388 1185, 41 Main Street, Hahndorf, provides brochures on all the attractions.

WHAT TO SEE AND DO

The architecture of many buildings and cottages in the Adelaide Hills is typically German. In **Hahndorf**

many of the original structures have been preserved and the German heritage of the gabled village is evident everywhere. The original Lutheran community built two fine old churches: **St. Michael's** constructed in 1858, and **St. Paul's**, constructed in 1890, both still used by the local community. The **Blacksmith's Shop** and neighboring buildings were also built in the nineteenth century. Some authentic German restaurants and cafés are scattered around the town.

Bridgewater, folded into the hills just off the South East Freeway, began its life as a tiny fording settlement. In 1860 a flour mill was established and was worked until the 1950s. Now restored it houses an excellent wine cellar and one of South Australia's best restaurants, **Peteluma's Bridgewater Mill** ((07) (08) 8339 3422, Mount Barker Road. The restaurant is open for lunch only Thursday to Monday, but some of Australia's finest wines can be tasted seven days a week between 10 AM and 5 PM. The **Old Clarendon Gallery** ((08) 8383 6219, in Clarendon, has regularly changing exhibitions, while **Paris Creek Pottery** ((08) 8388 3224, in the town of Meadows, sells local crafts.

The **Warrawong Sanctuary** ((08) 8370 9422, Stock Road, Mylor, is home to an assortment of smaller indigenous animals such as brush-tailed bettongs, wallabies and rainbow lorikeets. Its main claim to fame is a breeding colony of platypuses, the only such colony in existence. The best time to see the wildlife is at dusk, and the management organizes walks every evening at sunset. Reservations are required.

In the expensive to very expensive price range, but for something really completely different, try **Thorngrove Manor** ((08) 8339 6748 WEB SITE www .slh.com / thorngro.com.au, at 2 Glenside Lane, Stirling, a Gothic castle-like structure, that has surprises around every corner. The elaborate suites are as different from each other as they are daring. The **Adelaide Hills Country Cottages** ((08) 8338 4193 WEB SITE www.ahcc.com.au has five unique residences dotted about the farm. Choices include French provincial, English country, and the Australian-style Gum Tree cottage (moderate to expensive).

There are some pretty B&Bs tucked away in the hills at Aldgate. Within easy reach of good

Mount Lofty Summit, only 20 minutes from the city within the Mount Lofty Ranges, has the best panoramic views of Adelaide and its surrounding area. The summit is dominated by an **Obelisk** built in 1885, the information center, and a café/restaurant. The 1,500-km-long (932-mile) **Heysen Trail** cuts through the range, beginning at **Parachilna Gorge** in the Flinders Ranges. From there the trail winds its way south, following the Mount Lofty Ranges, and ends at Cape Jervis on the Fleurieu Peninsula. The **Office for Recreation and Sport** WEB SITE www.recsport.sa.gov.au has detailed information and good links for the Heysen Trail.

WHERE TO STAY

Rather than stay in Adelaide many travelers prefer the serenity of one of the charming guesthouses or B&Bs in the Adelaide Hills.

restaurants, art galleries and wineries, the moderately priced **Aldgate Lodge B&B** ((08) 8370 9957 FAX (08) 8370 9749, 27 Strathalbyn Road, is a home-style retreat. Also in the moderate price range is the conventional but comfortable **Hahndorf Inn Motor Lodge** ((08) 8388 1000 TOLL-FREE (1800) 882 682 FAX (08) 8388 1092.

HOW TO GET THERE

The Adelaide Hills region is about 30 km (19 miles) from the city and can be reached by taking the signposted turn-off on the South-Eastern Freeway. Hills Transit ((08) 8339 1191 run services between Adelaide and Mount Barker, Strathalbyn and Hahndorf.

A local game of cricket in the Adelaide Hills.

FLEURIEU PENINSULA

The Fleurieu Peninsula, just south of Adelaide, is close enough for day-trips and has long been a favorite family holiday area, with fishing and water sports the main activities. Inland there's plenty of rolling farmland with some lovely vineyards in the McLaren Vale region and historic towns scattered around the countryside. The beauty of the surrounding hills, uninhibited rural vistas, pristine beaches and coastal scenery has over the years attracted artists and crafts people to the district. Their creative work is displayed at a number of galleries around McLaren Vale. Warm, dry summers moderated by cooling breezes from the Gulf create favorable conditions for varied agricultural endeavors. Avocados, olives, almonds, stone fruits and berries all grow well in the temperate Mediterranean climate and are featured in many local restaurants.

GENERAL INFORMATION

For all information concerning wineries contact the **McLaren Vale and Fleurieu Visitor Centre** ((08) 8323 9944 E-MAIL visitors@fleurieu.com.au, Main Road. For specific information on each area try the **Victor Harbour Tourist Information Centre** ((08) 8552 5738, 10 Railway Terrace; **Strathalbyn Tourist Information Centre** ((08) 8536 3212, South Terrace; and the **Goolwa Tourist Information Centre** ((08) 8555 1144, Cadell Street.

WHAT TO SEE AND DO

Low hills run down the center of the peninsula, where historic towns dot the landscape. Their placid appearance belies their past: Smugglers once worked the region, evading customs officials as they landed spirits and tobacco illicitly. Many a gang of contraband runners rowed their illegal merchandise up the **Onkaparinga River** and hid in **Old Noarlunga**.

Victor Harbour

Located 83 km (52 miles) south of Adelaide, Victor Harbour was once the main port on the South Australian coast and the access point for all goods traveling up and down the Murray River. Now it's South Australia's most popular beach resort.

The first European settlers moved into the area in 1839 and some of the historic buildings include **Adare House**, built in the 1860s by Governor Hindmarsh's son John; **Saint Augustine's Church of England**, built in 1869; and **Warringa Guest House** ((08) 8552 5970, built in the early part of the twentieth century. The **Victor Harbour National Trust Museum** ((08) 8552 5388, 2 Flinders Parade, in the Old Customs and Station Master's House contains memorabilia of the town's early

history and the Fleurieu Peninsula. It also has a good walking map of the major historic buildings in town. A chairlift operates on weekends and school holidays, weather permitting, giving breathtaking views of the peninsula and coast.

A causeway links the town to **Granite Island**. Visitors can take a horse tramway, constructed in 1882, across the bridge to see penguins parade on the island's rocks at dusk. The **Penguin Interpretive Centre** ((08) 8552 7555 take visitors on guided walks with a penguin specialist every evening at dusk.

Another way to explore the peninsula is to take the **Cockle Train** ((08) 8391 1223 along the coast from **Goolwa** to Victor Harbour, a 30-minute journey. The train runs Sundays and during school vacations.

Victor Harbour overlooks **Encounter Bay**, where from May to September migrating southern right whales can be seen swimming close to shore. For more whale information contact the **South Australian Whale Centre** ((08) 8552 5644, 2 Railway Terrace.

McLaren Vale

McLaren Vale, at the northern end of the peninsula, is not as well-known a wine-making region as the Barossa Valley. Its moderating maritime climate and a long summer/autumn ripening period, however, make it one of Australia's premium grape growing regions. Vale red wines, particularly Shiraz (Syrah), display pronounced fruit and are notably soft, spicy and ripe. The dominant white variety is Chardonnay, which produces rich, peachy and buttery wines. The area also produces fine flinty, delicate Rieslings.

A few of Australia's best wines are produced here. **Wirra Wirra** ((08) 8323 8414, **Andrew Garrett** ((08) 8323 8911, and **Geoff Merrill** ((08) 8381 6877 are all names to look out for on good wine lists. When you're in the region though, it's worth taking the time to search out some of the smaller vineyards that survive on hard-earned reputations, selling premium wine from their cellar doors. At **Noon's** ((08) 8323 8290, Rifle Range Road, Drew and Raegen Noon produce small quantities of Grenache from some of the oldest dry-grown bush vines in the Vale. These grapes, as well as their Shiraz, are made into superb wines that can be enjoyed young, due their richness, yet will live and improve with time.

At **D'Arrenberg** ((08) 8323 8206, Osborn Road, Chester Osbourne produces a broad range of wines in McLaren Vale's tradition. These simply-made wines owe their success to low yield and value for money. The cellar door offers a wonderful view of the vale, while their restaurant, **D'Arrys Verandah** ((08) 8323 8710 overlooks the vineyards and serves classic French cuisine showcasing local products (expensive). Book well ahead. **BRL Hardys Tintara** ((08) 8323 9185 uses grapes from many different regions of Australia, and innovative techniques produce well balanced wines typical of the McLaren Vale style. The cellar door is a short distance from the main road, in the heart of the township. In a classic Australian setting with soaring eucalypti and great views, **Coriole** ((08) 8323 8305, Chaffeys Road, produces quality wines including the Italian variety Sangiovese. They also grow olives, and sell their own excellent olive oil and a wide range of local cheeses.

WHERE TO STAY AND EAT

Smugglers ((08) 8552 5684, 16 Crozier Road, Victor Harbour, is a warm and welcoming guesthouse. The **Anchorage Guest House** ((08) 8552 5970,

cuisine, using mainly local produce (expensive). Their well-stocked cellar boasts rare and aged wines from the region. Open for lunch Thursday to Tuesdays, and dinner Fridays and Saturdays. Bookings are essential.

HOW TO GET THERE

By car the peninsula starts 22 km (14 miles) south of Adelaide, taking Main South Road following the coast.

An enjoyable way to reach the Fleurieu Peninsula is aboard the *Southern Encounter* ((08) 8391 1223, a steam train that winds its way from Mount Barker in the Adelaide Hills on to Strathalbyn,

21 Flinders Parade, listed on the state's heritage register under it's original name of Warringa Guest House, is one of South Australia's few surviving nineteenth-century guesthouses. It still offers exquisite inexpensive to moderately priced rooms. The luxurious **Whalers' Inn** ((08) 8552 4400, The Bluff, overlooking Encounter Bay (expensive), welcomes guests with a complimentary bottle of champagne on arrival. The splendid view of the bayside and Granite Island from its waterfront seafood restaurant is an added bonus.

The excellent **Star of Greece** ((08) 8557 7420, The Esplanade, Port Willunga, sits on the cliff top overlooking the coast. They dish out the best in fresh South Australian seafood, cooked to perfection, in a wonderfully relaxed atmosphere (moderate). The **Salopian Inn** ((08) 8323 8769, at the corner of McMurtrie and Willunga Roads, McLaren Vale, has been highly praised for its incredible

Goolwa and Victor Harbour. The train operates from May to November with reservations necessary. **Premier Roadlines** ((08) 8415 5555 runs coaches to Goolwa daily, departing from the terminal at 111 Franklin Street, Adelaide.

KANGAROO ISLAND

Kangaroo Island was first sighted by Europeans in 1802, when Matthew Flinders was circumnavigating the continent. He sent crew members ashore to replenish the dwindling supplies. The French, for a while, were also interested in southeast Australia and in 1803 Kangaroo Island was visited by their navigator, Nicholas Baudin, after whom several landmarks around the island were named. Its early history is also closely connected

Friendly Kangaroo Island kangaroos are smaller than those on the mainland.

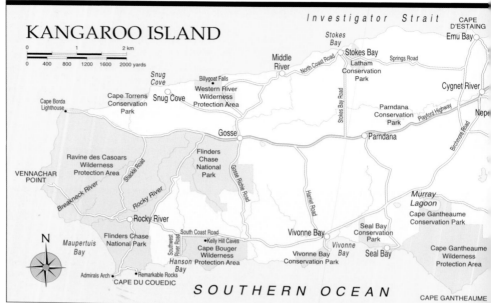

with the sealing and whaling industries in the southern waters off Australia. Since these industries were banned, the seal population is thriving and sightings of whales in the southern oceans are becoming ever more frequent.

Although the island shows archeological traces of Aboriginal inhabitation, it seems no one had lived there permanently since it separated from the mainland 9,000 years earlier. The Kaurna people on the nearby mainland referred to the island as *Kartan*, from *karta*, meaning kangaroo, suggesting they did visit on hunting expeditions; and hence the English name.

Today Kangaroo Island is a nature lover's paradise and an ideal place to get away from it all. This huge island supports the most diverse abundance of wildlife — some extremely rare and beautiful — thanks to its lack of predators. The Kangaroo Island kangaroo, a subspecies of the western gray, is smaller, darker and has longer fur. It shelters in the bush during the day, coming out to graze as dusk approaches. The tammar wallaby is abundant here but almost extinct on the mainland. Koalas are so widespread on the island (close to 5,000 at last count) they have become a problem. They overeat and over-breed, and thus deplete their own food supply too rapidly and starve in drier months. A sterilization project has been introduced to keep the numbers down.

Australia and New Guinea are the only places in the world where monotromes — egg-laying mammals — are found. There are three types of monotromes: two echidnas and the platypus. The long-beaked echidna is endemic to New Guinea, the short-beaked echidna is widespread through-

out Australia and found in the lowlands of New Guinea, while the platypus is endemic only to Tasmania, Victoria and Australia's east coast. Kangaroo Island harbors the short-beaked echidna, which resembles a hedgehog, but sightings are unpredictable. The platypus has been introduced in Flinders Chase, although to see one takes patience and dedication.

For bird-watchers, 251 varieties have been recorded on the island. One of the most brilliant is the superb fairy-wren; the bright blue male is easily spotted. Cockatoos, lorikeets and parrots can be seen and heard screeching in big flocks all over the island. Penguins and pelicans are found in a number of coastal areas.

Diving enthusiasts should be content with the many shipwrecks that scatter the reefs here. Some of their salvaged cargo and fittings are on display in the island's museums. At about 20 m (65 ft) walls of Gorgonia corals and red, orange and white sponges are easily visible. A diving highlight would be to see the illusive leafy sea-dragon, endemic to these waters.

GENERAL INFORMATION

The **Kangaroo Island Gateway Information Centre** ((08) 8553 1185, Howard Drive, Penneshaw, is open seven days a week. **National Parks and Wildlife** ((08) 8553 2381, 37 Dauncey Street, Kingscote, also supplies information on camping and nature tours. There are fees for entry into parks and for tours. An **Island Parks Pass** covers most places of interest, they're available from any of the National Parks offices on Kangaroo Island.

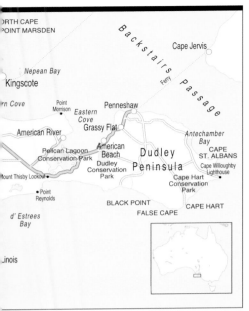

to **Reeves Point** (old Kingscote), South Australia's most famous heritage site. A mulberry tree planted here in 1836 still bears fruit that is made into jam each year. The **Hope Cottage Folk Museum** built in the 1850s is surrounded by buildings with exhibits depicting the pioneer history of the island. The well-maintained **Kingscote Cemetery** is also an interesting source of historical information. From the **jetty** you are almost always guaranteed to catch a decent feed of King George whiting, garfish or snook. For safe swimming there is the rock-bound sea-water pool in front of the town, and **Little Brownlow Beach** in front of the yacht club is ideal for shallow swimming and wading. **Little penguins** have established themselves in the sandstone and clay cliffs in front of the town and guided tours leave from the Ozone Hotel at dusk. **Pelicans** are fed daily at 5 PM just north of the wharf area, and the feeder gives an informative talk. **Emu Bay**, about 18 km (11 miles) north of Kingscote, is one of the most popular spots on the island for safe, clear-water swimming. **Surf-fishing** here brings in bull salmon of up to five kilograms (11 lbs).

Penneshaw

If coming across from Cape Jervis on the mainland, the ferry arrives in the Cornish-style settlement of Penneshaw on the **Dudley Peninsula**. After being neglected until recently, the **Hog Bay Jetty**, built in 1902, has been restored to its former splendor with the introduction of the ferry. The jetty is famous on the island as a well-stocked fishing spot. The clean beaches of **Hog Bay** are safe for swimming and have great views to the mainland. On the eastern end of the beach is **Frenchman's Rock**, where a sailor with the French Baudin expedition of 1803 carved a memento into the rock, which can still be seen. There are plenty of penguins here too, with tours departing at dusk from the **Interpretive Center** at the **Lloyd Collins Reserve**. The **Ligurian honey** cultured near here is unique in the world. The strain has remained pure since 1881, when August Fieburg brought 12 hives from the Italian province of Liguria. Early legislation ensured the bees on Kangaroo Island, unlike their cousins in Europe, had no contact with other bee varieties.

American River

Named after American sealers who settled here in 1803, American River's good fishing and safe beaches made it a popular holiday destination as early as the 1890s. The town is at the entrance to **Pelican Lagoon** and the **American River Aquatic Reserve**, popular with birdwatchers. **Pelican Lagoon Research Centre** is a private research facility used by Dr. Peggy Rismiller for long-term wildlife studies. The center has a fascinating display on her research into echidnas.

The **Tourism Kangaroo Island** WEB SITE is at www.tourkangarooisland.com.au.

The island has no public transportation, but visitors can bring a vehicle over on the ferry or rent a car or four-wheel drive on arrival from **Budget Rent a Car** ((08) 8553 3133 FAX (08) 8553 2888 or **Hertz** TOLL-FREE (1800) 088 296. Several companies on the island organize day and half-day bus tours, including **Sealink's Wildlife Day Tour** (131 301 or (08) 8202 8688, which connects with ferry arrivals and departures and will pick up and drop off at local hotels.

WHAT TO SEE AND DO

The island is sparsely populated and primarily a destination for those interested in its wildlife and flora. It does have long stretches of beautiful coastline and pristine beaches, and sports fishing is popular around American River and Penneshaw. The three major roads are paved, as are the connecting roads to Seal Bay, American River and Emu Bay. Otherwise all roads on the island are gravel or dirt. They're generally fairly good, as long as drivers keep below 40–50 km/h (25–30 mph), which is also a good way to avoid hitting the animals you've come to see.

Kingscote

The commercial center, Kingscote has a population of 1,500 and is about as hectic as it gets on the island. There are excellent views over **Nepean Bay** from here to the mainland. To the north, steep cliffs offer a panoramic view of the boat-studded harbor and **Western Cove**. The cliffs drop steeply

Seal Bay and Cape Gantheaume

A highlight of a trip to Kangaroo Island is visiting the large breeding colony of **Australian sea lions** at Seal Bay Conservation Park, whose ancestors managed to survive the savagery of early sealers. Australian sea lions are the only endemic species of seal in Australia — they're unusual in having an exceptionally long gestation period of 18 months, and pups are suckled for 18 more months. Visits are controlled and under strict supervision of a National Parks Ranger, to protect the sea lions as much as visitors, as bulls can become aggressive if they feel threatened.

Apart from the wooden steps leading down to it, the beach has been left entirely in its natural state: a crescent of white sand with cliffs at either end, home to numerous varieties of sea birds and backing onto the Seal Bay Conservation Park and Cape Gantheaume Wilderness Protection Area. Cape Gantheaume has a large population of Kangaroo Island kangaroos and a lovely stretch of beach at D'Estrees Bay. Murray Lagoon, the island's largest body of fresh water, is home to a range of birds including the blue-billed duck, the western whipbird and the black-winged stilt.

Kelly Hill Caves

An extensive area of sinkholes and caverns of ornate calcite formations, some covered with iron-rich red bands. The caves are named after a horse, Kate Kelly, which is credited with discovering them when she fell through the roof of one of the caverns in the 1880s. Other animals over the centuries have shared Kate Kelly's fate, and the remains of Tasmanian devils, spotted-tail quolls and brush-tailed phascogales have been found in the caves — all of which disappeared from the island thousands of years ago. The wetlands around the caves harbor a range of wildlife.

Flinders Chase National Park and Ravine des Casoars Wilderness Area

The wildlife protection area is one of Australia's most significant, due to its natural state, the variety of wildlife found here and the lack of introduced predators. There are many fine walks in the area. The **visitor center** ((08) 8559 7235, at Rocky River, has detailed maps and plenty of information. This is a good spot to take a stroll and spot koalas, tammar wallabies and Cape Barren geese. Built in 1909, Cape du Couedic **lighthouse** is now fully automated — leaving the keeper's residences' available for inexpensive accommodation (see WHERE TO STAY, below). A steep but short walk from here leads to **Admirals Arch**, where a colony of playful chocolate-brown **New Zealand fur seals** can be seen bodysurfing and slapping around on the rocks. **Remarkable Rocks**, a cluster of granite boulders sculpted by the weather and perched on a granite dome rising steeply from the ocean,

are only five kilometers (three miles) east of here. Another historic light station is now available for accommodation at **Cape Borda**, at the far north west end of the park. If staying here, it is well worth taking the splendid **Ravine des Casoars**, a five-kilometer (three-mile) return loop trail that passes along creek banks and climbs high above the valley floor, providing memorable views.

WHERE TO STAY AND EAT

The renovated **Ozone Seafront Hotel** ((08) 8553 2011 FAX (08) 8553 2249, on the foreshore at Kingscote, has enormous and comfortable high-ceilinged rooms, and a modern bar and bistro (and poker machines — this is South Australia) downstairs overlooking the Western Cove.

A moderately priced old-fashioned guesthouse in Kingscote, **Ellson's Sea View Motel and Guest House** ((08) 8553 2030 E-MAIL ellsons@seaview .net.au, Chapman Terrace, also has inexpensive modern motel rooms and an Internet café.

The moderately priced **Wanderers Rest of Kangaroo Island** ((08) 8553 7140, Bayview Road, overlooks American River from its hillside perch. This place is very relaxed and secluded, the only noise coming from native birds welcoming the dawn. **Wisteria Lodge** ((08) 8553 2707 E-MAIL wisteria @kin.on.net, 7 Cygnet Road, Kingscote, has moderately priced rooms with ocean views and Jacuzzis. Their **Beachcomber** restaurant offers a good à la carte menu, which includes a little French, a little Italian and lots of seafood.

Wilderness Lighthouse Accommodation offers inexpensive cottages in light stations and heritage buildings away from the towns, in Cape du Couedic, Cape Borda, Rocky River and Cape Willoughby. It is run by the **National Parks and Wildlife Service** ((08) 8559 7235 FAX (08) 8559 7268. The indispensible **Kangaroo Island Holiday Letter Agents** (/FAX (08) 8553 2340 has all types of accommodation on its books, from host farms, motels to backpacker hostels.

HOW TO GET THERE

Kangaroo Island Sealink (131 301 or (08) 8202 8688, 440 King Street, Adelaide, and **Kangaroo Island Ferry Connections** TOLL-FREE (1800) 018 484 run ferries between Cape Jervis and Penneshaw; the trip takes 30 minutes. **Kangaroo Island Fast Ferries** ((08) 8295 2688 links Glenelg with Kingscote in a two-hour trip. **Coachlines of Australia** ((08) 8332 2644 connects with the Kangaroo Island Sealink ferries. They pick up and drop off passengers from hotels throughout Adelaide.

Kendell Airlines (131 300 TOLL-FREE (1800) 338 894 and **Emu Air** TOLL-FREE (1800) 182 353 have flights from Adelaide to Kingscote.

THE SOUTHEAST

If you're driving the splendid coastal route between Adelaide and Melbourne, the Mount Gambier region can be an interesting area to explore; notable for caves and other volcanic formations, fossils, and the narrow strip of remarkable rich *terrain*, Coonawarra, which produces many of Australia's best reds.

MOUNT GAMBIER

Mount Gambier township not only has a large number of attractive, historic buildings, but is quite

at its deepest point, inexplicably turns a brilliant blue from the end of November until March, then reverts back to a dull gray for the remainder of the year. The three-and-a-half-kilometer (two-mile) road and walking track around the lake provides access to many spectacular viewing points. **Aquifer Tours (** (08) 8723 1199 takes visitors to the surface of Blue Lake: tours descend the crater via the original limestone bore-well in a glass-paneled elevator; from the bottom a tunnel leads onto a pontoon at the lake's surface.

The Blue Lake is the most famous of the region's lakes, but others including **Little Blue Lake, Browne's Lake, Valley Lake** and **Leg of Mutton Lake** (now dry and wooded over), grouped together

unique in Australia, been built on the slopes of an extinct volcano. The first settlement was established in 1841. Today it's a large rural center surrounded by rich farming and dairy country and one of the largest pine plantations in Australia.

General Information

Drop into **the informative and fun Lady Nelson Discovery Centre (** (08) 8724 9750, Jubilee Highway East, dominated by a full-size replica of the *Lady Nelson*, the brig in which Lieutenant James Grant first sighted and named Mount Gambier in 1800. The center has all the information you could want on the region.

What to See and Do

The most magnificent of the several crater lakes in the region is undoubtedly **Blue Lake**. Still a scientific mystery, the water, which is 85 m (279 ft)

to the west of Blue Lake, are well worth exploring too. Walkers are rewarded with often breathtaking views.

A walking track leads to the summit of the extinct volcano, **Mount Schank**, 12 km (seven miles) south of town on the Port MacDonnell Road. The two-and-a-half-hour walk starts at the car park and ascends to the edges of the volcanic crater, which another path encircles. The views are magnificent; it's also possible to descend into the crater itself.

A huge network of limestone caves under the city of Mount Gambier was first recorded in 1884. Cave divers regularly explore this site and have put together maps showing the massive extent of this underground cave system. **Engelbrecht Cave**, formed some 30 to 40 million years ago, extends under seven city streets. Hourly conducted tours

Kangaroo Island's Remarkable Rocks.

follow passages through which water makes its way towards the Blue Lake. The visit includes a number of chambers, two of them used by divers to enter the water and explore under the city. The major viewing platform is 27 m (89 ft) below the surface. On the Jubilee Highway **Umpherston Cave**, a sinkhole landscaped with palm trees, has terraced gardens hanging over its edges, all beautifully floodlit at night.

Tantanoola Cave, 33 km (20.5 miles) northwest of Mount Gambier, is a single cave formed in an ancient coastal cliff, notable for its excellent columns, shawls and helictites. There's easy access, even for wheelchairs. While in town drop in to see the **Tantanoola Tiger** on display in the Tantanoola Hotel. Ask the publican about the beast and you're in for some colorful local yarns.

Back on the surface, Mount Gambier has some fine examples of colonial dolomite and limestone buildings. The **Old Court House,** built in 1865, now contains a local museum incorporating law records and a photographic history of the town. The 1866 **Jail** was used through 1995. It's now available for budget accommodation. The **Riddoch Art Gallery** houses a permanent collection of nineteenth- and twentieth-century paintings, sculptures and Aboriginal art from central Australia. There's also the **Town Hall** (1862) with its prominent clock tower, now a community arts center, a wonderful old **Post Office** (1865) and three nineteenth-century churches. A heritage walking trail booklet is available from the Discovery Centre.

There are several classic old pubs in town; two of the best are the **Mount Gambier Hotel** ℂ (08) 8725 0611, built in 1862, Commercial Street West, and **Jens Hotel** ℂ (08) 8725 0188, built in 1884. Jens has a beautiful cast-iron balcony and sits prominently in the town center. Both offer inexpensive to moderately priced accommodation.

It's a decent walk up to **Centenary Tower**, perched 190 m (623 ft) above sea level, but spectacular views of the lakes, city and the lush countryside are ample reward. Opened in 1904, the tower includes an extensive display of early photographs of the lakes area.

PENOLA

Penola, fifty-two kilometers (32 miles) north of Mount Gambier, is famous in Australia as the town where the Blessed Mary MacKillop founded the order of the Sisters of St. Joseph of the Sacred Heart. The **MacKillop Schoolhouse**, built in 1867, and the memorial rose garden are open to visitors. Contact the **Interpretive Center** ℂ (08) 737 2092, corner of Portland Street and Petticoat Lane, for admission and tourist maps. Petticoat Lane contains well-restored and maintained examples of slab and hewn cottages, including **Sharam Cottage**, built around 1850. The grand **Yallum Park**

(*circa* 1880) is a magnificent sandstone mansion built for John Riddoch, a pioneer of the district.

For information specific to Penola and the Coonawarra wine region contact the **Penola Tourist Information Centre** ℂ (08) 87 372855, 27 Arthur Street, Penola.

COONAWARRA

Just north of Penola, the Coonawarra wine region produces some of Australia's finest red wines, particularly its excellent Cabernet Sauvignons, Merlots and Cabernet Francs. Coonawarra's first vines were planted in these rich *terra rossa* soils in the 1890s. Well-known wineries here include **Wynns Coonawarra Estate** ℂ (08) 8736 3266, **Lindemans** ℂ (08) 8736 2613, **Riddoch** ℂ (08) 8736 3380, and one of my all-time favorites, **Katnook Estate** ℂ (08) 8737 2394. The nearby **Padthaway Estate** ℂ (08) 8765 5039 produces excellent wines too. Its beautifully restored 1882 homestead has a hotel (expensive) and a restaurant (moderate) on the property and cellar-door sales from the historic wool shed.

NARACOORTE

Naracoorte, 50 km (30 miles) north of Penola, contains two World Heritage-listed areas: **Naracoorte Caves Conservation Park** and **Bool Lagoon Game Reserve**. Many of Naracoorte park's 26 caves contain extensive fossil deposits, dating back 500,000 years. These have yielded fossils of extinct animals such as the thylacoleo, a marsupial lion; the zygomaturus, a marsupial resembling an ox; and the procoptodon, a three-meter kangaroo. A series of interconnecting chambers and galleries within the caves exhibit impressive natural formations. A large fossil deposit can be seen on a guided tour of **Victoria Fossil Cave**, and the ancient bones are brought back to life in a hi-tech display at the **Wonambi Fossil Centre**.

Over 150 species of birds visit or inhabit Bool Lagoon, a massive seasonal wetland area. During the wet season, water birds flock in the thousands to breed here, some from as far away as Siberia. Birds can be viewed from boardwalks and established hides. Even in drier times a keen watcher can spot up to 50 species in a day. The **Naracoorte-Sheeps Back-Tourist Information Centre** ℂ (08) 8762 1518, MacDonnell Street, has details of tours and other points of interest (the center itself is a converted 1870 flour mill and houses a wonderful museum and craft shop).

ROBE

The picturesque coastal town of Robe, 105 km (65 miles) southwest of Naracoorte, has been a popular seaside resort for more than 150 years. **Guichon Bay** has plenty of safe swimming beaches, good fishing and sheltered areas for smooth sailing. The biggest attraction for many people, though, are the incredible lobsters caught here from October to May — they don't get much better than here. Robe was an important port from 1846 until the early twentieth century, originally exporting wool and horses. The town center contains several buildings of historical note. The **Robe Tourist Information Centre** ((08) 8768 2465 is located in the **Robe Library**, Victoria Street.

WHERE TO STAY

Although there's generally no shortage of accommodation possibilities in the southeast, it's recommended to book ahead in the summer high season. The **Mount Gambier International Motel** ((08) 8725 9699 offers luxurious accommodation at moderate prices. Some rooms have private Jacuzzis. Facilities include an indoor heated pool, sauna and a large Jacuzzi.

The region has many fine B&B and cottage style accommodation available at very reasonable rates. **Berry Hill B&B** (/FAX (08) 8725 9912 WEB SITE www.berryhill.com.au, off Cafpirco Road, Mount Gambier, is a tranquil rural retreat and, as the name suggests, David and Denise grow their own raspberries, blackberries and boysenberries on exquisite grounds. They serve a hearty country breakfast; prices are moderate. Guests at **Koonara Cottage** ((08) 8736 3267 E-MAIL vreschke@hotmail.com, Tricia Reschke Road, Coonawarra, have an old cottage all to themselves in this premium red-wine growing district. Moderate to expensive. The three guest rooms at **Dartmoor** ((08) 8762 0487 WEB SITE www.rbm.com.au/dartmoor, 30 MacLay Street, Naracoorte, are spacious and furnished in antiques. A gracious old homestead built during the 1890s, the large guest lounge features an open fireplace and breakfasts are gourmet standard (prices are moderate). **Robe House** ((08) 8768 2770 WEB SITE www.robe.sa.gov.au/robehouse, Hagen Street, Robe, was the first house built in this historic port in 1846. It has been meticulously restored and has three self-contained guest rooms with all modern comforts, at moderate prices.

The region also has a huge selection of hotels, motels, caravan parks and campsites, offering a wide choice to suit all budgets. Contact the local tourist information centers for details.

HOW TO GET THERE

Mount Gambier is 439 km (273 miles) southeast of Adelaide on the Princes Highway, National Route 1, just before the Victoria border.

Premier Stateliner Coach Group ((08) 8415 5555 has daily services to Mount Gambier from Adelaide, **Kendell Airlines** ((08) 8725 7888 has daily flights from both Adelaide and Melbourne.

THE BAROSSA VALLEY

The Barossa is Australia's richest and best known grape-growing and winemaking region. The area comprises both the Barossa and Eden valleys, and is only a one-hour drive north of Adelaide.

Soon after the colony of South Australia was proclaimed in 1836, German mineralogist Johann Menge surveyed the ranges north of the infant city. His report couldn't have been more accurate: "I am certain that we shall see…vineyards and orchards and immense fields of corn throughout all (of this) New Silesia…." Meanwhile a Lutheran Pastor, August Kavel, had arranged to have his congregation migrate to Australia to escape religious persecution by the King of Prussia. In 1838, 468 Prussians, Silesians and Pomeranians made the journey to the Barossa, where they worked the vineyards and fields and developed a typical agrarian Prussian village named Bethany in 1842. Subsequent waves of German-speaking settlers started other villages such as Langmiel and Lyndoch, while English free settlers tended towards Angaston and the Barossa Ranges.

Today approximately 9,000 ha (22,200 acres) of vineyards are under cultivation, producing approximately one third of Australia's total wine output.

GENERAL INFORMATION

To make the most of your vineyard visits, drop into the **Barossa Valley Wine & Visitor Centre** ((08) 8563 0600 WEB SITE www.barossa-region.org, Coulthard House, 66 Murray Street, Tanunda. They know their wines almost as well as the producers. In Adelaide, the **Gawler Visitor Centre** ((08) 8522 6814, 2 Lyndoch Road, is very helpful too.

WHAT TO SEE AND DO

The Barossa is best known for its glossy black Syrah grapes, known in Australia as Shiraz: rich and full bodied with an intensely concentrated fruit flavor, often mellowed by small oak maturation. One of the only premium international grape-growing areas not ravaged by phylloxera in the 1800s, the Barossa remains as the repository of the world's oldest Syrah vineyards. Cabernet Sauvignon has long been a classic red grape variety in the region too, producing dense fruit flavors and soft tannins. Perfect for "putting down," some of Australia's most respected wines have been made from Barossa Cabernet, and 40-year-old classics are still smooth and alive when opened today. Many wineries have also made expert blends with Grenache and Mourvèdre, which are slightly higher in alcohol, have crisp acidity and make excellent wines to be enjoyed with a variety of food.

Of the whites, the Semillons and Chardonnays both ripen easily producing full-bodied wines with citrus and honey flavors and crisp freshness — a perfect match to seafood on a hot summer's day. Exceptional Rieslings are produced in the Barossa's Eden Valley and in neighboring Clare Valley. Ideal conditions develop wines delicately perfumed with hints of spice and citrus, with a lingering, refreshing acidity. After 20 or 30 years of age these Rieslings develop classic honey, toast and spice.

Wineries

The wineries listed include several of the bigger producers that offer interesting historical and viticulture tours, as well as my favorite smaller vineyards. Cellar doors are open seven days a week unless otherwise indicated.

Seppelt Wines ((08) 8568 6200, Seppeltsfield, the Barossa's most historic operational winery, was established in 1851 and has more than 10 million liters (2,200,000 gallons) maturing in the cellars. Best known for sparkling and fortified wines, they also produce some good red and white table wines. Tours of the winery, grounds and gardens are conducted Monday to Friday. The imposing Seppelt family mausoleum sits atop a small hill — climb the steps for wonderful views over Seppeltsfield. **Penfolds** ((08) 8560 9408, Tanunda Road, Nuriootpa, is a major vineyard owner in the valley and also an important buyer of grapes from independent growers. Originally established in 1844 in the suburbs of Adelaide, they moved to their present location in 1974. Penfolds produces a full range of red and white table wines and fortified wines.

My favorite of the smaller wineries, and well worth a visit, is **Rockford Wines** ((08) 8563 2720, Krondorf Road. Very "traditional" wines are made here in the restored 1850s buildings, using an old Bagshaw crusher run by a vintage petrol engine, and old wooden basket presses. They make a wonderful sparkling Burgundy and their Basket Press Shiraz is full bodied and notable. **St. Hallet Wines** ((08) 8563 2319, St. Hallet's Road, Tanunda, specializes in premium red and white table wines. Their Old Block Shiraz, made with fruit from 100-year-old vines, is particularly exceptional. **Yalumba Wines** ((08) 8561 3200, Eden Valley Road, Angaston, founded in 1849, has beautiful buildings, lawns and gardens surrounded by horses; the owner is a keen racer. Their premium red and whites are well priced. **Saltram Wine Estates** ((08) 8564 3355, Angaston Road, Angaston, an historic (1859) and attractive winery, produces high-quality wines. They're also well known for their varietals. Saltram's bistro makes for a good lunch break. **Turkey Flat Vineyard** ((08) 8563 2851, Bethany Road, Tanunda, is a small family-owned winery specializing in full bodied dry table wine. The winery is one of the oldest in Australia (1847) — the cellar door still has its original paint.

Villages

One of the most picturesque towns in the Barossa Valley is **Tanunda**, which features old buildings and cottages built in architectural styles common in Germany in the mid-nineteenth century. Tanunda has several beautiful churches with stained-glass windows, ornate statues and impressive pipe organs. Traditional games such as German skittles are still a favorite pastime. Other evidence of the region's German heritage can be seen in the **Barossa Historical Museum** ((08) 8563 0507, 47 Murray Street. The historic **Château Tanunda Estate** ((08) 8563 3888, Basedow Road, an imposing French-style château built of Bethany blue-stone has been painstakingly restored to include art galleries; they also host wine tasting and sales. A fun side-trip in Tanunda is to **Norm's Coolies Performing Sheep Dogs** ((08) 8563 2198, Gomersal Road, where Norm Keast's extraordinarily

skilled sheep-dogs round-up the herds and show off their intelligence.

For the some of the best views of the Barossa take the Menglers Hill Road eight kilometers (five miles) east of Tanunda to the **Menglers Hill Lookout**. The park in front contains contemporary stone sculptures.

A walk down the shady street of **Bethany**, the valley's oldest village, founded in 1842, is rewarded with streets of thatched barns and pretty rustic cottages of an earlier, more romantic period. **Herbege Christi Church** is the focal point, alongside the old school buildings and opposite the **pioneer cemetery**, the church is distinctive for its nineteenth-century revivalist ornamentation. Australian artists are well-represented at the **Bethany Art and Craft Gallery** ((08) 8564 3344, 12 Washington Street, in the historic former courthouse and police station.

Angaston, in the northeastern corner of the valley, was popular with middle-class English settlers, and it still retains a touch of Northern England in its sandstone architecture. Angaston's well-established parks are lovely for picnics and a creek meanders through the town. Nearby at the **Lindsay Park Stud** ((08) 8564 2424 visitors can tour the stables of the prominent Hayes Family and see some of the finest racing horses in Australia. **Angus Park Fruit Co.** ((08) 8564 2052, 3 Murray Street, sells a huge array of South Australian food products with dried and glazed fruit, nuts, chocolates and much more.

At the southern end of the Barossa, **Lyndoch** has one of the noisiest museums in Australia. Set among the grapevines, the **Museum of Mechanical Music** is alive with the sounds of antique music

The Barossa Valley.

boxes, phonographs, mechanical singing birds and pianolas. The **Lyndoch Bakery** offers a range of traditional German breads and pastries, including *brezen* and *bienenstich*.

WHERE TO STAY

Nestled in undulating hills between Lyndoch and Tanunda, the **All Seasons Barossa Valley Resort** ((08) 9301 2756 WEB SITE www.allseasons.com.au, Golf Links Load, Rowland Flat, has luxurious moderate to expensive, air-conditioned apartments. Facilities include a heated outdoor pool and a well-equipped gymnasium with Jacuzzi and sauna. The resort is set in a peaceful natural amphitheater overlooking Jacob Creek and the North Para River, with beautiful sunset views of the surrounding vineyards. **Woodlands Vineyard Homestead** ((08) 8524 4511, at the corner of Barossa Valley Way and Altona Road, Lyndoch, has two luxurious self-contained three-room suites in a restored homestead on the vineyard, with superb views and open fires.

In the heart of the Barossa, the **Nuriootpa Vine Inn** ((08) 8562 2133 FAX (08) 8562 3236, 14-22 Murray Street, Nuriootpa, and the **Karawatha Guest House** ((08) 8562 1746, Greenock Road, Nuriootpa, are both moderately priced and very comfortable. **Stonewell Cottages** ((08) 8563 2019 E-MAIL stonewell @dove.net.au, Stonewell Road, Tanunda, is literally in the middle of 198 ha (80 acres) of vines. The cottages are modern and purpose-built, but very tastefully done. Only five kilometers (three miles) from Tanunda, **Lawley Farm** (/FAX (08) 8563 2141, on Krondorf Road, is run by Bruce and Sancha Withers, who do everything they can to make their collection of nineteenth-century stone cottages comfortable for guests.

Collingrove Homestead ((08) **8524 5353, Eden Valley** Road, Angaston, built in 1854 for the pioneering Angus family (after whom the town of Angaston is named), has the best in Victorian-style accommodation (expensive) and includes a cedar hot tub and tennis court. The inexpensive **Vineyards Hotel** ((08) 8564 2404, Stockwell Road, Angaston, is centrally located.

WHERE TO EAT

In the tradition of generations of peasant farming, the early settlers brought with them skills such as smoking meats, preserving fruit and making cheeses. Today Barossa's butchers, bakers and food producers continue these skills.

Maggie Beer's **Pheasant Farm** ((08) 8562 4477, Pheasant Farm Road, Nuriootpa, is simply a foodie's heaven. Although the restaurant is no longer, it is well worth going to enjoy an antipasto and to taste her seasonal treats and regional specialties. Open Thursday to Monday, 10:30 AM to 5 PM.

Landhaus ((08) 8563 2191, Bethany Road, Bethany, is one of the best in contemporary provincial fine dining in the Barossa. Local pork, hare and duck feature on the set menu and the wine list includes rare local vintages. Open for dinner only, Wednesday to Saturday from 7 PM (expensive). **Vitner's** ((08) 8564 2488, Nuriootpa Road, Angaston, one of the Barossa's premier restaurants, specializes in regional produce with a Mediterranean edge, served in either the casual brasserie or the slightly more formal dining room (moderate). The moderately priced **1918 Bistro and Grill** ((08) 8563 0405, 94 Murray Street, Tanunda, serves well-prepared modern Australian meals in a convivial atmosphere in either the rustic indoor

dining rooms or, weather permitting, in the lovely garden. The **Café Heidelberg** ((08) 8563 2151, 8 Murray Street, Tanunda, is a good inexpensive family restaurant serving traditional German and Australian home-cooked meals. It is also a pleasant spot for afternoon teas and light snacks.

HOW TO GET THERE

The Barossa Valley can be reached from Adelaide by taking the Main North Road to Gawler, and then turning right towards Lyndoch. The first wineries appear along the road within 70 minutes' driving.

The **Barossa–Adelaide Passenger Service** ((08) 8564 3022 runs regular rail services to Lyndoch, Tanunda, Nuriootpa and Angaston. The **Barossa Wine Train** ((08) 8212 7888 WEB SITE www .barossawinetrain.com.au, three refurbished 1950s *Bluebird* carriages with large comfortable lounge seats in true Old World style, departs Adelaide Railway Station Tuesdays, Thursdays, and Sundays at 8:50 AM, arriving in Tanunda 90 minutes later, from where it departs at 3:10 PM. The picturesque journey passes through Gawler, Lyndoch and Rowland Flat, and passengers have the option of joining a coach or personalized tour from Tanunda Station.

Tour the vineyards in true style with **Barossa Daimler Tours** ((08) 8524 9047 WEB SITE www .barossadaimlertours.com.au, who propose one-to three-day tours in vintage Daimler luxury limousines. The one-day tour starts at $210 per person. You can also tailor your own tour. **Barossa Experience Tours** ((08) 8563 3248 E-MAIL barex @dove.net.au offers full-day ($110 including lunch) and half-day ($55) tours of the Barossa's attractions and its wineries. Visitors meet with a few of the winemakers, who discuss their wines with passion. Personalized tours are also available.

BURRA

Burra, one of Australia's oldest mining towns, is 156 km (97 miles) north of Adelaide. Approximately 50,000 tons of copper were extracted from the hills around here between 1845 and 1877. The boom attracted miners from Wales, Scotland and Cornwall. Even small communities of Germans and Chileans came. In the mid-nineteenth century Burra was in fact the largest inland town in Australia. Many of the original buildings remain intact.

Burra is one of the undiscovered gems of South Australia and deserves more attention than it has received. The very fact that it has been ignored means that its nineteenth-century town and village streetscapes are intact.

GENERAL INFORMATION

The **Tourist Information Centre** ((08) 8892 2154, 2 Market Square, has a wealth of historic information on the town. The center organizes tours when enough people show interest.

WHAT TO SEE AND DO

For the visitor who doesn't mind wearing out some shoe leather, the 11-km (seven-mile) **Heritage Trail** around Burra is the best way to see most of the points of interest: historic churches, the graveyard, colonial buildings and the copper mines.

To familiarize yourself with its history, pay a visit to the **Market Square Museum** ((08) 8892 2154, 9 Market Square, which includes a re-creation of a general store and post office of the 1870s. A more extensive museum on the mining history of Burra is located in the **Bon Accord Mine Complex** ((08) 8892 2056, in Railway Terrace, which was once a working mine.

The scars of open cut mines are scattered all around Burra, the water in them stained green by copper salts. Miners here lived within their own ethnic communities. The row of stone houses along Kingston Street is where the Cornish miners lived: **Paxton Cottage Number 1** has had its original furnishings restored and is open to the public on weekends and public holidays. Other cottages in Paxton Square have been modernized and converted into visitors' accommodation (see WHERE TO STAY, below). Cornish miners also lived along the river, in caves dug into the bank. Extensions to accommodate additions to the family were easily accomplished by simply excavating another room. Best of all, they didn't pay rent. It's estimated that 1,800 of these thrifty people lived along a five-kilometer (three-mile) stretch of river, where several of the dwellings remain intact and can be visited as part of the Heritage Trail tour.

Another highlight of the Heritage Trail is **Hampton**, an English village built in 1857 that remained unchanged until it was abandoned in 1960. Ruined houses in various states of disrepair line its single street, and cows graze about its outskirts.

WHERE TO STAY

For a taste of the real Burra stay at **Paxton Square** ((08) 8892 2622 FAX (08) 8892 2555, in Kingston Street, which provides refurbished 1850 miners' cottages at moderate rates. **Tivers Row** ((08) 8892 2461, in Truro Street, also offers moderately priced rooms, and the **Burra Caravan and Camping Park** ((08) 8892 2442 has powered sites and on-site vans.

HOW TO GET THERE

From Adelaide you can drive to Burra along Main North Road and Barrier Highway. **Bute Buses** ((08) 8826 2110 provides regular bus service from Adelaide Wednesday to Sunday, Greyhound Pioneer services the same route daily, departing Adelaide at 8 AM.

FLINDERS RANGES

On a hot day, the Flinders Ranges shimmer from a distance, changing color from red and orange to blue and purple depending on the time of day and the season. After spring rains, a carpet of golden wildflowers bursts across the landscape.

These jagged, weathered mountains are not high, but their rugged beauty is accentuated by the plain surrounding them. They begin near Crystal Brook, 200 km (124 miles) north of Adelaide, and stretch north into the desert interior of South Australia — a distance of around 400 km (248 miles).

In South Australia, the country's driest state, windmills draw water from deep bores.

The Flinders Ranges National Park encompasses the lovely Edeowie and Brachina gorges, Aroona and Bunyeroo valleys and Wilpena Pound, an extraordinary 90-sq-km (35-sq-mile) natural basin encircled by slopes that rise to 55 m (180 ft). Wildlife includes rare western gray kangaroos, emus, wedge-tailed eagles and flocks of colorful parrots. The Flinders Ranges have the biggest population of the endangered yellow-footed rock wallabies in Australia, perhaps the prettiest of Australia's marsupials. Honey gold with a white belly, its tail is banded in deeper brown and its ears are tipped with ocher and a white streak wraps around its gray face.

Legend has it that Akurra, the Rainbow Serpent, created the ranges and formed the gorges by wriggling across the countryside. He then slithered westward to Lake Frome and drank it dry, which would explain the absence of water there. It is said that Akurra now sleeps in the Yacki water hole in the Gammon Ranges.

GENERAL INFORMATION

As with any trip into Australia's outback, don't go unprepared. Distances are great, and unless you're with an experienced guide, a detailed map is essential. Always carry water and hats.

Flinders Ranges and Outback South Australia ((08) 8373 3430 WEB SITE www.outback.aus.com, 142 Gawler Place, Adelaide, are the best people to talk to. If you're planning to venture further than Wilpena, especially north to the Gammon Ranges National Park or Mount Painter Sanctuary, take the time to discuss your plans in detail. The **Port Augusta Tourist Information Centre** ((08) 8641 0793, 41 Flinders Terrace, Port Augusta, is housed in the excellent **Wadlata Outback Centre** (see PORT AUGUSTA, page 224). **Peterborough Tourist Information Centre** ((08) 8651 2708, Main Street, Peterborough, and the **Quorn Tourist Information Centre** ((08) 8648 6419, 3 Seventh Street, Quorn, are extremely knowledgeable on the area. A good **web site** for a general overview of the Flinders Ranges, with handy links, can be found at WEB SITE www.flinders.outback.on.net.

QUORN TO WILPENA

Quorn was once an important junction for the Ghan narrow-gauge railway before the standard-gauge railway opened in 1956, bypassing it. Today the town is a dusty outpost. The **Pichi Richi Railway** ((08) 8648 6598 or (08) 8395 2566, through Pichi Richi Pass to Woolshed, provides a feel for the romance of the long-past era of the steam train. The round trip takes about three hours. Unfortunately, the train only runs between March and November on the second and fourth Sunday of the month, although additional trips are arranged

during the tourist season. Quorn is 40 km (25 miles) northeast of Port Augusta.

From Quorn it is a 67-km (42-mile) drive north to Hawker. A turn-off 42 km (26 miles) from Quorn leads to the ruins of **Kanyaka Homestead**. The family property once supported 70 farmhands and their families, and ran 50,000 head of sheep. The homestead's history illustrates the folly of transposing European farming practices to such a harsh environment. Its original owner, Hugh Proby, survived service with Admiral Nelson at Trafalgar and on the Nile, only to drown in a flash flood at Willochra Creek. His grave is a 30-km (19-mile) drive off the main road. Over 20,000 sheep died in the three-year draught of 1864–1867, the rest were driven south to safety. Although its owners continued battling their environment for 21 years, they finally abandoned the homestead in 1888. **Yourambulla Caves**, 11 km (seven miles) south of Hawker, contain fine Aboriginal rock paintings and carvings. It's a three-kilometer (two-mile) walk to the caves from the road.

Hawker is the true gateway to the Flinders Ranges. Like Quorn, the township suffered at the loss of the Ghan and survives (barely) today on tourism to the Flinders Ranges. **Hawker Motors Mobil Service Station** ((08) 8648 4014, at the corner of Wilpena and Cradock roads, doubles up as a tourist information service. The entrance to the Flinders Ranges National Park is 40 km (25 miles) northeast.

Twenty kilometers (12 miles) after Hawker, in a beautiful setting at the foot of Rawnsley Bluff, **Rawnsley Park Station** ((08) 8648 0008 WEB SITE www.rawnsleypark.com.au is a working sheep station open to visitors, with demonstrations of sheep shearing and working cattle-dogs. They also lead horseback rides riding through the station. Comfortable inexpensive to moderate accommodation is available for those wanting an extended outback experience.

THE FLINDERS RANGES NATIONAL PARK

Wilpena Pound

Ten kilometers (six miles) into the Flinders Ranges National Park, Wilpena Pound is an immense elevated basin whose rocky walls and cliffs encircle an oval bowl, 20 km (12.5 miles) long and eight kilometers (five miles) wide. The only way in is along a walking track through a narrow gorge above Sliding Rock. The bowl itself is covered with scrub, and in spring wildflowers grow in profusion. Five walking tracks snake across the basin, slopes and ridge-tops — most will take a good day's hike round trip, although there are also shorter walks on marked tracks. Red kangaroos and euros (hill kangaroos) are common, and several types of venomous snakes live throughout the ranges (wear shoes and socks). If you're willing to clamber up to the Pound's highest point, **Saint Mary's Peak** (1,170 m or 3,840 ft), there is a marvelous view of Wilpena Pound from the top.

The **information center** ((08) 8648 0048 (just before the Wilpena Pound Resort) can provide maps of the basin and its bush-walks. They also organize Aboriginal cultural treks (from $50 per person), 20- or 30-minute **scenic flights** over Wilpena Pound and the Flinders Ranges National Park (from $60 per person) or full- or half-day **four-wheel-drive tours** of the surrounding area (from $70 per person). For further tour details call TOLL-FREE (1800) 805 802.

Scenic Drives

While roads through the national park are unpaved, they are generally accessible to standard two-wheel drive vehicles as long as the floor-plan isn't too low. Following heavy rain roads may become mud-ridden and dangerous.

Twenty kilometers (12 miles) south of the entrance to the Flinders Ranges National Park, the **Moralana Scenic Drive** cuts through the hills, with views of Wilpena Pound. There are generally a lot of kangaroos and emus in this area. The 30-km (19-mile) drive connects with State Road 83, from where you can continue north to Parachilna, Leigh Creek and Arkaroola, or take the first turn right onto the **Brachina Gorge Geological Trail**, a convoluted and extremely rocky drive which eventually leads back to Wilpena Pound. There are good views from **Brachina Lookout**, on the left before the entrance to the national park. Eight kilometers (five miles) into the park, you have the option of turning right onto the more picturesque but winding and rocky **Bunyeroo Gorge Trail** to Wilpena, or continuing to the T-intersection (left to Arkaroola, right to Wilpena).

Another option is to drive north from Wilpena Pound to Arkaroola. After leaving the Pound and turning left onto the main road, a seven-kilometer (four-mile) track to the right leads to **Sacred Canyon**, where there's some Aboriginal rock art. A little past the art site, water tumbles down over the rocks at very narrow neck of the canyon.

On the main road, 18 km (11 miles) past the beginning of the track to Sacred Canyon, **Stokes Hill Lookout** provides a dramatic panorama of Wilpena Pound. The road continues to Blinman South, from where it's a three-hour drive to Arkaroola (fill up the tank at Blinman), following signs to the Gammon Ranges National Park. Driving through Wearing Gorge you'll see the brilliant white of the usually dry Lake Frome's saltbed.

ARKAROOLA

The 61,000-ha (145,000-acre) **Arkaroola-Mount Painter Sanctuary and Historic Reserve** is a privately owned wildlife sanctuary in the northern

Flinders Ranges, northeast of the Gammon Ranges National Park. There are some excellent drives and walks through the sanctuary, which has a range of arid bush wildlife similar to that of the Flinders Ranges National Park: wallaroos, yellow-footed rock-wallabies, western gray kangaroos, possums and marsupial mice, emus, ducks, parrots, galahs and cockatoos. The rugged country features quartzite razorback ridges above long valleys that were once a seabed (fossilized marine animals are often found here). Lovely **waterholes** in the valleys and gorges are well worth a visit, and by this stage a dip is generally much appreciated. Some of the prettiest are Nooldoonooldoona, Bolla Bollana, Arkaroola, Stubbs and Bararranna waterholes.

The focus of the sanctuary, which the current owners bought in 1968, is **Arkaroola Village** TOLL-FREE (1800) 676 042, which has motel accommodation, camping, a shop, gas station, restaurant and bar and an information center. The management organizes a number of different tours, including **scenic flights** (from $65), **bush tucker and Aboriginal medicine walks**, led by Aboriginal people from the nearby Nepabunna community ($25) and the **Ridge-Top Tour**, a four-wheel-drive adventure that leaves Arkaroola Village at 8 AM and 1 PM daily (adults $65, children $38).

The clear skies of Australia's outback are a boon to those not used to the southern constellation. Subject to weather conditions, tours of the **Arkaroola Astronomical Observatory** ($25) are run nightly, and the observatory's 360-mm (14.2-in) telescope is open to visitors. There is also a display of astronomical charts.

WHERE TO STAY AND EAT

The **Mill Motel** ((08) 8648 6016, 2 Railway Terrace, Quorn, has inexpensive rooms and a reasonably good restaurant. The restored **Bruce Railway Station** ((08) 8648 6344, 20 km (12.5 miles) southeast of Quorn, is now a moderately priced B&B. Inexpensive accommodation in Hawker is available at the **Hawker Hotel-Motel** ((08) 8648 4102 FAX (08) 8648 4151, 80 Elder Drive, and the **Outback Chapmanton Motel** ((08) 8648 4100 FAX (08) 8648 4109, 1 Wilpena Road. **Rawnsley Park** ((08) 8648 0030, Hawker Road, provides moderately priced cabin accommodation and has campsites and on-site caravans.

Wilpena Pound Resort TOLL-FREE (1800) 805 802 WEB SITE www.wilpenapound.on.net, near the Pound's entrance, has moderately priced motel units, some with kitchenettes, and a swimming pool. They also have campsites. **Camping** within the park is allowed; a permit costs $7, available from the entrance stations or the Wilpena Pound Resort information center. Some sites have basic facilities. In Parachilna (population seven), the **Praire Hotel** ((08) 8648 4895 has inexpensive rooms and budget cabins and is famous for its restaurant, which serves a unique blend of pub grills, bush tucker and feral meats. Expect the menu to include kangaroo steaks, emu pâté, goat, camel and lamb, with bush seasonings and native fruits. Open seven days a week, prices are moderate. **Arkaroola Village** TOLL-FREE (1800) 676 042 has inexpensive rooms and a good-value restaurant serving standards and native meats.

HOW TO GET THERE

Quorn is 313 km (194 miles) from Adelaide. The most scenic routes are from the north through Burra and Peterborough, or via the Clare Valley through Clare, Gladstone, Melrose and Wilmington. Port Wakefield Road runs directly from Adelaide to Port Augusta; the Quorn turnoff is at Stirling North. Many of the roads through the Flinders Ranges are unpaved and subject to flash floods: it's best to discuss your trip with the tourist office. For information on the state of any road in South Australia call ((08) 11 633.

Premier Stateliner Coach Group ((08) 8415 5555 has two services a week to Quorn, Hawker and Wilpena Pound.

EYRE PENINSULA

The Eyre Peninsula is a vast region stretching 1,000 km (621 miles) from Port Augusta to Western Australia, and 400 km (248 miles) north–south from the Gawler Ranges to Port Lincoln. The Spencer Gulf borders the eastern edge of the peninsula, with white-sand beaches and small fishing villages. The west coast is exposed to the full force of the Southern Ocean, offering some of the most spectacular coastal scenery in Australia. After dark, the large number of kangaroos in the area constitute a major road hazard. It's best not to drive at night, but if you have no choice, the only way to avoid a collision is to drive very slowly — no more than 30 km/h (10 mph).

The peninsula's climate is generally hot and dry, although winters are a little milder on the southern coast, and the land supports a sizeable wheat industry — giant wheat silos dominate the landscape in parts. Its other major industry is fishing. Bluefin tuna, striped tuna, southern rock lobster, western king prawn, whiting, shark, snapper and salmon are all fished commercially. Coffin Bay oysters are the best in the state, and abalone and scallops are also harvested in the area.

GENERAL INFORMATION

The helpful staff at the **Port Lincoln Visitor Information Centre** ((08) 8683 3544 TOLL-FREE (1800) 629 911 E-MAIL plvic@camtech.net.au, 66 Tasman Terrace, Adelaide, has a wealth of detailed infor-

mation on the Eyre Peninsula and will help with tour and accommodation suggestions. Other information centers include **Port Augusta Tourist Information Centre** ((08) 8641 0793, 41 Flinders Terrace, Port Augusta; **Whyalla Tourist Center** ((08) 8645 7900 E-MAIL tourist.centre@whyalla .sa.gov.au, Lincoln Highway, Whyalla; Ceduna's **Gateway Visitor Information Centre** ((08) 8625 2780 TOLL-FREE (1800) 639 413, 58 Poynton Street, Ceduna; and the **Baird Bay Center** ((08) 8688 2584, in Hales Mini Mart, 1 Bratten Way, Streaky Bay.

Budget Rent a Car ((08) 8682 1072, 4 Blackman Place, Port Lincoln, has reliable late-model vehicles at very reasonable rates.

The best **Internet** facility in Port Lincoln can be found within the local TAFE College at the end of Tasman Terrace.

PORT AUGUSTA

Port Augusta is the state's major crossroad: roads from here lead south to Port Lincoln; north to Flinders Ranges, Coober Pedy, Alice Springs and Darwin; west to Perth; and east to Adelaide, Broken Hill, Sydney and Melbourne. Otherwise the town holds little appeal, apart from the excellent **Wadlata Outback Centre** ((08) (08) 8642 4511 on Flinders Terrace (in the same building as the tourist information office). Wadlata uses hands-on audiovisual displays, film and music to present a wealth of information on South Australia's flora and fauna (including nasties), history, geology and geography, and Aboriginal culture and Dreamtime mythology. Open daily, adults $8, children $5, families $18.50. Next door, the airy **Outback Tucker Box** café looks out to a rock-pool and a windmill, and serves inexpensive lunches and snacks.

WHYALLA TO TUMBY BAY

Whyalla is the first center on Alternative Highway 1, the spectacular coastal road around the peninsula, and a seaside town with an outback feel. The area offers excellent fishing — Whyalla hosts the Australian amateur snapper fishing championship each Easter, drawing competitors from all over Australia. For diving enthusiasts, May and August see thousands of giant cuttlefish spawning along the rocky shores of **Black Point** and **Point Lowly**. The extensive gardens of the **Maritime Museum** ((08) 8645 7900 are a great place for a picnic. The museum houses an interesting collection of curios and artifacts and a monstrous 650-ton ship, the *Whyalla*. The beach offers safe fishing in shallow waters, and the jetty sees good catches of Tommy ruff, garfish and squid. The **Whyalla Wildlife and Reptile Sanctuary** ((08) 8645 7044, west of town off the Lincoln Highway

---

The entrance to Talia Caves on the Eyre Peninsula.

near the airport, is a strange mixture of free-ranging kangaroos, koalas, wallabies and emus, a walk-through aviary and a zoo section with imported monkeys, hyenas and celerse black apes. Open daily, 10 AM to dusk.

Cowell, 111 km (69 miles) from Whyalla, is primarily a fishing destination, although there are good swimming beaches at Lucky Bay, 16 km (10 miles) east of town. **Jade** is mined in the nearby Minbrie Ranges and cut, graded and processed in Cowell. If you're interested in a purchasing some, rough jade is sold at the Gemstone Corporation compound on the northern Lincoln Highway.

Point Gibbon, 20 km (12.5 miles) south, has a lovely stretch of beach with huge white sand hills.

a semi-submerged viewing platform enables visitors to watch the frenzy as the tuna are fed. For the more adventurous, **Calypso Star Boat Charter (** (08) 8364 4428 E-MAIL calypsostar@nbw.com.au specializes in white pointer shark cage-diving and game fishing.

Covering the southern tip of the Eyre Peninsula, **Lincoln National Park** is a magnificent nature area of contrasting land- and seascapes. The sheltered open spaces and quiet bays are ideal for camping, fishing and day-trips. Parrots, emus and kangaroos are common throughout, while osprey and sea eagles frequent the coast. **Memory Cove** is a beautiful sheltered inlet near the southernmost tip of the Eyre Peninsula. Popular sites for picnics

It's a short walk south from the car park to the point, where a small colony of sea lions often doze at the water's edge.

and sightseeing with vehicles include **Surfleet Point**, **Spalding Cove**, **Cape Donnington** and **Taylor's Landing**.

PORT LINCOLN

Almost 280 km (174 miles) south of Whyalla, the bustling little township of Port Lincoln sits on the edge of the clear blue waters of the enormous **Boston Bay**. Just off the coast, **Boston Island** is ringed by a vast expanse of sheltered water, idyllic for small boat fishing and sailing, while further out lie the **Joseph Banks Group of Islands**, for more of the same. **Triple Bay Charters (** (08) 8682 4119 operates relaxing full- and half-day fishing and sightseeing tours of the bay. For skippered yacht cruises contact **Yacht-Away Cruising Holidays (** (08) 8684 4240. **Dangerous Reef Explorer II (** (08) 8682 2425 takes visitors to the tuna farms, where

COFFIN BAY TO STREAKY BAY

Coffin Bay National Park features white-sand beaches and azure waters. Spring is the best time to visit, for the wildflowers and native heaths. Large numbers of western gray kangaroos and emus inhabit the park, and ospreys and white-bellied sea eagles frequent the coastline. Entry permits and camping permits are available at the park entrance.

There are some striking views of the cliffs and cerulean blue waters at a few points just off the drive to Streaky Bay. **Cummings Monument Lookout** is just past Kiama, and affords an uninterrupted view from Point Drummond in the south to the rugged cliffs of Sheringa in the north. It's also home to a family of osprey who nest on a craggy pinnacle adjacent to the lookout. **Locks Well** and **Sheringa Beach** are known for superb surf fishing, consistently yielding large salmon. There's a 120-m (394-ft) wooden staircase at Locks Well to access the beach, with a lookout at the top. The cliff-top scenic drive to Anxious Bay leads to **Blackfellows**, one of the best surf breaks in Australia. It's not uncommon to share the waves with a school of dolphins who also enjoy the surf (watch out for sharks too). Nearby **Talia Caves** is one of the most beautiful spots along this coast, with limestone caves, granite rockface and formations, magnificent white-sand dunes and a beautiful beach.

inquisitive, but to have them glide past and around you is well worth the (chilly) plunge. Contact Alan and Trish who organize this memorable eco-tour at **Baird Bay Dolphin and Sea Lion Tours** (/FAX (08) 8626 5017 E-MAIL sealions@bigpond .com.au. There are places for those who want to watch from the boat, and they also organize sightseeing trips to Cape Radstone Cliffs or the Investigator Islands.

Streaky Bay is the next main town. The water here has beautiful bands of color caused by the oils given off by the seaweed and plenty of safe shallow swimming. There are sea lions and dolphins in the waters here too, although Streaky Bay is best known for its less-friendly great white sharks.

Venus Bay is a quiet fishing community on a narrow peninsula overlooking the bay and its islands. A short drive past the houses, **Needle Eye Lookout** offers views of towering cliffs and booming surf. David and Mandy Masters run the **Venus Bay Caravan Park and General Store** ((08) 8625 5073, on the waterfront near the wharf, and organize budget cabin accommodation, rent boats and fishing tackle, and help you to spot dolphins and whales.

Venus Bay is a good base for trips to **Baird Bay**, where visitors can swim with sea lions and dolphins in their natural habitat. Point Labatt, which separates the bay from the ocean, has the only permanent colony of sea lions on the Australian mainland. Inquisitive sea lions press their noses to your mask and rest their flippers across your shoulders. They sumersault around you and leap out of the water. The dolphins are a little less

WHERE TO STAY AND EAT

Derhams Foreshore Motor Inn ((08) 8645 8877, Watson Terrace, Whyalla, has moderately priced air-conditioned units and a swimming pool, and an inexpensive restaurant serving Thai food and pasta. **Cowell Jade Motel** ((08) 8629 2002, Lincoln Highway, Cowell, has inexpensive rooms, a swimming pool, and also sell jade jewelry, marble and jade carvings, and emu eggs. The **Franklin Harbour Hotel** ((08) 8629 2015, 1 Main Street, Cowell, serves enormous counter meals including great fish and chips, and has a dining room with more upmarket offerings.

OPPOSITE: Pelicans coming in for a feed as fishermen clean their catch at Venus Bay.
ABOVE: Swimming with the fur seals at Baird Bay.

Most of the best places to eat and stay in Port Lincoln are on Tasman Terrace, running along the foreshore. All have bay views. The **Grand Tasman Hotel** ((08) 8682 2133, 94 Tasman Terrace, has inexpensive rooms above a busy bar-restaurant-gaming lounge complex. The quieter **Limani Hotel** ((08) 8682 2750, 50 Lincoln Highway, has inexpensive and moderately priced comfortable, modern suites with balconies overlooking the bay. The restored former farmhouse and lighthouse at **Cape Donnington** in Lincoln National Park has been fully furnished for inexpensive rental accommodation, with fine views over Boston Bay. Bookings are taken at the Port Lincoln visitor information center. Port Lincoln has a good selection of restaurants, cafés and pubs serving well-prepared local produce, the specialty of course being a vast array of seafood. The moderately priced **Moorings Seafood Restaurant** ((08) 8682 2133, in the Grand Tasman Hotel, serves the best available produce and has a good inexpensive bistro or counter meals. The hotel also has comfortable, moderately priced rooms. The best café in town is **Café Flix** ((08) 8683 1199, 3 Hallett Place, at the old restored **Flix Cinema**. Café Flix makes huge gourmet sandwiches and has incredible cakes flown in fresh daily from Adelaide.

For some of the best oysters in Australia drive 49 km (30.5 miles) west to Coffin Bay. A good place to try them is at the **Coffin Bay Oyster Farm** ((08) 8685 4009 on the Esplanade, which also serves the succulent local lobster. Fisherman also bring in some of the best abalone, scallops and prawns I've ever tasted. Two of the best spots to cast a line and try your own hand are at **Snapper Point** and **Crinolin Point**, where you are almost guaranteed a catch. **Siesta Lodge** ((08) 8685 4001, in Coffin Bay, have basic inexpensive units (designed for anglers) with sea views and air-conditioning.

Venus Bay Caravan Park and General Store ((08) 8625 5073 can help with inexpensive cabin and holiday home accommodation. The **Streaky Bay Hotel** ((08) 8626 1008, 33 Alfred Terrace, overlooks the bay and has the best accommodation (inexpensive) in town, and some hearty, inexpensive bistro meals.

HOW TO GET THERE

Kendell Airlines ((08) 8231 9567 or 131 300 WEB SITE www.kendell.com.au operates frequent and direct daily flights from Adelaide to Port Lincoln and Whyalla. A luggage restriction of 14 kg (six pounds) is strictly enforced on the tiny Saab 340 planes — excess luggage may be left at Morgan's Corner Newsagency at the domestic terminal of Adelaide Airport for a small charge. **Lincoln Airlines** TOLL-FREE (1800) 018 234 has flights between Port Lincoln and Adelaide, and **Whyalla Airlines** TOLL-FREE (1800) 088 858 has flights from Adelaide

to Whyalla, Cleve and Wudinna. **Airlines of South Australia** ((08) 8682 5688 (or call Qantas (131 313) also operates daily services between Port Lincoln and Adelaide.

Premier Stateliner Coach Group ((08) 8415 5555 runs daily overnight and daylight coaches from Adelaide to Port Augusta, Whyalla, Port Lincoln and Streaky Bay.

Car rental in Port Lincoln is available through **Avis** ((08) 8682 1072, **Budget** ((08) 8684 3668, **Hertz** ((08) 8682 1933, or **Thrifty** ((08) 8683 0540.

CROSSING THE NULLARBOR

The Nullarbor is a vast treeless plain (hence the name) literally falling away in the south into the Great Australian Bight, where sheer limestone cliffs drop directly into the pounding surf. Ceduna is pretty much the last town in South Australia, before the long drive westward into Western Australia. A hot, dry town on the shores of Murat Bay, its name is derived from the Aboriginal word "chedoona" meaning "a resting place" — aptly as that's what most people stop here for on the long drive from Adelaide or Perth.

The **Ceduna Community Hotel/Motel** ((08) 8625 2008 TOLL-FREE (1800) 655 300, on the foreshore, offers inexpensive rooms and has a bistro, a restaurant and two bar areas (and the ubiquitous gaming machines).

Penong is 75 km (47 miles) west of Ceduna, where it would be difficult to miss the **Penong Hotel** ((08) 8625 1050, Main Street, which serves counter meals and offers inexpensive accommodation. There's also a store and gas station here. Surfers turn off at Penong to **Cactus Beach** where diehard wave-catchers camp out in coastal caves. Ask for directions at Penong. Camping costs $6 and the owner drives around the campsites every evening supplying firewood. It's an interesting community, living off the abundance of fish caught off the local jetty and the welcome smoothies and veggie burgers sold at the store that opens for two hours daily. James Spitzkowsky organizes tailor-made **camel safaris** ((08) 8625 1093 in the area, which last anything from two days to two weeks.

The only other fuel and refreshment stops on the long, hot drive across the Nullarbor to Eucla in Western Australia are the **Nundroo Roadhouse** ((08) 8625 6120, **Yalata Roadhouse** ((08) 8625 6986, the **Nullarbor Hotel-Motel Inn** ((08) 8625 6271, and **WA-SA Border Village** ((08) 9039 3474. All offer basic inexpensive accommodation. Most of the land between the Nundroo and Nullarbor roadhouses is Aboriginal-owned, and a permit is required to leave the highway (see ABORIGINAL LANDS, page 319 in TRAVELERS' TIPS). Permits are sold at the Yalata Roadhouse (adults $8, children under 16 free).

The white sand dunes and beaches meet the Bunda Cliffs at the **Head of Bight**, on the Yalata Aboriginal Lands 78 km (48.5 miles) west of Yalata. Head of Bight is a major whale breeding ground for the southern right whale — from June to October it is one of the best whale-viewing areas in the world. lucky visitors have even seen calves being born here.

The White Well Ranger Station ((08) 8625 6201, the Yalata Roadhouse, or the Ceduna Gateway Visitor Information Centre all issue permits to enter the Aboriginal lands and have information on where to spot whales. **Whale Air** ((08) 8625 6271 offers half-hour scenic flights departing from the Nullarbor Roadhouse daily between May and October over Nullarbor caves and blowholes and the Bunda Cliffs and Nullarbor Plain. The highlight is viewing southern right whales, bottle-nose dolphins, seals and great white sharks.

HOW TO GET THERE

Kendell Airlines ((08) 8231 9567 or (131 300 WEB SITE www.kendell.com.au has daily flights between Adelaide and Ceduna. **Premier Stateliner Coach Group** ((08) 8415 5555 runs daily overnight and daylight coaches from Adelaide to Ceduna, and Greyhound's Adelaide–Perth bus service passes through Ceduna and Penong.

Ceduna Rent-A-Car ((08) 8625 2085 specializes in four-wheel-drives. There's also a **Budget** ((08) 8625 2742 office in Ceduna.

COOBER PEDY

On the edge of the Great Victoria Desert, in the middle of nowhere, Coober Pedy is 863 km (535 miles) northwest of Adelaide and 687 km (430 miles) south of Alice Springs. The town derives its name from the Aboriginal phrase "kupa piti," which loosely translated means "white man's burrow." With most of the population living in subterranean coolness, the surface is a strange, deserted lunar-like landscape, making it one bizarre township. In the 1980s, Mel Gibson's *Mad Max* films made the most of Coober Pedy's stricken, desolate appeal to portray a post-apocalyptic future world (thereby launching Gibson into international stardom).

The town was built on the wealth of opals, discovered in the area in 1915 and today yielding 85% of Australia's total. See also SPECIAL INTERESTS, page 53 in YOUR CHOICE.

GENERAL INFORMATION

The **Coober Pedy Tourist Information Centre** ((08) 8672 3474, is in the Council Office in Hutchison Street, and is open 9 AM to 5 PM weekdays, 9 AM to noon Saturday and 2 PM to 5 PM Sunday.

WHAT TO SEE AND DO

On the surface the landscape is desolate; mines and diggings cover a radius of 50 km (31 miles) around the town. Thousands upon thousands of small pyramids of white sand two to three meters (six to nine feet) in height are piled up beside old diggings. Care should be taken walking around Coober Pedy: old mines have been known to collapse in drops of up to 30 m (100 ft).

While not as close to the Almighty as they could be, the **Catacomb Church** in Catacomb Street and **Church Saints Peter and Paul** are both underground and a good deal cooler than had they been built along more traditional lines, soaring to the heavens. Both can be inspected daily and services are conducted on Sunday. In 1993 the **Serbian Church** opened in Potch Gully, its walls covered in fine religious carvings by Norm Ashton.

Also underground is the **Umoona Opal Mine and Museum** ((08) 8672 5288, in Hutchison Street, which is a complex of chambers. It incorporates a museum with exhibitions on opal mining and Aboriginal culture, as well as an impressive display of opals. The **Old Timer's Mine** ((08) 8672 5555, in Crowder's Gully Road, is another museum which gives an intriguing insight into opal mining and includes an original 1918 miner's home. Across the road is **The Big Winch**, a giant mine winch overlooking the town. Below it is an opal and art gallery, displaying famous black opals. A **Coober Pedy Discovery Tour** ((08) 8672 5028 is a good introduction to the town and opal mining. Another way to explore Coober Pedy is to take the **Gem City Opal Tours** ((08) 8672 5333, where Trevor McLeod, a crusty ex-miner himself, shows you around the town and the surrounding countryside.

Within **Breakaway National Reserve**, the **Painted Desert** draws visitors to its ever-changing colors. You can get there by taking Alice Springs Road for 28 km (17 miles) out of Coober Pedy.

WHERE TO STAY

Very sensibly, there are several underground hotels in Coober Pedy. **Opal Inn** ((08) 8672 5054 FAX (08) 8672 5911, Hutchinson Street, and the **Desert Cave** ((08) 8672 5688 TOLL-FREE (1800) 088 521, Hutchinson Street, are both moderately priced.

HOW TO GET THERE

Kendell Airlines (131 300 has one flight a day from Adelaide. Most coaches between Alice Springs and Adelaide stop in Coober Pedy. **Premier Stateliner Coach Group** ((08) 8415 5555, McCafferty's and Greyhound Pioneer all run services along this route.

Western Australia

WESTERN AUSTRALIA HAS ALWAYS BEEN SOMEWHAT SET APART FROM THE REST OF THE COUNTRY. Even though European settlement occurred here before Victoria or South Australia, it has a feeling of newness. The state exemplifies the pioneer mentality of other isolated parts of the country, and its citizens have a chauvinism that is parochial — more Western Australian than Australian.

From the start, its geographical isolation required Western Australia to be self-reliant, a task made easier by its healthy mining industry. The state experienced its first growth spurt when gold was discovered in Coolgardie and Kalgoorlie in the early 1890s. More discoveries of mineral wealth were to follow.

The state's relationship with the rest of Australia has not always been harmonious. On April 8, 1933, Western Australia held a referendum on whether to secede from the rest of the country. There was overwhelming support for the proposal, with 138,653 voting "yes" and just 70,706 voting "no." Western Australians objected to the federal government's high tariff policy which disadvantaged their state's exports. In particular, the high price of sugar that protected Queensland's growers raised their ire. To dramatize their point the Fremantle Sugar Party was planned to emulate the famous Boston Tea Party, threatening to dump sugar into Fremantle Harbour. This not very original act of defiance never took place and the west soon lost its enthusiasm for secession.

Over the last few decades of the twentieth century, Perth was the fastest-growing city in Australia. Its skyline shot up, reflecting the state's confidence. Unfortunately many of the new developments were promoted by homegrown entrepreneurs, who in the 1980s had used borrowed money to take over companies. The bubble finally burst in the early 1990s and thousands of small investors lost their savings. It's Western Australia's immense mineral wealth that keeps it going, though — from diamonds in the Kimberley to the Pilbara's iron mountains and gold and nickel in the Kalgoorlie–Kambalda area. Gas reserves recently discovered within the North West Shelf off Port Hedland are believed to be the world's largest. There have been other booms and busts in the state's history. Each time the irrepressible Western Australians bounced back to new heights.

More than any other place in Australia, Western Australia sees its future in Asia, hardly surprising when you consider that Perth is closer to Singapore than to Sydney.

Western Australia covers a third of the continent, over 2.5 million sq km (about 965,000 sq miles), most of it desert which comes alive each spring with a carpet of wildflowers. When visiting a state as vast as this, one has to be selective. Distances are almost incomprehensible and the essentially arid climate inhospitable, with tropical monsoons (and occasionally hurricanes) in the north and sudden heavy rainfall further south causing flash floods and making roads impassable. The population numbers just 1.76 million, two-thirds of whom live in the Perth region. On many, many roads, weeks can go by without a single car passing. This is not a state to visit for those short on time or patience.

The state can be roughly divided into three main regions: the Kimberley to the north; the middle area of the Pilbara, Gascoyne and the Mid West; and the wheat belts and gold fields of the south. Each area has distinctive landforms and remarkable indigenous flora and fauna. The northern portion of the state is watered by monsoons, receiving between 500 and 1,000 mm (20 to 40 in) of rain between December and April. The narrow coastal strip south of Perth is the only temperate part of the state; here timber, fishing and a burgeoning wine industry are supplanted by tourism, primarily from Perth residents and avid surfers, although Australians from "The East" visit from August to November, the spring wildflower season.

For the visitor, the southeast and the far north hold most attractions. But even a visit confined to these areas is daunting. It's very easy to lose perspective when the combined area of Austria, Belgium, Denmark, France, Portugal, Spain, Switzerland, Germany, Italy, Luxembourg, The Netherlands, Norway and the United Kingdom is 25,647 sq km (9,902 sq miles) *smaller* than Western Australia. In fact, if Western Australia were a country, it would be the world's ninth largest.

PERTH

Perth, "the most isolated city in the world," enjoyed short-lived international recognition when Alan Bond won the America's Cup yacht race in 1983. It seems content since to have returned to anonymity and just to bask in the sun — it has more sunny days per year than any city in Australia. Founded in 1829, Perth straddles a wide expanse of the Swan River bank, between the Indian Ocean and the Darling Ranges. Perth is a modern city of sleek multi-story buildings intermingled with early colonial structures and wide highways that never experience traffic jams. The river and beaches are safe and clean, as all heavy industry is kept well out of the city. Life is alfresco and healthy, most nights streets are alive, while on the weekends Perth's beaches, boardwalks, tennis courts and sidewalk cafés are crowded.

GENERAL INFORMATION

The **Western Australian Tourist Centre** ((08) 9483 1111 WEB SITE www.westernaustralia.net, at the corner of Forrest Place and Wellington Street, has a good selection of brochures and can arrange

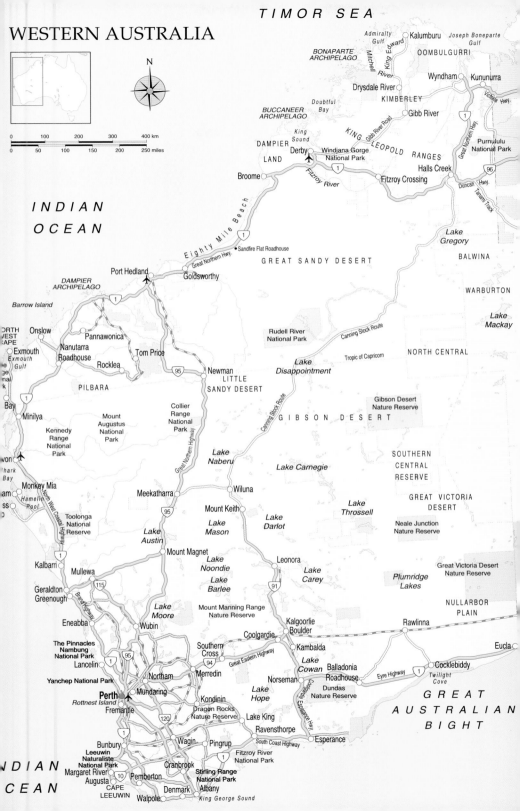

accommodation and tours. For details of national parks contact the **Western Australia Department of Conservation and Land Management** ((08) 9367 0333 or the **Conservation Council of Western Australia** ((08) 9321 4507.

The **Traveler's Club Tour and Information Centre** ((08) 9226 0660, 499 Wellington Street, allows customers 15 minutes free **Internet** access and provides complimentary tea and coffee. Other services include photocopying, faxing, and printing. The **Perth Tourist Lounge** ((08) 9481 8303, 2 Carillon Arcade, 680 Hay Street Mall, has coin-operated access to the Internet at $2 per 15 minutes. Both can help with tours and accommodation throughout Western Australia. In Fremantle, the **Net Trek Café** ((08) 9336 4446, Bannister Street Mall, offers Internet access for $5 per half hour.

Perth's **GPO** ((08) 9326 4444, Forrest Place, provides a postal service between 8 AM and 5:30 PM Monday to Friday, 9 AM to 12:30 PM Saturday and midday to 4 PM Sunday.

For medical services contact the **Royal Perth Hospital** ((08) 9224 2244, Victoria Square, or the **Traveler's Vaccination and Medical Clinic** ((08) 9321 1977, 5 Mill Street.

GETTING AROUND

Getting around the city is free on buses and trains within the bounds of Kings Park Road, Thomas Street, Newcastle Street, the Causeway and Barrack Street Jetty. The "Perth Tram" is in fact a bus that does a circuit of Perth's attractions: a day-pass costs $15. For information on all of Perth's transport services call **Transperth Service Information** (132 213 weekdays from 6:30 AM to 9 PM and weekends from 7 AM to 7 PM. Their office is in the Plaza Arcade off Hay Street. For country and interstate trains phone (136 213.

There are **taxi** ranks throughout the Perth central business district, or cabs can be ordered by telephoning the major operators: Swan Taxis (131 388, Black and White Taxis (131 008 or Independent Taxis ((08) 9375 7777. You can also hire a qualified taxi driver to conduct your own personal guided tour of Perth.

The **Royal Automobile Club of WA (RACWA)** ((08) 9421 4444, 228 Adelaide Terrace, Perth, offers maps and touring advice. Its **Breakdown Service** (131 111 operates all hours. Members of an affiliated overseas auto club receive reciprocal membership.

Perth and Fremantle have an interesting network of cycle-ways which provide an excellent opportunity to view some of the most picturesque parts of the cities from the saddle. Booklets detailing routes around the river, along the coast and from Armadale to Perth are available from the **Department of Sport and Recreation** ((08) 9387 9700, or **BikeWest** ((08) 9320 9301. It's illegal in Western Australia to ride a bicycle without a helmet.

WHAT TO SEE AND DO

Perth is situated on a broad stretch of the **Swan River**. The river's almost lake-like proportions give a sense of spaciousness; the city provides a sleek backdrop to the colorful sailing boats bobbing on the waters.

Overlooking the Swan River is **King's Park**, 400 ha (1,000 acres) of gardens and bush on the western edge of the central business district. The park was reserved by explorer/politician John Forrest in 1872 for children "a thousand years hence to see what the bush was like when Stirling arrived." In spring the park is a mass of beautiful wildflowers, a living example of the wisdom of Forrest's bequest. If the weather is not too hot, a good way to see it is on a bicycle; **Koala Bicycle Hire** ((08) 9321 3061 are tucked behind the pleasant Garden Restaurant.

The park overlooks **Narrows Bridge** and the colony's first flour mill. At the south end of the bridge a Perth landmark, the 1835 **Old Mill** ((08) 9367 5788, contains relics of the pioneer days. It is open from 10 AM to 4 PM daily.

St. George's Terrace is Perth's main thoroughfare. Strolling along "the Terrace," you pass a mixture of the city's oldest buildings and the glittering glass towers erected during the last boom of the 1880s. Down at your feet are more than 150 bronze plaques which have been embedded into the sidewalk. Each one honors a Western Australian who made an outstanding contribution to the life of the state's first 150 years. Running along the southern side of the Terrace is **Stirling Gardens**, which stretches east from Barrack Street and stops just short of Victoria Street. These are a popular venue for concerts and art shows. Facing them and opposite Pier Street is **Government House**, the official residence of the Governor built between 1859 and 1864. Described as Jacobean Mansion revival-style, it is set in elegant English-style gardens. Across the road is the **Deanery**, built in the late 1850s and retaining its shingle roof. **Old Perth Boys' School**, west up the Terrace and near King Street, was built between 1852 and 1854 as Western Australia's first and Australia's second oldest school. You can enter the fine sandstone building, which contains a café and souvenir shop. At the corner of Hay and Barrack streets is Perth's **Town Hall**, built by convicts in the 1860s in the fashion of an English Jacobean market hall.

Exhibitions relating to different aspects of the state's history are on display the **Western Australian Museum** ((08) 9328 4411, Francis Street, Northbridge. The pride of its collection is the 11-ton Mundrabilla meteorite; opening hours on weekdays and Sunday are from 10:30 AM to 5 PM and on Saturday and public holidays from 1 PM to 5 PM. Admission is free. The museum is part of the **Perth Cultural Centre** that also contains the **Art Gallery of Western Australia** ((08) 9328 7233, with one of the best collections of Aboriginal art in Australia, and the **Perth Institute of Contemporary Art** ((08) 9227 6144.

One of the best ways to see Perth and its environs is from a river cruiser; there is a good selection of trips to choose from, most of which start the **Barrack Street Jetty**. The **Transperth Ferry** ((08) 9221 2722 departs daily for tourist destinations near Perth and along the Swan River. A pleasant short trip is to the **Perth Zoo** ((08) 9367 7988, 20 La Bouchere Road, South Perth, which is set in beautifully landscaped gardens.

Perth's suburban **surf** beaches are some of the best in the country. On a fine day those between North Fremantle and Scarborough are crowded with sun seekers.

In the sheltered waters of the Swan River hundreds of **yachts** and **sail boards** catch the Fremantle Doctor, a cool breeze that blows most afternoons. You can rent a sailboard from the Pelican Point Windsurfing Hire ((08) 9386 1830, 126 Broadway, Nedlands, or from Funcat Hire TOLL-FREE (1800) 926 003, Coode Street Jetty, South Perth.

The waters around Perth are also popular with **scuba** divers. About 25 km (16 miles) from Perth is the Marion Marine Park ((08) 9448 5800, accessible from Hillarys Boat Harbour, that features

SPORTS AND OUTDOOR ACTIVITIES

With such good weather year round, it is no surprise that so many of Perth's attractions are sports or outdoors related. Its climate is perfect for **golf**, and more than 20 courses are close to the city. Forty-five minutes south of Perth is the Meadow Springs Country Club's Collier Park Golf Course ((08) 9581 6360, Meadow Springs Drive, where you can play 18 holes on a course bounded by a pine plantation with a couple of lakes to keep the game interesting. If your appetite for golf is not sated, then drive five minutes down the road to the Secret Harbour ((08) 9357 0993, a nine-hole course where you can send balls sailing along its fairways between sand dunes and enjoy the ocean views. For details about other courses contact the Western Australian Golf Association ((08) 9367 2490.

limestone reefs and the wealth of sea life living off them. Off Rottnest Island are eighteenth-century wrecks to explore and some spectacular underwater caves. The Mindarie Diving Academy ((08) 9305 7113, in the Mindarie Keys Marina, organizes charter trips to reefs near Perth and runs beginner courses.

WHERE TO STAY

Expensive

The **Perth Parmelia Hilton** ((08) 9322 3622 TOLL-FREE (1800) 222 255 FAX (08) 9481 0857, Mill Street, in the heart of Perth's business and shopping district, is a stroll to Kings Park and has good views of the Swan River. In the center of town, all rooms at the **Hyatt Regency** ((08) 9225 1234

Perth's pedestrian-only shopping center.

TOLL-FREE (1800) 222 188 E-MAIL hyatt@hrp.com.au,
99 Adelaide Terrace, have river views and access
to all the facilities one would expect. The Hyatt
also boasts several fine restaurants. **Rydges of
Perth** ((08) 9263 1800 E-MAIL reservations_perth
@rydges.com, corner of Hay and King Streets, a
lovely first-class hotel, has great year-round package deals that are well worth inquiring about. The
Broadwater Pagoda Hotel ((08) 9367 0300
TOLL-FREE (1800) 650 222 E-MAIL pagoda@agn
.net.au, 112 Melville Parade, Como, in South Perth,
is a relaxed hotel with a beautiful swimming pool,
a gymnasium and sauna. Its elegant colonial-style
Pagoda LongBar and excellent restaurant, built in
1922 and faithfully restored, is the perfect place
to sip a cocktail on one of Perth's balmy evenings.

Overlooking the Indian Ocean and only 15 minutes from the city in Scarborough the **Radisson
Observation City Resort Hotel** ((08) 9386 1155
E-MAIL reservation@debretts.com.au, The Esplanade, has several good bars and all rooms have
private balconies.

Only 35 minutes out of town in the wine growing region of the Swan Valley, the **Novotel Vines
Resort** ((08) 9297 3000 WEB SITE www.novotelvines
.com.au, Verdelho Drive, is regarded as Western
Australia's finest luxury resort. Select from one
of their "seven deadly sins" package deals for total
decadence.

Moderate

The **Criterion Hotel Perth** ((08) 9325 5155 E-MAIL
criterion@E-MAIL.upnaway.com, 560 Hay Street,
with its wonderful art deco façade, has been recently refurbished and offers style without the high
price. At around the same price, the centrally located, **City Waters Lodge** ((08) 9325 1566 TOLL-FREE
(1800) 999 030 E-MAIL perth@citywaters.com.au,
118 Terrace Road, offers comfortable fully equipped
self-contained studios. The **Best Western Indian
Ocean Hotel** ((08) 9341 1122 TOLL-FREE (1800)
998 106, 23–27 Hastings Street, Scarborough, has
deluxe rooms with ocean views at very reasonable
rates. Breakfast is included, and they have some of
the best package deals in town. **Annabelle Cottage**
((08) 9227 6855, 246 Lake Street, Northbridge, provides home comforts in a relaxed atmosphere.

Inexpensive

Guests at the **Cottesloe Beach Hotel** ((08) 9383
1100 FAX (08) 9385 2482, 104 Marine Parade, enjoy the bonus of having one of Perth's best beaches
just across the road. For those with a car, it's well
worth going just two kilometers (one mile) west
of Perth to the **Murray Lodge Motel** ((08) 9321
7441 FAX (08) 9321 7282, 718 Murray Street, which
offers excellent amenities for the price. In the city,
Backpackers International ((08) 9227 9977,
FAX 9384 6741, 110 Aberdeen Street, Northbridge,
is one of the more popular with budget travelers.

WHERE TO EAT

One of the great pleasures of dining in Perth is the
abundance of outdoor tables on city sidewalks and
overlooking the Swan River. The array of seafood
is overwhelming, but carnivores and even vegetarians are reasonably well catered to these days.
Wines from Margaret River are recognized as some
of Australia's best and feature in better restaurants.

Expensive

Bibendum ((08) 9388 8333, 388 Hay Street, Subiaco,
has an excellent six course tasting menu that exemplifies the chef's diversity and creativity with
contemporary cuisine. **Campo Foiori** ((08) 9316
3600, 22 Kearns Crescent, Ardross, has the best in
simple Italian cuisine served in rather ostentatious
surroundings, although it is in fact very casual.
The help-yourself antipasti is delicious and their

signature dish of tender roast baby lamb is served with a finger bowl and bib to remove all formality. **Fraser's Restaurant** ((08) 9481 7100, Fraser Avenue, Kings Park, West Perth, has one of the best views over the city, sitting indoors or out. Their menu changes daily to take advantage of the best available produce. **Friends** ((08) 9221 0885, 20 Terrace Road, in the Hyatt Center, is best known for its outstanding wine list of over 500 wines. The large menu features modern international fare with extreme attention to detail. This is definitely one of Perth's true fine dining establishments.

Moderate
Northbridge, especially around James and Lake streets, is the heart of Perth's café and restaurant scene. There are, literally, hundreds of restaurants where you can find Italian, Greek, Chinese, Thai, and many other cuisines all within a four block

radius. **Toledos** ((08) 9227 5282, 35 Lake Street, serves a very good Spanish tapas, with an outside dining terrace popular in the evenings. For a casual ambiance take an outside table at **Fishy Affair** ((08) 9328 6636, 132 James Street; the atmosphere inside is a little more intimate. Oysters are good here, and for main course their sensational seafood platter is a must. Open 24 hours a day seven days a week **Oriel** ((08) 9382 1886, 483 Hay Street, Subiaco, serves modern Australian dishes and is one of the best breakfast and brunch spots (inexpensive) in Perth. Also in Subiaco is **Mead's Fish House** ((08) 9380 0868, 222 Hay Street, a bustling seafood restaurant with a sunny courtyard where perfectly fresh fish are deftly prepared and cooked. **No. 44 King Street** ((08) 9321 4476 has over 60 wines available by the glass and an imaginative

Perth has grown rapidly over the past few decades, adding ever-taller buildings to its skyline.

menu that changes daily; this is a place for boisterous lunches and intimate dinners at incredibly reasonable prices — one of Perth's best. **E'Cucina** ((08) 9481 1020 Hay Street is stylish with its polished dark-wood floors and views onto native gardens. The regularly changing menu has good pastas and risotto and usually some choice beef and fresh seafood.

Inexpensive
At the **Sparrow Indonesian Restaurant** ((08) 9328 5660, 434A William Street, meals start at a ridiculously low $4 for a main, but quality and authenticity remain high. Favorites include the flavorsome beef and potato cakes, and the fish cakes. **Viet Hoa**

((08) 9328 2127, 314 Williams Street, Northbridge, is the place to go for great full-flavored soups, noodles and rice. There always seems to be a crowd at **Mamma Maria's** ((08) 9328 4532, on the corner of Aberdeen and Lake streets, enjoying well-prepared Italian meals.

NIGHTLIFE

Nightlife in Perth centers around Subiaco and Northbridge, where local bands play in the areas' many bars from Thursday to Sunday nights, often for free. For information on upcoming concerts and theater in Perth check the entertainment pages of the daily *West Australian*. The free *X Press* WEB SITE www.xpressmag.com.au and *Hype* WEB SITE www.hypemag.com.au are gig guides with music and event reviews. Their web sites keep everyone up to date on who's playing where.

The **Subiaco Hotel** ((08) 9388 9816, on the corner of Hay Street and Rokeby Road, is a favorite with locals, and the lively and friendly bar has music on Friday and Saturday nights. Another popular bar is the more upmarket **Black Tom's Bar** ((08) 9380 0898, 226 Hay Street, with great bar snacks and good wines. Possibly Perth's grooviest nightspot, **Club Red Sea** ((08) 9382 2022, 88 Rokeby Road, has live music and DJs and is open until late on Friday and Saturday. The **Saphire Bar** ((08) 9380 4470, 298 Hay Street, has an extensive wine list and hip decor, with dancing on weekends.

Northbridge, just over the railway line from the city center, is the main nightclub area, with around 20 nightclubs, 10 pubs, and over 100 restaurants all within a few blocks. **Metropolis** ((08) 9228 0500, 134 Roe Street in Northbridge, is Perth's largest, with six levels of bars and dance floors. **Post Office** ((08) 9228 0077, 133 Aberdeen Street, Northbridge, plays eclectic world music in a fairly slick atmosphere, while **Havana**, 69 Lake Street in Northbridge, plays dance music until 5 AM.

Globe ((08) 9481 2521, 393 Murray Street, Perth, **Connections** (gay and lesbian), 78 James Street, and **O2 Bar and Night Club** ((08) 9328 7447, 139 James Street, are three popular clubs in the center of town. Other favorites include **The Church**, **The Jackal**, **Redheads**, **Club A** and **DC's**. For some lively jazz drop into the **Hyde Park Hotel** 331 Bulwer Street, Monday or Tuesday night.

The **Perth Concert Hall** ((08) 9231 9900 in St. George Terrace features anything from opera to rock concerts, while the concert hall at the **University of Western Australia** campus in Nedlands is essentially a contemporary music venue. The **Burswood Resort Casino** ((08) 9362 7777, on the Great Eastern Highway, incorporates a top-class hotel and 14,000-seat entertainment center. The casino is open until 3 AM.

The Swan River is its prettiest at night, surrounded by the skyline lights of Perth. See it on an evening cruise offered by **Boat Torque Cruises** ((08) 9221 5844, aboard the *Star Flyte* where you can take in the shimmering sights over a meal and then spend the rest of the evening dancing. Dinner cruises depart Friday and Saturday evenings at 7:45 PM.

HOW TO GET THERE

Perth is a terminus for one of the world's great train journeys: the transcontinental *Indian-Pacific*. The journey takes 64 hours from Sydney including 482 km (300 miles) of absolutely straight track through the Nullarbor Plain.

There are direct flights every day into Perth from all capital cities and Alice Springs.

By road Perth is a long way from anywhere: the drive from Adelaide takes about 32 hours, and from Darwin 46 hours.

AROUND PERTH

FREMANTLE

Spread around the mouth of the Swan River, Fremantle, 19 km (12 miles) downstream from Perth, was once a humble work-a-day seaport. Almost a suburb of Perth today, "Freo," as it is known to the locals, retains many buildings dating back to the first half of the nineteenth century when it was an unpretentious seaside town, the place to go for an inexpensive meal, a walk along the foreshore or to visit an art gallery.

There's a **tourist booth** located in the Town Hall Arcade ((08) 9336 6636.

What to See and Do

In 1987 the America's Cup defense was held in the waters off Fremantle, thrusting the town into the international limelight. A powerful lot of money was spent doing up the town, and some of the eyesores along the foreshore were tastefully renovated. The development included a boardwalk, built where waterfront restaurants cluster. Several hotels were built to accommodate the yachting crowd and fortunately do not spoil the feel of Freo.

At the south end, near the river's mouth, the **Round House** ((08) 9430 7351 was built in 1831. This 12-sided building, the oldest in Western Australia, was first used to jail minor offenders. When convicts first arrived in 1850, it accepted more serious offenders. Part of the building is now a café.

Further up High Street, towards the city center, is the **Town Hall**. In 1884 the municipal council put itself in hock for fifteen years to pay for this building, with its ornate façade and elaborately decorated balconies and balustrades. Admission to the **Western Australian Maritime Museum** ((08) 9431 8444, Cliff Street, is by donation. Pride of place is given to the restored stern section of the Dutch treasure ship *Batavia*, wrecked in 1629 off the Western Australian coast near Geraldton, 330 km (206 miles) north of Perth. The museum is open every day from 10:30 AM to 5 PM.

The **Fremantle Arts Centre** ((08) 9335 8244, 1 Finnerty Street, has three downstairs galleries showing works mainly by Western Australian artists. Exhibitions change every four weeks and works are for sale. The upstairs gallery has a permanent collection of the work from local artists and craftspeople. Open daily from 10 AM to 5 PM.

There is no better place to start an evening out in Fremantle than South Terrace, otherwise known as "Cappuccino Strip," where buskers entertain and pavement artists display their latest works. There are also some great pubs in Freo. Drop into the **Sail & Anchor Pub Brewery**, 64 South Terrace, for a drop of one of the local ales, which have sprightly names like Redback, Dogbolter and Iron Brew; some are brewed on the premises. The younger crowd looking for lively music goes to **Metropolis Concert Club**, 58 South Terrace.

Where to Stay

In Fremantle, the **Esplanade Hotel** ((08) 9432 4000 TOLL-FREE (1800) 998 201 E-MAIL reservations@ehf .com.au, at the corner of Marine Terrace and Essex Street, is a grand old hotel that was refurbished in 1988 without losing its character. Most rooms open out onto a verandah where breakfast can be served in summer.

On the river, the moderately priced **Riverside B&B** ((08) 9336 2209, 15 John Street, North Fremantle, includes a pool and has some rooms overlooking the beach. A selection of B&B accommodation is offered in and around Fremantle by **Fremantle Homestay** ((08) 9336 4864, 1 Norfolk Street, while **Fremantle Colonial Accommodation** ((08) 9430 6568 FAX (08) 9430 6405 E-MAIL colonial@fremantle.com, 215 High Street, Fremantle, have a choice of B&B and charming heritage-listed cottages.

Where to Eat

For sophisticated Japanese dining, **Chunagon** ((08) 9336 1000, 46 Mews Road, Fremantle, stands alone (expensive). All the classics are there — tempura, teriyaki, sashimi, and sushi — and they have several set-priced crayfish menus prepared in a number of tantalizing ways. Many of the dishes have sensible wine recommendations and customers get to enjoy incredible views of the harbor; screened private rooms are available.

Great seafood restaurants with million-dollar views abound on Fremantle Harbour. At **Sails** ((08) 9430 5050, 47 Mews Road, second floor, all meals can be taken as starters or mains. Best dishes include drunken mussels flamed in cognac served with a garlic cream sauce, and calamari marinated in fresh herbs, olive oil then pan sizzled. The wine list includes well-priced local wines. **Red Herring** ((08) 9339 1611, 26 Riverside Road, East Fremantle, sits on the water with river views and offers oysters alone or in combinations such as with fish roe with wasabi dressing. Their bouillabaisse is legendary. Both restaurants are moderately priced.

How to Get There

There is a regular commuter train service between Perth and Fremantle; a round-trip ticket costs $6. An alternative is to take the daily ferry down the Swan River from Barrack Street Jetty, which costs $18 one way.

Looking across the Swan River from the Royal Perth Yacht Club.

ROTTNEST ISLAND

Rottnest Island, a low, sandy island 19 km (12 miles) from Fremantle, provides a range of vacation attractions and is best known for its abundant wildlife. Rottnest is reasonably large at 11 km long and five kilometers wide (seven by three miles), making an overnight stay worthwhile to fully appreciate all it has to offer.

Background
In the seventeenth century, Dutch explorer Willem de Vlamingh landed on a small island off the west coast of Australia. Believing it to be infested with

What to See and Do
There are no private cars on Rottnest Island, so your choices for traveling around are by foot, bike or minibus. A great way to see the island is on a bicycle, **Rottnest Bike Hire (** (08) 9372 9722 is behind the Rottnest Hotel (also known as the Quokka Arms). Most of the terrain is flat but there are some low hills to ensure that you keep trim. You are pretty much guaranteed to come across friendly **quokkas** after a few kilometers on the road, particularly around Lake Baghdad and Herschel Lake. Peacocks and pheasants were introduced in the nineteenth century, and also inhabit these areas. The series of lakes attract a huge variety of birds and reflect a mosaic of colors at sunset.

rats, he named it *Rottenest* ("rats nest") Island. The island is home to perhaps the least known but most endearing of Australia's marsupials — the quaintly named quokka. Quokkas, a species of short-tailed wallaby, once roamed the southwest tip of Australia, but are now mainly confined to Rottnest and Bald Islands.

As fighting between the white settlers and the state's Aboriginal population increased, in 1838 a prison settlement was established on Rottnest to hold Aboriginal offenders, often under inhumane conditions. The prison was finally closed in 1903.

General Information
The **visitor center (** (08) 9372 9752 is located opposite the ferry terminal in Thomson Bay. From September to the end of April, two-hour coach tours of the island leave from here at 11:15 AM and at 2:15 PM daily.

A three-kilometer (1.8-mile) railway line connects Thomson Bay and **Oliver Hill**, where visitors can tour the old gun emplacements and tunnels. There are good views from here, and from nearby Lookout Hill. The rest of Rottnest Island offers a variety of activities from fishing along its coastline to swimming, scuba diving among shipwrecks, and surfing. **Dive, Ski and Surf (** (08) 9292 5167, in Thomson Bay, rents boards, snorkels and boats and fishing tackle. A glass-bottomed boat, the **Underwater Explorer**, leaves Thomson Bay Jetty every hour for a 45-minute tour that includes shipwrecks, reefs and rainbow-colored fish.

Where to Stay and Eat
The prison, known as the Quad, is an octagonal limestone building now questionably transformed into the **Rottnest Lodge Resort (** (08) 9292 5161, with its cells converted into moderately priced

tourist lodging. In the center of the Quad stood the gallows, since removed, perhaps in consideration for the sensibilities of guests. The lodge's restaurant, the **Garden Lake**, serves the best food on the island, although it is pricey. Moderately priced accommodation is available at the **Rottnest Hotel (** (08) 9292 5011 FAX (08) 9292 5188, Bedford Avenue, which was built in 1864 as the summer residence of the Governor of Western Australia. The hotel serves reasonable counter meals, including good fish and chips.

The **Rottnest Island Authority (** (08) 9372 9300, located in "E" Shed, Victoria Quay, Fremantle, can help with reserving self-catering houses and units and provides general information. Camping or cabin rental from **Rottnest Camping (** (08) 9372 9737 provides inexpensive alternatives.

How to Get There

Rottnest Island can be reached by daily ferry services from **Barrack Street Jetty (** (08) 9211 5844 in Perth; **Hillary's Marinas (** (08) 9246 1039; or off **Northport Rous Head (** (08) 9430 5844, Fremantle. Taking the ferry from Perth means that you can enjoy a 45-minute trip down the Swan River. The island can also be reached by a 15-minute flight from Perth Airport with **Rottnest Airlines (** (08) 9292 5027. **Kookaburra Air (** (08) 9354 1158 FAX (08) 9354 5898 E–MAIL aka@iinet.net.au has day-trips to Rottnest from Perth as well as fly there/sail back deals from $120, children from $65.

YANCHEP NATIONAL PARK

Yanchep National Park, 51 km (32 miles) north of Perth, is an area of natural bush incorporating a wildlife sanctuary. There's a large population of kangaroos in the park, and an introduced but thriving population of koalas. In spring the whole park comes to life when it is covered in wildflowers. Cave formations and Waugal monoliths (giant limestone sculptures depicting Aboriginal ancestral beings) are interesting to explore, and there's a safe swimming beach six kilometers (just under four miles) west of the park.

General Information

At the **Yanchep National Park Visitor Center (** (08) 9561 1004, pick up a visitors guide, detailing activities, times and features of the park.

What to See and Do

Yanchep features the **Yonderup** and **Crystal caves**, which are filled with 1,000-year-old stalagmites and stalactites. A colony of koalas lives near the lake of **Loch McNess**, where rowboats are for rent. The one-hour **Yanjidi Walk trail** leads through the heart of the Loch McNess wetland. For a shorter walk, the half-hour **Boomerang Gorge Trail** follows the base of a limestone gorge. **Balga Mia**

Village displays local Aboriginal culture and traditional lifestyle. The new **wildflower gardens** give visitors a chance to wander through a collection of native plants that includes banksias, feather flowers, kangaroo paws and hakeas.

How to Get There

To reach Yanchep, take the Wanneroo Road north from Perth, past Wanneroo, and then follow the Yanchep National Park signs.

THE SOUTHWEST

The spectacular southwest coastline has some of Australia's best surfing beaches, a lot of them so relentless in their pounding they are suitable only for the very experienced. The powerful waves have carved impressive cliffs along this coast, where extensive cave systems, particularly between the towns of Margaret River and Albany, provide an interesting escape from the midday sun. Inland, the area is defined by the towering hardwood forests and downy-looking heathland of Cape Leeuwin Naturaliste Park. The Margaret River area is becoming one of Australia's most successful wine-growing regions, particularly known for vibrant whites.

CAPE LEEUWIN NATURALISTE PARK

Cape Leeuwin Naturaliste Park extends down the east coast between Cape Naturaliste and Cape Leeuwin, the most southwesterly point of Australia. The park contains dramatic coastal scenery, heathland and hardwood forests of karri, marri, jarrah and blackbutt. The tip of Cape Leeuwin has a towering limestone **lighthouse** and the nearby **water wheel** has gone unused for so long it is turning to stone. To get there take the Caves Road north to Dunsborough. Along the way make a stop at Yallingup and tour the **Ngilgi Cave**, which is associated with an Aboriginal legend that describes the battle between a good spirit (Ngilgi) and an evil spirit (Wolgine). An interpretive center details the cave's history, and there are semi-guided tours. For the more adventurous three-hour cave tours explore the inner chambers. To book an adventure tour call **(** (08) 9755 2152 or E–MAIL ngilgi@downsouth.com.au.

MARGARET RIVER

I first went to Margaret River long before it was considered suitable for grapevines, when it still existed solely as a service town for the dairy and timber industry. It was the classic sleepy hollow with some of Australia's best surfing. But the

Sturt's desert pea, Western Australia's state flower, takes its name from the nineteenth-century explorer who died in Australia's central deserts.

enormous success of the wineries has changed all that. The town woke up and, while the rest of Australia was having a recession, Margaret River and its surrounding district boomed. Thankfully the town has retained its country feel.

General Information
The **Margaret River-Augusta Tourist Office** ((08) 9757 2911, corner of Bussel Highway and Tunbridge Road, has a good guide to the wine areas and plenty of information on the region.

What to See and Do
Just out of town, Yallingup is a Mecca for surfers from around the world and a great place to watch

north of Margaret River, on the Bussel Highway. Here you can taste the region's wines, decide which you prefer, and plot out a wine trail for yourself with the help of experienced staff.

One of the better known wineries is **Leeuwin Estate** ((08) 9757 6253 E-MAIL winery@leeuwinestate .com.au, Stevens Road, which produces one of the most exceptional and characteristic Chardonnays in Australia. It has won many international awards and much critical acclaim. The excellent restaurant (expensive) on the property makes the perfect spot to dine at the end of a hard day touring the vineyards. **Vasse Felix** ((08) 9755 5242 E-MAIL info@vassefelix.com.au, corner Caves Road and Harmans Road, South Willyabrup, produces a

them in action. If this inspires you it may be wise to take a few lessons with **Josh Palmateer's Surf Acadamy** ((08) 9757 1850, in Margaret River. Josh is a world touring veteran and can usually get you standing (more or less) in two hours. If you think you've mastered the sport grab a copy of *Down South Surfing Guide* from the tourist office for a complete list of the many breaks in the region.

Margaret River wines have a reputation for distinguished character and quality, and have been awarded numerous Australian and international awards. The association of favorable climatic conditions, excellent soil, and talented, passionate winemakers consistently results in superb varietals and blends, producing intense Chardonnays, rich Semillons, robust Cabernets and soft Merlots.

A good place to start is at the **Margaret River Regional Wine Centre** ((08) 9755 5501, 9 Bussel Highway, Cowaramup, about 12 km (seven miles)

powerful Cabernet Sauvignon typical of the region, although it has a subtlety others can't quite match. The restaurant here is also very good (moderate), particularly at lunch for the panoramic vineyard views. One of my long time favorites is the superb **Cape Mentelle** ((08) 9757 3266 E-MAIL info@capementelle.com.au, off Wallcliffe Road. The Chardonnay and Semillon Sauvignon Blanc are among Australia's best, the potent Shiraz always first class, and the berry and spice Zinfandel stands alone in Australia.

Where to Stay
Cape Lodge ((08) 9755 6311, on the Margaret River, is set on six hectares (13 acres), a quarter of it under vine, and overlooks an attractive small lake. **Basildene Manor** ((08) 9757 3140 E-MAIL stay @basildene.com.au, Wallcliffe Road, a National Trust listed building, is Old World and stylish, with

jarrah timber staircases and balustrades and a majestic main hall to relax in. They have some rooms just within the moderate range but most are expensive. Also on Wallcliffe Road, the **Emerald Colonial Lodge** ((08) 9757 2633 TOLL-FREE (1800) 622 336 E-MAIL mr@emeraldhotel.com.au has moderately priced, large rooms (some with Jacuzzi; expensive), a swimming pool, all modern hotel facilities and a good restaurant. **Margaret River B&B** ((08) 9757 2118, 28 Fearn Avenue, has comfortable inexpensive rooms in the heart of town. Rooms with en-suite creep into moderate prices. Inexpensive accommodation on the beach is available at the **Surf Point Lodge** ((08) 9757 1777 E-MAIL office@surfpoint.com.au, Riedle Drive, Gnarabup Beach. Dorms start at $21, doubles $52 and a deluxe double with en-suite at $68. The lodge is clean and spacious with many facilities and a free courtesy bus to and from Margaret River.

How to Get there
Margaret River is 290 km (180 miles) south of Perth on National Route 1.

Westrail (132 232 has daily **buses** from Perth to Margaret River via Busselton and Yallingup, and then on to Augusta.

AROUND MARGARET RIVER

Only five kilometers (three miles) south of the town of Margaret River, **Eagles Heritage** ((08) 9757 2960 rehabilitates injured birds of prey (raptors) for release back to the wild. Those not healthy enough to return are kept for educational displays and breeding purposes.

The Capes region boasts about 350 caves of all shapes and sizes, some as old as 500,000 years. Several are open to visitors. About fifteen minutes by car south of Margaret River, **Mammoth Caves** are suitable for all — they even have easy wheelchair access. Nearby **Lake Cave**, with extensive formations reflected in the underground lake, is also easily accessible. The 25,000-year-old remains of a Tasmanian tiger were found in **Jewel Cave**, where massive karri tree roots extend a staggering 42 m (138 ft) underground.

Augusta, only 29 km (18 miles) south of Margaret River, sits on the slopes of Hardy Inlet overlooking the mouth of the Blackwood River and broad ocean beaches on the other side. It is one of the oldest settlements in Western Australia and popular with vacationers for its fishing, swimming and boating.

GREAT SOUTHERN REGION

Rimmed by unspoiled, rugged coastline, the Great Southern Region of Western Australia saw the first brig of British convicts and settlers, the *Amity*, in 1826 at Albany. The temperate climate and a history

that combines an ancient Aboriginal culture, convicts, whaling and sailing ships make the area an interesting side-trip from Perth.

In Western Australia everything appears larger than life, and nowhere is this more obvious than in its southern forests, where the trees dwarf every other specimen in the country. The karri is the tallest tree in Australia and the third tallest in the world. These massive trees measure up to 75 m (200 ft) in height, weigh about 200 tons fully grown and are only found in the southwest corner of Western Australia. They have long slender trunks, whitish gray in color, and take up to 200 years to reach full size. There is no better way to see the tall timber forests than by tram. A rail line built in the Depression now operates as a tourist tram between Pemberton and Northcliffe, offering a lovely trip among the towering karri and the shorter but still impressive jarrah and marri trees. The tram travels through the heart of karri country, traversing streams on wooden trestle bridges, passing ancient forests and winding its way through pretty countryside along its 36-km (22-mile) route. The best time to see the forest is in early summer, when it becomes a colorful blaze of wildflowers.

GENERAL INFORMATION

The impressive **Albany Tourist Bureau** ((08) 9481 1088 WEB SITE http://worf.albanyis.com.au, Proudlove Parade, is located in the old train station, and is a monument in itself. The helpful staff can supply a good walking tour brochure of the town and information on the region's natural wonders. The **Esperance Tourist Bureau** ((08) 9071 2330, Dempster Street in the municipal museum, (worth a look in), is open daily from 9 AM to 5 PM.

WHAT TO SEE AND DO

Pemberton
Karri trees are impressive when viewed from the ground, but the view is spectacular from near the top. Three kilometers (two miles) from Pemberton, visitors can climb a spiral ladder, made out of wooden karri pegs and steel spikes, 61 m (180 ft) up a fire lookout tree called the **Gloucester Tree**. If that's still not quite high enough for you, then climb the slightly higher 68-m (200-ft) **Bicentennial Tree** located in the Warren National Park, 17 km (10 miles) north of Pemberton.

Karri trees only flower once every three years, and the honey produced from their nectar is delicious. Jars can be bought from the **Lavender and Berry Farm** (/FAX (08) 9776 1661, on Browns Road, two kilometers (one mile) north of Pemberton. They

A pony grazes contentedly among the vines near Margaret River.

have a cozy café and cottage accommodation. In Jamieson Street, Pemberton, you will find the studio of world-renowned wood craftsman **Peter Kovacsy** (/FAX (08) 9776 1265. He uses local timber to make beautiful handcrafted furniture and turned-wood products.

Albany

West Australia's oldest town, Albany's streets are lined with some fine examples of colonial architecture. Stirling Terrace at the base of the main street has some wonderful Victorian shop fronts and most of the best preserved buildings. The **Albany Residency Museum**, built in the 1850s, originally home to the resident magistrates, has historical and environmental exhibits. Next to the museum is a full scale replica of the *Amity* — the brig that brought Major Lockyer and a party of convicts to establish the settlement in 1826. The **Old Gaol** built in 1851 is now a folk museum; entry includes a visit to the **Patrick Taylor Cottage**, Western Australia's oldest dwelling. Built in 1870, Albany's restored Post Office is now the **Inter-Colonial Museum**. The intercontinental telegraph started here in 1875 and the museum displays a collection of communications equipment from this era. The **Courthouse**, begun in 1896, has two impressive arched doorways that are quite unique in their design and perfect symmetry. The historic **Old Farm** at Strawberry Hill on Middleton Road, established in 1836, is set in the oldest garden in the state. The house and garden are open daily from 10 AM to 5 PM; closed in June. The tearooms here serve light lunches and good cakes.

Dog Rock, an outcrop resembling a dog's head, is the most photographed of the natural wonders in the Albany area. The **Gap** is a 24-m-deep (79-ft) chasm in the rock face of the southern coastline in Torndirrup National Park. Waves rush into the Gap and explode upwards in an exhilarating display, viewed from the safety of a fenced platform. Also in the park is the **Natural Bridge** of giant granite, carved by the powerful seas.

Ellen Cove, located next to Middleton Beach, has some of the best views of **King George Sound**. A boardwalk winds its way around the city from **Emu Point** along the coast as far as **Frenchman Bay**. Numerous vantage points look onto some of the best scenery in the region and are especially popular during whale-watching season. **Mount Clarence**, which is a hefty walk from town or a quick drive up Apex Drive, has the best panoramic views of the town. **Whale-watching cruises** operate daily from the town jetty from July to mid-October. Contact the visitors' center for details. **Whaleworld Museum** ((08) 9844 4021, at Cheynes Beach Whaling Station, 25 km (16 miles) southeast of Albany, has videos, exhibits and hourly tours of Australia's last whale station. Open daily 9 AM to 5 PM; adults $9, children $7.

In spring the **Stirling Range National Park**, 90 km (56 miles) north of Albany, comes alive with a richly colored carpet of wildflowers. Walking tracks provide easy access to the park's wildlife and 4,000 plant species. **Bluff Knol** (1,073 m or 3,520 ft) rises abruptly from the surrounding agricultural ground and dominates the park; it is popular with climbers. Alternately, the western access via Tourist Drive No. 253 from Cranbrook leads along the Salt River Road to Red Gum Springs Road and into the heart of the national park. Picnic areas with barbecue facilities are located throughout the park.

Denmark

Only 55 km (34 miles) west of Albany, Denmark was originally a timber milling town and in the surrounding area forests of towering karri trees sweep down to meet the southern ocean. **Anvil Beach** and **Parry's Beach** are best for swimming and are also good surf fishing spots. For the best surf go to **Ocean Beach**. **Shadforth Scenic Drive** is a pretty drive west to **William Bay National Park** and the lovely **Greens Pool**, **Madfish Bay** and **Waterfall Bay**. William Bay National Park has impressive dunes, karri forests, and beaches strewn with mini-Ulurus — monstrous granite boulders that seem to have fallen from the sky. The **tourist office** ((08) 9848 2055 on Strickland Street in Denmark has brochures listing heritage walks and safe swimming beaches in the area.

Esperance

The Esperance region offers a comparatively temperate climate (for Western Australia) and sugar-white sand bordered by brilliant blue-water bays. The area spectacular coastal scenery, hundreds of islands and extensive national parks are home to an abundance of wildlife including seals, dolphins, whales, emus and sea eagles. It is also one of the few places I have seen kangaroos sunbathing on the beach.

The **Municipal Museum** displays pieces of **Skylab**, the space station that fell to earth over Esperance in 1977, alongside its collection of antique machinery, furniture and farm equipment.

Perfect for diving and snorkeling, crystal-clear waters surround **Recherche Archipelago**, which consists of some 200 coastal islands. Take the Bay of Isles Wildlife Cruise with **McKenzie Cruises** ((08) 9071 5757 and get close to the region's wildlife as you make your way across to the **Woody Island Wildlife Sanctuary**, where there is simple but comfortable accommodation, a visitor's center and kiosk and excellent walking trails. Sea lions, fur seals, dolphins and sea eagles are generally sighted on these cruises. Cruise bookings can also be made at the tourist bureau.

Along the 38-km (24-mile) circular loop of the **Great Ocean Drive** are some idyllic sheltered beaches safe for swimming. Try **Twilight Beach**. Almost 100% pure table salt is "harvested" from solar ponds on the eastern end of **Pink Lake**. The color is attributed to high concentrations of a salt-tolerant algae and sometimes even turns purple, depending on weather conditions. Huge salt stock-piles can be seen from Pink Lake lookout. Other lookouts on the drive include the **Rotary Lookout** on Doust Street — with great views of the town and the archipelago — and **Observatory Point**. A pleasant walking and cycling trail runs from the Rotary lookout to **Salmon Beach**.

WHERE TO STAY AND EAT

Flinders Park Lodge ((08) 9844 7062 E-MAIL doug @parklodge.com.au, corner of Lower King and Harbour roads, Albany, has eight moderately priced guest rooms with fine views, an Old World style, and rates include breakfast. The **New London Hotel (** (08) 9841 1040 E-MAIL london@omninet .net.au, 160 Stirling Terrace, Albany, was actually built last century and has great facilities for the low price. Rooms start from $18 per person and the restaurant is a good place to fill up cheaply.

In Esperance, the **Bay of Isles Motel (** (08) 9071 3999 E-MAIL bluegum@emerge.net.au, at 32 The Esplanade, has moderately priced, air-conditioned rooms, a swimming pool, Jacuzzi and a restaurant catering for vegetarians. The **Esperance Seaside Apartments (** (08) 9072 0044 E-MAIL ianhay @comswest.net.au, 15 The Esplanade, has moderate to expensive luxury apartments, each having balconies with panoramic views. Nearby, the **Crokers Park Holiday Resort (** (08) 9071 4100 E-MAIL crokerspark@bigpond.com.au, 817 Harbour Road, Esperence, has inexpensive to moderately priced cabins and inexpensive powered camp sites.

HOW TO GET THERE

The quickest route by road from Perth is the Albany Highway (Route 30), a 400-km (249-mile) inland route.

THE GOLDEN MILE

Gold found at Coolgardie in 1892 triggered the Western Australian gold rush. Eleven months later, nearly 100 ounces of gold were found at Mount Charlotte near the Kalgoorlie-Boulder by Paddy Hannan, Tom Flanagan and Daniel Shea. Their discovery set off a rush that was to uncover the richest square mile in the world, hence the area's sobriquet, the Golden Mile.

Like most of Western Australia, the Golden mile is hot and arid. Many early miners and their families died of thirst and from the heat and the often unsanitary conditions. Fresh water had to be trucked in to the gold fields until a pipeline was

opened in 1903, supplying water from a dam at Mundaring, 565 km (350 miles) away, pumping 27,300 cubic meters (35,800 cubic yards) across every day. This is still the longest water pipeline in Australia. It did not, however, fully quench the diggers' thirsts — that was left to Kalgoorlie's 93 pubs and eight breweries, for 30,000 thirsty miners. Coolgardie too once boasted 23 hotels and three breweries.

To date, a staggering 1,800 tons of gold have been extracted from the Golden mile, but the days of people picking up gold nuggets off the ground are long gone. There are still small-time prospectors in Kalgoorlie, though, combing the ground with metal detectors and hoping to find another

rich lode. In fact, rising gold prices worldwide has recently seen increased interest in the area. These men, who spend a lot of time in the bush, can be found in town propping up the bar ready to tell a tall tale.

The area is impossibly hot in summer. The best time to visit is in spring, when wildflowers from here to the coast are among the state's most spectacular, particularly the everlasting daisies. It's still warm enough to appreciate the nearby beaches at Esperance too — nearby in local terms anyway: Esperance is 400 km (248 miles) south of Kalgoorlie.

GENERAL INFORMATION

The **Kalgoorlie-Boulder Tourist Centre (** (08) 9021 1966, 250 Hannan Street, Kalgoorlie, and the **Coolgardie Tourist Information Centre (** (08) 9026

A statue pays tribute to Kalgoorlie's lost miners.

6090 FAX (08) 9026 6008, 62 Bayley Street, Coolgardie, are both open daily. Kambalda's **Tourist Bureau (** (08) 9027 1446, in Irish Mulga Drive, Kambalda, opens weekdays from 9 AM to 5 PM.

WHAT TO SEE AND DO

Coolgardie

At its peak, there were about 15,000 people, 23 pubs and six banks in Coolgardie. Recently the population dropped to fewer than 200, making it almost a ghost town, although now it has reached 2,000 with recent renewed interest and tourism. The **Goldfields Exhibition (** (08) 9026 6090, 62 Bayley Street, in the original Warden Courts building, tells of the rise and fall of Coolgardie. A 35-minute video "Gold Fever" complements the exhibition, which is open daily from 9 AM to 5 PM; an admission fee is charged.

The magnificent three-story **Warden's Court** in Bayley Street now houses Coolgardie's museum, where detailed dioramas give an idea of life in Coolgardie during its heyday. An old tree on Hunt Street with chains attached to it is a comment on the speed with which this wild town started. Before the gaol was built prisoners were simply chained to this **Gaol Tree** to await trial. The chains are replicas. The **Old Coolgardie Railway Station** in Woodward Street (1896) has been restored to its former grandeur, complete with an old steam train and antique carriages. An exhibition inside the station details the famous "Varischetti rescue." In a drama that captured world attention in 1907, a sudden downpour trapped miner Modesta Varischetti underground for nine days. Rescuers battled to bail the water out of the mine's maze of tunnels, while divers desperately attempted to get to the miner.

Walking around the town and the surrounding area, 150 historical markers, illustrated with photographs from the period, help visitors identify the main landmarks and appreciate Coolgardie's history. Traces of workings can still be seen. Much of the early transportation was provided by camels, and these contrary beasts are available for one-hour rides or for the more hardy, two-day safaris from the **Camel Farm (** (08) 9026 6159, three kilometers (two miles) west of Coolgardie on the Great Eastern Highway. Reservations are essential for treks more than a day long.

Kalgoorlie–Boulder

One of Kalgoorlie's most famous migrant workers was Herbert Hoover, who spent years working here as a mining engineer in 1898 before going on to become the thirty-first President of the United States. He found the place too rough for his taste, describing Kalgoorlie as being only "three yards inside civilization." The description still stands.

The thoroughfares of the twin towns of Kalgoorlie and Boulder still have that rough-and-ready feel they had 100 years ago. Kalgoorlie is still very much a man's town, and often a woman's nightmare. The pubs are filled with hard-drinking men, fights are not uncommon, and entertainment runs between satellite television and topless barmaids. The best-known street in Kalgoorlie is **Hay Street**, where prostitutes stand outside tin shacks waiting for customers. The police politely turn a blind eye to this illegal trade. Serious drinking goes on behind the Edwardian façade of the **Palace Hotel**, with wooden verandahs and wrought-iron balconies. Its **Shaft Bar** nightclub continues until dawn. The **Golden Mile Museum**, incorporating the tiny former British Arms Hotel, has a good display on the heady gold-rush years.

Seven kilometers (four miles) north of Kalgoorlie on Menzies Road is a **Two Up School**, where visitors can play this traditional game of chance. Danny Sheehan tosses pennies in the air in a bush tin shed and punters stand in a circle betting on the fall of the two coins. Two up has been played in Australia for over 100 years, despite being illegal — that is except in Kalgoorlie, where you can enjoy the game from about 4 PM to 7 PM any day of the year without fear of a run in with the law.

Hannans North Tourist Gold Mine ((08) 9091 4074, on the Eastern Bypass Road, five kilometers (three miles) north of Kalgoorlie, has various displays and demonstrations that tell the story of gold mining and extraction. Visitors can go underground to see mining work in progress, or take a short bus tour to the "Super Open Pit." Hour-long railcar tours on the **Golden Mile Loopline (** (08) 9093 3055, Boulder City Station, depart Monday to Saturday at 10 AM.

Kambalda

There was a short-lived gold rush in Kambalda in 1906, after which the town rested peacefully until nickel was discovered in 1966. The town is on Lake Leroy, a salt pan popular for land-yachting. The surrounding countryside can best be viewed from **Red Hill Lookout** on Gordon Adams Road.

WHERE TO STAY AND EAT

Kalgoorlie–Boulder is the best place to base yourself for a tour of the gold fields. During the spring wildflower season it's best to book ahead. **Mercure Hotel Plaza Kalgoorlie (** (08) 9021 4544 TOLL-FREE (1800) 090 600 FAX (08) 9091 2195, 45 Egan Street, and **Sandalwood Motor Inn (** (08) 9021 4455 TOLL-FREE (1800) 095 530 FAX (08) 9021 3744, Hannan Street, provide comfortable, moderately priced accommodation.

There are moderately priced motels in town, but for a bit more character and class try the

Exchange Hotel ((08) 9021 2833, 135 Hannan Street, or the Palace Hotel ((08) 9021 2788 FAX (08) 9021 1813, on the corner of Hannan and Maritana streets. Both are inexpensive and serve good counter meals. Kambalda Motor Hotel ((08) 9027 1333, Blue Bush Road, is moderately priced, as is the Coolgardie Motor Inn Motel ((08) 9026 6002 FAX (08) 9026 6310, on the Great Eastern Highway. For inexpensive accommodation try the Railway Lodge ((08) 9026 6166, 75 Baley Street, Coolgardie. All three towns have caravan parks with vans that can be rented cheaply. For more detailed information contact the Kalgoorlie-Goldfields Accommodation Information Service ((08) 9091 1482 FAX 9091 1484.

twice-weekly coach service from Perth. Westrail (132 232 operates a regular coach service between Kalgoorlie and Esperance three days a week and has services between Esperance and Perth.

THE WEST COAST

Heading north along the North West Coastal Highway by car is a challenge. Although the coastline is spectacular in parts, with untouched beaches and turquoise waters, distances are enormous — 2,318 km (1,440 miles) separate Perth and Broome via the North West Coastal Highway. Few towns interrupt the long stretches of straight road running through endless arid plains and often desert.

Hannan Street has a range of inexpensive to moderate eating places, and most of the town's pubs serve enormous steaks with chips.

HOW TO GET THERE

Qantas flies to Kalgoorlie–Boulder from Perth and Adelaide, connecting with flights from other states. Ansett flies direct from Perth.

The *Prospector* train leaves from the East Perth Terminal ((08) 9326 2222 daily. Great Southern Railways ((08) 8213 4444 FAX (08) 8213 4480 run the *Indian–Pacific* between Adelaide and Perth, with a twice-weekly stop in Kalgoorlie.

Australian Coaches and Westliner Coaches run a **bus** service from Perth twice a week. The Adelaide–Perth Greyhound Pioneer runs daily through Kalgoorlie, Coolgardie and Kambalda, and the Goldfields Express ((08) 9021 2954 is a

The country become more barren the further north you travel. Fuel stops should be planned carefully, and always carry plenty of water. Much of the road goes through unfenced areas where wildlife and stock roam freely, and driving at night can be dangerous. Driver fatigue is another real danger.

This coast boasts the first European settlement in Australia — following a Dutch shipwreck off the Abrolhos Islands in 1629. The highlights, though, are from the natural world: the Pinnacles Desert near Cervantes, Monkey Mia's friendly dolphins and the ancient stromatolites of Hamelin Pool, and the weighty dugongs and enormous whale sharks at Shark Bay and Ningaloo Reef.

Greyhound Pioneer has coach services from Perth all the way to Darwin, via Geraldton and Broome. If your time is limited, flying is an easier

Limestone pillars in the Pinnacles Desert.

way to visit places like Shark Bay or Ningaloo Marine Park. Broome is far closer to Darwin than to Perth, and it often makes more sense to visit the northern part of Western Australia from there or from Alice.

PINNACLES DESERT

Thousands of limestone pillars, some five meters (16 ft) tall, stand in the surreal landscape of the Pinnacles Desert within **Nambung National Park**, 250 km (160 miles) north of Perth off the Geraldton Highway, 29 km (18 miles) south of Cervantes and two kilometers (one mile) inland from the beach. The structures formed underground 30,000 years ago by rain soaking through dunes made up of lime-rich shells, dissolving some of the lime, which later hardened into the cement-like pinnacles. Over thousands of years, strong winds removed the surrounding sand, uncovering the formations. Nambung National Park stretches for 26 km (16 miles) along the coast. Dutch sailors saw these limestone outcrops from the sea and thought they were the remains of an ancient city.

The dirt road from Cervantes may be washed out after heavy rains, check with the **Cervantes Tourist Information Centre (** (08) 6952 7041 before driving it in a conventional vehicle. **Kookaburra Air (** (08) 9354 1158 FAX (08) 9354 5898 E–MAIL aka@iinet .net.au offers scenic flights over the Pinnacles from Perth, including a two-hour driving tour among them, for around $200 per person. For $100 more they'll add an afternoon on Rottnest Island.

Cervantes Pinnacles Motel ((08) 9652 7145, 227 Aragon Street, has inexpensive and comfortable rooms.

GERALDTON

Geraldton, 420 km (261 miles) north of Perth, is the largest town on the west coast (population 25,000). A lot of ships have been wrecked on the reefs off the coast along here, particularly those of the Dutch East Indies company en route to Indonesia in the seventeenth and eighteenth centuries — the wreck of the *Batavia* in 1629 resulted in the first (recorded) European settlement in Australia. The ship was carrying 316 people to Batavia (now Jakarta) when it went down. Most passengers survived and set up camp on a nearby island. Captain Francisco Pelsaert and 47 of the survivors rowed the ship's boat to Batavia, returning six months later to rescue the other stranded survivors. In the mean time, however, a Lord of the Flies-like situation had developed, and a group of mutineers had murdered 125 of their fellow survivors. Captain Pelsaert executed the ringleaders and punished others by cutting off their hands. Two mutineers were marooned on the mainland at Bluff Point, south of Kalbarri,

becoming the first European inhabitants of the mainland, although how long they survived is anyone's guess. A full-size replica of the 24-gun *Batavia*, built by 55 shipwrights and craftsmen in the Dutch seaport of Lelystad using seventeenth-century techniques and materials, served as the flagship of the Dutch presence in the 2000 Sydney Olympics.

The **Geraldton-Greenough Tourist Bureau (** (08) 9921 3999 is opposite the train station in Geraldton, within the Bill Sewell Complex on Chapman Road.

What to See and Do

Housed in the Old Railway Building the **Geraldton Museum (** (08) 9921 5080, 244 Marine Terrace, has exhibits ranging from local Aboriginal history and culture to European exploration and settlement. Upstairs is a quirky flora and fauna museum featuring stuffed animals and piped-in animal and bird sounds. Next door, the fascinating **Geraldton Maritime Museum (** (08) 9431 8444 has relics from ship parts and cannons to navigational aids and maps from wrecks including the *Batavia*, the *Zuytdorp*, which went down near Kalbarri in 1712, and the *Zeewijk*, which struck a reef south of the Abrolhos Islands in 1727. Both are open daily, admission free (donations welcomed).

Three blocks back from the foreshore, **Saint Francis Xavier Cathedral** on Cathedral Avenue is one of the most unusual in Australia. It was designed and built by eccentric architect-priest Monsignor John Hawes, who constructed a large number of churches and church buildings in the Central West. The cathedral took 23 years to build and was completed in 1938. Its process was hampered by disagreement on the eclectic design, which incorporates a French Renaissance main doorway, Romanesque columns, an Italianate central cupola and a surprising orange-and-gray striped interior, reminiscent of Eastern Orthodox churches. The twin towers are similar to those on Santa Barbara's Californian Mission Church.

Author Randolph Stow was born in Geraldton in 1935. Stow has written extensively about the area, particularly in his semi-autobiographical *The Merry-go-round in the Sea.*

More than 100 islands make up the **Houtman Abrolhos Islands**, 60 km (37 miles) off the coast of Geraldton, a protected area administered by the Western Australian Department of Conservation and Land Management. Although the thriving rock lobster industry supports small communities on the islands, visitors are prohibited from staying overnight. The islands harbor a variety of bird life — this and the surrounding spectacular coral reefs (and shipwrecks) attract keen birdwatchers and divers. Tours can be organized through the tourist bureau in Geraldton, or the Western Australian Tourist Centre in Perth.

A ghost town until the National Trust took over in the 1980s, **Greenough**, 24 km (15 miles) south of Geraldton, had a population of over 1,000 primarily wheat farmers in the mid-nineteenth century. A series of natural disasters — floods, draught, crop diseases and a severe hurricane in 1872 — lead to the town's near-desertion by 1900. Many buildings have been remarkably well-preserved. The National Trust administers the **Greenough Hamlet** ((08) 9926 1140: eleven buildings in the center of town including churches, the goal, police station and courthouse and a small school. Open from 9:00 AM to 5 PM daily, with tours leaving the National Trust Office regularly. The Greenough Heritage Trail identifies 25 sites of interest outside the Hamlet, including the Wesley Church, Clinch's Mill, convict-built Gray's Store and the Pioneer Cemetery. The restored 1863 Hampton Arms Inn now houses a fairly good restaurant.

The entire west coast experiences powerful winds, evidenced around Greenough by river red gums bent almost parallel to the ground.

Where to Stay and Eat

The **African Reef Resort Motel/Hotel** ((08) 9964 5566, 5 Broadhead Avenue, has large air-conditioned rooms at inexpensive to moderate prices. The **Mercure Wintersun Hotel** ((08) 9923 1211 TOLL-FREE (1800) 642 244 FAX (08) 9923 1411, 41 Chapman Road, and the **Batavia Motor Inn** ((08) 9921 3500 FAX (08) 9964 1061, 54 Fitzgerald Street, are similarly priced.

Boatshed Seafood Restaurant ((08) 9921 5500, 357 Marine Terrace, has excellent seafood with views of the foreshore. **Lemon Grass Restaurant** ((08) 9964 1172, 18 Snowdon Street, serves good-value, inexpensive Thai food. The friendly **Beach Break Bar and Grill** ((08) 9964 3382, 166 Chapman Road, is the best place for a relaxed early evening drink on the foreshore.

How to Get There

Skywest (131 300 has daily flights to Geraldton from Perth and Broome. In addition to the Greyhound Pioneer service, **Westrail** (132 232 has coach services to Geraldton.

SHARK BAY

Shark Bay was named by William Dampier on his second voyage to Australia in 1699. The area is the biggest draw on the coast, and the subject of great controversy. The dolphins at Monkey Mia are at the root of it all, as many people feel their contact with humans may be detrimental to the dolphins' natural development. The dolphins are not the only attraction around the bay, which is now a listed World Heritage Area and is being developed as a marine park in an attempt to lessen the impact of visitors on the dolphins and the natural

environment in general. The beautiful stromatolites at Hamelin Pool are some of the most accessible in the world, and Shark Bay has the most secure colony of dugongs left on earth. Steep Point near the town of Useless Loop is mainland Australia's most westerly point.

General Information

Information about tours to Monkey Mia or Dirk Hartog Island can be obtained from the **Shark Bay Tourist Centre** ((08) 9948 1253 in Denham. They also organize scenic flights and boat trips to view dolphins and dugongs.

What to See and Do

Denham, on the Péron Peninsula, is the base for visits to **Monkey Mia** and the Shark Bay World Heritage Area and Marine Park. Monkey Mia (pronounced Myah) is another 26 km (16 miles) northeast, on the other side of the peninsula.

Dolphins have been regularly coming up to the shallows of the beautiful stretch of white-sand beach at Monkey Mia since the wife of a local fisherman began feeding them in the early 1960s. Today small groups of dolphins, all well-known and identified by their distinctive dorsal fin markings, come in a few times on most days, generally between 7 AM and noon, although their movements are by no means regular, particularly during the November mating season. The dolphins are exceptionally friendly, playing and nudging waders, and flipping themselves into the air. A separate section of the beach is set aside for visitors to swim with the dolphins and observe their antics and family interactions. The area is also a base for dolphin researchers, who investigate different aspects of dolphin ecology, reproduction and behavior, ranging patterns, community structure, habitat and diet.

Environmental problems in the area have been exacerbated in recent years by the number of visitors, which can reach 1,000 a day, and continuing efforts are being made to control problems of pollution and other environmental damage. There is a dolphin information center at the beach, where rangers are available to assist tourists. Rangers also patrol the beach and hand out information on how to behave with the dolphins. Very strict controls apply to the feeding of dolphins within the Monkey Mia area: it is illegal to feed them unless under ranger supervision. The local AM radio station, 666-6LN, broadcasts a "dolphin report" every day between 7:45 AM and 8:15 AM.

Faure Sill separates Shark Bay from the landlocked marine basin of **Hamelin Pool**, where single-cell cyanbacteria (blue-green algae) is protected from its normal fish predators. The bacteria has produced enormous calcareous stromatolites on the water's edge, domed formations growing at a rate of one millimeter per year, which date back to the Precambrian era, 3.5 billion years ago.

Over 10,000 enormous **dugongs** live around Eagle Bluff, 20 km (12.5 miles) south of Denham. The dugong is one of two surviving sirenians, the other being the manatee found in areas of the Caribbean, the Amazon and West Africa. In summer months dugongs come close to shore to graze on the sea-grass, hence their common name, sea cows. Monkey Mia Dolphin Resort organizes cruises to observe the dugongs, which depart from the Monkey Mia jetty at 1 PM daily. Just south of Eagle Bluff, **Shell Beach** is entirely covered in a thick layer of multi-colored shells.

Where to Stay and Eat

Monkey Mia Dolphin Resort ((08) 9948 1320 FAX (08) 9948 1034 WEB SITE www.monkeymia.com .au/resort, on Monkey Mia Road, provides accommodation from inexpensive on-site caravans and cabins to moderately priced apartments. In Denham, **Mala Villas Chalets** ((08) 9948 1323, in Fry Court, and the **Shark Bay Hotel Motel** ((08) 9948 1203, 43 Knight Terrace, are both moderately priced.

Dirk Hartog Island Homestead ((08) 9948 1211 WEB SITE www.dirkhartogisland.com has doubles for $300, which includes all meals and activities.

How to Get There

Denham is 120 km (74.5 miles) off the coastal highway from the Overlander Roadhouse. **Western Airlines** TOLL-FREE (1800) 998 097 has flights to Kalbarri three times a week, with connections to Monkey Mia's tiny airport. Greyhound Pioneer's Perth–Darwin service stops at the Overlander Roadhouse, from where they have a coach connection to Denham a few days a week. Scenic coastal flights from Perth to Monkey Mia, which spend the morning on the beach with the dolphins and fly off in search of sharks before returning to Perth, are offered by **Kookaburra Air** ((08) 9354 1158 FAX (08) 9354 5898 E-MAIL aka@iinet.net.au. The day-trip costs around $600 per person; they offer two-day tours too.

NINGALOO REEF

The remote Ningaloo Reef, stretching 260 km (160 miles) along the Western Australian coast from Amherst Point to North West Cape near Exmouth, is not nearly as well known as the Great Barrier Reef. This is pristine water and, because of the small number of visitors, Ningaloo has not suffered the destructive development that has occurred along the Great Barrier Reef. The northern 180 km (112 miles) of reef is protected as part of the Ningaloo Marine Park — home to humpback whales, manta rays, whale sharks and dugongs. Green, loggerhead and hawksbill turtles nest on its sandy beaches from November to January.

Coral Bay is on the central region of Ningaloo Reef, just north of the Tropic of Capricorn and about

1,150 km (715 miles) from Perth. The tiny town is a good base for snorkelers or scuba divers wanting to explore the reef. The other option is to stay in Exmouth, at the northern end of the reef, the largest town in the region, with a population of 3,500.

General Information

The **Exmouth Tourist Bureau** ((08) 9949 1176 is in Payne Street, Exmouth, and the **Coral Bay Supermarket** ((08) 9942 5988 handles tourist information and inquiries too. Both can help book reef trips.

What to See and Do

Accessing Ningaloo Reef — the largest coral fringing reef in the world — from the coast is easy. At some points it is only meters from the beach. Common fish on the reef include butterfly fish, angelfish groupers and parrot-fish, but the area supports over 550 species of fish and more than 200 species of coral. The most beautiful time to appreciate Ningaloo Reef is during the **coral spawning** period, which lasts for only a few nights a year, usually beginning about a week after the full moon in March. It is an amazing sight.

Although harmless, **whale sharks** are the largest of the sharks — reaching lengths of up to 18 m (59 ft) and weights of up to 40,000 kg (18,144 lb), although they average around 12 m (39 ft). They're rarely seen in shallow coastal seas, but up to 20 whale sharks come in to Ningaloo Reef daily from March to late June, to feed on plankton in the nutrient-rich waters. Flights and boat trips take visitors to see the whale sharks, and those looking for an ever bigger thrill can join them for a swim. In spring, **manta rays** come into the reef, and snorkelers wanting more speed can grab on for a tow, while from August to October colossal **humpback whales** migrate along the coast. The only way to explore the reef is underwater. Snorkeling and diving gear can be rented from **Coral Coast Dive** ((08) 9949 1004, in Yardie Creek Road, Exmouth. **Exmouth Dive Centre** ((08) 9949 1201, in Payne Street, Exmouth, and their Coral Bay branch, **Ningaloo Reef Dive** ((08) 9942 5824 E-MAIL ningaloo @bigpond.com, organize diving and snorkeling trips and give lessons (leading to PADI certification). In whale-shark season they employ a light aircraft to fly overhead throughout the day to spot each shark and guide the boat to it. They're extremely knowledgeable about whale sharks and other marine inhabitants and provide careful instruction on how to approach and swim with them with caution and respect.

Cape Range National Park extends along the west coast of North West Cape. The national park features rugged limestone ridges, scrub and heathland, with a number of marked walking tracks. The **Milyering Visitor Centre** ((08) 9949 2808 at the park entrance has walking maps and details on local ecology.

Although Exmouth Gulf was used during World War II as a base for Australian and United States' submarines, the town of Exmouth was not born until the Harold E. Holt United States Naval Communication Station was established at North West Cape in the 1960s. The base is now controlled by the Australian Navy (part of it has been converted to backpacker accommodation), but there is still a sizeable United States service personnel. Big game fishing is another drawcard here, although fishing in the marine park is restricted.

Where to Stay and Eat

The **Ningaloo Reef Resort (** (08) 9942 5934, E-MAIL whaleshark@bigpond.com.au, 1 Robinson Road, on the edge of Coral Bay, has moderately priced, air-conditioned units and a large swimming pool. Their bar-restaurant serves well-prepared simple classics. The resort also operate **Coral Bay Backpackers** next door.

In Exmouth, **Ningaloo Lodge (** (08) 9949 4949 TOLL-FREE (1800) 880 949, Lefroy Street, and the **Potshot Hotel Resort (** (08) 9949 1200, Murat Road, both have moderately priced, air-conditioned rooms and swimming pools. **Whaler's Restaurant** on Kennedy Street is a friendly place with hearty meals. Their shady broad veranda adds to the appeal.

How to Get There

Greyhound Pioneer coach service to Exmouth departs Perth Wednesday, Friday and Sunday. There are daily Ansett flights into Exmouth.

Skywest (131 300 has daily flights to Learmonth Airport, 35 km (22 miles) south of Exmouth. A shuttle bus meets each flight servicing Exmouth and Coral Bay, and taxis are also available. **Kookaburra Air (** (08) 9354 1158 FAX (08) 9354 5898 E-MAIL aka@iinet.net.au offer flexible charter flights from Perth; whale-shark spotting flights can be included. Prices start at $600 per person, plus the pilot's food and accommodation costs.

THE KIMBERLEY

The Kimberley, a group of mountains and plateaus in the sparsely populated northwest corner of Australia, is almost as big as Texas. Its population, however, numbers fewer than 30,000, most of whom live in towns such as Broome, Derby and Kununurra. Kimberley Range has a rugged beauty well worth the voyage to this far off part of the continent: Rivers that run rapidly during the wet season have carved deep gorges into the countryside; the coastline is lined with steep cliffs, some 250 m (800 ft) high.

William Dampier visited the Kimberley in 1688 and made unflattering observations about the infertile land he found. The first European expedition into the Kimberley was led by Lieutenant George Grey in 1837. On his first day ashore Grey almost came to grief when he tried to swim Prince Regent River, and while he just failed to lose his life he did succeed in losing his trousers in the attempt.

In the 1890s the Bunuba Aborigines waged a guerrilla war against white settlers under the leadership of Jundumurra, who was known by the whites as Pigeon because he was shorter than other Bunuba men, and fast-footed. Jundumurra started by spearing the invaders' sheep and cattle but was captured and taken in chains to Derby. Jundumurra's reputation among the Bunuba grew after he escaped from custody, and when he killed Constable William Richardson in 1894 and freed Bunuba prisoners he became the indisputable leader of the local resistance around Fitzroy River.

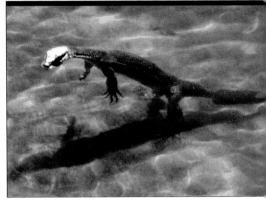

Jundumurra captured a cache of guns and began training his warriors and conducting successful ambushes. Wounded and weakened from hunger, Jundumurra was finally hunted down in 1897 at Tunnel Creek.

Touring the Kimberley it's easy to see how a skilled bushman could evade the whites for such a long time. Few tourists explore off the beaten track, where wildlife is rich and natural land forms give the Kimberley's wide open spaces their majesty.

GENERAL INFORMATION

Broome Tourist Bureau ((08) 9922 2222 is at the corner of Broome Road and Bagot Street. The **Tourist Information Centre (** (08) 9191 1426, 2 Clarendon Street in Derby, is open Monday to Saturday. To plan your trip call **Kimberley Tourism (** (08) 9193 6660 TOLL-FREE (1800) 000 088 for a copy of the helpful *Kimberley Holiday Planner*, or check their WEB SITE www.ebroome.com/Kimberley.

A reliable four-wheel-drive vehicle is needed for many roads in the Kimberley. In fact, the area is so isolated it's not recommended to travel off the main roads without a second vehicle and a working radio (in the wet season, from November

A lizard escapes Western Australia's relentless heat.

to March, much of the area is impassable even with a four-wheel-drive vehicle). A guided four-wheel-drive tour is the safest bet; various operators run trips from Broome, Kununurra or Darwin. Check with the **Royal Automobile Club of Western Australia (** (08) 9421 4444 or **Western Australia Main Roads Department** for up-to-date road conditions before driving into the Kimberley.

The climate is hot year-round, and unbearably so during the humid months that run from November to March.

WHAT TO SEE AND DO

Most travelers to the Kimberley pass through its very southern edge only, missing out on the extraordinary natural beauty and rich Aboriginal heritage of the sandstone ranges and valleys, and the craggy, twisted coastline of its central and northern areas. To explore these areas though requires time and planning, but a number of excellent tours are offered from Broome and Darwin.

Purnululu (Bungle Bungle) National Park contains some of the world's strangest landforms: enormous, striped, hive-shaped sandstone domes. Only in the past 20 years has this area became known to people other than locals. Although there are now basic camping facilities, it remains a true wilderness area. Purnululu is rich in Aboriginal rock art galleries. Wandjina representations of heads with large eyes and "halos" have been interpreted by some as drawings of extraterrestrial beings.

Most sightseers choose to view the Bungle Bungles from the air, in a **scenic flight** from Kununurra. Those who do take the long road journey can still opt for an aerial view with the locally based helicopter. There are thousands of surreal, striped "bee-hives" with narrow passages of small bright green trees between them. From the ground those same bee-hives are strange and formidable mountains, ringed with alternating layers of red and black. The passages between them are gullies with rocks and tall palms. Broome Aviation **(** (08) 9192 1369 has **scenic flights** over the Bungle Bungles on weekdays, or try an overnight **camel safari** with Kimberley Bushwalks **(** (08) 9192 7077 (see BUZZ THE BUNGLE BUNGLES, page 13 in TOP SPOTS).

From Fitzroy Crossing, the 800-km (497-mile) long Gibb River Road is the one real "artery" of the Kimberley. It leads to the rough Kalumburu Road, and the start of the **Mitchell Plateau**. These roads are often inaccessible during the wet season. The flat, grassy plateau leads on to the craggy ranges, caves and waterfalls of the rocky northern area. Just after the wet season, wildflowers color the grassy plains, and grevillea and wattle trees burst into fiery shades. Beautiful pink water-lilies float on lagoons hidden in rocky gullies. Many tours to the area include a day's canyoning along

the Mitchell and King Edward rivers, which involves rock-climbing, rafting and caving between sheer cliffs of dark red rock.

The Kimberley abounds with **animal life**. It has 70 species of native mammals, 39 of them found on the Mitchell Plateau. Many are nocturnal and unique to this area and Arnhem Land. The bats, rare tree rats and rock ringtail possums hide themselves well in daytime, but walkers will often spot rock wallabies, goannas and lizards, and birds such as black grass-wrens and blue-winged kookaburras.

At the northeast edge of the Kimberley, Wyndham is on the Cambridge Gulf and has Australia's most concentrated native crocodile population. Proud of their claim to fame, a model of an 18-m (16-ft) crocodile stands at the town entrance. There's a crocodile lookout in town too.

The Kimberley has the world's largest diamond mine. Argyle diamonds are internationally renowned for their brilliance and color, and tours to the **Argyle Diamond Mine**, a major producer and home of the rare pink diamond, are offered daily (for details contact Kimberley Tourism).

Broome

Broome is something of an oasis between the Indian Ocean, the vast scrub plains of the Great Sandy Desert, and the Kimberley to the north. The start of the "dry tropics" Broome is a frontier town, with outback characters galore and a Wild West atmosphere. Don't be surprised to see heavy-drinking macho-types holding up the bar in the town's pubs ready to entertain a crowd with tales of outback life. **Cable Beach** is pristine, clean, and one of the last opportunities — if you're continuing your travels north — for safe swimming in the sea. Saltwater crocodiles infest coastal waters beyond.

From about 1880 until 1930, Broome was the world's leading exporter of mother-of-pearl shell, used before plastic to make buttons. In its heyday a fleet of 300 pearling boats was headquartered here, and the lucrative pearling industry attracted divers and adventurers from many countries: Aborigines, colonial Brits and Europeans, Malaysians, and Japanese populated the wealthy streets as fortunes were made and lost overnight in the high-stake business of collecting shell. This boom-town developed a face as much Asian as European.

Broome's pearl-lugging history is a focus of the tourism industry. Some 900 headstones mark the graves of Japanese pearl divers in the **Japanese Cemetery**, and part of the Broome Historical Society Museum, the **Pearl Luggers Exhibition (** (08) 9192 1562 includes a guided tour of an authentic pearl lugger. The tour guide, Salty, is a storehouse of old sailor yarns. Sunset cruises

A tropical oasis hidden among the craggy ranges of the Mitchell Plateau.

on the restored *Willie* ((0418) 919 781, a 24-m (80-ft) pearl lugger, are a relaxing way to wind down and enjoy the cool sea breeze. The *Willie* also takes small groups out on afternoon boom-netting cruises. **Pearl Sea Coastal Cruises** ((08) 9193 7375 offers similar cruises. A number of shops along **Dampier Terrace** sell local pearls. The dark blue, almost black harvest pearls are the more highly prized. Broome's multicultural population is a remnant of the pearling days. There are some nice multicultural architectural touches too, with pagoda-topped public phone booths serving Chinatown. While cultured pearl farming remains an important local industry, and divers still dive for shell, these days tourism is the major force in the local economy.

Flaktrak Tours ((02) 9192 1487 organizes four-wheel-drive trips to Cape Leveque that stop at several remote Aboriginal communities. Highlights include the Scared Heart Church with a mother-of-pearl altar in Beagle Bay, completed in 1918 by Palatine monks and the local Lombadina Aborigines, and a swim at the gorgeous beach in Kooljaman. Spring low-tides reveal **dinosaur footprints** thought to be 130 million years old on the rocks at **Gantheaume Point**. Cement casts of the prints are on display at the top of the cliffs.

A number of organizers run fishing trips from Broome, which include ocean trips out to the reef, fishing and mud-crabbing tours up the nearby mangrove creeks. Even if you've never cast a line in your life, you're almost guaranteed to bring in enough to feed a family of eight on one of these trips. **Dampier Creek Boat Cruises** (0408 922 055 runs great sightseeing, fishing and mud-crabbing tours.

For drive-in buffs, trade in your car seats for deck chairs and enjoy true open-air viewing. **Sun Pictures** is reputed to be the oldest operating picture garden in the world, running since 1916. Movies start at 7:55 PM. At **Astrotours** ((08) 9193 5362, idiosyncratic local astronomer Greg Quicke takes visitors out under the extraordinarily clear Kimberley night sky several evenings a week.

Derby

The local authorities in Derby made an unusual use of the area's distinctive baob tree, the trunk of which is shaped like a fat skittle. Seven kilometers (four miles) from town, the Prison Tree is a 1,500-year-old specimen, its circumference 14 m (46 feet) in diameter. The tree's hollow trunk is reputed to have housed 20 lawbreakers in one night. Derby Tourist Information Centre can give directions to the tree. The awe-inspiring rock formations of **Windjana Gorge**, a mere 149 km (92.5 miles) from Derby on the Gibb River Road, provide shelter and water for a prolific bird life and a large population of freshwater crocodiles. Although these crocs are up to two to three meters

(six and a half to ten feet) long, they're timid and considered harmless. I wouldn't tempt them, though. **Tunnel Creek National Park** is 30 km (19 miles) past Windjana Gorge; here visitors can wander through a 750-m (half-mile) cave system.

WHERE TO STAY AND EAT

In Broome, luxury accommodation is provided by the **Cable Beach Resort** ((08) 9192 0400 TOLL-FREE (1800) 095 508 E-MAIL reserve@broome.wt.com.au, Cable Beach Road. The resort's bungalows have latticework and verandahs modeled after old pearl masters' homes. They are scattered in lush gardens and the grounds are intersected by canals. The resort's restaurant serves thick sirloin steaks and native meats like emu, crocodile and kangaroo. There's also the option of taking the evening seafood buffet. The **Blue Seas Resort** ((08) 9192 0999

E-MAIL bluseas@tpg.com.au has very comfortable self-contained apartments, two swimming pools and is moderately priced all year round. For a friendly guesthouse atmosphere try the inexpensive **Broometime Lodge** ((08) 9193 5067 FAX (08) 9192 2429, 59 Forrest Street. It's close to town with easy access to Cable Beach.

The **Derby Boab Inn** ((08) 9191 1044 E-MAIL derbyboabinn@wn.com.au, Loch Street, Derby, has both moderately priced and budget accommodation, or for real outback accommodation try **Mount Elizabeth Station Guest House** (/FAX (08) 9191 4644, an authentic working cattle station 370 km (230 miles) northeast of Derby.

Broome's **Last Resort Youth Hostel** ((08) 9193 5000 WEB SITE www.yha.com.au is one of the best in Western Australia, with an open-air bar and dining room, big balconies and a swimming pool set in a tropical garden.

HOW TO GET THERE

Greyhound Pioneer and McCafferty's both have daily bus services from Perth to Darwin that stop at Broome.

There are Ansett flights daily to Broome from Perth, and Qantas operates daily services from Perth and Darwin. **Qantas Holidays** (131 415 often has good-value packages from Sydney and other major cities including return airfare to Broome and seven days four-wheel-drive rental. Kookaburra Air offers charter flights to Broome, and packages incorporating scenic flights over the Kimberley.

By road, Broome, can be reached from the Great Northern Highway. Broome is 1,870 km (1,162 miles) from Darwin and 2,230 km (1,386 miles) from Perth.

A cool rock proves perfect for a mid-afternoon siesta in the Kimberley.

Northern
Territory

THE NORTHERN TERRITORY IS A PLACE OF GREAT DISTANCES. Away from Darwin and Alice, the doctor comes by plane, children take their classes by short-wave radio, and cattle are rounded up using motorbikes or helicopters. While the state is generally bewilderingly arid, the weather is tropical and can shift violently from drought to flood. There seems to be nothing in between. The landscape of the territory can only be described as bizarre. Over eons nature and geological forces have played havoc with the earth's surface to create flamboyant rock masterpieces in red and ocher. Rivers have sliced deep gorges through sandstone plateaus. Spectacular waterfalls tumble down vertical rock faces. And there is a lot of very flat terrain too… an awful lot!

This is one of the planet's last untamed places, and with its harsh ranges, hazardous wetlands and great central dry plains, it will probably remain as such. The northern portion of the state is watered by monsoons, receiving between 500 and 1,000 mm (20 to 40 inches) of rain between December and April, otherwise water is scarce throughout the territory. But spring-fed rock pools provide welcome relief from the heat, while gorges and wetlands areas contain an enormous diversity of flora and fauna species. The territory's nasties range from huge saltwater (estuarine) crocodiles to death adders and hand-sized bird-eating spiders.

There are few towns in the territory. Of its 173,500 residents, 78,000 live in Darwin and 22,000 in Alice Springs. The Northern Territory has the highest proportion of Aboriginal people of any of Australia's states and territories: 22% of the total population. The Aboriginal Lands Rights Act of 1976 returned large tracts of land to the traditional owners, including Uluru (Ayers Rock) and Kata Tjuta (the Olgas). These and other parks in the territory have a special richness and beauty. The gradual return of lands to their traditional custodians has helped reaffirm Aboriginal cultural practices and ties to their people's "country"— there are desert people and saltwater people, people of the stone country and people of the islands. Each

has its own creation ancestor, language, ceremonies and laws. Many areas encompass Aboriginal sacred sites, in addition to harboring cave paintings and other art works. Aborigines often accompany tours into the bush, teaching about Aboriginal culture and relationship with the land, from traditional bush tucker and medicines to art and craft techniques and local Dreaming creation mythology.

DARWIN

There have been two serious attempts to demolish Darwin. The first was during World War II when the Japanese conducted 64 bombing raids causing a loss of 243 lives. The second came on Christmas Eve of 1974 when a hurricane, Cyclone Tracy, unleashed four hours of destruction, flattening much of Darwin, injuring thousands and leaving 66 dead.

Darwin has recovered from both of these catastrophes, a tribute to the spirit of its inhabitants. Such persistence in the face of repeated disasters is evidence, for many southerners, that its inhabitants must truly be "madmen." But for the people of Darwin, living anywhere else would truly be out of the question. Every setback only reinforces their ties to this bizarre tropical town.

Set on a peninsula, Darwin's lush fertility, tropical nonchalance and suburbs set in a colorful sea of bougainvillea, frangipani and poinsettia provide an exotic backdrop to Australia's most northerly capital city.

The best time to visit the territory is during the dry season, between May and October, when the days are warm, the weather stable and the humidity relatively low. The rest of the year is the wet season, when monsoons bring rain and attendant lightning storms late in the afternoon and overnight, making the days humid.

GENERAL INFORMATION

Darwin Regional Tourism Association ((08) 8981 4300 WEB SITE www.nttc.com.au, 38 Mitchell Street, is open weekdays from 8:30 AM to 6 PM, on Saturdays from 9 AM to 3 PM and on Sundays from 10 AM to 2 PM. **Australia's Northern Territory and Outback Centre** ((02) 9283 7477, 27 Harbour Street, Darling Harbour, Sydney, has experienced and knowledgeable consultants and provides interactive information kiosks.

The **GPO** is on the corner of Cavenagh and Edmund Streets.

Internet access is available at Darwin Global Gossip ((08) 8942 3044, 44 Mitchell Street, open from 8 AM to midnight seven days and Territory Internet Services ((08) 89414600, Shop 24 Paspalis Centrepoint Arcade, Smith Street Mall, open 9 AM to 5:30 PM weekdays and 10 AM to 3 PM Saturday and Sunday.

The MGM Grand Darwin Casino.

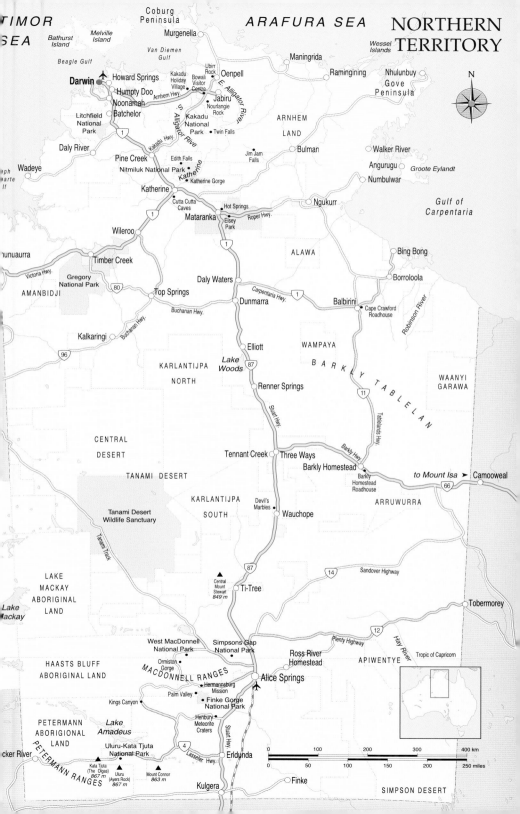

The **Automobile Association of the Northern Territory**, **AANT** ((08) 8981 3837 FAX (08) 8941 2965, MLC Building, 79–81 Smith Street is a good place for touring tips and road maps. For **roadside service** call ((08) 8941 0611 or (131 111.

The **Darwin Private Hospital** ((08) 8920 6011 operates 24-hour medical assistance and is a part of the **Royal Darwin Hospital** ((08) 8922 8888, at Rocklands Drive, Tiwi, which is on the northern side of Darwin.

GETTING AROUND

Darwin is very compact. While most attractions are within easy walking distance, "walking distance" in the Northern Territory is a relative term. Often Darwin's heat and humidity can turn what might seem a relatively short walk into an exhausting and dehydrating ordeal.

Darwin's **public bus service** ((08) 8999 6540 runs every day but Sunday. For information and timetables the city terminus is on Harry Chan Avenue. An **airport shuttle service** ((08) 8981 5066 runs for every flight and costs $6 one way or $10 return. *The* **taxi** number is (131 008.

Renting a car is not expensive in Darwin, and the always inclusive air-conditioning provides a welcome relief. Some of the better companies in town are Budget Rent a Car ((08) 8981 9800, Delta Car Rentals ((08) 8941 0300 and Cheapa Rent a Car ((08) 8981 8400.

WHAT TO SEE AND DO

Much of Darwin has been rebuilt since Cyclone Tracy. Its central business district covers the northwest corner of the peninsula, jutting into Darwin Harbour, where the main shopping area is along Smith Street mall between Bennett and Knuckey streets. A well-paced stroll through town is the best way to get a feel for the place.

The modern **Christchurch Anglican Cathedral** stands at the northeast end of Smith Street. Built after the havoc of Tracy, the design incorporated the original porch, which was all that survived the hurricane. The Chinese community was similarly devastated when its temple was ripped apart by Tracy's 280-km/h (175-mph) winds. A new **Chinese Temple** was erected on the site at 25 Woods Street; it retained the outline of the original structure built in 1887. Open to the public on weekdays from 8 AM to 4 PM and on weekends from 8 AM to 3 PM, admission is free, but tourists are requested to respect the sanctity of this place and the dignity of its worshipers. Next door to the temple, the **Chung Wah Society Museum** provides interesting information on the history and everyday life of Chinese immigrants in Australia.

Most of the historic buildings spared by Cyclone Tracy are to be found towards the harbor end of town. **Government House** is on the Esplanade overlooking the harbor. It is not open to the public. The century-old building has lived through Japanese bombing raids, a succession of cyclones and even an attack of white ants. Nevertheless, with its grand verandahs and gables the whole edifice has a colonial elegance now rare in Darwin.

Since gaining limited statehood in 1994, the territory government has built itself a magnificent $120 million **Parliament Building** to house just 25 members.

At the other end of Esplanade, near the corner of Daly Street, **Doctor's Gully** sees hundreds of fish swim into the shallows at high tide, where they know they'll get a free feed from visitors. **Aquascene** ((08) 8981 7837, 28 Doctor's Gully, lets visitors participate in this spectacle. It's advisable to call ahead to find out feeding times, which change depending on the tides. Admission is $4 for adults and $2.50 for children.

The **Botanical Gardens** off Gilruth Land have a collection of over 400 species of tropical and subtropical plants. An amphitheater serves as the setting for cultural events varying from classical concerts to Aboriginal dance performances. Open daily from 7 AM to 7 PM; entry is free.

The **East Point Reserve**, a long stretch of white-sand beach, offers safe swimming in **Lake Alexander** and great views from the sandstone cliffs, where an old World War II gun turret still stands. At sunset lots of wallabies come out for a hand-feed in the picnic areas.

A superb collection of Aboriginal artifacts and Oceanic art is on show at the **Museum and Art Gallery of the Northern Territory** ((08) 8999 8201, Conacher Street, Fanny Bay, about four kilometers (two and a half miles) out of town. There is also a good collection of modern works by Aboriginal and non-Aboriginal Australian artists in the gallery. Open 9 AM to 5 PM weekdays and 10 AM to 5 PM weekends, entry is free.

Off the Stuart Highway on the Cox Peninsula Road, Berry Springs, the **Territory Wildlife Park** ((08) 8988 7201 shows off the territory's animals in their native habitat. At 10 AM every day, wedge-tailed eagles and other birds of prey soar around park handlers. At 1:30 PM, greedy pelicans go into a feeding frenzy at Wader Lagoon. It generally takes at least three hours to look around this immense reserve. The entrance is open daily from 8:30 AM to 4 PM, gates close at 6 PM. **Darwin Day Tours** ((08) 8981 8696 has a package that includes transport from Darwin hotels and the park entry fee.

The **Darwin Crocodile Farm** ((08) 8988 1450, at Noonamah along the Stuart Highway, 40 km (25 miles) out of Darwin, has more than 10,000 crocs at various stages of growth, from chicks crawling out of eggs to jaw-snapping monsters. The farm is open 10 AM to 4 PM daily, admission costs $9.50 for adults and $5 for children.

To celebrate Australia Day on January 26, a race is held around the entire country: the competitors are cockroaches and the course is a replica of Australia with a race track around the edge. The **Cockroach Race** is held at the **Darwin Sailing Club (** (08) 8981 1700, which also has decent counter meals (no roaches) served on outdoor tables by the beach.

TOURS

The **Blue Banana (** (08) 8945 6800 TOLL-FREE (1800) 245 680 WEB SITE www.octa4.net.au is a jump-on, jump-off backpacker bus service that departs from Darwin four times a week on a circuit of the Top End. Places visited include Kakadu National Park, Nitmiluk National Park and Litchfield National Park. Darwin to Darwin round trips cost $170 and are valid for three months. The service doesn't operate during the wet season.

Coo-ee Tours ((08) 8981 6116 E-MAIL coo-ee @dayworld.net.au are the Litchfield Park specialists, taking in all the major sights at a relaxed pace with informative guides.

Darwin is well geared up for **fishing**, and the Top End is famous for its barramundi (known locally as "barra"). These freshwater fish are cunning and provide anglers with a good fight. While there is reasonable barra fishing near Darwin, anglers willing to travel to find the best take camping safaris into the outback to find the prime spots can be and catch 18-kg (40-lb) barra. The best time of year for barramundi fishing is from March to May. **Obsession Fishing Charters (** (08) 8941 6193 E-MAIL obsessbarra@ozemail.com.au and **Hotspot Fishing Tours** TOLL-FREE (1800) 809 035 E-MAIL ajuliusfm@octa4.net.au know the best spots around Darwin for barra fishing, and organize day-trips as well as extended safaris for serious anglers. Expect to pay about $200 a day for an all-inclusive tour.

WHERE TO STAY

The **MGM Grand Darwin (** (08) 8943 8888, and the **Beaufort Darwin (** (08) 8943 8888 FAX (08) 8943 8999, on the Esplanade, have the best in luxury accommodation; both have ocean views.

The **Poinciana Inn (** (08) 8981 8111 FAX (08) 8941 2440, 84 Mitchell Street, in the center of town has comfortable, clean rooms. The **Mirambeena Tourist Resort (** (08) 8946 0111, 64 Cavenagh Street, has a wonderful landscaped swimming pool. Both are moderately priced.

Darwin is popular with backpackers so there is also a wide selection of inexpensive accommodation in town. In hostels check the rooms first for cleanliness and make sure the air-conditioning is not only working but not so noisy it will keep you awake all night. The **Tiwi Lodge Motel (** (08) 8981 6471 FAX (08) 8981 3285, 53 Cavenagh Street, is clean and reasonably quiet. A little out of town,

the **Banyon View Lodge (** (08) 8981 8644 FAX (08) 8981 6104, 119 Mitchell Street, Larrakeyah, is set in tropical gardens and reflects the informality typical of Darwin: guests mingle around an evening barbecue. The **Air Raid Motel (** (08) 8981 9214, 35 Cavenagh Street, has basic rooms with private baths.

WHERE TO EAT

The best restaurant in town **Crustaceans on the Wharf (** (08) 8981 8658, Stokes Hill Wharf (moderate to expensive), has relaxed open-air dining, serving a variety of perfectly prepared local seafood. The interior is so large that they have a complete Indonesian refugee boat in it and a popular upstairs bar/club. Open 6 PM until late Monday to Saturday and seven days in July and August.

For a menu offering exotica such as buffalo, camel and crocodile, visit the **Magic Wok (** (08) 8981 3332, 48 Cavenagh Street (moderate), or the **Terrace Restaurant (** (08) 8981 5388, 122 Esplanade (moderate).

If Darwin weather is not hot enough for you, sample the heat of a Thai curry at the moderately priced **Hanuman Thai Restaurant (** (08) 8941 3500, 28 Mitchell Street.

NIGHTLIFE

The tropical heat ensures a regular revenue for the many pubs in town, many of which liven up when the sun goes down. On weekends most places are open until late.

Packed with backpackers most nights **Kitty O'Shea's Irish Pub** on the corner of Mitchell and Herbert Streets, usually has some dancing going on, with more of the same at **Shenanigans** on Mitchell Street. A quieter place for a chat and sip a cocktail is the **Roma Bar**, Cavenagh Street, which plays predominately ambient music.

Weather permitting — and it usually is except during the rainy season — head to the under-the-stars **Deckchair Cinema (** (08) 8981 0700 and watch a film on the cliff edge at Stokes Hill Wharf. On Thursday and Sundays, visit the sunset market at **Mindil Beach**, open throughout the dry season (May to October). Plays and performances, from the mainstream to the fringe, are held in an historic 1885 stone building at **Brown's Mart Community Arts Theatre (** (08) 8981 5522, 12 Smith Street.

Overlooking Mindil Beach, the squat, pyramid-shaped **MGM Grand Darwin Casino**, on Gilruth Avenue, offers gambling, regular live shows, and dancing at **Sweethearts Downunder**. The casino also provides jazz concerts on its lawns at sunset during the dry season.

Friday's edition of the *Northern Territory News* has a gig guide listing all that's on at night in Darwin.

How to Get There

Ansett and Qantas both have regular flights between Darwin and Australia's major cities.

Driving to Darwin is a major undertaking, the closest capital city is Adelaide, 3,020 km (1,888 miles) away. The main (Stuart) highway from Adelaide to Darwin passes through Alice Springs — the Red Centre of Australia.

LITCHFIELD NATIONAL PARK

Litchfield is a relatively new park which features fantastic waterfalls, sandstone escarpments, clear refreshing water-holes, patches of monsoon rainforest and intriguing **"magnetic" termite mounds** — three-meter-high (10-ft) narrow mounds that are always constructed in perfect north-south alignment. Access to the main attractions is made easy on well-sealed roads; a four-wheel-drive allows you to reach the more remote locations, including the **Lost City**, with its strange sandstone formations, and **Tjaynera Falls**.

There are numerous walks through the park, ranging from 20-minute jaunts to extended wilderness walks. Cycads — short palm-like trees that are throwbacks to the Jurassic period — abound, and small frilled-neck lizards scamper over the hot rocks. Within minutes of stepping from your vehicle, you'll want to plunge into the nearest rock pool. **Buley Rockhole's** cool clear water cascades over rocks into a series of natural pools, some bath-sized, others the size of a small swimming pool. A short walk upstream leads to other less populated small pools. Some of the best falls within easy access are **Wangi**, **Tolmer** and **Florence falls**. Water plummets from heights of 100 m (328 ft) into large deep pools, perfectly safe for swimming.

Litchfield Park is a two-hour drive from Darwin. Camping is allowed in designated areas.

KAKADU NATIONAL PARK

In the heart of the "Top End," the 19,804 sq km (7,648 sq miles) of wilderness in the Kakadu National Park is a spectacular landscape. Dominated by half the length of the 1,000-km-long (620-mile) Arnhem Land escarpment, with great gorges carved out by monsoon rains, and four rivers and numerous creeks tumbling off it into waterfalls, Kakadu's lowlands and floodplains have more than half of all the bird species found in Australia. Enormous numbers of raucous birds, including the jabiru and kingfisher, magpie geese, cockatoos and gorgeously colored parrots, thrive on the water life of fish, reptiles, frogs, insects and plants. Many of these animals and plants are unique to Kakadu. Underneath the pretty pink water-lilies and apparent peace are more sinister creatures: man-eating saltwater crocodiles.

Most tourists choose to visit Kakadu in the cooler dry season, from April to September. But Kakadu is really at its best during the Wet or at the beginning of the Dry, when its magnificent waterfalls are in full fury. The impressive lightning storms at this time of year are an unforgettable sight. Although some of the falls at these times can be pretty well inaccessible, it's still easy to reach the UDP Falls in the South, the area where the film *Crocodile Dundee* was shot.

Despite the abundant eucalyptus and malaluca trees, Kakadu can become dusty during the latter part of the Dry. A good compromise is to visit late-April to early June, missing the violence of the monsoons, but before the the the wetlands and waterfalls dry up. From late June to the end of August is the most popular time to visit, particularly for Australians from the south seeking a winter break. It's the coolest time of the year in the Top End too — which means hot and dry rather than extremely hot and humid. This is a good time for birdwatchers in particular, as much of the park's waterways have dried out, obliging the waterbirds to congregate in enormous numbers around the remaining billabongs.

General Information

Most of Kakadu is Aboriginal land, leased to the Territory government. An admission fee of $15 covers a visit of up to 14 days, payable at the information booth on the Arnhem Highway at the entrance of Kakadu National Park. Children 16 and under are allowed in free of charge. A yearly ticket ($60) admits one vehicle and its passengers to the park — with it they are then exempt from paying camping fees at any of Kakadu's campsites.

It is a further 80 km (50 miles) to the **Bowali Visitor Centre (** (08) 8938 1121, which provides a comprehensive collection of *Park Notes*. These explain the ecology of Kakadu and include maps of major Aboriginal art sites. The center, which includes a café and a good gift store, is open from 8 AM to 5 PM. There is also a tourist information center in **Jabiru (** (08) 8979 2548.

What to See and Do

Kakadu has been inhabited by Aborigines for at least 60,000 years and has some of the world's best examples of prehistoric rock art. There are as many as 5,000 recorded sites scattered throughout the park — some are forbidden to tourists because of their traditional significance. The most accessible sites are **Ubirr** (previously known as Obiri Rock) and **Nourlangie Rock**. These ancient galleries reveal splayed hand stencils, hunters carrying barbed spears, and creation beings Namarrgon and

Waterfalls tumble into a deep rockpool in Litchfield National Park.

Ngalyod, the Rainbow Serpent. "X-ray" drawings of animals show internal organs and bone structure.

Aboriginal culture is still very much alive in Kakadu. The traditional Aboriginal connection with the land confronts Western industrial society head on at the **Jabiluka uranium mine**. Though a tiny area within the huge park, the mine is a focus of much controversy. After visiting this unique wilderness you may want to contact Greenpeace WEB SITE www.greenpeace.org to find out what you can do to help stop unnecessary destruction.

The **Warradjan Cultural Centre**, four and a half kilometers (three miles) off Kakadu Highway, near **Cooinda**, presents the **Bininj** people's Dreaming through art and story. Admission is free.

During the dry season Kakadu's water recedes to a network of lagoons and billabongs which attract thousands of birds. Along the coast, tidal mudflats and mangrove forests provide yet another habitat, contrasting with the rest of the park. Six kilometers (just under four miles) off Kakadu Highway near Cooinda, the **Yellow Water Billabong** is a wonderful wilderness spot supporting large flocks of birds, fish and fruit bats. **Boat trips** ((08) 8979 0111 leave regularly from just past the small settlement of Coinda. Here, close to where we had just boarded our small boat, an enormous crocodile devoured a large goose it had caught in the brush. Saltwater crocodiles really are man-eating, and warrant care when walking near any water.

The park includes a broad flood plain backed by the high ramparts of the Arnhem Land escarpment. Accessible only in the dry season, and even then by four-wheel-drive only, waterfalls thunder off the plateau. The most breathtaking are the 200-m (650-ft) drop of **Jim Jim Falls** and the smaller **Twin Falls**. Along the banks, sandy beaches are surrounded by dense forest filled with wildlife. Both falls are reached off the Kakadu Highway along rather bumpy dirt roads. Check with a tourist office first to see if conditions are suitable for conventional vehicles.

TOURS

Kakadu Dreams TOLL-FREE (1800) 813 216 runs two-, three- and five-day tours to Kakadu Park, while **Kakadu Gorge and Waterfall Tours** ((08) 8979 0111 FAX (08) 8979 0148 takes full-day canoeing tours of Jim Jim and Twin Falls.

Another way to get a view of the park, particularly if you don't have much time, is from the air. **Kakadu Air** ((08) 8979 2411 TOLL-FREE (1800) 089 113 E-MAIL kakair@kakair.com.au has daily departures from Darwin and within Kakadu itself, taking in the region around Jim Jim and Twin falls. The same company also run Guluyambi East Alligator River cruises, 75-minute informative cruises down the ribbon of water that separates Kakadu from Arnhem Land.

WHERE TO STAY

Most of Kadadu's accommodation is in Jabiru or Cooinda, close to the park center.

Cooinda has the advantage of being handy to Yellow Water Billabong. **Gagadju Lodge Cooinda** ((08) 8979 0145 has moderately priced units and very basic and inexpensive cabins, and offers powered campsites. The lodge has a restaurant and a bar/barbecue area where salads and deserts are offered as well as raw meat for you to cook up on the grill.

In Jabiru, **Gagudju Crocodile Hotel** ((08) 8979 2800 TOLL-FREE (1800) 800 123 FAX (08) 8979 2707, Flinders Street, is an enormous luxury hotel in the shape of a crocodile (why not?). Rates run from moderate to expensive. In the moderate range, **Kookaburra Lodge** ((08) 8971 0257 E-MAIL kookaburra @nt-tech.com.au, at the corner of Lindsay and Third streets, has clean and comfortable dorms and twin share, along with good guest facilities. **Kakadu Lodge and Caravan Park** ((08) 9301 2756 E-MAIL info@northernterritory.com, Jabiru Drive, has lodges and cabins (moderate) and camping and caravan facilities (inexpensive).

ARNHEM LAND

Arnhem Land's central plateau is a mosaic of outcrops and bushlands interspersed with paperbark-lined creeks. Like Kakadu, the Wet sees creeks turn into powerful fast-flowing rivers, and vast areas become unpassable flood plains. At all times Arnhem Land is abundant in native wildlife — cockatoos, wallabies, crocs and dingos. Visiting Arnhem land is neither easy nor inexpensive, but for the visitor to Australia seeking to learn more of its Aboriginal heritage and to make direct contact with its remotest Aboriginal communities, this vast area occupying 100,000 sq km (39,000 sq miles) will definitely repay the effort required.

Arnhem Land is particularly rich in ancient rock art (see ABORIGINAL ART, page 42 in YOUR CHOICE), and tours to cave art sites at Maningrida, Oenpelli, Ramingining and Elcho Island feature on most itineraries. Many of Arnhem Land's Yolngu communities produce outstanding contemporary work that continues the artistic tradition of their ancestors — milkwood carvings (unique to the region), bark paintings, screen prints and woven baskets and mats. **Nambara Arts and Crafts** ((08) 9872 8111 at Nhulunbuy sells a good selection of these contemporary works.

All of Arnhem land is Aboriginal land, and a permit from the **Northern Land Council** ((08) 8920 5100 FAX (08) 8945 2633 WEB SITE nlc.org.au, PO Box 42921, Casuarina NT 0811, is required to travel through it, although visitors can fly in to Nhulunbuy (Gove) without a permit. Both Qantas and Ansett have daily flights into Gobe Airport from both Cairns and Darwin. As different roads pass through different clan lands, numbers on many are tightly regulated. In some areas this means you should apply for the permit up to a year in advance. The easiest way to make the most of a visit to Anrhem Land is to take an organized tour, in which case the tour operator will handle all permits. A number of possibilities are discussed in SPECIAL INTERESTS, page 53 in YOUR CHOICE.

There are a few places to stay in Nhulunbuy. The best is **Walkabout Lodge** ((08) 8987 1777 E-MAIL kay@walkaboutlodge.com.au WEB SITE www .walkaboutlodge.com.au, PO Box 221, Nhulunbuy NT 0881, 12 Westal Street, which overlooks the

DARWIN TO ALICE

The Stuart Highway, known simply as the "Track," bisects the Northern Territory, from Darwin to Alice Springs 1,530 km (950 miles) to the south and then another 290 km (180 miles) to the South Australian border. Along this route are found some of the most remarkable and varied landscapes, many of these in Aboriginal land where permits are necessary.

GENERAL INFORMATION

The **Katherine Region Tourist Association** ((08) 8972 2650 is on the Stuart Highway on the corner

waterfront (expensive). Walkabout has a reasonably good restaurant , the all essential swimming pool, and organizes sportsfishing trips (the peninsula's barramundi draw keen anglers) as well as a range of tours into Arnhemland — they can arrange permits too, but it's best to give them a few weeks' notice. Another good accomadation option is the **Gove Peninsula Motel** ((08) 8987 0700, 1 Matthew Flinders Way, with comfortable, moderately priced, air-conditioned rooms and a swimming pool.

For more information about traveling in Arnhem Land contact the **Darwin Regional Tourism Association** ((08) 8981 4300 WEB SITE www .nttc.com.au, 38 Mitchell Street, Darwin, or the **East Arnhem Land Tourist Association** ((08) 8987 2255 FAX (08) 8987 2288 E-MAIL arnhemland@ealta.org web site www.ealta.org.au, PO Box 1212 Nhulunbuy NT 0881.

of Lindsay Street. The **Tennant Creek Region Tourist Association** ((08) 8962 3388 E-MAIL tcrta@topend .com.au is in Peko Road.

Two good **web sites** for tour and accommodation bookings and general information are www .northernterritory.com and www.nttc.com.au.

NITMILUK (KATHERINE GORGE) NATIONAL PARK

Katherine, 345 km (214 miles) south of Darwin, is the next main town on the highway, and famous for the Nitmiluk National Park, which is located 32 km (20 miles) out of town. It's a great place for canoeing, swimming, bush-walking, or for just relaxing on a cruise through these mighty cliffs.

Freshwater crocodiles sun themselves on the banks of Yellow Water Billabong in Kakadu National Park.

Gecko Canoeing WEB SITE www.geckocanoeing .com.au, takes one-, three- and six-day fully catered adventure canoeing tours along the rivers of the gorge. Before setting off bush-walkers need to contact the ranger and make sure that their pathway is known.

Going through these gorges is venturing into prehistory, through rocks formed some 16 million years ago. In the past, this was the home of the great reptiles. The freshwater crocodile is still here, but unlike its saltwater cousin, is not a hazard to people. More recent animal species abound: goannas, tortoises, monitor lizards, along with many species of fish and birds. For the budding botanist, over 400 different plant species exist here.

The main geological structure is split up into 13 sandstone gorges. On either side of the Katherine River are 70-m (230-ft) walls which change color according to the weather and time of day. The best time to see them is first thing in the morning. In the other direction is the sheer face of **Jedda's Leap**, where legend has it that a couple jumped to their deaths because they were not allowed to wed. A two-hour boat ride up the first two gorges is probably the best way to appreciate their beauty, although there are longer rides that take in additional gorges. **Katherine Gorge Boat Tours** ((08) 8972 1253 FAX (08) 8971 1044 makes trips ranging from two to eight hours, with the longer trips involving some cross-country hiking.

Edith Falls, a superb chain of falls in the park, can be reached from the Katherine Gorge by very dedicated bush-walkers. It's an arduous trek, and it's important to check with the ranger for a permit to go through the Aboriginal land. You'll be rewarded with a swim in the large natural pool below the falls. Sunsets and sunrises are a breathtaking sight here, with the glowing red cliffs contrasting with white waterfalls. An easier way to Edith Falls is simply to drive there, taking the 20-km (12-mile) sealed road from the Stuart Highway. Edith Falls has accommodation and ample camping facilities.

Manyallaluk Aboriginal Community

It is possible to visit the Manyallaluk Aboriginal Community, about 100 km (62 miles) southeast of Katherine. Manyallaluk Cultural Tours ((08) 8975 4727 TOLL-FREE (1800) 644 727 FAX (08) 8975 4724 provides tourists with the opportunity to learn about the Aboriginal culture in a genuine family setting. They have one- and two-day organized tours and a one-day self-drive tour option. You can have a go a at throwing spears or try some traditional basket weaving. Accommodation is in tents or in the caravan park with all modern amenities.

MATARANKA (ELSEY PARK)

About an hour and a half south of Katherine is one of nature's little bonuses: the brilliant, clear thermal pool near Mataranka. Fed by spring water bubbling to the surface at a warm 34°C (93°F), the spring supports a veritable oasis, a small pocket of palms and lush tropical forest in a landscape otherwise almost bare of vegetation. This region is called the "Never Never" — those who live here can never leave it.

The adjacent **Elsey Park** is being developed by the Mataranka people as an area of both natural beauty, with its forest, river and waterfalls, and as the historic homeland of the Mataranka people. This was also the site of Elsey Station, a nineteenth-century homestead known as the setting for A. Gunn's books *The Little Black Princess* and *We of the Never Never*.

Woodland gives way to the scrub and red earth of Australia's interior at **Renner Springs**, 500 km (310 miles) south of Katherine. This change marks the limit of the monsoons and the beginning of the dry center.

Daly Waters, 584 km (365 miles) from Darwin, provides a break from driving for an ice cold drink in the oldest pub in the territory.

TENNANT CREEK

Tennant Creek is the site of the last gold rush in Australia, which began in 1932. The creek itself is 11 km (seven miles) out of town. Convenience overrode good intentions when, in 1933, Joe Kilgariff made his way to the area with a cart carrying supplies and materials for the construction of a pub. Caught in a sudden downpour and bogged in the mud, Kilgariff unloaded his wagon and built the pub on the spot. The thirsty miners chose to build their town next to the pub rather than near the water supply of the creek. Tennant Creek is currently the third-largest gold producer in Australia.

On guided tours of the **Gold Stamp Battery** overlooking the town you can see and hear the rhythmic sound of the 130-year-old stamps as they crush the ore.

The **Ngalipanyangu Cultural Centre and Gallery** displays and sells some hiqh-quality local works. To get the feel of life on a cattle station, try the **Juno Horse Centre (** (08) 8962 2783 FAX (08) 8962 2199 four-hour cattle-mustering trip, which costs only $55. Bookings must be made at least 48 hours in advance.

Devil's Marbles

About 105 km (65 miles) south of Tennant Creek, the Devil's Marbles straddle the highway — hundreds of giant spherical granite boulders, some of which balance precariously on others. Aborigines believed they were eggs laid by the rainbow serpent during the Dreaming, and this is a registered sacred site. Geologists suggest the Marbles are the weathered remains of a huge, shattered, crystallized granite formation. The best time to view the Devil's Marbles is at dusk, when the sun's rays bring out the colors of red, yellow and brown minerals present in the granite.

Central Mount Stuart, a low, round hill to the west of the highway 65 km (40 miles) past Barrow Creek, is more or less at the geographical center of the continent.

WHERE TO STAY

There is moderately priced accommodation along the Track, although most of the smaller towns offer little choice.

In Katherine, the **Pine Tree Motel (** (08) 8972 2533 TOLL-FREE (1800) 089 103 FAX (08) 8972 2920, 3 Third Street, and the **All Seasons Frontier Katherine Motor Inn (** (08) 8972 1744 FAX (08) 8972 2790 are both air-conditioned and moderately priced, with fairly standard restaurants. Both have small swimming pools, almost a necessity in the Northern Territory.

Mataranka Homestead Tourist Resort ((08) 8975 4544 FAX (08) 8975 4580, on Homestead Road, also provides moderately priced accommodation, and guests can relax in a thermal pool filled with natural spring water.

Until recently accommodation choices in Tennant Creek were limited, but an upturn in tourism has led to the opening of a few new motels. The **Safari Lodge Motel (** (08) 8962 2207 FAX (08) 8962 3188, 12 Davidson Street, offers both moderately priced rooms and inexpensive bunkrooms. The **Eldorado Motor Lodge (** (08) 8962 2402 FAX (08) 8962 3034, Paterson Street, has moderately priced rooms with all the necessary facilities for a comfortable stay (both motels have swimming pools). There are also several inexpensive caravan parks with camping facilities in and around Tennant Creek; the **Outback Caravan Park (** (07) 8962 2459, on Peko Road just east of town, also offers inexpensive air-conditioned cabins and has a small swimming pool.

THE RED CENTRE

To many visitors this arid center, stretching from the Great Sandy Desert to the Simpson Desert, is the real Australia: ethereal, unmerciful, and unique. To Australians this red earth and its monolithic geological formations — Uluru (Ayers Rock), King's Canyon, the Devil's Marbles and the 36 domes of Kata Tjuta (the Olgas) — can inspire a sentimental, almost familiarial, fondness (although Australians often prefer seeing them from the comfort of an airplane seat on the way to Bali).

Uluru-Kata Tjuta National Park is managed jointly by the Australian Conservation Agency and the Anangu people, the traditional custodians of the area, whose ties to the land go back over 25,000 years. The park has the distinction of being a listed World Heritage Site not only for its unique physical beauty but also for its cultural significance. Uluru is the most famous feature of the Red Centre, and one of the country's most important tourist attractions. Its domed silhouette is as distinctly Australian as the Pyramids are Egyptian or the Eiffel Tower French.

While tourism to the famous rocks is centered in the small town of Yulara, on the edge of the Uluru-Kata Tjuta National Park, Alice Springs, known simply as "the Alice," is the unofficial capital of the Red Centre. In a country where the spirit of the outback is revered, Australians have a soft spot in their hearts for the Alice.

GENERAL INFORMATION

The **Central Australian Tourism Industry Association (** (08) 8952 5800 E-MAIL visinfo@ catia.asn.au, 60 Gregory Terrace, Alice Springs, is open from 9 AM to 6 PM weekdays, and 9 AM to 4 PM weekends. The office has an extensive range of information on the area, the desert environment, and incorporates a Parks and Wildlife desk. This is a good place to pick up maps and information on all parks and reserves in the Red Centre. The **Parks and Wildlife** main office **(** (08) 8951 8211 is five kilometers (just over three miles) south of town on the Stuart Highway.

For medical assistance call the **Alice Springs Hospital (** (08) 8951 7777; the emergency admissions desk is open 24 hours a day.

Outback Auto Rentals ((08) 8953 5333 FAX (08) 8953 5344, 78 Todd Street, rents reliable new cars from $45, and **Boomerang Rentals (** (08) 8955 5171 FAX (08) 8955 5276 rents late model four-wheel-drive vehicles at reasonable rates.

Byte Me Internet Lounge ((08) 8952 8730, 94 Todd Street, (at Melanka Backpackers) has 18 computers, a lounge area with free tea and coffee plus friendly helpful staff. Open 9 AM to 10 PM seven days.

As the suns rays lower, the Devil's Marbles redden to shades of rich ocher.

ALICE SPRINGS

Alice Springs is at the foot of the **MacDonnell Ranges**, whose ever-changing colors provide an attractive backdrop. The town is built in an area traditionally inhabited by the Arrernte people around the junction of two rivers, known to the Arrernte as Anthelke Ulpeye and Lhere Mparntwe. A waterhole was discovered in the bed of the usually dry Lhere Mparntwe, and in 1871 a telegraph station was built, a link in the first telegraph line across the continent, which was completed the following year. The new settlers renamed the rivers the Charles and the Todd, after Sir Charles Todd, who had overseen the construction of the Overland Telegraph Line.

The town itself wasn't established until 1888 and was originally given the name of Stuart. Early on, however, a small spring near the waterhole had been named after Alice Todd, Sir Charles's wife. This name gradually took hold, and in 1933 the town was officially renamed Alice Springs.

The population of the Alice is today over 23,000, supported mainly by tourism, which has boomed since the world discovered the Red Centre.

What to See and Do
The **Aboriginal Art and Culture Centre** ((08) 8952 3408 WEB SITE www.aboriginalart.com.au, 86 Todd Street, has a "Didjeridu University," an Aboriginal music museum and an art and craft gallery.

Built between 1870 and 1872, the **Telegraph Station Historical Reserve** ((08) 8952 3993, on the Stuart Highway, contains a reconstruction of the stone repeater station that was a vital link in the 3,000-km (1,860-mile) Overland Telegraph Line. The historic reserve has guided tours daily from May to September. To get a greater appreciation of the history of central Australia visit the **Old Timer's Folk Museum** ((08) 8952 2844, on the Stuart Highway south of Alice Springs, which displays relics from the early pioneer days. Open from 2 PM to 4 PM with a small admission fee charged.

Unfortunately only a few headstones remain at the **Old Pioneer Cemetery** on George Crescent. Buried here are two men who are part of the Red Centre's colorful history. One of them, Harold Lasseter, set out into the desert in 1930 with two camels, never to return. His last diary entry tantalizingly declared that he had found a fabulously rich gold reef, which subsequently no prospector has ever succeeded in finding. The other, Albert Namatjira, immortalized many features of the MacDonnell Ranges in vivid watercolor paintings. Although his work is universally admired he died a tragic figure in 1959, unable to claim the fundamental human rights white Australians take for granted. You can see works by this great Australian artist in the **Araluen Centre for Arts and Entertainment** ((08) 8952 5022, Larapinta Drive, which also showcases

exhibitions of Central Australian artists and hosts the annual Desert Mob Art Exhibition that highlights artwork from Aboriginal communities. The **Strehlow Research Centre** ((08) 8951 8000, Larapinta Drive, is a fascinating repository for the life's work of TGH Strehlow who spent many years with the Aranda people recording their songs, ceremonies, legends and the complex rules which govern their society.

The **Henbury Meteorite Conservation Reserve** ((08) 8951 8211, 150 km (93 miles) southwest of Alice Springs, contains a series of craters formed 4,700 years ago when a shower of meteorites struck the Earth at about 40,000 km/h (25,000 mph). The largest is 183 m (600 ft) wide and 15 m (50 ft) deep. A four-wheel-drive vehicle is recommended.

Tours
Pitchi Richi Aboriginal Cultural Tours ((08) 8952 1931 have Dreaming and bush tucker guided tours by local Aborigines, which include spear- and boomerang-throwing instruction, artifact displays and historical stories. Another way to learn about Aboriginal people and their lifestyle is to join a postman in delivering mail to some of Central Australia's most remote Aboriginal communities. **Ngurratjuta Air** ((08) 8953 5000 FAX (08) 8953 5060 is an Aboriginal-owned company with half- and full-day flights meeting locals from all over the state. The red-earth scenery viewed from above is spectacular.

John and Rex Spencer of **Spencer Tours** (/FAX (08) 8952 2639 have worked with some of the caner's original pioneering cattlemen, as well as having a lifetime of learning from their Aboriginal elders. They offer a range of short and extended tours with an emphasis on nature-based and cultural visits.

For true adventurers, the Queensland-based **Outback Camel Company** ((07) 3854 1022 FAX (07) 3854 1079 WEB SITE www.outbackcamel.com.au has 12- to 23-day treks into the real outback. No back-up vehicle and no permanent camps, just you the camels and the highly experienced guides. Although even the treks they consider easy are a physical and mental challenge, people of all ages say it is one of the most rewarding experiences they've ever had. For the slightly less adventurous who would nevertheless enjoy a camel ride, **Frontier Camel Tours** ((08) 8953 0444 FAX (08) 8955 5015 WEB SITE www.cameltours.com.au offers several pleasant one-hour camel rides along the banks of the Todd River.

8956 9823, Ross Highway, 85 km (53 miles) out of Alice Springs, where guests stay in timber slab cabins. Prices are generally inexpensive. Several adventure trips are organized from the Homestead and boomerang-throwing lessons are given by Mike Turner at 10 AM every day — it usually takes a few — but when it finally comes back, look out!

Situated on the banks of the Todd, the quiet **Outback Motor Lodge** ((08) 8952 3888 WEB SITE www.outbackmotorlodge.com.au, South Terrace, has adequate moderately priced rooms. The nearby **Gapview Resort Hotel** ((08) 8952 6611 WEB SITE www.gapview.com.au, at the corner of Gap Street and South Terrace, has comfortable moderately priced and inexpensive self-contained units.

Ossie's Outback Horse Tours ((08) 8952 2308 WEB SITE www.ossies.com.au runs small group, nature-based guided horseback tours from three hours to overnight campouts. **Alice Springs Air Charter** ((08) 8955 5200 has flights over the MacDonnell Ranges, the Ross River area and Simpsons Gap.

Where to Stay

The luxurious **Plaza Hotel Alice** ((08) 9281 1450 E-MAIL reservation@australiahotels.net, Barrett Drive, offers the best accommodation. Near the casino, **Vista Alice Springs** ((08) 9281 1450 WEB SITE www.alicesprings-vista.com.au has 140 moderately priced, first-class air-conditioned rooms. **Lasseter's Hotel Casino** TOLL-FREE (1800) 808 975 WEB SITE www.lasseters.com.au, 93 Barrett Drive, has moderately priced rooms with all comforts.

For authentic outback accommodation try the **Ross River Homestead** ((08) 8956 9711 FAX (08)

Where to Eat

Alice has several excellent bush-food restaurants. A good place to sample some indigenous delicacies is the **Red Ochre Grill** ((08) 8952 6914, 11 Leichhardt Terrace, which proposes one of Alice's more interesting bush-tucker menus. Dishes include crocodile confit, yam gnocchi, territory buffalo fillet and wallaby mignon. Prices are moderate.

Many other nationalities represented in Alice prepare first-class food at moderate prices. **Keller's Swiss and Indian Restaurant** ((08) 8952 3188, Gregory Terrace, in the Diplomat Hotel building, may serve an unlikely combination of cuisines, but it's actually very good. With Swiss sausage salad and Indian masala butter chicken on the menu, there's sure to be something here for everyone. **Oscar's** ((08) 8953 0930, Todd Mall, combines Spanish, Portuguese and Mediterranean food.

Uluru, the world's biggest rock.

THE MACDONNELL RANGES

Most people who visit Alice Springs focus their attention on traveling to Uluru (Ayers Rock). However, the drive into the western MacDonnell Ranges, which are much closer to Alice, is equally interesting. This route offers some lesser known, but spectacular scenery, with a series of deep gorges cutting through the hills. There's a lot to cover in one day so it's best to start early.

Simpsons Gap National Park, 22 km (14 miles) west of Alice Springs on the MacDonnell Ranges Scenic Drive, is the start of **West MacDonnell National Park**. Later in the afternoon or early in the

Larapinta Drive. At **Hermannsburg Mission** — the first Aboriginal mission in Northern Territory, established in 1887 — there is a turn-off to **Palm Valley**, an oasis of ancient cycads that are part of the **Finke Gorge National Park**, 155 km (96 miles) west of Alice Springs. The oldest river in the world carved **Finke Gorge** into the surrounding plain. Note the cabbage palms, a vestige of when the area was much wetter. The gorge can only be explored by foot, and after rain a series of rock pools form along its length.

For an aerial view of the MacDonnell Ranges, **Spinifex Ballooning** ((08) 8953 4800 TOLL-FREE (1800) 677 893 offers a 60-minute sunrise balloon flight for $175 (including a champagne breakfast), or a 30-minute champagne flight for $110.

morning you're likely to see black-footed rock wallabies scampering nimbly about the rock slopes. Take **Ghost Gum Walk** for a closer look at the native plants of this arid region. Another short walk to **Cassia Hill** gives excellent elevated views of the ranges and **Simpsons Gap**. For cycling enthusiasts, a sealed bicycle path meanders for 17 km (10 miles) between Simpsons Gap and **John Flynn's Grave**.

Take the turn-off to **Standley Chasm** further into the park through forests of stately ghost gums. Aim for midday to see the chasm's walls flame red. Go back to the main road and take the right fork along Namatjira Drive for 82 km (51 miles) to the turnoff to **Ormiston Gorge**. An underground spring feeds the stream that flows through the gorge and the deep water hole provides welcome relief from the heat. In the sun, the gorge's near vertical cliff face shimmers red, punctuated by white ghost gums rising from ledges. The road curves round to the south to join

ULURU/KATA TJUTA NATIONAL PARK

In 1985, the Northern Territory government handed the Pitjantjatjara and Yankunytjatjara people freehold title over the 132,566 ha (327,574 acre) of land surrounding Ayers Rock. They immediately changed the name back to its original "Uluru." The rock's important Aboriginal history means the national park is one of only two places in the world recognized as a World Heritage Site because of its living cultural significance.

Uluru (Ayers Rock)

Uluru was first sighted by Europeans in 1873, by surveyor William Gosse during an expedition to map the 2,400 km (1,500 miles) of desert between Alice Springs and Perth. This single rock, the peak of a buried mountain, rises 384 m (1,260 ft) from the surrounding plain. The perimeter is some nine kilometers (five and a half miles) at its base. Its flanks are etched with deep gullies which fill with rushing water when it rains.

The sandstone monolith is rich in the crystalline mineral feldspar, giving the rock its vibrant colors, which vary with the time of day and the weather. On sunny days it's an orange-red; when wet, it changes to black, white or shades of purple. Even a novice photographer can take stunning photographs at dawn or sunset when the colors are most vivid.

Sacred to Aborigines, Uluru abounds in Aboriginal legends; every crevice and contoured shape has a Dreamtime story attached to it. Take the southside indentations, scored by spears in a battle between the poisonous snake people, the Leru, and the sleeping lizard people, the Loongardi.

Although the traditional Aboriginal owners (Anangu) prefer visitors to respect the cultural significance of Uluru by not climbing it, it is possible to climb to the top; there are handrails and guide chains on the more difficult sections. The round-trip to the summit takes about two hours, although many turn back at a place called "chicken rock." The climb becomes positively dangerous in windy conditions, and near the top in any conditions. The rock is "closed" in unsafe weather conditions.

Kata Tjuta (The Olgas)
The unique beauty of Kata Tjuta National Park, a collection of giant weather-beaten, red-domed rocks, with fissures, gorges and valleys carved between them, impresses some visitors more than Uluru. Kata Tjuta (Mount Olga) itself is higher than Uluru, rising 546 m (1,790 ft) above the surrounding plain. Like Uluru, the Olgas hold their own spectacular light show at sunset.

Experienced walkers can take the three- to four-hour walk through the impressive **Valley of the Winds**. In summer it's advised to drink two liters of water per hour in this arid heat, and to only attempt these walks in the cooler early morning hours. An easier alternative is the **Olga Gorge (Walpa Gorge)** walk, which takes approximately one hour. There is also a sealed road to and around the Olgas.

Tours
For those who want to learn more about Aboriginal mythology of Uluru, **Anangu Tours** ((08) 8956 2123 WEB SITE www.users.bigpond.com/lbanangu offers a variety of informative guided tours. Anangu guides tell creation stories thousands of generations old and demonstrate bush survival skills taught to them by their grandparents. All tours are conducted in the guide's own traditional language, translated into English by interpreters.

A scenic flight over Uluru and the Olgas is an unforgettable experience. Both **Professional Helicopter Services** ((08) 8956 2003 E-MAIL phsrock @topend.com.au and **Rockayer** ((08) 89555 5200

E-MAIL astp@ozemail.com.au offer a range of different flights and flight–tour combos.

Where to Stay and Eat
Ayers Rock Resort ((Sydney) (02) 9339 1040 WEB SITE www.ayersrockresort.com.au is the only place there is to stay within the park. Fortunately it offers a wide range of accommodation. The resort consists of two luxury hotels — **Desert Gardens** and **Sails in the Wind** — the expensive **Emu Walk Apartments**, the moderate to inexpensive **Outback Pioneer Hotel and Lodge**, the inexpensive **Spinifex Lodge**, and an excellent camping ground. It also has fine dining restaurants and quick food outlets.

For a unique meal under the stars of the southern sky, **Sounds of Silence** ((08) 8957 7888 (departs from Ayers Rock Resort) transports you into the desert in time for magnificent sunset views of the Olgas and Uluru. A candlelit table awaits under the stars, with the menu encompassing the best of local bush food and some less-adventurous options.

HOW TO GET THERE

Qantas and Ansett have daily **flights** into Alice Springs and Yulara's Uluru airports from Darwin, Adelaide, Cairns, Melbourne, Sydney and Perth and offer frequent service between Uluru and Alice Springs airports. Both Qantas and Ansett have offices in Alice Springs on the corner of Todd and Parsons streets.

Greyhound Pioneer and McCafferty's run **bus services** between Adelaide and Darwin. Alice Springs is roughly halfway between these two capitals — around 20 hours from either by bus. Both companies have daily services from Alice to Uluru.

The **Ghan** (132 232 train connects Alice and Adelaide, leaving Adelaide at 2 PM, Monday and Thursday, and arriving in Alice at 10 AM the following day. The return trip departs from Alice at 2 PM, Tuesday and Friday. Ghan coach class fares are slightly more than the bus — around $200 one-way. Prices double for a shared sleeper ($380) and triple for a first-class private sleeper with bathroom and meals ($590). Named after the Afghan cameliers who used to transport supplies and people across these deserts, the Ghan began in 1877, although until 1928 it only went as far as Oodnadatta; from where camel trains took over. The new Ghan opened in 1980.

Uluru is 470 km (290 miles) southwest of Alice Springs. It's reached by taking the turnoff from the Stuart Highway onto the Lasseter Highway (the route is well signposted). A lot of commercial package **tours** of Uluru and Kata Tjuta are available from Alice Springs (see TOURS, page 269 above, or contact the Central Australian Tourism Industry Association in Alice Springs).

After a hard day's trekking, a camel beds down for the night.

Queensland

COASTAL QUEENSLAND AND ITS CORAL SEA ISLANDS are the number-one vacation destination for Australians. Queensland's balmy tropical climate, white-sand beaches and turquoise waters attract everyone from high school kids on summer break to retirees escaping the winter chills of the south. And like most Australians, whenever I visit Queensland I find myself contemplating a move there. Adventure seekers gravitate to the almost inaccessible rivers and national parks of the Cape York Peninsula and along the Gulf of Carpentaria. For nature lovers, Queensland's tropical and subtropical rainforests harbor hundreds of endemic species of flora and fauna, including the electric blue Cairns birdwing butterfly, the two-meter-tall (six-and-a-half-foot), prehistoric-looking flightless cassowary and the less innocuous estuarine crocodile.

While the Gold Coast's more recent tourist developments include Warner Bros. Movie World, Wet 'n' Wild Water World, Sea World and Dreamworld, Queensland's true Magic Kingdom is half the size of Texas and predates Disneyland by 100,000 years. A wonderland of color and movement, home to the beautiful, the exotic and the grotesque, the Great Barrier Reef is a 2,300-km-long (1,400-mile) underwater theme park, the largest living organism on the planet, and with its coral cays and islands forms a playground for sun-seekers and thrill-seekers, water-sports enthusiasts and those who prefer to just sit back and take it all in.

Of course, Queensland is not just coast. The Great Dividing Range, the spine of eastern Australia, stretches the length of the state, all the way up to the tip of Cape York. In fact, the Torres Strait Islands are its final northern peaks. While to the east these mountains fall away to rainforests and the verdant slopes and valleys of the Pacific coast, to the west they flatten out into hinterlands and tablelands, then ease down to the broad arid plains of the outback.

To most Australians, the north is another country. Its inhabitants are stereotyped as slow-talking and extremely conservative, and there's some truth in this. Although Queenslanders are in general as warm and friendly as the climate, racist attitudes are far more prevalent here than in the southern states — issues of Aboriginal land rights, racial equity in general and liberal or artistic values can spark off some uncomfortable discussions. Be prepared.

BRISBANE

Although Brisbane saw a building boom in the 1990s, rapidly losing its old big-country-town feel, homes in the suburbs only minutes from the center have large gardens adorned with mango trees and banana palms. Older houses are built "Queensland style" — on stilts to allow cooling breezes to circulate on sweltering days.

BACKGROUND

Soldiers and recalcitrant convicts first established a settlement on Moreton Bay in 1824, but it proved to be an unsuitable site. The following year they moved up the Brisbane River to the spot where the city center stands today. The convict population never exceeded 1,000, and by 1839 their number had reduced to 29; on February 11, 1842, Brisbane became a free settlement.

In 1859, the Moreton Bay District separated from New South Wales to become a colony in its own right.

In the early days there was constant friction between the local Aborigines and the white settlers. In 1845 several tribes forged an alliance under the leadership of Dundalli, who led a guerrilla campaign against the colony for the next nine years.

Once the hinterland had been opened — despite determined opposition from the Aboriginal population — the wealth of natural resources helped Brisbane grow. Cattlemen from New South Wales drove their herds north to the wide plains and tablelands and occupied large tracts of grazing land. The discovery of gold and the establishment of a successful sugar industry added to the colony's wealth. However, it was the expansion of coal exports after the World War II and the state's tourist boom that made Queensland a powerhouse in Australia's economy and Brisbane its third-largest city.

GENERAL INFORMATION

Tourist Information booths are located at the Queen Street Mall ℂ (07) 3229 5918 and the Brisbane City Hall, open Monday to Thursday, 9:30 AM to 5:30 PM, Friday until 9 AM to 9 PM, Saturday 9 AM to 4 PM and Sunday 10 AM to 4 PM. You can also contact **Brisbane Tourism** ℂ (07) 3221 8411 FAX (07) 3229 5126 WEB SITE www.visitbrisbane.com.au, PO Box 12260 Elizabeth Street, Brisbane, Queensland, for all inquiries about your Brisbane stay.

The **Queensland Government Travel Centre** ℂ 131 801 or (07) 3874 2800 FAX (07) 3221 5320 WEB SITE www.queensland-holidays.com.au, 243 Edward Street (at the corner of Adelaide Street), provides information and takes bookings for attractions, accommodation and package vacations throughout Queensland. The center is open weekdays 8:30 AM to 5 PM and Saturday 8:30 AM to midday. For information on national parks phone the **Queensland Department of Conservation and Heritage** ℂ (07) 4227 7111 or the **National Parks Association of Queensland** ℂ (07) 4367 0878 FAX (07) 4367 0890.

Brisbane's **General Post Office** is on Queen Street and is open weekdays only from 7 AM to 6 PM.

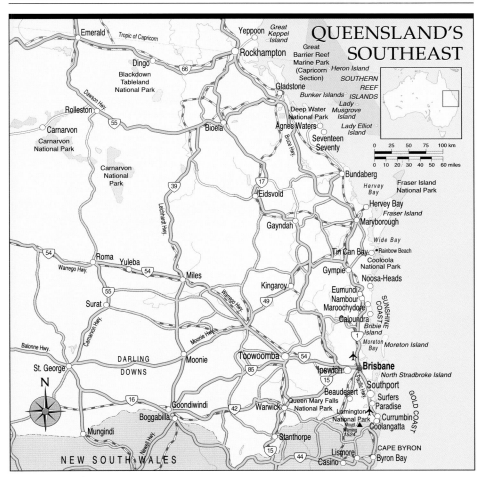

On weekends the Post Shop on the second level of the Myer Center, off the Queen Street Mall, is open 10 AM to 4 PM, and will handle most postal functions.

There's no shortage of **Internet** services in Brisbane. The IYSC (International Youth Service Center) ((07) 3229 9985, Level 2, 69 Adelaide Street, has 40 stations, with friendly and helpful staff. They serve cheap vegetarian meals and beverages too. Open 9:30 AM to 11 PM Monday to Saturday and 10 AM to 6 PM Sunday. Opposite the transit center, Backpacking Round Australia ((07) 3236 5802, 158 Roma Street, has full Internet services along with fax, photocopying and scanning. They're also good for cheap tours and air and coach tickets.

The **RACQ (Royal Automobile Club of Queensland)** ((07) 3361 2444, 261 Queen Street, can supply touring maps and provide driving accessories, tips and warnings.

For **medical assistance** contact the Travelers' 24-hour Medical Service ((07) 3211 3611, 245 Albert Street (second floor); the Royal Brisbane Hospital

((07) 3253 8111, Herston Road, Herston (if you're on the North side of Brisbane); or Princess Alexander Hospital ((07) 3240 2111 (on the South side).

GETTING AROUND

The combined **City Sights Bus and River Cat Tour** ((07) 3407 2330, which lets you tour the city at your own pace, provides a good way to familiarize yourself with Brisbane from the land and the water. Passengers get on and off whenever they like, catching the next bus or catamaran at 30-minute intervals. A non-stop tour with commentary takes about 80 minutes and costs $15 per adult.

River Queens Paddlewheelers ((07) 3221 1300 FAX (07) 3229 6334 runs two old Mississippi-style paddlewheelers up and down the Brisbane River, with lunch cruises at 12:45 PM and dinner cruises at 7:30 PM. The boats leave from Eagle Street Pier, and it's a good idea to book in advance.

For information on Brisbane's buses, ferries and trains call **TransInfo** (131 230.

WHAT TO SEE AND DO

The imposing **City Hall** on the corner of Adelaide and Albert streets was once the city's tallest structure. Corinthian and Ionic columns dominate the entrance and tall clock tower. It has a free lift to an observation platform, which gives a fairly good overview of the city center, but is unfortunately a bit lost in a cluster of modern high-rise offices that now dominate the skyline. City Hall is open weekdays from 8:30 AM to 4:30 PM and Saturdays from 10 AM to 4:30 PM.

The **Old Windmill** overlooks the city in Wickham Terrace as a reminder of the city's convict past.

now part of the Queensland University of Technology at the bottom of George Street. It is also home to the National Trust of Queensland. On the Point is the French Renaissance-style **Parliament House** ((07) 3406 7562, built in 1868. There are free guided tours when Parliament is not in session. Call for tour times. The **Parliament House Annexe** is the nondescript modern tower block behind overlooking the river.

Behind Parliament House are the **Old Botanic Gardens** (Brisbane's "new" Botanic Gardens are at Mount Coot-tha, five minutes northwest of the city center, see AROUND BRISBANE, below). First used by convicts to grow vegetables, the southern tip jutting into the river is still known as **Garden Point**.

Built in 1828 to crush corn, it failed to function because of a design fault; whereupon, the sails were removed and convicts put to work on a treadmill to get the job done. Offenses as trivial as using "disgusting language" and "insolence" earned convicts 14 hours of backbreaking shifts on the treadmill.

The grand sandstone **Customs House** ((07) 3365 8999, 299 Queens Street, was built in 1884 and houses an Art Gallery. Its licensed Brasserie Gallery is fine for light lunches or afternoon tea and cake. The building is open from 10 AM to 4 PM. Along George Street you will find the restored **Lands Building** which now houses the Conrad International Hotel (see WHERE TO STAY, below) and the **Treasury**, an impressive Italian Renaissance structure built of local gray sandstone which is now the Treasury Casino. Originally Brisbane's first university, **Government House** is a good example of a well restored classic colonial building and is

The first Director of the Botanic Gardens laid them out much as they appear today, and you can still walk down the avenue of bunya pines he planted. Free guided tours of the gardens leave from the rotunda south of Albert Street at 11 AM and 1 PM, every day except Monday.

Just over Victoria Bridge, the Queensland Cultural Centre houses the **Queensland Art Gallery** ((07) 3840 7303 with a good collection of colonial-era paintings (open 10 AM to 5 PM, admission is free). The **Queensland Museum**, the **Performing Arts Complex** and the **State Library of Queensland** are all here too. Tours leave on the hour from 10 AM to 4 PM, Monday to Saturday.

A bit further down the river, the **South Bank Center** stretches along the Brisbane River. It includes everything from the **Brisbane Convention and Exhibition Center** and **Opera** to residential apartments and a wide range of restaurants, cafés and retail outlets. Visitors are free to wander around the **Gondwana Rainforest Sanctuary** and other ecosystems set up within the parkland. The artificial lagoon has a long sandy beach area, while the nearby **Formal Gardens** show off Brisbane's tropical flora among ornamental fountains. There's even a **Nepalese Pagoda**. On Fridays the **Parklands Night Markets** open from 5 PM to 10 PM, while on weekends a **Crafts Village** pops up from 11 AM to 5 PM Saturday and 9 AM to 5 PM Sunday. The **Piazza** serves as a venue for a diverse range of entertainment including concerts, sporting events — in winter it's converted into an ice rink and snow-play area. On the corner of Grey and Melbourne Streets is the fun and fashionable **Queensland Museum of Wearable Art** open 9:30 AM to 5 PM daily. The **Southbank Information Centre** ((07) 3867 2051, on the Piazza, is open seven days a week from 8 AM to 8 PM. The parklands are open daily, 6 AM to midnight. Admission is free, although there may be an entrance fee for special events.

WHERE TO STAY

Brisbane looks after its guests well. You don't have to pay a fortune to stay close to the city center and to enjoy what most establishments here consider standard. Almost all hotels, in all price categories, have air-conditioning and swimming pools. Those seeking luxury pampering have ample international-standard hotels to choose from. There are also numerous well-priced B&Bs and budget hotels close to the city.

Expensive

The recently renovated **Carlton Crest** ((07) 3229 9111 TOLL-FREE (1800) 777 123 FAX (07) 3229 9618 E-MAIL res@carltoncrest-brisbane.com.au, King George Square, is in a centrally located, elegant old building. Guests have a choice of modern rooms or Old World style. **Conrad International** ((07) 3306 8888 FAX (07) 3306 8880, in Brisbane's original Lands Building, is another top-of-the-range hotel with the added attraction of its colonial charm. The Conrad is close to the river and the central business district — handy to theaters and the convention center.

The **Sebel** TOLL-FREE (1800) 888 298, at the corner of Albert and Charlotte Streets, is an unpretentious world-class hotel commanding some inspirational views of Brisbane — all rooms have large balconies. The downstairs restaurant and wine bar opens to the street, in the thick of downtown Brisbane. The Sebel has a few rooms in the moderate range as well.

Moderate

Thornbury House ((07) 3832 59850 FAX (07) 3832 7255 WEB SITE www.babs.com.au/qld/thornbury, 1 Thornbury Street, Spring Hill, is a B&B set in an elegant colonial residence. The house is in a quiet, leafy street within easy walking distance of the city, and rooms are furnished with the feel of an old-fashioned country estate. An entirely modern complex in the same area, **Astor Apartments** ((07) 3839 9022 FAX (07) 3229 5553, 35 Astor Terrace, Spring Hill, has 14 floors of reasonably priced one- and two-bedroom units. Only the two-bedroom units have baths, but its central location and low price make up for any minor inadequacies.

Centerpoint Central Apartments ((07) 3832 3000 TOLL-FREE (1800) 061 359 FAX (07) 3832 1842 E-MAIL llitster@pradella.com.au, 69 Leichhardt Street, Spring Hill, only 800 m (875 yards) from the city center, has large one-, two- or three-bedroom apartments, all with private balconies. The one-bedroom apartments start at $135, and all have fully equipped kitchens and baths.

In the center of an area famous for its cafés, bars and restaurants, **Merthyr Astoria B&B** ((07) 3254 1615 FAX (07) 3254 4494 E-MAIL rshera@gil.com.au, 19 Merthyr Road, New Farm, combines historic charm with modern comforts. Tall palms and exotic flowers adorn this two-story colonial building, making it a very welcoming sight after a day of tiring sightseeing. Lower rates apply for a stay of two days or more, but as they have only two rooms, it is advisable to book well ahead.

Ryan's on the River ((07) 3391 1011 FAX (07) 3391 1824, 269 Main Street, Kangaroo Point 4169, is not the most beautiful building, but that's of little consequence once you walk out onto your private balcony looking across the river to the city. The starting price of $99 includes a light Continental breakfast and facilities including a sizeable saltwater swimming pool.

Even the executive and deluxe two-bedroom suites at **City Park** ((07) 3839 8683 FAX (07) 3839 8616, 251 Gregory Terrace, Spring Hill, fall into the moderate price range — as close as it gets to luxury accommodation without the hefty price tag. A basic double falls just over the inexpensive range. More facilities than you could possibly ever use make this one of Brisbane's best-value accommodation options. **Parkview Motel Southbank** ((07) 3846 2900 FAX (07) 3846 4933, 41 Russell Street, South Brisbane 4101, has daily serviced studio units at $85 per unit. The Parkview is only one kilometer (half a mile) from the heart of Brisbane and a short stroll from the Southbank parklands.

Inexpensive

Close to Southbank and only two kilometers (one mile) from the city center, the **Ambassador Motel** ((07) 3844 5661 FAX (07) 3846 2031 E-MAIL ambass@eis.com.au, 180 Gladstone Road, Highgate Hill 4101, has clean, modern units. Its off-the-street location guarantees a good night's sleep, and prices from $55 a night represent great value.

Brisbane's Old Botanic Gardens, close to the city center.

Modern, comfortable studios and one- and two-bedroom apartments are a steal at **Milton Motel Apartments** ((07) 3876 2360 FAX (07) 3876 2359 WEB SITE www.milton-motel.com.au, 12 and 19 Sheehan Street, Milton. All units have covered balconies with outdoor settings and fully equipped kitchens. The trendy Park Road eateries are within easy walking distance. **Annie's Shandon Inn** ((07) 3831 8684 FAX (07) 3831 3073, 405 Upper Edward Street, Brisbane, is a quaint 19-room B&B that has been run by the same family for over 100 years. Exceptionally friendly and welcoming, at only $50 a night for a double, Annie's is affordable inner-city accommodation.

In the heart of one of the more happening districts in Brisbane, **Balmoral House** ((07) 3252 1397 FAX (07) 3252 5892, 33 Amelia Street, Fortitude Valley, has clean, comfortable rooms from $45 a double. There's no pool (there are two Olympic pools close by) and rooms have overhead fans only, but the money saved on accommodation would be well spent in one of the area's superb restaurants and cafés.

WHERE TO EAT

In recent years, dining out in Brisbane has caught up impressively with the other culinary capitals of Australia, perhaps even surpassing some for quality and value. The agreeable climate allows open-air and sidewalk dining most of the year.

Expensive

With a beautiful location right on the river, **Bretts** ((07) 3868 1717, 449 Kingsford Smith Drive, is my pick for a romantic dinner. Getting there adds to its charm: Bretts is a 10-minute cruise by City Cat water taxi from the city center — but if you're not rushed take one of the slower, older boats. The restaurant specializes in seafood. Start with delicious and unusual sautéed soft-shell Moreton Bay bugs and succulent char-grilled tiger prawns with feta cheese and black olives. Follow with an over-the-top combination seafood platter for two, perfect with the Trilogy Semillon, Sauvignon Blanc. Service is professional but friendly and casual. Open all year round from 11 AM until late.

Multiple award-winning **Il Centro** ((07) 3221 6090, Shop 1, Eagle Street Pier, serves the best modern Italian cuisine in Brisbane. Their signature mud-crab lasagna is a definite winner. The wine list has been well chosen to match the food. Bookings are essential. Open for lunch Sunday to Friday midday to 3 PM and for dinner seven days from 6 PM until late. Everything at **Siggi's at the Heritage** ((07) 3221 1999, Edward Street, is pretty well top class. At the top of a carved, polished mahogany staircase is the Heritage's magnificent old colonial bar, adjacent to it is the beautiful dining room, specializing in contemporary takes on French classics.

The tasting menu is highly recommendable and it is not difficult to see why Siggi's has received many prestigious awards over the years. Open Tuesday to Saturday, dinner only from 6:30 PM until late.

For some of the best Asian cuisine in town, **Marco Polo** ((07) 3306 8744, second floor, Treasury Casino, George Street, serves authentic Chinese, Malaysian, Indonesian, Japanese and Indian food. The mud-crab bisque with Chinese rose-wine and the abalone, pork and shitake lasagna demonstrate their dedication to originality; both are excellent. Open for dinner only from 6 PM until late, seven days. For fine dining that keeps to the moderate side of expensive, **Augustine's on George** ((07) 3221 9365, 40 George Street, Brisbane central, has been packing in the corporate set since 1985. Discreet white-gloved waiters offer a constant supply of warm freshly baked bread to enjoy with your meal. Indulge in some of their seafood specialties.

Moderate

Palettes ((07) 3224 3528, corner of Albert and Charlotte streets, has appetizing lunch and dinner specials which are hard to beat for central city casual dining. The creative à la carte menu is extensive, with a wine list to match, and the set menu for around $25 for two courses and a glass of wine represents great value. Open for lunch midday to 3 PM and dinner 6 PM to 10 PM Monday to Thursday and until 11 PM Friday and Saturday, with a snack menu between 12 PM and 5 PM on weekends and bar snacks available every day from 3 PM to 8 PM. **Pages On Mary** ((07) 3229 6606, 169 Mary Street, Brisbane central, is a charming heritage-listed restaurant and bar a block from Eagle Street Pier. The menu is broken up into à la carte, grazing and bar. This is a good place for some serious wine tasting too, with bar staff waiting to share their extensive knowledge of Australian wines. **Pier Nine** ((07) 3229 2194, Eagle Street Pier, 1 Eagle Street, is probably the best known seafood restaurant in Brisbane. Its informality makes all welcome and the constantly changing menu ensure a regular return trade. All the produce is regional so freshness is guaranteed. If you haven't tried mud crab yet this is the place to do so. Keep an eye out for the excellent specials board and be sure to book ahead.

Set in a cute little cottage, **Chow** ((07) 3368 1969, 55 Railway Terrace, Milton, surprises with a New York-style interior: a slick bar, a cherry-red dining room with touches of dark blue, polished floorboards, minimal wall art and modern lighting. The creative cuisine includes duck cottage pie and oxtail borscht. For these alone Chow is well worth seeking out. It's licensed and BYO; open Tuesday to Friday midday to 3 PM and Tuesday to Saturday 6 PM to 10 PM.

Sailboats on Brisbane River.

An informal and relaxed café that has recently (and very successfully) become more ambitious, **gertie's Bar and Restaurant** ((07) 3358 5088, 699 Brunswick Street, New Farm, has an imaginative à la carte menu including some really innovative tapas. Try the warm truffled asparagus tarts with rocket (arugula) and parmesan, or the fusili pasta with wild mushrooms, olives, onion, and olive oil. For dessert (which should not be missed) the best option is to order a "variation plate." The cheese platter too is excellent. **Bravo Wine Bar And Bistro** ((07) 3852 3533, 445 Brunswick Street, Fortitude Valley, has one of the best wine lists in Brisbane with knowledgeable staff only too happy to make recommendations. Their signature dish is

snacks, salads and a few more substantial hot dishes. Open for breakfast and lunch seven days.
Senso Unico ((07) 3358 6644, 92 Merthyr Road, New Farm, draws in an arty crowd, attracted by classic Mediterranean food that doesn't burn a hole in their pockets. Close by is **Aix** ((07) 3358 6444, 83 Merthyr Road, New Farm, an extremely popular café-bistro that serves simple snacks and good chargrills in its open and airy dining room.

HOW TO GET THERE

Qantas and Ansett have flights into Brisbane's domestic airport from all state capitals, and the international terminal is serviced by more than

seared salmon on lemon oil-infused sourdough and almond puree — it deserves all the accolades it has received. Open seven days until late and Sunday brunch from 9 AM.

The **Summit Restaurant** ((07) 3369 9922, Sir Samuel Griffith Drive, Mount Coot-tha, is open seven days and has spectacular city views at night. Regional and seasonal ingredients are used to produce contemporary Australian cuisine with an Asian edge.

Inexpensive

With one of Brisbane's best river views, **Vino's Cellar Bar and Café** ((07) 3221 0811, Level 1, Eagle Street Pier, has great-value pastas, hearty mains and enormous salads with a comprehensive wine list to match. Vino's is an affordable place to sample some of Australia's best wines. **City Gardens Café** ((07) 3229 1554 in the Botanic Gardens serves delicious specialty breads, gourmet sandwiches, light

20 airlines. Brisbane airport is 15 km (just over nine miles) from the city center. Regular buses operate to the Brisbane Transit Centre and to most major hotels.

Queensland Rail (132 232 has passenger services to Brisbane from towns throughout the state, with connections to New South Wales rail services.

Inter- and intra-state buses operate daily into Brisbane's **Transit Centre** ((07) 3236 4444, in Roma Street, close to the city center.

AROUND BRISBANE

Only 11 km (seven miles) from Brisbane, the **Lone Pine Koala Sanctuary** ((07) 3378 1366, Jesmond Road, Fig Tree Pocket, has a large variety of Australian animals including wombats, Tasmanian devils and kangaroos, in a natural bush setting. The 'roos are entirely happy to be hand-fed and, yes, visitors can "cuddle a koala" here. A launch leaves Hayles Wharf at North Quay on the Brisbane River daily at 1:15 PM, with additional departures on Sunday. Alternatively, take a bus from "Koala Platform," which leaves the Myer Center hourly.

A few kilometers past the sanctuary, **Mount Coot-tha Botanic Gardens** ((07) 3403 2533, on Mount Coot-tha Road, mixes parklands and forest. As Australia's largest subtropical gardens, they're most remarkable for the inordinate number of bearded lizards lazing in the Queensland sun. The gardens are home to over 20,000 species of plants. Native bush and rainforest plants encircle lagoons and ponds connected by small streams, and part of the gardens is devoted to vegetation found

in Queensland's arid zones. At Mount Coot-tha's peak there's a breathtaking panoramic lookout point across Brisbane, Moreton Bay and its islands, and sometimes as far as the Glass House Mountains to the north and the mountains of the Gold Coast Hinterlands to the south. The gardens include the once futuristic-looking domed **tropical display house**. Look for the one-kilometer-long (half-mile) Aboriginal Art Trail, along which some interesting works are displayed by local Aboriginal artists. The gardens' **Sir Thomas Brisbane Planetarium**, the largest in Australia, accommodates 144 people. The show starts off like most others but quickly becomes a brilliant array of special effects depicting the more spectacular cosmic occurrences (children under six are not admitted). Programs are shown in the afternoon and evening Wednesday to Sunday. The gardens are open daily from 8 AM to 5 PM, tours can be reserved by calling ahead.

Moreton Island is the world's second-largest sand island after Fraser Island, a little further up the coast. There's relatively no development here. The island has the world's highest sand dunes — Mount Tempest standing at an impressive 280 m (920 ft) — which makes sand-tobogganing very popular. Freshwater lakes, wetlands and forest attract a wide range of birds and small marsupials, but the most popular animals here are the wild dolphins who visit the shallows every evening. **Tangalooma Wild Dolphin Resort** ((07) 3268 6333 WEB SITE www.tangalooma .com.au, Moreton Island, has packages (minimum two nights stay) from $195 per adult and $78 for children; the price includes accommodation, breakfast, transfers and dolphin feeding. One-day tours don't include dolphin feeding, but there are plenty of amusing pelicans who'll gladly take a bite.

Also contained within Moreton Bay are the ever popular **North Stradbroke**, **South Stradbroke** and **Bribie** islands. Their long-stretching golden beaches and tucked-away bays attract anglers, snorkelers and family day-trippers from Brisbane.

Mr. Day Tours (/FAX 3289 8364 E-MAIL mrdaytou @powerup.com.au organizes full- and half-day tours of Brisbane and its surroundings. They offer a lovely afternoon mountain-and-rainforest drive, sharing their wealth of knowledge with small groups only.

THE GOLD COAST

Australia's answer to Miami begins an hour's drive south of Brisbane along the Pacific Highway. The Gold Coast is Australia's most famous playground, providing visitors with an abundance of sun, surf and sand. This glitzy, brash and unashamedly hedonistic resort region caters to the wealthiest and the most pedestrian vacationer — and everyone in between.

For decades the Gold Coast has been colonized by southerners seeking escape from the rigors of winter, bringing an explosion of development along its magnificent beaches — some would say too much. The number of summer visitors attracted to this popular vacation destination exceeds the year-round population of Queensland, and the area's population is further boosted by retirees moving north in search of a permanent place in the sun.

GENERAL INFORMATION

The **Gold Coast Visitor and Convention Bureau** ((07) 5593 1199 is at 105 Upton Street, Bundall. There are also tourist information kiosks in Cavill Mall, Surfers Paradise, and Marine Parade, Tweed Heads.

E-mail Express ((07) 5539 9433, Shop 126, Ground floor, Paradise Centre, Surfers Paradise, offers **Internet** services.

The artificial lagoon in Brisbane's Southbank Center proves a popular spot to cool off.

WHAT TO SEE AND DO

Theme Parks

The Gold Coast has more major manmade attractions than any other tourist region in Australia.

Sea World ((07) 5588 2222, WEB SITE www.seaworld .com.au, The Spit, Main Beach, is three kilometers (two miles) north of Surfers Paradise. A monorail takes visitors around the park, which features dolphin shows, marine displays, and rides. It's open 9:30 AM to 5 PM daily. Admission is $50 for adults and $30 for children. As with Florida, the Gold Coast's consistently sunny weather and huge tourist flow made it the ideal location for **Warner Bros. Movie World** ((07) 5573 3999 WEB SITE www.movieworld.com.au, 16 km (10 miles) north-west of Surfers Paradise at Oxenford. Along with stunt shows and rides there are tours of special-effects studios and displays of movie paraphernalia ($50 adults, $31 children). Literally next door is **Wet 'n' Wild World** WEB SITE www.wetnwild .com.au, with a massive wave pool, water-slides from the friendly to the terrifying, and rides for all ages. They promise a "a whole world of splash-tacular fun and entertainment" ($28 adults, $19.50 children). **Dreamworld** ((07) 5588 1111 WEB SITE www.dreamworld.com.au, 17 km (10 miles) north of Surfers Paradise at Coomera, has more than 35 rides, shows and attractions including an IMAX cinema ($49.80 adults, $30.80). **Cable Ski World** ((07) 5537 6300 WEB SITE www.cableskiworld .com.au, Runaway Bay, is a massive complex of five freshwater lakes with Australia's highest bungee jump as well as cable water skiing, jet skiing, go-karting and lots more.

In all Gold Coast theme parks, children's prices refer to children up to 13 years of age.

Beaches

The Gold Coast boasts 42 km (26 miles) of golden, unpolluted beaches stretching from **Southport** in the north to **Coolangatta** in the south, with a lush subtropical backdrop of the hinterland, although this is sometimes obscured by the encroaching high-rise hotels. Some of the better surf beaches include **Main**, **Surfers**, **Mermaid**, **Miami**, **Burleigh Heads**, **Palm**, **Currumbin** and **Kirra**.

Wildlife Sanctuaries

Fleay's Fauna Reserve ((07) 5576 2411 WEB SITE www .env.qld.gov.au, West Burleigh Road, Burleigh Heads, has saltwater crocodiles, the only Lumholtz's tree kangaroo in captivity in the world, an exceptional nocturnal house filled with rarely-seen animals, and a four-kilometer (two-and-a-half-mile) walk through rainforest and mangroves. Another wild-life reserve well worth visiting is **Currumbin Sanctuary** ((07) 5534 1266 WEB SITE www.currumbin -sanctuary.org.au, 28 Tomewin Street, Currumbin

Beach, 19 km (12 miles) south of Surfers Paradise, where visitors can hand-feed the flock of cheeky wild lorikeets that frequent the park. Kangaroos, wallabies and other native animals wander freely around the reserve.

National Parks

Burleigh Heads National Park, a prominent head-land on the southern end of the Gold Coast, offers an extensive system of marked walks along easy tracks through the park's rainforest, as well as pandanus groves, tussock grassland, coastal heath, rocky foreshore, mangroves, creeks and ocean beaches. In wintertime, humpback whales can be seen off this stretch of the coast. For further information contact

the **Burleigh Heads Information Centre** ((07) 5535 3032, on the Gold Coast Highway.

Lamington National Park ((07) 4533 3584, 54 km (33 miles) southwest of Surfers Paradise, features wet eucalyptus and subtropical rainforests. See the park on foot by way of its 160 km (100 miles) of walking paths, taking time to visit some of its 500 waterfalls, picnic beside crystal clear streams, explore cliffs and fern-filled gullies and wonder at mountain lookouts with spectacular views.

Tamborine Mountain affords beautiful views on both sides of the ranges and has a number of rainforest areas with quiet streams and attractive waterfalls. From the ridge are clear views to both the west and the east. Of the many easy walking tracks within the seven national parks dotted around its slopes, one of the most delightful is the short track down to **Cedar Creek Falls**, which tumbles gently down into a gully in **Cedar Creek**

National Park. For maps and information drop in to the **North Tamborine Information Centre** ((07) 5545 1171, Doughty Park, North Tamborine.

Sun, wind, water and ice sculpted **Girraween National Park's** boulder-strewn hills and valleys from the ancient granite mass of the New England Tableland. Girraween means "place of flowers" in the local Aboriginal language, and in late winter and spring the bush provides a spectacular display of wildflowers. Girraween's eucalyptus forest and granite heaths are home to many species of birds including the relatively uncommon turquoise parrot and the attractive diamond firetail. Hike past **Bald Rock Creek** to **Granite Arch**, a natural granite formation where one huge boulder

several scenic cruises around the islands and estuaries of the northern Gold Coast, with options such as paraflying and seaplane flights. One tour cruises upriver into the Hinterland for a real Aussie experience.

WHERE TO STAY

Although they may lack character, the ocean views from the upper floors of high-rise hotels and apartments along the Gold Coast add an element of hedonism. Outside school vacation periods there is keen competition among hotels: you should be able to pick up significant out-of-season discounts and package deals all along the Gold Coast.

is supported by two others which act as pillars. If it's warm enough take a dip in the rock pools. A little further on is the gravity-defying **Balancing Rock**, a granite monolith impossibly balanced on top of a peak overlooking the entire national park. A closer inspection reveals a remarkably small "foot" area, where the rock rests upon the ground. While the park is good for rock climbing, a few areas have climbing bans, so check first. For information contact the **park ranger** ((07) 4684 5157.

TOURS

Mountain Trek Adventures ((07) 5524 1090 WEB SITE www.bigvolcano.com.au, offers canal cruises, one-day tours of Lamington National Park, Tamborine Mountain Tours and night discovery tours.

Island Queen Showboat Cruises ((07) 5557 8800 WEB SITE www.islandqueen.com.au has

In Surfers Paradise, the luxurious **ANA Hotel** ((07) 5579 1000 TOLL-FREE (1800) 074 440 FAX (07) 5570 1260, 22 View Avenue, and **Ramada Hotel** ((07) 5579 3499 TOLL-FREE (1800) 074 317 WEB SITE www.ramada.com.au/reef, Gold Coast Highway, have enormous apartment-style rooms with spectacular ocean or hinterland views. Expensive to moderate rates apply depending on the season; both offer good package deals worth inquiring about.

Two reliable moderately-priced motels are **Coomera Motor Inn** ((07) 5573 2311, next to Dreamworld just 20 minutes from Surfers Paradise, and **Broadbeach Motor Inn Holiday Apartments** ((07) 5570 1899, 2651 Gold Coast Highway.

O'Rielly's Guesthouse ((07) 5544 0644, in the middle of the Lamington National Park, has been welcoming people since 1926. O'Rielly's offers

Despite miles of high-rise development, sand and surf dominates the shoreline at Surfers Paradise.

several very attractive package deals, some including all meals and tours.

If you decide to stay on the Gold Coast for a week or more, renting a self-contained apartment is an inexpensive option. Prices start at $200 a week for a two-bedroom unit. Reservations for apartments can be arranged through **Broadbeach Real Estate (** (07) 5539 0000 FAX (07) 5538 3280, 2703 Main Place, and **Coolangatta Realty (** (07) 5536 2000 FAX (07) 5536 1084, 72–74 Griffith Street. It is best to book well in advance.

WHERE TO EAT

Several of the larger hotels go for all-out gourmet dining. **Cristel's (** (07) 5592 9972, in the Park Royal Hotel, Surfers Paradise, is well known for terrific fresh seafood dishes and their distinctive salads. The Sheraton Mirage, **Horizons Restaurant (** (07) 5591 1488, Main Beach, has a very chic and formal dining room, serving modern Australian cuisine with a French edge. They have two tasting menus for those who can't make up their mind. Both restaurants are in the expensive category.

A Tavola Caffe Cuccina e Bar ((07) 5528 3777, 14 Tedder Avenue, Main Beach, does excellent homemade pastas and a hearty fish stew, and always includes a few vegetarian options. **Kairo Café (** (07) 5531 5868, corner of Surf Parade and Queensland Avenue, Broadbeach, has a creative modern Australian menu enhanced by daily blackboard specials, indoors or alfresco. Both are moderately priced.

For cheap eats 24 hours a day, seven days a week, try the **Beachside Café (** (07) 5592 2360, Elkhorn Avenue, Surfers Paradise, which has particularly good breakfast deals. There are also three inexpensive restaurants in **Imperial Plaza (** (07) 5538 3211, on the corner of Gold Coast Highway and Elkhorn Avenue, Surfers Paradise — one Chinese, one Japanese, and the third Mediterranean.

HOW TO GET THERE

There are two ports of entry for domestic flights to the Gold Coast: Coolangatta Airport and Brisbane Domestic Airport. Ansett and Qantas have daily services into both.

It's approximately a one-hour drive from Brisbane city to Surfers Paradise — the Gold Coast Highway branches off the Pacific Highway at Gaven. Regular interstate coach services with Greyhound Pioneer and McCafferty's stop at the Surfers Paradise Bus Station and Brisbane City Transit Centre, and both Sunbus and Airporter offer 24-hour door-to-door coach service from Brisbane to the Gold Coast's major hotels and resorts.

An electric train operates between Brisbane and Helensvale. For details and reservations contact **Queensland Rail Reservations Centre (** 132 232, or **(** (07) 3235 1122.

> ## MATILDA HIGHWAY AND OUTBACK QUEENSLAND

Cutting through the outback, the Matilda Highway runs 1,800 km (1,118 miles) from the New South Wales border north of Bourke to Karumba on the Gulf of Carpentaria. This is the land of weather-beaten shearers and stockmen, of stations — ranches — the size of Kentucky, and the birthplace of Australia's unofficial national anthem, Banjo Patterson's "Waltzing Matilda." When Patterson writes "I love a sunburnt country, a land of sweeping plains, of rugged mountain ranges, of draughts and flooding rains," this is the Australia he means: a land "where churches are few, and men of religion are scanty."

Three roads make up the Matilda Highway. The **Mitchell Highway** takes you from Barringun in New South Wales to Augathella; from there to Cloncurry you're on the Landsborough Highway; the last stretch to **Normanton** and **Karumba** is part of the Bourke Developmental Highway. From Normanton, the Bourke Developmental Highway cuts east across the Atherton Tableland to join the Kennedy Highway, 270 km (165 miles) southwest of Cairns.

You can join the highway from Brisbane, Rockhampton or Townsville, or from the Northern Territory through the ming town of **Mount Isa**. But wherever you are on the highway, you're literally miles from anywhere. This is a trip for those with plenty of time and a love of the open road. You don't need a four-wheel drive for the trip — the road is paved for its entire length — but I'd definitely recommend a reliable vehicle with air-conditioning. And always carry plenty of water.

If you're thinking of driving this hinterland route, it's a good idea to discuss your plans with the knowledgeable people at the **Royal Automobile Club of Queensland (RACQ) (** (07) 3361 2444, FAX (07) 3252 3587 261 Queen Street, Brisbane. The **Australian Automobile Association's (AAA)** WEB SITE www.aaa.asn.au has a lot of information on this and other outback routes. For more on outback driving see DRIVING HAZARDS, page 322 in TRAVELERS TIPS.

In the heart of the Gulf Country is one of the most curious train tracks in the world. It leads nowhere and serves no practical purpose. Starting at **Normanton**, the *Gulflander* winds 152 km (94 miles) inland to **Croydon**, once a gold mining town. It is a leisurely journey, and unscheduled stops are not because of mechanical breakdowns but rather the driver's desire to show his passengers something of interest near the track. The train leaves Normanton on Wednesday and returns from Croydon on Thursday. Reservations can be made at Normanton Station **(** (07) 4745 1391, or at the **QR Travel Centre (** (07) 4052 6249, in Cairns. In 1993 the Queensland government tried to close down the *Gulflander* but decided otherwise in the face of the ensuing public outcry.

SUNSHINE COAST

The Sunshine Coast, which begins an hour north of Brisbane, has several pleasant resort towns, a string of beautiful beaches and rocky headlands, a fertile hinterland, and a free-and-easy charm that's far less commercialized than the Gold Coast. This is an area of great natural beauty, from the Glass House Mountains rising dramatically from emerald-green-cloaked valleys to magnificent coastal scenery and good surf breaks. Noosa is the

Pumistone Passage. In town there's an impressive replica of Captain Cook's HM *Endeavour*, (two-thirds the size of the original) at 3 Landsborough Parade, open daily from 9 AM to 4:30 PM.

Caloundra is also a good base to visit the mysterious **Glass House Mountains** and the **Blackall Range**. Steeped in Kabi Aboriginal folklore — for whom the mountains are petrified forms of a family fleeing the incoming tide — the Glass House Mountains are a series of spectacular volcanic plugs rising dramatically from the coastal plain. Popular with rock climbers, professional and novice alike, they offer an interesting inland detour. To get there take Route 24 west (Landsborough exit) off the Bruce Highway and follow the well posted signs. If you

most fashionable resort on Queensland's coast, its perfect beaches complemented by a series of coastal parks and waterways waiting to be explored.

GENERAL INFORMATION

Tourism Noosa Incorporated ((07) 5447 4988 is on Hastings Street, Noosa; **Caloundra Tourist Information** ((07) 5491 0202 is at 7 Caloundra Road, Caloundra; and the **Maroochy Tourist Information Centre** ((07) 5479 1566 is on the corner of Aerodome Road and Sixth Avenue, Maroochydore.

WHAT TO SEE AND DO

Caloundra
The first port north of Brisbane, Caloundra is an excellent place for well-protected sailing, windsurfing, fishing and swimming on the blue waters of the

happen along the **Mike Moss Tea House** it's worth a stop to chat with Mike for local tips, passionate political discussions and tasty homemade treats. For outstanding views of the coast continue through Landsborough and take the Maleny Road to the southern edge of the Blackall range. **Howells Knob** near Reesville has an outstanding 360-degree view of the mountains and valleys.

Maroochydore
Heading back east towards the coast through Nambour, where it would be difficult to miss the domineering "**Big Pineapple**" ((07) 5442 1333 — which houses agricultural-themed exhibits, games and rides. Continue east to reach Maroochydore, the largest beach resort and business center of the Sunshine Coast, with some beautiful beaches.

Sunshine Coast lifeguards demonstrate their rescue skills, as part of the Surf Carnival.

Excellent fishing in the **Maroochy River** also attracts many visitors to this town. **Sunshine Coast Eco-Tours (** (07) 5476 5745 WEB SITE www.cruise maroochyeco.com.au has several interesting nature-based tours of the region, highlighting the environment, Aboriginal culture and local history.

Noosa

Further north is the relaxing, stylish town of Noosa, which makes a pleasant base to explore the Sunshine Coast. With a brilliant conservation policy which dictates that no building shall be higher than the tree-line, Noosa has fortunately been spared the towers of hotels that dominate other regions. Noosa is actually a series of small linked centers incorporating Sunshine Beach, Noosa Junction, Noosa Heads, and Noosaville. While it has always been popular for surfers, these days Noosa also caters to an upmarket crowd of travelers. There are plenty of rental services for anglers, divers and surfers; information is available from the tourist information office and in almost every hotel or guesthouse. Surf skis and catamarans are rented out on Main Beach, while other centers rent jet skis, canoes and dinghies. For those who don't suffer vertigo, paraflying allows great views of the region. Call **(** (07) 5449 9639 for details or just head down to Main Beach, Noosa, where they take off throughout the day, seven days a week.

Noosa Heads is the most popular shopping and eating area, with an impressive array of high-standard, and not cheap, open-air sidewalk restaurants, cafés and boutiques along Hastings Street (the main drag). The warm night air keeps the streets alive with people until late, making for interesting sidewalk entertainment. Noosa Heads attracts a fairly ritzy crowd, but there's ample accommodation and eateries for all tastes and budgets here, or in any of the satellite centers close by.

The small but lovely **Noosa National Park** extends for about two kilometers (one mile) in each direction from the headland and has fine walks around a dramatic rocky coastline dotted with sheltered beaches and coves. Enter the park at the northeast end of Hastings Street. A path leads along the cliffs to **Granite Bay** with its pebble beach and the popular nudist beach at **Alexandria Bay**. A series of tracks through the national park alternate between tranquil rainforest, open forest, wallum headlands, scrubland and grasslands, where birds and small marsupials find refuge in the native flora. **Clip Clop Treks (** (07) 5449 1254, on Lake Weyba, just south of Noosa, organizes short and long horseback riding and camping trips along lakes and beaches and into the wilderness areas surrounding Noosa.

Noosa River begins at Cooloola, making its way through the **Cooloola National Park** and past **Kinaba National Park**. The still, dark upper waters create magnificent reflections as the river flows past dense banks lined with sedges. Expect to see pelicans, cormorants, ibises, blue cranes and osprey eagles among the varied bird life. The river then enters **Lake Coothharaba** which is perfect for sailing and windsurfing. Meandering south, it cuts a channel through **Lake Cooroibah**, then flows on to **Tewantin**. There's a car-ferry at Tewantin to cross the river. A gravel road leads to **Teewah Beach**, famed for its colored sands. The sandy cliffs, which reach 200 m (656 ft) in height, are made up of as many as 72 different colored sands, produced by combinations of iron oxide and leached vegetable dyes. An Aboriginal legend attributes their formation to the destruction of a rainbow by a huge boomerang. Noosa River continues past **Lake Doonella**, then through Noosaville and Noosa, where it is joined by Weyba Creek and eventually flows out into Laguna Bay by Noosa's Main Beach. The **Everglades Water Bus Co. (** (07) 5447 1838 TOLL-FREE (1800) 688 045 has four-, six- and eight-hour all-inclusive cruises taking in all the sights along the river, combined with inland four-wheel drive on the eight-hour tour. **Total Adventures (** (07) 5474 0177 organizes trips for those interested in canoeing, kayaking, abseiling and mountain biking.

If you're around on a Saturday, **Eumundi's market** is perhaps the best in Queensland. Besides a huge variety of stalls selling local crafts and produce, there are rides for the kids and usually some live entertainment. The tiny subtropical rainforest village retains century-old timber houses and public buildings, lovingly restored and painted. Practically everyone from the surrounding region is here so don't miss out. If getting there is a problem call **Henry's (** (07) 5474 0199, a shuttle service that picks up passengers from their hotels.

WHERE TO STAY

Prices change dramatically in Noosa from low to high season — by as much as 100% between December and January. Be sure to verify current prices before booking.

The luxury hotels are along Hastings Street facing Laguna Bay. Two beautiful resorts on this strip are **Sheraton Noosa (** (07) 5449 4888 E-MAIL noosa _reservations@sheraton.com and **Netanya Noosa (** (07) 5447 4722 WEB SITE www.netanyanoosa.com.au. Both offer international-standard accommodation and direct access to the beach.

Moderately priced accommodation is available in Noosaville at **Sandy Beach Resort (** (07) 5474 0044 WEB SITE www.sandybeachresort.com.au, 173-175 Gympie Terrace, but minimum stays may apply. If you are willing to travel five kilometers (three miles), Noosaville has inexpensive motel accommodation at **Palm Tree Lodge (** (07) 5449 7311, 233 Gympie Terrace, and **Noosa Gardens Riverside Resort (** (07) 5449 9800, 261 Weyba Road. At the end of Hastings Street is the inexpensive **Noosa Tewantin Caravan Park (** (07) 5449 8060

FAX (07) 5474 1171, which has powered camping spots and on-site vans.

The year-round good weather makes Queensland a nudist's Nirvana, and there are numerous secluded resorts from which to choose. **Pacific Sun Friends (** (07) 5498 8333 WEB SITE www.nha.com.au, Quinn Road, Donnybrook, close to the Sunshine Coast, has excellent facilities, including a swimming pool, communal kitchen and recreation pavilion. The resort incorporates bush trails for walking and a tidal stream for swimming and boat trips.

WHERE TO EAT

Noosa has the best selection of restaurants and cafés on the coast. Choosing is difficult, and the traditional way to select one is to allow an hour or so to wander the length of Hastings Street, checking out the menus and stopping for the occasional coffee or cold drink. The last time I was in Noosa the choice was so difficult and took so long, suddenly all were either full or the kitchen had just closed (around 10 PM). I ended up at the spacious and inexpensive **Aromas Café (** (07) 5474 9788, Hastings Street, and thoroughly enjoyed an assortment from their vast evening tapas selection. The wine list is limited but well chosen. Aromas also does incredible breakfasts, great salads and gourmet sandwiches, and serves the best teas and coffee in town. Open 7 AM to midnight, seven days. At the popular **Eduardo's on the Beach (** (07) 5447 5875, 25 Hastings Street, we enjoyed an excellent seafood curry and grilled reef fish (expensive). Definitely worth popping in earlier to book a table on the beachfront deck. Open seven days for breakfast, lunch and dinner. **Berardo's Restaurant (** (07) 5447 5666, 50 Hastings Street, does excellent seafood (expensive). Particularly good are the linguini with mud crab and the roast fillet of swordfish. They also serve choice beef, lamb and chicken and have good vegetarian alternatives.

In Maroochydore, the **Grapevine (** (07) 5443 1579, 55 The Esplanade, has an excellent international menu with an over-the-top seafood platter for two. Their two-course dinner menu for $22 is great value, and there are stunning views from the verandah.

HOW TO GET THERE

Maroochy Airport, across the Maroochy River from Maroochydore, is served by daily Qantas and Ansett flights from Brisbane, Sydney and Melbourne. There are regular shuttle buses into Noosa, a half-hour drive from the airport.

By bus, **Suncoast Pacific (** (07) 5443 1011 FAX (07) 5443 9731 runs five daily services from Brisbane's Roma Street **Transit Centre (** (07) 3236 1901 along the Sunshine Coast to Noosa Heads, approximately a three-hour trip. They also pick up travelers from

Brisbane's domestic and international airports. **Tewantin Buses (** (07) 5449 7422 run a regular service between Tewantin and Noosa Heads, and down to Maroochydore.

The Sunshine Coast is about a 60-minute drive along an excellent divided highway, the Bruce Highway, part of National Route 1. Noosa is another 30 minutes along at the northern end of the coastline.

FRASER ISLAND AND HERVEY BAY

World Heritage-listed Fraser Island is where the surf stops and the reef begins. With access to the island and ample activities of its own, Hervey Bay is becoming one of the fastest-growing tourist destinations in Queensland. The ideal conditions allow for year-round beach activities. In addition to swimming or sailing, more adventurous options include water skiing, jet skiing, sea kayaking, parasailing, diving and combined scenic flight/sky dive.

The coastal waters are home to turtles, dolphins and dugongs, and between August and October the magnificent humpback whale can be spotted resting and giving birth to calves here. Calves are three and a half meters (11.5 ft) long at birth; to feed her calf a mother produces up to 600 liters (132 gallons) of milk every day.

GENERAL INFORMATION

Hervey Bay Tourist & Visitors Centre ((07) 4124 4050, 63 Old Maryborough Road, Pialba, and **Hervey Bay-Fraser Island Visitors Centre (** (07) 4124 8741, Maryborough Road, Hervey Bay, can supply maps and general information and book whale-watching tours, transport to Fraser Island, and accommodation. **Safari Four-Wheel Drive (** (07) 4124 4244 TOLL-FREE (1800) 689 819, 102 Boat Harbour Drive, Pialba, has a wide range of fully-equipped vehicles for rent for self-drive touring of Fraser Island. Four-wheel-drive rental is popular, but Fraser Island's sands can be a challenge to even the most experienced driver. If you're considering this option, discuss it through with the rental company or the tourism office. **Fraser Coast Holiday Centre (** (07) 4124 9685, 463 The Esplanade, Hervey Bay, can arrange bookings for eco-tours and accommodation on Fraser Island and in Hervey Bay.

WHAT TO SEE AND DO

Fraser Island
Fraser Island takes its name from Eliza Fraser, who, with her husband Captain Fraser and his crew, was shipwrecked here in 1836. Captured by Aborigines, the survivors were used as slaves. Only Eliza got away, escaping after three weeks in captivity. Her ordeal unhinged her so gravely that she was eventually committed to a lunatic asylum.

Fraser Island is the largest sand island in the world. At 124 km (77 miles) long and covering 163,000 ha (400,000 acres), the island comprises long surf beaches of giant colored dunes (some towering to 240 m or 790 ft), cliffs and gorges, freshwater lakes, extensive mangrove and thick rainforest. Over 230 species of birds live on the beaches and in the forests, and the island's isolation from the mainland has preserved the purity of the dingo population, who are present here in greater numbers than anywhere else in the country. The island's impressive brumbie (wild horse) herds run freely around too. The **Great Sandy National Park** preserves the northern part of the island, while the 110-km (70-mile) ocean beach is the main freeway

the bay are a strip of loosely connected villages including Gatakers Bay, Urangan, Torquay, Scarness, Pialba, Burrum Heads and Point Vernon, mostly comprising small shopping centers and a run of holiday accommodation of all types. Hervey Bay's great attraction lies in the almost year-round perfect weather and the variety of activities it caters to, including whale spotting, water skiing, scuba diving, and excellent fishing. **Torquay Beach Hire** ((07) 4125 5528 rents surf skis, sailboards and organize water skiing and more. **Divers Mecca** ((07) 4125 1626 TOLL-FREE (1800) 687 178 runs an excellent dive course for only $149 that includes four boat dives, with two of them around ship wrecks.

and the runway for regular tourist flights. Places of note include **Rainbow Gorge**, the splendid inland lakes **Wabby** and **Mackenzie**, the **Cathedrals Sandcliffs**, the **Maneno Shipwreck**, the **Satinay Rainforest** at Central Station, and the rare Angiopteris ferns in **Woongoolbver Creek**. These huge ferns belong to a type of ancient plant present on earth at the time of the dinosaurs and existing only as fossils outside of Queensland.

With so much to see and do organize at least an overnight stay on Fraser Island. **Fraser Island Top Tours** ((07) 4125 3933 WEB SITE www.fraserislandtours .com.au has $70 one-day and $165 two-day tours that include transfers, meals and accommodation.

Hervey Bay

On the coast opposite Fraser Island is Hervey (pronounced Harvey) Bay, a large area of protected water and a bustling city resort. Around

The most interesting time to be here is between August and mid-October, when humpback whales migrate from the south to warmer waters to mate and give birth. Hervey Bay is one of the best places in the country to see these great mammals and casual passers-by have even observed the birth of calves here. Due to its enormous popularity no fewer than 10 different companies operate boats out to the whales. One of the bigger operators is *Spirit of Hervey Bay* ((07) 4125 5131 TOLL-FREE (1800) 642 544, whose boat has underwater windows and a hydrophone so that you can hear the whales singing to each other.

Vic Hislop's White Death Shark Show ((07) 4128 6103, The Esplanade, Urangan, is a quirky tourist attraction: it displays a monstrous six-and-half-meter (22-ft) white pointer that Vic caught and details the challenge he went through to bring it in. **Neptune's Reefworld** ((07) 4128 9828, Dayman

Point, displays living coral, tropical fish, a shark pool and Basil the performing seal.

The one-kilometer-long (half-mile) pier at Urangan is a good fishing spot if you don't have a boat. It's the site of Hervey Bay's annual fishing festival in September.

WHERE TO STAY

One of the most congenial places to stay on Fraser Island is **Kingfisher Bay Resort and Village** ((07) 4120 3333 TOLL-FREE (1800) 072 555 FAX (07) 4127 9333, which has indulgent one-, two- and three-bedroom villas (moderate to expensive). They also offer guided walks and four-wheel-drive tours. For moderately priced accommodation on Fraser Island try **Happy Valley** ((07) 4127 9144, whose wonderful timber cottages are close to the beach, or **Eliza Sands** ((07) 4127 9132, with comfortable, self-contained flats. The **Eurong Beach Resort** ((07) 4127 9122 is a good, inexpensive accommodation option.

In Hervey Bay, **Great Sandy Straits Marina Resort** ((07) 4128 9999 WEB SITE www.greatsandy straits.com.au, Buccaneer Drive, has uninterrupted bay views from the large and comfortable rooms, at moderate to inexpensive prices. **Kondari Resort** ((07) 4128 9702, 49 Elizabeth Street, offers inexpensive motel rooms, moderate studio suites and self-contained lakeside villas.

The beachfront of Hervey Bay is lined with inexpensive camping and caravan grounds. Among them are **Fraser Lodge** ((07) 4125 1502 and **Shelley Beach** ((07) 4125 1105. No one is particularly better than the other, so contact the tourism center for a detailed list. For budget travelers there's the **Colonial Backpackers** ((07) 4125 1844 and **Koala Backpackers** ((07) 4125 3601.

The **Hervey Bay Accommodation Centre** ((07) 4124 2424, 139 Boat Harbour Drive, Hervey Bay, has numerous accommodation options on their books to suit all budgets.

HOW TO GET THERE

Driving to Hervey Bay take the Bruce Highway (National Route 1) north from Brisbane 269 km (167 miles) to Maryborough. Hervey Bay is 34 km (21 miles) northeast of Maryborough. **Suncoast Pacific** ((07) 5443 1011 FAX (07) 5443 9731 has daily bus departures from Brisbane's Roma Street Transit Centre ((07) 3236 1901 to Hervey Bay via the Sunshine Coast.

THE GREAT BARRIER REEF

Queensland's tropics begin at the Tropic of Capricorn, which crosses through Rockhampton. The Great Barrier Reef's southern tip is off the coast here, prevented from extending further south by

the drop in water temperature. From here the reef continues north for some 2,500 km (1,554 miles) north, ending in Torres Strait, just south of Papua New Guinea.

From Mission Beach to Cooktown the Great Barrier Reef moves close to the coast. Water depths are much shallower than further south and the reef can be easily and safely explored by even a first-time snorkeler. The water here is never too cold, but those who prefer to stay dry can opt for a tour in a glass-bottomed boat, often only a few feet above the profusion of variegated corals, with swarms of neon-colored fish and the odd turtle or giant ray gliding silently below. The options for day-trips, overnight trips or three- or four-day cruises to coral cays and the outer reef from Cairns or Port Douglas are endless, and most have a marine biologist on board to help visitors understand more about this beautiful marine environment. If you've ever considered scuba diving, this is the place to do it; there's no shortage of qualified instructors.

CAPRICORN COAST

The waters of the Capricorn Coast are dotted with islands and coral cays, home to a variety of exotic marine and bird life. Several islands are national parks with nothing more than basic campgrounds for adventurers, while others are owned by plush resorts, offering an enormous range of land and water activities.

WHAT TO SEE AND DO

Bundaberg

Bundaberg on the Burnett River is one of the few sugar towns that all Australians have heard of, not because of the sugar directly, but through another sugarcane product: Bundaberg Rum, a hearty dark spirit from a distillery attached to one of the town's five sugar mills. A visit to Bundaberg would not be complete without a stop at the **Rum Distillery** ((07) 4152 4077, Avenue Street. Here visitors follow the processing operation of the renowned rum. This tour is informative but hazardous as it ends with a sampling of the distillery's product. There are guided tours on the hour from 10 AM to 3 PM weekdays and 10 AM to 1 PM on weekends; $5.

Fourteen kilometers (nine miles) northeast of Bundaberg is **Mon Repos Beach**, Australia's largest, most accessible turtle rookery, where many species of turtles come ashore from November to February to lay their eggs. At the **Mon Repos Turtle Rookery**, loggerhead, green, leatherback and flatback turtles can be seen making their way up the beach one hour before high tide or up to two hours afterwards, laying their eggs at the top of

One of the many island resorts dotted along the Great Barrier Reef coastline.

the beach on a grass-covered bank. From January to the end of March you can observe the hatchlings emerging from their eggs. Contact the **Queensland National Parks and Wildlife Service (QNPW)** ((07) 4159 1652, which is open daily from 7 PM to 6 AM during the season — as the best time to see the turtles laying is around midnight.

Seventeen Seventy and Agnes Waters
Captain James Cook and his party first stepped on mainland Queensland here in 1770 — his second landing on Australian soil. This historic occasion is commemorated by the **Captain Cook Memorial** at nearby **Round Hill Head** in the laid-back seaside town of (you guessed it) Seventeen Seventy. There are pleasant beaches to be found, good fishing spots and living reef to explore. Most cruise, tour and rental agencies for the region are located here. **1770 Adventure Tours** ((07) 4974 9470 has half-day, full-day, and overnight guided tours which explore the area around Seventeen Seventy and Eurimbula National Park. **Downrite Adventures** ((07) 4974 9539 take diving and snorkeling excursions and fishing charters. They will also organize camping transfers to Lady Musgrave Island.

Agnes Waters is just a little south and like Seventeen Seventy and has not been commercialized yet — but is becoming increasingly popular. Nearby are **Deepwater National Park** and **Eurimbula National Park**, covered in rainforest, native shrubs, open heathland, swamplands, and plenty of native animals and bird life. There are some lovely secluded beaches here, safe for swimming and good for beach and rock-fishing. A camping permit is required for the parks and is available from the **Seventeen Seventy National Parks Office** ((07) 4974 9350. The **Discovery Centre** ((07) 4974 7002, in the Endeavour Plaza, Agnes Waters, is the local visitor information bureau and can assist with accommodation, tour bookings and other local information.

Access is via Miriam Vale on the Bruce Highway, 63 km (39 miles) southwest of Seventeen Seventy. The road from here takes you straight to Agnes Waters and on to Seventeen Seventy.

Lady Elliott Island and Lady Musgrave Island
The "Two Ladies of the Reef," Lady Elliot Island and Lady Musgrave Island (both small coral cays) lie 50 km (31 miles) northeast of Seventeen Seventy and are ideal straight-off-the-beach diving and snorkeling spots. There's a good chance of seeing the big but harmless manta ray, as well as turtles, giant clams, colorful parrot-fish and ship wrecks. For those who don't snorkel, the resort provides suitable footwear for reef walking. At low tide, starfish, coral and clams become exposed. Both of these islands are also popular with bird watchers who observe terns, egrets, plovers and gulls in their natural habitat. The uninhabited Lady Musgrave

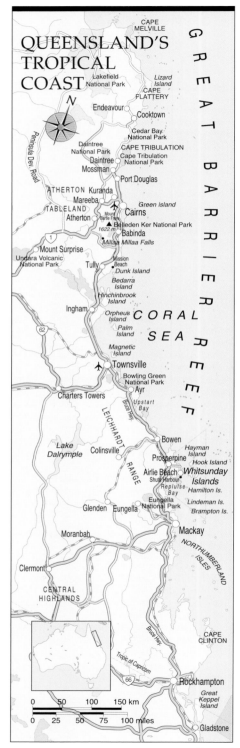

Island has a massive tropical lagoon that is a haven for marine life. You can stay here but the island only supports completely self sufficient camping (bring your own drinking water) for up to 50 people, so be prepared to rough it.

Lady Elliot Resort ((07) 4156 4444 TOLL-FREE (1800) 072 200 WEB SITE www.ladyelliot.com.au is the only accommodation here. It has moderately priced tent cabins and reef units, as well as expensive suites. Costs include breakfast and dinner. Whitaker Air Charters offer day-trips to Lady Elliot from Bundaberg and Hervey Bay for $130, which includes lunch and snorkeling gear. Book flights through **Sunstate Travel** ((07) 4152 2322. Day cruises depart from Bundaberg Harbour Monday to Thursday and Saturdays at 8:30 AM aboard the *MV Lady Musgrave* and the *MV Spirit of Musgrave* and cost $125 for adults and $63 for children plus a $4 environmental management charge. For bookings call ((07) 4159 4519 TOLL-FREE (1800) 072 110 or browse their WEB SITE www.lmcruises.com.au.

Heron Island

Tiny Heron Island, 72 km (45 miles) northeast of Gladstone, is also a coral cay, with the wonders of the reef lying just off its beaches, making it a Mecca for divers. From December to April thousands of turtles use Heron Island as a breeding ground and in the winter months large numbers of whales can be seen passing through the channel between the cay and Wisteria reef. The **Heron Island Resort** (132 469 E-MAIL resorts_reservations @poaustralia.com caters to a maximum of 300 people, starting at $150 a person including meals, but you can tack on another $150 for the return catamaran trip from Gladstone, as there are no day-trippers allowed to Heron.

Rockhampton

Rockhampton is the Capricorn region's main town and is a good place to rest up for the next leg of the journey. A laid-back and welcoming town, the historic **Criterion Hotel** ((07) 4922 1225 E-MAIL cri@cyberinternet.com.au, 150 Quay Street, a Rockhampton landmark since 1858, makes Rockhampton a good place for an overnight stay. It was a rough and rollicking frontier tavern until 1889, when the Parker family decided to build a genteel hotel for people of class. Many famous people have passed through its elegant doors since, including General MacArthur, and today it retains all its original charm. Here you can eat one of the best steaks in Australia and afterwards retire to one of their comfortable terrace rooms, where a basic double costs only $46 a night.

With its lovely orchid house and exotic zoo, Rockhampton's century-old **Botanic Gardens** makes an ideal place for a barbecue. Nearby, the **Mount Archer Lookouts** and **Park** offer panoramic views across the surrounding countryside. If the

heat gets to you, go underground at **Olsen's Capricorn Caverns** ((07) 4934 2883, 23 km (14 miles) north of Rockhampton. Walks within the cave system range from easy to adventure caving, and you may even spot a rare ghost bat. Only seven kilometers (four miles) north, the **Dreamtime Cultural Center** ((07) 4936 1655 displays and sells Aboriginal and Torres Straight Islander art works. Open 10 AM to 3:30 PM.

Great Keppel Island

Forty-two kilometers (26 miles) northeast of Rockhampton is the sleepy seaside town of Yeppoon, the access point for Great Keppel Island (although boats for Great Keppel actually leave from Rosslyn Harbour, seven kilometers, or four miles, south of Yeppoon). Although Great Keppel Island is very popular, it is still possible to find deserted beaches with the aid of a dinghy, or by walking through the island's National Park. A lot of activity centers on the island's resort and shops, where watersports facilities and the swimming pool are available to both guests and day-trippers. The island is not on the reef, but there are regular boat trips to it for snorkelers and scuba-divers.

Keppel Tourist Services ((07) 4933 6744 TOLL-FREE (1800) 356 744 can book resorts and tours on the island. They also run tours to Middle Island, one and a half kilometers (one mile) from Great Keppel, where an **Underwater Observatory** gives excellent coral viewing through panoramic windows.

Great Keppel Island Resort ((07) 4125 6966 TOLL-FREE (1800) 245 658 WEB SITE www.gkeppel .com.au has four styles of accommodation and often offers attractive package deals. **Keppel Haven** ((07) 4933 6744 provides inexpensive accommodation, but is a bit of a family place.

WHITSUNDAY COAST

The 74 Whitsunday Islands are in fact the tips of a long-submerged mountain range, where extensive growths of fringing reefs have formed in the shallower waters. Named by Captain Cook on Whit Sunday, 1770, the beautiful islands now boast a number of expensive resorts, attracting visitors as much for the idyllic tropical environment as for the reef and other natural attractions. Sailing these waters on either an organized cruise or a skippered or bare-boat charter is the ultimate getaway holiday. Most of the islands have safe coves to moor in, and evenings can be spent on the boat, on your own private beach or cove, or visiting one of the many restaurants or poolside bars on the resort islands.

MACKAY AND EUNGELLA NATIONAL PARK

Lying roughly halfway between Brisbane and Cairns, the Mackay district combines stunning rainforest, lush mountain gorges and rich fertile plains.

Mackay itself is a major launching point for the reef and its islands, although otherwise it's not particularly interesting to the visitor. This is Queensland's largest sugar-producing region, and what appears to be endlessly long cane trains frequently clatter along the old lines.

What to See and Do

Sugarcane has been cultivated in the surrounding fields since 1885, and today Mackay produces a third of Australia's total production. At **Poistone Cane Farm** ((07) 4959 7359, Homebush Walkerstone Road, 20 km (12.5 miles) inland from Mackay, visitors can see every stage of sugar production and finish the day with a cool drink of sugarcane juice. Back in town, see the exquisite blooms of orchids in the conservatory at **Queens Park**, which also showcases ferns and colorful tropical flowers. Mackay is doing its best to restore what is left of its historical buildings, and along with attractive streets, community street art makes it quite an appealing place to rest and have a bite to eat, while waiting for a boat to the islands.

Eungella (Aboriginal for "land of clouds") **National Park**, 95 km (59 miles) west of Mackay, is Queensland's largest national park, and is a highly recommendable inland day-trip. Waterfalls flow into crystal clear streams and natural waterholes, making a pleasant respite from the tropical heat. **Broken River** is one of the few places where you are almost guaranteed to see a platypus in its natural habitat. Flora varies from grassy eucalyptus woodland to tropical rainforest with exceptional fern growth. The two-and-half-kilometer (one-and-a-half-mile) track along the gorge to the **Wheel of Fire Falls** and swimming hole is one of the most rewarding wilderness tracks I've taken. The diverse wildlife includes the leaf tailed gecko, the rare gastro brooding frog, turtles, possums, kingfishers, the stunning Ulysses butterfly, and of course the endearing (but shy) platypus. The 16-hour trek to **Mount Dalrymple** (1,280 m or 4,200 ft) and **Massy Gorge** is rewarded with exceptional coastal views. **Mackay Tourism and Development Bureau** ((07) 4952 2677, 320 Neebo Road, Mackay, can organize tours and accommodation in the region.

Brampton and Carlisle Islands

Surrounded by coral reefs, these two mountainous islands, 32 km (20 miles) from Mackay, are both national parks and wildlife sanctuaries, with lush forests, palm trees and fine white beaches. The islands are connected by a sandbank that can be crossed at low tide — there are some excellent coral reefs to explore just off this passage. Graded trails ramble through forests to secluded bays and the islands' interior heights. Carlisle has the highest peak, **Mount Skiddaw** at 389 m (1,276 ft), while Brampton's **Brampton Peak** measures only 219 m

(719 ft). If you're walking these tracks, look out for ancient cycad palms and mounds of rotting leaves built by the scrub fowl to incubate their eggs.

The luxury price-tag of the **Brampton Island Resort**, operated by the P&O group ((02) 9299 2477 (Sydney office) TOLL-FREE (1800) 737 678 WEB SITE www.poresorts.com.au, includes all meals and a host of activities. Brampton island doesn't cater to day guests, and its intimate resort is a perfect getaway for romantic couples. Carlisle Island is uninhabited and really only suitable for the adventurous camper.

Qantas and Ansett have daily flights from all major Australian capital cities to Mackay or Hamilton Island. Brampton Island Resort guests are then shuttled to meet their boat to the island. Boats to Carlisle Island leave from the Mackay marina (not Tuesdays or Wednesdays).

Coastal waters north of Great Keppel Island are visited by **box jellyfish** from late November to March. Swimming is only advisable on beaches protected by "stinger nets." Swimming on the reef and islands is generally safe, but ask the locals first.

How to Get There

Greyhound Pioneer and McCafferty's coaches stop at Mackay Bus Terminal ((07) 4951 3088 in Milton Street on their Brisbane to Cairns routes — fares are around $100 from Brisbane, $85 from Cairns. Both the *Sunlander* and the *Queenslander* stop here too, although they're double the price of the bus. Mackay Airport has regular flights from major Queensland towns, connecting at Brisbane with interstate flights.

AIRLIE BEACH

Walking down the esplanade of Airlie Beach you will hear conversations being spoken in half a dozen European languages. This small but lively place, internationally known as a backpackers town and an inexpensive base to island hop, also offers a broad range of accommodation and places to eat. It's a good place to learn to dive or to charter a yacht and take up sailing.

General Information

Tourist information on the islands can be obtained at Airlie Beach from **Whitsunday Visitor and Convention Bureau** ((07) 4946 6673 WEB SITE www.whitsundayinformation.com.au, at the intersection of Shute Harbour and Mandalay roads; open weekdays only. There are several **Internet** cafés in Airlie Beach. The one with the best services and prices is Airlie Net Café ((07) 49464022, Shop 5 Beach Plaza, The Esplanade.

What to See and Do

Innumerable shops, eating places, pubs and bars only a few meters from the beach keep the place buzzing, but Airlie Beach exists primarily as a jumping-off point for visitors to the Whitsunday Islands. Most of the tour operators and travel agents are based here.

Only eight kilometers (five miles) west of town, the **Billabong Wildlife Sanctuary** ((07) 4778 8344 WEB SITE www.billabongsanctuary.com.au is home to an enormous variety of Australian fauna in fastidiously reproduced habitats. There is also a swimming pool with water slides and interactive displays for the kids. Open daily from 8 AM to 5 PM.

To the south of Airlie Beach is the rugged **Conway Range National Park**, with some fine nature walks through the rainforest. **Mount Roper Lookout**, a two-and-a-half-kilometer (one-and-a-

had a taste of scuba you'll wonder why you hadn't done it sooner. **Fantasea Cruises** ((07) 4946 5111 TOLL-FREE (1800) 650 851 WEB SITE www.fantasea .com.au is the largest operator in the Whitsundays, with a fleet of air-conditioned, high-speed catamarans crisscrossing the reef and islands. They have some of the best deals for combined reef/diving tours. They also do eco-tours and whale-watching trips (July to September). Another reputable company is **Whitsunday All Over Cruises** ((07) 4946 9499 WEB SITE www.whitsundayallover.com.au, with some great reef snorkeling/dive package deals; the company also runs the popular Yellow Sub, with panoramic underwater windows in its hull for those who don't want to get wet.

half-mile) walk from the car park, has great views across to the Whitsunday Passage and islands. A short drive takes you to the beautiful **Cedar Creek Falls**, which tumble 12 m (39 ft) among ferns and vines into a stream that is ideal for swimming.

Most tour boats and water taxis to the islands leave from Shute Harbour, eight kilometers (five miles) east of Airlie Beach, or from the Abel Point Marina, one kilometer (half a mile) west. A frequent shuttle bus from Airlie Beach meets the boats.

Scuba Diving and Reef Trips

A trip to the Whitsundays would not be complete without at least one diving or snorkeling trip to the reef. People of all ages try scuba for the first time here. Most of the resorts on the islands offer scuba lessons and reef trips to their guests, non-guests are better off organizing a trip through one of the many operators in Airlie Beach. Once you've

Sailing

If you're not in any hurry then sailing is the best way to get around the Whitsundays. Conditions are nearly always perfect. At only $77 including lunch for a day sailing and snorkeling the reef, Australia's fastest commercial sailing catamaran, *On the Edge* with **Prosail** ((07) 4946 5433 FAX (07) 4948 8609 WEB SITE www.prosail.com.au represents great value (scuba diving is a $48 optional extra). The crew are loads of fun and well informed, and when the wind picks she really moves. Prosail operate quite a few yachts, some taking guests on extended cruises of up to six nights.

You don't have to have a permit or any previous experience to sail the Whitsundays; with a little instruction many people take off on their

Hamilton Island is the biggest resort in the Whitsundays. The center swimming pool features an island cocktail bar.

own for the experience of a lifetime. **Australian Bareboat Charters** ((07) 4946 9381 FAX (07) 4946 9220 WEB SITE www.ozemail.com.au/~bareboat has a variety of fully equipped skipper-yourself yachts and cruisers. Training is given and they offer guides for the first few days if required. They will even stock up the boat with gourmet provisions and can supply diving gear and other water-sport accessories. Bare-boat prices are seasonal and range between $350 and $650 per night, depending on the vessel; boats are normally rented for a minimum of five days.

If you would prefer to be skippered around the islands, **Queensland Yacht Charters** ((07) 4946 7400 TOLL-FREE (1800) 075 013 WEB SITE www.yacht charters.com.au provides fully-crewed yachts, catamarans and cruisers anywhere within the Whitsunday Islands.

Where to Stay

Laguna Quays Resort ((07) 4947 7777 TOLL-FREE (1800) 812 626 WEB SITE www.lagunaquays.com.au, Kanapipi Springs Road, 20 minutes south of Proserpine on the Whitsunday coast, is set in natural bush. Accommodation ranges from deluxe lodge rooms to fully self-contained villas alongside the resort's golf course. All the facilities you could need are on hand, with starting prices in the expensive to luxury range. **Coral Sea Resort** ((07) 4946 6458 WEB SITE www.coralsearesort.com.au, 25 Oceanview Avenue, includes a gym, massage room, and pool and has stylish expensive and moderately-priced suites with Jacuzzis on private balconies overlooking the ocean.

Airlie Beach Hotel ((07) 4946 6233 WEB SITE www.airliebeachhotel.com.au, corner of the Esplanade and Coconut Grove, offers moderately priced rooms with beach views. Other good choices in the moderate range include **Wanderers Retreat** ((07) 4946 6446 FAX (07) 4946 6761 E-MAIL cross@whitsunday .net.au, Shute Harbour Road, set within a beautiful tropical garden, and **Club Crocodile** ((07) 4946 7155 FAX (07) 4946 6007 E-MAIL airliebeach @clubcroc.com.au, Shute Harbour Road, a relaxed and social place with nightly entertainment and good facilities, although it can be noisy at night.

There are numerous hostels in town for the budget traveler. One of the better ones is **Club 13 Begley Street** ((07) 4946 7376, 13 Begley Street, which has great bay views and is clean and modern. Some rooms even have a Jacuzzi.

How to Get There

Ansett and Qantas have daily flights into Proserpine from Brisbane, and flights six days a week from Adelaide, Rockhampton and Cairns. It takes about 22 hours by train from Brisbane to Proserpine, the nearest railway station to the Whitsundays. Greyhound Pioneer and McCafferty's coaches stop at Airlie Beach on their Brisbane to Cairns routes.

WHITSUNDAY ISLANDS

Although resorts have been established on a handful of islands in the beautiful Whitsunday group, most of the 74 islands remain almost untouched. Lying along a similar latitude to Mauritius and New Caledonia, the islands are cloaked in deep green forests harboring exotic flora and fauna and rimmed with sugar-white beaches and sapphire-blue seas. Add to this the accessibility of the reef, and you'll understand why visitors to the Whitsundays find it such a memorable experience. The range of accommodation varies from world-class, international-standard, five-star luxury to rustic beach front cabins and Parks and Wildlife-operated campsites. Each island has something different to offer, so it is just a matter of deciding which is right for you.

General Information

Contact **Tourism Whitsundays** ((07) 4946 6673 FAX (07) 4946 7387 WEB SITE www.whitsunday information.com.au, for ferry timetables and all other information concerning the Whitsundays.

Island Hopping Adventures from Airlie Beach offer economical six- to fifteen-night packages for those who want to stay over on several different islands in a limited time. **Fantasea Cruises** ((07) 4946 5111 WEB SITE www.fantasea.com.au organizes eco-tours, whale-watching cruises, overnight stays at Reefworld and day-trips to several of the islands including Whitehaven Beach.

Whitsunday Island and Hook Island

The largest island in the group is Whitsunday Island, home to the unadorned rock wallaby and an important rookery for brahminy kites, ospreys, white-bellied sea eagles and peregrine falcons. The six-kilometer-long (3.7-mile) Whitehaven Beach is renowned for its snowy-white sands, and most day-trips stop here at some point. There is no resort on the island, but it does have several Queensland National Parks and Wildlife Services-controlled camping areas (((07) 4721 2399).

Just north of Whitsunday Island, tiny Hook Island is a popular scuba-diving spot, sheltered from the southerly weather. Book scuba trips to Hook with **Club Whitsunday** ((07) 4946 6182 TOLL-FREE (1800) 679 755 FAX (07) 4946 6890, 346 Shute Harbour Road, Airlie Beach, who also arrange day-trips to many of the islands in the group and extended cruises. The **Hook Island Wilderness Resort** ((07) 4946 9380 has inexpensive, basic lodge rooms and camping facilities.

Hayman Island

Touted as one of the world's premier resorts, **Hayman Island Resort** ((07) 4940 1234 WEB SITE www.hayman.com.au, with its luxurious accommodation, perfect white-sand beaches and more

than ample facilities, is the place to go if you want to be cosseted in a tropical paradise. Behind the resort, trails weave through eucalyptus forests to secluded bays and the island's lofty interior. Hayman's luxury price-tag makes it one of the most exclusive in the Whitsundays — there are no day-trips to the island. Prices do include an enormous tropical (or traditional, if you prefer) breakfast, as well as many of the activities that cost extra on other resorts. For more on Hayman see LIVING IT UP, page 37 in YOUR CHOICE.

Lindeman Island

Lindeman Island is the most southerly in the group, and the other 73 islands can be clearly seen from the peak of its 210-m-high (689 ft) **Mount Oldfield**. Most of the island is national park, noted for its birds and butterflies and is crisscrossed with over 20 km (12.5 miles) of walking tracks. The most eco-friendly resort in the Whitsundays, **Club Med**

Lindeman Island ((07) 3229 3155 TOLL-FREE (1800) 258 2633 WEB SITE www.clubmed.com has three restaurants, four bars and a multitude of land- and water-based sports, including a nine-hole golf course and five floodlit tennis courts.

Hamilton Island

Hamilton Island Resort **(** (07) 4946 9999 WEB SITE www.hamiltonisland.com.au is one of Australia's largest resorts, with options for a broad range of budgets. It's a small, self-contained village, where guests putt around to and fro in golf carts between the island's beaches, tracts of forest, swimming pools and cafés, shops and hilltop vistas. There are 10 restaurants, seven bars, six pools, 24 specialty shops and a supermarket, and sporting possibilities include go-karting, squash and floodlit tennis

What Palm Bay Hideaway on Long Island lacks in modern facilities it makes up for in simple charm.

as well as a plethora of water sports. Prices start at $200 a double for bungalow accommodation but go well into the expensive price range.

Hamilton's airport has regular direct flights from Sydney and Brisbane with Ansett and Qantas, or it's a 30 minute ferry ride from Shute Harbour.

South Molle Island

South Molle Island Resort ((07) 4946 9433 FAX (07) 4946 9580 is one of the oldest in the Whitsundays. In the 1930s South Molle was used for school groups on week-long natural-science field trips; the island's national park remains popular among visitors seeking to discover more of tropical Australia's flora and fauna. The resort is cheaper than most, especially given that all meals and many activities are inclusive in the moderate-to-expensive rates. Day visitors are welcomed and can use most facilities. South Molle is a 30-minute trip from Shute Harbour by water taxi.

Daydream Island

Daydream Island Resort ((07) 4948 8488 FAX (07) 4948 8499 WEB SITE www.daydream.net.au has managed to create a modern complex and still retain most of its natural surroundings, providing a unique island vacation experience. Accommodation and most facilities are contained in one central complex at the northern end of the island, overlooking the Whitsunday Passage — you don't get your own bungalow here, but the upside is that the island's national park is lush and unspoiled, and provides plenty of opportunity to completely escape. **Sunlovers Restaurant**, overlooking the central atrium, has an impressively understated menu, predominately Tuscan-style, with an emphasis on the quality of the produce used. Day visitors are welcome at the southern end of the island, where there's a café, swimming pool (the main resort pool is at the north end) and water-sports equipment for rent, and the island's open-air **Under The Stars** cinema, screening nightly. Regular ferries from Shute Harbour stop at Daydream.

Long Island

A recluse's hideout in the true sense, **Palm Bay Hideaway** ((07) 4946 9233 FAX (07) 4946 9309 has no in-room telephones or televisions to disturb you. The moderately priced resort has only 14 comfortably equipped bungalows, each with a hammock swaying out towards a small lagoon. When the seclusion gets too much, guests meet at the rustic dining room for simple buffet-style meals or a quiet drink. Pretty brown-faced wallabies hop past the pool, and bush turkeys and other birds wander freely around the bungalows. In fact, there are over 50 species of birds and four varieties of wallabies on the island, and the bushland surrounding the resort has 20 km (12.5 miles) of walking tracks for those keen to spot some of the local inhabitants.

TOWNSVILLE AND MAGNETIC ISLAND

With a population of 102,000, Townsville rates as Queensland's fourth largest city. It's an important port catering to northern Queensland's immense inland production of beef, fruit and other crops. Its geographical position in the "dry tropics" means that Townsville enjoys on average 320 days of unbroken warmth and sunshine. Just off the coast, Magnetic Island offers 25 spectacular beaches and a dramatic coastline studded with magnificent hoop pines and huge granite boulders. Although there are four villages on the island, two-thirds of it remains national park, with large populations of koalas, rock wallabies and possums.

GENERAL INFORMATION

For tourist information head to the **Flinders Mall Information Centre** ((07) 4721 3660, Flinders Mall. The **Queensland National Parks & Wildlife Service Information Office (QNPW)** ((07) 4721 2399 is in Great Barrier Reef Wonderland, 2–68 Flinders Street. For accommodation inquiries in Townsville contact **Townsville Enterprise Ltd.** ((07) 4771 3061 E-MAIL tel@tel.com.au.

The **Internet Den** ((07) 4721 4500, Shop 5, Alexandra Arcade, Flinders Mall, has up-to-date equipment and decent coffee.

WHAT TO SEE AND DO

In the center of town, **Flinders Mall** has some beautifully restored buildings dating back to the region's European settlement in the late nineteenth century. On Sundays the mall transforms into the huge **Cotters Markets**, selling specifically North Queensland arts, crafts and produce.

Townsville's multicultural population celebrates with the **Townsville Cultural Festival** in August and the **Australian/Italian** festival in May. The town's ethnic diversity is also reflected in its restaurants, which utilize a plentiful supply of fresh and exotic produce. Head down to **Palmer Street** for the best array of eating choices.

The biggest attraction in Townsville is **Great Barrier Reef Wonderland** ((07) 4750 0800 FAX (07) 4772 5281 WEB SITE www.reefhq.org.au, 2-68 Flinders Street. The main, two-and-a-half-million-liter (660,400-gallon) tank houses a self-supporting coral reef ecosystem, which visitors can walk through via an underwater viewing tunnel. There are 100 varieties of coral and 200 species of fish on display. Other tanks include a touch pool where some of the hardier marine specimens can be handled, an observation deck and a "predator tank" with sharks, and rays gliding around through a sunken replica of the SS *Yongala* shipwreck. For cinema fans, there is also a monsterous **Omnimax Cinema** in the complex. Adjacent is the **Museum of Tropical Queensland** ((07) 4726 0600, with a wing focusing on the HMS *Pandora* — the ship sent in search of the Bounty mutineers — and a good natural history museum with an interesting collection of Aboriginal artifacts. **Castle Hill**, a 300-m (980-ft) red-granite outcropping that rises steeply immediately behind the business district offers the best view of Townsville, a growing city which has nonetheless succeeded in retaining much of its colonial elegance.

To escape the heat there is a free artificial rock pool along the **Strand** beachfront drive, which ensures year-round safe swimming.

The most popular reason to visit Townsville, though, is the fact it is only 20 minutes by catamaran to **Magnetic Island**. The 2,000-strong permanent population gives Magnetic Island the feel of a small community rather than just a tourist resort. This still leaves two thirds of the island as national park, which makes it easy to get away to one of its 23 golden-sand, palm-fringed bay beaches, or to explore the many trails that lead into the island's hills.

Magnetic Island supports a prolific koala population. The three-kilometre (two-mile) **Forts Walk** is the best trail to spot these well-hidden cuties. Rent a Mini Moke, a fun and inexpensive means of transportation, to get around the island and its main town of **Picnic Bay**.

The **Magnetic Island International Resort** ((07) 4778 5200 TOLL-FREE (1800) 079 902 FAX (07) 4778 5806, on Mandalay Avenue, set on the side

of a hill in a pretty bush setting, has a vast assortment of moderately priced accommodation, from luxury private cottages to resort rooms of exceptional value.

HOW TO GET THERE

Townsville has an international airport, with services from Europe and Southeast Asia. There are also frequent daily domestic flights from the southern states.

Sunferries ((07) 4771 3855 has terminals at both 168–192 Flinders Street East (City Terminal) and on Sir Leslie Thiess Drive (Breakwater Terminal) and runs regular ferry service between Townsville and Picnic Bay on Magnetic Island. The crossing takes approximately 20 minutes, for $16.50 return. **Magnetic Island Car Ferries** ((07) 4772 5422 has a service to Geoffrey Bay on Magnetic Island, a 40-minute crossing that costs $112 return for a standard car with up to six passengers, or $13.20 return for foot passengers (and bicycles). Their terminal is at Ross Street in South Townsville.

CASSOWARY COAST

Extending from Cardwell to Cairns, the lush splendor of the Cassowary Coast is a fitting introduction to the Wet Tropics. And wet is the word. This strip of coast boasts the wettest place in Australia — Tully measures its rain in meters, making it the country's whitewater rafting and kayaking capital.

The region earns its exotic name from Australia's second-largest bird. The cassowary stands up to two meters high (six and a half feet), its bright blue head crowned by an over-sized, yellow bony outgrowth. The species is endangered, but most of the remaining birds live in this area. Unfortunately a lot fall victim to road accidents. If you're driving forested lanes around here at dawn or dusk, keep the speed down and your eyes peeled. Cassowaries are generally pretty calm, although once the female has laid her eggs she leaves the male in charge of incubating them and caring for the young — at this time males can get edgy if they feel threatened. They should never be approached, as their sharp outer talons can disembowel an adult. From here on, too, estuarine crocodiles become a reality in saltwater creeks and rivers. Look out for signs warning of their presence and don't swim anywhere you're unsure of.

GENERAL INFORMATION

The **Rainforest and Reef Centre** ((07) 4066 8601 in Cardwell issues permits to visit Hinchinbrook Island and has information on other parks in the

The cassowary is Australia's second-tallest bird, reaching up to almost two meters (six and a half feet) in height.

area. Open daily. **Tully Information Centre (** (07) 4068 2288, on the Bruce Highway just south of Tully, can book rafting and canoeing trips. Open 9 AM to 5 PM Monday to Saturday, Sunday 1 PM to 5 PM. **Mission Beach Visitor Centre (** (07) 4068 7099, Porters Promenade, Mission Beach, opens 9 AM to 5 PM Monday to Friday, 9 AM to noon on weekends.

WHAT TO SEE AND DO

The Bruce Highway passes some of the north's most spectacular scenery along the coast here. Byways lead to coastal holiday villages, island resorts, rivers for whitewater rafting and gentle canoe trips, sugar and fruit plantations, crocodile farms, rainforest walks and the jungle wilderness beneath mist-topped mountains. **Cardwell** is of most interest as a jumping-off point for Hinchinbrook Island, although the Hinchinbrook Channel here is popular for fishing, crabbing and shrimping, and dugongs can occasionally be seen grazing on the sea-grass of its sheltered waters. **Whitewater rafting** trips down the Tully River in Cardston National Park (grade-4 rapids) can generally pick up passengers in Mission Beach, Cairns or Tully. One of the most established companies, R'N'R Rafting **(** (07) 4051 7777 TOLL-FREE (1800) 079 039 has packages combining rafting with ballooning, jet boating, helicopter flights or bungee jumping.

The **Mission Beach** area, a series of four villages — Bingil Bay, Mission Beach, Wongaling Beach and South Mission Beach — along a 14-km (nine-mile) stretch of palm-fringed beaches, combines reef, rainforest, tropical islands and excellent fishing. Cruises leave Clump Point Jetty at the northern end of Mission Beach for the reef and the resort islands of Dunk and Bedarra. The other seven Family Islands are uninhabited, but accessible on regular and charter cruises. Sea-taxis to the islands take just 10 minutes — ask at the information center next to the jetty. As one of the few places parachutists can land on the beach, **skydiving** is offered by Jump the Beach TOLL-FREE (1800) 638 035, from Castaways Resort right on the beach. Castaways also rents catamarans, boats and paddleskis, and skydivers can use the pool and bar to relax after free-falling over the Great Barrier Reef and islands.

The outer reef is only 40 km (25 miles) offshore here: **cruises** and **snorkeling trips** are offered by Dunk Island Cruises **(** (07) 4068 7211 or Friendship Cruises **(** (07) 4068 7262. For those interested in **scuba-diving**, Mission Beach Dive Charters TOLL-FREE (1800) 700 112 runs day-trips and exploratory expeditions, including dives to the 108-year-old wreck of the *Lady Bowen*. They offer PADI courses up to dive-master levels, and introductory dives to Beaver and Taylor reefs. Quick Cat Dive **(** (07) 4068 7289 is a smaller company offering pretty much the same thing. **Sea-kayaking** is more of a tranquil experience here than the surf-kayaking

offered further south, but paddling next to turtles, dolphins, manta rays and possibly even dugongs makes up for that. Most popular is the five-kilometer (three-mile) paddle from Mission Beach to beautiful Dunk Island. Sunbird Adventures **(** (07) 4068 8229 E-MAIL sunbird@znet.net.au has full-day ($70) kayak tours to Dunk Island and half-day ($40) coastal trips. They also have a fun night walk in the local jungle for $20.

There are some magical walking tracks into the **Licuala State Forest** off Mission Beach–Tully Road, west of the South Mission Beach turnoff. The rainforest is home to many exotic birds and butterflies, and to the cassowary: walkers should keep a watchful eye out for this beautiful and rare flightless bird. A four-kilometer (two-and-a-half-mile) circuit walk from Bingil Bay into Clump Mountain National Park passes by a lookout over the islands at Bicton Hill. The visitor center organizes morning and evening **rainforest walks**, guided by Clump Mountain Aboriginal people, who explain the plants' uses for food and medical purposes. Mission Beach Adventure Tours **(** (07) 4068 8850 organizes similar full-day walkabouts, and offer **horseback safaris**. Bush 'n Beach Horserides **(** (07) 4068 7893 also has horseback tours. **Crocodile-spotting safaris** are organized through the visitor center too, or try a Crocodile Country River Rat Night Cruise **(** (07) 4068 8400.

Paronella Park and **Heritage Gardens (** (07) 4065 3225 WEB SITE www.paronellapark.com.au, Japoonvale Road, Meena Creek, 20 minutes north into the rainforest, are listed National Trust Heritage sites. A Spanish-styled castle and elaborate exotic gardens established here in the 1930s have long-since fallen victim to the tenacious tropical jungle. Visitors can sway on the suspension bridge over **Meena Falls** or swim in the creek below. The secret garden's tropical flowers and plants mingle with the local palms, ferns, vines, strangling figs and epiphytes, climbing over the enchanting ruins colored by forest moss and lichens. Entrance costs for $10 adults, $5 children. It is well worth making use of their inexpensive camping facilities or cabin accommodation.

Driving north to Cairns, look out for **Mount Bartle Frere**, on the left about 20 km (12.5 miles) past Innisfail in the Bellenden Ker National Park. It's Queensland's highest mountain (1,622 m or 5,321 ft) and a challenge even to experienced bushwalkers. Permits are available from the ranger station at Josephine Falls. North of **Mirriwinni** the highway passes through a narrow valley between rainforest-covered mountains, side roads leading to streams and waterfalls.

Hinchinbrook Island

Hinchinbrook, Australia's largest island national park, covers an area of 39,350 ha (97,200 acres) — a pristine wilderness of rainforests, everglades and mountains with a small resort. One of the most beautiful islands along the coast, Hinchinbrook hasn't suffered from over-development, and to protect its delicate ecology, its management restricts the numbers of visitors to the island.

Exploring by foot has its rewards, as the terrain changes from coastal mangroves and sandy beaches to fertile mountains in the interior. **Mount Bowen** at 1,142 m (3,745 ft) is the highest point. At **Missionary Bay** watch for dugongs. These rare mammals look like overfed seals, but in the water they glide gracefully among the extensive sea grass beds in the area, where they graze. They grow up to three meters (18 ft) in length and weigh up to 420 kg (1,000 lbs).

Hinchinbrook Island Adventures ((07) 4066 8270 TOLL-FREE (1800) 682 702 has daily cruises to the island from Cairns. Guides take you through some of the prettiest parts of the island's national park, imparting their astute knowledge of the flora and fauna of the area and narrating its colorful Aboriginal and early European history. From Cardwell, **Hinchinbrook Island Ferries** TOLL-FREE (1800) 682 702 have daily service to the island most of the year, less often in the Wet. The island can also be reached by water taxi from Cardwell (ask at the Rainforest and Reef Centre).

The secluded **Hinchinbrook Island Resort** TOLL-FREE (1800) 777 021 FAX (07) 4066 8742, at Cape Richards, is small and exclusive and definitely for the well-heeled. **Camping** is permitted at Macushla near Cape Richards and The Haven at the northern end of the island. The **Thorsborne Trail** on the eastern coast is an outstanding four- to five-day wilderness walk for the fit. The number of people undertaking this walk is limited, so book early. For information contact the Department of Environment and Heritage's **Rainforest and Reef Centre** ((07) 4066 8601 in Cardwell.

Dunk and Bedarra Islands

The only inhabited islands in the Family Islands Group, Dunk and Bedarra are both resort islands run by P&O Resorts. Dunk is accessible to day-trippers, unlike the more exclusive Bedarra.

Famous for its amazing number of butterflies, Dunk is best place to spot the sapphire-winged Ulysses butterfly. The island offers beautiful rainforest walks and spectacular views from **Mount Koot-ta-loo**. The enormous **Dunk Island Resort** (132 469 WEB SITE www. poresorts.com.au has 148 rooms offering suites, units or private cabanas with a choice of beach or rainforest views, all well-designed to complement the rainforest environment (moderate to expensive). No buildings are above tree-top level. Resort guests have an ample selection of activities to make their stay as active — or inactive — as desired. The well-equipped water sports area and the Spit Bar near the jetty are available to day-trippers, but prior

arrangements are required for use of other facilities, including the resort's restaurant, bar and swimming pool.

Bedarra Island (same contact numbers as Dunk Island Resort) is a few kilometers south of Dunk. The emphasis here is on luxury, relaxation, exquisite dining and the sense that you have the island to yourself. Accommodation and resort facilities are of a high international standard with inclusive extras such as your own motor-powered dingy to explore deserted beaches, with gourmet picnic hampers included. Guest numbers are limited on Bedarra, and privacy is assured. Both resorts organize regular flights from Cairns Airport for resort guests. For more on Bedarra see LIVING IT UP, page 37 in YOUR CHOICE.

WHERE TO STAY AND EAT

Both set in pristine rainforest with beautiful ocean and forest views and beach access, **Lugger Bay** ((07) 4068 8400 E-MAIL lugger@ozemail.com.au and **The Horizon** ((07) 4068 8154 WEB SITE www.the horizon.com.au are two expensive resorts on Explorers Drive in South Mission Beach. They offer similar facilities, with rainforest walks, designer swimming pools and excellent restaurants. In the moderate range, **Castaways** ((07) 4068 7444 E-MAIL castaway@4k2.com.au, on the beach at the corner of Pacific Parade and Seaview Street, Mission Beach, has clean, comfortable, motel-style units opposite Dunk Island. The cocktail bar and appealing hourglass-shaped swimming pool overlook coconut palms and the beach (with a stinger net from November to April).

Perhaps I was particularly hungry when I ate at **Toba** ((07) 4068 7852, but it couldn't have been better. The Indonesian cuisine is perfect in Mission Beach's sultry climate, the fresh assortment of fish is caught locally and the chef grows her own herbs, which she uses deftly. Tropical flowers subtly perfume the outdoor seating area.

HOW TO GET THERE

Cardwell and Tully are on the Brisbane–Cairns railway line; for information call **Queensland Rail** (132 232. Greyhound Pioneer and McCafferty's coaches stop at Cardwell, Tully and Mission Beach on their Brisbane to Cairns routes. **Coral Coaches** ((07) 4031 7577 have regular daily services up and down the coast from Mission Beach to Cairns, Port Douglas and Mossman, with transfers from Cairns Airport.

Cardwell is just under halfway between Townsville and Cairns on the Bruce Highway, roughly 170 km (106 miles) or two-hours' drive from either. Tully is 48 km (30 miles) north. Mission Beach is 11 km (seven miles) off the Bruce Highway, turn at Tully from the south or at Al Arish from the north.

CAIRNS

Tropical North Queensland is a destination on its own. Most of its attractions are found in its two World Heritage-listed areas, which lie side-by-side along the east coast: the Great Barrier Reef and the Wet Tropics. Cairns is a definitely lively mixture of backpackers and other tourists, fruit pickers and sailing and diving fanatics, and professional shrimp and big-game fisherman. It's not the most attractive town on the coast, but with a busy international and domestic airport and over 700 tour options available each and every day, Cairns is definitely the gateway to the north. Interspersed with generic modern buildings are remnants of Cairn's early days as a goldfields' port: colonial, broad-verandahed public buildings and classic Queenslander homes standing high off the ground on stilts to keep them cool.

Accommodation and restaurants here have more competition than the northern beaches or Port Douglas and tend to be a little cheaper. Over the past decade or so, Cairns has made an effort to scrub itself up a little, and as more and more visitors decide to stay on, the town is slowly developing a cosmopolitan feel. It hasn't, however, lost its rougher edge, particularly in some of the bars around the port area.

GENERAL INFORMATION

Tourism Tropical North Queensland ((07) 4051 3588 FAX (07) 4051 0127 WEB SITE www.tnq.org.au, at the corner of Grafton and Hartley streets, is open daily and can help with information on Cairns and the entire York Peninsula.

The **Gulf Savanna Tourist Organisation** ((07) 4051 4658, 55 Macleod Street, provides information on attractions in the Gulf of Carpentaria. The **Cape York and Gulf Savannah Hotline** TOLL-FREE (1800) 629 413 operates 8:30 AM to 5 PM daily.

Student Uni Travel ((07) 4041 4500, 39 Lake Street, is a good place to find cheap flights and coach deals; they also offer free e-mail access. There's an **Internet** café at Shop 1/345 Sheridon Street in North Cairns. For a Black and White **taxi** call ((07) 4051 5333.

City 24-Hour Medical Centre ((07) 4052 1119 offers emergency and general medical assistance; they make house (hotel) calls.

GETTING AROUND

Sunbus ((07) 4057 7411 has regular services throughout Cairns and the northern beaches to Palm Cove. They also run a night bus that drops passengers off at their accommodation.

There are plenty of **car rental** companies in Cairns, but those planning to drive into the Daintree or to Cape Tribulation should discuss this clearly when selecting a car. A four-wheel-drive vehicle is needed for most of the cape north of Mossman. Two reputable rental companies specializing in **off-road vehicles** are Get Lost Self Drive Safaris (0427 135 245, 21 Victoria Street, and 4wd Hire Service ((07) 4032 3094, 440 Sheridan Street. Thrifty Car Rental ((07) 4051 8099 is at the corner of Sheridan and Aplin streets.

WHAT TO SEE AND DO

As with other towns along this coast, Cairns' major attractions are the rainforest behind it and the Great Barrier Reef out front. Tour operators here have something for everyone, from simple cruises and reef snorkeling trips to adventure safaris into the northern wilderness. It's a good idea to shop around for reef trips and other tours — some of the best combine a variety of activities. Cairns also offers shopping, restaurants, a Saturday market, numerous bars and nightclubs, a casino and some good galleries.

Cairns Museum ((07) 4051 5582, at the corner of Shields and Lake streets, has an interesting display of photographs from the gold-rush and timber-cutting days. The museum also houses a good collection of Aboriginal artifacts from the Irukandji, Konkandji and Idindji Aboriginal tribes who lived in the area before Europeans arrived, and from the Atherton Tableland Tjapukai, Djabugay and Yirrgandyji. **Cairns Regional Gallery** ((07) 4031 6865, in a beautiful colonial mansion at the corner of Shield and Abbott streets, showcases the work of local artists, including Aboriginal and Torres Strait Islander art.

Flecker Botanical Gardens ((07) 4050 2454, in Collins Ave, Edge Hill, are open daily from 7:30 AM to 5:30 PM, admission is free. The gardens showcase an extensive array of tropical shrubs, trees and palms, flowers, vines and ferns, and include an Aboriginal plant-use section. There's a small restaurant, a Fernery, and an Orchid House, all of which close at 4:30 PM. A boardwalk through the wetlands connects the area with **Centenary Lakes Park**, a series of saltwater and freshwater lakes that attract a variety of bird life. Also in Edge Hill, the **Royal Flying Doctor Service** ((07) 4053 5687, 1 Junction Street, is open daily 9 AM to 4:30 PM. The Flying Doctors have provided medical service to isolated outback homesteads and communities since 1928. Hudson Fysh, a fighter pilot in World War I, founded the service when he realized the potential for aircraft in Australia's great outback. Fysh went on to found Qantas, Australia's national airline. The Cairns center includes a museum and a slide and video show portraying a typical day in the RFDS.

Collecting to save the forests, at the Eumundi Market not far from Noosa.

Cairns' **Undersea World Aquarium** ((07) 4041 1777 WEB SITE www.iig.com.au/underseaworld, Pier Marketplace, has 20 different reef habitats and over 1,200 marine creatures on display. It's a good place to learn a little about the reef and its inhabitants before taking the plunge. Open daily 8 AM to 8 PM; the sharks and fish are hand-fed by divers at 10:30 AM, noon, 1:30 PM and 3 PM. If inclined, visitors are welcome to dive with the sharks too.

Marlin Jetty is at the mouth of **Trinity Inlet**, a mangrove-fringed waterway favored by saltwater crocodiles. **Crocodile-watching cruises** slink slowly along the inlet daily. Redbank Crocodile Farm, operated by the Pormpuraaw Aboriginal Community, is Australia's largest. Croc Cat Tours ((07) 4041 0977 WEB SITE www.CrocCat.com.au leave from Marlin Marina D through the mangroves. They also have dinner and spotlighting cruises. Croc-watching cruises on the SS *Louisa* ((07) 4051 1145, a Mississippi-style paddle-steamer, are also good-value.

The **Tjapukai Dance Company** first began in Kuranda in 1987 and is now the most successful in Australia: the troupe was one of the highlights of the 2000 Sydney Olympics opening ceremony. With dance performances every hour, **Tjapukai Aboriginal Cultural Park** ((07) 4042 1246, E-MAIL tjapukai@tjapukai.com.au, WEB SITE www.tjapukai.com.au Caravonica Lakes, Cairns 4870, combines theater, film, dance, contemporary and ancient art in a fascinating presentation of Tjapukai Aboriginal culture and dreamtime mythology. At the impressive **Creation Theater**, live actors interact with giant holograms to explain the spiritual and traditional beliefs of the Tjapukai people (translated into eight languages through head-sets). In the **encampment** area, visitors are taught to throw a boomerang and spear, or you can take a bushwalk with a guide explaining how the plants are used in traditional bush foods and medicines. The park is a few kilometers north of Cairns, at the base of the Kuranda Skyrail. Many tour operators in Cairns have organized packages combining the two.

VISITING THE REEF

With so many options, choosing a reef trip can be daunting. If you're here for the snorkeling or scuba, and not prone to sea-sickness, I'd recommend a smaller boat, which offers more personalized attention and a friendly, familial atmosphere. The larger cruises have more horsepower and can reach the outer reef (where the coral is generally more spectacular) far more quickly and with less turbulence — although you could find yourself snorkeling with a crowd. Larger operators do offer extras that can be attractive, especially to groups with mixed requirements. The Quicksilver's pontoon and underwater observatory, for example, is

ideal if you have non-swimmers in your party. Whichever you choose, take plenty of sunscreen and apply it regularly; on every trip I've been on, at least half the passengers end up painfully sunburned. A lot of Port Douglas' reef cruises, including Quicksilver, pick up in Cairns too. Note that an environmental management charge of $4 is levied on all adults and children entering the Great Barrier Reef Heritage Area. The money goes to the long-term sustainability and protection of the reef and is collected on all reef trips in addition to the cruise fare.

The reef spawns almost simultaneously during the full moon of November, producing one of the most colorful of natural spectacles to be seen. **Deep Sea Divers Den** ((07) 4031 2223 WEB SITE www.divers-den.com, 319 Draper Street, is one of the most experienced reef tour operators in Cairns. They have 14 moorings on the outer reef and offer snorkeling and diving cruises, as well as PADI instruction to dive-master level. **Great Adventures Outer Reef Island Cruises** ((07) 4051 5644, on Wharf Street, runs day-trips to Green Island, Lizard Island, and other attractions along the reef. **Sunlover Cruises** ((07) 4050 1333 TOLL-FREE (1800) 810 512 WEB SITE www.sunlover.com.au, Trinity Wharf, also has good-value day-trips to the outer reef and Fitzroy Island, and a range of rainforest-and-reef packages.

Great Adventures ((07) 4051 0455 WEB SITE www.greatadventures.com.au specializes in trips to Green and Fitzroy islands and has a pontoon on the outer reef. Their prices are competitive, and in addition to snorkeling and scuba, optional extras range from parasailing and sailboarding to windsurfing and rainforest walks. Operating in conjunction with Great Adventures, **Cairns Heli-Scenic** ((07) 4031 5722 E-MAIL heliscenic@iig.com.au, Cairns City Heliport, The Pier Marketplace, has helicopter flights to Green Island and to Great Adventures' pontoon on the outer reef. They offer packages combining flights and snorkeling or scuba-diving, some with rainforest walks on Green Island and use of the island's swimming pool. For those who'd prefer to sail to the reef, **Silver Sail Cruises** ((07) 4031 3488 FAX (07) 4035 2585 sails the 19.5-m (64-ft) restored pearl lugger *Falla* to a sandy cay on the outer reef daily, with snorkeling and scuba diving included.

Captain Cook Cruises ((07) 4031 4433 WEB SITE www.captaincook.com.au offers the most magical cruises I've found. The *Reef Endeavour* sails once a week from Cairns to Fitzroy Island, Cooktown, Two Isles, Lizard Island and Ribbon Reef. The four-day voyage allows it to reach more isolated snorkeling locations. Hikes into the islands' rainforests and a tour of Cooktown are optional, and the ship is luxuriously appointed with Jacuzzis, sauna, a gym, swimming pool and a restaurant and bar. Once back in Cairns, the *Reef Endeavour* sets off on a three-day tour south to Dunk and Hinchinbrook Islands and Hedley Reef. This second voyage focuses more on island wildlife.

Ocean Spirit Cruises ((07) 4031 2920 TOLL-FREE (1800) 644 227 WEB SITE www.oceanspirit.com.au, 33 Lake Street, offers three-hour dinner cruises leaving Marlin Marina A at 7:30 PM daily.

SPORTS AND OUTDOOR ACTIVITIES

Fishing charters also leave from Marlin Jetty, to the reef to catch coral trout and red emperor, or up the river estuaries for king salmon, mangrove Jack and the much-sought-after barramundi. The game-fishing season for black marlin is from September to December, when the fish migrate along the outer reef. Big-game anglers from around the world congregate in Cairns for the November **Marlin Meet**. Black marlin here can reach four meters (14 ft) in length and weigh over 730 kg (1,700 lbs), in which case they are known as "granders." Contact the Cairns Game Fishing Club ((07) 4051 5979 if you're interested in joining in.

Hikes and shorter walks with experienced guides are the best way to discover the rainforest. One of the most knowledgeable around is the **Adventure Company** ((07) 4051 4777 FAX 4051 4888 WEB SITE www.adventures.com.au, based in Cairns, with guided walks, hikes and canoeing trips into virgin rainforest led by experienced and friendly naturalist guides. Tours range from half-day to four days or more and cost around $100 a day, including meals, transfers and hammock camping. Another reputable company that offers four-wheel-drive safaris with shorter walks into the rainforest is **Jungle Tours and Trekking Australia** ((07) 4032 5611 TOLL-FREE (1800) 817 234 WEB SITE www.jungletours.com.au. They're also based in Cairns.

Amity Tours TOLL-FREE (1800) 620 022 has one-day flights along the reef to Blue Lagoon on Lizard Island, which include a walking tour of the island and time to swim and snorkel. They also offer two-and three-day "air safaris" over the tip of Cape York Peninsula to the Torres Strait Islands, and across into the Gulf Savannah region, or short scenic flights over the reef and rainforest. **Hot Air** ((07) 4054 4488 TOLL-FREE (1800) 800 829 WEB SITE www.hotair.com.au and **Raging Thunder Adventures** ((07) 4030 7990 WEB SITE www.ragingthunder .com.au both offer balloon flights over the coast and rainforest, with binoculars supplied for wildlife-spotting. Flights begin at $125, with good-value day-trips combining ballooning with practically any other tour option (reef trips, safaris, rafting, Tjapukai, Kuranda Skyrail). Skydiving over the Great Barrier Reef is another way to see the coral from above. **Skydive Cairns** TOLL-FREE (1800) 444 568 offers tandem skydives, with solo jumps for the experienced.

If you must bungee jump in Queensland, then this is the right place to do it. **A.J. Hackett Bungy** TOLL-FREE (1800) 622 888 has a purpose-built platform surrounded by rainforest in the hills off the coastal highway five kilometers (three miles) beyond Smithfield. With airborne time, including rebounds, at only a matter of seconds, it's the climb up to the tower and steeling yourself to take the plunge into what looks like a fish pond that gets the adrenaline going. For the truly adventurous, A.J. Hackett, Skydive Cairns and Raging Thunder Rafting have put together a "triple challenge" packet. **Cairns Parasail and Watersport Adventures** ((07) 4031 7888 E-MAIL parajet@cairns.net.au offers parasailing, jet-ski and jet-boat rides from Marlin Marina.

Wild World Australia ((07) 4055 3669, at Palm Cove north of Cairns, has an exceptional collection of snakes and other reptiles, koalas, kangaroos, saltwater crocs, wombats, dingoes, cassowaries and emus. You can also go horseback riding at beautiful Palm Cove, with **Blazing Saddles** ((07) 4059 0955. Just off Redlynch Intake Road, 20 km (12.5 miles) west of Cairns, **Crystal Cascades** is a narrow forest gorge gushing with rapids, small waterfalls, and swimming opportunities. It's somewhere to picnic rather than explore — the large, pale-green, heart-shaped leaves of stinging trees, common on the sides of the paths here, are definitely best to be avoided.

SHOPPING

The Esplanade is the focus of the city, with an eclectic mix of cafés and restaurants. It's opposite the harbor, at high tide anyway. The tide recedes to expose broad mudflats. The **Pier Marketplace** has the advantage of extending into the harbor past the mud, and in Cairns' incessant humidity an air-conditioned shopping center can suddenly become appealing. The complex has art and craft stores, including a good Aboriginal art and artifacts outlet, and stores selling snorkels and dive gear, swimsuits, towels, hats and light cotton and linen clothes suited to the tropics. This is a good place to stock up on sunscreen too. The Food Court at the back overlooks the harbor, it's one of the best places in town for an inexpensive lunch. Further down the Esplanade, Cairns' **Night Markets** ((07) 4051 7666 are open every night of the week from 5 PM to 11 PM, making the most of the cooler evening air. Shops and stalls sell everything from clothes and food to artworks, with musical entertainment and artists working while you watch.

Cairns Central on McLeod Street is the town's largest shopping complex; otherwise it's similar to the Pier. Outside the complex, the weekend market, **Rusty's Bizarre**, showcases regional produce and local arts and crafts, with buskers providing entertainment. **Cairns Hatters** ℂ (07) 4031 6392 E-MAIL hatter@fastinternet .net.au, Shop 6, Ground Floor, Orchid Plaza, sells original Australian bush gear, including Akubra hats, oilskin coats, boots, belts and kangaroo- and crocodile-skin products.

WHERE TO STAY

As one would expect in a large tourist center such as Cairns, there is a wide range of accommodation to choose from. Staying in the center is the cheapest option, and you'll be close to bars and restaurants, but the beautiful northern beaches offer a more tranquil tropical experience.

erately priced B&B accommodation just north of town, in a white colonial-style two-story building with wide wooden verandas and a swimming pool, set within a tropical palm-fronded garden near the beach. With similar prices, **Galvins Edge Hill B&B** ℂ (07) 4032 1308 E-MAIL jessup@ozemail.com.au, 61 Walsh Street, Edge Hill, has only two guest rooms in a beautiful "Queenslander" house on stilts with an established garden and a small pool; it's close to the Flecker Botanical Gardens. **Lilybank** ℂ (07) 4055 1123 WEB SITE www.lilybank.com.au, 75 Kamerunga Road, offers similar accommodation, a little closer to the beach. **Nutmeg Grove** ℂ (07) 4039 1226 E-MAIL ingrid@ozemail.com.au, a grand old "Queenslander" on a rainforest valley property surrounded

Expensive

Most of Cairns' best hotels are along the Esplanade, overlooking the harbor. The **Pacific International** ℂ (07) 4051 7888 is at the corner of Spence Street and the Esplanade, and **Sunshine Tower Hotel** ℂ (07) 4051 5288 is at 140 The Esplanade. Both have swimming pools and Jacuzzis, and views over the harbor and marina.

Moderate

The **Fig Tree** ℂ (07) 4041 0000 WEB SITE www.figtree lodge.com is a welcoming Irish bar and tropical hotel in the heart of Cairns. Its bright spacious rooms are tastefully decorated, and the swimming pool and garden make it a relaxing place to stay at very reasonable prices.

Beaches at Holloways ℂ (07) 4055 9972 E-MAIL bookings@beaches-at-holloways.com, 2 Marietta Street, Holloways Beach, offers inexpensive to mod-

by mountain ranges, with a large swimming pool and a Jacuzzi, is the perfect choice for birdwatchers. The **Flying Horseshoe Motel** ℂ (07) 4051 3022 FAX (07) 4031 2761, 281-289 Sheridon Street, is moderately priced and close to town.

Inexpensive

Sugar Shack ℂ (07) 4055 7224 E-MAIL sugarshack @iig.com.au, 16 Buckley Street, Yorkeys Knob, is a simple B&B with a swimming pool and small garden, adjacent to the beach and yacht club. The centrally-located **Flag Inn Club Crocodile Hides Hotel** ℂ (07) 4051 1266 TOLL-FREE IN THE US (877) 668 9330 WEB SITE www.bestlodging.com, in a restored nineteenth-century heritage building at 87 Lake Street, is a cross between a hostel and a hotel and offers budget prices and lots of activities, as well as a swimming pool and complimentary light breakfast. **Castaways BackPackers** ℂ (1800) 243

944, 207 Sheridan Street, is a good, cheap option for travelers wanting to party. Rooms are clean and bright, and Castaways has built its reputation on linking travelers up with good-value tours and offering unbeatable deals on outdoor adventure activities.

WHERE TO EAT

Cairns' balmy climate is ideal for alfresco dining. Stylish restaurants and cafés along Shields and Grafton streets and the Esplanade offer high-quality seafood and tropical fruit dishes, with hearty steaks another specialty. Barramundi, crocodile and Moreton Bay bugs are on many menus.

Although the **Red Ochre Grill** ((07) 4051 0100, 43 Shields Street, Cairns, serves fine fish, beef, veal and poultry, their specialty is bush food using rainforest fruits, nuts and spices and indigenous meats from wallaby and kangaroo steaks and stews to grilled crocodile or smoked emu (expensive).

A classy little Italian bistro with a seasonal menu making the most of Tableland veal, lamb, beef and vegetables, and of course local fish, **Café Milano** ((07) 4041 6600, 20 Lake Street, is open 10 AM to late, seven days a week. Prices are moderate; they also do a mean (inexpensive) pizza and good coffee. Right on Trinity Inlet, with views of the Tablelands, **Mondo Café Bar and Grill** ((07) 4052 6780, in the Hilton Hotel on Wharf Street, is a laid-back local favorite; its inexpensive prices are surprising given the location. Meals are huge and ingredients always fresh.

HOW TO GET THERE

More and more flights these days enter Australia via Cairns International Airport. Qantas and Ansett have domestic flights into Cairns from all major Australian cities; Sunstate operates flights within Queensland.

Cairns is 1,807 km (1,130 miles) from Brisbane. The main rail line ends at Cairns, as does the Bruce Highway. Both the *Queenslander* and the *Sunlander* trains make the Brisbane-to-Cairns journey, following the Bruce Highway along the coast. The cheaper *Sunlander* leaves Brisbane every Tuesday, Thursday and Saturday at 9:55 AM, arriving in Cairns at 4:10 PM the following day. The more luxurious *Queenslander* departs Brisbane every Sunday at 10:55 AM, arriving in Cairns Mondays at 4:10 PM. For bookings and all inquiries call **Queensland Rail** (132 232.

The Trinity Wharf Coach Terminal is the hub for most bus services. Greyhound Pioneer and McCafferty's run services from Brisbane, or to Mount Isa and Northern Territory via Townsville and Charters Towers.

KURANDA

Known for its markets (held four days a week), artists, indigenous culture and magnificent rainforest scenery, tiny Kuranda sits on the edge of the Atherton Tableleand, at the top of Barron Gorge — spectacular in the wet season when the river rages down the falls, but otherwise tamed by a hydroelectric dam upstream. A constant stream of visitors arriving from the coast seems to have turned it into a stereotypical resort village — something this once atavistic community was keen to escape. But despite expanding development and heavy market-day tourism, it's hard not to like the place.

GENERAL INFORMATION

Tourism Tropical North Queensland ((07) 4051 3588 FAX (07) 4051 0127 E-MAIL information@tnq.org.au WEB SITE www.tnq.org.au, in Cairns, books tickets on Kuranda Railway and Skyrail and have details of the myraid tours to Kuranda offered from Cairns.

WHAT TO SEE AND DO

The **Kuranda Railway** ((07) 4052 6249 provides a leisurely way of seeing the rainforest. From Cairns Railway Station, the 100-year-old train sluggishly winds its way up through 15 tunnels to Kuranda's ferny colonial station, a trip of 34 km (21 miles). The track clings to the face of the escarpment, passing

A sweeping view from Kuranda Skyrail across to Cairns and the Coral Sea.

through lush forest and over 40 bridges. The old beast wheezes past the edge of **Barron Falls** which, after heavy rain, becomes a thundering torrent plunging hundreds of meters into a gorge colored with rainbow-flecked mist. When in full flow, **Stoney Creek Falls** is so close to you that its spray envelopes the track. The other option is to soar above the treetops on the world's longest gondola cableway, **Skyrail**, which allows hundreds of thousands of visitors a year to see the World Heritage rainforest with minimum impact on its sensitive ecology (for more information, see UNDER THE CANOPY, page 21 in TOP SPOTS).

Walk through Kuranda Market Arcade on the main street to reach **Kuranda Market**. Ninety stalls provide a vast range of handmade local crafts plus Australian opals and other gemstones, "bush-clobber" clothing, Aboriginal crafts and didjeridus, and crocodile and kangaroo leather goods. At the far end are a few refreshment stalls and an open area where musical acts perform on and off throughout the day. The market opens from 9 AM to 4:30 PM on Wednesday, Friday and Sunday.

Kuranda's **Butterfly Sanctuary** ((07) 4093 7575 WEB-SITE www.australianbutterflies.com.au, 8 Rob Veivers Drive, is open from 10 AM to 4 PM seven days a week. The sanctuary houses 2,000 free-flying tropical butterflies: giant Ulysses and strikingly bright blue Cairns birdwing butterflies are the most obvious of the dozen local species protected by their breeding programme. **Birdworld**, behind the markets, is a superb aviary with tree-lined paths and free-flying birds. The aviary includes 45 Australian tropical bird species and 25 other species from threatened world rainforests. Kuranda also has a **Noctarium** ((07) 4093 7344 at the upper end of Coondoo Street, with a collection of nocturnal animals native to Australia, including various possums and other marsupials and fruitbats (which cling to the side of the caged area to have visitors rub their noses). All three sanctuaries charge around $10 entrance fee. There's also a huge colony of **flying foxes** to see, hear and smell opposite the BP garage at the top of Coondoo Street.

There are a number of lovely **rainforest walks** around Kuranda. For a short introduction to the rainforest, follow the trail behind the Noctarium down to Jumrum Creek (about one hour). For a longer foray into the jungle, there's a good trail following the road from **Barron Falls Lookout** (two kilometers from town at the end of Barron Falls Road) to **Wright's Lookout**, continuing into dense forest along **Surprise Creek** and to the power station. A steep and in parts slippery walking track descends from Barron Falls Lookout to cool swimming spots along the river.

Kuranda Rainforest Tours ((07) 40937 476 or (015) 159 216 run 45 minute cruises into the rainforest, departing from the riverside landing below the Railway Station regularly from 10:15 AM till 2:30 PM. To reach the landing, cross the railway foot bridge and follow the stairs into the forest. The cruise

operators often rent out canoes too, and a one-hour guided rainforest walk departs from here at 11:45 AM. **Rainforestation Nature Park** ((07) 4093 9033 WEB SITE www.rainforest.com.au, a rainforest-themed theme park 10 km (six miles) out of Kuranda runs tours into the rainforest on an amphibious Army Duck. The park also presents the Pamagirri Aboriginal Dancers and has demonstrations of spear and boomerang throwing and other bush skills.

WHERE TO STAY AND EAT

Kuranda is not a place where many people stay overnight, and there's not a lot of accommodation. Staying here though adds a lot to the experience, as the town almost empties of tourists with the last Skyrail and train down to Cairns.

There are several choices of moderately priced accommodation. The **Cedar Park Rainforest Resort** ((07) 4093 7077 FAX (07) 4093 7841, 1 Cedar Park Road, is about 15 km (nine miles) out of town. Off the main road, this resort is filled only with the noises of the rainforest: the gurgling of the Clohesy River, the wind in the trees, and the occasional screech of a sulfur-crested cockatoo. With a mixture of moderately priced cabins and inexpensive motel accommodation, the **Kuranda Rainforest Resort** ((07) 4093 7555 E-MAIL kuresort@ozemail.com.au, on the Kennedy Highway, offers good value. Set in tropical rainforest and landscaped gardens with a magnificent mountain backdrop, it features its own private rainforest walk and a wallaby sanctuary. Next to the split-level swimming pool and Jacuzzi, the resort's **Fernery** restaurant has been desig ned to reflect the natural environment; featuring natural slate floors, large interior ferns and palms. Kuranda is a 25-minute walk from the resort, which runs regular shuttles into Kuranda and Cairns. In town, near the rail station, **The Bottom Pub** ((07) 4093 7206 serves good counter meals and has basic rooms at inexpensive prices.

Friendly **Kuranda Van Park** ((07) 4093 7316 E-MAIL kur.vanp@internetnorth.com.au is a real find. Two kilometers from Kuranda (it's a lovely walk along the river, or a short drive), it offers cabins, vans and campsites surrounded by rainforest, as well as a swimming pool and courtesy bus service (inexpensive). **Tentative Nests** ((07) 4093 9555, 26 Barron Falls Road, has a series of on canvas-canopied treehouses in the rainforest for $60 per person.

HOW TO GET THERE

Getting to Kuranda is half the fun. While it's just a 25-minute drive from Cairns, and buses leave Cairns' Trinity Wharf Coach Terminal twice daily, most visitors take the Kuranda Scenic Railway or *Skyrail* cable car.

Feeding time for Charley, at Hartley's Creek Crocodile Farm.

THE ATHERTON TABLELAND

The magnificent highland rainforests of the Atherton Tableland, which begin less than an hour's drive into the mountains west of Cairns, encompass waterfalls, crystal-clear crater lakes and stupendous examples of tropical curtain figs — which grow from branches at the height of the canopy, sending a mesh of roots to the ground that eventually completely strangle their host. Remaining tracts of ancient forest provide refuge for many unique species of birds and other animals. Some, like the tree-climbing kangaroo, which lives in the heights of the rainforest above the sheltering canopy, are relics of an ancient fauna whose history dates back to Gondwana. Behind the rainforest are tiny time-forgotten townships, almost unchanged since the heady gold-rush days.

For those with a car, the Tablelands can be visited easily on day-trips from Cairns, Kuranda or Port Douglas. Otherwise, the best way to visit the area is to take a tour from Cairns or Port Douglas, many of which include river cruises and horseback riding.

GENERAL INFORMATION

Tourist offices in Cairns and Port Douglas have ample information on the Tableland and touring possibilities. For more information contact the **Atherton Tableland Promotion Bureau** ((07) 4091 4222 WEB SITE www.athertontableland.com, in the Old Post Office Gallery Information Centre, Herberton Road, Atherton.

WHAT TO SEE AND DO

The Atherton Tableland is one of the most popular **bird-watching** areas in Australia, with over 300 species enjoying the cool, tropical highlands. One outstanding location is **Hasties Swamp**, just past Atherton, which has waders and water birds such as jacanas and large flocks of whistling ducks. Migratory birds vary with the season — from late June, brolgas and sarus cranes fly in. The cool rainforest environment of **Mount Hypipanee Crater**, 25 km (16 miles) from Atherton, shelters Macleay's and bridled honeyeaters, fern-wrens, golden bowerbirds, lesser sooty owls and spotted catbirds. In the crater itself, sheer granite walls plunge 120 m (394 ft) to a still pool 70 m (230 ft) deep. Nearby **Dinner Falls** is a beautiful series of falls tumbling through the rainforest, perfect for a paddle and a picnic. Along **Wongabel Botanic Walk** you're likely to see tooth-billed bowerbirds and other birds, and occasionally tree kangaroos.

Millaa Millaa is one of the oldest villages on the Tablelands, renowned for the series of spectacular waterfalls along the lovely **Millaa Millaa Waterfall Circuit**. The 13-km (eight-mile) circuit off the main highway west of the village passes by the Millaa Millaa Falls first, the biggest on the circuit, then Zillie Falls and finally Elinjaa Falls. The Falls Teahouse awaits at the end of the circuit. Heading east from Atherton on Highway 52 towards **Yungaburra** (a quaint town with many of the original buildings still in use), are the twin **Crater Lakes**, Barrine and Eacham. Both are extinct volcanic craters full of cool, refreshing water, offering a great break from the heat.

Exhilarating half-hour **balloon flights** over the Tablelands with Raging Thunder Adventures ((07) 4030 7990 include transfers from Cairns and a chicken-and-champagne breakfast, for around $120. Raging Thunder also offers whitewater rafting trips down the Barron River. For more action, there's **whitewater rafting** in the Barron Gorge — wild fun despite it being a conveyor-belt business: as you pick yourself out of the river, the raft is dragged back for the next busload.

WHERE TO STAY

Arriga Park (/FAX (07) 4093 2114, Dimbulah Road, Mareeba, has moderately priced farm-stay accommodation in a colonial homestead in the heart of the Tableland. The property has lush tropical gardens and a Jacuzzi and offers horse and pony riding; rock wallabies are frequent visitors. For a budget B&B in the Tableland, **Banchory Gardens** ((07) 4095 3147, 27 Bunya Street, Yungaburra, is a relaxing small property in the heart of the village with prize-winning tropical gardens. Hosts Jenny and Wally Coutts will help guests discover local bird life and platypuses.

PORT DOUGLAS

Port Douglas is the jewel of one of the most scenic sections of the Far North Queensland Coast. It's a tropical haven with million-dollar yachts and world-class resorts, while a short drive north is a wilderness of rainforest inaccessible to all but the most experienced adventure travelers.

A tiny township jutting into the Coral Sea 96 km (60 miles) north of Cairns, this is a quiet resort and the closest town to the Great Barrier Reef. The town backs onto the soaring forest-clad Daintree, with lovely Four Mile Beach along its southern approach. Nets protect swimmers from jellyfish during the dangerous months from November to April.

Port Douglas is also a convenient gateway to the Cape York Peninsula. Several tours are available north to Cape Tribulation and Cooktown, or rent a car (try a Moke, the ubiquitous Aussie holiday runabout) and drive up to Mossman Gorge for delightful walks through the rainforest. Several tours of the Daintree and further north operate from Port Douglas, taking you into true Crocodile Dundee Territory. For information on these see the following sections: THE DAINTREE AND CAPE TRIBULATION and NORTH TO COOKTOWN.

There is a small **Tourist Information Office** ((07) 4099 5599 at 23 Macrossan Street.

WHAT TO SEE AND DO

Although he's not the biggest croc they have, Charley is the star at **Hartley's Creek Crocodile Farm** ((07) 4055 3576, just south of Port Douglas on the Cook Highway at Palm Cove. Charlie has been a resident at Hartley's since his capture in 1934. A breeding farm for salt and freshwater crocodiles, Hartley's also has snakes, cassowaries, emus, dingoes, koalas and flying foxes. This is a family-run business, and

There is no shortage of golfing greens in idyllic locations around Port Douglas. Within the same course the first nine holes can be by the mountains and the next nine by the ocean. Others have a stunning rainforest backdrop, with tropical birds swooping across the sky. **Tropical Golf Tours** ((07) 4098 3448 E-MAIL tropgolf@tnq.com.au organizes golfing packages for all levels at three of the best links: Mossman, Paradise Palms and the Sheraton Mirage.

Odyssey Bound Tours (0149 798 183 E-MAIL odysseybound@intenetnorth.com.au WEB-SITE www.odyssey-bound.com.au organizes adventure safaris in comfortable air-conditioned four-wheel-drive vehicles from Port Douglas into the Wet Tropics World Heritage Area and the outback of Cape York.

the croc keepers have grown up among the reptiles. Keepers chat and joke while hand-feeding some of the biggest of them. Open daily 8 AM to 5 PM.

The MV *True Blue* takes fishing and cruising charters and a popular sunset cruise, spotlighting crocodiles and jumping fish. The evening includes a delicious seafood barbecue in true Australian tradition. Cruises last three hours, or they'll take you fishing along the estuaries for up to four hours. They also offer a children's special if you need a few hours' break. Contact **Port Douglas Cruise and Fishing Centre** ((07) 4099 4966, Shop 3, 1 Ashwood Avenue, or e-mail the boat's operators directly at trueblue@internetnorth.com.au. **Trinity Sport Fishing** ((07) 4099 5031, 18 Macrossan Street, offers half-day ($80), full-day ($150) and night-time ($80) fishing charters with an experienced guide. Trips include complimentary soft drinks, sun block and insect the all neccessary repellent.

Odyssey Bound's tours are relaxed, informal and educational. A one-day safari costs around $160 and the two-day safari starts at $495.

VISITING THE REEF

Like Cairns, the number and variety of reef trips offered from Port Douglas can be overwhelming. When shopping around, ask about any hidden costs. For example, some operators charge extra for snorkeling tours with a marine biologist, which on most is included in the fare. Introductory scuba-dives are offered as an extra on most trips; again, ask about the cost and time allowed. Smaller boats can take longer to reach the outer reef, but fewer passengers make it a more personalized experience. For more on reef trips, see the Cairns section.

Mandalay's serviced apartments in Port Douglas offer luxury accommodation at moderate prices.

The biggest and most well known of the many cruise operators, *Quicksilver* ℂ (07) 4099 5500 E-MAIL reservations@quicksilver-cruises.com WEB SITE www.quicksilver-cruises.com, Marina Mirage, has daily trips to the outer reef from Port Douglas. They run a shuttle bus for passengers from Cairns and Palm Cove, or there's the option of taking their Wave-piercer connection instead. Quicksilver has a permanent, multi-level pontoon at Agincourt Reef, from where visitors snorkel and dive the reef (with professional divers and marine biologists at hand). Visitors can also view the reef through an underwater observatory and small semi-submersible vessels. Short helicopter flights also leave from the pontoon.

The *Poseidon* ℂ (07) 4099 4772 E-MAIL poseidon @internetnorth.com.au WEB SITE www.poseidon-cruises.com.au is an impressive, custom-designed catamaran that speeds to the outer reef in no time at all, to some of the best snorkeling and diving spots off this part of the coast. We went to three different reef sites, giving a great personal overview of what this bewildering reef has to offer. *Poseidon* takes a maximum of 25 passengers — far less crowded than many others.

Adventure Diving and Research Expeditions ℂ (07) 4099 5911 E-MAIL undersea@ozemail.com.au WEB-SITE www.undersea.com.au run scuba-diving trips to the reef and coral atolls, including a six-day Coral Sea-Osprey Reef and Cod Hole expedition. Depending on the time of year, divers encounter marine life from whales (mid June to early August) to sharks (selected weeks). Their purpose-built research boat, the *Undersea Explorer*, is an impressive and comfortable vessel and the crew have had a lot of experience in sailing and diving these waters.

For a reef cruise with a difference, board the authentic Chinese Junk *Shaolin* ℂ (07) 4099 4650 FAX (07) 4098 5470 and sail off to the Blue Lagoon. After sailing the South China Sea for 16 years, she was brought to Australia and refitted throughout for a very soft-style adventure cruise. *Shaolin* is quite a sight to see when her blue bat-wing sails are hoisted. The all-inclusive day cruise costs $90 for adults and $50 for children. *Shaolin* leaves Monday to Saturday from berth C2 Marina Mirage at 9:30 AM, returning around 4:30 PM.

For those who'd like to learn more about the reef environment before taking the plunge, Marine biologists at **Marine Life Education** ℂ (0412) 726 472 E-MAIL coralbrief@tnq.com.au give audio-visual presentations of coral formations, aquatic plants, and the reef's intriguing fish and mammal species ($20 adults and $15 children).

WHERE TO STAY

Port Douglas offers a plethora of luxury accommodation, and the town has a reputation as a resort for the wealthy. Surprisingly, though, there's
Sailboats at Port Douglas's small marina.

a youth hostel in the center of the main street, and some other budget options including out-of-town camping. There are some good moderately-priced alternatives in town, and it is advised to book well ahead for these.

Luxury

At the top of the range is the exclusive **Sheraton Mirage Resort** ((07) 4099 5888 TOLL-FREE (1800) 073-535 FAX (07) 4098 5885 E-MAIL sheraton@poresorts .com.au WEB SITE www.poresorts.com.au, which has the biggest swimming pool — "swimming lagoon" — I have ever seen, as well as beach frontage, a golf course, a well-equipped gym and spa, and numerous restaurants. Bill Clinton and family had a break from it all here, in one of the resort's private double-storey bungalows, after winning a second term in 1996. **Radisson Treetops** ((07) 4099 4324 E-MAIL treetops@ozemail.com.au, just outside Port Douglas, is world-class resort with a rainforest theme, with another large, irregularly shaped pool — this one is in a jungle setting, and a realistic-looking waterfall tumbles into one end. The hotel restaurant, on stilts among the treetops, serves elaborate and delicious French-style meals. Both resorts offer full facilities, from water sports and golf to reef trips and organized tours into the Daintree Rainforest.

Expensive

Club Tropical Resort ((07) 4099 5885 FAX (07) 4099 5868 E-MAIL info@uniqueresorts.com.au, corner Macrossan and Wharf streets has a variety of simple suites in a choice of tropical, Balinese, Japanese or Indian theme. The rock-sculptured pool has a Jacuzzi tucked away in a cave with soft underwater lighting. A terraced dining area above is serenaded by the calming notes of the gentle cascade below. Very romantic.

Moderate

The best value-for-money accommodation in Port Douglas, beautiful **Mandalay** ((07) 4099 6188 FAX (07) 4099 3461 E-MAIL mandalay@portdouglas.tnq .com.au WEB SITE www.mandalay.com.au, at the corner of Garrick and Beryl streets, is perfectly located in quiet seclusion, only 50 m (55 yards) across a walkway to the white sands of Four Mile Beach. The 25 two- and three-bedroom, self-contained, serviced apartments have expansive living areas and the attention to detail — with tasteful designer furnishings and fixtures — is faultless. With its tennis court and decadent outdoor swimming pool/Jacuzzi and patio area, you won't want to leave except to venture out to the reef or into the Daintree. Next door is the newly opened sister property **Shalimar** (same contact details), which has similar apartments and access to all the same facilities.

Hibiscus Lodge ((07) 4099 5315, on Mowbray Street, has six comfortable units (inexpensive out of season) in a central location.

Inexpensive

In the center of town, **Port Douglas Backpackers** ((07) 4099 4883, 8 Macrossan Street, has dorm beds for $20. **Port o' Call Lodge** ((07) 4099 5422 in Wharf Street, one kilometer (half a mile) south of town, is a YHA-associated hostel with beds in four-bed dorms for $18. Each dorm has its own bathroom, and the hostel has a swimming pool, a kitchen, bar and restaurant, and offers courtesy coach service to Cairns Monday, Wednesday and Saturday.

Kulau Caravan Park ((07) 4099 5449, 24 Davidson Street, is the most central in Port Douglas, with sites from $14 and cabins from $50.

WHERE TO EAT

Port Douglas boasts quite a few excellent restaurants, and some fairly slick bars and cafés. Most are along Macrossan Street.

Spacious and airy inside with a large cocktail bar and a broad sidewalk eating area, moderately priced **Swallows** ((07) 4099 6100, corner of Macrossan and Wharf streets, serves Asian-influenced meals — crispy duck wantons served with a spicy pawpaw salad are perfect in the steamy tropical heat. Barramundi poached in coconut milk is another delicious option. The well-selected wine list complements the varied menu perfectly.

Salsa Bar and Grill ((07) 4099 4922, 38 Macrossan Street, has a diverse menu with classic dishes like herb-crusted rack of lamb or simple but very tasty char-grilled swordfish (moderate). They also have an extensive wine list. **Sardi's Italian Restaurant and Bar** ((07) 4099 5266, 123 Davidson Street, serves modern Italian food with interesting pizza variations at inexpensive prices. Their very original selection of antipasti and crostini is a tasty light meal in itself.

THE DAINTREE AND CAPE TRIBULATION

The Daintree refers to the entire area from Mossman to Cape Tribulation in the north, much of which was cleared by early settlers to plant banana and sugarcane plantations. Part of the Wet Tropics World Heritage Area, **Daintree National Park** begins near Mossman, 15 km (nine miles) north of Port Douglas. This is the true rainforest, with limited access even for walkers away from a few marked trails. At Daintree Village a passenger and vehicle ferry crosses the Daintree River to Cape Tribulation Road. From here the road winds through lowland and thick tropical rainforest and climbs over high capes, often with glorious coastal views, to **Cape Tribulation** — perhaps the most beautiful place in Australia.

In the dry season, conventional vehicles with high road clearance can now make it through to Cape Tribulation. Although the river and creek crossings

Curtain figs send a mesh of roots to the ground, eventually completely strangling their hosts.

have bridges or causeways (unlike those past Cape Tribulation), these are subject to flooding in the wetter months from November to April. Thrifty Car Rentals in Cairns are one of the few to allow conventional rental cars as far as Cape Tribulation, and most visitors rent a four-wheel-drive vehicle (which also permits you to take some of the tiny tunoffs along the way) or visit Cape Tribulation on an organized tour from Cairns or Port Douglas.

WHAT TO SEE AND DO

Just south of **Mossman** is a turnoff to **Mossman Gorge**, four kilometers (two and a half miles) away at the edge of the Daintree National Park. Walking trails here pass through rainforest and excellent swimming holes, and the luxury-priced Silky Lodge resort is a good place to stop for lunch.

Daintree Village is 17 kilometers past Mossman. **Daintree River and Reef Cruise Centre ℓ** (07) 4098 6115 are among a small number of local operators here taking cruises along the river and its estauries, where saltwater crocodiles tend to dissuade swimming. **Daintree Connection ℓ** (07) 4098 6120 FAX (07) 4098 6176 TOLL-FREE (1800) 658 333 have similar cruises departing from the Daintree ferry crossing daily at 1:30 PM. Also near the ferry crossing, at the Big Croc Café, **Daintree River Estaury Cruises** TOLL-FREE (1800) 658 833 have cruises deep into mangrove-lined creeks to the mouth of the river.

Daintree National Park teems with life, and over 400 species of birds have been recorded in the region, among them are the dancing Victoria's rifle bird, scrub fowls (the worlds biggest nest builder), brolgas, bustards, jabirus, emus and cassowaries. Rare orchids bloom from September onwards, and epiphytes, ferns, giant Banyan tees and pencil cedar all fight for space in the dense growth. Tours with qualified guides are the best way to learn about the forest. Many leave from Cairns or Port Douglas, but a good local company is **Forest Park Rainforest Walks ℓ** (07) 4096 6146 on Stewart's Creek Road a few kilometers out of Daintree Village.

Eight kilometers (five miles) before Daintree Village, **Wonga Beach Trail Rides ℓ** (07) 4098 7583 take small groups horseback riding into the rainforest and along the northern sweep of broad Wonga Beach. Their horses are well cared for and very responsive — suitable for even inexperienced riders. Rides depart daily at 8:30 AM and 3 PM.

The **Daintree Ferry ℓ** ((015) 630 494 operates from 6 AM to midnight, seven days a week. Shortly after crossing the ferry the real adventure begins. The road quickly enters the rainforest and climbs over the heights of Mount Alexandra, becoming narrow and winding with sharp bends and few places to pull to the side. Drive slowly and watch constantly for oncoming traffic.

For those with the time, there is an interesting detour at the base of the mountain to the beach at

Cape Kimberley, opposite Snapper Island. Past this turnoff it's uphill to **Alexandra Lookout**, then down to the informative **Daintree Rainforest Environmental Centre**, which has a boardwalk into the forest. Look out for the double-eyed fig parrot, found only in this part of Queensland. A green and yellow parrot with a pale blue face, it has a realistic-looking third "eye" above its beak (and eats mainly figs). Tucked into the rainforest just past the center is a restaurant, a hotel and motel and **Floravilla Art Gallery Tea Gardens**, who provide light meals in a tropical garden and tourist information. A little further on, the **Daintree Ice Cream Company** sells tropical-fruit ice-creams to help you in your battle against the heat.

The road then heads across **Cooper Creek** before turning back to meet the coast at **Thornton Beach**, with pristine sands and a small café-restaurant, **Café on Sea ℓ** (07) 4098 9118. A walk along this perfect beach, against the backdrop of Thornton Peak and the rainforest and with little Struck Island just off the coast, may well convince you never to return to city life. A little further north is the parking area for the **Marrdja Botanical Walk** through the forest to the mangroves at **Noah Head**. This is a beautiful self guiding walk with sturdy crocodile protection at the end.

Cape Tribulation is a few kilometers further on. Like **Mount Sorrow** behind it, the small peninsula was named by Captain Cook after the *Endeavour* ran into the reef nearby. A long swing of white-sand beach separates dense, emerald-green forest from impossibly blue waters to create this most photogenic of coastlines. Cape Tribulation National Park blankets the cape, and walks into the rainforest here can also afford glimpses of the Coral Sea. The Cape Trib area offers rainforest accommodation from friendly guesthouses to backpacker and luxury resorts.

TOURS AND SAFARIS

Australian Wilderness Safaris ℓ (07) 4098 1666 is a private operation that works in conjunction with Silky Oaks Lodge near Mossman (see WHERE TO STAY, below). They pick up from Mossman and Port Douglas, with a naturalist on board to take walks into the lowland rainforest. The day includes a cruise on the Daintree River and the afternoon at Cape Trib, ending with a swim back at Silky Oaks.

De Luxe Safaris ℓ (07) 4098 2097 WEB-SITE www.deluxesafaris.com.au is run by a husband and wife photo-journalist team who know Cape York like no-one else. They offer full-day tours in a seven-seater Land Cruiser to Mossman Gorge, along the Daintree River and into the rainforest, and on past Cape Tribulation. Tours leave from Port Douglas. **Jungle Tours ℓ** (07) 4032 5600 WEB-SITE www.jungletours.com.au have a selection of organized one- to seven-day tours into Cape Tribulation. Among the many options they offer are scuba-diving, horseback riding, bushwalks and sea kayaking.

Native Guide Safari Tours ((07) 4098 2206 FAX (07) 4098 1008 departs Monday to Saturday from Port Douglas ($105 per adult) (catamaran connections from Cairns $115) visiting Mossman Gorge, Daintree, and Cape Tribulation. The tour is owned and operated by Hazel, of the far north Queensland Gugu people, who guides you through the aboriginal culture and ecology of the rainforest.

Odyssey Bound Tours ((0149) 798 183 WEB SITE www.odyssey-bound.com.au offer adventure safaris to the wet tropics, rainforest, world heritage areas and the outback of Cape York in comfortable air-conditioned four-wheel-drive vehicles. The packages include all meals and accomodation and are informal and educational. They also offer charters (minimum of two people).

WHERE TO STAY AND EAT

Silky Oaks Lodge ((07) 3876 4644 FAX (07) 3876 4645 E-MAIL visitors@greatbarrierreef.aus.net is an idyllic retreat alongside Mossman Gorge. The main lodge overlooks a rainforest lagoon, and from their private patios, guests have an armchair view of one of the most diverse ecosystems on this planet. **Daintree Wilderness Lodge** ((07) 4098 9105 WEB SITE www.internetnorth.com.au/dwl, on Cape Tribulation Road at Alexandra Bay is a second resort offering luxury accommodation in the thick of the rainforest. Both resorts organize a plethora of river cruises, reef trips, and rainforest walks and incorporate excellent, if expensive, restaurants.

Daintree Manor ((07) 4090 7042, on Forest Creek Road, just past the Daintree Ferry, is a moderately-priced B&B with spacious rooms and panoramic forest views. Another good choice in the moderate range is the **Rainforest Retreat Motel** ((07) 4098 9101 near the turnoff to Cow Bay, with self-catering units and a swimming pool. The **Cow Bay Hotel** ((07) 4-98 9011 is across the road, with moderately-priced accommodation, hearty bistro meals and a bar.

Crocodylus Village (07 4098 9166 is a YHA hostel deep in the rainforest back from Cape Tribulation. Accommodation is in canvas bungalows on raised wooden platforms, with a choice of dormitory or a few doubles or small-group cabins. The resort has a swimming pool and a small restaurant and bar. Inexpensive.

NORTH TO COOKTOWN

From Cape Tribulation roads become rough tracks passable only in four-wheel-drive vehicles. If you plan to take this journey on your own, take the time to discuss your itinerary with the tour office in Cairns or Port Douglas. Part of the trip involves crossing the broad and tidal **Bloomfield River**. Tide times are listed on a blackboard outside the **Café**

on Sea in Thornton Beach, before Cape Tribulation. The crossing is an interesting experience for those unused to seeing people driving through significant water. The waters are infested with crocodiles, who are remarkably adept at lying concealed. A sign warns that it will cost $200 if you have to get a tractor to drag you out of the river.

Cooktown is where Captain Cook first landed on mainland Australia — he put in to make repairs on the *Endeavour* after running aground on a coral reef. Gold was discovered near here in 1883, and Cooktown went from a one-horse town to a boomtown that supported 68 bordellos, 64 bars, and numerous gambling dens — an indication of the miners' priorities. At the time it was the second-largest town in Queensland (after Brisbane). Once the goldmines were exhausted, though Cooktown became a backwater: today its population is just 1,500.

The main attraction in town is the **James Cook Historical Museum** ((07) 4069 5386, at the intersection of Helen and Fureaux streets. The building is typical of early Queensland architecture, with wide verandahs and airy rooms, and displays include fascinating early photographs of the miners and the local Aboriginal people.

A few operators have safaris up to and past Cooktown, including **Oz Tour Safari** ((07) 4055 9535 WEB SITE www.oztour.com.au.

LIZARD ISLAND

Lizard Island (132 469 WEB SITE www.poresorts .com.au is the most northerly resort on the Great Barrier Reef, 90 km (56 miles) north of Cooktown. Captain Cook visited in 1770, seeking a way through the reef. When he climbed to the highest point on the island, he saw the outer reef — only 15 km (nine miles) away — where waves pound the edge of the continental shelf. Cook named the island after its prehistoric-looking monitor lizards.

Lizard Island Lodge has 40 rooms, all with private balcony, king or twin beds, air-conditioning, ceiling fans and private bathroom. Rates are in the luxury category, although they include all meals and most activities — tennis, windsurfing, water-skiing, catamaran sailing, glass-bottom boat trips, paddle skis, outboard dinghies, and fishing and snorkeling gear. This is a true tropical-island getaway, with long stretches of squeaky white sand backed by tropical gardens leading to airy private bungalows with polished pine floors.

Resort guests are flown to the island from Cairns. **Amity Tours** TOLL-FREE (1800) 620 022 has day tours flying along the reef to Blue Lagoon on Lizard Island. The trip includes a walking tour of the island and time to swim and snorkel. They also offer two- and three-day "air safaris" over the tip of Cape York Peninsula to the Torres Strait Islands, and across into the Gulf Savannah region, or short scenic flights over the reef and rainforest.

Travelers' Tips

GETTING THERE

The "land down under," Australia is a good distance from just about anywhere else. Seasons are the reverse of the United States and Europe, and getting there involves many fatigue-inducing flying hours across many thousands of kilometers — as well as a fairly expensive ticket. They don't call those flights "long haul" for nothing. Shopping around for a good deal on your flight is almost as exhausting as the journey itself, although on-line ticket operators have taken some of the pain out of the process, and competition has brought prices down in recent years.

of Immigration and Multicultural Affairs, whose offices are located in most capital cities.

Visitors over 18 years of age may bring into Australia 200 cigarettes or 250 g (8.75 oz) of cigars or tobacco, and 1,250 ml (two pints) of alcohol — this includes wine and spirits. Strict prohibitions apply on bringing weapons and drugs into Australia. Prescription drugs should be accompanied by a doctor's certificate and should not exceed one month's supply. If you plan on bringing in any type of knife, even a small pocket-knife, pack it in your check-on baggage. If you have a valid reason to bring guns, hunting knives or any other weapons into Australia, tell this to your local Australian consulate when applying for a visa.

Most international flights enter through Sydney and Melbourne, and more recently Cairns. Nonstop flights from Los Angeles take about 14 hours, while flights from London take 24 hours or more, usually via Southeast Asia.

ARRIVING (AND LEAVING)

All visitors require a passport and visa to enter Australia, except for New Zealanders who require only a passport and are given a visa on arrival. Visa applications should be made before entering the country, at the nearest Australian consulate or embassy. Visitors must hold fully paid onward or return tickets to a country which they have permission to enter, and sufficient funds to maintain themselves during their stay. Tourist visas are usually valid for a maximum of six months. Applications for extensions are made through the Department

Australia is extremely strict about protecting local wildlife from imported pests. There are rigid regulations about the import of animal fur or hair, plants, seeds, insects and most foodstuffs. It is prudent to declare any food, plants or seeds that you have in your luggage. Even products made out of plant material, such as bamboo hats, should be shown to the custom officials. When you arrive, customs officials may spray the interior of the aircraft as you remain seated. It's harmless for humans.

WORKING VACATIONS

Working Vacation visas are available to commonwealth citizens up to the age of 28 years, who must apply before arriving in Australia. The visa entitles you to work for up to three months with any one employer anywhere in Australia. For details contact the **Department of Immigration and**

Multicultural Affairs (131 881 WEB SITE www.immi .gov.au, 88 Cumberland Street, The Rocks, Sydney 2000. On arrival in Australia with any type of working visa you should contact the nearest **taxation office** to apply for a Tax File Number. For addresses call TOLL-FREE 132 861.

ABORIGINAL LANDS

If traveling independently through Aboriginal lands you must obtain a permit. (This will be arranged for you if you're on an organized tour.) It is the right of the traditional owners of the land to refuse anyone. Inquires should be directed to the relevant land council or Aboriginal affairs authority, some of which are listed below. Applications must state the reason for entry, the dates and duration of your intended stay, the names of all members of your group, your itinerary and all the routes you intend to take while on these lands. Permits can only be issued after consultation and approval of the relevant Aboriginal landowners. Allow four to six weeks for processing.

The exemption on permit provisions for public roads that cross Aboriginal land applies only to the immediate road corridor. If it is likely you will need to make fuel stops, seek transit permits from the relevant land councils.

Commercial photography is not permitted on Aboriginal lands at any time without prior permission. You may take photos for personal use, but if these photos involve the people who live in these areas, please observe courtesies you would normally expect for yourself.

To learn more of the Aboriginal view of the land visit WEB SITE whoseland.com, which has links to hundreds of other Aboriginal sites on the web.

Contact the following associations for permits:

Northern Territory
Alice Springs and Tennant Creek regions: Central Land Council ((08) 8951 6211 FAX (08) 8953 4343 WEB SITE www.clc.org.au, PO Box 3321, Alice Springs NT 0871.
Anangu Pitjanjatjara lands: Pitjantjatjara Yankunytjatjara Land Council ((08) 8950 1511 FAX (08) 8950 1510 WEB SITE www.waru.org/ap/PMB Umuwu via Alice Springs NT 0872.
Darwin, Nhulunbuy (Arnhem Land) and Katherine regions: Northern Land Council ((08) 8920 5100 FAX (08) 8945 2633 WEB SITE www.nlc.org.au, PO Box 42921, Casuarina NT 0811.

Queensland
North Queensland Aboriginal Land Council ((07) 4031 4779 FAX (07) 4031 7414, PO Box 679N, Cairns QLD 4870.
Cape York Land Council ((07) 4051 9077 FAX (07) 4051 0097 WEB SITE www.cylc.org.au, PO Box 2496, Cairns QLD 4870.

South Australia
Aboriginal Lands Trust ((08) 8226 8907 FAX (08) 8226 8919, 22 Pulteney Street, Adelaide SA 5000.
Maralinga Tjarutja ((08) 8625 2946 FAX (08) 8625 3076, PO Box 435, Ceduna SA 5690.

Western Australia
Aboriginal Affairs Planning Authority ((08) 9235 8000 FAX (08) 9235 8088, 35 Havelock Street, West Perth WA 6005.
Kimberley Land Council ((08) 9193 1118 FAX (08) 9193 1163, PO Box 337 Derby WA 6728

EMBASSIES AND CONSULATES

Detailed information on Australian embassies and consulates abroad and foreign embassies and consulates in Australia can be found at WEB SITE www.dfat.gov.au.

AUSTRALIAN EMBASSIES AND CONSULATES ABROAD

Australian embassies and consulates abroad include:
Canada: Australian High Commission ((613) 236 0841 FAX (613) 236 4376, 7th Floor, Suite 710, 50 O'Connor Street Ottawa, Ontario K1P 6L2; Consulate ((416) 323 1155 FAX (416) 323 3910, Suite 314, 175 Bloor Street East Toronto, Ontario M4W 3R8.
Ireland: Australian Embassy and Consulate ((353-1) 676 1517 FAX (353-1) 678 5185, Fitzwilton House, Wilton Terrace, Dublin 2.
Netherlands: Australian Embassy and Consulate ((31) 070 310 8200 FAX (31) 070 310 7863, Carnegielaan 4, 2517 KH The Hague.
New Zealand: Australian Embassy and Consulate ((09) 303 2429 FAX (09) 377 0798, 7th and 8th Floor, Union House, 132-138 Quay Street, Auckland.
South Africa: Australian High Commission ((021) 419 5425 FAX (021) 419 7345, 14th Floor, BP Centre, Thibault Square, PO Box 4749, Cape Town 8000; Consulate ((021) 208 4163 FAX (021) 209 4081, Lee Chem Laboratories, 24 Buro Crescent, Mayville Durban.
United Kingdom: Australian High Commission ((0207) 379 433 FAX (0207) 240 5333, The Strand, London WC2B 4LA; Consulate ((0161) 228 1344 FAX (0161) 236 4074 Chatsworth House, Lever Street, Manchester M1 2QL.
United States: Australian Embassy ((202) 797 3000 FAX (202) 797 3168, 1601 Massachusetts Avenue NW, Washington DC 20036; Consulate ((212) 408 8400 FAX (212) 408 8401, Suite 420, International Building, Rockefeller Center, 630 Fifth Avenue, New York, New York 10011.

In Tasmania the remnants of Port Arthur's large church, built in 1837, are testament to the convicts' skills. The youths in the boys' prison carved the stone blocks and some of its fittings.

FOREIGN EMBASSIES AND CONSULATES IN AUSTRALIA

Useful foreign embassies in the Australian Capital Territory include:

British High Commission ((02) 6270 6666 FAX (02) 6273 3236, Commonwealth Avenue, Yarralumla ACT 2600.

Canadian High Commission ((02) 6273 3844 FAX (02) 6273 3285, Commonwealth Avenue, Canberra ACT 2600.

Irish Embassy ((02) 6273 3022 or (02) 6273 3201 FAX (02) 6273 3741, 20 Arkana Street, Yarralumla ACT 2600.

Netherlands Embassy ((02) 6273 3111 FAX (02) 6273 3206, 120 Empire Circuit, Yarralumla ACT 2600.

New Zealand High Commission ((02) 6270 4211 FAX (02) 6273 3194, Commonwealth Avenue, Canberra ACT 2600.

South African High Commission ((02) 6273 2424 FAX (02) 6273 3543, Rhodes Place, Yarralumla ACT 2600.

United States Embassy ((02) 6214 5600 FAX (02) 6214 5970, Moonah Place, Yarralumla ACT 2600.

TOURIST INFORMATION

The **Australian Tourism Commission** has offices worldwide, although I've found their excellent WEB SITE at www.aussie.net.au to be a lot more helpful. It offers a superabundance of facts for the international visitor and information on cities, regions, special interest activities, itineraries, and travel package deals.

State tourist boards are excellent resources when planning your trip, and all capital cities have information offices for visitors to their state. Their web sites, listed below, will get you started:

Countrylink NSW Travel Centre ((02) 9224 4744 or 132 077 WEB SITE www.tourism.nsw.gov.au, 31 York Street, Sydney NSW 2000.

Sydney Visitor Centre ((02) 9255 1788 WEB SITE www.sydneycity.nsw.gov.au, 106 George Street, The Rocks, Sydney NSW 2000.

Canberra Visitor Information Centre ((02) 6205 0044 TOLL-FREE (1800) 026 192 WEB SITE www.canberratourism.com.au, 330 Northbourne Avenue, Dickson ACT 2602.

Victoria Visitor Information Center ((03) 9658 9972 or 132 842 FAX (03) 9653 9744 WEB SITE www.visitvictoria.com, Melbourne Town Hall, Swanston Street, Melbourne VIC 3000.

Tasmanian Travel and Information Center ((03) 6230 8233 WEB SITE www.tas.gov.au/tourism, 20 Davey Street, Hobart TAS 7001.

South Australian Tourism Commission Travel Centre ((08) 8212 1505 TOLL-FREE (1800) 882 092 WEB SITE www.tourism.sa.gov.au, 1 King William Street, Adelaide SA 5000.

Western Australian Tourist Centre ((08) 9483 1111 WEB SITE www.westernaustralia.net, Forrest Place, Perth WA 6000.

Darwin Regional Tourism Association ((08) 8981 4300 WEB SITE www.nttc.com.au, 38 Mitchell Street, Darwin NT 0800.

Central Australian Tourism Industry Association ((08) 8952 5800 E-MAIL visinfo@catia.asn.au, 60 Gregory Terrace, Alice Springs NT 0870.

Queensland Government Travel Centre (131 801 or (07) 3874 2800 FAX (07) 3221 5320 WEB SITE www.queensland-holidays.com.au, 243 Edward Street, Brisbane QLD 4000.

Many state tourist boards also have branches in other states. For addresses of these, contact the head offices.

Almost every town in Australia has a tourist information office, all with trailer-loads of printed information for the taking.

The web site **www.ozemail.com.au/~fnq/rta/** is useful with links to pretty well all of Australia's tourism organizations.

GETTING AROUND

BY AIR

Given the vast distance between destinations in Australia, flying is often the most efficient way to get around the country, particularly if you are short on time. There are two major domestic airlines — **Ansett** (131 300 and **Qantas** (131 313 — with services to over 100 destinations. Around 20 small regional airlines are associated with one of these two major carriers; one of the biggest is **Kendell Airlines** ((08) 8725 7888, with flights in South Australia, Victoria, Tasmania and southern New South Wales.

In 2000, Virgin Blue (136 789 started a low-cost, no-frills service between Sydney, Brisbane and Melbourne, which has broken the Qantas/Ansett monopoly and brought down the prices of internal flights considerably.

BY RAIL

Train travel in Australia is not necessarily a cheaper alternative, particularly since the arrival of Virgin, which has created a much applauded price-discounting war among airlines.

Trains connect all state capitals except Hobart and Darwin. Reservations for all can be made on (132 232. Details of rail services within each state can be obtained from the following state rail authorities:

New South Wales (132 232.

Victoria (132 232.

South Australia ((08) 8231 4366.

Queensland (132 232.

Western Australia ((08) 9326 2222.

all meals, activities and even child-minding. Some are very exclusive, and a few cater especially to couples wanting a romantic break — children are not permitted. If you plan to spend a reasonable length of time at any resort it is worth asking about their package deals, which can reduce the cost somewhat. Queensland has the highest concentration of resorts in Australia, keeping prices very competitive. There are even several that cater primarily to backpackers.

HOTELS

All state capitals have world-class international hotels, most of which have toll-free 1800 numbers and web sites through which reservations can be made anywhere in Australia. Many also offer reward programs and special-rate package deals: it's worth checking their web sites carefully for these. Some of the major international hotel chains are listed below.

Hilton TOLL-FREE (1800) 222 255 WEB SITE www .hilton.com
Sheraton TOLL-FREE (1800) 073 535 WEB SITE www .sheraton.com
Hyatt WEB SITE www.hyatt.com
Radisson TOLL-FREE (1800) 1800 333 333 WEB SITE www.radisson.com
Regent WEB SITE www.regenthotel.com
Holiday Inn WEB SITE www.basshotels.com/holiday-inn
Intercontinental WEB SITE www.interconti.com
　　Many top-quality private hotels offer a combination of luxury and character unmatched by the larger chains. Smaller hotels, often referred to as "boutique" hotels, combine luxury with intimacy. Some of those recommended throughout this book are also of historic interest.

A surfer demonstrates acrobatic skills on a wave crest. In Australia, good surf attracts aficionados from hundreds of miles around.

Two services that take reservations for independent hotels around the country are **Country Comfort** TOLL-FREE (1800) 065 064 and **Choice Hotels** TOLL-FREE (1800) 090 600.

MOTELS

Considering Australia's dependence on the car, it is not surprising that the backbone of the accommodation business is the motel. These are dotted along most highways, particularly on the roads into and out of towns.

Motel prices are usually in the range of $60 to $100 for a double, while a top one should cost no more than $160. Always ask about special deals.

Golden Chain Motor Inns TOLL-FREE (1800) 023 966 WEB SITE goldenchain.com.au.

PUB STAYS

When you're on the road, don't overlook the famous Australian institution, the country pub. Sometimes it may be the only choice anyway. Pubs offer cold beer, basic meals, and simple but comfortable accommodation, from only $35 a night. It's here you'll meet the dinky-di Aussies — colorful, boisterous characters full of yarns and great for local tips. Many pubs are wonderful old historic buildings; some beautifully restored and others that haven't seen a lick of paint in years. Most pubs are

An average motel (motor-inn) is clean and comfortable, with air-conditioning, a television, an electric kettle and everything else you need to make a cup of tea or coffee. Breakfast is usually not included in the tariff, but can be ordered the night before. Some have a restaurant but these are not necessarily the best places in town to eat. Many, particularly those further north, have swimming pools. Jacuzzis are also becoming increasingly popular.

Reservations with the four largest motel chains can be made by contacting the following numbers or through their web sites, which will also give motel locations and links. Sticking with one chain can give you sizeable discounts:

Budget Motel Chain TOLL-FREE (1800) 811 223 WEB SITE www.budget-motel.com.au.
Flag (132 400 WEB SITE www.flagchoice.com.au.
Best Western (131 779 WEB SITE www.bestwestern.com.au.

easy to find and advance reservations are usually not unnecessary, but bear in mind that standards may vary considerably according to the type of pub and its location. It is by no means impolite to ask to see the room before deciding to stay.

BED AND BREAKFAST AND FARM-STAYS

Bed-and-breakfast (B&B) accommodation is not new to Australia, and is growing as increasing numbers of tourists are looking for intimate places to stay, often in out-of-the-way places. Some B&Bs are quaint colonial cottages in the city center, while others may be restored lighthouses or rooms in Victorian mansions on huge country properties. The enormous variety of possibilities and reasonable rates make this a very attractive option. This industry is well organized and booklets listing B&B places are readily available from tourist information offices.

Bed-and-breakfast accommodation is also offered on farms, where you may be encouraged to take part in or observe daily farm activities. Before you know it you'll be rounding up cattle on horseback! Accommodation on farms ranges from self-contained cottages on the property to a room in the main homestead, where you are guaranteed fresh, hearty meals.

Tourist organizations have lists of farm-stays in their state. **Bed & Breakfast Australia (** (02) 9498 5344 FAX (02) 9498 6438 WEB SITE www.bnba.com.au is an Australia-wide organization with thousands of B&Bs and farm-stays on their books.

YOUTH HOSTELS AND CAMPING

Youth hostels have come a long way in Australia, offering a high standard of inexpensive accommodation not just to backpackers in dorms, but also to travelers wanting comfortable and spacious twin, double and family rooms. Their facilities are more than ample, with swimming pools and air-conditioning common in the warmer regions, and helpful staff who organize tours and transport. All have amenities for self catering and are generally clean and well supervised and often well located. Most will collect guests from bus or train stations and airports if you give them enough notice. Fees average $15 per night.

The **YHA Australia (** (02) 9261 1111 FAX (02) 9261 1969 WEB SITE www.yha.org has over 150 hostels around Australia, and membership also entitles cardholders to a host of discounts worldwide. Membership of Hostelling International should be obtained in your country of origin, although visitors can join Australia's YHA on arrival.

Nomads Australia ((08) 8363 7633 TOLL-FREE (1800) 819 883 FAX (08) 8363 7968 WEB SITE www.nomads world.com/oz is a network of quality budget accommodation linking the main travel destinations of Australia. They also have some great arrival package deals worth asking about and organize low-cost tours throughout the country.

Backpackers Travel-Centre TOLL-FREE (1800) 020 007 E-MAIL information@backpackerstravel .net.au has offices in Victoria, New South Wales, and Queensland and has an information and travel advice service for the independent traveler concentrating on the most popular destinations in Australia.

Three good **web sites** with information and contact details for hostels in Australia are: www .ozbackpack.com.au, www.backpackers.com.au, and www.hostels.com/au.

Camping grounds and **caravan parks** are plentiful across the nation. Many are near beaches and rivers and in national parks. You will also find them on the fringes of major cities and towns. Facilities vary, but basic amenities include electricity hook up, hot and cold water, showers, toilets and laundry facilities. Sites cost from $8 to $15 per day for two people. At many caravan parks you can rent on-site vans or cabins from $16 to $65. In most cases, linen and blankets can be rented; if you're lucky they will be included in the price. Australian state motoring organizations and the State Government tourist offices produce guides to camping and caravan parks, and can direct you to camping equipment suppliers.

DINING OUT

Prices in this book are based on the average cost of a three-course meal per person, not including drinks:

Expensive   over $60, or a main course over $26.
Moderate $35 to $60, or a main course between $15 and $26.
Inexpensive   under $35, or a main course under $15.

Although Australians in rural areas may eat as early as 6 PM, it is more common in urban areas to eat at around 8:30 PM or later. Most city restaurants open for lunch at midday and for dinner at 7:30 PM, but in country towns it may all be over by 9 PM. There will always be several cafés who run continuously from breakfast to dinner if your eating habits don't follow a routine.

American visitors should note that in Australia, as in France and Great Britain, the first course of a meal is the entrée. This is followed by the main course — often referred to just as the main. Because of the confusion experienced by visitors from the United States, some restaurants eschew the term entrée completely, offering starters and mains.

TIPPING

While there is no obligation to tip in Australia, tipping is used to show your appreciation of good service. Restaurants and hotels don't add service charges, although in Sydney Melbourne and Canberra, and in more upmarket restaurants and resorts, tips of 5% to 10% are customary, if not necessarily expected. When buying drinks in pubs it is acceptable to leave small change for the bartender; rounding the fare to the nearest dollar in taxis is also common. Hairdressers are not tipped.

BASICS

TIME ZONES

Time differences between Australia and the rest of the world are a bit of a hoary chestnut. Many travelers admit defeat and preface all international calls with "Did I wake you up?" You can always send e-mails instead.

After laying her eggs, the female emu leaves the hatching and raising of her chicks to their father.

Australia has three time zones: Queensland, New South Wales, Victoria and Tasmania are on **Eastern Standard Time** (EST), which is 10 hours ahead of Greenwich Mean Time, 15 hours ahead of United States' Eastern Standard Time, and 18 hours ahead of Vancouver or Los Angeles. **Central Standard Time** in South Australia and the Northern Territory is a half hour behind EST, and **Western Standard Time** in Western Australia is two hours behind EST.

This would be easy enough, but to complicate matters, daylight saving is adopted by Victoria, New South Wales, South Australia and Tasmania, and not by Western Australia, the Northern Territory or Queensland. In these states clocks are put forward an hour at the end of spring (late October) and back again in autumn (March). Tasmania's daylight savings period is longer than that of other states, operating from early October to April.

As daylight savings periods are the reverse of those in northern hemisphere countries, time differences between Sydney and North America or Europe, for example, can change twice in a matter of weeks.

WEIGHTS AND MEASURES

All measures in Australia are metric. For approximate conversions: Centigrade to Fahrenheit multiply by two and add 30 — 20°C is about 70°F; one kilogram equals about two pounds; four liters to a gallon; a meter to a yard; one kilometer to five eighths of a mile.

ELECTRICITY

Australia's AC electricity supply operates at 240 volts. Most modern electronic gear will accept input voltage anywhere from 110 volts to 240 volts (read the equipment label) so all that is needed is a plug adapter. A typical travel voltage converter may be suitable for hairdryers and the like, but a good voltage converter is recommended for portable computers and more expensive equipment.

Australian plugs have either two or three flat, angled, prongs.

MONEY

All prices listed in this book are in Australian dollars. Australia uses a decimal system of currency, expressed in dollars and cents. Silver-colored coins increase in size with value — with 5, 10, 20 and 50 cent denominations. The two gold-colored coins — one- and two-dollar pieces — are smaller than the 20-cent piece, which can sometimes be a little confusing.

Plastic notes come in different colors and are available in denominations of $5, $10, $20, $50 and $100.

Travelers' checks present no problems and can easily be cashed at international airports, hotels and motels, money changers, and banks. Banks are open Monday to Thursday from 9:30 AM to 4 PM and until 5 PM on Friday. Some banks in capital cities are also open Saturday morning. Money can be withdrawn 24 hours a day from automatic tellers, which are located outside banks and in many shopping centers.

International credit cards are accepted in most places: MasterCard and Visa cards are most widely accepted, followed by American Express, Diners Club and Carte Blanche.

At the time of writing the United States dollar to Australian dollar **exchange rate** was:
AU$1.82 to US$1.
US$0.55 to AU$1.

A controversial 10% Goods and Services Tax (GST) came into being across the country in June 2000. This is included by law in the quoted price, unless stated otherwise. Visitors cannot reclaim refunds on this tax, although when a supplier agrees to export a major item to a visitor's home address, GST will not be charged on either the goods or the freight.

COMMUNICATION AND MEDIA

POST

Post offices are open from 9 AM to 5 PM on weekdays, and will hold mail poste restante for visitors. Outside of these hours, state capital cities have post office shops open on Saturday morning and some newsagents also sell stamps.

Mail posted from anywhere in Australia costs $0.45 for a standard letter while aerograms are $0.60. The rate for postcards is less than air-mailed letters, and these vary depending on their destination.

TELEPHONES

Local calls cost 40 cents from pay-phones and are not timed. Pay-phones generally take telephone cards, which are sold at tourist information centers, newsagents and pharmacies. Some public telephones still take coins too, particularly the small orange telephones often found in pubs and camping grounds.

Australian telephone numbers are generally 10 digits long. Most begin with a two-digit state prefix, which can be omitted when making local calls but is needed for interstate calls. New South Wales and Canberra numbers begin with (02), Victoria and Tasmania with (03), South Australia, Western Australia and Northern Territory numbers with (08), and Queensland numbers commence with (07). The far southwest of New South Wales falls into the (08) zone.

The symbols Ⓕ *FAX* Ⓣ *TOLL-FREE* Ⓔ *E-MAIL* Ⓦ *WEB SITE refer to additional contact information found in the chapter listings.*

337

The symbols Ⓕ *FAX* Ⓣ *TOLL-FREE* Ⓔ *E-MAIL* Ⓦ *WEB SITE refer to additional contact information found in the chapter listings.*

339

The symbols **(F)** FAX **(T)** TOLL-FREE **(E)** E-MAIL **(W)** WEB SITE *refer to additional contact information found in the chapter listings.*

The symbols Ⓕ *FAX* ⓣ *TOLL-FREE* Ⓔ *E-MAIL* ⓦ *WEB SITE refer to additional contact information found in the chapter listings.*

The symbols Ⓕ *FAX* Ⓣ *TOLL-FREE* Ⓔ *E-MAIL* Ⓦ *WEB SITE refer to additional contact information found in the chapter listings.*

345

The symbols ⓕ *FAX* ⓣ *TOLL-FREE* ⓔ *E-MAIL* ⓦ *WEB SITE refer to additional contact information found in the chapter listings.*

347

The symbols Ⓕ FAX Ⓣ TOLL-FREE Ⓔ E-MAIL Ⓦ WEB SITE *refer to additional contact information found in the chapter listings.*

The symbols Ⓕ FAX Ⓣ TOLL-FREE Ⓔ E-MAIL Ⓦ WEB SITE *refer to additional contact information found in the chapter listings.*

351

The symbols Ⓕ FAX Ⓣ TOLL-FREE Ⓔ E-MAIL Ⓦ WEB SITE *refer to additional contact information found in the chapter listings.*

353

The symbols Ⓕ *FAX* Ⓣ *TOLL-FREE* Ⓔ *E-MAIL* ⓦ *WEB SITE refer to additional contact information found in the chapter listings.*

355

The symbols Ⓕ *FAX* Ⓣ *TOLL-FREE* Ⓔ *E-MAIL* Ⓦ *WEB SITE refer to additional contact information found in the chapter listings.*

359

The symbols Ⓕ FAX Ⓣ TOLL-FREE Ⓔ E-MAIL Ⓦ WEB SITE *refer to additional contact information found in the chapter listings.*

The symbols Ⓕ *FAX* Ⓣ *TOLL-FREE* Ⓔ *E-MAIL* Ⓦ *WEB SITE refer to additional contact information found in the chapter listings.*

363

The symbols Ⓕ FAX Ⓣ TOLL-FREE Ⓔ E-MAIL Ⓦ WEB SITE refer to additional contact information found in the chapter listings.

The symbols ⓕ *FAX* ⓣ *TOLL-FREE* ⓔ *E-MAIL* ⓦ *WEB SITE refer to additional contact information found in the chapter listings.*

367

Photo Credits

All photographs by **Roberto Rossi**, with exception of the following:
Adina Amsel: page 245
Australian Tourist Commission: pages 14, 15 *(bottom)*, 39 *(bottom)*, 41 *(bottom)*, 42, 49 *(bottom)*, 62, 74,
78-79, 117, 141, 143, 168-169, 186-187, 266, 268-269.
Douglas Baglin: page 200-201
Alain Evrard: pages 134-135, 146-147, 178, 195, 236-237.
Dallas & John Heaton: pages 84, 258, 288, 175.
Geoff Higgins: pages 48-49, 129, 164-165, 171, 238, 256-257.
Tony Nolan: page 325
Paul Steel: pages 247, 282-283.
Carl Wolinsky: page 253